D0026315

GENERAL DEFENCES IN CRIMINAL LAW

The law relating to general defences is one of the most important areas in the criminal law, yet the current state of the law in the United Kingdom reveals significant problems in the adoption of a consistent approach to their doctrinal and theoretical underpinnings, as exemplified by a number of recent developments in legislation and case law. A coherent and joined-up approach is still missing. This volume provides an analysis of the main contentious areas in British law, and proposes ways forward for reform.

The collection includes contributions from leading experts across various jurisdictions. Part I examines the law in the United Kingdom, with specialist contributions on Irish and Scottish law. Part II consists of contributions by authors from a number of foreign jurisdictions, all written to a common research grid for maximum comparability, which provide a wider background of how other legal systems treat problems relating to general defences in the context of the criminal law, and which may serve as points of reference for domestic law reform.

Substantive Issues In Criminal Law

Series Editors:
Alan Reed and Michael Bohlander

Substantive Issues in Criminal Law presents a series of volumes that systematically address areas of the criminal law that are in need of reform or which belong to the core areas of law where doctrinal abstraction or greater analysis is required. One part of each book is dedicated to an in-depth look at the situation in the UK, with individual chapters analysing points of current interest. A second feature of each volume is a major comparative section of other domestic jurisdictions. These international contributions are written to a uniform research grid provided by the editors in order to ensure a maximum degree of ease of comparison. The key purpose of the series is to produce a major library of reference works to which all actors in the wider criminal justice and policy community in the UK and elsewhere will have recourse for academic, judicial and policy purposes.

General Defences in Criminal Law

Domestic and Comparative Perspectives

Edited by

ALAN REED
Northumbria University, UK

and

MICHAEL BOHLANDER
Durham University, UK

with

NICOLA WAKE
Northumbria University, UK

and

EMMA SMITH
Northumbria University, UK

ASHGATE

© Alan Reed, Michael Bohlander and contributors 2014

All rights reserved. No part of this publication may be reproduced, stored in a retrieval system or transmitted in any form or by any means, electronic, mechanical, photocopying, recording or otherwise without the prior permission of the publisher.

Alan Reed and Michael Bohlander have asserted their right under the Copyright, Designs and Patents Act, 1988, to be identified as the editors of this work.

Published by
Ashgate Publishing Limited
Wey Court East
Union Road
Farnham
Surrey, GU9 7PT
England

Ashgate Publishing Company
110 Cherry Street
Suite 3-1
Burlington, VT 05401-3818
USA

www.ashgate.com

British Library Cataloguing in Publication Data
A catalogue record for this book is available from the British Library

Library of Congress Cataloging-in-Publication Data
Reed, Alan (Matthew Alan), author.
  General defences in criminal law: domestic and comparative perspectives / by Alan Reed and Michael Bohlander.
    pages cm. — (Substantive issues in criminal law)
  Includes bibliographical references and index.
  ISBN 978-1-4724-3335-0 (hardback: alk. paper) — ISBN 978-1-4724-3336-7 (ebook) — ISBN 978-1-4724-3337-4 (epub)
  1. Defense (Criminal procedure)—Great Britain. 2. Criminal law—Great Britain. 3. Defense (Criminal procedure) I. Bohlander, Michael, 1962– author. II. Title.
  KD8358.R44 2014
  345.41'05044—dc23

2014015810

ISBN 9781472433350 (hbk)
ISBN 9781472433367 (ebk – PDF)
ISBN 9781472433374 (ebk – ePUB)

Printed in the United Kingdom by Henry Ling Limited,
at the Dorset Press, Dorchester, DT1 1HD

Contents

Notes on Contributors

Kai Ambos is Chair of Criminal Law, Criminal Procedure, Comparative Law, and International Criminal Law at the Georg-August-Universität Göttingen, Germany (since May 2003). Head of the Department of Foreign and International Criminal Law, Institute of Criminal Law and Justice at the University of Göttingen, and Director General of the Centro de Estudios para Derecho Penal y Procesal Penal Latinoamericano (CEDPAL). Judge at the Provincial Court (*Landgericht*) of Lower Saxony in Göttingen (since 24 March 2006). Legal education at the universities of Freiburg im Breisgau (Germany), Oxford (UK), and Munich (Germany). First State Exam, 1990. Legal Preparatory Service, 1992–94. Second State Exam, 1994. PhD 1992 (Munich). Habilitation (Post-Doc) 2001 (Munich). *Venia legendi* in Criminal Law, Criminal Procedure, Criminology, Comparative Law, and Public International Law. Former senior research fellow at the Max Planck Institute for Foreign and International Criminal Law, Freiburg im Breisgau, Germany, in charge of the sections 'International Criminal Law' and 'Spanish-Speaking Latin America' (1991–2003).

Petter Asp is Professor of Criminal Law at Stockholm University and the present holder of the Torsten and Ragnar Söderberg Chair in Legal Science.

Mirko Bagaric is a professor at the Deakin Law School. He is the author or co-author of over 25 books and 100 refereed articles. He is the editor or co-editor of several law journals, including Australia's leading criminal law journal, *The Criminal Law Journal*. His main research areas are sentencing, evidence, substantive criminal law, and moral and legal philosophy. He is also a practicing lawyer.

Stefanie Bock is a senior research assistant of Professor Dr Kai Ambos, Department for Foreign and International Criminal Law, University of Göttingen, and an Assistant Professor at the same department. She has studied law at the University of Hamburg and holds a PhD in criminal law from the same University. Prior to taking up her current position, she worked as a research assistant at the Universities of Hamburg and Göttingen and as an intern at the International Criminal Court. Her main fields of research are international criminal law, European criminal law, and comparative criminal law.

Michael Bohlander is the Chair in Comparative and International Criminal Law at Durham Law School.

Luis E Chiesa is Professor of Law and Director of the Buffalo Criminal Law Center, SUNY Buffalo Law School. Chiesa earned his J.D. at the University of Puerto Rico School of Law (graduating first in his class), then his master of laws and doctor of juridical science degrees at Columbia University. He clerked for Hon. Federico Hernández Denton, chief justice of the Puerto Rico Supreme Court, and taught at Pace Law School before joining SUNY Buffalo Law. Previously, Chiesa was the Rembe Distinguished Visiting Professor at the University of Washington; a visiting professor of criminal law at the Torcuato Di Tella University in Buenos Aires, Argentina; and a member of the visiting faculty at Sergio Arboleda University in Bogota, Colombia. Chiesa's writings have been published in the *Washington & Lee Law Review*, the *Utah Law Review*, the *Ohio State Journal of Criminal Law*, and the *New Criminal Law Review*, among other journals. Furthermore, Chiesa often publishes in some of the leading European and Latin American criminal law reviews. In addition to his teaching and scholarship, he directs the Buffalo Criminal Law Center. Chiesa's research interests focus on substantive criminal law, criminal procedure, comparative law, and animal cruelty laws.

John J Child has been a lecturer at Sussex Law School since September 2013. Prior to this, John was a Lecturer (2010–11) and Senior Lecturer (2011–13) at Oxford Brookes Law School. Before moving to Oxford Brookes, John completed his PhD at the University of Birmingham whilst working as a postgraduate teaching assistant. He also worked as a research assistant on the Criminal Law Team at the Law Commission for England and Wales. His research interests centre on criminal law theory, and particularly the internal structuring of offences and defences within general part of the criminal law, encompassing outputs in *The Criminal Law Review*, *Legal Studies*, *Northern Ireland Legal Quarterly*, and the *Journal of Criminal Law*.

Claire de Than, BA (Hons), LLB, LLM is a senior lecturer in law and Director of Student Experience at City University, London, having previously held appointments at two London University colleges. A graduate of Queen Mary, University of London, she is the author or co-author of more than 15 books, including de Than and Heaton, *Criminal Law* (OUP 2013) and de Than and Shorts, *International Criminal Law and Human Rights* (Sweet and Maxwell 2004). She has also published articles in a variety of national and international journals, including the *Modern Law Review*. Her research fields include criminal law, human rights law, media law, and disability law. She has advised several governments and many organisations on criminal law, human rights, and law reform issues, with specialisms in the law of British Overseas Territories and Crown Dependencies and in the law of consent.

Susan Edwards is Professor of Law and Dean of Law of Buckingham Law School. She is currently University Dean of Research and is a practising barrister and a Door Tenant 1 Grays Inn Square Chambers London. She has acted as an expert witness in both civil and criminal cases relating to domestic violence and ethnicity as well as gender and dress, and also acted in a consultancy capacity with regard to domestic violence in Europe and in the Middle East. Her work on domestic violence and homicide spans several decades, during which time she has advised the police, the CPS, and also trained police forces in Denmark, Spain, and Germany. Her work explores the interface of gender and culture, ethnicity, and identity, as these concepts impose themselves on the construction and interpretation of criminal and Human Rights Law.

Catherine Elliott, LLB, barr., DEA is a senior lecturer at City University London. She has written extensively on both English and French criminal law. Her publications include a successful textbook, *Criminal Law* (Pearson, 2010); now in its ninth edition; a monograph, *French Criminal Law* (Willan 2001); and a chapter on French criminal law in *The Handbook of Comparative Criminal Law* (Stanford University Press 2011).

Jesse Elvin graduated with a PhD in law from the University of London in 2005. He is a Senior Lecturer in Law at City University London, where criminal law is one of his specialist fields. He has published in a number of leading journals, including the *Modern Law Review*, the *Cambridge Law Journal*, the *Law Quarterly Review*, the *King's Law Journal* (formerly known as the *King's College Law Journal*), and *Feminist Legal Studies*.

Erik Gritter, LLM, is senior lecturer in criminal law and criminal procedure at the University of Groningen, the Netherlands. He has a broad experience in teaching substantive criminal law and criminal procedure. The focus of his research is mainly on substantive criminal law. In this field of law, he has published several papers and book contributions. His PhD thesis (Groningen 2003) concerns a comparative analysis of the impact of considerations of effectiveness on the enforcement of regulatory law and on the origins and development of certain aspects of criminal liability (e.g., the fault principle and criminal liability of corporations).

Mohammad M Hedayati-Kakhki graduated from Durham University in 2008 with a PhD in Middle Eastern Politics and Law. He qualified from Shahid Beheshti University in Tehran in 1990 with a Law Degree, and completed a Master's in International Law at the University of Shiraz, Iran, in 1999. He practised in both civil and criminal law as a First Class Attorney within the Islamic legal system of Iran. Alongside teaching LLM modules including Islamic Law at Durham Law School, he continues his involvement in legal practice by acting as an expert in cross-border criminal and commercial litigation, human rights, and immigration cases. He is frequently appointed to conduct research and provide commentary into varying aspects of Islamic law. He is also a legal consultant for Amnesty International, a Special Advisor to the Centre for Criminal Law and Criminal Justice at Durham University, and was the co-founder and Associate Director of the Islam, Law and Modernity Research Group in Durham from 2011–2014.

Jonathan Herring is a fellow in law at Exeter College, Oxford University, and Professor of Law at the Law Faculty, Oxford University. He has written on family law, medical law, criminal law, and legal issues surrounding old age. His books include: *Caring and the Law* (Hart 2013); *Older People in Law and Society* (OUP 2009); *European Human Rights and Family Law* (Hart 2010) (with Shazia Choudhry); *Medical Law and Ethics* (OUP 2013); *Criminal Law* (6th edn, OUP 2014); *Family Law* (6th edn, Pearson 2014); and *The Woman Who Tickled Too Much* (Pearson 2009).

Gerhard Kemp, BA, LLB, LLM, LLD (Stellenbosch), ILSC (Antwerp), is Professor of Criminal Law and International Criminal Law in the Faculty of Law, University of Stellenbosch, South Africa, and advocate of the High Court of South Africa. He is visiting lecturer in International Criminal Law at the Nelson Mandela Metropolitan University, Port Elizabeth. Gerhard is the author of various books, chapters in books, and journal articles in the fields of criminal justice and international criminal law. He is editor of the *African Yearbook on International Humanitarian Law* and serves on the editorial board of the *Law & Justice Review* (Turkey). Gerhard also serves on the board of directors and the executive committee of the Institute for Justice and Reconciliation (Cape Town) and serves as expert consultant to the Institute for Security Studies' Southern Africa curriculum development project for training courses in international criminal justice.

Arlie Loughnan is Associate Professor and ARC Research Fellow in the Faculty of Law, University of Sydney. Her research in this collection is supported by the Australian Research Council grant, Responsibility in Criminal Law (No. DE130100418). She is the author of *Manifest Madness: Mental Incapacity in Criminal Law* (OUP 2012). Arlie is a graduate of the University of Sydney (BA Hons 1, LLB Hons 1), New York University Law School (LLM), and London School of Economics (PhD).

Claire McDiarmid is a Reader at the University of Strathclyde. In criminal law, Claire has a particular interest in homicide and defences, and has published on both the partial defence of provocation ('Don't Look Back in Anger: The Partial Defence of Provocation in Scots Criminal Law' in J Chalmers, L Farmer and F Leverick (eds), *Essays in Criminal Law In Honour of Gerald Gordon* (Edinburgh University Press, 2010), and the *mens rea* of murder ('"Something Wicked This Way Comes": The *Mens Rea* of Murder' [2012] *Scots Law 2012 Juridical Review*), and is co-author of *Scots Criminal Law: A Critical Analysis*. She has also worked extensively on the age of criminal responsibility and on aspects of the Scottish children's hearing system, and has a particular interest in the criminal capacity of the child and in the difficulty for law in dealing with child criminals—individuals who are, simultaneously, vulnerable and in need of protection as children and, also, offenders.

Christopher J Newman is a Reader in Public Law at the University of Sunderland. Dr Newman has published in the fields of public order, policing, and the constitutional and human rights implications of legislation designed to regulate protest, and has worked with academics from Germany on comparative approaches to free speech.

R Murat Önok, BA (Izmir Dokuz Eylul University, 2000), LLM (Izmir Dokuz Eylul University, Social Sciences Institute, 2002), PhD (Izmir Dokuz Eylul University, Social Sciences Institute, 2005), is currently an assistant professor in the Law School at Koç University, Istanbul, and Vice President of the Turkish Press Council. Dr. Önok's fields of research are criminal law, human rights law, international criminal law, and international law. Dr Önok is author of two books (*The International Criminal Court and its Historical Perspective* (Turhan 2003) and *The Crime of Torture Within its International Dimension* (Seckin 2006)), and co-author of three textbooks (*Theory and Practice of the Special Part of Penal Law* (10th edn, Seckin 2013), *International Criminal Law* (2nd edn, Seckin 2014), and *Handbook on Human Rights* (4th edn, Seckin 2011). He has also written four book chapters, including 'Penal Law' in *Introduction to Turkish Law* (6th edn, Kluwer International 2011).

Alan Reed graduated from Trinity College, Cambridge University with a First Class Honours Degree in Law and was awarded the Herbert Smith Prize for Conflict of Laws and the Dr Lancey Prize. Cambridge University awarded him a full Holland Scholarship to facilitate study in the United States, where he obtained an LLM (Comparative Law) at the University of Virginia. After completion of the Law Society Finals Examinations, he spent three years in practice in London at Addleshaw Goddard, and also acted as a Tutor in Criminal Law at Trinity College, Cambridge. He spent seven years as a lecturer in law at Leeds University, and then engaged as Professor of Criminal and Private International Law at Sunderland University. Since April 2012 he has acted as Associate Dean (Research and Innovation) in the Faculty of Business and Law at Northumbria University. Alan has published over 200 monographs, textbooks, and articles in the substantive arena in leading journals in England, Australia, New York, Florida, and Los Angeles. For the last 10 years he has been editor of the *Journal of Criminal Law*.

Kent Roach is a Professor of Law and Prichard-Wilson Chair of Law and Public Policy at the University of Toronto Faculty of Law, with cross-appointments in criminology and political science. He is a graduate of the University of Toronto and of Yale, and a former law clerk to Justice Bertha Wilson of the Supreme Court of Canada. Professor Roach has been editor-in-chief of the *Criminal Law Quarterly* since 1998. In 2002, he was elected a Fellow of the Royal Society of Canada and in 2013 he was one of four Canadians in the social sciences awarded a Trudeau Fellowship. Professor Roach's books include *Constitutional Remedies in Canada* (winner of the 1997 Owen Prize for best law book), *Due Process and Victims' Rights: The New Law and Politics of Criminal Justice* (short-listed for the 1999 Donner Prize for best public policy book), *The Supreme Court on Trial: Judicial Activism or Democratic Dialogue* (short-listed for the 2001 Donner Prize), *September 11: Consequences for Canada* (named one of the five most significant books of 2003 by the Literary Review of Canada), and (with Robert J Sharpe) *Brian Dickson: A Judge's Journey* (winner of the 2004 JW Dafoe Prize for best contribution to the understanding of Canada). He is also the author of *The Unique Challenges of Terrorism Prosecutions: Towards a Workable Relation Between Intelligence and Evidence* (2010), *Criminal Law* (5th edn, 2012), and co-author (with Robert J. Sharpe) of *The Charter of Rights and Freedoms* (5th edn, 2013), co-author (with Ken Jull and Todd Archibald) of *Regulatory and Corporate Liability: From Due Diligence to Risk Management* (2005), and co-author (with Bibi Sanga and Robert Moles) of *Forensic Investigations and Miscarriages of Justice*. His most recent book is *The 9/11 Effect: Comparative Counter-Terrorism* (Cambridge University Press 2011). Professor Roach is also the co-editor of several collections of essays, including: *Global Anti-Terrorism Law and Policy* (2nd edn, 2011), *Taking Remedies Seriously* (2010), *Access to Care: Access to Justice* (2005), and *The Security of Freedom* (2001), as well as several published casebooks. He has also written over 160 articles and chapters published in Australia, China, Hong Kong, India, Israel, Italy, Singapore, South Africa, the United Kingdom, the United States, and Canada.

John E Stannard is a graduate of Oxford University, and has been on the staff of the Queen's University of Belfast since 1977. He has written widely on criminal law topics in a variety of journals including the *Irish Jurist*, *Legal Studies*, and the *Law Quarterly Review*, and is the author of a textbook on Northern Ireland criminal procedure. He is a member of the Society of Legal Scholars, of the Irish Legal History Society, and a Fellow of the Institute of Teaching and Learning. He is also a past president of the Irish Association of Law Teachers.

Bob Sullivan is emeritus professor of law, University College London. His research interests are in the fields of substantive criminal law and criminal law theory. He is co-author of Simester and Sullivan's *Criminal Law: Theory and Doctrine* (5th edn, Hart 2013) (with Simester, Spencer, and Virgo). He has published widely in the leading general and specialist journals.

Julia Tolmie, LLB ((Hons) (Auckland)), LLM (Harvard), is an Associate Professor at the Faculty of Law, University of Auckland. Prior to taking up her position with the University of Auckland in 1999, she was an academic on the Faculty of Law, University of Sydney for ten years. She has been the chair of the New Zealand Family Violence Death Review Committee since December 2011.

Magnus Ulväng is Professor of Criminal Law at Uppsala University.

Nicola Wake is Senior Lecturer in Law at Northumbria University and Convenor for the Criminal Justice Section of the Society of Legal Scholars. Nicola's research interests lie in the complex inter-relationship between traditional intoxication doctrine and mental condition defences. She is nationally and internationally published in this particular arena. Nicola co-organised and co-chaired the first UK conference on controversial governmental reforms to the concessionary defences: 'Coroners and Justice Act 2009—Panacea or Pandora's Box for Partial Defences?' and subsequently 'Mental Disorder and Criminal Justice' (2013).

William Wilson is Professor of Criminal Law at Queen Mary, University of London. He is the author of *Criminal Law: Doctrine and Theory* (4th edn, Longmans, 2010) and *Central Issues in Criminal Theory* (Hart, 2002).

Introduction

In broad terms, the prosecution in a criminal case bears the burden of proving not only that the defendant acted with the relevant fault ingredient for the individuated crime in question, but also to disprove any defence in support of which evidence is propounded. Defences apply consequentially to ensure that only the blameworthy are punished in accordance with culpability thresholds, and that blameless individuals are not unjustly punished for propagating a social harm. Exculpatory evidence may be adduced as justification (necessity or self-defence), by way of total excuse (duress or insane automatism), potentially as partial excuse (intoxication or diminished responsibility), or mitigation.

General defences have developed in England and Wales in a solipsistic ad-hoc manner, and haphazardly rather than in a coherent structure. Extant law reveals significant problems in adoption of consistent approaches to doctrinal and theoretical underpinnings of general defences. This has been exemplified by a plethora of recent jurisprudential authorities revealing varying degrees of confusion and vacillation. A variety of Law Commission proposals for bespoke defences, although emboldening the debate, have yet to be adopted in any logical template. This book's chapters by individual contributors, domestic and comparative, explore the fundamental precepts of general defences and cover a range of key issues within the spectrum of exculpatory behaviour. This includes England and Wales, Scotland and Ireland, as well as alternative approaches from several foreign jurisdictions.

In Chapter 1, 'How Criminal Defences Work', William Wilson considers the various attempts made to establish some core unifying rationale to criminal defences capable of providing a blueprint for both their development and constituent elements. In this chapter, it is argued that it may be more helpful to draw attention to those constant elements in the constitution of criminal defences which quite understandably, if erroneously, have lent support to the view there is a unified rationale rather than a collection of different claims to avoid punishment. These constant elements typically include requirements such as reasonableness, immediacy, and a triggering condition, which serve to distinguish true defences from quasi-defences rooted in the defendant's personality or psychological make-up. Crucially, these constant elements support the alternative view that the various rationales of criminal defences complement, rather than compete with, each other. They create the conditions by which the actor may support the actor's claim that his conduct was justified; that he lacked the capacity or fair opportunity of conforming to the standards demanded; that he did not betray the standards of character which we have come to expect of ordinary decent citizens; or that his conduct was truly out of character.

Bob Sullivan, in Chapter 2, 'Avoiding Criminal Liability and Excessive Punishment for Persons Who Lack Culpability: What Can and Should Be Done?', argues that a finding of culpability requires proof that the defendant (D) stands in some form of blameworthy relationship with a wrong. A wrong requires some setback or threat of imminent setback to the legally protected interests of individuals, organisations, or society at large. (The wide ranging content of modern criminal law includes many offences which may be committed without instantiating a wrong in the sense identified above. These offences fall beyond the scope of the chapter. Offences of strict liability which encompass wrongs in the sense identified above are within the scope of the chapter.)

Situations will arise where D appears to be in some form of blameworthy relationship with a criminal wrong. To deflect findings that he was culpable, he may claim that defining elements of the wrong were not present, or that aspects of his personhood undermine any blame for his wrongs, or that because of the circumstances in which he found himself, conformity with the criminal law was not to be expected. Alternatively, he may assert that what ordinarily would constitute a wrong was in the circumstances the right thing to do. The scope and content of the general defences made available under English criminal law will be assessed in terms of their reliability as indicators of non-culpability for wrongs. Cases of underinclusiveness will be identified and some inclusionary proposals will be made. However, not all forms of non-culpability can be accommodated within a rule based system of criminal law.

In Chapter 3, 'Prior Fault: Blocking Defences or Constructing Crimes', John Child highlights that when assessing D's liability, the orthodox approach of the criminal law is necessarily narrow and precise in its focus. We do not ask, for example, whether D satisfies an offence *mens rea* 'at some non-specific point in D's life', or whether, 'all things considered', we believe she is deserving of a defence; such questioning may help us assess D's moral character, but is too general and too subjective to drive the enquiries of criminal law. However, without some flexibility, this approach is vulnerable to creating unwanted results, most obviously in relation to criminal defences. For example, D decides to kill her enemy V (victim). D taunts V in order to elicit a violent reaction. V attacks D (as D anticipated) and D kills V in 'self-defence'. In this case, D has created the conditions of her own defence in order to commit a serious wrong, and thus her defence must be blocked. This 'blocking' is achieved through the doctrine of prior fault.

The doctrine of prior fault has attracted considerable academic comment, with much of this criticising perceived inconsistencies within the doctrine. In this chapter, the aim is to discuss and evaluate both the doctrine of prior fault itself and those claims of inconsistency. The chapter begins by rationalising the areas of law where issues of prior fault arise, distinguishing its application to defences (where it can act to block a defence) from its application to rules of offence construction (where it becomes an inculpatory rule). By recognising and highlighting the different contexts within which the doctrine of prior fault operates, the chapter is able to justify certain inconsistencies (between categories) whilst exposing other problematic issues and inconsistencies (within categories).

Chapter 4, 'Transfer of Defences', by Michael Bohlander, aims first to focus on analysing the existing judicial authorities on the matter of transferred malice and the transfer of defences, as well as the academic commentary, within English law. It then tries to address the underlying structural issues of the transferred malice doctrine to find out whether the current English and Welsh approach is defensible or in need of rethinking: in other words, whether the stress on the idea of a 'transfer' is really appropriate and helpful or rather misleading, and what the consequences of a departure from the idea of a transfer of intent are for the transfer of defences.

Jonathan Herring, in Chapter 5, 'Consent in the Criminal Law: The Importance of Relationality and Responsibility', explores the moral work undertaken by consent. It highlights the importance of not simply asking was there a 'yes' or 'no' but also the relational context within which any alleged consent was obtained. This approach highlights the responsibilities that can arise between the parties, which will depending on the context of their relationship. This might mean in some cases that an apparent consent cannot be relied upon by a defendant if they have not fulfilled their responsibilities in obtaining the 'consent'. The relational obligations may also mean that in some contexts the 'consent' is insufficient to justify the wrongdoing of the defendant.

In Chapter 6, 'The Claims of Necessity: Good and Harm, Excuses and Justifications and the Moral Narratives of Necessity', Susan Edwards explores the way in which the legal doctrine of necessity is shaped in accordance with time, place, and cultural context, producing an historical and cultural fluidity as judges as grand masters of necessity balance certain goods and harms in producing a 'lesser of two evils' outcome. Legal theorists have struggled to unearth some operating rationale and schema in the case law decisions, to discover only one certainty: that killing can never be defended by necessity, and even here the rule seems open to challenge. The role of articulated motives as they surface either as justifications or excuses for conduct has also been investigated for evidence of some abiding pattern. The impact of the 'doctrine' works to mitigate the harshness of law where prosecutorial discretion has failed to sift out cases where prosecutions would otherwise produce absurd outcomes. Since the defence of necessity presents as heresy to the rule of law, it has received limited approval, resulting in many defendants' pleas being shoehorned into other defences. The rule of necessity, in its own internal search for objectivity, is guided by precepts of reasonableness, proportionality, and commensurability—all of which, when interpreted, are socially constructed in accordance with class, culture, power, (private power and state power), rights, and gender of the day, time, and place. What passes as a legitimate necessity argument is determined by prevailing public policy, sieved and sifted through the judicial lens.

In Chapter 7, 'Duress And Normative Moral Excuse: Comparative Standardisations And The Ambit Of Affirmative Defences', Alan Reed notes that the affirmative defence of duress engages the argument that the defendant effected the crime in order to avoid unlawful physical threats made by a third party or via situational circumstances. As such, it does not negate a defendant's *mens rea* or offence-specific fault element, but rather an exculpatory excuse applies to negate a conclusion of guilt and to relieve a degree of responsibility for conduct. It is submitted in this chapter that duress should be standardised as an emotional excuse to culpability, and that to provide a defence to crime the defendant, contrary to extant law, ought to bear the burden of proving this affirmative defence. The defence may be analogised as a concession to human frailty and predicated upon 'confession and avoidance'. The defendant admits the completion of the *actus reus* with the attendant *mens rea* (confession), but seeks to excuse his conduct to deny criminal liability (avoidance). The defence involves a concoction of excuse, moral involuntariness and human frailty—the salutary lessons from recent jurisprudence show that a more compassionate and logical approach, which reflects on enhanced role for jury determination of excusing conduct, must be established. The chapter locates the defence within apposite classificatory boundaries and considers the paradigm ambit and threshold elements of duress. It is contended that duress as an excusatory defence ought to require the law to consider the type of conduct legitimately expected of our fellow citizens, who are threatened by dire consequences and coerced into completely atypical behaviour that is morally repugnant to them and their previous code of conduct. Optimal reform pathways are set out, reflecting a novel template for adoption.

In Chapter 8, 'Of Blurred Boundaries and Prior Fault: Insanity, Automatism, and Intoxication', Nicola Wake and Arlie Loughnan examine the relationship between intoxication and insanity, and intoxication and automatism. This relationship is currently oriented around the defendant's prior fault, which structures the law on intoxicated offending, and, by its absence, the law on insanity and automatism. The sharp boundaries, neat distinctions, and clear moral lines around prior fault which structure the current law are coming under some pressure. Through a discussion of the relevant case law, and the recent proposals for reform advanced by the Law Commission for England and Wales, Wake and Loughnan examine the fault lines between intoxication and insanity, and intoxication and automatism. They suggest that the difficulties associated with co-morbid defendants raising insanity, and the challenges of accommodating an increasingly differentiated group of defendants beneath the scope of the *Majewski* approach to intoxication, are putting pressure on the neat distinctions currently structuring this area of criminal law, and on the notion of prior fault that constitutes the centrepiece of the law.

Chapter 9, by Claire De Than and Jesse Elvin, is entitled 'Mistaken Private Defence: The Case for Reform'. This chapter examines the complex and contradictory position of the current law on mistakes in relation to self-defence, defence of property, and the similar statutory defences. The Law Commission proposals from 2009 on intoxicated mistakes will be considered critically, in particular their recommendation that the rule from *O'Grady* [1987] QB 995, now codified in section 76 of the Criminal Justice and Immigration Act 2008, should remain in place (Law Commission, Intoxication and Criminal Liability (Law Com No 314, 2009, 3.53–3.65)). The chapter will further argue that reasonable mistakes about the existence of exculpatory factors should found a general defence based on 'acting reasonably' regardless of intoxication, and assess the merits of the current subjective test under *Gladstone Williams* and statute. Recent proposals, such as the Conservative manifesto pledges, will be subjected to critical evaluation and testing through the use of hypothetical case studies. The approach of other jurisdictions and the impact of international law on these issues will be examined as part of the search for coherent and logical principles.

In Chapter 10, 'Statutory Defences of Reasonableness: Inexcusable Uncertainty or Reasonable Pragmatism', Christopher J Newman highlights that there are a number of criminal offences within the English legal system where the defendant can rely on the reasonableness of his actions to exculpate conduct which otherwise would have attracted criminal liability. This chapter examines the operation of such defences and the inherent limitations of leaving decisions as to whether the conduct was reasonable to the finders of fact at trial. It is contended that the statutory ambiguity inherent in construction of the 'reasonable excuse' defence places an undue interpretive burden upon the courts. This has resulted in courts indulging in an ad-hoc limitation of acceptable excuses to the point where the certainty of the defence may well be being compromised.

The discussion considers these issues using the prism of public order law and terrorism law but will also consider the broader statutory context in which the defence of reasonable excuse can operate. There is a subsequent analysis of the synergy between reasonable excuse and the defence of lawful excuse, seeking both connections and separations between these two excusatory defences. The chapter concludes with a series of suggestions for reform of this area of law and demonstrates that the difficulties in relying on a broadly drafted, generic defence means that such a defence is, by its very nature, subject to the ad-hoc decision making process at play in the lower courts. What is missing is clarity that can only come with Parliamentary intervention or clearer guidelines being issued by an appellate court.

In Chapter 11, 'How Do They Do That? Automatism, Coercion, Necessity, and *Mens Rea* in Scots Criminal Law', Claire McDiarmid identifies that, in relation to murder, the case of *Drury v HM Advocate* [2001] SLT 1013, was regarded by academic commentators as potentially disruptive of the relationship between mens rea and defences in Scots criminal law. Specifically, there was a concern that proof of the absence of defences (self-defence and provocation) would now be required to establish the mens rea of wicked intention to kill. Contemporaneous and subsequent cases (*Galbraith v HM Advocate* [2002] JC 1 (diminished responsibility) and *Lord Advocate's Reference No 1 of 2000* [2001] JC 143 (necessity)) were closely scrutinised to determine whether the trend was borne out in relation to other defences and other crimes. Though this appeared not to be the case, the issue itself remains worthy of scrutiny.

This chapter examines the issue more generally, from a normative perspective, in relation to necessity, coercion, and automatism in Scots law. It seeks to identify the existing relationship between mens rea and these defences and to consider how this might best operate.

John Stannard, in Chapter 12, 'In a Spirit of Compromise: The Irish Doctrine of Excessive Defence', notes that, for the most part, the criminal law of Ireland, especially in relation to general defences, closely reflects that of England and Wales. However, one notable exception is its acceptance of the doctrine of 'excessive defence'. This doctrine was imported from Australia by the Supreme Court in 1972 in the case of *People (Attorney-General) v Dwyer*, and provides that a defendant who kills by using excessive force, but no more force than he or she honestly believed to be necessary, should be guilty of manslaughter rather than murder. Though this doctrine no longer applies in Australia, it still forms part of Irish law, and it has been argued on several occasions that the law of Northern Ireland would benefit from adopting a similar approach, most notably in cases involving killings by the police and members of the security forces. The aim of this chapter will be to consider the coherence of this doctrine, and to ask to what extent its adoption would be of benefit to the criminal law.

The domestic chapters are complemented in Part II by the chapters on several foreign jurisdictions which were written to a common research grid, in order to allow a maximum of comparability between them. They set out the basic doctrine of the law on general defences and where appropriate, aspects of special interest. They will thus allow domestic lawyers to get a quick overview of the salient issues in these countries, which may also aid in efforts of law reform and in the evaluation of parallel domestic concepts on a more general level.

PART I

Chapter 1
How Criminal Defences Work

William Wilson

Introduction

Most communities are constituted by rules of conduct breach of which renders the individual susceptible to censure and/or penalty, depending upon the nature of the relationship and the nature of the rule. Censure, in this context, operates primarily as a communicative tool designed to reinforce normative expectations. Penalty, as in criminal punishment, is either an expression of that censure[1] or, as in sport or regulatory offences, simply a logical embodiment of the imperative nature of the rule. Susceptibility to censure and/or penalty varies, therefore, according to the nature of the relationship. As such it must accurately convey a message which is recognised by all parties as their due both in terms of the expectations it describes and in the manner in which these expectations have been confounded. Unjust or unfair censure generates conflict, which may harm not only the interests of censurer and censuree but also those of third parties who are connected to the relationship. The urge to censure, therefore, must be sensitive to the relationship, which requires consideration to be taken of the context, the capacities, motives and emotions of the individual. This is perhaps most evident in relation to the family. Family life engenders norms embodying expectations as to how each member of the family should behave. Such expectations typically vary according to the role and status of the family member. What is censurable behaviour for offspring will not necessarily be censurable for a sibling. What is censurable behaviour for a 10-year-old will not necessarily be censurable behaviour for a five-year-old. And, of course, what is censurable behaviour for a 15-year-old will not necessarily be censurable behaviour for a parent or spouse.

This relational nature of responsibility has other consequences.[2] In particular, it sets up a structure for dialogue between affected parties concerning the basis and propriety of censuring incidents, on the one hand and, on the other, for the kind of response that is appropriate for the censuree, be it contrition, righteous indignation, or reasoned explanation. Using the family again as our test bed, children quickly learn to understand not only the rules of behaviour to which they are subject but also the kinds of considerations which affect the responses of parents and siblings to the breach of these rules. At an early stage this may bring an appreciation that accidents and other involuntary behaviours affect the disposition to censure, that deliberate wrongdoing elicits a different response from accidental or involuntary wrongdoing. 'I didn't mean it' is the five-year-old's trump card, a card which progressively loses power with growing maturity. As normative expectations become more sensitive to age and capacity, distinctions may be drawn between the accidental and the careless, between the careless and the reckless, between the reckless and the deliberate, and so on. As it does so, the initial one-way nature of the communication may give way to a dialogue in which the censuree's perceptions of fairness and justice may feed back into the process of communication, with associated potential, if not always realised, for resolving conflicts of interest, opinion and perception. At this stage matters pertinent to cognition, such as whether the censuree knew what was expected, or deliberately flouted norms or expectations, or was careless may be enriched by more contextual and personal considerations taking into account, ordinary human dispositions such as indignation, anger, fear, fatigue, and contrition, and ordinary human conditions such as gender, intelligence, physical and mental capacities, and so on.

---

1   J Feinberg, 'The Expressive Function of Punishment' (1965) 49 Monist (Philosophy of Law) 397.

2   For extended discussion of this idea, see RA Duff, *Punishment, Communication and Community* (OUP 2003) ch 2 s 4.1 and ch 3 s 2.2.

The relationship policed by the criminal law is necessarily different from that existing between family members, clubs, societies, or other communities of interest. In its paradigm form of core crime, it embodies obligations which depend for their authority not upon the existence of the rule itself and their uncritical internalisation, as in sport or games, or the need to foster and maintain the integrity of a close relationship as in families, but upon a generalised acceptance of the truth of the standards concerned. This can sometimes be seen when parents give up their offspring to the police upon discovery of an act of serious wrongdoing. It is not simply because those parents do not care, cannot forgive, or want to teach a lesson. It is because they acknowledge that they do not own the wrong which has been committed and of the authority of the State to take action on behalf of the community affected. People who kill, hurt, steal, and defraud are appropriately made the subject of public condemnation. No other mechanism than punishment can express this condemnation and only the State has the authority to punish on behalf of the affected community.[3] For all these reasons susceptibility to censure punishment explains the requirement of *mens rea*. Quite apart from considerations of utility, or maintaining trust within a relationship, censure is unpleasant, and punishment unpleasant and harmful. It is simply not appropriate to denounce and punish someone who has done wrong unless they are at fault in so doing.[4] The premise here is that the criminal law has a function to perform over and above declaring wrongs or compensating victims, namely to limit its impact to those who defy the values embodied in criminal norms and thus deserve to have their conduct denounced as a public wrong.[5]

Because the State, rather than those directly affected, owns the wrong, however, matters such as context and motivation are inevitably of lesser importance than basic questions of responsibility in deciding questions of desert. At a basic level this can be understood as reflecting the lack of social unanimity concerning the ethical foundations of appropriate action. Modern societies lack the cultural and ideological homogeneity necessary to produce a common notion of right and wrong. People who support the same political party, follow the same religion and football team, enjoy the same books, drink together in the same pubs, and structure their lives around the same moral values may nevertheless disagree even on what the law of murder should comprise. Is abortion/euthanasia a matter of personal choice, of the best interests of all concerned, or inviolable moral obligation?[6]

The state's primary role, in this context, therefore, is to specify clearly the rules which govern cases where the balance of reasons for and against action may be misunderstood. Where, as in core crimes such as murder and other crimes of violence, the conduct element embodies a moral proscription, lending an actor's reasons for violence a defining role in the offence would be self-defeating. By relegating context and motives to the 'realm of supervening defences', the clarity of the moral principle—hurting people is wrong—can be sustained. It is a principle which generates its own reason to conform. It may well appear to an individual on the horns of a dilemma that to kill 'mercifully' is the best option and it is just because it may so appear that criminal offences and defences are structured in the way they are.[7] Criminal prohibitions demand obedience even in the face of compelling reasons for disobedience. They have clarity of purpose, which enable us to know what is the 'right' thing to do without our having to engage in complex moral inquiry. If the special context or the motive of the actor is capable of providing a countervailing reason not to conform that reason must first be evaluated from the point of view of the proscribing society rather than that of the actor himself or his immediate moral audience. In this way full moral consideration can be given to it.[8]

This refusal to allow context and motive a greater say in the construction of criminal liability points out, however, a general systemic problem which no amount of judicial tinkering at the edges can hope to resolve: namely, how best to reconcile the needs of society on the one hand and justice/fairness to the individual on the

---

3   G Lamond, 'What is a Crime?' (2007) 27 OJ LS 609; A Lee, 'Public Wrongs and the Criminal Law' (May 2013) Crim L & Philos <http://link.springer.com/article/10.1007%2Fs11572-013-9231-z>, makes the point that a public wrong is not one which necessarily 'harms' the public but rather one which the public, via the State, ought to punish.

4   See generally HLA Hart, *Punishment and Responsibility* (OUP 1968).

5   G Lamond (n 3).

6   R Dworkin, *Life's Dominion* (Penguin 1993); W Wilson, *Central Issues in Criminal Theory* (Hart 2002) ch 2.

7   See J Raz, *The Authority of Law* (OUP 1979) ch 1 and generally; see also A Norrie, *Punishment Responsibility and Justice* (Clarendon Press 2000).

8   J Raz, op cit 19–26.

other where public and private interests and perceptions collide.[9] In the context of this chapter, this problem can be restated as questioning whether it is possible to generate a basic blueprint for criminal defences by which defences meet for recognition can be judged and the elements of defences already recognised identified and evaluated. These concerns have had the most profound impact in murder. The mandatory sentence makes it morally imperative, rather than simply desirable, for criminal defences effectively to patrol the boundaries between the most heinous killings and those which may be excusable or partially excusable.[10] And yet, as seen in the way the defence of duress has been removed from murder; how central constitutive features in the human condition such as mercy and despair do not figure in the construction of criminal identities; and how the impact of everyday emotions and psychologies have been attenuated by the partial defence of loss of self-control, questions inevitably arise as to whether the present balance is entirely right.

The Role of Criminal Defences in the Construction of Liability

Rather than engage in general moral evaluation of the defendant's conduct for the purpose of assessing the defendant's fitness for condemnation and punishment, the criminal justice system makes its decision via an analytical prism, which fractures the fault and wrongdoing elements in criminal liability into more basic elements. This prismatic approach aims to effect a separation of the objective facts out of which a criminal prohibition and its attendant mental element is constructed, from the contextual variables which may serve to excuse or justify its breach.[11] The point of compartmentalising the conduct and fault element in this way is, as has been explained, to exercise control over the contextual variables which do or do not affect criminal liability and to minimise the scope for ambiguity and dissent governing what is and what is not censurable behaviour. Historically this analytical division was reflected in a criminal process in which prosecution and defence bore separate burdens.[12] The prosecution bore the burden of proving the basic (inculpatory) elements of the offence and the defence those matters which, like self-defence, operated to exculpate the defendant from liability for that offence. Once upon a time, whether a defence was categorised as an excuse or justification was potentially of great moment. A killer excused of homicide nevertheless forfeited his possessions to the Crown. A justified killer did not. Formal consequences no longer attach to categorising defences in this way. Perhaps they should do. Suppressing the distinction serves to suppress important moral and penological functions of defence doctrine such as the provision of secure labels for different forms of wrongdoing.[13] For example, a person who kills another under the mistaken belief the other was about to commit serious violence, or robs a bank under conditions of duress presently receives an unqualified acquittal. In a sense this is undeserved. After all, in each case the actor has done something which, while understandable and excusable, is nevertheless to be deplored. It might make more sense, then, to register excused wrongdoing with a special verdict, say, 'not guilty by reason of excuse'.[14] It might also justify different evidential or procedural conventions such as a reversal of the burden of persuasion coupled perhaps with a lower standard of proof.[15] Not only would such outcomes chime better with the equivocal moral response which excused wrongdoing tends to elicit it is possible that there would be a greater readiness to accept marginal excuses, such as killing for reasons of compassion, if the consequence was not an outright acquittal. It could also serve as a basis for grafting onto the not guilty verdict enforceable conditions designed to reduce the likelihood that such wrongdoing would be repeated.[16] The defence of automatism is an obvious case in point. In England, the courts, largely for reasons of social defence, have often strained to implement the special verdict of not guilty by reason of insanity or

---

9 Lacey, 'Space, Time and Function: Intersecting Principles of Responsibility Across the Terrain of Criminal Justice' (2007) 1 Crim L & Philos 233, 235.

10 See B Mitchell and J Roberts, *Exploring the Mandatory Life Sentence for Murder* (Hart 2012).

11 RA Duff, *Answering for Crime: Responsibility and Liability in the Criminal Law* (Hart 2007).

12 G Fletcher, *Rethinking Criminal Law* (Little, Brown 1978) ch 7; J Langbein, *The Origins of Adversary Criminal Trial* (OUP 2003) 59.

13 Fletcher (n 12).

14 P Robinson, 'Criminal Law Defences: A Systematic Analysis' (1982) 82 Colum L Rev 199, 209.

15 See A Stein, 'Criminal Defences and the Burden of Proof' (1990) 28 *Coexistence* 82–86.

16 The offence of handling stolen property provides something of a prototype in this respect.

even convict in cases where, although, lacking definitional fault, the wrongdoer shows himself in need of treatment, supervision, or other corrective measures.[17] Clearly the impetus to engage in such practices would be lessened if a different form of acquittal were available which gave courts the powers necessary to minimise the dangers posed by a given excused wrongdoer. Such reasoning will not necessarily apply in cases where the defendant's conduct is justified in the sense of being socially desirable or permissible. Here an unqualified acquittal may be appropriate reflecting the fact that no wrongdoing is attributable to the defendant.[18]

In theory, then, criminal defences operate in tandem with the *mens rea* requirement, refining 'the wording of (offence definitions)' to ensure that the moral purpose of a criminal prohibitions is realised.[19] This is particularly so for justifications, whose normative structure complements and support that of the offences themselves. A simplified analysis of crimes of violence, for example, illustrates why a system of prohibitions grounded in moral norms presupposes also a systematic means of justifying infringements. Crimes of violence, for example, fulfil the dual function of supporting individual autonomy and also upholding the moral principle that hurting people is wrong. The former function plays the major structuring role in the makeup of the offences. Violence is proscribed largely, though not entirely, because it will generally involve an unjustified attack upon individual autonomy. Where autonomy is not unjustly compromised, violence itself is easier to justify. Accordingly, consent, self-defence, and medical necessity usually negate the wrongdoing implicit in acts of violence—cancelling, as one might expect, the duty to be guided by the reasons informing the rule.[20] The same reason—the need to secure individual autonomy—explains the reason not to use force against another and also the reason why that reason is defeated when the other consents, is incapable of consenting where the use of force is in his best interests, or is himself subjecting the other to unjustified force. It explains also why that reason is not defeated if it is contrary to the known wishes of the patient[21] or, in the case of temporarily incompetent patients, if it pre-empts a reasoned choice when the patient recovers consciousness. In each case the moral source (and force) of the offences would make no sense without their corresponding justifications and their own intrinsic limitations.

The idea that criminal defences and offences are different sides of the same coin[22] has prompted the view that the conditions of liability are better analysed without resort to the somewhat artificial categories of *actus reus*, *mens rea*, and defence. Not all of the doctrines comprehended by the phrase *actus reus* refer to the objective state of affairs proscribed by a criminal prohibition. The voluntary act requirement, for example, describes, in a similar manner to excuses, the circumstances under which a person is fairly answerable for a harmful occurrence. Correspondingly, the definitional mental element sometimes helps define the wrongdoing rather than what makes the actor responsible for it. Again, not all questions of fault or responsibility are settled by the *mens rea* doctrines but require resort to the principles governing defences and causation. This replacement of the tripartite separation into the more fundamental separation of the conditions of liability into those of wrongdoing and attribution underpins Fletcher's categorisation of defences into justifications and excuses. The former are relevant to wrongdoing, that is, whether their admitted violation of the rules is in fact an instance of wrongdoing for which they must account. The latter are relevant to attribution, that is, whether the defendant is responsible for their wrongdoing. Although the usefulness of this analysis has subsequently been questioned[23] there is probably no better way of rendering intelligible the fact that those who assist a person acting in a justified fashion, say in self-defence, but not in an excused fashion, say under coercion,

---

17   See, for example, *Lipman* [1969] 3 All ER 410; *R v Sullivan* [1984] AC 156; *Burgess* [1991] 2 All ER 386.

18   Even here, however, there is some dissent. See Fletcher (n 12) ch 6.

19   P Robinson, 'Criminal Law Defences: A Systematic Analysis' (1982) 82 Colum L Rev 199, 209.

20   J Raz (n 7).

21   *St George's Healthcare NHS Trust v. S* [1998] 3 All ER 673; *Re C* [1994] 1 All ER 819; *Malette v Shulman* (1988) 63 OR (2d) 243; *Re W (a minor) (medical treatment)* [1992] 4 All ER 627.

22   RA Duff (n 11). Cf A Loughnan, 'Diminished Responsibility as Hybrid Legal Form' (Mental Disorder and Criminal Justice Conference, Northumbria University, October 2013).

23   For discussion, see P Greenawalt, 'The Perplexing Boundaries of Justification and Excuse' (1984) Colum L Rev 1847; P Robinson (n 19); JC Smith, *Justification and Excuse in the Criminal Law* (Sweet & Maxwell 1989); Fletcher (n 12) ch10; D Husak, 'On the Supposed Priority of Justification to Excuse' (2005) 24 L & Philos 557; J Gardner, 'In Defence of Defences' in *Offences and Defences, Selected Essays in the Philosophy of Criminal Law* (OUP 2007); AP Simester, 'On Justifications and Excuses' in L Zedner and J Roberts (eds) *Principles and Values in Criminal Law and Criminal Justice: Essays in Honour of Andrew Ashworth* (OUP 2012) 95.

also escape criminal liability. Again, it renders intelligible the fact that justified force (no wrongdoing) cannot lawfully be resisted while excused force (wrongdoing without responsibility) can lawfully be resisted.[24]

Perhaps the most important by product of this analysis, however, is that it is capable of affording normative guidance to citizens as to what is they must or must not do in order to avoid state punishment. Antony Duff has based his call for a dual code containing one part for citizens and the other for officials on just such a separation. Justificatory defences, since these serve to qualify the notion of wrongdoing, are properly contained in the code for citizens. Doctors need to know, for example, when they can legitimately perform surgery, or when it is lawful to administer drugs which will accelerate the death of a patient. Ordinary citizens need to know when the use of force is lawful including cases of purposely causing harm. On the other hand, matters going to attribution, such as excuses and principles of causation, should be in the officials' code directing them how to decide whether a person bears responsibility for a given infringement, how it should be graded, or otherwise when it would be inappropriate to prosecute, convict or punish notwithstanding the infringement of a given rule. In principle this should not be included in the citizen's code. The fact that one is coerced, or is provoked, or is suffering from mental abnormality should not be a matter to which a citizen has regard in deciding what he/she is permitted to do, if only because it might alert her to how best to escape punishment. Although Fletcher's wrongdoing/attribution distinction is unable to help with all these questions it seems to provide a basic framework for what should appear in either code.

The Role of Criminal Defences in the Avoidance of Liability

Following this separation of the defences into excuses and justifications, what, if at all, should follow in terms of their constituent elements?[25] I have argued elsewhere that central to the constitution of criminal excuses is the occurrence of some form of crisis of a nature to block the usual inference that those who infringe a primary norm of behaviour manifest the kind of bad character which fits them for condemnation, punishment and the attribution of fault. This is not to take sides in the character versus choice/capacity debate on criminal responsibility.[26] Instead it involves the uncontroversial assumption that for most excuses the considerations which elicit the conclusion that an actor lacked the capacity or fair opportunity to act as the law requires[27] must elicit also the conclusion that they lacked also the bad or dangerous character which fits them for punishment,[28] whether retributive or reductive. There is, however, a meta-theoretical basis for preferring one to the other which is often overlooked. This is that capacity theory endorses, in a way character theory arguably does not, the idea that State Punishment is, at root, problematic.[29] In rooting criminal defences in the absence of the capacity or fair opportunity to conform to a criminal prohibition capacity theory avoids making any link between the fact of criminal responsibility and desert in punishment. It commits itself only to the view that without culpable wrongdoing punishment cannot be deserved and inserts a further precondition for state

24   For discussion see W Wilson (n 6) ch 10.

25   See generally RA Duff (n 11).

26   W. Wilson, 'The Filtering Role of Crisis in the Constitution of Criminal Excuses' Canadian Journal of Law and Jurisprudence Vol. XVII, no. 2 (July 2004) at pp.387–416. For discussion see P Arenella, 'Character, Choice and Moral Agency' in EF Paul, FA Miller and J Paul (eds), *Crime, Culpability and Remedy* (Clarendon Press 1990); N Lacey, 'Character, Capacity, Outcome: Towards a Framework for Assessing the Shifting Pattern of Criminal Responsibility in Modern English Law' in MD Dubber and L Farmer (eds), *Modern Histories of Crime and Punishment: Critical Perspectives on Crime and Law* (Stanford University Press 2007) 14–41; N Lacey, 'The Resurgence of Character: Criminal Responsibility in the Context of Criminalisation' in RA Duff and S Green (eds), *Philosophical Foundations of Criminal Law* (OUP 2013) 151–178.

27   Hart (n 4).

28   Fletcher (n 12).

29   See generally A Brudner, *Punishment & Freedom: A Liberal Theory of Penal Justice* (OUP 2012) and a special issue of the New Criminal Law Review devoted to its analysis: (2011) 14 New Crim L Rev 427; see also RA Duff, 'Blame, Moral Standing and the Legitimacy of the Criminal Trial' (2010) 23 Ratio 123; A Norrie, *Punishment Responsibility and Justice* (Clarendon Press 2000) ch 1; N Lacey, 'Punishment, (Neo)Liberalism & Social Democracy' in J Simon and R Sparks (eds), *The Sage Handbook of Punishment and Society* (Sage Publishing 2012) 260–280.

intervention, namely that the State is not acting oppressively or unfairly.[30] Neither of the competing theories of defences proceed from this premise. For one, if the subject's wrongdoing is in character—for the other, if the subject's wrongdoing is objectively unreasonable—no further condition for State condemnation and punishment is needed. Be that as it may, each theory proceeds from an acknowledgement of the basic building blocks of crisis, and reaction thereto, which structure core criminal defences. The excuses are grounded in the recognition either that the reaction of the defendant was reasonable or that the most balanced amongst us can, in extreme conditions such as trauma, terror, or anger, lose touch with that basic core of reasonableness which invites conformity with legal rules.[31] The basic excuse template uniting these defences ensures, in a manner comparable to defences of reasonable reaction, that it is only these 'one-off' reactions to crisis which are capable of blocking the attribution of morally discreditable behaviour.[32] The importance of crisis is not however, limited to structuring criminal excuses. It also has a role to play in justifications where, we shall see below, in its absence the subject's free and informed choice to breach a primary obligation is less easy to reconcile with the moral and political purpose of the criminal prohibition. [33]

Crisis marks the moral limits within which a workable system of norm enforcement can be achieved. In the case of affirmative defences such as duress, self-defence and necessity crisis helps mark the parameters for the need for, and proportionality of, a subject's action or reaction. For the purpose of the defences of loss of self-control, involuntary intoxication, and physical or mental involuntariness crisis may also deprive individuals of their susceptibility to conform their behaviour to rules. Its major constitutive function in both sets of defences is in ensuring that this susceptibility is rooted in the characteristics of human beings generally rather the specific possibly antisocial or dangerous characteristics of the individual actor.

The Equivocal Role of Crisis in Structuring Criminal Defences

A key function of crisis in the constitution of criminal defences is in the way it helps to structure defences according to shared moral organising themes. Thus, it operates in a comparable way for duress, necessity, and self-defence, ensuring that breaches of a criminal prohibition for the purpose of avoiding harm pose no systemic threat to the rule of law. Its influence can be seen in the way, over time, doctrinal differences for defences with supposedly similar rationales have been ironed out. A notable example involves the doctrinal convergence of coercion and provocation, where for the past 40 years the appellate courts have taken pains to ensure that the reasonableness of the defendant's response to the trigger for action, be it provocation or coercion—was evaluated in the same way, that is according to the objective strength of the trigger rather than the personalised response of the individual. The newly reformed partial defence of loss of self-control takes this affinity to another level by requiring this trigger to be the fear of serious violence, or words or deeds of such gravity as to induce a justifiable sense of being seriously wronged.

This example points up the equivocal nature of crisis in structuring defences, in that it may serve to conceal or misrepresent the appropriate moral basis to a given defence. Although capacity, character and reasons theory each have strengths at the analytical level, their differences at the normative level are considerable.

---

30   See generally RA Duff, *Answering for Crime: Responsibility and Liability in the Criminal Law* (Hart 2007). For recent discussion, see V Tadros, *The Ends of Harm: The Moral Foundations of Criminal Law* (OUP 2011); cf S Uniacke, 'Punishment as Penalty' (2013) Crim L & Philos [online version not yet assigned to issue].

31   For criticism of the view that all excuses reduce to the claim that the defendant's action was reasonable, see J Horder, *Excusing Crime* (OUP 2007); V Tadros, *Criminal Responsibility* (OUP 2005) 286; and W Wilson, 'The Filtering Role of Crisis in the Constitution of Criminal Excuses' (2004) Can JL and Jur XVII. See also D Klimchuk, 'Excuses and Excusing Conditions' in F Tanguay-Renaud and J Stribopoulos (eds), *Rethinking Criminal Law Theory: New Canadian Perspectives in the Philosophy of Domestic, Transnational, and International Law* (Hart 2012) 118.

32   W Wilson, ibid.; W Wilson, 'The Structure of Criminal Defences' [2005] Crim LR 108; P Westen, 'An Attitudinal Theory of Excuse' (2006) L & Philos 289.

33   This is not to say, of course, that this is an invariable rule. Certain excuses or defence groupings, for example, are clearly grounded in individual moral or practical bases, which necessarily exclude the operation of the template. For example, the defence of voluntary withdrawal for accessorial liability requires a very different kind of organising rationale from other excuses and justifications—one based essentially in societal needs rather than fairness to the individual beset by crisis.

In relation to both duress and loss of self-control, for example, it is by no means clear that at the normative level the claim to avoid responsibility is *unequivocally*, as with self-defence, 'my action was a reasonable reaction' to crisis or, as with diminished responsibility, 'my unreasonable action should be excused as a concession to my human frailty'. With loss of self-control, given that it is a partial excuse serving primarily to provide judges with the sentencing discretion which most commentators consider they should have anyway, it is arguable that its doctrinal kin is—and should be—diminished responsibility rather than duress.[34] Both defences deny full responsibility for an action which, on one view, can have no justification, partial or otherwise, on the basis of a behavioural trigger so powerful as to diminish the actor's susceptibility to control by rules. For the one defence the trigger is external. For the other it is internal. The arguable injustice attached to the newly formulated defence is the false logic involved in moving from the premise that the subject's loss of self-control was objectively unjustified, partially or otherwise, to the conclusion that, therefore, the State is justified in punishing.[35] The State must also ensure that the demands it makes on its human subjects are neither oppressive nor unfair.[36] We cannot expect human beings with the constitutional weaknesses of ordinary human beings always to measure up in times of extreme stress, and it would be inappropriate for the state not to recognise this fact.[37] The better alternative, perhaps, would have been to permit the defendant to raise evidence of extreme emotional disturbance triggered by an overpowering event[38] and that, in that context, her failure to adhere to a rule diminished her responsibility for her reaction.[39]

Duress is also usually characterised, like self-defence and necessity, as a defence of reasonable reaction. But this characterisation is out of step with its presentation in doctrine as a defence of moral involuntariness allowed as a concession to human frailty.[40] Indeed, judges often conflate these quite different rationales. Typical is the following statement of Lord Hailsham in *Howe*: 'as a concession to human frailty . . . a reasonable man of average courage is entitled to embrace as matter of choice the alternative which a reasonable man could regard as the lesser of two evils'. If the choice is, from the point of view of reasonable people, the lesser of two evils then it should not be thought of as a concession to human frailty.[41] By contrast, if duress is truly a concession to human frailty, it should be applicable, within limits, even though the choice is not reasonably viewed as a lesser of two evils so long as the circumstances were of a nature to overwhelm the subject's capacity for reasoned choice. People act unpredictably under conditions of extreme stress.[42] This conflation is also indicative of a more general confusion surrounding the interface of duress of circumstances and necessity, one which might well be attributable to the reluctance of judges to state explicitly that necessity exists otherwise than in its excuse form[43].

In fact, this latter confusion serves an important function. It is an easy mistake to make that because a family of defences have similar doctrinal components, they therefore have the same or similar rationale. It is clear to me at least, however, that duress involves two distinct rationales, both of which are served by the same defence structure. The first is that the defendant acted reasonably, if not justifiably. A bank teller who

---

34   R McKay and B Mitchell, 'Provoking Diminished Responsibility: Two Pleas Merging Into One?' [2003] Crim LR 745; cf J Dressler, 'Battered Women Who Kill Their Sleeping Tormentors' in Shute and Simester, *Criminal Theory: Doctrines of the General Part* (OUP 2002).

35   MN Berman, 'Rehabilitating Retributivism' (2013) 32 L & Philos 83; B Rosebury, 'Moore's Moral Facts and the Gap in the Retributive Theory' (2011) 5 Crim L & Philos 361.

36   M Zimmerman, *The Immorality of Punishment* (Broadview Press 2011); N Levy, 'Zimmerman's *The Immorality of Punishment*: A Critical Essay' (2013) Crim L & Philos [online version not yet assigned to issue].

37   This view forms the basis of the corresponding provision of the American Model Penal Code Clause 210.3(1)(b). For further discussion, see V Tadros (n 31) and V Tadros, 'The Characters of Excuse' (2001) 21 OJLS 495, 517.

38   See J. Horder, 'Reshaping the Subjective Element in Provocation' (2005) OJLS 123.

39   See KJM Smith and W Wilson, 'Impaired Voluntariness and Criminal Responsibility' (1993) 13 OJLS 69 and J Horder, 'Pleading Involuntary Lack of Capacity' [1993] CLJ 298.

40   'Threats of immediate death or serious personal violence so great as to overbear the ordinary power of human resistance should be accepted as a (personal) justification for acts which would otherwise be criminal'. Lord Edmund-Davies in *DPP v Lynch* [1975] 1 All ER 913, 917, approving the statement of Murnaghan J in *Whelan* [1934] IR518, 526; cf *R v Rahman* [2010] EWCA 235.

41   cf *Rahman* ibid.

42   V Tadros (n 37).

43   See for example *Pipe* (2012) All ER (D) 238 (May); *Pommell* (1995) 2 Cr App Rep 607; *R v S and L Ltd* (2009) EWCA Crim 85. See notes 66 and 67

calmly and deliberately hands over the contents of a till to an armed robber under threats to her life can avail herself of duress whether or not, through fear, she lost the capacity to resist and so, surely, can her colleague at the neighbouring till who to minimise the stress and danger involved helps her to do so. The second is the more basic claim, considered above, that the State cannot fairly condemn and punish a person simply for manifesting human weakness in the face of crisis. The more valuable issue is how common structural defence elements support such distinct moral claims to avoid punishment since this will advance understanding of their broader role in the constitution of criminal liability. In particular, it may enable a measure to be identified by which to distinguish between true defences from quasi-excuses rooted in the defendant's personality, upbringing, or psychological makeup. And, crucially, it may invigorate those claims to avoid liability which, cut loose from their true rationale have had their ability to do justice unjustifiably attenuated.[44] The view, which is advanced here, is that the common structure ensures that the various rationales of criminal defences complement rather than compete with each other. In short, it illuminates the conditions under which it may be appropriate to excuse an actor for lacking the capacity or fair opportunity of conforming to the standards demanded, or which may reassure us that they did not betray the standards of character which we have come to expect of ordinary decent citizens, or that their action was truly out of character.

The common elements structuring the majority of criminal defences operate to annul the wrongdoing element in a criminal prohibition or block the attribution of morally discreditable behaviour, by virtue of the occurrence of a 'one-off' reaction to crisis which manifests no broader antisocial or dangerous disposition. This, as will now be outlined, involves, in the usual case, some form of direct connection between the prompt and the reaction in the manner of a behavioural 'trigger' rather than a simple normative breakdown. The anti-social disposition in the cases of duress, loss of self-control, self-defence, and necessity is filtered through their respective rationales to require reasonableness and proportionality of reaction (almost) always and in the case of coercion and the remaining defences an absence of prior fault.

The Basic Template

The Trigger

The majority of core defences, including involuntary behaviour, automatism, loss of self-control, duress, necessity, and self-defence are operational only upon proof of an external trigger. This operates whether the basis of the defence is a justification or an excuse and whether the moral claim is whether the defendant acted reasonably as in self-defence or necessity, as reasonably as could be expected as in duress or loss of self-control, or the more profound claim that the trigger deprived the State of any basis upon which to evaluate the behaviour of the actor as in involuntary behaviour or automatism. In each case the trigger performs two key functions. First, it structures the defence in terms amenable to proof.[45] Second, it provides criminal excuses with their moral and political validation. Both of the ruling theories of criminal responsibility, character and capacity theory are united in the rejection of any idea that a person's general life conditions or social context are relevant in deciding his fitness for punishment. We have free will and we must take responsibility for our choices or character however determined they are by factors outside our control. It is only in response to crisis that it is plausible to claim that our choices and character are not authentically ours, as in automatism or involuntary intoxication, or, if authentically ours, nevertheless not indicative of censurable indifference to the interests of others as in the affirmative defences.

In general, the fact that one's situation, or something like it, has been deliberated upon in advance at a collective level sustains a duty of compliance, however much the individual may be (rationally) disposed to disagree. In times of crisis, this reasoning will often not apply. Typically crisis will deprive the actor of recourse to official protection and/or guidance and he/she will be uniquely placed to grasp exactly what needs to be done, or, alternatively, be so overcome by the enormity of the situation that norms of behaviour lose

---

44   Such claims include involuntary intoxication operating as an affirmative defence (*R v Kingston* [1993] All ER 373 Court of Appeal) rather than a failure of proof defence (*R v Kingston* [1994] 3 All ER 353 House of Lords), brainwashing, and mercy killing.

45   *R v Shayler* [2001] EWCA Crim 1977.

all power. The constituent elements of the trigger for each of the affirmative defences are, therefore, broadly similar. There must be an evil or threat of harm to be avoided (necessity, self-defence, duress and loss of self-control), or objectively provocative words or deeds (loss of self-control). For each defence, the criminal conduct which it is sought to justify or excuse must be directly attributable to the threats or evils which are relied upon. The defences are unavailable if the action taken was for ulterior reasons. A person cannot rely on either self-defence or loss of self-control if motivated by revenge rather than the triggering event.[46] A person cannot rely on duress if, although the subject of a mortal threat, the true trigger for action was blackmail.[47] Further, a person cannot rely on duress or necessity if they are unable to point to any specific threat, and its source, which prompted the reaction.[48] Similarly, a person cannot rely on loss of self-control if the defence are not able to point to any specific provoking words or deeds which prompted the reaction.[49]

With affirmative defences the trigger provides the moral focus, for the actor's claim that he acted reasonably (self-defence, necessity), or could not, with justice, reasonably be expected to react any better than he did, in breaching the primary norm (duress, provocation). This point is made clearly in *R v Shayler* in relation to duress of circumstances and necessity, which were the basis of the defendant's case in answer to a charge under the Official Secrets Act:

> [I]t is inherent in the defence that it has ingredients which Mr Shayler is not in a position to establish. He cannot identify the action by some external agency which is going to create the imminent (if not immediate) threats to the life and limb of members of the general public as a result of the security service's alleged abuses and blunders. This is a fundamental ingredient of the defence. Without it, it is impossible to test whether there was sufficient urgency to justify the otherwise unlawful intervention. It is also impossible to apply the proportionality test. Furthermore, if it is possible to identify the members of the public at risk this will only be by hindsight. This creates difficulty over the requirement of responsibility. Mr Shayler's justification for what he did lacks the required degree of precision. There is no close nexus between his disclosure and the possible injury to members of the public. Putting it simply there was no necessity or duress as those words are ordinarily understood.[50]

The trigger also serves, therefore, to escape both the free will conundrum and also the rule of law problem which informed Lord Denning's rejection of a general defence of necessity in *Southwark*[51] and which later released from the confines of that defence the less compromising claim of duress of circumstances. If all our choices are determined in one way or another, it still makes moral and political sense to require the critical determinant in any excuse or justification to be rooted in the characteristics of human beings generally rather the specific, perhaps antisocial or dangerous, characteristics of the actor.[52] The trigger facilitates the making of such a judgement.

The trigger performs a comparable role in the defence of loss of self-control. Indeed, in domestic law the word first appears in this context in a criminal statute. In *Dawes, Hatter, Bowyer*[53] the Lord Chief Justice distinguished between (general) determinants and (specific) 'triggers' by reference to events issuing from a marriage breakup: Although the fallout from the breakup of a relationship might well create a qualifying trigger, as where the deceased makes particularly wounding deeds or remarks,[54] the mere fact of the breakup of a relationship, of itself, would not normally constitute circumstances of a sufficiently grave character to render

---

46   *R v Ibrams and Gregory* (1981) 74 Cr App R 154; *R v Hussain & Hussain [2010]* EWCA Crim 94.

47   *Singh* [1972] 1 WLR 1600; *Valderrama-Vega* [1985] Crim LR 220.

48   *Shayler* (n 44).

49   *Acott* [1997] 1 All ER 706, House of Lords; *R v Grant* [2010] EWCA Crim 3339; *R v Bowyer* [2013] EWCA Crim 322.

50   Para 66.

51   *Southwark LBC v Williams* [1971] Ch 734, 746.

52   So, in *R v Rodger* [1998] 1 Cr App R 143, Sir Patrick Russell said that to allow duress of circumstances in the absence of an external trigger would amount to a 'licence to commit crime dependent on the personal characteristics and vulnerability of the offender'.

53   [2013] EWCA Crim 322.

54   As occurred in *Clinton, R v (2012) EWCA Crim 2* and to which the Lord Chief Justice referred in reaching this conclusion.

this determinant a 'qualifying' trigger.[55] A marriage breakup, particularly those involving 'sexual infidelity', is always fraught with tension and difficulty, with the possibility of misunderstanding and the potential for apparently irrational fury (stemming) from a sense of betrayal and heartbreak, and crushed dreams.[56] That this is an understandable response does not mean that it is appropriate to attribute it to a triggering event.

This is so also in relation to automatism where the criminal law has sought to filter involuntary behaviours which are genuine one-offs from those which are not and so are apposite for either punishment,[57] or some form of preventive/therapeutic regimen.[58] It does so by requiring the excusing trigger to be an external event rather than an internal condition.[59] Many supposed internal conditions which may dispose to criminal wrongdoing can, of course, be triggered by external factors. For example, sleepwalking can be triggered by alcohol, medication, or stress. Since these are normal human conditions which can be expected to reoccur, the determinant has been interpreted as the internal condition rather than the external prompt which gave rise to it.[60] Diabetes provides another example. In *Hennessy* the defendant, a diabetic, took a motor car without consent whilst disqualified from driving. He was suffering hypoglycaemia at the time due to a failure to take insulin, attributable to stress and depression. These determinants were induced by external factors, namely the breakup of the defendant's marriage and problems at work. The Court of Appeal ruled that although these were external factors, they 'lacked the feature of novelty or accident' necessary to replace the internal condition of stress and depression as the imputable cause of the defendant's failure to take insulin and the consequences which ensued. In other words the trigger must be direct, immediate and overwhelming to explain the failure to take insulin and excuse the defendant's consequent forgetfulness rather than just a powerful determinant.[61] Here it was not. He was 'just depressed'. In theory, at least, sleepwalking or hypoglycaemia following post-traumatic stress, for example, being the victim of a car crash or physical violence should be treated as externally triggered.

Thus a threshold is created, albeit a somewhat vague one, between behavioural frailties signalling a potentially antisocial or otherwise dangerous disposition and those attributable to being a normal human being. It is only 'one-off' reactions to external crisis which are capable of blocking the attribution of morally discreditable or otherwise objectionable behaviour. If the reaction is not a normal response to crisis then this must be reflected in the nature of the defendant's claim to avoid censure and punishment.

The Reaction

Central to the idea of a 'trigger' is an event which is of a nature to excite a reaction. Accordingly, all the affirmative defences require, albeit to varying degrees, the reaction to be a spontaneous one. Again the variations are controlled by the rationale of the defence. The relationship between the rationale and the nature of the reaction has been explored most thoroughly in relation to loss of self-control and its progenitor and precursor, provocation.[62] The rationale of each distinguishes those whose behaviour is triggered by a socially condonable emotion—fear or justified moral outrage—rather than a considered desire to avenge or to protect oneself from further instances of violence. The former sentiment would offer no excuse of any kind. The latter would need to conform to the strictures of self-defence for it to be consistent with respect for the rule of law. Although the reaction must be attributable to a triggering event it is now clear that it need not follow immediately.[63] This is because loss of self-control is, by definition, a personalised response to stress. As

---

55   '(W)e agree with Judge Goldsack that the reality of this case was that the death of the deceased was a direct consequence of the appellant's response to the breakdown of the relationship, and that there was no particular feature of the evidence to suggest any justifiable sense in the appellant of being seriously wronged'. *Dawes, Hatter, Bowyer* at para 65.

56   ibid.

57   See, for example, *Quick and Paddison* [1973] QB 910.

58   *Bratty v A-G for Northern Ireland* [1963] AC 386.

59   *Bratty* ibid; *Kemp* [1957] 1 QB 399; *Sullivan* [1984] AC 156; *Hennessy* [1989] 2 All ER 9.

60   Compare causation doctrine where, as *Blaue* [1975] 1 WLR 1411 illustrates, intervening causes are counterposed to conditions. In the case of both defence and causation doctrines, this distinction operates to isolate everyday determinants from those of a sufficiently extraordinary character to block normal channels of attribution.

61   ibid.

62   Law Commission, *Partial Defences to Murder* (Law Com No 290, 2004); Law Commission, *Murder, Manslaughter and Infanticide* (Law Com No 304, 2006).

63   *Ahluwalia* [1992] 4 All ER 889.

such, it can be triggered in different ways depending upon the individual, the context, and the nature of the triggering event. A typical example of a delayed loss of self-control is that experienced by the victims of domestic violence. Judge LCJ explained this in *R v Dawes* as follows:

> Provided there was a loss of control, it does not matter whether the loss was sudden or not. A reaction to circumstances of extreme gravity may be delayed. Different individuals in different situations do not react identically, nor respond immediately. Thus for the purposes of the new defence, the loss of control may follow from the cumulative impact of earlier events. For the purposes of this first ingredient, the response to what used to be described as 'cumulative provocation' requires consideration in the same way as it does in relation to cases in which the loss of control is said to have arisen suddenly.

Immediacy or suddenness is, however, of constitutive importance to duress, although here, once again, we must qualify this by reference to the form of duress, that is, if it is one of moral involuntariness or of reasonable reaction to crisis. In the case of the former, which will typically involve duress by threats, in the absence of an emergency which requires immediate action, the basis of the excuse, which is that it would not be just to expect the defendant to overcome his fear, is annulled. If the threat is not an immediate one there is no reason to credit the claim that the defendant's normative resources were overpowered. Contrast this with duress of circumstances and necessity where the defendants moral claim will generally be one of reasonableness, that is, that it was reasonable for an ordinary human being to choose a course of action which did not sacrifice his life or limb or that of another for whom he is responsible, or, in the case of necessity, was a reasonable means of avoiding a greater evil. For these two defences the trigger necessarily is more flexible, acting more by way of the turning of a tap, which in time but not immediately will cause the drowning of the victim, rather than the pressing of a trigger of a gun which will strike immediately. In *Pommell*[64] the defence was held available to protect a defendant for possessing a firearm without a certificate when, on his account, he was in possession of the gun to prevent its owner from using it for a revenge killing. Although arguably more a case of necessity than of duress of circumstances it is clear, in either case, that imminence, rather than immediacy, of threat was sufficient to admit the excusing trigger.[65] Another example is *R v S and L*[66] The defendants' defence to a charge under the Private Security Industry Act for employing unlicensed guards was that this was done to address the risk of terrorist attack on their premises. They contended that there was no alternative means for protecting those who might be passing by or those who were in those premises from death or serious injury other than by protection to be afforded by the guards. The Court of Appeal, allowing the appeal, agreed that if these steps were necessary to guard against an immediate or imminent threat of a major terrorist attack on a retail store and there was no other way of avoiding the risk to those in the store or passing by, then this could ground a defence of necessity.

The American Model Penal Code's definition of necessity has no immediacy or imminent risk requirement, legitimating defiance of a criminal prohibition if this is a lesser evil than 'the harm or evil sought to be avoided by such conduct'.[67] More generally, however, it is almost axiomatic that necessity's core cases do involve one-off emergencies of a character similar to duress. The actor pushes the victim out of the way of the oncoming car, breaks the speed limit to get a dangerously ill relative to hospital, throws cargo from a ship which would otherwise sink, moors his boat in another's dock in the teeth of a storm. The individual reacting to a one-off emergency of this character does not appoint himself as a legislator in his own cause and his conduct has no implications for future cases. By contrast, where there is no immediate necessity the individual, as has been explained, must allow himself to be guided by society's *ex ante* collective decisions. We may disagree, as we may well be disposed to if **we** are homeless, starving, or the victim of some other cruel circumstance, but we must be guided by the law's rather than our own ideas of the guiding principles obtaining in a given predicament. In *Re F*, however, the justificatory effect of the trigger was acknowledged with regard to medical necessity, and with it, the acknowledgment that dire emergencies are not always of the essence so long as

---

64 [1995] 2 Cr App Rep 607.
65 See note 44
66 ibid
67 Neither does Brooke LJ's definition of necessity in his judgement in *Re A (conjoined twins)* [2001] 2 WLR 480.

there is no challenge to the rule of law and were in the best interests of the patient. Thus operations on those incapable of consenting, as well as other interventions, may be justified even if performed for other than immediately necessary clinical reasons;[68] 'these might include such humdrum matters as routine medical or dental treatment, even simple care such as dressing and undressing and putting to bed'.[69] Significantly, in *Pipe*, which was not a case of medical necessity, the defence was held to potentially justify the action of a father who broke the speed limit in order to get his injured son promptly to hospital, although the injury was by no means life threatening.[70]

The political and moral underpinnings of self-defence also imply immediacy. Again we distinguish between action taken in response to an attack, or threatened attack, and angry aggression. At the political level, the privilege afforded by self-defence to 'take the law into our own hands' must be a privilege which is consistent with the generalised subjection of individuals to governance by rules. It would not be if respect for autonomy allowed us to take strategic decisions to oppose non-existent or uncrystallised threats with violence or engage in angry retaliation. Doctrine effects the balancing act between respect for autonomy and the rule of law by again requiring the trigger to be of sufficient urgency to justify defensive action without requiring the threat always to have crystallised. Three distinct situations can be identified. First, where a threat is not immediate a pre-emptive strike may be permissible if it is nevertheless imminent. In the words of Lord Griffith[71]: 'A man about to be attacked does not have to wait for his assailant to strike the first blow or fire the first shot; circumstances may justify a pre-emptive strike'. Second, where a threat is as yet uncrystallised pre-emptive action may be taken so long as it falls short of the actual deployment of force. So arming oneself with petrol bombs[72] or threatening to kill someone[73] may be legitimate defensive action in the face of a future threat of violence. Third, in cases of law enforcement, preventive force may be used to prevent the probable commission of future offences.[74]

Immediacy is inevitably not of the essence of automatism. As with loss of self-control, the subject's reaction inevitably varies with the nature of the trigger and the effect this has on the subject's mental processes. It is inevitably a less precisely focussed excuse than loss of self-control or duress, operating, much as the defence of infancy arguably does, as a kind of exculpatory wild card. For crimes of *mens rea*, at least, it seems enough that the defendant can adduce evidence that his responsiveness to the specific reasons why he should act as the rule requires may have been affected. Here the basic excuse template is doing much of the exculpatory work—the undeniable fact of external trauma simply serves to block the attribution of wrongdoing to the actor, whether or not the evidence stacks up that the defendant did not know what she was doing, whether it was wrong, whether her action was at all out of character, and so on. Its ambivalence— unlike insanity or diminished responsibility, automatism floats relatively unchecked in the space between denials of capacity, denials of fair opportunity, and denials of bad character—allows its use to bridge the evidential gap occurring wherever, for crimes of *mens rea*, some external trauma precedes some form of erratic antisocial behaviour by the defendant. This is particularly necessary given the absence of the kind of normative connection between the trigger and the reaction appearing in duress and loss of self-control. In duress the crime is committed because of the threat and it is framed by the threat. In loss of self-control, similarly, the crime is committed because of the trigger and is framed by the provoking trigger. By contrast, with automatism, a person may escape liability for robbery simply upon the basis that she has been raped or hit on the head despite the absence of any conceptual connection between the two events.[75] In this context the subject's mental abnormality can tell us nothing more about what prompted the reaction other than that she may have been temporarily unresponsive to the reasons why she should not act as she did. The excuse is

---

68   Cf *Re Eve* (1986) 31 DLR (4th) 1 CSC.
69   *Re F* [1989] 2 All ER 545, HL at 564.
70   [2012] All ER (D) 238 (May).. See note 44.
71   *Beckford v The Queen* [1988] AC 130.
72   *A-G's Reference (No. 2 of 1983)* [1984] 1 All ER 988.
73   [1986] 2 All ER 449.
74   s 3(1) Criminal Law Act 1977.
75   See, for example, *R v T* [1990] Crim LR 256.

operational—in other words, notwithstanding any clear indication as to the mental processes or lack of them which led to the wrongdoing.[76]

The Reaction Must Not Manifest an Antisocial Or Otherwise Dangerous Disposition

The trigger and reaction elements in the criminal defence template are inevitable constituents of the traditional liberal notion of responsibility rooted in individuated wrongful action. So, a person is guilty of murder if he/she intentionally kills another, *unless* this reaction is triggered by an event which blocks her community's disposition to hold her to account. By this epitome, it becomes clear that although the trigger and the reaction are preconditions of fairly holding someone to account for their harmful actions this is not the full story. The subject of criminal sanction is not an isolated individual whose actions affect unrelated others. He/she is one who lives in a community whose values define and constitute her as a person and as a subject. Inevitably, therefore, both offences and defences typically manifest those values in the determination of wrongfulness and in the determination of blame.[77]

All the affirmative defences are constructed to require either reasonableness of reaction, or alternatively in the case of duress, sometimes, and loss of self-control, always, a reaction which does not indicate an inherent susceptibility to overreact to the triggering event. Provocation demanded a reaction to the trigger which is not out of line with what we have come to expect from ordinary people. Its replacement, loss of self-control, exaggerates this excusing feature by removing explicitly from the potential coverage of the excuse reactions which display socially discreditable attitudes, thus withdrawing from the jury any power to condone them. The trigger is qualified by assuming the reactor to have the capacity and fair opportunity to control his/her reaction in anything other than extreme conditions—fear of serious violence to himself of another, or otherwise words or deeds of exceptional gravity. As a measure of this emphasis on the need for the reaction to be consistent with reasonableness defined as evincing proper respect for the autonomy and physical welfare of others, sexual jealousy or possessiveness is explicitly identified as an attitude which will not justifiably trigger a loss of self-control.

There are comparable restrictions on the reactions characterising the other affirmative defences, each of which is tailored to the respective rationale of the defence. For duress the trigger is inoperative if it acts only because the defendant lacks the courage and/or steadfastness of the ordinary citizen. On the fact of it this may seem unjust. If moral involuntariness, as well as reasonableness of reaction, lies at the heart of the defence, why should it matter whether the fear was reasonably entertained or not or whether the reaction was a reasonable response thereto? Either moral involuntariness does not lie at the heart of the defence or there is another reason why excuses demand reactions to measure up to objective standards of courage. The usual reason given is that duress, like all excuses, operates by denying moral blame. Moral blame is not negated by claiming one is unduly susceptible to fear any more than it is, on a charge of theft, that one is a slave to temptation.[78] The more relevant insight, for the purpose of this chapter, is that defences are structured in this way for a purpose—to rid defence claims of their susceptibility to collapse under the weight of the free will conundrum. Specifically, to ensure that determinants of action whose consequences do not follow a predictable cause and effect sequence are ignored, or else are deflected into capacity based excuses such as diminished responsibility. The structure of all core defences follows this route, demanding the defendant's action to be within striking distance of what we have come to expect from those facing a crisis even if, through

---

76   It goes without saying that the courts are unwillingly to acknowledge this. See most recently *R v Coley*; *R v McGhee*; *R v Harris* [2013] EWCA Crim 223, in which the Court of Appeal, while acknowledging that to raise automatism the behaviour must be involuntary, and that if it is not involuntary but irrational this can only affect liability if *mens rea* is absent, did not explain how questions of intention can be isolated from questions of rationality.

77   For general discussion see RA Duff, 'Punishment, Communication, and Community' (2003); Sandel, *Liberalism and the Limits of Justice* (Cambridge University Press 1982); Walzer, 'The Communitarian Critique of Liberalism' [1990] Political Theory 6–23; Etzioni, 'The Responsive Community: A Communitarian Perspective' (1996) 61 ASR 1–11.

78   Being 'unnaturally cowardly . . . is the very ground for blaming him. It could hardly serve as an excuse. Such defences are not accorded in moral any more than in legal judgment'. S Kadish, 'Excusing Crime' (1987) 75 Cal L Rev 257, 276.

personal weakness or vulnerability, that expectation is unrealistic.[79] The criminal law's only concession is to build into the characteristics of the subject to be judged those which, unlike mental illness or lack of moral fortitude, are not authentic expressions of who they are but are characteristics which could be visited upon any rational person such as a reduced capacity to threats attributable to cumulative violence at the hands of the coercer.[80]

Again, the threats of the coercer do not amount to an operative or qualifying trigger if, placed as (s)he was, (s)he could have avoided being in the line of fire by avoiding the company of dangerous criminals.[81] In either case the subject of the criminal prohibition is the socially responsible and conscientious citizen. In each case the claim to avoid punishment—that it is unjust to be required to make a personal sacrifice for the sake of conformity to the law—is trumped by the subject's failure to avoid the crisis by acquitting themselves responsibly.[82] For duress of circumstances we have seen that there must be no other way of avoiding the threat, although clearly this restriction is qualified by reasonableness.[83] In necessity, where a threat of immediate harm is not the only qualifying trigger, what is 'needed' to advance the common good will often be open to interpretation and so the question as to whether the action was necessary is also examined through the conceptual filter of reasonableness. So the legitimacy of performing a sterilisation operation on a woman lacking mental capacity was not decided on the basis that the operation was a true 'necessity' in the duress sense of there 'being no other option' as it might have been for clinical reasons, but whether it was a reasonable means of preventing an undesirable pregnancy. For necessary action, we can, in other words, substitute 'reasonable' or even 'not unreasonable'.[84]

By contrast with duress, there are good reasons intrinsic to the defence why, for self-defence, the threat qualifies as a trigger to action, irrespective of the actor's ability to retreat and irrespective of his own responsibility for provoking the crisis.[85] This is because the socially responsible and conscientious citizen is not expected to sacrifice his own autonomy or interests in the face of an unjustified threat of harm. What he may not lawfully do is sacrifice the autonomy or interests **of another person**. Self-defence, by contrast with duress, is, in other words, a claim of right. The subject of such a claim does not seek to excuse his conduct but insists that his autonomy is respected both by those who would seek to undermine it and the State whose function it is to support it. Respect for autonomy means that human beings cannot be expected to retreat in the challenges thereto.[86]

Automatism is also responsive to the doctrine of prior fault, indicating that, unlike insanity, and like duress, it is a true excuse, rather than—as it is sometimes characterised—an exemption from liability. As with duress, action is morally involuntary only if it is an *unavoidable* reaction to crisis. Responsibility is not avoided simply because the accused was temporarily not a mistress of her own body at the moment of performing the *actus reus*. Intoxicant-induced automatism does not negate voluntariness any more than it can be used to support duress or mistake. Responsibility is avoided only where, on the basis of a broad interpretation of the time-frame surrounding the fatal event, it is inappropriate to attribute authorship of the relevant event to the accused because of the overwhelming influence of some other factor without the defendant's control. So, if a lorry driver falls asleep at the wheel due to a failure to take sufficient rests, liability for a consequent traffic offence is justified on the basis that the latter chose to bring about the conditions which he is now claiming

---

79   See, for example, *(Tony) Martin* [2001] EWCA Crim 2245.

80   *Emery* (1993) 14 Cr App R (S) 394.

81   *R v Hasan* [2005] UKHL 25; *Mullally* [2012] EWCA Crim 687.

82   See P Robinson, 'Causing the Conditions of One's Own Defence' (1985) 71 Va L Rev 1; cf Larry Alexander, 'Causing the Conditions of One's Defense: A Theoretical Non-Problem' (2013) Crim L & Philos [online article not yet assigned to an issue].

83   See *R v S and L Ltd* [2009] 2 Cr App R 171.

84   *Re F* [1989] 2 All ER 545, HL; *R v Bournewood Community and Mental Health NHS Trust* [1998] 3 All ER 289.

85   So, in *Field* [1972] Crim LR 435, the defendant was permitted to rely on self-defence although he had had ample opportunity to escape a threatened attack. The court concluded that the defendant had no duty to quit premises he was lawfully inhabiting simply to avoid attack. By contrast, in *Gill*, the defence was not available where the defendant had been afforded a good opportunity to raise the alarm and escape the threat. *Gill* [1963] 2 All ER 688.

86   The victim of coercion has then two means of doing the right thing, either to seek police protection or to meet coercion with defensive force.

to support his defences. As with duress he voluntarily traded in the promise of future freedom from State coercion for freedom now.

Proportionality

For all the affirmative defences, a requirement of proportionality serves to underwrite the requirement that the defendant's action or reaction be consistent with the conduct and character of the socially responsible legal subject. Proportionality is intrinsic to the notion of necessity, with its demand that the action taken is proportionate to the evil sought to be avoided. If it were not it could not serve to advance the common good which is necessity's basic rationale. This is most obvious in necessity's classical utilitarian form which balances on a cost/benefit basis the social harm which will result if the rule were honoured against that which will result if it were not. In *Re A (conjoined twins)*[87] this cost/benefit analysis was stated as follows:

- The act is needed to avoid inevitable and irreparable evil;
- No more should be done than is reasonably necessary for the purpose to be achieved; and
- The evil inflicted must not be disproportionate to the evil avoided.

In truth, however, while proportionality on a lesser of two evils basis is necessary it is not in itself enough to constitute the justification. This is because of the moral priority afforded to individual rights over collective interests. It is not, and in the foreseeable future, never will be lawful to force an individual to give blood although many lives might thereby be saved. As a basic minimum requirement, therefore, a commitment to proportionality must ensure that the action taken does not involve a deliberate victimisation of an innocent person. Notwithstanding Brooke LJ's statement of principle, the central justifying feature in *Re A* was not simply that it was necessary but that the essence of the act to be performed was a lifesaving operation on the stronger twin, Mary; that the death of Jodie, the weaker twin, would occur by way of double effect; and that, because Jodie's continued existence was dependent upon the continued existence of Mary, the choice to be taken was to permit the death of both children or only one.[88] The operation was justified, in other words, because the setback to Mary's interests would not take the form of a direct attack on her person and autonomy using her as a means to an end. In this latter respect the restriction shows some structural affinities with self-defence where, again, the act's justified purpose is directed at protecting the autonomy of A rather than the harming of B. It is this non-utilitarian feature in self-defence which explains why, although proportionality of a kind is necessary, it is not thought proper to insist upon a lesser of two evils measure. So while the defender is generally permitted to kill if fatal force is necessary to prevent being killed herself, or raped or maimed she may not, with impunity, kill to defend her possessions, her home, or less serious interference with her physical interests even supposing this was the only means available to her.

The requirement of proportionality in self-defence is, by contrast with the other defences, problematic, however. If, as seems likely, the defence is so constituted as to vindicate a general right to autonomy and freedom from unwarranted interference it is not immediately obvious why the victim of an attack or threatened attack on his person or property should need to look beyond that which is necessary to fulfil that aim. The necessary supposition here, reflected also in the organisational bifurcation of criminal law into regulatory (harm preventing) and core (autonomy-sustaining) offences, is that autonomy is only one among many interests protected by the criminal law. Accordingly, self-defence, as with other justificatory defences which accord individuals the permission to take 'the law into their own hands', must reflect and express the overall structure of values by which our system of criminal offences is ordered.[89] Those values include

---

87   ibid (n 65) 1052.

88   In the words of Walker LJ, the 'operation was an act of necessity to avoid inevitable and irreparable evil; that its purpose was to preserve the life of J and not to cause the death of M'. For discussion, see M Bohlander, 'Of Shipwrecked Sailors, Unborn Children, Conjoined Twins and Hijacked Airplanes – Taking Human Life and the Defence of Necessity' (2006) JCL147; T Hoernle, 'Hijacked Airplanes: May They be Shot Down?' (2007) 10 New Crim L Rev 582.

89   See discussion above (nn 19–22).

the respect accorded to individual autonomy but also, ultimately, the sanctity of life, and the general moral principle that hurting people is wrong. If consent is no defence to murder or duelling it is because society's moral values do not ultimately reduce to an uncomplicated respect for individual autonomy. Likewise, what would it tell us about the hierarchy of values supporting criminal doctrine if fatal force could be used to repel an attack on property if not that property rights took priority over the value of human life?[90] A defender must, in other words, look to matters other than her understandable desire to protect her interests against unjustified attack in settling upon the appropriate mode of response. She must balance the threat to her own autonomy and physical interests against the setback to the other's interests were that threat to be successfully repelled. In balancing that threat she must acquit herself as befits a socially responsible subject, properly alert to the values by which the common good is advanced, including respect for human life. An aggressor does not forfeit the protection of the criminal law entirely. His interests in life and bodily security are valued as highly as those of the aggressee, but if all else fails, respect for the aggressee's interests permits her to put her interests before those who pose an unjust threat to the limited degree necessary to sustain the moral credentials of the criminal law.

Both forms of duress have a more exacting proportionality requirement rooted in necessity's 'lesser of two evils' requirement. The difference between coercion and necessity in this context is that with the latter the choice taken is not objectively the lesser of two evils—if it were we would be dealing with a case of necessity—but because from the defendant's point of view and others who may be caught in his predicament it certainly seems to be. The apparent basis to the defendant's claim to escape liability is that since reasonable people might have acted similarly, it does not merit blame. However, this analysis might be questioned in the light of the widespread death or serious injury requirement in duress. After all, it may be thought that any harm is proportionate for the point of view of the defendant if the threat is enough to make the reasonable person do as the accused did. Again this points to the as-yet-under–theorised idea that the courts are conflating two different claims to avoid punishment, either of which, in theory, should be sufficient. These are, as in typical cases of duress of circumstances, that the action was objectively reasonable without being justifiable and, alternatively, as in typical cases of duress by threats, that although objectively unreasonable the State would be asking too much to expect the actor to sacrifice himself for the greater good. In short, it is not the reasonableness of the defendant's reaction to coercion which excuses but rather the sheer futility and/or moral impropriety of demanding an impossible sacrifice.

Conclusion

All the core defences manifest a similar structure. This has encouraged the belief that defences share a common rationale whether that rationale be, in the case of core excuses, that the defendant's wrongdoing was out of character, was as reasonable as could be expected in the circumstances or was not the product of a fair and reasoned choice. These various rationales tend to hinder our understanding of how defences work. It encourages us to find moral affinities between defences where there are none. It encourages inappropriate doctrinal convergences between defences rooted in different claims to avoid punishment and in so doing compromise their ability to deliver criminal justice. A better way of understanding the common structural elements in core defences is to see these as central to any effective rule enforcement system. The core criminal defences of self-defence, duress, necessity, provocation, and automatism differentiate those things which happen to us by virtue of who we are and the things which happen to us opportunistically, where we are singled out by an unruly fate to cope with emergency.[91] In the case of affirmative defences such as duress, self-

---

90   The recent amendment to the proportionality requirement in self-defence in relation to householders under threat in their own home challenges this supposition. Section 43 of the Crime and Courts Act 2013 adds a new subsection (5A) to section 76 of the 2008 Act. The effect of subsection (5A) is to apply a lower standard of reasonableness of reaction to the householder, than for the defence generally, to give householders 'greater latitude in terrifying or extreme situations where they may not be thinking clearly about the precise level of force that is necessary to deal with the threat faced.' Only if the reaction is grossly disproportionate will the householder be denied the defence.

91   This is not to say, of course, that this is an invariable rule. Certain excuses or defence groupings, for example, are clearly grounded in individual moral or practical bases which necessarily exclude the operation of the template. As an

defence, and necessity crisis helps mark the parameters for the need for, reasonableness of, and proportionality of a subject's action or reaction. For the purpose of physical or mental involuntariness crisis may also deprive individuals of their susceptibility to conform their behaviour to rules. Its major constitutive function in these defences, is in ensuring that this susceptibility is rooted in the characteristics of human beings, generally rather the specific possibly anti-social or dangerous characteristics of the actor. In consequence, the common structure affords a means of escaping the free will conundrum by ensuring that triggers rather than simple determinants are required for moral responsibility to be compromised, and ensuring also an effective and just balance between the rule of law and fairness to the individual in cases where public and private interests collide.

---

simple illustration the defence of voluntary withdrawal for accessorial liability requires a very different kind of organising rationale from other excuses and justifications—one based essentially in societal needs rather than fairness to the individual beset by crisis.

Chapter 2

Avoiding Criminal Liability and Excessive Punishment for Persons Who Lack Culpability: What Can and Should Be Done?

Bob Sullivan

Introduction

A criminal conviction is typically followed by some form of punishment.[1] The term 'punishment' indicates some hard measure, some setback to core interests of the person punished. Such a hostile intervention by the state against a subject (D) should rest on proof that D has done something or failed to do something and this puts him in a bad light. In other words he is at fault for what he has done or failed to do. Finding D to be at fault entails that his conduct was a wrong, a wrong for which he is culpable. Criminal convictions and culpability should be bedfellows. Except, of course, they are not necessarily bedfellows, as things stand now in English and Welsh criminal law.

As every criminal lawyer knows there are thousands of strict liability offences, which do not require proof of any culpability or a limited culpability that encompasses only some of the elements of the offence.[2] The many reverse burdens of proof allow convictions where culpability is suspected rather than proved.[3] These pervasive features of modern criminal law are unlikely to change any time soon, if they ever do. In any critique of this state of affairs it is important to keep a sense of proportion. Suppose D receives a huge and wholly unexpected tax demand, entailing the cancellation of an important business project. He may be far more aggrieved about the tax he has to pay than the speeding fine he paid with barely a shrug because if he had not exceeded speed limits on that day he would have missed his holiday flight. Yet it remains the case that the criminal justice system can do things to persons subject to its jurisdiction far more grievous than any tax demand. If D is a person of 'positively good character'[4]—an honest man disinclined to use violence in his interactions with others—to such a person, the threat of imprisonment must seem to be merely theoretical. But despite his confidence in the security of his liberty such a man may find himself in prison not through any miscarriage of justice but under due process of law. Moreover, the events that lead to his imprisonment may leave his 'positively good character' intact in terms of morality, if not in law.

Below there will be analysis and critique of two Court of Appeal cases which exemplify great variation in the importance attached to culpability in terms of liability and punishment.

---

1 Sometimes there will be no retributivist or deterrent aspect as with absolute or conditional discharges.

2 It seems that 45% of offences triable in the Crown Court in England and Wales have a strict liability element. Andrew Ashworth and Meredith Blake, 'The Presumption of Innocence in English Criminal Law' [1996] Crim LR 306. See also James Chalmers and Fiona Leverick, 'Tracking the Creation of Criminal Offences' [2013] Crim LR 543.

3 See Ashworth and Blake (n 2).

4 This was the description given to the two defendants in Rehman and Woods [2005] EWCA Crim 2056, who were each convicted of a serious crime and imprisoned.

Culpability and the Court of Appeal: Two Contrasting Approaches

(1) In *Rehman and Woods*,[5] D (1) and D (2) were convicted and imprisoned for possession offences under the Firearms Act 1968.[6] Both defendants were men of positively good character, with no previous criminal convictions. D (1) was a recent graduate of Imperial College London and prior to his imprisonment was a highly thought of employee working for Customs and Excise. D (2) was a successful business man who among other things gave training in the use of firearms to the police. It was accepted that neither man had any criminal project in respect of the weapons they possessed. How then did they end up in prison?

D (1) bought a replica weapon online. He was a collector of miscellaneous objects which he would mount on the walls of the family home. He was undecided how he would display the replica in his collection of objects and, pending his decision, put it under his bed in its wrapping. He was unaware that the replica could be adapted into a firearm. The fact that it could be converted made its possession an offence of strict liability punishable with a minimum term of five years unless there were 'exceptional circumstances'.[7] The Court of Appeal found that exceptional circumstances existed and reduced his sentence of five years to one year.[8]

D(2) was a keen weapons collector and pursuit of this hobby led to convictions for minor offences under the Firearms Act 1968 which did not carry the minimum five year sentence. However some twenty years previously he had taken possession of a shortened shotgun from his grandfather which he put in his attic where it remained *in situ* until found in a police search.[9] He received a five year sentence for possession of this weapon, the Court of Appeal confirming that there were no exceptional circumstances.[10]

(2) In *R v L, HVN, THN T v R*,[11] the four defendants were found to be trafficked into the United Kingdom. For each defendant, the offences they were charged with (for three of the defendants' offences relating to the production and supply of cannabis, for the fourth, use of a forged passport) were found to be integral to the trafficking process. Subjection to trafficking and the attendant vulnerability was found to 'extinguish' culpability. For each defendant the Court of Appeal ruled that this lack of culpability should have led to a successful abuse of process challenge to the jurisdiction of the trial court. Accordingly, all the convictions were quashed.

What is remarkable about this case is the determination of the court to avoid a conviction for a person who satisfied all the definitional requirements of the offence charged, has no nominate defence to raise, but may nonetheless not be culpable for what he or she has done. This case takes the abuse of process doctrine into new territory. Hitherto, any response to a lack of culpability despite grounds to convict has been through the sentencing process.[12] There had never been any suggestion that abuse of process challenges could impinge on merely a prosecutorial decision to proceed in cases likely to result in a conviction. If the doctrine were stretched to include such cases one would anticipate that ample latitude would be left to the prosecutor: the

---

5   *Rehman and Woods* (n 4).

6   Sections 1, 5, 51(A).

7   Firearms Act 1968, ss 5, 51(A).

8   His possession of this replica firearm came to light because of police surveillance of the French website from which it was purchased. The prosecution accepted that it was acquired *qua* collector with a lack of awareness that it could be adapted into a firearm. D (1) and his parents with whom he lived were wholly co-operative and open with the police. It is noteworthy that D (1)'s employers stood behind him and left his post open until he was imprisoned, his line manager expressing astonishment that the law could take such a course.

9   His weapon-collecting enthusiasm had attracted police surveillance.

10   For what reason he took possession of the shortened shotgun from his grandfather does not emerge in the judgment of the Court of Appeal.

11   [2013] EWCA Crim 991.

12   Arguably, complaints of entrapment raised in cases such as *Loosely* [2001] UKHL 53 raised under the abuse of process doctrine could be said to involve matters of personal culpability, but the emphasis is on the acceptability or otherwise of the police conduct. In such cases, all the definitional elements of the offence are satisfied and no issue other than police entrapment is in play. If the entrapper had been a private person not acting under police authority or direction, liability would have ensued.

prosecution should be stayed only if the decision to proceed was manifestly unreasonable. But where the challenge is based on lack of culpability, according to *R v L and others*, the test to be applied was whether the court agreed with the decision to prosecute.[13]

The three drug offence defendants in *R v L* are of particular interest.[14] In each case there was a considerable degree of obscurity about the circumstances of the trafficking and uncertainty as to their respective ages.[15] Being trafficked does not raise *per se* any nominate defence.[16] The position adopted in substance by the Court of Appeal was that once a reasonable possibility that a defendant was trafficked was raised, the defendant would be taken to be trafficked unless the contrary was proved.[17] And a further assumption was that the circumstances of the trafficking, whatever they were, 'extinguish' culpability, at least for offences associated with the trafficking process.[18] Contrasting the non-trafficking case of *Wilson*,[19] where D, a thirteen year old boy, assisted his father in the latter's fatal assault on V, is instructive. As duress was unavailable,[20] an attempt was made to reflect the fact that D was 'swept along' by his father's 'uncontrolled aggression' by arguing that in such circumstances it could not be safely assumed that D intended to kill or cause serious harm. The argument cut no ice with the trial court or the Court of Appeal. It is assumed here that any challenge at the time of *Wilson* to the jurisdiction of the court by raising abuse of process would have failed too. Must that assessment be revisited in the light of *R v L*?

How Influential is *R v L* Likely To Be?

Theoretically, *R v L* could be cited in support of the following, sweeping principle, namely that where the circumstances surrounding D's offence 'extinguish' his culpability, any prosecution against D for that offence will be stayed as an abuse of process if the trial judge disagrees with the prosecutor's decision to prosecute. The unreality of subscribing to that proposition can be demonstrated by attempting to apply it to cases already discussed above. In *Wilson*, D could not attempt to raise evidence of a lack of culpability because of the non-applicability of the defence of duress in murder. Suppose that in *Wilson* there was evidence that D participated in a killing perpetrated by his father because he acted under a threat of death if he disobeyed his father by not assisting him. Could evidence of that kind be raised post *R v L* to stay the prosecution as an abuse of process in a similar case? Surely such an argument would have gone nowhere: it would be a blatant attempt to get around the restrictions imposed at the highest appellate level on the defence of duress.[21]

There would be great attractions in using *R v L* in cases such as *Rehman and Woods*.[22] The case shows modern criminal law at its absolute worst.[23] To be sure, there is a compelling public interest in suppressing the possession and circulation of firearms. The number of firearms in circulation is gratifyingly low and strict

---

13   ibid (n 11) [17].

14   The fourth defendant, a trafficked woman in her thirties, had clearly been coerced to work in the sex trade and the forged document was an essential part of her cover should she asked to explain her presence in England. It is highly likely that these circumstances would have given rise to a defence of duress.

15   ibid (n 11) [45], [54], [67].

16   It must surely be the case that the circumstances of trafficked persons vary and that some members of that class do have a degree of voluntariness and agency with respect to the crimes they commit in the United Kingdom. It would be much better to have a specific statutory defence applicable to trafficked persons setting out in terms those circumstances relating to trafficking that undermine any judgment of culpability for offences committed by a trafficked person. Arguably the United Kingdom is legally obliged to provide such a defence by becoming a party to the Council of Europe Convention on Action against Trafficking on Human Beings and protecting its Victims and under the terms of Directive 2011/36/EU on Preventing and Combating Trafficking on Human Beings and Protecting its Victims.

17   ibid (n 15).

18   ibid (n 11) [20], [33], [45], [56].

19   [2007] EWCA Crim 1251.

20   *Howe* [1987] AC 417.

21   ibid.

22   *Rehman and Woods* (n 4).

23   For a searching critique of the unfairness of risk based possession offences see Andrew Ashworth, *Positive Obligations in Criminal Law* (Hart 2013) ch 6.

gun control laws must surely play a part in bringing about that satisfactory state of affairs.[24] But there is no need to send non-dangerous persons of 'positively good character' living successful and productive lives to prison. The argument used by the Court of Appeal to justify imprisonment, the argument that the weapons were dangerous even if the defendants were not, does not wash. The number of weapons that circulate in criminal circles by way of takings from the homes of persons of positively good character must surely be at most miniscule.[25]

But again the prospect of avoiding such outcomes by way of abuse of process is more or less zero. For good or ill, Parliament has chosen to make strict liability the standard for firearm offences and also provided a minimum sentence for these offences of five years imprisonment. To allow this recent and frequently updated draconian regime[26] to be outflanked by the abuse of process doctrine has its attractions in terms of fairness and retributivist justice. Yet, of course, there are weighty separation of powers objections to be raised against such a prospect.[27] Even if the harsh sentences of imprisonment that are the all too predictable consequence of current firearms law might embolden a judge to be sympathetic to an abuse of process plea in a particularly harsh firearms case, it is difficult to see how this could be doctrinally restricted to firearms offences but not for other crimes where D might face imprisonment following conviction for a strict liability offence. Resort by Parliament to strict liability even for serious offences is a significant cause of convictions and punishment untethered to proof of culpability.[28] It requires a vast imaginative leap to envisage large inroads into the extent of strict liability in English criminal law by way of abuse of process. It is noteworthy that none of the experienced counsel that represented the four defendants in *R v L* raised abuse of process. It was the Court of Appeal that informed them that an abuse of process challenge would have succeeded.

R v L is a case about crimes committed by D after he was trafficked and it seems safe to assume that its reasoning will be confined to trafficked defendants.[29] While such fact based confinement of the impact of cases is meat and drink to practitioners, it is not attractive to persons of a theoretical bent who strain to find some conceptual/normative proposition at the heart of every decided case. Yet the conceptual/normative principle that can be abstracted from this case—prosecutors cannot lawfully maintain a prosecution against persons even if their conduct falls within the terms of an offence if their culpability was extinguished by circumstances relating to the commission of the offence—is far too disruptive if given any general application. If proof of culpability is necessary to establish liability, the time and place to resolve the presence or absence of the culpability element is the trial. If proof of culpability is not necessary to establish liability, matters relating to the moral culpability of the defendant arise at the sentencing stage. At the heart of *R v L* is the fact that the United Kingdom Government has made treaty commitments to the Council of Europe and incurred obligations under EU law to protect vulnerable trafficked persons,[30] but has made no provision to shield from criminal liability trafficked persons who have been conscripted into illegal activities such as growing cannabis

---

24 For the years 2008–09, 2009–10, and 2010–11, there was an average of 47 homicides involving guns, a tiny number by international standards. Home Office Statistical Bulletin, *Homicide, Firearm Offences and Intimate Violence* (2011).

25 Of course the statement in the text is unsupported by any attempt to verify. Yet the opinion of the Court of Appeal that the weapons in the hands of these peaceable defendants constituted a public danger is completely implausible.

26 Firearms Act 1968; Firearms (Amendment) Act 1988; Firearms Amendment Act 1997; Anti-Social Behaviour Act 2003 s 39; Violent Crime Reduction Act 2006 s 34; Crime and Security 2010 s 46.

27 The frequent updating of the gun control legislation to wider and harsher effect leaves no doubt that any judge made dilution of the regime would be contrary to what Parliament intends.

28 Of particular note is the strict liability offence of rape of a child, contrary to s 5 of the Sexual Offences Act 2003, which has a maximum sentence of life imprisonment. In *G* [2008] UKHL 37, the House of Lords confirmed the 15-year-old D's conviction for the rape of V, a 13-year-old girl, while accepting that he had reasonable grounds for believing V to be 15. He was sentenced to 5 years youth custody and was placed on the sex offenders registry for life.

29 There was nothing at stake for any of the defendants in L save for the quashing of their convictions. Each defendant had completed the sentence imposed. The appeals were brought after interventions by the Child Protection Agency and the United Kingdom Borders Agency. One is left with the impression that the audience addressed in the appeal were officials of the Crown Prosecution Service who will, post-L, be far more circumspect about bringing criminal proceedings against trafficked children and young persons.

30 ibid (n 16).

or using false passports.[31] What is refreshing about the case is the determination of the Court of Appeal to ensure that such persons are helped rather than prosecuted. It is the spirit of the decision that is important but general resort to abuse of process to avoid criminal liability for the non-culpable is not feasible.

What can be done more generally to protect persons who lack culpability from criminal convictions and excessive punishment following a conviction? Quite a lot if judges are prepared to work creatively within the institutional and doctrinal limits of criminal law. In examining the scope for judicial activity in this regard, it will be argued that some of the injustice associated with strict liability offences can be mitigated if courts insist that even for strict liability offences there must be some underlying responsibility on which liability can rest and that general defences are applicable to strict liability offences. It will be further argued that courts should refrain from using imprisonment for strict liability offences wherever possible. In the final section the judicial approach to developing defence doctrine will be examined and the suggestion will be made that defence doctrine could be developed and extended on a more liberal basis.

Strict Liability: Responsibility, Defences, and Punishment

Strict liability is a long-standing and wide-ranging presence in English criminal law.[32] The most common form of strict liability is exemplified by the myriad of statutory offences regulating vast swathes of economic, transportation, municipal, social, and other public activities. There is a tendency to downplay this vast body of law as a form of regulatory, quasi-administrative law, not the real criminal law,[33] yet many of these offences carry sentences of imprisonment despite the fact that in their typical form proof of any culpability is unnecessary. Moreover, some very serious offences are offences of strict liability such as rape of a child[34] and possession of a firearm.[35]

Responsibility and Strict Liability

The point is often made that strict liability is not absolute liability. The point is important. All forms of criminal liability should rest on some form of responsibility on the part of D for some act or omission which brought about or contributed to bringing about the external elements of the offence charged against D.[36] So if D, a butcher, is charged with selling meat unfit for human consumption, a sale of unfit meat by him or someone with D's authority to sell his meat must be proved. Imagine that a municipality, concerned by some serious cases of botulism, enacts a bylaw to the effect that if one butcher doing business in the town is found guilty of selling unfit meat all other butchers established in the town will also be deemed to have committed the same offence. The idea behind this draconian law is that it will goad butchers to apply pressure on other butchers to meet hygiene standards. The question of whether such a law could be validly enacted will not be addressed.[37] Yet even if the validity of this law is conceded, surely a *criminal* offence has not been created. Can instances of criminal liability be deemed into existence, triggered by the action of a third party over which the convicted person has no authority or control? To do so would be to divorce responsibility from liability.

---

31   s 53(A) of the Sexual Offences Act 2003 does make it an offence for D to pay for the sexual services of V if V was forced or deceived into prostitution. The plight of trafficked women informs the offence but it does not offer any direct protection or assistance to such women.

32   For general discussion and critique, see AP Simester (ed), *Appraising Strict Liability* (OUP 2005).

33   'Offences that require mens rea are the real crimes, strict liability crimes are regulatory matters that are almost always exclusively forward looking in their intent: they hope to shape conduct not to punish it.' Michael Moore, 'The Specialness of the General Part of the Criminal Law' in Dennis J Baker and Jeremy Horder, *The Sanctity of Life and the Criminal Law: The Legacy of Glanville Williams* (Cambridge University Press 2013) 69, 88).

34   Sexual Offences Act 2003 s 5.

35   ibid (n 26).

36   See GR Sullivan, 'Conduct and Proof of Conduct: Two Fundamental Conditions of Criminal Liability' in Kaiyan Kaikobad and Michael Bohlander (eds), *International Law and Power, Perspectives on Legal Order and Justice: Essays in Honour of Colin Warbrick* (Koninklikje Brill NV 2009) 205–253.

37   Clearly all manner of legal objections might be in play relating to the legislative authority of the municipality, Article 6 of the European Convention for Human Rights and private law issues too.

A frequently prosecuted offence in England and Wales is the offence of being a parent of a child of compulsory school age, a child who is failing to attend regularly.[38] There is no question that this is an offence of strict liability. But it goes further. Frequently this offence doles out criminal liability on an absolute basis.[39] The courts have invariably enforced this offence where the non-attendance of the child (frequently a strong-willed 14- or 15-year-old) is a state of affairs completely and blamelessly beyond the control of the parent.[40] As with the butcher example above, this is to divorce responsibility from liability. It will be objected immediately that parental liability for this offence is nothing like the butcher hypothetical. You may not be your fellow butcher's keeper but you are indubitably the parent of your child and one of your prime parental obligations is to ensure your child's education.

There is undeniably a strong parental obligation of that kind and indeed a parent, otherwise acting in good faith, may be liable for this offence even if she has given of her absolute best, beyond what it was reasonable to ask, to ensure her child's attendance yet there remained things to be done that might have ensured attendance. The obligation is a strict duty to do everything possible to ensure attendance, a duty which may involve a commitment that exceeds normal expectations. But once the limits of the possible have been reached, no more can be asked even on a strict standard. The limits of responsibility must be bounded by what human beings, taken in the round, can do even though exceptional effort may be required. But there are limits: for instance it would be absurd to impose a duty on males under twenty five to run a mile within four minutes. Some members of that cohort could perform the duty; for the vast majority of the group the best advice would be not to even try. That too, *mutatis mutandis*, would be the advice to a mother who is in hospital or in prison whose daughter is sure to be absenting herself from school while mother is unavoidably away.[41] But it seems the mother will commit the truanting offence, at least according to some judges.[42]

Absolute liability is not confined to parental obligations. It seems that some decades ago at least, that it was not possible to can peas without from time to time canning some green caterpillars as well. Even a company that was a state of the art in terms of canning vegetables and whose procedures were beyond criticism might yet face criminal proceedings should a (harmless and late) caterpillar be spotted in the tin.[43] The stakes are higher where the unavoidable concomitant of lawful and essential activities is in statistical terms serious injury and death. Persons employed in inherently dangerous activities such as construction, transportation, mining and emergency services are entitled to maximum legal protection against employers who skimp on safety measures. But in the nature of these activities accidents will occur which were unpreventable. Preventing the unpreventable is beyond the bounds for what even an employer should be made responsible. That was overlooked by the House of Lords in *Chargot*,[44] where D Ltd was found in breach of health and safety law following the death of its employee V, who died when his dumper truck overturned on a building site. The obligation that D Ltd was found to have breached was to provide as safe a system of work as was reasonably practicable.[45] No criticism could be made of the defendant's safety measures and practices. No explanation could be offered as to why the accident occurred. The House of Lords ruled that in the absence of any explanation for the accident, its cause must be imputed to some breach of the obligation to provide a safe system of work. This ruling absolved the prosecution from proving an event for which D Ltd could be held responsible. Absolute rather than strict liability was applied.

---

38   Education Act 1996 s 441.

39   See GR Sullivan, 'Parents and Their Truanting Children: An English Lesson in Liability Without Responsibility' (2010) 12 Otago L Rev 285.

40   As in *Alison Barnfather v London Borough of Islington, Secretary of State for Education and Skills* (2003) 1 WLR 2318; *New Forest Education Authority v E* [2007] EWHC 2584 (Admin).

41   It might be argued that this is to let parents off too lightly, that there is responsibility for the fact that the daughter is disinclined to attend school because better parenting might have inculcated a better attitude towards education. But it would be grossly unfair to insist that all deficiencies in the child can be traced back to the parents. Alternatively, responsibility could be engaged by going back to the choice to have children: parents at that point voluntarily assume the risk that the child at some future point might truant. But that would make the choice to have children akin to acquiring some animal that requires control. If these points are accepted then there is a strong affinity between the butcher hypothetical and the liability that is imposed on parents by this offence.

42   *Barnfather* (n 40).

43   *Smedleys v Breed* [1974] AC 489.

44   [2008] UKHL 73.

45   Health and Safety at Work Act 1974.

It is submitted that absolute liability has no place in criminal law. It would be perfectly possible for judges to read in a responsibility requirement for all offences, however strict, as has been done consistently in other Anglophone jurisdictions.[46] If useful benefits might arise in certain circumstances through the imposition of absolute liability, those benefits should be sought through civil and administrative processes.

Strict Liability and the Availability of Common Law Defences

The term defences is used loosely to cover denials of *mens rea* as when it is said that voluntary intoxication is a 'defence' to crimes of specific intent. And of course when the term defence is used to denote a lack of *mens rea*, there is no application to crimes of strict liability. The same does not apply to 'defences' which deny the presence not only of *mens rea* but also of *actus reus*, such as automatism, whether arising from a disease of the mind or from some external factor. Thus it was an error for McGowan LJ to assert in *DPP v H*[47] that the defence of insanity had no application to offences of strict liability because the defence establishes a lack of *mens rea*. If for whatever reason D wishes a special verdict for a crime of strict liability she could, according to circumstances, say her conduct was involuntary and not an *actus reus* because of a state of automatism arising from an internal condition, or, if she was conscious and capable of choice, she was nonetheless unaware that her conduct was wrong. As for what may be called the supervening defences which deflect liability despite the presence of the definitional elements of the offence, modern appellate authority clearly recognises the defence of duress, whether by threats or circumstances, applies to strict liability offences.[48] The same should apply to the defences of necessity and self-defence. Allowing these defences will not do much to alleviate the injustice that strict liability may give rise, but none the less injustice may be avoided on particular occasions.

Strict Liability and Punishment

A finding or conceding of liability is the penultimate step to the imposition of punishment upon D for the crime he has committed. Sometimes punishment may not be imposed. Even where the crime is serious—manslaughter for instance—the sentencing judge may regard the crime as the product of particular and non-recurrent circumstances and see no point in adding a fine let alone imprisonment to the other measures she invokes at the sentencing stage.[49] Indeed there are even murder cases such as *Ibrams*,[50] where, despite the mandatory sentence, the Court of Appeal did what it could to avoid punishing the prisoner.[51] Lack of culpability can and should be taken into account at the sentencing stage to fill in the gaps that rule based defences inevitably leave.

The picture changes where strict liability offences are concerned. Even crimes of the most regulatory/ administrative character may carry sentences of imprisonment in addition to fines. When Parliament has declined to make culpability a matter going to liability, it follows, alas, that matters of culpability raised at the sentencing stage will, unless the circumstances are exceptional, at most mitigate rather than avoid any penalty. If an offence is created that requires proof of culpability, a court may well be sympathetic at the sentencing stage if culpability in the moral sense is lacking or much diminished, even though in the defining terms of the offence, culpability is legally present. Offences of this kind are, after all, about punishing culpable persons and from time to time even offences that require culpability will overreach. The default position for all criminal offences, strict or otherwise, is that liability entails punishment unless there is a strong reason

---

46   See references in Sullivan (n 39).

47   [1997] 1 WLR 1406.

48   *Martin* (1989) 1 All ER 652.

49   As was sometimes the case when a manslaughter verdict on the grounds of the old version of diminished responsibility was agreed between the defence and the prosecution on the expectation that the judge would not impose any sentence of imprisonment. Whether the current version of diminished responsibility will prove amenable to this practice may be doubted. See further AP Simester, JR Spencer, GR Sullivan, GJ Virgo, *Simester and Sullivan's Criminal Law* (5th edn, 2013) 734–735.

50   (1982) 74 Cr App R 154.

51   The presiding Judge Lawton LJ took the unusual step in the course of a judgment confirming a murder verdict, of announcing that he would be writing to the Home Secretary to urge the immediate release of the prisoner.

not to impose punishment. Lack of culpability cannot be a strong reason not to punish a crime where proof of culpability was unnecessary. But even the most tough-minded consequentialist should accept one major constraint on this logic, namely that non-culpable persons should not be sentenced to imprisonment. Liability to pay large sums of money can be a major setback and if it comes by way of a fine it carries a coating of stigma. But it does not compare with going to prison, a prospect which fills most persons with horror.[52] It is a peculiarly hard fate for a non-culpable person who has unwittingly infringed the criminal law.

It will be recalled that that was the fate of D in *Rehman*.[53] The trial judge accepted that D was an innocent at large, a person of positively good character who at worst had acted with a degree of naiveté. But that fact coupled with his openness and honesty with the investigating police did not save him at trial from a five year sentence prescribed as the minimum for unlawful possession of a firearm. The Court of Appeal reduced the sentence to one year, which is half a loaf. What it should have done, on finding that 'exceptional circumstances' were present, was to lay down firm guidance that a complete lack of culpability entails a finding of 'exceptional circumstances', which preclude imprisonment as a sentencing option. There are other examples of strict liability offences of great seriousness where the courts have imprisoned persons lacking the culpability that warrants imprisonment.[54] This is regrettable and avoidable.[55]

Judicially Developing Defences

It has been noted already that the term defence can be used when raising a plea that a definitional element of the offence is missing. In this section the term will be confined to what may be termed supervening defences—true defences which may be raised to avoid liability—even though the defining elements of the offence are present. These defences are available for crimes of *mens rea* and strict liability.[56] The argument will be made that supervening defences should be made more widely available by the judges in developing and, on occasion, even creating new defences. Criticism will be offered of the judicial reluctance to make incremental expansion of existing defences let alone venture into novelty. This stems from a mistaken view that judicial creativity in the field of defence doctrine is as problematic as creativity in the expansion of the scope of criminal offences.[57] However, before these criticisms are made, recognition should be made of the limits imposed by a system of rules on the capacity of judges at the liability stage of the trial to

---

52   For a compelling argument that strict liability should be removed from all imprisonable offences, see Ashworth (n 23) ch 4.

53   [2005] EWCA Crim 2056.

54   See, e.g., G [2008] UKHL 37.

55   In *Reference Re Section 94(2) of the Motor Vehicle Act (BC)* [1985] 2 SCR 486, the Supreme Court of Canada ruled that strict liability offences that carried sentences of imprisonment offended the fundamental principles of justice. And to similar effect see *City of Levis v Tetreault* [2006] SCC 12. At one time similar judicial refusal to allow even fines (unlimited) for strict liability offences was raised, extra-judicially, by LJ Arden in 'Criminal Law at the Cross Roads: The Impact on Human Rights from the Law Commission's Perspective and the Need for a Code' [1999] Crim LR 439, 450. The article has not proved prescient.

56   Supervening defences will most obviously cover defences such as necessity, duress, self-defence, reasonable mistake, insanity, infancy, and, for those jurisdictions that recognise them, mistake/ignorance of law and involuntary intoxication. The division between supervening defences and matters which go to denial of the definitional elements of offences is not always clean. The key to the distinction is that supervening defences can come into play when the definitional elements of the offence have been proved but there will be occasions where unstable conventions as to what is to be regarded as a definitional element blur the distinction.

57   For a recent example of sensitivity to the distinction between construing offence definitions and resolving the limits of defences, Hughes LJ excluded extreme intoxication as a recognised medical condition for the purposes of the partial defence of diminished responsibility despite the fact that it was a recognised medical condition in the standard glossaries published respectively by the World Health Organisation and the American Medical Association: *Dowds* [2012] EWCA Crim 281 [34–5]. When reaching this perfectly sensible conclusion, his lordship observed that the rule of strict construction was not an inhibiting factor. That, with respect, is perfectly correct: there are no fair warning worries when the availability of diminished responsibility is checked because nobody consults the boundaries of this partial defence as a guide to future conduct. But it goes both ways: strict construction has no application when the boundaries of a defence are expanded.

recognise all forms of non-culpability. Certain states of moral innocence can only be accommodated by way of prosecutorial discretion or at the sentencing stage.

Some Things That Defences Cannot Do

A major constraint on the competence of judges to give full recognition to what she considers a condition of non-culpability are the definitional parameters of criminal offences, however contested and unstable the core values enshrined in the offence may be. The offence of assisted suicide provides a salient example of this constraint. The core value—would-be suicides should not be helped or encouraged to die—is now contested in certain cases by public opinion and in practice. Indeed, any prosecution must now comply with Crown Prosecution Service guidelines concerning when a prosecution may be brought, otherwise the prosecution will be stayed.[58] Should the guidelines disfavour the bringing of a prosecution, effectively the enforcement of the law is blocked by way of the abuse of process doctrine. Suppose a prosecution permissible under the guidelines is brought against D but strongly disapproved of by the presiding judge, who has nothing but sympathy for D, whom she considers blameless. She has no choice but to apply the law of assisted suicide. She cannot create a new guideline for the case in hand nor fashion some novel form of defence based on the facts of the case. Culpability or its absence must be judged in the light of the offence as drafted and not by reference to some credo of the judge.

When developing and expanding defences care must be taken to work within a conception of law as a rule based method of imposing the strictures of the criminal law. Inevitably this means that persons who may be blameless or lack a culpability warranting conviction for an offence must on occasions be convicted of the offences with which they have been charged. A rule-based system of defences cannot anticipate or accommodate all forms of blamelessness. The last point is of particular importance. There will be occasions where D may contravene the core values enshrined in the offence but may do so in circumstances which make for understanding and compassion. Such circumstances almost invariably have to be accommodated by a decision by the prosecutor or at the sentencing stage, but not when determining liability. Take D, recently deserted by her partner P, who took for himself all the money in their joint account. Her house is burgled the day before Christmas Eve and all the presents she has bought for her children are taken. Unable to face the disappointment of her children, she buys them presents using a credit card, aware that there is no more credit on the card and that her prospects of paying off the debt are for practical purposes non-existent. Up to this point in time, she has been a person of exemplary character.

It is to be hoped that no judge would send this woman to prison. But he could not direct an acquittal on a charge of fraud by false representation.[59] There might be a temptation to ask a jury whether they considered her dishonest given the emotional and economic pressures she was under when buying replacement presents. But if buying goods you know you cannot pay for is not dishonest in the terms of the law, it is difficult to know what is. This melancholy example shows that the criminal law at the liability stage is concerned with episodes of conduct and the state of mind of D at the time of her conduct. At this stage of proceedings D appears before the court as an abstracted juridical person until more is revealed at the sentencing stage.

To reinforce this point consider D, a man devastated by the recent desertion of his partner and under enormous pressure at work. Under the guise of sympathy V, a work colleague and jealous rival, persuades D to join him for a drink, although usually D abstains from alcohol. During the evening their conversation takes a bad turn, with V telling D in the most unpleasant way that he is bad at his job and even worse at sustaining relationships. Disinhibited by the alcohol, D lashes out at V, punching him several times in the face. If the case were to reach court, a conviction of D for at least assault by beating is inevitable. Unless one is threatened with physical attack, the stresses of life must be endured without resorting to violence.[60] But suppose D had

---

58   *Purdy* [2009] UKHL 45; *R v Ministry of Justice, Director of Public Prosecutions, Attorney General etc.* [2013] EWCA Civ 961.

59   Fraud Act 2006 s 1.

60   One of the major difficulties with the old defence of provocation and also, to some extent, with the replacement defence of loss of control is finding some cogent normative basis for partially condoning violence which is the product of anger rather than a response to danger. Given the mandatory sentence for murder struggling with this issue is required but not for other offences. See further Alan Reed and Michael Bohlander (eds), *Loss of Control and Diminished Responsibility: Domestic and International Perspectives* (Ashgate 2011).

only bought for himself and asked to be bought by V soft drinks but V had surreptitiously fortified D's drinks with vodka in the hope that he could goad the intoxicated D into being violent, in order to discredit him at work. Now the incident is something beyond the normal parameters of social life. D has been entrapped and destabilised by V in a way that is not acceptable. The incident is distinctive and its details could inform the creation of a rule based defence which would exempt the involuntary intoxicated from some offences if not the most serious offences.[61] The English Court of Appeal was receptive to a defence of involuntary intoxication though perhaps in a manner that was too broad and undiscriminating.[62] Be that as it may, the House of Lords refused to countenance a new defence of involuntary intoxication.[63] It is this judicial reluctance to develop and create rule based defences that will now be addressed.

Developing Defences

The judicial role is well suited to developing and even on rare occasions creating defences. When interpreting the definitional elements of offences, respect for the text is a paramount virtue in terms of separation of powers and to maximise *ex ante* guidance for subjects. Defences are different. Persons seeking greater latitude for their conduct by seeking the shelter of defences are likely thereby to forfeit any protection the defence affords. Judges should be free to accommodate a lack of culpability by extending or even creating rule-based defences which leave the definitional elements of the offences charged intact. Lord Wilberforce, in agreeing the extension of the defence of duress to murder had this to say of the judicial role in the matter of defences:[64]

> I have no doubt that it is open to us on normal judicial principles to hold the defence admissible. We are in the domain of the common law: our task is to fit what we can see as principle and authority to the facts before us and it is no obstacle that the facts are new. The judges have always assumed authority for deciding questions of principle relating to criminal liability and guilt and particularly for setting the standards by which the law expects normal men to act.

But the same case also contains a very different approach advised by Lord Simon:[65]

> I can hardly conceive of circumstances less suitable than the instant for five members of the appellate committee of your Lordships' House to arrogate to ourselves so momentous a law-making initiative.

Unfortunately, it is Lord Simon's approach that currently seems in the ascendancy. There are striking examples of restricting or rejecting defences rather than extending defences. This contrasts with the boldness that courts have shown in using procedural devices of uncertain ambit and applicability to protect vulnerable defendants. As already discussed the abuse of process doctrine has been interpreted in a manner to provide what is in substance a defence for trafficked persons.[66] Convictions of asylum-seekers for using false documents have been avoided by findings that deficient legal advice rendered guilty pleas a nullity.[67] The Director of Public Prosecutions has twice been required to draft guidelines to alert persons assisting the suicide of others as to the circumstances likely to result in prosecution.[68] This last example is particularly noteworthy. The

---

61   GR Sullivan, 'Involuntary Intoxication and Beyond' [1994] Crim LR 272.

62   *Kingston* [1994] QB 81. It was taken to be a general defence applicable to all offences. There must be some reservation about the availability of the defence to crimes such as rape and murder if D, despite his intoxication, is able to form mens rea.

63   *Kingston* [1995] 2 AC 355.

64   [1975] AC 653 AT 684.

65   ibid 696.

66   *R v L and others* [2013] EWCA Crim 991.

67   *R v Koshi Mateta and others* [2013] EWCA Crim 1372.

68   See references (n 58). And see also Jonathan Rogers, 'Prosecutorial Systems, Prosecutorial Policies and the Purdy Litigation' [2010] Crim LR 543.

terms of the offence were redrafted and indeed strengthened some few years earlier.[69] Avoiding the application of the offence in any case of assisted suicide whatever the degree of compassion aroused by particular facts by way of a rule based supervening defence would have been doctrinally out of the question as that would have involved contradicting the core terms of section 2 of the Suicide Act 1961. One can understand, indeed applaud, the creativity of the appellate committee of the House of Lords in finding a legal basis for obliging the Director of Public Prosecutions to provide guidelines for the offence of assisting and encouraging suicide and in setting the ground for the enforcement of the guidelines by way of abuse of process.[70] That is a better outcome for many observers than consistently prosecuting those relatives and friends who help persons settled on suicide to reach countries where assisting suicide is lawful or condoned. The point being made here is that judges should show the same appetite for the liberal interpretation of defences. That is something less radical than fashioning a new regime for the enforcement of an offence like assisting suicide, which is so freighted with strong emotions and strong opinions. Defences do not fight with the values or policy of offences: they allow convictions to be avoided where there are compelling reasons of fairness and justice to do so.

For instance, a more liberal approach to the interpretation of the *M'Naghten* Rules would have resulted in an insanity defence more fit for purpose.[71] The defence of infancy was stripped down to a matter of being under ten years old, with *doli incapax* swept away.[72] A defence of involuntary intoxication could have been recognised, as it fleetingly was by the Court of Appeal,[73] and developed to accommodate other forms of blameless destabilisation.[74] Duress was almost extended to all forms of participation in murder but then completely withdrawn as a defence to that offence.[75] Duress was also held to be inapplicable to what may be termed 'state of affairs' offences.[76] Furthermore a responsibility requirement has not been read-in to offences of this kind to avoid their worst excesses.[77] The enormous range and complexity of modern criminal law has not led to recognition of a mistake/defence of law defence despite the fact that contravening the terms of even a serious offence may come as a complete surprise to the reasonable, honest and non-aggressive person who has unwittingly broken the law.[78] There is plenty of judicial work to be done to improve the condition of defences. Whether it will be done is anyone's guess.

---

69   s 59 of the Coroners and Justice Act 2009 reformulated s 2 of the Suicide Act 1961 into a new and broader offence. There need no longer be a suicide or attempt at suicide, it suffices that D did an act capable of assisting or encouraging suicide on the facts as he took them to be.

70   It was remarkable how Article 8 of the European Convention for Human Rights was pressed into service as the legal basis for controlling the Director of Public Prosecutions.

71   In *Sullivan* [1984] AC 156, the House of Lords refused to go beyond the original language of the M'Naghten Rules, language which as judicially interpreted leaves persons with severe mental illness outside the scope of the insanity defence as well as including within its scope persons who are obviously sane. For a further example of rigid adherence to a narrow interpretation of the rules, see *Johnson* [2007] EWCA Crim 1978.

72   *R v JTB* [2009] UKHL 20.

73   ibid (n 62).

74   As argued by GR Sullivan, 'Making Excuses' in AP Simester and ATH Smith (eds), Harm and Culpability (OUP 1996) 131.

75   *Lynch* [1975] AC 653; *Abbott* [1977] AC 755; *Howe* [1987] AC 417.

76   *Hampshire County Council v E* [2007] EWHC 2584 (Admin). A remarkable case where it was accepted that if P's mother D had tried to ensure P's attendance at school, P a 15 year old drug dealer would have inflicted serious harm on her. Duress was denied to her on the singular ground that liability for the offence of failing to ensure P's attendance at school was triggered by the conduct of P.

77   ibid (n 36) and associated text.

78   See, for examples of cases with those features and for a powerful argument favouring an effective mistake/ignorance of law defence, Andrew Ashworth, 'Ignorance of Law and Duties to Avoid It' (2011) 74 MLR 1.

Chapter 3
Prior Fault:
Blocking Defences or Constructing Crimes

J.J. Child[1]

When assessing a defendant's (D's) liability, the orthodox approach is necessarily narrow and precise in its focus. We do not ask, for example, whether D satisfies an offence *mens rea* 'at some non-specific point in D's life', or whether, 'all things considered' we believe she is deserving of a defence; such questions may help us assess D's moral character, but they are too general and too subjective to drive the enquiries of the criminal law. Rather, criminal liability is event-specific: asking whether D satisfied the *mens rea at the time* of completing the conduct required for the *actus reus*, and whether the circumstances *at that time* give rise to a defence. In this manner, the law assesses and criminalises D for her role in the particular event, not for her more general character.[2]

In certain cases, however, the narrow focus of the orthodox approach can become problematic, and this is never more apparent than in relation to so-called 'prior fault' cases. Consider the following examples:

1) D decides to kill her enemy V. Fearing that she may lose her nerve, D becomes heavily intoxicated in V's company, knowing that she becomes violent when drunk. While intoxicated and out of control, D kills V.
2) D decides to kill his enemy V. D taunts V in order to elicit a violent reaction. V attacks D (as D anticipated), and D kills V in 'self-defence'.
3) D voluntarily becomes intoxicated. Whilst drunk, D decides to play with her new gun and accidentally shoots and kills V. D is unlikely to have made the mistake if sober.
4) D voluntarily becomes intoxicated. Whilst drunk, D mistakenly believes that V is about to attack him. D shoots and kills V in self-defence. D is unlikely to have made the mistake if sober.

In each example, if we apply the orthodox approach, it is difficult to conclude that D should be liable for the death of V. This is because, at the point of D's conduct that directly causes death, D either lacks physical control and/or *mens rea* as to causing harm (1 and 3), or appears to have a valid exclusionary defence (2 and 4). However, this conclusion does not appear acceptable. D's behaviour when acting to directly cause death (T2) may be defensible in isolation, but when considered in light of his prior fault at the earlier point (T1: when planning to lose control in order to kill (1); when planning to manipulate criminal defences (2); or when choosing to lose partial control or faculty through intoxication (3 and 4)), such exculpation is intuitively much less justifiable. Thus, we are inclined to question the orthodox approach—not necessarily to reject it completely (we do not want to punish D for *unrelated* activities or thoughts), but rather to expand it in certain cases to allow for consideration of D's behaviour at T1 where that behaviour is intimately linked to her behaviour at T2.

The task for legal theorists is to construct a set of rules that will allow for T1 to be considered in cases of this kind, but to do so fairly, and without undermining the coherence and appropriate standing of the wider orthodox approach. In doing so, because of the structural similarities between prior fault cases (such as those in our examples above), commentators have generally looked for a single solution to apply consistently

---

1   Thanks to Adrian Hunt and Amir Paz-Fuchs for comments on a draft of this chapter. A draft was also presented at the University of Sussex as part of the Criminal Law, Criminal Justice and Criminology Group within the Centre for Rights and Responsibilities.
2   Except, of course, to the extent that her character is revealed through the event.

between each.[3] As we will discuss, the failure of any single approach to provide the mechanism required for these cases is important in a normative sense: we need a robust and defensible method for finding liability in appropriate cases. However, the criticism of such proposals, and their varying strength in relation to different examples of prior fault, are also interesting for what they tell us about the structure of the problem, and indeed, the wider offence/defence distinction.

It is the contention of this chapter that, if we begin with a principled separation of offences and defences, the 'single' problem of prior fault becomes four separate problems.[4] Matching our four examples above, this separation marks the difference between:

1) Specific prior fault and the construction of offences;
2) Specific prior fault and the blocking of defences;
3) General prior fault and the construction of offences; and
4) General prior fault and the blocking of defences.

This four part separation is vitally important and will be justified more fully as we discuss each category in turn below. The contention of this chapter is that the four category separation is essential to recognise structural differences in the operation of offences and defences, to recognise the different principles engaged in each context within the prior fault problem, and therefore to recognise the need for different (potential) solutions in each case. However, the discussion is equally important in its search for coherence and consistency *within* each category. In this manner, where Robinson criticises the current law in America for its remarkably inconsistent approach to prior fault[5] (a criticism that can be levelled at English law with equal force[6]), this chapter seeks to explain and justify a degree of (principled) inconsistency, whilst agreeing with his criticism in the narrower contexts of our four identified categories.

Category I: Specific Prior Fault and Constructing Offences

Prior fault cases in Category I are those in which D possesses the *mens rea* for an offence at T1, but lacks *mens rea* (including voluntary movement[7]) at T2. The classic example of this involves voluntary intoxication:

> D decides to kill her enemy V. Fearing that she may lose her nerve, D becomes heavily intoxicated in V's company, knowing that she becomes violent when drunk (T1). While intoxicated and out of control, D kills V (T2).

Category I (often referred to as 'grand schemer' cases[8]) represents the paradigm and foundationary example of prior fault doctrine: *actio libera in causa* (a state resulting from voluntary action).[9] It is generally agreed

---

3   See, for example, Paul Robinson, 'Causing the Conditions of One's Own Defence: A Study in the Limits of Theory in Criminal Law Doctrine' (1985) Va L Rev 1; Larry Alexander, 'Causing the Conditions of One's Own Defence: A Theoretical Non-Problem' (2013) Crim L & Philos 623. The single solution approach is also reflected in current leading textbooks, for example, Andrew Ashworth and Jeremy Horder, *Principles of Criminal Law* (OUP 2013); Andrew Simester, John Spencer, Bob Sullivan, and Graham Virgo, *Simester and Sullivan's Criminal Law* (Hart 2013) 121.

4   A similar line, rejecting a single approach (and, thereby, a single problem), is also pursued by several authors in recent proceedings from a conference on '*Actio Libera in Causa*' in Pennsylvania (2011), published in [2003] Crim L & Philos (2013).

5   Robinson (n 1) part 1.

6   English law does not include the added problem of inconsistency between State Codes, but its inconsistent approach to prior fault between different defences is plain. For example, compare the very strict approach within duress that will disqualify the defence on the basis of negligent association (*Hasan* [2005] UKHL 22), with the comparatively narrow requirement of 'incitement' or planning needed to disqualify a loss of control defence; Coroners and Justice Act 2009, ss 55(6)(a) and (b). See remarks in *Oye* [2013] EWCA Crim 1725 [43].

7   I prefer to analyse the voluntariness of movement as a *mens rea* element. However, as little turns on this for present purposes, it will not be pursued in this chapter.

8   This is because, unlike standard intoxication cases, here D is actively planning to commit an offence while out of control.

9   As we will see, this approach has since been expanded to the other categories of prior fault.

that, in cases of this kind, D should not be allowed a defence at T2 (despite her lack of capacity) and will therefore be liable for the offence (in our example, murder). This position is reflected in the current law in *AG for NI v Gallagher*,[10] where Lord Denning made clear (in now widely accepted *dicta*) that English law would allow no defence in such circumstances regardless of whether the offence committed was one of basic or specific intent.

The result of this approach, a finding of liability, is uncontroversial. However, two problems have emerged. The first is one of legal principle: how can we justify finding liability for D's acts at T2 if those acts are not performed voluntarily? This problem begins to hint at our contention that this category is better analysed in terms of constructing offences as opposed to blocking defences, but more on this below. The second problem is one of consistency: would/should the same approach apply, in the same way, if D lacked capacity as a result of a non-intoxicating external factor (involving potential automatism) or internal factor (involving potential insanity)?

Beginning with the problem of legal principle and theoretical underpinning, several commentators have offered potential explanations. These explanations have generally come within three types. The first type, exemplified by the traditional interpretation of *actio libera in causa* within German law, will only find liability where D has the requisite *mens rea both* at T1 and at T2.[11] This approach will find liability where D becomes intoxicated, for example, to lose all inhibitions. However, it is too narrow for present purposes. English law will already allow for liability in the context of intoxicated Ds that do not lack *mens rea* at T2 (an intoxicated *mens rea* is still a *mens rea*[12]); the problem case (exemplified above) concerns D who *lacks mens rea* at T2. Here, it seems that the traditional German approach will not help us.

The second potential explanation accepts a lack of capacity at T2 (viewed in isolation), but finds liability by re-describing D's conduct to include both T1 and T2.[13] D's liability is thereby constructed upon a more general complex act description. Thus, for example, if we can describe D's complex act as 'becoming intoxicated and then killing V', where this description is both accurate (in causal terms) and acceptable (in descriptive terms), then D's actions (including those at T2) become the product of her agency.[14] Although this approach offers a route to liability in our example, it is not an attractive one. First, this is because the re-description approach is overly subjective: speaking of acceptable act descriptions in moral terms is one thing, but to base criminalisation on them (without specific criteria), and to explain the process to a jury, would be quite another. Second, it is difficult intuitively, even as part of a complex act description, to accept that D's actions at T2 are anything other than involuntary: D, at this point, is not in control of his own body. In this manner, the re-description approach seeks to create something of a legal fiction in order to find liability, an approach that the criminal law should (where possible) avoid.

The third potential explanation, outlined by Robinson[15] and (more recently) Dimock,[16] allows a defence at T2 (intoxication or automatism) but finds liability through T1. For Robinson, in line with his more general theory, D commits the offence because D is culpable in causing the conditions of his defence. In this manner, D's acts at T1 are presented as similar to the use of an 'innocent agent',[17] or even to a conspiracy with one's later-self,[18] and are (as such) deserving of criminalisation. Dimock reaches a similar conclusion, stressing that although D cannot be liable for involuntary conduct at T2 alone, if we can 'trace' the harm caused at T2 back to voluntary and culpable conduct at T1, then (in common with innocent agency, conspiracy, corporate liability, etc.) it should be possible to construct liability.[19] This approach then leads Dimock, echoing

---

10   [1963] AC 349.

11   Joachim Herrmann, 'Causing the Conditions of One's Own Defence: The Multifaceted Approach of German Law' (1986) BYU L Rev 747, 763–765.

12   *Kingston* [1994] 3 WLR 519.

13   Claire Finkelstein, 'Involuntary Crimes, Voluntarily Committed' in Stephen Shute and Andrew Simester (eds), *Criminal Theory: Doctrines of the General Part* (OUP 2005) 143, 163–169.

14   ibid 165–166.

15   Robinson (n 1) 1.

16   Susan Dimock, 'Actio Libera in Causa' (2013) Crim L & Philos 549.

17   Robinson (n 1) 34. Similar logic has also appeared in consecutive editions of Smith and Hogan's Criminal Law.

18   Leo Katz, 'Entrapment Through the Lens of the Actio Libera in Causa' (2013) Crim L & Philos 587, 591.

19   Dimock (n 15) 565–567.

Robinson, to discuss what manner of culpability should be required at T1, including: a 'strong' causal link with T2; foresight of T2; *mens rea* as to future offending; and so on. As Dimock concedes, 'in the context of criminal liability, the devil will be in the details'.[20]

The explanations of Robinson and Dimock are the most intuitively plausible of those we have considered (and come closest to the approach favoured in this chapter) in that they accept (*to some extent*) that the focus of liability should be moved from T2 to T1. However, it is contended that in each case the analysis offered is *unnecessarily* complex, seeking for the creation and introduction of special rules that are not required to find liability.[21] For Robinson, it is contended that such complexity is the result of his one-size-fits-all approach to the problem of prior fault, an approach that prevents him focusing on the unique factors at play within this category. Equally, for Dimock, there may be similar issues in relation to her emphasis on tracing liability *from* T2, as opposed to focusing more directly on T1.

In relation to Category I prior fault cases (where D acts with *mens rea* at T1, and involuntarily at T2), it is contended that there is no need for special rules relating to prior fault at all. In these cases, D is not causing the conditions at T1 for a defence at T2, but rather committing acts at T1 that she hopes will lead to harms at T2 that she will not be responsible for (i.e., that she will not commit an offence at T1 or T2). However, by acting in this manner, our standard rules of legal responsibility (and liability) should *already* lead to the conclusion that D is straightforwardly liable.

As T1 is the last occasion in which D acts voluntarily, this becomes our only focus for potential liability. To find *actus reus*, we ask whether D's conduct (at T1) was performed in the required circumstances, and caused any relevant results (in our example, the killing of V). In line with standard causation rules, D's acts need not be an especially 'strong' cause (as suggested by Dimock), but simply a 'but for' cause, which has a more than de minimis impact.[22] The actions of D after T1 should not be analysed as separate or independent causes (as they are, to varying extents, by Robinson and Dimock). Rather, after T1, D's uncontrolled body becomes nothing more than a *tool* of his prior conduct, more accurately compared to a bullet in flight or (acknowledging the likely unpredictability) to the release of stampeding cattle. In such examples, D's act (shooting the bullet; releasing the cattle) would be presented as causing the harm by bullet or cattle even though D loses control of each before harm is brought about. We need not pretend that the bullet or cattle act as an innocent agent, form a conspiracy with D, or require a tracing of culpability. Rather, unconscious objects of this kind, and equally the uncontrolled body of D, are simply tools (a means to an end).[23] As Williams remarked:

> Suppose ... that a man sets a time-bomb to kill people, and is asleep when it goes off; obviously he is guilty of murder. Similarly, if he fuddles himself with drink in order to commit murder, he turns himself into a kind of human time-bomb.[24]

Once we accept that D's behaviour after T1 can be (most accurately) presented in this manner, it is clear that her satisfaction of *actus reus* elements will not require any special rules of *prior* fault. Our focus shifts to *mens rea*, and to question whether D had the required *mens rea* when performing the conduct required for the offence (i.e., at T1). Where this is the case, as it is with our intoxicated killer, D will be liable. D may raise the issue of intoxication to demonstrate that he was not in control at T2, but this will not undermine his liability at T1; in fact, her lack of control at T2 (the fact she becomes a simple tool) is a necessary factor for us to find liability at T1.

It is contended that this is the best approach to Category I cases, constructing liability through the application of standard rules. However, there are two areas of criticism that require brief discussion: that the

---

20   ibid 566.

21   Robinson recognises the complexity of his approach, but justifies it by comparison to equally complex (and unfair) operation of the current law. Whilst we agree with this analysis, it is contended that the approach in this chapter reaches the same conclusion as Robinson (in terms of liability), but through a more logical and straightforward mechanism.

22   *Adams* [1957] Crim LR 365.

23   Robinson acknowledges this approach but, wedded to his wider thesis, does so only in analogy with his own approach. Robinson (n 1) 37.

24   Glanville Williams, *Textbook of Criminal Law* (Sweet and Maxwell 1978) 422.

preferred approach is descriptively flawed in that the conduct of (for example) becoming intoxicated cannot be presented as the conduct element of an offence, and that it is flawed in casual terms because there may be an insufficient link between the conduct of (for example) becoming intoxicated and the later harms at T2.[25] In response, it is useful to separate result crimes, conduct crimes, and strict liability offences.

In relation to result crimes (such as murder in our example), the causal criticism maintains that D's conduct at T1 is not the proximate cause of harm at T2: essentially, that D's lack of control will break the chain of causation.[26] However, just as the flight of D's bullet, or the stampede of released cattle would not break the causal chain, it is not accepted that D's uncontrolled movements would be any more likely to do so. Importantly, this would *not* lead to unchecked causation and the potential for over-criminalisation. This is because D's liability will also be contingent on proof of *mens rea* at T1: proof that D (in our example) acted with the intention to kill or cause GBH, not in general terms, but *through that conduct*. Thus, for example, if D lost control through intoxication whilst considering or even intending to kill V in the future, and then did cause death whilst out of control, he would not commit murder: he did not possess *mens rea* at T1.

The descriptive criticism likewise, for result crimes, has little impact. This is because result crimes merely require D to perform *conduct* that causes the result. As the type of conduct is often unspecified, it is therefore easier to describe D's conduct of (for example) becoming intoxicated, as the conduct causing death. This may seem unintuitive at times, particularly if we consider D's criminal attempt at a stage just short of losing control,[27] but this is not a conclusive criticism: many attempts will involve otherwise innocent behaviour.[28]

For conduct crimes, the causal criticism raises some concern. For example, let us imagine D that would like to have intercourse with V, but knows that she will not consent. Where D becomes intoxicated (*not* planning to rape V), would our approach find liability where D has non-consensual intercourse with V whilst out of control? After all, we do not seem to have a result element that must be intended *by these acts* at T1. The answer is 'no'. This is because, even for 'so called' conduct crimes, D must possess *mens rea* as to conduct. D will not be liable for rape in this example because the *mens rea* for rape requires D to intend to penetrate V *by this conduct*, an intention that D lacks in our example. Thus, for both result and conduct crimes, liability will be controlled by the requirement of *mens rea* at T1.

Perhaps more problematic, for conduct crimes, will be the descriptive criticism. Conduct offences do not require a non-specific act causing a result, but provide some level of detail that may not match D's conduct at T1. For example, for rape, how can we describe D's conduct at T1 (becoming intoxicated) as the conduct of sexual penetration?[29] The answer, of course, is that we cannot. However, rather than seeing this as a conclusive criticism of our approach (it is a criticism that also applies to alternative approaches[30]), it is perhaps better presented as a criticism of the prevailing interpretation of conduct crimes. For example, if the conduct element of an offence was interpreted narrowly in terms of bodily movement (or omission), then almost all conduct crimes can be described in causal terms (for example, conduct causing penetration) and the criticism is avoided.[31] D's conduct when becoming intoxicated is not the conduct *of* penetration, but (like firing the bullet or releasing the cattle) it is conduct *causing* penetration.

Strict liability offences (whether result or conduct crimes) create no further descriptive problems. However, they require separate consideration because of the unique impact of the causation criticism. Take the example of D who has an unexpected seizure while driving, crashes, and causes death. Could D be liable for a (hypothetical) strict liability homicide offence?[32] At T2, when D's car hits V, D is not acting voluntarily. However, if we apply the preferred approach, we must acknowledge that at T1 (just before the seizure) D is acting voluntarily with the *mens rea* (none) required for the offence. This can be seen as (yet another) reason to question strict liability within the law, but it is a problem that the preferred approach must be able to cope with.

---

25 These criticisms are forcefully made in an excellent article by Finkelstein (n 12) 143.
26 ibid 146–153.
27 Katz (n 17) 594; Herrmann (n 10) 747.
28 For example, the act of releasing the cattle in our example of causing death by a directed stampede.
29 Katz (n 17) 529; Finkelstein (n 12) 145, 153–156.
30 Recognised by Finkelstein at 167.
31 This response leads to a discussion of action within the criminal law that cannot be perused here.
32 Finkelstein (n 12) 146–153.

To avoid a finding of liability, we must either concede that D's lack of control breaks the chain of causation (undermining the preferred approach), or focus on alternative causation rules: for example, foreseeability and/or blameworthiness, and look for a break in the causal chain in cases of this kind only. With regard to this second option, which must be preferred, the concern is that requiring foreseeability and/or blameworthiness is to incorporate fault into offences that are designed not to include it.[33] However, such an approach can be kept within bounds. For example, it would be possible to maintain that where D loses control between conduct and result (be this control of her body, or through the use of a bullet or cattle etc.), legal causation of the harm requires this lack of control to be foreseeable. Where D acts through a bullet or cattle etc., this assumes that D must have a basic understanding of the tool (understanding that his actions could lead to uncontrolled results) in order to be the legal cause of any harm that results from it. In the same way, where D's tool is his own unconscious body, the same principle would require a basic understanding at T1 of the potential for losing control. Thus, strict liability offences will only come within Category I where D's involuntariness was at least broadly foreseeable.

Having discussed the theoretical underpinnings of this approach, it is important to acknowledge its potential for internal consistency *within* this category of 'prior fault'. Category I includes all cases in which D has *mens rea* at T1 and brings about criminal results (whilst lacking control) at T2. In this manner, the reason for D's lack of control (intoxication; a non-intoxicating external factor; or an internal factor) should be irrelevant.[34] For example, where D acts at T1 with the intention *by those acts* to cause death, whether she plans to lose control through intoxication (our paradigm example), through hypnosis, or through an omission to take medication, her culpability remains the same, and the preferred route to liability will be equally consistent. The inconsistent approaches (*within* this category) of the current law should therefore be criticised and amended.[35]

Category II: Specific Prior Fault and Blocking Defences

Our second prior fault category involves cases in which D manufactures events at T1 so that when he commits an offence at T2 (satisfying both *actus reus* and *mens rea*), he may avail himself of a criminal defence. For example,

> D decides to kill his enemy V. D taunts V in order to elicit a violent reaction (T1). V attacks D (as D anticipated), and D kills V in 'self-defence' (T2).

Unlike Category I cases, there is no issue here of constructing the missing elements of an offence: D's *actus reus* and *mens rea* at T2 are uncontroversial. The question is rather, having satisfied that *offence*, should D's conduct at T1 undermine the availability of a *defence* at T2?

Unsurprisingly, the current law's answer has been to block D's defence in these circumstances, leaving D liable for the offence (in our example, murder). This is not only the case where D culpably manufactures circumstances of self-defence,[36] as in our example, but equally in the case of duress,[37] necessity,[38] and the partial defence of loss of control.[39] In this manner, unlike Category I cases, the current law relating to Category II cases is reasonably consistent in result *and* method (blocking defences). As discussed further below, the same method is favoured in this chapter. However, despite this broad level consistency, the precise circumstances

---

33   ibid 148–149.

34   Echoed in Dimock (n 15) 561.

35   For a discussion of that inconsistency, see, Ronnie Mackay, 'Intoxication as a Factor in Automatism' (1982) Crim LR 146; Edward Mitchell, 'Culpability for Inducing Mental States: The Insanity Defence of Dr Jekyll' (2004) J Am Acad Psy & L 63.

36   *Rashford* [2005] EWCA Crim 3377 [19].

37   *Hasan* [2005] UKHL 22.

38   This is likely through analogy with duress. It may also support Lord Denning's famous dicta about the limits of necessity in *Southwark London Borough v Williams* [1971] 2 All ER 175.

39   Coroners and Justice Act 2009, s 55(6).

leading to the blocking of a defence remain worryingly unclear, as well as inconsistent depending upon which defence is at issue. Before we move to the analysis of these circumstances (assuming the preference for a 'blocking' approach), it is useful to consider two alternatives approaches in the literature.

The first alternative is the general approach to prior fault outlined by Robinson. Consistent with his analysis of Category I cases, Robinson would allow a defence at T2 (in our example, self-defence), but would find liability (in our example, for murder) on the basis of D's prior fault at T1. The main advantage of this approach, according to its supporters, is that liability can be found without undermining D's defence at T2. In this manner, D is still allowed (and even encouraged) by the available defence to act in an appropriate manner: to defend himself in our example, or (more convincingly) to choose a lesser evil in circumstances of necessity.

> Assume that an actor sets a fire that threatens a nearby town to create the conditions that will justify his using his enemy's farm as a firebreak. Denying a justification defence might dissuade him from undertaking such a scheme, but if it fails to dissuade him, the unavailability of the defence may reduce his incentive to set the firebreak and save the town.[40]

It is further contended that as an intervening third party would be justified in setting the firebreak, or in defending D from V's attack, it would be illogical to block D's defence in the same circumstances.[41] In fact, the strength of this logic led Larry Alexander to label the whole discussion a 'theoretical non-problem', seeing the Robinson-type approach as self-evident.[42]

Although Robinson's method provided our lead into the preferred approach for Category I cases, that is not true for Category II cases. First, this is because liability (for Robinson's approach) relies on a faulty causal link between D's acts at T1 and the harm at T2. Unlike Category I cases, where D's body becomes the unconscious tool of his acts at T1, Category II cases involve potentially intervening acts by a conscious D at T2 (in our example, the act of 'justified' killing), as well as the potentially intervening voluntary acts of V (in our example, attacking D).[43] Secondly, and perhaps more importantly, for cases in Category II, Robinson's analysis becomes unintuitive to the point of incoherence. This is because, *even if* a causal link could be formed between D's conduct at T1 and the harm at T2, Robinson's approach requires us to view the harm (in our example, killing) as *at once* a criminal act resulting from T1, *and* a justified act resulting from T2.[44] Robinson sees the justification at T2 as an incentive for D to 'do the right thing', and yet D has already forfeited the right to the defence from his conduct at T1, so where is Robinson's incentive? Any incentive is as functionally empty as the promise of the defence: D's justified (T2) and unjustified (T1) conduct will always lead to liability.

A second alternative that would also allow for a defence at T2 has been offered by Farrell.[45] Under Farrell's approach, D's conduct at T1 will not undermine the defence at T2, but will qualify it considerably: D may perform minimum acts of self-preservation as valid self-defence at T2, but may not go beyond this (even if such conduct would otherwise be justified by the standard rules of self-defence).[46] In this manner, Farrell does not rely on a causal link from D's conduct at T1, or the unintuitive conclusion that the same result is both justified and unjustified. However, his approach remains problematic. Although Farrell talks of a moral right to self-defence,[47] there is little to suggest why this should be reflected as a legal right. Fundamentally, it seems wrong that D should be able to make use of a defence in order to cause harm to V at T2 (even within Farrell's restrictive terms[48]), when this is exactly what D has culpably procured from his conduct at T1.

---

40   Robinson (n 2) 28. For a similar example, see Alexander (n 2) 623–624.

41   Alexander (n 2) 626.

42   ibid.

43   This point is highlighted by Kimberly Ferzan, 'Provocateurs' (2013) CrimL & Philos 597, 603; Katz (n 17) 593; Daniel Farrell, 'What Should We Say About Contrived 'Self-Defence' Defences?' (2013) Crim L & Philos 571, 578.

44   Ferzan describes this position as 'rather odd'. Ferzan (n 42) 603.

45   Farrell (n 42) 571.

46   ibid 582. This approach also gains some support from German law. Herrmann (n10) 756.

47   Farrell (n 42) 585.

48   Setting Farrell's new standard of minimum (as opposed to reasonable) force would be another difficulty of this approach.

It is this final criticism of Farrell's approach, building upon our discussion of Robinson's alternative, which (I believe) lies at the heart of the Category II cases (and their distinction from Category I cases). The first category of prior fault cases centred on potential problems with coincidence, with the harm at T2 lacking physical control (at that time). Thus, our challenge was to find a point at which coincidence could be found in order to attribute full criminal responsibility to D in order to construct and identify the criminal wrong within a single event. Cases in Category II are different. For these cases, we have our criminal event (D completes the *actus reus* and *mens rea* at T2), and there are no problems with coincidence. Our focus is on the availability of a defence, and thus, rather than looking at the basis for offence liability (as Robinson arguably does), we need to consider the theoretical basis for criminal defences.

Criminal defences (as opposed to inculpatory rules such as intoxication and automatism) accept that D has committed a wrong, but prevent (or mitigate) liability on the basis of secondary considerations. These considerations (defences) vary considerably in their detail, but each holds to certain general principles that are helpful to us here. One such principle, most often discussed in relation to excusatory defences (for example, duress), is that D should be allowed a defence where his offending does not reveal a vicious character but rather an unlucky fate; that she was trapped; in crisis; that she demonstrated an understandable, or reasonable, human frailty; where 'there but for the grace of God go I'.[49] Indeed, although less often discussed, this requirement of 'crisis' is equally central to justificatory defences (for example, self-defence): D is never justified to commit an offence in general; she is justified *in these circumstances*. In each case, D is not allowed to choose to take the law into his own hands, to become a vigilante, but where choice is removed through crisis, we can accept that certain exceptions must be permitted. It is on this basis that D's potential defence at T2 can (and should) be blocked in Category II cases. D's acts at T1 (in our example, taunting V) have artificially created the 'crisis' at T2 (in our example, the need for physical defence): D's prior acts change his normative position,[50] she is not a victim of circumstance, she has chosen, and a common-sense morality would deny him a defence on that basis.[51]

As we have highlighted, this common-sense morality is already generally reflected by the current law. However, within this category of cases, both the clarity of rules governing when defences will be blocked, as well as the consistency of rules between defences, are very poor.[52] Although we do not have scope to explore these in detail, it is useful to sketch a potential way forward to demonstrate the importance of these rules and the danger of continued ambiguity. It is contended that, before D's defence is blocked at T2, she must have been reckless at T1 in relation to two core facts:

1. <u>D must be reckless as to causing the circumstances of the defence</u> (in our example, causing V to attack). In this manner, D has at least *chosen* to risk manufacturing the crisis that would otherwise give rise to a defence. D's foresight of his causal role is also vital to avoid difficult cases such as the executioner that might otherwise be blocked from a defence of killing in line with his job, or violence involved in police work: in each case, D may foresee their offending and their use of a defence, but they will not (if acting legitimately) foresee themselves as the cause of the unlawful actions of V;[53]

2. <u>D must be reckless as to his own offending</u> (in our example, as to killing V). Again, before we can say that D has manufactured his defence at T2, it is logical to require that he should foresee his future offence. This requirement would also allow courts some discretion in duress cases, for example, where D might foresee threats to commit minor offences but is then threatened to commit serious offences. Where the disparity is very great, D's defence may not be blocked on the basis of his failure to foresee the type of offending later completed.[54] Dimock contends that, for the defence to be blocked, D should have the *mens rea* for the offence at T1.[55] However, a requirement of full *mens rea* is surely

49   William Wilson, 'The Structure of Criminal Defences' (2005) Crim LR 108.
50   David Ormerod, *Smith and Hogan's Criminal Law* (OUP 2011) 392, quoting from *Keane* [2010] EWCA Crim 2514.
51   Ferzan (n 42) 605. In this case, *both* D and V are wrongdoers (615).
52   See (n 5).
53   Ferzan (n 42) 618.
54   See discussion in Dimock (n 15) 558.
55   ibid 558.

unnecessary: we are not constructing liability at T1 (as we were for Category I cases), we are merely seeking criteria that undermine D's defence based claim of being trapped in a crisis.

A standard of 'recklessness' has been chosen because it is the minimum fault requirement demonstrating some *choice* on D's part (here, a choice to risk), procuring the conditions of a defence.[56] Through choice, of course, the claim of being trapped is likely to be undermined. However, unlike an 'intention' to procure a defence, it could be argued that recklessness has the potential to block defences too widely. For example, where D wears provocative clothing on a night out, or D (a black woman) walks through an area known for race-related violence, she may foresee attack from V and she may foresee the use of defence. If D is attacked in these circumstances and causes harm to V in self-defence, will the defence be blocked?[57] The answer is no. This is because recklessness incorporates a reasonableness standard within the second limb: to be reckless, it must be unreasonable for D to have taken the risk foreseen.[58] Thus, where D wears provocative clothing in our example, or walks through a violent area, she may foresee attack from V; she may foresee the use of defence; but she will not (usually) be reckless to either because her running of the risk is not unreasonable. D's defence will only be blocked where she acts with intention (she becomes a vigilante),[59] or her running of a foreseen risk is unreasonable in the circumstances.

A further potential objection is that although D may have been reckless as to procuring the defence, the recommended scheme will block the defence even where D has not (in fact) caused the events foreseen. For example, if D taunts V (as in our example) to provoke a reaction, and V attacks, should D's defence still be blocked if it transpires that her provocation had no effect on V who was planning to attack anyway? D may be reckless at T1, but she did not create a risk.[60] Although there is some force in this point, it is not sufficient to add a complex and burdensome additional causal requirement. It is contended that, in these very few cases, even when D has not in fact created the circumstances of his own defence, his attempt to do so is still a reasonable basis for denying that he has been trapped in a crisis, and denying him a defence.

Category III: General Prior Fault Constructing Offences

Category III of prior fault, as with Category I, involves D that does not commit an offence at T2 because of a lack of *mens rea* and (potentially) a lack of voluntary movement. However, unlike Category I cases, D's offence cannot be located at T1 because D does not have the *mens rea* for an offence at this stage either. For example,

> D voluntarily becomes intoxicated. Whilst drunk, D decides to play with his new gun and accidentally shoots and kills V. D is unlikely to have made the mistake if sober.

Finding liability in these cases creates serious difficulties; requiring the construction of an offence (in our example, a homicide offence) without essential offence elements at any time in the event.[61] Indeed, recognising

---

56   It is on this basis that I object to blocking defences on the basis of negligence, as we see in the current law of duress. See minority speech of Baroness Hale in *Hasan* [2005] UKHL 22; and discussion in Ferzan (n 42) 615–616.

57   Concern about these cases is discussed in Robinson (n 2) 40; Herrmann (n 10) 753–755; and Ferzan (n 42) 599, 617, 621.

58   *G* [2004] 1 AC 1034.

59   The only exception is boxing in relation to offences against the person and the defence of consent: here we would not want to block D's defence despite intentionally procuring the circumstances of the defence (arranging the boxing match) and intentionally harming V (in the boxing match). However, rather than seeing this as a criticism of the recommended scheme, this may be better presented as a (further) criticism of place of boxing within the law and/or the presentation of 'consent' as a defence. Neither can be pursued here.

60   Paul Robinson, 'Prohibited Risks and Culpable Disregard or Inattentiveness: Challenge and Confusion in the Formulation of Risk-Creation Offences' (2003) Theor Inq in L 367, 376–77.

61   Reminiscent of the dispute in *Brown* (1994) 1 AC 212, the question is not: 'Do we allow a defence where D is intoxicated?'; rather, the question is: 'Does D commit a crime on the basis of her intoxication'? Andrew Simester, 'Intoxication is Never a Defence' (2009) Crim LR 3.

this as a separate category of prior fault is useful to insulate the previous categories from problems and criticisms in this area.

The current law, through the intoxication rules, will construct liability at T2 (allowing D's voluntary intoxication to substitute for a lack of *mens rea*) for offences classified as basic intent, but not for offences classified as specific intent.[62] Although the results of this approach are defensible,[63] the principles underlying them are intensely problematic. First, this is because it appears to be based on the widely discredited idea that becoming voluntarily intoxicated at T1 is *equivalent* to foresight of a specific risk (recklessness) at T2,[64] and even more difficult, that it is *equivalent* to intentional movement at T2 (we refer to this below as the 'equivalence thesis').[65] The equivalence thesis is problematic in its own right, but the latter (equivalence with intentional movement) also creates problems of application: leading to inevitable debate and confusion about what constitutes intentional conduct (the lack of which can be replaced by intoxication), and what constitutes intention as to surrounding circumstances and/or results (the lack of which cannot be replaced by intoxication).[66] A second focus of criticism, for the current law, is the lack of coherence between the treatment of intoxication and the treatment of other potentially culpable reasons for lacking *mens rea* and/or voluntariness. For example, negligence leading to non-intoxicated automatism will also lead to the construction of liability at T2,[67] but such rules are not modelled on intoxication and do not distinguish between basic and specific intent (allowing for the substitution of *any mens rea*).[68] Negligent insanity (for example, resulting where D fails to take medication, leading to a lack of *mens rea*) could be viewed similarly.

Below we outline a number of alternative approaches that seek to make sense (and potentially reform) the rules on intoxication. Having done so, we will then sketch a preferred approach, and show how this could be used as a model for the rationalisation of other inculpatory rules in this category.

There are three main alternative approaches to intoxication in the literature. The first, exemplified by recent Law Commission recommendations, would maintain a basic claim of equivalence in line with the current law (criticised above), but would seek to make the separation of basic and specific (or, to use the language of the Commission, 'integral' and 'non-integral') more precise and consistent.[69] This approach must be rejected for its continued reliance on flawed and problematic equivalences, as well as other aspects discussed elsewhere.[70]

The second alternative is best illustrated by Robinson's general approach to prior fault.[71] Robinson rejects the language of the equivalence thesis, but his approach (liability for causing the conditions at T1, for a defence at T2) still requires some *mens rea* at T1 that can be constructed upon. Thus, as D lacks *mens rea* in Category III cases, Robinson needs to establish some manner of equivalence between D's intoxication and his missing fault, or no liability can be found. This creates an obvious problem for Robinson's attempt at a universal approach to prior fault and leads him (somewhat grudgingly, and with little commitment) to consider several options. Most interesting is the option of a presumption of *mens rea* at T1: justified by its potential for rebuttal by D; and, potentially, by its reclassification as a defence rather than offence element.[72] It is an approach that must be rejected on its own terms, but it is also a useful illustration of our contention that prior fault should be considered separately in its four different guises. Essentially, Robinson's approach is an attempt to force cases within this category (where D lacks *mens rea* at T1 and T2) into Category I cases (where D has *mens rea* at T1, and Robinson's approach has most appeal). Where D has *mens rea* at T1, there

62   *DPP v Majewski* [1977] 1 AC 443.

63   Jeremy Horder, 'Sobering Up? The Law Commission on Criminal Intoxication' [1995] Mod L Rev 534.

64   See discussion in Robinson (n 2) 14–17; Douglas Husak, 'Intoxication and Culpability' [2012] Crim L & Philos 364, 366–368; Rebecca Williams, 'Voluntary Intoxication – A Lost Cause?' (2013) LQ Rev 264, 266–271.

65   *Lipman* [1970] 1 QB 152.

66   See *Heard* [2007] EWCA Crim 125, and the discussion of intentional 'touching'.

67   *Quick* [1973] QB 910. See discussion in John Rumbold and Martin Wasik, 'Diabetic Drivers, Hypoglycaemic Unawareness, and Automatism' [2011] Crim LR 863.

68   Mackay (n 34) 153–156.

69   Law Commission, *Intoxication and the Criminal Law* (Law Com No 314, 2009).

70   John Child, 'Drink, Drugs and Law Reform: A Review of Law Commission Report No 314' [2009] Crim LR 7.

71   Robinson (n 2).

72   ibid 58–63.

is no need for a presumption.[73] However, where D lacks *mens rea* at T1 (as in our example), any presumption of *mens rea* must be rejected if we respect the presumption of innocence and reject the equivalence thesis. This position is not affected by the (equally objectionable) presumption of *mens rea* within the current law, or by the potential to re-classify the presumption as a defence.[74]

The third alternative is the only one to reject the equivalence thesis completely, contending that D's liability should be captured in a new intoxication offence.[75] It is therefore the most appealing, and forms the basis for the preferred approach. A detailed attempt to design such an offence has recently been put forward by Rebecca Williams.[76] Williams creates a general offence (structured similarly to inchoate liability), in which D is liable for 'committing the *actus reus* of offence X [in our example, a homicide offence] while intoxicated'. Williams' approach is able to find liability (in line with public policy expectations), and to do so by explicitly focusing on D's blameworthy intoxication rather than trying to transform it into *mens rea* for a principal offence (in our example, for murder or manslaughter). It captures the unique aspects of prior fault in this category; labelling and punishing D for what he has done (causing harm whilst intoxicated) rather than what he has not done (D has not committed an offence with *mens rea*).

This final alternative (a separate intoxication offence) offers the most promising option for reform. However, the approach outlined by Williams will require modification. This is because, although Williams is correct that her approach accurately labels D (*actus reus* plus intoxication), this does not mean that D is accurately or appropriately criminalised. Under the equivalence thesis, this second question of appropriate criminalisation does not arise: if intoxication is equivalent to the missing *mens rea*, then appropriate criminalisation of the 'offence with *mens rea*' will be equally applicable in the intoxication (equivalent) context. However, once it is accepted that intoxication is *not* equivalent to *mens rea*, then the wrongs captured by the new offence become quite different and require separate justification: leading us to question whether *actus reus* plus intoxication is always sufficiently wrongful to be criminal?

The problem for Williams' approach is a general one, with every combination of *actus reus* and intoxication capturing a new combination of wrongs that are simply assumed (within her approach) to be deserving of criminal sanction. However, the potential for over-criminalisation is most obvious in relation to two types of offences where *mens rea* is central to the substantive wrong. The first type of offences, partially recognised by Williams, are inchoate offences or (more accurately) any offence including an ulterior *mens rea* element. As the focus of these offences is the mind of D (as opposed to a harmful *actus reus*), Williams acknowledges that the '*actus reus* plus intoxication' offence may not be appropriate.[77] She suggests that a list of statutory exceptions may resolve this. However, such lists are prone to inaccuracies,[78] and her choice not to rule out theft (which includes an element of ulterior *mens rea*), is demonstration of exactly that risk:[79] the law does not recognise the *actus reus* of theft as deserving of criminalisation without D's ulterior intention to permanently deprive (even where V suffers the same loss[80]), so why should it do so where D is intoxicated? It may, but this requires *separate* consideration. The second type of offence to highlight problems for the Williams approach, building upon the first, is any offence where a *mens rea* of intention or knowledge is required: for example, knowledge for complicity; intentional touching for sexual offences; knowledge that the victim is

---

73   It may be difficult to prove that D had *mens rea* at T1 where some time has passed, but this is not novel for the law, and certainly no reason to shift the burden of establishing *mens rea*.

74   A similar approach is offered by Husak, who would allow for objective recklessness at T1 to construct liability at T2. Husak (n 63) 371.

75   First articulated by Smith and Williams in the Criminal Law Revision Committee, *Offences Against the Person* (1980) 113–114.

76   Williams (n 63).

77   ibid 284.

78   John Child, 'The Structure, Coherence and Limits of Inchoate Liability: The New Ulterior Element' (2013) LS, discussing the inadequacy of statutory lists used to limit infinite inchoate liability.

79   Williams (n 63) 283.

80   Williams highlights that from 'the victim's point of view' a deprivation is theft (279). This is true, but the criminal law is concerned with the defendant: where a sober person takes without the intention to permanently deprive there is no theft (despite the victim's deprivation), and thus, without a claim that intoxication is equivalent to such an intention, this does not justify the application of Williams' offence.

human for homicide; and so on.[81] Here, again, the *actus reus* of the offence is only deemed to be deserving of criminalisation where a high level of *mens rea* is present, and the assumption that *actus reus* plus intoxication will be sufficiently blameworthy is on weak footing.[82]

These two illustrations represent the tip of a critical iceberg, and one that does not 'vanish' on recognition that D is being charged with a new intoxication offence.[83] D may be appropriately labelled by Williams' approach, but the question of appropriate criminalisation remains unanswered. Some use could be made of a part of her policy not yet remarked upon: that D will not be liable where a 'sober and reasonable person' may have done likewise. However, although this is useful to address problematic facts (for example, while intoxicated D trips on a wire that he would not have seen even if sober), it is insufficient as a tool for evaluating the wrongfulness of offence *actus reus*, not least because (as our examples above illustrate) the law is full of unreasonable conduct that we only see as deserving of criminalisation where D has a specific *mens rea*.[84]

The preferred approach, therefore, attempts to capture the many benefits of the Williams approach, but to start from the opposite end: identifying and criminalising '*actus reus* plus intoxication' only where a case for such criminalisation can be made.[85] Core offences are likely to include causing property damage whilst intoxicated, causing harm against the person whilst intoxicated, and so on.[86] Where the current law criminalises for basic intent offences despite a lack of *mens rea* (through the equivalence thesis) and acquits for specific intent offences despite D's voluntary intoxication, the preferred approach will only find liability for the (appropriately labelled) intoxication offence.

The potential for the preferred approach to apply consistently within this category of prior fault (i.e., beyond intoxication) leads to an interesting debate. In the context of negligent automatism,[87] and even negligent insanity,[88] it is contended that the preferred approach has considerable promise. As with voluntary intoxication, rather than working on an inaccurate and inconsistent model of equivalence in order to find liability for current offences,[89] a discrete offence involving certain harms combined with negligent automatism or negligent insanity would bring coherence to the law. This could either be achieved within the intoxication offence (specified harm plus voluntary intoxication *or* negligent automatism *or* negligent insanity), or alongside it as a separate (but consistent) offence. Debate arises, however, in cases where D's (non-intoxicated) negligence leads to a lack of *mens rea* but not an automatic state (using our example, where D accidentally shoots the gun due to extreme fatigue rather than intoxication). The question becomes, is the new offence best designed to target harm caused by extreme negligence (in the sense that it causes complete loss of control) and common negligence (as with intoxication), or are we uncovering a more general belief that negligently caused harms should be criminalised?[90] In either guise, the separation of liability within a new offence appears to offer the logical way forward.

---

81   I have not included examples where an alternative offence (with the same *actus reus*) allows for a lesser *mens rea* (e.g., intention to kill or cause GBH for murder). The examples given are those where intention or knowledge is required for D's conduct to be considered criminal at all.

82   This point is used by Horder to defend the current specific/basic intent distinction. Horder (n 62).

83   Williams (n 63) 283.

84   For example, a reasonable person would not *risk* sexual contact with minors, and yet the law only criminalises intentional contact (Sexual Offences Act 2003). Whether it should criminalise intoxicated contact requires, again, independent consideration.

85   *Actus reus* plus intoxication, in this context, includes cases where D lacks *voluntary control of her body* due to intoxication.

86   Whether these core examples are deserving of criminalisation, and any other examples beyond them, would be the subject of individual consideration.

87   For example, where D drives while very tired and falls asleep.

88   For example, where D negligently fails to take her medication and loses control.

89   Mackay (n 34); Mitchell (n 34) 63.

90   This would represent a considerable extension of the current law, but perhaps one that we see through the proliferation of negligence offences and the expanding use of prior fault in automatism cases. Rumbold and Wasik (n 66).

Category IV: General Prior Fault Blocking Defences

The final category of prior fault, as with Category II, focuses on D that completes the *actus reus* and *mens rea* of an offence and is seeking to rely on a defence. However, unlike Category II cases, where D's defence at T2 was blocked on the basis of his foresight and manipulation at T1, Category IV cases involve no specific anticipation from D. For example,

> D voluntarily becomes intoxicated. Whilst drunk, D mistakenly believes that V is about to attack him. D shoots
> and kills V in self-defence. D is unlikely to have made the mistake if sober.

The availability of defences, where D is intoxicated, varies considerably within the current law. For example, where a defence (such as duress) requires reasonable belief and fortitude then D's intoxicated mistake will obviously undermine his defence;[91] indeed, even where a subjective test is employed (as with self-defence), D's intoxicated mistake may still undermine his defence.[92] However, for certain statutory defences, this will not be the case.[93] A similar debate has emerged in relation to honest (subjective) belief in self-defence, where such belief is based on insane or insane-like delusions.[94]

It should be clear that D's lack of foresight (of his future offence, or the potential defence) makes this category of prior fault very different from Category II. However, as with Category II, we are again considering the availability of defences (as opposed to the construction of offences) and so the same principles should be applied.

Most interesting are defences (such as self-defence) that will allow D's defence to be based upon an unreasonable but honest belief, but not upon an intoxicated mistake. We must ask whether the general fault displayed by D's voluntary intoxication is sufficient (and sufficiently different from other forms of unreasonable belief) that it should undermine his defence? Our focus is not whether D is trapped in a crisis as it was for Category II cases (D is mistaken and therefore, in reality, is not trapped). Rather, our focus is on what we want or expect of D where he *thinks* he is trapped. As in our example, where D mistakenly believes he is under attack (or that another is under attack), do we want him to act in defence (in which case the defence should be allowed) or not (in which case it should be blocked)?

This question leads to three potential ways forward. First, it may be that we want to block D's defence because *any* unreasonable mistake undermines the basis for criminal defences. Something like this approach is supported by Williams, and would require all criminal defences to employ a reasonableness standard.[95] Secondly, it could be contended that D's defence should be allowed, that we would want (or at least excuse) D's defensive acts. This approach leads us to consider those defences where an objective standard is employed, asking whether these should be amended or on what basis defences like self-defence should be distinguished. It also leads to consideration of the proposed intoxication offence; whether an intoxicated mistake could form the basis for a defence to this new offence. Finally, it could be contended that a subjective test should be preferred (for some or all defences), but that reliance on intoxicated mistakes are so unreasonable that they should continue to be exempt. This approach, similar to the principled inconsistency discussed when concluding our Category III discussion, requires more work on why intoxication is different from other negligent mistakes, leading us to question whether any others (for example, insane-like delusions) should be similarly exempt.

Clarified in this manner, the question is an appealing one. However, in want of a settled preference, it is one that will have to await further consideration.

---

91   *Hasan* [2005] UKHL 22.

92   *Hatton* [2005] EWCA Crim 2951.

93   *Jaggard v Dickinson* [1981] 3 All ER 716.

94   *Oye* [2013] EWCA Crim 1725, where the Court of Appeal commented obita that an insane delusion could not be the basis for an honest belief in self-defence.

95   Williams (n 63) 285–286.

Conclusion

Categorising and grouping issues within the criminal law can be a rewarding process, both to identify the principles that underlie such groupings (allowing for more effective evaluation), and to expose internal inconsistencies (requiring justification or change). However, such categorisation must be undertaken with great care. Indeed, it was the perceived similarity between the four categories of prior fault discussed in this chapter that led to the inappropriate expansion of the 'actio libera in causa' doctrine,[96] and commentators such as Robinson criticising general inconsistencies and proposing general solutions.[97]

This chapter has attempted to identify four distinct categories of prior fault cases: distinguished as to the inculpatory or exculpatory rules at issue, as well as in relation to the specific or general character of D's prior fault. In doing so, it has rejected criticism of inconsistency between categories, demonstrating that such inconsistency is inevitable and beneficial, but sought to challenge any inconsistency within categories. At each stage, we have looked to move the debate forward, proposing alternative or adapted approaches in light of clarified problems. Each proposal requires further discussion, of course, but it is hoped that such discussion can now take place more fruitfully within the identified categories.

---

96 Dimock (n 15) 550–552.
97 Robinson (n 2).

Chapter 4
Transfer of Defences

Michael Bohlander[1]

Introduction

D wants to shoot V1 but hits V2, who is standing next to V1, by mistake. D's intent to harm or kill V1 is 'transferred' to V2.[2] The traditional reasoning behind this principle is straightforward: the offence of murder requires the killing of another human being, not of a *particular* human being; Jeremy Horder calls this the 'impersonality principle'.[3] D wanted to kill a human being; the fact that he did not manage to kill the one he intended to kill does not enter into the equation. Consider this variation: D is being attacked by V1, D shoots at V1 to defend himself, misses, and hits V2 instead. The conventional approach to this example is that the intent is transferred to V2, but so is apparently any defence that D had vis-à-vis V1, if indeed he had one. The case that is commonly cited for this proposition is *Gross*[4]: provoked by blows from her husband V1, D shot at him intending to kill him, but missed and killed V2 instead. However, *Gross* is not much of an authority as far as the rank of the source in the judicial hierarchy is concerned. It is also far from clear whether the example of provocation, which aims at excusing a loss of self-control, that is, an uncontrolled act, can simply be extended to other more relational defences such as duress, necessity, or self-defence, and so forth. This chapter will highlight some of the inconsistencies produced by the traditional doctrine. There is a structural clash between the *abstract* impersonality approach underlying the transferred malice doctrine that creates normative intentional liability for factually unintended results, and the *concrete* relational approach to relational defences based in one way or another on the behaviour of an *individual* victim: D may under law be considered as having an intent to kill a generic human being V, but he will have such a relational defence only against a particular human being V—the idea of a 'generic right to self-defence' regardless of the conduct of the victim, is patently absurd.

Individual Problems

Problem 1: Cumulative Results

The traditional transferred intent doctrine creates dogmatic problems when there is a result with the intended *and* the unintended victim: D shoots at V1 with intent to kill, and because V1 can duck away, the bullet merely grazes his arm but hits V2 in the head and kills her. Here, D would clearly be guilty of wounding V1 with intent as a lesser included offence to murder, and indeed, with attempted murder—unless the intent for the lethal result that did not materialize in V1 was transferred to V2. But can one split the intention of D? If one cannot, is there any intent 'left' for the wounding charge, or can we not transfer anything at all, even though the intent went wider than the result in V1? Can D possibly be reckless with regard to V1 at the same time as intending to kill V2 under the transferred malice doctrine? Does D have a general intent to kill any human

---

1 This chapter is a substantially shortened and modified version of my previous publication, 'Transferred Malice and Transferred Defences: A Critique of the Traditional Doctrine and Arguments for a Change in Paradigm' [2010] 13 New Crim LR 555. References have been largely omitted for reasons of space and the reader is referred to that paper.

2 See the cases of *R v Latimer* [1886] 17 QBD 359 and *R v Pembliton* [1874] LR 2 CCR 119.

3 Jeremy Horder, 'Transferred Malice and the Remoteness of Unexpected Outcomes from Intentions' [2006] Crim LR 383.

4 *R v Gross* [1913] 23 Cox CC 455.

being affected by his actions, regardless of the number of potential victims? Can we *extend* the intention to V2 rather than *transfer* it? The definition of murder does not require that only *one* person is killed in one act, and indeed, if D as a terrorist were to place a bomb in a public place with at least the *Woollin*[5] intent to cause the death of an unspecified number of persons, would anyone doubt that he would be taken as having that intent for each and every one of the eventual victims and consequently be convicted of murder on as many counts as there are victims? However, does D's modus operandi not already tell us something about the nature of D's *actual* rather than *legal* intent? Should the modus operandi have an impact on how the *law* treats the intent?

Problem 2: Remoteness of Result and Unforeseen or Modified Causal Chains

Jeremy Horder[6] has argued that the transferred malice doctrine should not attach to results that are so remote from the original act of the perpetrator that they appear non-attributable to her. However, is the following already a remote result? D shoots at V1 with *Woollin* intent to kill in self-defence, but V1 is standing next to a large fuel truck, hidden by trees and entirely unrecognizable to D. The bullet misses V1, ricochets off a wall and hits the fuel truck which explodes, killing V1 as well as V2 through V100. Had D merely missed V1 and hit V2, with or without a ricochet, the traditional doctrine would cover the killing by self-defence. Structurally, there is no difference if D kills more than one person. Is D also justified in killing V2–V100? Let us remove the link by another degree: the tanker truck damages the main power line to a nearby nuclear facility. The nuclear plant's computer system suffers a short power outage that causes a malfunction which results in a leak and the contamination of the entire neighbourhood, affecting 20,000 people, 75 per cent of whom will die. Is this too remote for transferred malice to attach? Possibly. But by removing this course of events from the ambit of the transfer of liability, we also rob D of her transferred defence. She may now no longer be liable under criminal law because she may not be grossly negligent, but potentially she is still liable under tort law, even if she acted merely negligently. Had she still had the defence, she might also escape tort liability.

Problem 3: Crossed Defences

Furthermore, one can imagine cases of 'crossed defences' that may not be too far removed from real life: D is being seriously provoked by V1 and loses self-control; at that same moment V2, an accomplice of V1, attacks D with a samurai sword. If D shoots at V2 to fend off the attack, but hits V1 by mistake, the traditional view would transfer the self-defence to V1 and allow a full defence rather than a partial one, regardless of whether D wanted to kill or merely disable V2 at a level lower than GBH. If D shoots at V1 out of sheer rage from the provocation in the split-second before V2 attacks, and mistakenly hits V2, the transfer doctrine would shift the provocation defence to V2, which would merely provide a partial defence if D intended to kill or cause GBH, and none at all if D only intended to cause harm below the level of GBH. In addition, one might question whether in the second example D could argue self-defence at all, because he was not acting in the exercise of self-defence, so the subjective element[7] for self-defence might be missing. The confusion increases exponentially if D hits both of them in any of the two scenarios. Yet, if D had two guns and fired them at V1 and V2 at the same time, hitting both as intended, he might be acquitted of the murder of V2 and get a manslaughter conviction for V1; if we further accept that provocation applies to both V1 and V2 anyway and is not 'transferred', D will get a manslaughter conviction for V2 even if his self-defence plea for V2 fails. It is obvious that to leave the solution of these matters to the vagaries of the potential courses of events is deeply unsatisfactory.

---

5   *R v Woollin* [1999] AC 82.
6   ibid (n 2).
7   *Williams (Gladstone)* [1987] 3 All ER 411.

Problem 4: Response of the Innocent Victim

We need to be aware of another consequence of the transfer of defences: if D properly attacks V1 in self-defence but misses her, and his reaction is about to affect the innocent bystander V2, the transfer of self-defence to the relation D ⇔ V2 may mean that V2 cannot employ self-defence against D's attack on her, because there is conflicting authority on whether in principle there can be self-defence against an otherwise lawful action. This would seem to be an absurd consequence in our scenario because we cannot in all seriousness expect innocent V2 to stand by and suffer her rights and interests to be infringed, and maybe even get killed.

Problem 5: Partial Transfer of Defences

The fact that the law ties the transfer of the defence to the transfer of the intent produces another counterintuitive consequence. Because a transfer of intent is only allowed for objects of an identical nature and not for objects of differing qualities, the following scenario can arise: D is defending himself against an attack from V1 by hitting at him with a crow bar. He misses and hits V2 in the face, thereby also destroying her custom-made sunglasses. Although the intent and the defence for the facial injury may be transferred, depending on what the intent vis-à-vis V1 was, there is no transfer either of the intent or of the defence to the potential reckless criminal damage charge, or at the very least to the possible claim in tort by V2. This means D may be justified for the GBH done to V2 but not for the criminal damage that may have been an unavoidable side effect to his otherwise justified action, and is a much lesser offence into the bargain. Had D hit V1 as intended and broken his glasses, too, the damage to the glasses would have been covered by self-defence, and neither criminal nor civil sanctions or remedies would have been available to V1. We therefore realize that a defence may be only partially transferred.

Problem 6: Consent

The transferred defence model becomes even more suspect if we look at the example of consent. Imagine V1 who has debts to D, and consents to D taking £ 50 from his wallet. D by mistake grabs money from the wallet of V2. Or, to use an example from the Offences Against the Person Act (OAPA) 1861: D tackles football player V1 during a match, but by mistake wounds referee V2, who stands next to them. Consent operates within the *actus reus*, but would we say that the defence of consent by V1 in the theft example is transferred to V2, with the consequence that D lawfully acquires the money? In the second example, consent does not cover actual bodily harm (ABH) and above, unless the wider *Barnes*[8] criteria for implied consent in competitive sports are fulfilled, which may be hard to imagine for referees; in other words although it may be acceptable if the players in the heat of the match treat each other with a certain amount of roughness, this can as such never be the case for a referee. Will D now be justified in inflicting serious injury on the referee, if he had been covered under *Barnes* vis-à-vis another player?

The Domestic Development in English and Welsh Law

Provocation as a Starting Point for the Transferred Defence Principle?

Gross was concerned with a case of provocation. Consider in this context the case of *Davies*,[9] where the Court of Appeal made it clear that provocation may stem from a person other than the victim. The defence already implies a potential split between who or what may be its cause and thus the *potentially intended* victim, and who may suffer its consequences. It is also based on D's loss of self-control: his inability to conduct himself in accordance with what in a sober mind he would know to be right and wrong. Provocation, in its final analysis, is a defence based on an impairment of D's normal mental faculties. The reasonable man standard

---

8   *R v Barnes* [2005] Crim LR 381.
9   *R v Davies* [1975] 1 All ER 890.

in the second prong of the test is merely a public policy qualifier that says in effect nothing more than that society will tolerate such loss of control as a defence only if *anyone* would have been prone to react in that manner. Once we accept that *loss of control*, as provocation is now called under the Coroners and Justice Act 2009, is a partial defence because D is no longer able to comprehend fully the wrongness of her actions and act accordingly, we understand that *Gross* is not a case of transfer of a defence at all: just like a temporary mental disease may exempt *any and all* actions of D committed in that state from liability, a temporary loss of control exempts *any and all* actions committed under its influence. This is borne out by the reasoning of Darling J at the end of the judgment in *Gross*, a passage that is rarely if ever cited. After referring to the transferred intent doctrine for *intentional* homicide, he goes on to say that 'provocation was operating upon the mind of the prisoner':

> The reason of the distinction is that the ordinary balance of mind of the accused was so upset. As is often said, the law, in leniency and mercy, does not hold a person to the full consequences of an action committed in such circumstances.[10]

Similarly, it would be even more incorrect to speak of a *transferred* defence if D missed V1 and hit V2 in a state of insanity or intoxication. In those two scenarios, D is excused within the accepted parameters of these defences no matter what he does and which results he causes.

Law Reform

When drafting its recommendations for a Criminal Code of England and Wales in 1989, the Draft Code, the Law Commission had created the following provision in Clause 24:

> (2) Any defence on which a person might have relied on a charge of an offence in relation to a person or thing within his contemplation is open to him on a charge of the same offence in relation to a person or thing not within his contemplation.[11]

The justification given in the second volume of the report was:

> Subsection (2), providing for the transfer of defences, will be useful for the avoidance of doubt. It enables a person who affects an uncontemplated victim to rely on a defence that would have been available to him if he had affected the person or thing he had in contemplation.[12]

This paragraph has a footnote, no. 89, which refers to Appendix B in volume 1, example 24(iii). Example 24(iii) reads:

> D, under provocation, aims a shot at O with intent to kill him. The shot misses O and kills P. D may raise the plea of provocation. ...[13]

The Draft Code does not mention the case of *Gross* on which this example is clearly modelled. Under traditional transferred malice doctrine, the reference in Clause 24(2) to the 'charge of the same offence' is also somewhat misleading: if, under the application of Clause 24(2), D intended to kill V1 in justified self-defence but instead hit V2 in the chest, causing her GBH, surely the fact that vis-à-vis V1 he would have been charged

---

10   *R v Gross* (n 3) 456.
11   Law Commission, *A Criminal Code for England and Wales, Vol. 1, Report and Draft Criminal Code Bill* (Law Commission No 177, 1989) 53
12   ibid vol 2, Commentary [8.61].
13   ibid (n 10) vol 1, 159.

with murder would not rob D of self-defence on a charge of causing GBH vis-à-vis V2? The Law Commission revisited the above-mentioned reform proposals in 1993 in its report on offences against the person[14]:

> 42.1 Clause 25 of the Bill accompanying LCCP 122 [Law Commission Consultation Paper 122] restated, in the most general terms and not only in relation to offences against the person, the common law doctrine known as "transferred intent" (subsection (l)), and provided a corresponding rule for "transferred" defences. We received very little comment on the clause, and are satisfied, in particular, that the formulation of subsection (1) accurately represents the current law. Both subsections appear unchanged in clause 32 of the final draft Bill. Accordingly, the following explanation of the clause repeats in substance that which we gave in LCCP 122.
>
> Transferred defences
>
> 42.6 Clause 32(2) enables a person who affects an uncontemplated victim to rely on a defence that would have been available to him if he had affected the person or thing he had in contemplation. The provision will be useful for the avoidance of doubt.

Clause 32 in the attached Bill read:

> 32.-(1) In determining whether a person is guilty of an offence, his intention to cause, or his awareness of a risk that he will cause, a result in relation to a person or thing capable of being the victim or subject-matter of the offence shall be treated as an intention to cause or, as the case may be, an awareness of a risk that he will cause, that result in relation to any other person or thing affected by his conduct.
>
> (2) Any defence on which a person might have relied on a charge of an offence in relation to a person or thing within his contemplation is open to him on a charge of the same offence in relation to a person or thing not within his contemplation.

No serious analysis appears to have gone into the Law Commission's proposals, as they themselves admitted to having 'received very little comment on the clause'. In effect, the principle that was enunciated as being clear is, as we saw above, highly doubtful. More to the point, provocation is a bad example for the transferred defence principle because it is conceptually too far removed from relational defences such as self-defence, necessity, and duress.

Case Law

The most recent case that addresses the issue of transferred malice and defences is a tort law case heard in the Queen's Bench Division, *Bici and another v Ministry of Defence*.[15] The facts of the case were that:

> [A]t about midnight on July 2 1999, three British soldiers involved in a United Nations peacekeeping operation in Kosovo shot and killed two men, Fahri Bici and Avni Dundi, and injured another two. The men, all Kosovar Albanians, were travelling together in a car in the city of Pristina . . . The first claimant in this action, Mohamet Bici, was injured by a bullet which struck him in the face. It entered his mouth and exited the lower left side of his jaw. Apart from the not inconsiderable pain, it has also caused longer term problems with eating and speaking. The second claimant, his cousin Skender Bici, did not suffer any direct physical injury but alleges that he has suffered psychiatric illness as a consequence of being in the car, both as a result of being put in personal fear, and from witnessing the incident. Both claimants sue for damages both in negligence and trespass. The soldiers say that they were acting in self-defence being in fear of their own lives.[16]

---

14   Law Commission, *Legislating the Criminal Code: Offences Against the Person and General Principles* (Law Commission No. 218, 1993).

15   *Bici and another v Ministry of Defence* [2004] EWHC (QB) 786.

16   ibid 1.

The defendants claimed that they solely shot to kill Fahri Bici, who was allegedly pointing an AK-47 at them. The remaining victims would, from the defendants' point of view, thus be cases of unintended collateral damage that should be covered by the transferred defence doctrine, if and to the extent that their intended actions were covered under self-defence. The High Court ultimately rejected that defence and argued as follows:

> Second, he says that even although he was not the target of the soldiers' fire, in circumstances where he has been injured as a consequence of the deliberate act, the doctrine of transferred malice applies and permits him to sue the defendant. In support of this principle he relies upon the certain observations of Lord Hutton in *Livingstone v. Ministry of Defence* [1984] NILR 356. The facts were that the plaintiff was injured in Northern Ireland when a soldier fired a baton round after some soldiers were attacked by rioters. It was accepted that the round had been deliberately fired, although denied that it had been intended to strike the plaintiff. The claim was in negligence and assault and battery. The trial judge dismissed the claim in negligence but did not give a ruling on the question of battery. On appeal the Northern Ireland Court of Appeal allowed the appeal and ordered a new trial. Hutton J, giving the judgment of the court, rejected the argument that there could be no battery because the plaintiff was not the chosen target in the following terms (p 361):

> "In my judgment when a soldier deliberately fires at one rioter intending to strike him and he misses him and hits another rioter nearby, the soldier has "intentionally" applied force to the rioter who has been struck. Similarly if a soldier fires a rifle bullet at a rioter intending to strike him and the bullet strikes that rioter and passes through his body and wounds another rioter directly behind the first rioter, whom the soldier had not seen, both rioters have been "intentionally" struck by the soldier and, assuming that the force used was not justified, the soldier has committed a battery against both".[17]

The High Court accepted this approach[18] and the idea of transferred malice,[19] and as becomes clear from the next passage, would also have countenanced the transfer of self-defence:

> Of course, if the defendants were to have a defence of self-defence available to them with respect to the targeted individual, then it would run equally to the transferred claimant. The defendant can be no worse off in respect of the latter. However, since I have rejected that defence, it follows that the defendant is liable in this case to Mohamet Bici in trespass to the person as well as negligence.[20]

Modern Academic Commentary

The literature mostly contains brief references without much argument to the effect that if intent is transferred, so are any defences. In addition, hardly any make reference to the case law after *Gross*. Ormerod,[21] for example, states:

> If D shoots X with intent to kill, because X is making a murderous attack on him and this is the only way in which he can preserve his own life, he does not intend an actus reus (in the broader sense, above), for to kill in these circumstances is justified. If, however, D misses X and inadvertently kills V, an innocent bystander, he does cause an actus reus but he is not guilty of murder for there is no mens rea (in the broader sense) to transfer; the result which he intended was a perfectly lawful one.

---

17   ibid 68. The Irish Court referred to *James v Campbell* (1832) 5 Car & P 372 and to *Ball v Axten* (1866) 4 F & F.
18   ibid 71.
19   More interestingly, the court in Livingstone concluded that both victims had been intentionally struck, which is an important argument with regard to the question of whether anything was transferred, or whether the intent was not merely extended.
20   ibid 72.
21   D Ormerod, *Smith & Hogan's Criminal Law* (OUP 2011) 127–128.

This argument focusing on *mens rea* is not immediately clear: actus reus and mens rea in the broader sense apparently here refer to the purely offence-related elements—that is, killing a human being with intent, rather than the specific scenario of killing *V* with intent. However, even if that were accepted, I am not sure Ormerod's statement is entirely persuasive: If D acts in self-defence in the first example, then—as Ormerod rightly states—there is no *actus reus*,[22] and the question of what he intends to do becomes secondary. Yet, if D hits an uninvolved bystander, the logic of the argument must be as follows: if the case is one for which the doctrine of transferred malice applies, then *as a corollary, the defence is transferred* to the new victim, which in effect means there is no *actus reus*, either, because self-defence is a defence that goes to the *actus reus*. In other words, the transfer of intent theory is merely a doctrinal catalyst for triggering the transfer of the defence; the impact of that defence on *actus reus* or *mens rea* is determined by the nature of the defence, not by the nature of the catalyst.

Simester and Sullivan[23] also use an example of self-defence, yet merely refer to *Gross*; however, in a footnote[24] they say the following:

> Note that the transfer of a defence will not necessarily preclude liability for an independent offence. It may, for example, have been grossly negligent to shoot at Tom because of the risk of hitting Bill.

This 'independent negligence' scenario would not appear to be supported by the courts, especially the tort cases of *Livingstone* and *Bici*, which seem to say that for a defence to be transferred, no additional criteria apart from the transfer of the intent need to be fulfilled. The same can be said about the Law Commission's views. The gross negligence manslaughter variety, which Simester and Sullivan seem to have in mind, also presupposes a duty of care toward *V2*—a duty of care toward V1 cannot simply be transferred to V2, because the duties are an *objective* element and depend on whether *that particular V* was within the protective remit of the facts giving rise to a particular category of duty.[25] Gross negligence generally would seem to be excluded from the categories of *mens rea* transferrable under the transferred malice doctrine, although Simester and Sullivan emphasize that recklessness might be sufficient.[26] If D was justified in shooting at V1, the only discernible basis for such a duty toward V2, namely creating a dangerous situation (*Miller*[27]), fails because D is *allowed to behave dangerously*. It would be unusual to base a duty of care toward an unintended victim on that lawful dangerous act directed at someone else.

Conversely, if it was grossly negligent in the circumstances to shoot at V1, the defence in itself will very likely fail against V1 because then it may not have been reasonable force in the first place. Moreover, if, as Simester and Sullivan say, the reasonableness element in self-defence should be interpreted broadly and liberally[28] because of the frequent need for D to make a snap judgment in such circumstances, it is difficult to see when a jury would say that D's action was still within the ambit of reasonableness vis-à-vis V1 but *grossly* negligent vis-à-vis V2. They may agree that it was *negligent*, but that is not usually a basis for *criminal* liability under English and Welsh law, and by accepting it as an exclusion criterion for the defence, one would in fact be introducing simple negligence homicide through the back door. One has to be careful not to mix up two things here: under sec 76(4) of the Criminal Justice and Immigration Act 2008, some people may say that a negligent error might, in theory, rob D of the defence vis-à-vis the intended victim V1, so why should this not be the case with V2? The answer may be that as regards V1, D is already engaging in intentional or reckless dangerous conduct to ward off an attack, so he has an *actual mens rea* to cause harm to V1 independent of the mere belief supporting the defence. With V2, D has no *actual mens rea* at all but merely one based on *a legal fiction* (transferred malice doctrine). D may not even (be able to) see V2 and therefore

22 So clearly, e.g., Michael Jefferson, Criminal Law (9th edn, Longman 2009) 332.

23 AP Simester, GR Sullivan, JR Spencer and G Virgo, *Criminal Law: Theory and Doctrine* (3rd edn, Hart 2007) 157.

24 ibid 209.

25 This is supported by Glanville Williams, *Criminal Law: The General Part* (2nd edn, 1961) 137–138, who concludes that there can be no 'transferred negligence'.

26 ibid 156–157.

27 *R v Miller* [1983] 2 AC 161.

28 ibid 705–708.

not even be *actually* reckless or (grossly) negligent, and thus the *only actual fault* for the damage or injury resulting to V2 lies in D's negligence surrounding the modalities of the exercise of the defence.

Glanville Williams pointed out that even in transferred intent cases the law still requires proof of *actus reus* and *mens rea*, and so 'it follows that defences are in effect transferred with the malice'.[29] Although this would seem to support in principle what I said above with respect to the function of the transferred intent trigger as a mere catalyst for the transfer of defences that retain their nature, I am not sure whether it is entirely accurate to put it that way, unless one subscribes to a view that sees the *absence of defences* as *negative elements* of either the *actus reus*—for example, as an emanation of the word 'unlawful' often used in statutes to describe prohibited conduct—or the *mens rea* (compare to this the largely abandoned German theory of the *negative Tatbestandsmerkmale*[30]). Whereas in a trial it may be for the prosecution to disprove most defences once raised on the facts by the defence, that procedural issue should not cloud the fact that as a matter of substantive law, they are not really part of the offence description and thus of neither *actus reus* nor *mens rea*: murder, as commonly understood, is 'killing another human being with intent to kill or cause GBH', not 'killing another human being with intent to kill or cause GBH and without having either a justificatory or excusatory or partial defence'. If that were so, one might argue that the prosecution would *eo ipso* have to address the absence of any such defence even if the defendant did not raise them. However, Williams is right when he emphasizes that the accidental result is *in fact* always at best negligently caused. He explains by juxtaposing the example of D shooting at a duck and hitting V with D shooting at V1 and hitting V2. In the first case criminal liability arises only if D was grossly negligent with regard to V, in the second example D is immediately guilty of intentional homicide.[31] Stating that in his view the rationale for the transferred intent doctrine is merely an emotional one, Williams demands that the trend should be to accept a concretisation[32] of D's intent on the *physical* person he intends to attack. The result could be a charge of attempted murder to which D could, for example, plead self-defence, and potentially an independent charge of manslaughter or bodily harm if the requirements for that offence were fulfilled. That would, as Williams argues, concur better with the average person's moral attitude to the scenario.

Choice of Paradigm

Impersonality or Concretisation?

At the core of this matter is primarily the decision of each legal system about whether it uses an impersonality or concretisation approach in defining intent. In the first alternative, the categorical nature, not the identity, of the object of D's act is relevant for the decision whether categorical intent applies to an *in casu* unintended victim; in such a scenario it is perhaps better to speak of *replication* or *extension* of intent instead of *transfer*. In the second alternative, the intent is individualised because it is the individual identity *in addition to* the categorical nature of the object of D's act that matters; the logical consequence is a liability for attempt at V1 and a negligence liability vis-à-vis V2, if the criminal law allows for it. One will have to accept, however, that there is no logical preference to either way of approaching the premise of the problem: it is only the *consequences* that flow more or less directly and logically from each premise. The choice of the premise is hard to justify by way of *logical* argument: the arguments for or against impersonality lie at a stage before the legal argument; they are in the final analysis *moral* attitudes to what the law *should achieve* and relate to questions of due process and crime control models, as so often. Remember the above-mentioned approach of Glanville Williams, who saw this as an 'emotional' issue.[33] Moral attitudes are the building blocks of societal

---

29   ibid 132.

30   See my *Principles of German Criminal Law* (Hart 2009) 75.

31   Williams (n 24) 134.

32   ibid 134–135.

33   Williams, ibid 134–135. See also more recently, Shachar Eldar, 'The Limits of Transferred Malice' [2012] OJLS 633, who advocates a different model: 'I have drawn three conclusions. First, the common view that differentiates between the implications of bad aim and mistaken identity is misguided. Secondly, in both instances, transferred malice should be employed in cases of the cross border between offences that differ only in the subjective or culpability-based social harm that underlie them, and where the alternative of attempt liability is not available. Finally, the doctrine's application is best curtailed by the neglected qualifier of reasonable foresight'. (658)

conventions. Which attitude you have may be based on reasons that cannot really be described or critiqued by logic, but merely be criticized for violating or emulating other, possibly higher-order moral conventions. If you are a crime control person of a punitive disposition, you will tend to extend liability as far and as harshly as necessary, thus you are more likely to opt for the impersonality approach. Adherents to due process principles will favour the fair treatment of the offender, combined with concepts such as the harm principle, fair labelling, and the ultima ratio function of criminal law, toward a concretisation and foreseeability model. You may have good reasons for being either a crime control or a due process person, but it is difficult to establish a logical preference for either position.

The concretisation model has in my view the better argument on its side because I am fairly confident that the average person, the proverbial 'common man' for whose consumption the law is after all meant to be made, will have difficulty in understanding the idea that harming someone you did not want to harm at all or whom you did not even see when you acted, should be considered as having been encompassed by your intent. It simply seems too remote from the everyday perception of the moral character of what D does; in other words, it violates common sense. The concretisation approach also better synchronises intent and motive—concepts that even an educated layperson will not always be able to distinguish. The acceptance of any law will in the long run always depend on the degree of congruence with the average and reasonable law-abiding person's view of how the law should treat any given issue. The impersonality approach may appear to be a typical lawyer's solution, using the instrument of interpretation of existing norms to cover hitherto unforeseen scenarios when the professionals consider there to be an unjustifiable lacuna.

The Problem of Relational Defences

Applying the replication or extension variant in its unadulterated form in the context of relational defences entails the undesirable consequence that D can suddenly be liable for an intentional offence vis-à-vis unseen V2 when D's act would not have been an offence vis-à-vis targeted V1, because D has a defence vis-à-vis V1. The impersonality lawyer, beset by qualms about the law of unintended consequences, adopts the solution of transferring the defence along with the intent to avoid a monstrosity from arising, and it is here where the use of the word 'extension' instead of 'transfer' unmasks the problem: there is no cogent moral reason to extend the relational defence to innocent V2, and in fact, to do so is counterintuitive because the transfer doctrine is in its core a *crime control approach*, so nothing could be less desirable from its point of view than burdening the extended circle of protected persons with a relational defence to the creation of which they have not contributed anything. Extending the defence potentially robs the protected circle of their right to defend themselves. What the one hand gives, the other takes away.

Conclusion

The concretisation model typically results in an intent-negligence combination, unless D's intent already *actually* encompasses V2, in which case we have no unintended consequence to begin with. This works well with the continental figure of *dolus eventualis* but may present problems if transposed to the common law concept of recklessness, where one would probably have to require a high level of advertent recklessness, a kind of super-*Cunningham* type. This approach also makes a further discussion of a recklessness/negligence qualifier approach superfluous because unless there is negligence with regard to V2, there will be no liability regardless of the defence. The concretisation approach naturally provides no logical foundation for a *transfer* of a defence based on a transfer of the intent. It conceptually excludes all the problems mentioned in the example scenarios that have to do with the mechanical equation of 'transferred intent = transferred defence'. From its point of view, any harm to V2 must be addressed under the heading of 'collateral damage' arising from the act of D against V1. In the prime case of a relational defence, that of self-defence, the idea of covering any harm to V2 by self-defence to an attack by V1 jars with common sense. As I have argued elsewhere,[34] collateral damage scenarios are in effect instances of the defence of necessity, a balancing exercise to arrive

---

34   'In Extremis – Hijacked Airplanes, "Collateral Damage" and the Limits of Criminal Law' [2006] Crim LR 579.

at the choice of the lesser evil. Using necessity also has the advantage of removing the defence from some of the problematic consequences of the relational quality of self-defence: t no longer matters conceptually whether V2 contributed to the situation giving rise to the necessity dilemma or not. D has to make a choice, and the interests of V2 and her degree of contribution to causing the need for D's acts are mere factors D has to take into consideration. If he cannot take them into account, for example because he does not know of V2's existence or has to make a snap decision, that should not be held against him, but the question then is, of course, whether that justifies or merely excuses him, because *objectively* V2's interests are a factor that must be taken into account. A defence of collateral damage would have an objective nature coupled with the correct evaluation by D: if D gets the balancing exercise right, the defence applies, if not, the defence fails objectively. What possibly remains is a liability of D for negligence. In the 9/11 cases, where choices based on different numbers of identical victims must be made for the common good, I argued for a defence on the level of justification in principle, because in effect the state authorities must make the choice who lives or dies, and it would be undesirable in the context of such, on the one hand, highly prognosis-error-prone situations that present, on the other hand, a severe danger to the public, to refer the public officials making and executing such decisions to a potential criminal liability even if they honestly get it wrong. I acknowledge that this would conceptually rob the innocent victims of their right to defend and so save themselves, but the idea of a legal duty of self-sacrifice for a higher good is not an entirely unknown concept, and a pragmatic balance must be struck. If we include the situations of *private individuals not acting for the common good* but for their own good, the weight of the victim's interests increases dramatically. The idea of a duty of self-sacrifice has much less force, if any at all, when it is merely about D and V2. In this context, it would be undesirable to deny V2 the right to defend herself. With the defence of necessity failing, the innocent victim would (re-)gain her right of defence against D's actions. Any error on the part of D and V2 about the basis and the lawfulness of each other's actions could be balanced in a similar manner as in § 113(3) and (4) of the German Criminal Code. The threshold for an unavoidable error on the part of V2 should not be put too high. In the cases of crossed defences, the existence of a hypothetical defence vis-à-vis V2 clearly helps in the balancing exercise, unless one wishes to use the hypothetical defence directly[35]: D could in principle be treated as if the defence and *only* the defence vis-à-vis V2 applied to the harm caused unintentionally to V2 when reacting to V1. Thus if V2 merely provoked D, a potential self-defence vis-à-vis V1 should not be extended to V2 and vice versa, unless they acted in concert. D gets no acquittal under self-defence, but will, be convicted, if convicted at all, of the form of homicide of V2 provided under national law for cases of provocation[36]—which will often also be an acquittal from the murder charge and leave some form of (negligence) manslaughter, or a full acquittal if the domestic law does not provide for simple negligence homicide.[37] In these basic cases, D has no moral right to claim more of a defence against V2 than he would have had if V2 had attacked alone, and V2 cannot expect to be given a greater defence than she would have had if D had reacted to her alone; she is not in the same position morally as the entirely innocent victim and must accept some infringement of her interests. Purely personal and freely revocable 'defences' such as consent should remain with the person who gave the consent. From the point of view of public policy and the protection of personal autonomy, these cannot have effect with respect to other persons and should not even enter any necessity argument. If D acts on consent and unintentionally affects a non-consenting person, he must bear the risk of any liability. This is not unduly burdensome, as again under the concretisation model, it will normally mean either a mistake of fact that can negate the *mens rea* in any case, or a remaining liability for negligence, if the criminal law provides for it. The same applies to defences such as insanity, involuntary intoxication, diminished responsibility, and provocation which are not by their nature in need of transfer and thus fit well under the concretisation model. They apply regardless of the identity of the victim or damaged object, within their legal parameters, because D's capacity to act in accordance with the law is generally impaired, not merely vis-à-vis V1 or V2.

---

35   Using the hypothetical defence directly would follow the general principle that specific defences take precedence over general catch-all defences.

36   This solution avoids the problem mentioned above about gross negligence and self-defence in systems that do not provide for simple negligence homicide.

37   As is the case, for example, in England, which does, however, traditionally treat provocation-based manslaughter as voluntary —i.e., intentional—homicide based on the fact that provocation was essentially a mere sentencing mitigation for murder; this concept probably would have to be eliminated to avoid confusion.

In sum, based on the concretisation model, D will not normally be criminally liable for any harm done to V2 without intent, unless the domestic criminal law provides for negligence liability, which it may have to do under Article 2 of the ECHR. Situations where D is acting in a reckless or grossly negligent manner and still given a defence even against V1 are difficult to imagine. As far as D was negligent and not covered by a defence, V2 or V2's dependants may sue D in tort. Civil liability seems to be an acceptable level of addressing the competing interests of D and V2, especially if D had a defence that did not cover V2 under the criteria described above.

Chapter 5
Consent in the Criminal Law:
The Importance of Relationality and Responsibility

Jonathan Herring

Introduction

Consent plays a crucial role in the criminal law. In some cases it provides victims with the ability to permit acts which would otherwise be criminal offences. It can provide reassurance to professionals who need to touch patients that they will not be prosecuted. Consent is a huge and complex philosophical issue, as evidenced by the vast range of publications on the issue.[1] Much of the writing in the legal arena has focussed on what should or should not constitute consent and to which crimes consent should be a defence. These questions have produced lively debate. However, I suggest that much of this lacks a secure foundation because it fails to address what it is that consent does. While it is claimed that consent is 'morally transformative',[2] or even 'moral magic',[3] little attention is given on why that is so. What is it that consent is doing in moral terms to have its impact? Only once we understand what it is that consent does, can we then turn to the questions that trouble the criminal law.

In this chapter I will set out one theory, the one I find most convincing, of why it is that consent has its moral effect. The purpose of this chapter will not be to persuade the reader of the wisdom of that approach, but rather to focus on the significance of taking that particular approach to consent for the law.[4] I will draw out from that approach some general principles of application before addressing a few specific scenarios.

A Model for Consent

The model of consent I will adopt here is that propounded by Michelle Madden Dempsey in a recent important article.[5] In outline, the argument is as follows. Consent becomes relevant when D's act wrongfully harms another person's wellbeing thereby rendering the act a prima facie wrong. That requires the actor (D) to provide a reason justifying acting in the way he or she did. Consent can operate as providing a justifying reason. It gives D an option to decide to set aside the reasons against acting in a particular way which rest in V's well-being. Consent does that by allowing defendant (D) to assume that the act is not, all things considered, contrary to the wellbeing of the victim (V). That is because D is permitted to rely on V's assessment that the act is overall in V's best interests. In effect where consent is effective Madden Dempsey claims that D is entitled to say:

---

1 See, e.g., Joan McGregor, *Is it Rape?* (Ashgate 2005); Alan Wertheimer, *Consent to Sexual Relations* (Cambridge University Press 2003); Peter Westen, *The Logic Of Consent* (Ashgate 2004); Franklin Miller and Alan Wertheimer (eds), *The Ethics of Consent* (OUP 2010).

2 Alan Wertheimer, 'Consent to Sexual Relations in Franklin Miller and Alan Wertheimer (eds), *The Ethics of Consent* (OUP 2010)

3 Hedi Hurd, 'The,Moral Magic of Consent' (1996) 2 Legal Theory 121.

4 See also Jonathan Herring and Michelle Madden Dempsey, 'Rethinking the Criminal Law's Response to Sexual Penetration: On Theory and Context' in Clare McGlynn and Vanessa Munro (eds), *Rethinking Rape Law* (Routledge 2010)

5 Michelle Madden Dempsey, 'Victimless Conduct and the Volenti Maxim: How Consent Works' (2013) 7 Crim L & Philos 11.

This is [V]'s decision. He's an adult and can decide for himself whether he thinks the risk is worth it. In considering what to do, I will assume that his decision is the right one for him. After all, he is in a better position than I to judge his own well-being. And so, I will not take it upon myself to reconsider those reasons. Instead, I will base my decision of whether to [harm] him on the other relevant reasons.[6]

I would emphasise just a couple of points about this analysis. First, this is only true where there is full consent. As we shall see in the remainder of this chapter there may be cases of apparent consent which will not be true consent because it cannot do the moral work required.

Second, note that the consent offers D an 'exclusionary permission' to take up the reasons, but D does not have to take up the permission. D is perfectly entitled not to do what V has offered consent to. This point echoes the argument of Joseph Raz:

> The simplest case of giving an exclusionary permission is a case of a man who consents that another shall perform an act harmful to his interests. The permission does not alter the reasons against the action. It will still harm the person's interests. The intention and import of the permission is to allow the man who contemplates the action to disregard the interests of the person who granted the permission. The permission, it should be noted, is no reason for disregarding the interests of the person who gave it. It merely allows one to disregard them.[7]

Fairly obviously, if V says to D, 'you can punch me'; D is entitled to say, 'no thanks'. Less obviously, but crucial for medical law, if V says to a doctor I would like chemotherapy to treat my cancer, the doctor is entitled to say, 'no, I don't think that is appropriate'.[8] For all the talk of the pre-eminence of autonomy in medical law[9] it never has been the law that a patient's demand for a particular treatment had to be met. This is why consent does not completely 'negate' the reasons D has for not harming V. D is still entitled to rely on those reasons not to harm V. What consent does do is give D permission to rely on consent to take up the reasons offered by consent, if D so wishes.

Third, note the somewhat limited impact of consent. Heidi Hurd has famously argued that consent has moral magic and that it can transform 'trespasses into dinner parties … and rape into lovemaking … '.[10] That is clearly an exaggeration because as Michelle Madden Dempsey points out, 'turning a trespass into a dinner party requires, at least, dinner – while turning rape into lovemaking requires, at least, love'.[11]

There is more that can be said to develop these points,[12] but the main focus of this chapter is to explore some of the practical consequences of that approach for questions which have troubled the criminal law and so I will move on to those. I will start with some general observations on the role and nature of consent before addressing a few particular scenarios.

Consent and the Law

When is Consent Needed?

It will be clear form this model that consent is only needed when an act is a prima facie wrong. Where the act is not wrongful then D does not need reasons to do the act. Hence, consent is not needed to walk along a pavement as the act is not wronging anyone. Generally, looking at someone is not wrongful and does not require consent. So the fact an act is only lawful if performed with consent, indicates the act is a prima facie

---

6   ibid 20.
7   Joseph Raz, *Practical Reason and Norms* (OUP 1999) 96997
8   *R(Burke) v GMC* [2005] EWCA 1003.
9   See Charles Foster, *Choosing Life, Choosing Death: The Tyranny of Autonomy in Medical Ethics and Law* (Hart 2009).
10   Hedi Hurd (n 3) 122.
11   ibid (n 5).
12   ibid (n 5).

wrong which requires some justification. If it were not a prima facie wrong, there would be no need for consent. That provides one reason why Michelle Madden Dempsey and I were correct to claim that sexual penetration is a prima facie wrong.[13] We would not require or expect consent if the act of a sexual penetration was not itself a prima facie wrong.

The proposed model also explains whose consent is required. On the model outlined only V can provide D with the exclusionary permission to do the act. Fairly obviously, a third party cannot provide an adequate assessment of V's best interests, and D should seek consent from V. However, there are some exceptions relating to where V lacks capacity to consent. In such a case V's parent (if V is a child) or a holder of a power of attorney (if V is an adult lacking capacity) can provide the consent.

The Significance of 'No Consent'

The next point to emphasise is that there is a fundamental distinction between consent, 'no consent' and objection. Where the victim objects to the defendant acting in the harmful way proposed this generates a further reason why the defendant should not act in that way: not only are they causing the victim harm, but are doing so against the express wish of the victim. Where the defendant proposes a harmful activity and the victim does nothing (a 'no consent') then there is no change in the moral position. A 'no consent' is a nothing: it is the absence of something. It does not provide a reason against acting the way proposed and it certainly provides no reason in favour.

If the model proposed in this chapter is correct, then clearly a failure to object cannot be taken as an assessment by V that the act is in their well-being. That is why the courts are right to require consent as a positive act;[14] an 'agreement', as the Sexual Offences Act puts it.[15] It also is one reason for being concerned about the decision in *Aitken*,[16] where staying at the party while 'practical jokes' being played could be taken as consent to be the victim of a prank. There the 'no refusal' was improperly taken as consent.

Consent and Request

Michelle Madden Dempsey[17] argues that a request can be distinguished from consent in that as well as providing the permission that consent offers, a request provides a further positive reason that D acts in the way requested. This is helpful because it explains the error that is made by those who see consent as reflecting autonomy. Malcolm Thorburn[18] suggests:

> one plausible way to understand the law's many limits on the power to consent to bodily injury is that the law must be able to conceive of a person's consent as pursuing some genuine purpose of his own by doing so – say, playing a contact sport, engaging in physically intense sexual relations, etc. – rather than simply granting a licence to someone else to abuse his body.

But this is to confuse consent with a request. We can take it that all requests include consent, but not all consents are requests. A person may consent to medical student attempting to take an injection, but that is not to say that they are, in doing that, pursing their purpose. They are simply granting licence, not seeking to pursue a genuine purpose of their own, as Thorburn suggests. This distinction is particular relevant in sexual

---

13   Michelle Madden Dempsey and Jonathan Herring, 'Why Sexual Penetration Requires Justification' (2007) 27 OJLS 467.
14   *R(F) v DPP* [2013] EWHC 945 (Admin).
15   Sexual Offences Act 2003 s 74.
16   [1992] 1 WLR 1066.
17   ibid (n 5).
18   Malcolm Thorburn, 'Two Conceptions of Equality Before the (Criminal) Law' in François Tanguay-Renaud & James Stribopoulos (eds), *Rethinking Criminal Law Theory: New Canadian Perspectives in the Philosophy of Domestic, Transnational, and International Criminal Law* (Hart 2012).

context where Robin West makes the powerful case that unwanted sex may cause the victim a whole range of harms, even if it treated as being consensual.[19]

Consent and the Interests of Others

The consent of V in the model I am relying on only affects the decisions against acting which rest in the well-being of V. As explained above V's consent only gives D a reason for taking it that the act is not impermissible based on reasons vesting in V's well-being. Consent does not affect reasons against acting in the way proposed which rest on other concerns, in particular the interests of third parties. An example may clarify this claim. A asks B whether B is willing to consent to A using a racially offensive term and B consents. A uses that term. Under the model I have outlined, the fact that B has consented to A using the term in his presence means that those reasons that might exist which rest in B's welfare (e.g., that B will be offended) are negated. But B has no moral authority to affect other reasons that A may have against using the racially offensive term. Reasons resting in offence caused to other people who may have heard it; or arguments based on societal goods are unaffected by V's consent.

Applying this thinking to an assault, in so far as the reasons against A harming B rest in B's self-interest, then B's consent can in some cases negate those arguments resting in the welfare of B. But, it cannot affect other reasons against harming B that do not rest in B's best interests.[20] So V's consent to D harming her cannot provide a defence in a case where there is a public interest concern about the harm: e.g. that others will witness what has happened and be distressed or where there will be expenses incurred for the public.

D Must Seek to Act in V's Well-Being

Consent gives D a reason for accepting that the act is in the well-being of V, but D must act *for* that reason. John Gardner has helpfully explained that in order for a person to be justified, an act must be justifiable and the person is justified.[21] There must be an undefeated reason to engage in the conduct and D must act for that reason. That is true for consent too. Consider this:

> D, a doctor, determines that V needs a genealogical examination. D fancies V and so does this himself, rather than ask a nurse to do the examination, as he normally does. He does the examination properly but finds it sexually exciting.

Here although the examination is justifiable, D in performing the procedure is not acting for those reasons. He cannot claim to have used consent in the way described earlier in this article. It cannot, therefore, provide him with a justification.

The same will be true of a defendant who does not care whether the victim is consenting. A prostitute-user may well be using the prostitute for his sexual enjoyment, not caring, or not caring much, whether there is genuine consent. In such a case the consent of the prostitute is not properly playing its full force his reasons.[22] The user cannot claim to be acting on the reasons provided by the consent.

Michelle Madden Dempsey goes further with a more controversial example, where A, a sadist, punches B, a masochist, who consents to the punch:

> Despite B's consent, A keeps in play on his rational horizons (that is, A does not exclude) reasons he has not to punch B that are grounded in B's well-being, and A punches B, at least in part for reasons that are grounded

---

19   Robin West, 'Sex, Law and Consent' in Franklin Miller and Alan Wertheimer (n 1), although she is making that claim using a different understanding of consent to that used here.
20   ibid (n 5), where we use this argument to suggest that as some of the reasons why a man who penetrates a woman rest in reasons not connected to Von well-being more than consent is required to justify a sexual penetration. I will not develop that point further here.
21   John Gardner, *Offences and Defences* (OUP 2009).
22   Michelle Madden Dempsey, 'Rethinking Wolfenden: Prostitute-Use, Criminal Law, and Remote Harm' [2005] Crim LR 444.

in B's well-being. (That is, A's explanatory reasons include the fact that his conduct will cause B pain, injury, etc.) In such cases, despite B's consent, A's conduct nonetheless takes B as its victim; for, in virtue of A's sadistic explanatory reasons, B's consent failed to bear transformative normative force on the moral quality of A's conduct.[23]

Her argument is that A has not used B's consent in the appropriate way, in that A is acting positively in order to achieve some of the reasons against acting in B's well-being. That is a more difficult scenario. There is a fine line between A doing what B wants A to do, which includes the causing of pain, and where the causing of pain is an independent reason for A. It may be here that the distinction between consent and request becomes particularly relevant and a clear desire to meet the request of B may be sufficient to justify acting in this way, whereas meeting the consent would not.

Consent and Responsibility

One reason I am particularly drawn to the Madden Dempsey model of consent is that it emphasises two themes which I think are key to consent in this context. The first is that it reinforces the idea that if D is to wrong V, D has responsibilities to ensure that he or she has good reasons for so acting. The model acknowledges that D can accept V's assessment of their own well-being, but that consent can only be effective where it can be accepted as that. D must be acting in order to promote V's well-being and not for their own reasons.

There is often talk when consent arises (especially in the context of sexual offences) of the victim being to blame for putting themselves in the position where they were liable to be attacked or where D could have thought they were consenting. This is erroneous for many reasons, but one is that it overlooks the fact that D is choosing to do an act which is prima facie wrongful to V. D, therefore, has the responsibility to ensure that they are in fact not wronging V. The fact, for example, that V is so intoxicated she cannot indicate her views, of course, provides D with no justification for wronging V, indeed is a particularly strong case of where D has no good reason for wronging V. I will develop this point further shortly.

Consent and Autonomy

The language of autonomy is used to explain the role of consent. Unfortunately that can create mistakes. Professor Rubenfeld has recently written against the emphasis placed on sexual autonomy.[24] His points could also be made in relation to other touchings in the criminal law. He writes that:

> [G]uaranteeing everyone a right to sexual 'self-determination' is quite impossible. First, one person's sexual self-determination will inevitably conflict with others': John's will require that he sleep with Jane, but Jane's will require otherwise.

His argument points out the danger of talking of sexual autonomy in general. It would be far more helpful to talk of a right to sexual bodily integrity. That is because it is clear that the interference in John's autonomy if he cannot sleep with Jane, is very different from Jane's interference with her autonomy if John sleeps with her against her wish. This is why, as Nicola Lacey has pointed out, it is better to talk about sexual integrity than autonomy.[25] We have no right to have sex with anyone we want, any more than a patient has a right to demand a particular kind of treatment, or a customer that they be given a tattoo. What we do have is a strong right not to be sexually touched, be given medical treatment, or a tattoo, without consent. It is the right not to be touched without consent which is strongly protected by the law.

---

23   ibid (n 5).
24   Jed Rubenfeld, 'The Riddle of Rape-by-Deception and the Myth of Sexual Autonomy' (2013) 122 Yale LJ 1372.
25   Nicola Lacey, *Unspeakable Subjects* (Hart 1998).

Professor Rubenfeld[26] has another point. He notes we do not normally allow exercises of autonomy that harm others. Yet, he says:

> Paradigmatic exercises of sexual autonomy routinely do serious harm to others. A's refusal to have sex with B can cause B acute suffering.

Here again he is loose with the language. Properly understood we should say that autonomy cannot be exercised in a way which unjustifiably harms another. Of course an exercise of autonomy is permitted if it justifiably harms another. Otherwise a person could not exercise autonomy to use harm to another in self-defence. Once that is appreciated it is clear there is nothing unjustifiable in refusing to have sex with another and such a refusal does not unjustifiably harm another.

Criminal lawyers typically assume that by requiring 'consent' we are respecting a victim's autonomy. But, the issue is complex as the literature on autonomy shows. Phrasing the question as whether D can take V's consent as an assessment of V's well-being (broadly understood[27]) is helpful. That is because it is important to understand that autonomy can be understood in a range of ways. John Coggon has listed three versions of autonomy:

1) Ideal desire autonomy – leads to an action decided upon because it reflects what a person should want, measured by reference to some purportedly universal or objective standard of values.
2) Best desire autonomy – leads to an action decided upon because it reflects a person's overall desire given his own values, even if this runs contrary to his immediate desire.
3) Current desire autonomy – leads to an action decided upon because it reflects a person's immediate inclinations, i.e. what he thinks he wants in a given moment without further reflection.[28]

As this makes clear, we cannot assume that respecting autonomy is to respect an apparent consent made at the time of the incident, even accepting that there is free informed consent. The person may be consenting with current desire autonomy, but that not be reflecting best desire autonomy. And where the issue involves something as important as a serious wrong to V, we might want the deeper understanding of autonomy reflected by best desire autonomy, rather than current desire autonomy. Let us take an example.

> When Alfred gets down he sometimes engages in self-harm. His friend Steve has offered to help him cut himself. Alfred has recently received counselling and is determined to stop his self-harm. He accepts it does not do him any good and worsens his state of mind. He wants to find alternative ways of dealing with his feeling and has asked Alfred to help him. One evening he is feeling low. Steve suggests cutting and Alfred agrees. Steve cuts Alfred.

While Steve may claim that by cutting Alfred he is respecting Steve's current desires autonomy, he is not respecting his ideal or best desire autonomy. Understanding consent in the way proposed helps us see that Steve knows that this is not what Alfred thinks is in his well-being. This is momentary desire and not reflecting the true direction he wishes his life to take.

Catriona Makenzie and Wendy Rogers argue to be able to exercise autonomy we need the following:[29]

---

26   ibid (n 24).

27   Jonathan Herring and Charles Foster, 'Welfare Means Relationality, Virtue and Altruisma (2012) 32 LS 480.

28   John Coggon, 'Varied and Principled Understandings of Autonomy in English Law: Justifiable Inconsistency or Blinkered Moralism?' (2007) 15 Health Care Anal 235.

29   Catriona Makenzie and Wendy Rogers, 'Autonomy, Vulnerability and Capacity: A Philosophical Appraisal of the Mental Capacity Act' (2013) 9 Intl JL in Context 37.

- Self-determining: being 'able to determine one's own beliefs, values, goals and wants, and to make choices regarding matters of practical import to one's life free from undue interference. The obverse of self-determination is determination by other persons, or by external forces or constraints'. [30]
- Self-governing: 'being be able to make choices and enact decisions that express, or are consistent with, one's values, beliefs and commitments. Whereas the threats to self-determination are typically external, the threats to self-governance are typically internal, and often involve volitional or cognitive failings. Weakness of will and failures of self-control are common volitional failings that interfere with self-governance'.[31]
- Having authenticity: 'a person's decisions, values, beliefs and commitments must be her 'own' in some relevant sense; that is, she must identify herself with them and they must cohere with her 'practical identity', her sense of who she is and what matters to her. Actions or decisions that a person feels were foisted on her, which do not cohere with her sense of herself, or from which she feels alienated, are not autonomous'.[32]

As these examples show, even if V is appearing to consent, D may not be able to take that as a valid assessment by V of her well-being if she not able to self-determination, self-governance or authenticity. It is here that the relational context will be crucial.[33]

I would emphasise the importance of the relationship and the context of the encounter. In some cases D is not in a position to determine whether V's act does accord with their deeper values or they are fully able to exercise autonomy. They may be strangers and an investigation into this deeper understanding of autonomy could not to be expected. In other cases the fact the parties are strangers means that D has less ability to appreciate that V's wishes are inconsistent with the deeper values. V may appear to be making a fully free assessment of their wellbeing and D have no idea whether or not V is consenting. Contrast these two cases:

> Anne and Bob meet at a coffee bar and get chatting. After a lengthy conversation Bob suggests they go back to his house. Anne enthusiastically agrees. Bob suggests sex and Anne agrees. Unknown to Bob, Anne is deeply religious and strongly opposes sex before marriage. She later claims that her excitement of the moment meant that she could not consent. She is bitterly disappointed with herself the next morning.

> Charles and Deepa have been friends for a long while. Deepa has started the process to become a nun and has taken a vow of celibacy. Charles knows that Deepa has been struggling to keep the vow but is determined to do so. One night Deepa suggests sex.

In the first encounter we may conclude that Bob could not have known that Anne's decision was contrary to her deeper beliefs and values (assuming that did not come up in their conversation). He reasonably took Anne's consent to be her own assessment of well-being. Charles cannot, I would argue, do the same. He knows that Deepa's decision is a 'current desire autonomy', but does not reflect her true values and so is not an exercise of best desire autonomy, exhibiting self-governance. Of course, it may be that Deepa does later make a considered decide to depart from her vows of celibacy, but given Charles's knowledge of her he cannot take her consent as an authentic expression of her desires.

A proper respect for bodily integrity should allow the telling of a V's story of what happened before the incident, and the context within which it took place. This requires more than simply considering if there is a 'yes or no'. If D is to do an act which is a prima facie wrong against V then D can be expected to do a little more than that. Listening to what V is saying about the proposed act is likely to require appreciating how V understands the act within its wider relational and social meaning. Nicola Lacey,[34] writing in the context of

---

30 ibid.
31 ibid.
32 ibid.
33 Jonathan Herring, 'Relational Autonomy and Rape' in Shelley Day Sclater, Fatemeh Ebtehaj, Emily Jackson and Martin Richards (eds) *Regulating Autonomy* (Hart 2009).
34 ibid (n 25).

sexual behaviour, highlights the problems in simply asking whether the victim consented to 'the act'. She writes, discussing consent in the sexual context:

> The victim's consent responds to power by conferring legitimacy, rather than shaping power in its own terms: consent is currently understood not in terms of mutuality but rather in relation to a set of arrangements initiated, by implication, by the defendant, in an asymmetric structure which reflects the stereotypes of active masculinity and passive femininity.

This approach requires D, where appropriate, to consider V's whole story and place it in the context of her values and relationships. D should not to treat V as an object, little more than automatic barrier he is trying to get to raise. But D must recognise V as a person with desires, values and feelings, and understand their consent (their assessment of their wellbeing) in that context.

When the court is considering whether V's consent provides D with a defence, this involves looking at the encounter between the two people, how they understood and negotiated the act. Does the interaction indicate that D was seeking to let or enable V to make a free, informed decision about what was in her best interests or was D lying, threatening, pressurising V? The use of deceptions, pressures, manipulations and the like indicate that D was not seeking to use consent in the way promoted in this article, as an assessment by V of their wellbeing.

So understood, the question becomes less 'was there a yes?' or 'was there an intellectual understanding of the issues?' and, rather, 'was an interaction marked by mutuality and respect?', 'was it tender or exploitative?', 'was D truly seeking to find out and respect what V wanted or seeking to produce the answer D wanted?'.

Developing that last point, I would refer to a recent contribution to the debate by Leslie Green, who undertakes a sophisticated analysis of the interaction between law and morality in this area.[35] He, correctly I think, suggests the difficulties in the sexual arena around consent arise from the lack of clear rules of social interaction about sex. In some areas of social interaction we have well established rules which work well. A person gets into a taxi and asks to be taken to a destination. It is well known that by doing so the person is agreeing to pay. The newspapers are not full of stories of people getting into a taxi and not realising they are meant to pay. Green points out that similar conventions do not surround sex. Hence, there are sexual encounters where there has been a 'misunderstanding' about consent. He notes this may be surprising given that a simple question could normally determine consent, but he accepts that the failure to do so is normally due to 'nothing more than embarrassment or fears about what might 'kill the mood'. I am doubtful of that. I suspect the reason the question is not asked is fear the other person will say no. The defendant is very much wanting to have sex and if the signs are good has 'nothing to lose' by going ahead. Asking if the other person is happy to continue can only worsen his position, if the answer 'no' is returned.

Application of the Approach

Cases Where V is Mistaken

Some mistaken consent cases are best described as conditional consent cases. In *R(F) v A*[36] the court had to deal with a case where the woman agreed to sex but only if the man wore a condom. He had proceeded to have sex with her without a condom. At one point in the judgement the court described that a case where her consent was negated. In fact they were closer to the truth when they later said she did not consent to the act.[37] She had consented to a specific act: sex with a condom. The act done was not the act she consented to. Indeed more than that it was the very act she had said she did not consent to.

---

35   Leslie Green, 'Should Law Improve Morality?' (2013) 7 L & Philos 473.
36   [2013] EWHC 945 (Admin).
37   Both in para 26.

Others cases are less straightforward.[38] Imagine V is mistaken about a fact when 'consent' is given: for example, she thinks D belongs to a profession or is unmarried. If D knows that V is mistaken and that V would not have reached the same conclusion, D cannot take that consent. Quite obviously the work of consent as we have described it cannot be achieved where V is mistaken. D cannot take V's consent as an assessment of V's well-being because D knows that V would not think the act would promote V's well-being if she knew the truth. So, where D seeks to play a dangerous sport with V, but realises that V does not know the danger of the sport, then D cannot say, 'I assume V decided that the fun in the sport was worth the risk'. The consent that V has offered: 'I consent to this safe sport' is not consent to the dangerous sport.

To be clear this is not, of course, true for all cases where V is mistaken. If V is mistaken over a matter which would not affect their assessment then quite properly D can say, 'V has considered all the issues and determined that this is in her best interests. True V is mistaken over a particular fact, but I am sure that would not have affected their assessment'.

The point to remember is this: D is doing a wrongful act against V and needs the consent to provide him with reasons for believing that all things the act cannot wrong V. If he knows that V would not be consenting if V knew the truth then D clearly cannot rely on it as an assessment of best interests. In effect, in such a case, D is claiming to know better than V about what will be in V's interests. D is saying, 'V would not have consented had she known the truth about X, but I regard X as a trivial matter and V should not have cared about it and should have consented whether X or not were true'.

What is notable is that in other areas of the law we would not accept such an argument. Contrast these cases.

> V, a Chelsea Football club fan supporting pub owner, is offering half price beer to Chelsea fans. D, stating that he is a Chelsea fan, claims the half price beer. All would agree that V has not consented and that D has committed fraud.

> V, a Chelsea-loving woman, will only have sex with Chelsea fans. D, purports to be a Chelsea fan and V, who fancies D, agrees to have sex with him. In this scenario people find it hard to believe that V did not consent to sex.

Commentators are content to consider that V's reasons for only wanting to have sex with one class of people as 'trivial' or bizarre, in a way they never would with the fraud case.

Michael Bohlander[39] has responded to this point in the sexual context by stating:

> [T]ransactions in the property context take place in a *highly* ordered system of a mechanical exchange of goods and services based on public and more or less inflexible rules established to safeguard smooth commerce between participants in the system who may have had no prior contact. Being able to trust in the mere representations of the other side-with attendant severe sanctions for breach of that trust-is crucial for this commerce or the system will break down. None of this applies to sexual offences in our context.

But that is precisely my point: the current law fails to deal with breach of trust and deception in the sexual context, when it should. Enormous suffering has and is caused because men believe the 'seduction game' has no rules. Indeed, I would argue this is true generally where D is wishing to do a prima facie wrongful act against V it is not unreasonable to require D to ensure he has good reasons to act in that way. If he has had to use deceptions or breach trust to obtain consent that is a clear sign he does not have good reasons.

---

38 See Jonathan Herring, 'Mistaken Sex' [2005] Crim LR 511 for a fuller discussion.
39 Michael Bohlander, 'Mistaken Consent to Sex, Political Correctness and Correct Policy' (2007) 71 JCL 412.

Pressure

What if V is consenting under pressure? As will be obvious the approach advocated in this article will ask whether D can take V's consent to be that the proposed act will promote their well-being. That however might be problematic in this context.

First, if V has agreed to be wronged by D following a threat of death, can, on my approach, not D say that V's consent amounts to an all things considered assessment by V that the act is in her well-being. The error with that argument is that we need to consider the context of all that has taken place between D and V. Looked at as a whole V has not made the assessment that the wrong will promote her well-being. It is the avoidance of the threat that she has decided will promote her well-being. To explain further, if V would not consent to the wrong, but D then attempts to persuade V to consent by the use of threats or offers *independent of the act* D cannot claim to be seeking to assist V in assessing whether the act promotes well-being. Contrast this:

> Enid is interested in taking up fencing, but is nervous of taking up fencing as she is worried about being stabbed. Fred explains (truthfully) the risks and safety precautions that can be taken in attempt to reassure her that the risks of harm are small.

> Gavin is nervous about being set on fire as part of a stunt. Harry says that if Gavin does not do it he will make public embarrassing photographs of Gavin.

Fred is seeking to assist Enid in making a decision about whether the fencing is in her best interests. He is providing her with correct information and helping her focus on whether the act itself will promote her wellbeing. Harry is not seeking to assist Gavin in that assessment. He is seeking to persuade Gavin to consent by offering alternatives. Harry's conduct in this case indicates that he is not truly interested in Gavin making an assessment of Gavin's own best interests. Indeed the fact Harry is using a threat, indicates he realises the act is contrary to Gavin's best interests. Harry is interested in doing what he can to get Gavin to act in the way he wishes, not assisting Gavin reach his own decision.

The best response to cases of consent and pressure is to look at what is done in terms of whether it is consistent with D seeking to allow V to make a decision about whether the is in their well-being. Threats are clearly inconsistent with this. D is seeking to manipulate V into agreeing to the act in order to avoid the adverse consequence, rather than making an assessment about the value of the act. Similarly incentives too are likely to work in this way, particularly where the act is benefiting D. In such a case we expect that the incentive is offered at the level that D believes is a fair price for what is on offer. When D agrees a price with a prostitute he is little concerned with a calculation of whether the sum involved is such as to make the transaction in V's well-being, nor even concerned about whether V determines the sum is sufficient, he is likely to offer the price the service is to him. This indicates that he is not using V's consent in the acceptable way advocated in this article.

D's Assessment of Best Interest

I have described consent as operating by enabling D to rely on V's assessment of their own best interests, but understood in a rich way. I realise that this is a strict approach. It may mean that it is not easy for D be able to commit a prima facie wrongful act against V. But that should not surprise us. However, what of cases where V has given apparent consent, but it is not sufficient to amount a full assessment by V of her well-being? She is too pressurised or lacks sufficient evidence to give full consent. In that case D cannot rely on V's assessment of well-being to justify the act. Might, however, D be able to rely on D's own assessment of what is in V's best interest? I suggest yes in some cases. Distinguish these two scenarios:

> D, a tattooist, wants to give V a rose tattoo. He thinks V will look very pretty with it.

> D, a doctor, wants to give V a pain relieving injection, thinking that will greatly be in V's welfare.

Let us imagine in these cases that V's decision-making is impaired (e.g., she is drunk). As to the first case, there are two reasons why the tattooist's opinions should not be given weight, but the doctor's should. First, he has no expertise more than anyone else as to whether the tattoo will look good. His view on this is deserving of no weight (or only a tiny bit) as compared with anyone else. Indeed, the issue of whether a tattoo looks good is not capable of objective assessment. Contrast the position of the doctor who is able to make an assessment of what is in the well-being of the patient. This point is reflected in the Mental Capacity Act 2005 where if a person is lacking capacity a medical or personal care decision can be made by a medical professional or carer based on their best interests, but a personal decision (e.g. to marry, have sexual relations, etc.) cannot.[40]

A second point of distinction is that the doctor will make no personal gain from the transaction while the tattooist will expect payment. It is, therefore, where the decision-maker has a degree of expertise and a lack of self-interest that we can rely on their assessment of V's welfare, whereas in other cases we could not rely on D's assessment of what is in V's best interests. Where D gains personally from the decision it is hard to resist the conclusion that D is acting for self-interested purposes, rather than the best interests of V.

Conclusion

This chapter has sought to explore the significance of consent. It has, adopting the argument of Michelle Madden Dempsey, argued that consent operates by giving D an exclusionary permission to take V's consent as an assessment by V that the act is in V's well-being. If D chooses to take up that permission that allows D to set aside those reasons against harming V that rest in V's well-being. Most of this chapter has explored the significance of taking that approach. In this conclusion I want to bring out two particular consequences.

The first is that a proper assessment by V of their well-being requires not simply an awareness of facts but an ability to make the decision in accordance with the values they have chosen to adopt. What a person wants in the heat of the moment may not represent a true expression of autonomy. As explained in detail above, V needs self-determination, self-governance, or authenticity to be able to make an autonomous decision. If D is aware that the apparent consent of V in fact does not sit with their deeper values and decision then D is aware that the 'at the moment' consent cannot amount to a genuinely autonomous decision. The issue is harder where the parties are strangers. There, the nature of the act and the severity of the harm will determine whether it is appropriate for D to take the stranger V's current consent as being a sufficient assessment of their well-being.

The second consequence is that when D is going to do an act which is a prima facie wrong against V, D needs good reasons for committing the act. The consent of V can provide that good reason, but D has a responsibility to ensure that the consent is sufficient to authorize him to do the act. It should always be remembered that D has not right to commit a prima facie wrong against another person and is always free to walk away or wait until any uncertainty is resolved. In relying on consent D has the responsibility of giving V the time, information and freedom from pressure to provide that consent. Where D has used deceptions, pressure, manipulation or exploitation in order to obtain consent, this is inconsistent with D properly relying on consent as an expression by V of their assessment of their well-being. He has not been respecting the right to bodily integrity that gives V the right to self-determine whether an act is in their own well-being.

---

40 Mental Capacity Act 2005, s. 27.

Chapter 6

Good and Harm, Excuses and Justifications, and the Moral Narratives of Necessity

Susan Edwards

Introduction

The formalisation of a body of rules and regulations set out the structure necessary for the execution of a consistent law governing conduct. Max Weber, writing on the 'legality of enacted rules',[1] theorised the essentialness of rationalisation and structure. Simester and others agree that, 'The legal system will simply not work if its authority is optional'.[2] Of necessity, they say: 'Derogation from its rules is not permitted save in specific, confined circumstances'.[3] But Weber also recognised that with increasing rationalisation and formalisation legal rules can trap individuals in both an 'iron' and a 'figurative cage'. Contained in this critique of modernity and rationalisation are two considerations, first the morphological problem of over-rigid structures of authority which he addresses in his critique on bureaucracy and its limitations, and second, his exploration of conduct and action in which he attempts to offer an interpretive understanding of social action wherein he focuses on the intersubjective meaning of action for the individual and the social construction of motive. The recalcitrant and unintended consequences of the rigidity and inflexibility of bureaucracy and legal rules has been variously depicted in the nightmare scenarios imagined by Franz Kafka. In both *The Trial*[4] and *The Castle*,[5] Kafka envisages a labyrinth of enigmatic normative rules in a legal world from which there is no escape. The protagonist of *The Trial*, Joseph K, is a bank clerk, and significant to the plot, an ordinary man, who is arrested and prosecuted for a crime although neither he nor the reader discover what crime he has actually committed and so he finds himself trapped in a web of an abstracted and secretive legal system. The problem of this reification of law is also depicted by Lewis Caroll[6] through his characterisation of the Red Queen who, when Alice is giving evidence, traps her in a legal abstraction. Legal theorists have been enthralled by Kafka's prophetic vista where legality becomes fetishised, rendering the individual subject helpless. Such reification results in the consciousness of law becoming a thing, dislocated and cleaved from its moral and ethical foundation. Thus law if it becomes over-objectified can result in a banal law, a violent law, and an evil law. Law certainly reached banal and evil proportions in Nazi Germany when law became the absolute authority and was dislocated from morality, such that it became possible to implement laws that were positively harmful and, when authorised, promoted and legitimated hatred. For example, on September 15, 1935, the Nuremberg Laws revoked citizenship for Jews, prohibiting them from marrying or having sexual relations with persons of 'German or related blood'. Further example is provided where in South Africa, the Immorality Act of 1927 prohibited sexual relations between 'whites' and 'blacks', later followed by the Prohibition of Mixed Marriages Act 1949.

In everyday legal life, in jurisdictions where there is harmony between legal authority and morality, circumstances nevertheless arise where the enforcement of the legal rule would be palpably wrong, banal, even absurd. In the criminal law, an exemption is provided by the 'necessity' doctrine whose arguments respond in exceptional circumstances to valid moral claims and provide a defence for those who, when

---

1   Max Weber, *On Charisma and Institution Building* (Heritage of Sociology Series 1968) 215.
2   AP Simester, JR Spencer, GR Sullivan and GJ Virgo, *Criminal Law* (Hart 2013) 798.
3   ibid 799.
4   Kafka, *The Trial* (Penguin 2000).
5   Kafka, *The Castle* (Penguin 1970).
6   Lewis Caroll, *Alice's Adventures in Wonderland* (Wordsworth Edition 1993) 141. 'Let the jury consider their verdict', the King said, for about the twentieth time that day. 'No, no!' said the Queen 'Sentence first – verdict afterwards'.

conducting themselves in a particular way that is morally right in the circumstances, break the law. Perhaps Glanville Williams poses the question most appositely when he considers 'how far the notion of necessity can create new rules or serve as an excuse for dispensing with the strict law where the exigency requires it'.[7] The clearest legitimate application he identifies is where life is in danger.[8]

This chapter explores the ambit of the defence of necessity and raises some questions around the negotiation of the 'higher' moral claims exploring the reasoning informing the sanctioning of some claims and the rejection of others. What is at stake here then is the relation of law to moral and ethical questions, to public policy, to the judicial craft and to individual motives for exemption. The ambit of necessity is unclear since its legally accepted claims are shaped by context, in an historical and cultural fluidity, crafted by the judiciary who as necessity's arbiters balance typifications of goods and harms in particular cultural and historical milieus. What we see at the surface is the playing out of these values and claims, and at times correspondingly the suspension of law, as judges act as the grand masters of morals. Judges as grand moralists in 17th century took to divining whether hunting on another's private property was a breach of the law of trespass to be permitted in the circumstances of necessity.[9] In the 20th century, in *Leigh v Gladstone*,[10] Mrs Mary Leigh, a suffragette who had been forcibly fed whilst on hunger strike in prison brought an action against the Home Secretary. Lord Alverstone CJ, in his judgment directed the jury in favour of necessity, and said: 'It was the duty, both under the rules and apart from the rules, of the officials to preserve the health and lives of the prisoners, who were in the custody of the Crown. If they forcibly fed the plaintiff when it was not necessary the defendant ought to pay damages'.[11] The jury concurred, although doctors had argued that it was a question best decided by them.[12] As Williams points out, the doctrine of necessity 'becomes particularised in rules of law',[13] as is clear by the instances above, with regard to whether the invasion of private property or personal liberty. In exploring the panoply of social claims that can arise in a defence of necessity, consideration is also given to the authorisation in law of particular personal or intersubjective narratives. Here, the legally accepted narratives as they inform communication, and, for our purpose the shaping of motives for action, is also considered. In exploring necessity's motives the dominant discourses are considered not merely at the intersubjective level of actor's motives for conduct (as explored by Schutz's[14] reading of Weber, for example) but also as shaped by Foucault's[15] theorisation of discourse as preceding the subject. The significance of necessity's motive, either as a justification or as an excuse for infraction is specifically explored, concluding that necessity's motive is one of justification, which of itself presents a heretical challenge to law's authority providing a way out of both the iron and the figurative cage of law.

Legal 'Necessity'

'Necessity' provides an exemption to criminal infraction when the claim that s/he was compelled or impelled to act as s/he did permitting and allowing a disregard for the normative constraints of the law when a claim to a higher morality, or more weighty need or situation is the more desirable end. Both self-defence and duress are in fact sub species of a necessity defence. Clarkson argues in favour of collapsing the defences of self-defence, duress by threats, duress by circumstances and necessity into one general defence of necessity, termed

---

7   Glanville Williams, 'The Defence of Necessity' (1953) 6 Current Leg Probs 217–218.

8   ibid 219.

9   Y.B., M.12 H.8 10a,pl,2. Cited in Williams (n 7) 220–221.

10   [1909–1910] 26 TLR 139, cited in Glanville Williams, *Textbook of Criminal Law* (London Stevens and Sons 1978) 571. See later Bobby Sands, *One Day In My Life* (Mercier Press 2001); *Secretary of State for the Home Department v Robb* Family Division 4 October 1994 Case Analysis [1995] Fam 127; [1995] 2 WLR 722.

11   [My emphasis] ibid; *Leigh* 142.

12   Anyone reading the experience of suffragettes on the receiving end of forcible feeding may conclude with the medical profession at the time that it was an inhumane and disgusting practice. See Frank Moxon, 'What Forcible Feeding Means' (The Woman's Press) <http://www.brynmawr.edu/library/exhibits/suffrage/MoxonForcibleFeeding.pdf> accessed 1 January 1 2014; see especially pages 6–7 for a commentary on the Leigh case.

13   Williams (n 7) 222.

14   Alfred Schutz, *The Phenomenology of the Social World* (Heinemann London 1972).

15   Michel Foucault, *The Archealogy of Knowledge* (Routledge 2008).

'necessary action'.[16] This schema for conceptualisation has some support. Lord Woolf CJ in *Shayler*,[17] opined that the defences of necessity and duress of circumstance are 'simply different levels of the same thing … . None the less the distinction between duress of circumstances and necessity has correctly been by and large ignored or blurred by the courts'.[18] Chan and Simester,[19] in response to Clarkson's schema declare that such a general defence is not possible because the rationales for the various defences differ, either being a matter of justification, or a matter of excuse. They develop in some detail their objection to such classification and argue that there are in effect four categories of exculpation: (a) self-defence as justification; (b) duress where D may commit both a moral and a legal wrong where the pressure explains D's motivation; (c) necessity, where the pressure is motivated by a lesser evils defence; and (d) the best interests intervention of necessity— where the authors refer to examples of medical intervention.[20] Each of these defences, say the authors, has a different rationale. Stark,[21] in his review of Clarkson's proposal and Chan and Simester's argument, also considers excusatory necessity and justificatory necessity in his attempt to develop a rationalisation of the necessity defence as he rebuts the Clarkson thesis explaining why he considers it will not work. Whichever way the defences are cut—excuse or justification, or the infraction as weighed against the moral claim there are differences between them and in addition as Williams points out,[22] '[T]he language of necessity disguises the selection of values that is really involved'.

In both the circumstances of self-defence and duress the defendant breaks the law, and, in the case of self-defence[23] his conduct may be excused and may even be justified when he kills to ensure self-preservation, or (where duress applies) is compelled to commit a crime (murder excluded) following another individual's threats of serious harm or death. Both self-defence and duress, have in recent years, been further expanded. In the Martin case,[24] a farmer shot at intruders with a gun, loaded with birdshot, killing one of them. Pleading self-defence, he was convicted of murder. At the time, the law required no more than reasonable force to be used. Lord Woolf CJ said, 'In judging whether the defendant had only used reasonable force, the jury has to take into account all the circumstances, including the situation as the defendant honestly believes it to be at the time, when he was defending himself. It does not matter if the defendant was mistaken in his belief as long as his belief was genuine'.[25] Martin's conviction for murder was quashed and diminished responsibility manslaughter substituted on appeal.[26] Lord Woolf CJ identified the public mood. 'What has been the subject of debate is whether a defendant to a murder charge should be convicted of murder if he was acting in self-defence but used excessive force in self-defence'.[27] Section 76 of the Criminal Justice and Immigration Act 2008, provides further clarification to the common law and statutory defences by enshrining in statute the essentialness of a defence of self-defence. Section 76(3) sets out what had been the position in the common law—that the more unreasonable the belief, the less likely it will be considered to be honestly held. However, the much needed clarity is lost since whilst the degree of force used must be reasonable, Section 76(7) also recognises that a person may, in such circumstances of fear, surprise, alarm, be unable to 'weigh to a nicety' the exact measure of any necessary action.[28] Further attempts to refine the law on self-defence have followed in the Crime and Courts Act 2013 with the introduction of an amendment to Section 76. The force used may now be 'disproportionate'. This is qualified by the requirement—'but not grossly so', as provided in

---

16   CMV Clarkson, 'Necessary Action: A New Defence' [2004] Crim LR 81–95.

17   *R v Shayler* [2001] EWCA Crim 1977; 1 WLR 2206, *R v Shayler* [2002] UKHL 11 [2003] 1 AC 247.

18   ibid (CA) [52] and [55] respectively [emphasis added].

19   Winnie Chan and AP Simester, 'Duress, Necessity: How Many Defences?' [2005] 16 Kings Coll LJ 121–132.

20   ibid 127.

21   Findlay Stark, 'Necessity and *Nicklinson*' [2013] Crim LR 949.

22   Williams (n 7) 224.

23   *Beckford v R* [1988] AC 130. 'A defendant is entitled to use reasonable force to protect himself, others for whom he is responsible and his property … . It must be reasonable'. See also a plea under s 3 Criminal Law Act 1967. See also *Morris* [2013] EWCA Crim 436.

24   *R v Martin* [2001] EWCA Crim 2245 [5].

25   *Martin* ibid [5].

26   *Martin* (n 24).

27   *Martin* (n 24) [9].

28   *R v Bristow and others* [2013] EWCA Crim 1540.

Section (5A), such that, '[i]n a householder case, the degree of force used by D is not to be regarded as having been reasonable in the circumstances as D believed them to be if it was grossly disproportionate in those circumstances'. Such determinations will turn on the individual facts of each case in interpreting this confusing amendment 'disproportionate – but not grossly so'. Nicola Wake[29] has noted the opacity: 'Perplexed jurors will be required to engage in mental gymnastics in order to determine whether the defendant's conduct is to be regarded as reasonable, disproportionate or grossly disproportionate'.

Turning to the defence of duress there has been some welcome and rather more comprehendible expansion. Such a defence applies where the defendant is forced by another person or by circumstances (duress of circumstances) to commit a crime. The trigger for such compulsion is a threat of serious harm or death.[30] I have critiqued the gendered nature of the criteria required for this defence particularly with regard to the exclusion of the factual compulsion created for victims facing the predicament of domestic violence.[31] In this regard, the Court of Appeal judgment in *R v Coats*[32] is to be welcomed. Here, the appellant, C, had been involved in drugs importation. She pleaded guilty and was sentenced to a term of imprisonment. However, one of the group, W, had been convicted of a brutal murder whilst C was serving a prison sentence. W had been previously in a relationship with C. W was violent to her and this was supported in complaints that C made to the police although subsequently withdrew out of fear. C made an application to the Criminal Cases Review Commission who referred her appeal against conviction to the Court of Appeal on the basis of fresh evidence of battered woman's syndrome (BWS). The Court of Appeal did not accept that C was in fact suffering from BWS, but significantly, it did accept that BWS may be relevant to a defence of duress. What they did say was this. An accused would have to have suffered BWS in a severe form to be in a position where the will was overborne.[33] The Court of Appeal in recognising the effects of domestic violence on the will impliedly accepted the obiter remarks of Baroness Hale who in *Hasan* had attempted to educate their Lordships on just this specific form of duress.[34] Baroness Hale said: 'The battered wife knows that she is exposing herself to a risk of unlawful violence if she stays, but she may have no reason to believe that her husband will eventually use her broken will to force her to commit crimes. … The battered wife knows very well that she may be compelled to cook the dinner, wash the dishes, iron the shirts and submit to sexual intercourse. That should not deprive her of the defence of duress if she is obliged by the same threats to herself or her children to commit perjury or shoplift for food'.

The defence of 'necessity' is also part of this expansionist project but it is piecemeal and lacking in coherence. Simester et al. write: 'There is no unitary rationale of the necessity defence'.[35] Indeed, it is simply not possible to rationalise the exemption from liability provided by a necessity defence. As Lord Woolf CJ stated in *Shayler*:

> Any attempt at a definition of the precise limits of the defence is fraught with difficulty because its development has been closely related to the particular facts of the different cases which have come before the court … in 1953, Professor Glanville Williams said, in *Criminal Law, The General Part*, p 570, that the "peculiarity of necessity as a doctrine of law is the difficulty or impossibility of formulating it with any approach to precision".[36]

Stark[37] presents a valiant and at times persuasive attempt at conjuring an ex post facto rationale to its arbitrariness. But there is no one body of philosophy, ethics or morals that can be called upon to resolve

---

29   Nicola Wake, 'Battered Women, Startled Householders and Psychological Self-Defence: Anglo-Australian Perspectives' [2013] JCL 77, 433. See also *R v Dawes, Hatter and Bowyer* [2013] 2 Cr App R 3.

30   *R v Dao, Mai and Nguyen* [2012] EWCA Crim 1717, where threat of false imprisonment was not sufficient, reaffirming *Hasan* [2005] UKHL 22, where the House of Lords limited the defence to threats of death or grievous bodily harm.

31   Susan Edwards, 'The Straw Woman at Law's Precipice: An Unwilling Party' in Reed and Bohlander (eds), *Participation in Crime: Domestic and Comparative Perspectives* (Ashgate Publishing 2013) 59–77.

32   *R v Coats (Goldie Ann)* [2013] EWCA Crim 1472.

33   *Coats* ibid.

34   *Hasan* (n 30) [77].

35   Simester et al. (n 2) 799.

36   *Shayler* (n 17) [46E–F] 2223.

37   Stark (n 21).

whether, or when, the claim of a defendant should trump the claim of law. The judicial (and statutory) outcomes defy classification, rationalisation or formalisation, they are arbitrary, determined by location, culture, historical context and the ill defined and unruly horse of public policy.

Common Law to the Model Penal Code

In the UK, the legal defence of necessity still remains a matter for judges and the common law. In its draft Criminal Code, the Law Commission, when tasked with considering necessity, said, *'We are not prepared to suggest that necessity should in every case be a justification; we are equally unprepared to suggest that necessity should in no case be a defence'.*[38] The ad hoc development of the common law of necessity has resulted in the Law Commission trying to inject some consistency proposing that a general defence of necessity be introduced into English law, and by 1985 that a defence of necessity—'duress of circumstances' (excepting attempted murder and murder) should apply to all crimes.[39] The Draft Criminal Law Bill, 1993,[40] clause 26 provides:

> (1) No act of a person constitutes an offence if the act is done under duress of circumstances. (2) A person does an act under duress of circumstances if – (a) he does it because he knows or believes that it is immediately necessary to avoid death or serious injury to himself or another, and (b) the danger that he knows or believes to exist is such that in all the circumstances (including any of his personal characteristics that affect its gravity) he cannot reasonably be expected to act otherwise. It is for the defendant to show that the reason for his act was such knowledge or belief as is mentioned in paragraph (a). The defence would not apply to a person who knowingly and without reasonable excuse exposed himself to the danger known or believed to exist; the accused would have the burden of proving that he had not so exposed himself if the question arose.

By contrast, in the US, a necessity defence is part of the Model Penal Code (a proposed criminal code drafted by the American Law Institute and used as the basis for criminal law revision). Following the case of *The United States v Holmes*,[41] (discussed below) necessity is explicitly sanctioned and many US states have adopted some form of 'lesser evils' defence.[42] Section 9.22 specifically sets out the defence of necessity, where conduct is justified if:

> (1) the actor reasonably believes the conduct is immediately necessary to avoid imminent harm;(2) the desirability and urgency of avoiding the harm clearly outweigh, according to ordinary standards of reasonableness, the harm sought to be prevented by the law proscribing the conduct; and (3) a legislative purpose to exclude the justification claimed for the conduct does not otherwise plainly appear.[43]

California, for example, has laid down six criteria which are required before such a defence can be satisfied: (1) preventing significant bodily harm or evil; (2) no adequate legal alternative; (3) act did not create a greater danger; (4) actual belief that act was necessary; (5) reasonable to believe act was necessary; and (6) D did not substantially contribute to the emergency.

Whilst in the UK, the common law defence of necessity has relied on three principles. First, the balance of harms test requires the harm of breaking the law to be balanced against the moral good to be achieved. Second, breaking the law to meet the higher moral claim and conduct must be objectively reasonable. Third,

---

38   Law Commission, *Draft Criminal Code* (Law Comm No 177, 1989); Criminal *Law*: A *Criminal Code* for England and Wales (1989) 2 vols. See also Law Commission, *Legislating the Criminal Code* (1993) (Law Comm No 218, Cmnd 2370).

39   Law Commission (1993) ibid; see discussion at 77 para 40.1.

40   Law Comm 1993 (n 38). See discussion at 35.1–35.12; 35.3–35.7.

41   *United States v Holmes* (1842) 26 F Cas 360.

42   See Model Penal Code and Commentaries 3.02 cmt 5 (Official Draft and Revised Comments 1985), listing state statutes for 'general choice of evils defense'.

43   Penal Code Title 2; General Principles of Criminal Responsibility ch 9; Justification Excluding Criminal Responsibility sub ch A, General Provisions.

the principle of proportionality requires the breaking of the law to be proportionate to the higher moral good that will be accomplished. In both the cases of *Nicklinson*[44] and *Re A*,[45] these three requirements, originally uttered by Judge Sir James Stephen, were reiterated:

> [T]here are three necessary requirements for the application of the doctrine of necessity: (i) the act is needed to avoid inevitable and irreparable evil; (ii) no more should be done than is reasonably necessary for the purpose to be achieved; (iii) the evil inflicted must not be disproportionate to the evil avoided.[46]

These principles are indeed enigmatic and fluid. They have been left for judges to divine and interpret as and when ambitious and creative counsel place such arguments before them. However, in some limited circumstances necessity arguments have been accommodated in specific statutes. For example, Section 9 of the Midwives Act of 1951 makes it an offence for an uncertified person to attend a woman in childbirth other than under the supervision of a qualified medical practitioner but no offence is committed if attendance was given in a case of sudden or urgent necessity.[47]

Balancing the Incommensurable—Fur with Feathers

Balancing the goods and harms or in the words of the common law 'balancing evils' requires making moral and ethical judgments. Williams recognised the philosophical and social maze of weighing necessity claims to any moral nicety. 'Necessity in legal contexts involves the judgment that the evil of obeying the letter of the law is socially greater in the particular circumstance than the evil of breaking it'.[48] In the case of *Shayler*,[49] Lord Woolf CJ said: '[T]he act must be done only to prevent an act of greater evil: the evil must be directed towards the defendant or a person ... for whom he has responsibility ... the act must be reasonable and proportionate to the evil avoided'.[50] And so round and round we go, and all the recitations do not move us to a clearer place in an effort to identify any guiding rationale.[51] Necessity is presented with an incommensurability problem since it requires the weighing of one claim against another, a task of morals and ethics yet determined largely by judges of law and not of gnosis. Endicott expresses it thus: 'The incommensurability problem: if there is no rational basis for deciding one way rather than the other, then the result seems to represent a departure from the rule of law, in favour of arbitrary rule by judges'.[52]

Objectively Reasonable to Whom?

The second criterion founded on an objective test requires a consideration of whether the infraction is reasonable in the circumstances. The reasonable man of necessity, and the reasonable man of provocation (now loss of self-control), as the reasonable man elsewhere in the criminal law, is not an ahistorical man. He is indeed a time traveller, travelling through time, through culture, and through place. Clarkson recognises this historical contingency evident in the language he chooses to articulate the precept of reasonableness—'in our present society', 'culturally bound', 'present time bound' and 'in this present law'.[53] Was the action of Captain

---

44   *R (Nicklinson) v Ministry of Justice R (AM) v Director of Public Prosecutions Queen's Bench Division* (Administrative Court) 16 August 2012 [2012] EWHC 2381 (Admin) [2012] HRLR [64].

45   *A (Children) (Conjoined Twins: Surgical Separation), Re [2001] Fam 147; [2000] HRLR 721.*

46   *Nicklinson* (n 44) [64], *A (Children) (Conjoined Twins: Surgical Separation), Re*, ibid [225]. See also *Pipe v DPP* [2012] EWHC 1821(Admin).

47   Susan Edwards, 'In Whose Best Interest – Everybody's Talking 'Bout Ma Baby' The Leveller, November 1982, 22–23; see also PR Glazebrook, 'The Necessity Plea in English Criminal Law' (1972A) 30 Camb LJ 96.

48   Williams, *Textbook* (n 10) 553.

49   *S* [2001] 1 WLR 2206.

50   *Shayler* (n 17) CA 2224 [49].

51   For a wider discussion on incommensurability, see Joseph Raz, *The Morality of Freedom* (Clarendon Press 1988), John Finnis, 'Commensuration and Public Reason' in Ruth Chang (ed), *Incommensurability, Incomparability, and Practical Reason* (Harvard University Press 1997); see also Timothy Endicott, *Vagueness in Law* (OUP 2000).

52   See <http://denning.law.ox.ac.uk/news/events_files/Proportionality_and_incommensurability.pdf>.

53   Clarkson (n 16).

Tom Dudley and Mate Edwin Stephens (discussed later) reasonable? It would appear from all that is known about this case that their actions in eating the cabin boy were indeed reasonable not only to seamen[54] but also to the people of the seaport of Falmouth,[55] but unreasonable to the court of law in London, and no doubt to ordinary men and women unfamiliar with the perils of the sea.

Proportionate to What?

The third principle enunciated by Judge Stephen is that of proportionality. As with self-defence or duress, it is difficult to balance to a legal nicety a proportionate response especially in situations requiring an immediate decision, a decision taken in an emergency situation, or in extremis or a decision taken when the defendant is in a state of shock, or fear, or blind panic. What is proportionate to what? The perceptive Clarkson again, 'Of course, an assessment whether a response is reasonable and proportionate must incorporate society's moral and political judgments about what sort of emergencies or threats can be averted'.[56] Lord Goff acceded in *Richards*:[57] '[T]he scope of the defence is by no means clear'.

The Legal 'Rationale' of Excluded Claims

In applying these three considerations, English law, has set down, in a series of common law cases the imperfect ambit of necessity with the result that very few claims are recognised. Bohlander is of the view that successful cases should indeed be exceptional.[58] Simester and others also concur, 'necessity is a doctrine to be used sparingly … it is not a major organising principle of a modern legal system'.[59] Perhaps this parsimonious usage is because necessity is heretical to the rule of law itself. Williams asks, 'By what right can the judge declare some value, not expressed in the law, to be superior to the law'?[60] Indeed by what right! Past excluded claims simply tell us what necessity is not, not what necessity is!

Dudley and Stephens[61] is perhaps the most vigorous of all such rejections excluding murder from necessity's ambit. The case involved four men who found themselves in *in extremis* circumstances. Shipwrecked and 1,000 miles from land, without food for 18 days and exhausted, they decided to kill the weakest of their members: Parker. The stronger drew lots as to who should commit the actus reus, one of the remaining three opted out of the conspiracy to kill Parker. On the 20th day, Parker was killed, and in eating his flesh the two killers and the third man survived.

Captain Tom Dudley and Mate Edwin Stephens were prosecuted for murder at the Devon and Cornwall Winter Assizes. Huddleston B, by way of a special verdict, adjourned the case until 25 November at the Royal Courts of Justice. After a further adjournment to 4 December, the case was argued before five judges. Counsel for the defendants, relying on Judge Stephen, *Digest of Criminal Law*, art 32, argued: 'The facts found on the special verdict shew that the prisoners were not guilty of murder, at the time when they killed Parker, but killed him under the pressure of necessity. Necessity will excuse all acts which would otherwise be a crime'.[62] Coleridge CJ did not accede to defence argument. Dudley and Stephens were found guilty and sentenced to

---

54   See Neil Hanson, *The Custom of the Sea* (Doubleday 2000); AW Brian Simpson, *Cannibalism and the Common Law* (University of Chicago Press 1984) ('In spite of the frequent occurrence of survival cannibalism, often preceded by deliberate killing, and the abundant evidence of nautical custom legitimating the practice of killing under necessity the survivors of the *Mignonette* have always been regarded as the first and indeed only individuals who ever faced trial for murder for killing committed in such circumstances') 161. See also Donald McCormick, *Blood on the Sea* (Muller 1962).

55   Hanson ibid; AW Brian Simpson ibid.

56   Clarkson (n 16) 89.

57   *R v Richards* (unreported 10 July 1986), cited in Michael Jefferson, *Criminal Law* (8th edn, Pearson 2007) 268.

58   Michael Bohlander, 'Of Shipwrecked Sailors, Unborn Children, Conjoined Twins and Hijacked Airplanes – Taking Human Life and the Defence of Necessity Taking Human Life and the Defence of Necessity' **(2006)** JCL 70 (147).

59   Simester et al. (n 2) 807.

60   Williams (n 7) 224.

61   *Dudley and Stephens* [1884] 14 QBD 273 (known at the time as the case of the Mignonette).

62   *Dudley* (n 61) 273.

be hanged. Coleridge CJ ruled that necessity could never be a defence to murder. However, both AW Brian Simpson[63] and Neil Hanson[64] in their researches discovered that the residents of Falmouth considered the conduct of the defendants both reasonable and proportionate since three were saved whilst only one died. Indeed, it could be said that although Parker was 'designated' to die; he was, after all, the weakest and most probably the soonest to die and so Dudley and Stephens merely hastened his death. Their action in the same moment was both pragmatic and desperate, committed in circumstances of *in extremis* where proportionality and reasonableness cannot be weighed with any exactitude. Bohlander, in reviewing this case, questions whether it was more necessary to kill him Parker than one of the grown men? He asserts, 'To preserve one's life is generally speaking, a duty, but it may be the plainest and the highest duty to sacrifice it'.[65] It was perhaps not more necessary, but in my view an argument could be made since Parker was very probably going to die before the others. Like Mary in *Re A*,[66] she dying gave life to Jodie, so Parker dying gave life to Dudley, Stephens, and Brooks, as the fate of the men in the boat was conjoined in circumstances. Williams,[67] in his *Textbook of Criminal Law*, said of this case, it 'involved in a common disaster … the victim was alive, but his prospect of remaining alive for more than a short time was minimal, so that his 'right to life' was of a very small value'. Williams suggests that a defence of necessity could have been accepted. I agree.[68] Terence Morris and Louis Blom-Cooper, remarking on the case, also said, 'It is hard to understand why a man who is driven to killing as a result of acts of provocation from his victims commits manslaughter, whereas the person who kills to preserve his own life and the lives of others has no such defence to murder'.[69]

In the US case of *Holmes*,[70] the ship *William Brown* founded in icy seas and with only two lifeboats—all its 83 passengers could not be saved. Whilst some passengers died on board as the boat went down, further lives were lost as one of the two life boats was severely overcrowded and as water was coming in, Holmes, following the order of a mate, spent a gruesome night throwing 16 passengers overboard to lighten the load. Holmes was convicted of manslaughter since the grand jury refused to indict him for murder. The judge directed the jury that his act was illegal because the crewmen (and not the mostly Irish emigrant passengers) should have been so sacrificed and the choice as to which crewmen should have been forced off the boat was a matter to have been properly determined by the drawing of lots.[71]

More recent rejected necessity pleas have involved far less weighty considerations. In *Southwark London Borough Council v Williams*,[72] a number of homeless persons made an orderly entry into empty houses in Southwark owned by the council. The council's application to the court for immediate possession was granted.[73] The argument advanced by the homeless, that necessity was a defence, was rejected. The circumstances in *Buckoke v Greater London Council*[74] were also insufficient to exempt the defendants from liability. This case concerned whether the driver of a fire engine, when answering an emergency call, could cross a traffic light on stop. Lord Denning (obiter) set up a hypothetical situation: 'A driver of a fire escape with ladders approaches the traffic lights. He sees 200 yards down the road a blazing house with a man at an upstairs window in extreme peril. The road is clear in all directions. At that moment the lights turn red. Is the driver to wait for 60 seconds, or more for the lights to turn green. If the driver waits for that time, the man's life will be lost. I suggested to both counsel that the driver might be excused in crossing the lights to save the man. He might have the defence of necessity. Both counsel denied it. They would not allow him any defence

---

63   AW Brian Simpson (n 54).
64   Hanson (n 54) 250, 260, 262, 334, 389, 387.
65   ibid Bohlander (n 58).
66   *Re A* [2001] 2 WLR 480.
67   Williams (n 10) 561.
68   See (n 38): at 35.11, the Law Commission suggests that circumstances such as those in Dudley would be a matter properly for the jury.
69   Terence Morris and Louis Blom-Cooper, *A Calendar of Murder* (Michael Joseph 1964) 289.
70   *Holmes* (n 41).
71   Simpson ibid (n 54) 166–170. See also the case of the Euxine (1874) where lots were drawn and cannibalism followed. 188.
72   [1971] 2 All ER 175. *Southwark London Borough Council v Williams and Another, Southwark London Borough Council v Anderson and Another* [1971] Ch 734.
73   ibid 744.
74   [1971] Ch 655.

in law. The circumstances went to mitigation, they said, and did not take away his guilt. If counsel are correct – and I accept that they are – nevertheless such a man should not be prosecuted. He should be congratulated'.[75]

Where individuals have cultivated cannabis for medicinal use to alleviate their own pain and suffering and advanced a defence of necessity, the courts have held that necessity is not available.[76] Here, Alan Reed has this to say: 'The defence of medical necessity has been solipsistically deployed by the judiciary for reasons of policy rather than strict logic'.[77]

The Problem of the Door No Man Could Shut

In limiting the ambit of necessity, judges warn against the dangers of the misplaced development of this defence. In *Dudley and Stephens*,[78] Lord Coleridge warned that necessity could 'be made the legal cloak for unbridled passion and atrocious crime'. Whilst Denning J, a century later in *Southwark*, was at pains to point out that the doctrine so enunciated must be carefully circumscribed; otherwise, necessity would open the door 'to many an excuse'.

'Necessity would open a door which no man could shut. It would not only be those in extreme need who would enter. There would be others who would imagine that they were in need, or would invent a need, so as to gain entry. Each man would say his need was greater than the next man's. The plea would be an excuse for all sorts of wrongdoing. So the courts must, for the sake of law and order, take a firm stand. They must refuse to admit the plea of necessity to the hungry and the homeless: and trust that their distress will be relieved by the charitable and the good'.[79] Lord Edmund Davies in similar dissuasion said: '[T]he law regards with deepest suspicion any remedies of self-help, and permits those remedies to be resorted to only in very special circumstances. The reason for such circumspection is clear – necessity can very easily become simply a mask for anarchy'.[80]

But few accounts refer to the abuse of the defence of necessity that occurred in *Gregson v Gilbert*,[81] the *Zong* case, where 150 slaves were pushed overboard because water was running short (although Glanville Williams does indeed lead with this case in his article on necessity).[82] As slaves, the men were owned as chattel and had a property value, the loss of which could be estimated in monetary value. Thus, Gregson (the shipowners) brought a claim for the loss of their slaves (£30 each) from their underwriters (Gilbert) who refused to pay.

So, divining what passes as necessity is a matter for judges. On the one hand, to accede to the defence advanced in *Dudley and Stephens* was perhaps to allow conduct beyond the moral pail and villainous, whilst to break the law in *Buckoke* was a course of action for the hero. And so where is the rationale when questions inhabiting perhaps not the two ends of the spectrum of claims as above, are presented to the courts? Alan Reed,[83] writing on decision making in the context of drugs cases where necessity has been pleaded,[84] refers to what he calls the operation of a judicial divining rod: 'This body of jurisprudence is so inconsistent and policy themed that it seems to have come about by judicial divining rod'.

---

75   ibid 668A–C.
76   *R v Quayle (Barry) and others*, also known as *Attorney General's Reference (No.2 of 2004), Re* [2005] Court of Appeal (Criminal Division), EWCA 1415.
77   Alan Reed, 'Necessity: Supply of Cannabis for Medical Purpose' (2005) 69 JCL 464.
78   *Dudley* (n 61).
79   *Southwark* (n 72) 744 (CD).
80   *Southwark* (n 72) 740.
81   *Gregson v Gilbert* (1783) 3 Doug KB 232, 99 ER 629 (KB).
82   Williams (n 7) 224.
83   Reed (n 77).
84   *Quayle* (n 76).

Accepted Claims

Whilst there may be perfectly legitimate moral and ethical arguments pressing for an exemption from the force of the criminal law, including pleadings of poverty, starvation, homelessness, and sickness, it is only in a very restricted set of circumstances that necessity pleas have been accepted by the judiciary in judge made law as creating exonerable exemptions. So what claims have judges accepted? Lord Denning in The *Closing Chapter* sets out some of these circumstances where presumably these exceptional claims of necessity have inhabited a higher or weightier moral ground. Starting with a case from the Year Book of 1499, when a prison caught fire and a prisoner who broke the door down in order to escape from the fire was held to have a defence of necessity, 'for he is not to be hanged because he would not stay to be burned'. Denning then mentions the Great Fire of London in 1666, when it was lawful to demolish intervening houses in an effort to stop the fire from spreading,[85] and the jettisoning of cargo to save a ship from shipwreck on stormy seas in *Mouse*'s case.[86]

In *Cope v Sharpe (No 2)*,[87] '[T]he plaintiff, an owner of land, let the shooting rights over the land to one C, whose bailiff and head gamekeeper the defendant was. A fire broke out on the land, and, while men in the employ of the plaintiff were endeavouring to beat it out, the defendant set fire to strips of heather between the fire and a part of the shooting where there were some nesting pheasants, the property of his master. Shortly afterwards the plaintiff's men succeeded in extinguishing the fire. The plaintiff brought an action of trespass in the county court. The Court held: (1) 'Was the method adopted by the defendant in fact necessary for the protection of his master's property?' and (2) 'If not, was it reasonably necessary in the circumstances?'[88] Denning stated, 'There is authority for saying that in case of great and imminent danger, in order to preserve life, the law will permit of an encroachment on private property'. The claims of private property and chattels have surrendered in these circumstances.

Doctors' Duty and Necessity

In modern times, necessity has been pleaded with regard to a number of medical decisions as the authority of physicians in the modern world is increasingly recognised.[89] Physicians are in a very different position to others since 'their' necessity decisions involve the balancing of particular competing claims which inhabit the arena of ethical questions that are overlaid by religious precepts, matters of conscience, and in addition and most importantly their professional oath.[90] Chan and Simester describe physicians' claims to necessity as 'best interests interventions' which the authors claim involve some form of paternalism.[91] Stark,[92] in reviewing the necessity defence in this area of circumstances also speaks in the language of 'best interests interventions'. Physicians—in saving lives or preventing harm—have, on occasion, relied on the defence of necessity, aligning the physician's duty to alleviate human suffering[93] and the legal duty. In *R v Bourne*,[94] a doctor performed an abortion on an adolescent girl of 14 years of age who had been violently raped by five soldiers. It was his duty as a doctor to save life, both physical and mental, and to alleviate suffering. Yet, Dr Bourne

---

85   Tom Denning, *The Closing Chapter* (Butterworths 1983) 68.

86   (1608) 12 Co Rep 63.

87   [1912] 1 KB 496.

88   ibid 500–501.

89   See Ivan Illich, *Medical Nemesis* (Open Forum 1974).

90   The Hippocratic Oath is not just about patient confidentiality; it holds physicians to this duty: 'I will use treatments for the benefit of the ill in accordance with my ability and my judgment, but from what is to their harm and injustice I will keep them'.

91   Chan and Simester (n 19) 127.

92   Stark (n 21).

93   In life and death matters, this duty has been variously articulated as a duty to save life, and in wardship cases over the years it has been differently articulated moving from 'letting a child live' or 'letting a child die', then to express these two positions as 'treatment to live' and 'treatment to die', in an attempt to inscribe 'treatment to die' formerly expressed as 'letting a child die' with a positive inflection rather than a negative expression of an act of omission or failing. More recently, the medical approach has now centred not on the outcome of treatment with regard to life or death outcomes, but instead focused on the medical objective of easing of pain and suffering as the primary objective of medical health care.

94   *R v Bourne* [1939] 1 K.B 687.

was prosecuted (under Section 58 of the Offences Against the Person Act 1861).[95] The evidence submitted on behalf of the defence was that the girl would have become a 'mental wreck' had the pregnancy continued. Dr Bourne in evidence asserted that he considered it his duty as a doctor to perform the operation. The judge, MacNaghten J, in his summing up impliedly made the case for a necessity defence and said that Dr Bourne performed the operation 'unquestionably believing that he was doing the right thing, and that he ought, in the performance of his duty as a member of a profession devoted to the alleviation of human suffering, to do it'.[96] The judge drew on the provisions of the Infant Life Preservation Act 1929, which provided a defence to such a charge where it was carried out in good faith for the purpose of preserving the life of the mother. The jury acquitted Dr Bourne of performing an illegal abortion. However, in the case of *Attorney General v X*,[97] where a young adolescent who had been raped sought an abortion in England, public policy in Ireland, a Catholic country (albeit some 50 years later), took a different and more restrictive view. The Irish Supreme Court held 4–1 that it could be lawful in circumstances where there was risk to life as 'distinct from [risk to] the health' of the individual.[98] Culture and context, religion and ideology clearly influence the judicial divining rod with regard to the necessity defence where there are competing moral/ethical and religious interests. Interestingly, MacNaghten J in *Bourne* had also said this:

> On the other hand there are people who, from what are said to be religious reasons, object to the operation being performed under any circumstances. That is not the law either. On the contrary, a person who holds such an opinion ought not to be an obstetrical surgeon, for if a case arose where the life of the woman could be saved by performing the operation and the doctor refused to perform it because of his religious opinions and the woman died, he would be in grave peril of being brought before this Court on a charge of manslaughter by negligence. He would have no better defence than a person who, again for some religious reason, refused to call in a doctor to attend his sick child, where a doctor could have been called in and the life of the child could have been saved. If the father, for a so-called religious reason, refused to call in a doctor, he also is answerable to the criminal law for the death of his child. I mention these two extreme views merely to show that the law lies between them.[99]

He was, of course, referring to Protestant/Anglican/secular England and not to Catholic Ireland.

In cases involving those who are lacking mental capacity, or in the case of minors lacking legal capacity, the inherent jurisdiction or the wardship jurisdiction provides a shield of protection for doctors who in the case of adults and minors unable to consent to medical treatment otherwise might face prosecution. In the following cases involving the inherent jurisdiction the common law defence of necessity has been invoked. In *F v West Berkshire Authority*,[100] Lords Brandon and Goff held that necessity was a defence where a 35-year-old adult, who lacked mental capacity and was incapable of giving consent, was sterilized. The High Court made a declaration that the sterilization was not unlawful and no offence had been committed where it was performed out of necessity to protect the patient. In *Bournewood Community and Mental Health Trust*,[101] a mentally incompetent patient was informally admitted, and the admission was held unanimously to be justified in application of the 'doctrine' of necessity. In *AM v South London & Maudsley NHS Foundation Trust Upper Tribunal*,[102] the House of Lords held that there was a common law power under the doctrine of necessity to detain and restrain patients who lack capacity and where detention was necessary in their own best interests. The common law defence of necessity has also been invoked in cases where adolescent minors

---

95   Section 58 states: 'Administering drugs or using instruments to procure abortion. Every woman, being with child, who, with intent to procure her own miscarriage, shall unlawfully administer to herself any poison or other noxious thing, or shall unlawfully use any instrument or other means whatsoever with the like intent, and whosoever, with intent to procure the miscarriage of a woman, whether she be or be not with child, shall unlawfully administer to her or cause to be taken by her any poison or other noxious thing, or shall unlawfully use any instrument or other means whatsoever with the like intent, shall be guilty of a felony, and being convicted thereof shall be liable [. . .] to be kept in penal servitude for life [. . .]'.

96   ibid (n 94) 690.

97   *Attorney General v X* [1992] 1 IR 1, [1992] IESC 1, [1992] 1 IR 1.

98   *ibid* 53–54.

99   ibid (n 94) 693.

100   [1990] 2 AC 1.

101   [1998] 3 All ER 289.

102   Administrative Appeals Chamber, 6 August 2013 [2013] UKUT 0365 (AAC).

have been warded. The golden thread in the wardship jurisdiction lies with ensuring the best interests of the child.

The question of whether necessity might provide a defence in assisted suicide reflects changing values as they impact on the law and perhaps presents the greatest challenge. Underscoring its chimeric quality, Williams in 1953 wrote: 'Necessity involves a scale of values, and a judge in adjudicating upon the defence may have to make a decision of the greatest ethical difficulty'.[103] Whether there is a necessity defence for a family member assisting in hastening the death of an already dying/terminally ill loved one who pleads to die, or where a doctor assists in the death of already dying/terminally ill patient who pleads to die were questions raised in the case of *Nicklinson*.[104]At the heart of such actions lie conscience and the desire and necessity to end human suffering. That necessity, and, in the case of Heather Pratten,[105] that question of conscience and of duty was poignantly articulated and acted upon. At her trial she pleaded guilty to aiding and abetting the suicide of her son, Nigel Goodman, and was granted a conditional discharge:

> My son Nigel had the hereditary degenerative neurological disorder, Huntington's Disease. We'd both watched my husband die from the illness and knew the distress and agony it could cause. Nigel knew what was going on and that he did not want to be around to suffer anymore. On his 42nd birthday he told me the best present I could give him would be to end his life. He didn't want to die alone. I tried to persuade him against it but I would not let him die alone and promised him I would not let him fail. Looking back I still believe that it was his right to choose. Other people have tried to end their lives and failed and then been left in an even worse situation than they were previously in. I was put on bail for murder for being with Nigel and putting a pillow over his face when he lost consciousness from the overdose. In the end I was charged with aiding and abetting a suicide and received a conditional discharge for 1 year.[106]

In December 2013, the case of *Nicklinson and Lamb* was heard before nine Supreme Court judges, who considered whether a prohibition on assisted suicide provided in the Suicide Act 1961 is compatible with Article 8 right to respect for private and family life enshrined in the European Convention on Human Rights.[107] Counsel for Nicklinson (deceased) and Lamb argued that the law should include a defence of necessity. The Supreme Court delivered its in delivering it judgment[108] in June 2014 declined to uphold a right to die in dignity.

Behind Closed Doors and Beyond the Fringe: Necessity's Negotiations

The cases which have come before the courts, however, are indicative only of a fraction of the causes and cases in which a defence of necessity is pleaded, since the Crown Prosecution Service (CPS), especially in recent times, sifts through potential necessity pleas and takes the decision to prosecute, informed by conviction potential and also by public policy. The Law Commission[109] recognised that if the infraction was a minor one and necessity might be pleaded as a defence, then prosecutions were unlikely. In any event, Lord Shawcross the Attorney-General of England, in 1951, asserted with regard to the decision to prosecute, 'It has never been the rule in this country – I hope it never will be – that suspected criminal offences must automatically be the subject of prosecution'.[110] Although no research has been commissioned or conducted on this point, certainly some of the CPS discontinuances will be cases where although the test of sufficiency of evidence may be

---

103   Williams (n 7) 234.
104   *Nicklinson* (n 44).
105   'Caring Mother Helped Son Die – Woman Freed by Merciful Judge' The Journal (27 October 2000).
106   PA Newswire: Corporate Finance News (10 May 2013).
107   *The Times* (14 December 2013). See also Stark's argument that Nicklinson is not a case of necessity (n 21) 964.
108   R (on the application of Nicklinson and another) (Appellants) vMinistry of Justice (Respondent); R (on the application of AM) (AP) (Respondent)v The Director of Public Prosecutions (Appellant) [2014] UKSC 38, on appeal from [2013] EWCA Civ 961.
109   Law Commission Report on Defences of General Application No 83 (1977) 556 para 4.2.1 p 27.
110   See <http://www.dpp.gov.fj/default.aspx?page=decisionProsec> accessed 1 January 2014.

satisfied a realistic prospect of conviction is considered unlikely to follow, such that necessity arguments then may well be instrumental in decisions not to prosecute[111] and will subsequently impact on police decisions to prefer charges at the outset. For example, when the *Herald of Free Enterprise* capsized, killing some 193 passengers, it contained its own reality of a defence of necessity, especially when considering the measures adopted by the rescue crew who sought to save the lives of the shipwrecked. A clear example of necessity was detailed in the evidence submitted to the coroner's inquest in October 1987.[112] Remarking on this tragedy, Smith asserts: 'The law has lost touch with reality if it condemns as murder conduct which right-thinking people regard as praiseworthy'.[113] The incident was later recalled in the case of *Re A*,[114] by Lord Justice Brooke, 'At the coroner's inquest conducted in October 1987 into the *Zeebrugge* disaster, an army corporal gave evidence that he and dozens of other people were near the foot of a rope ladder. They were all in the water and in danger of drowning. Their route to safety, however, was blocked for at least ten minutes by a young man who was petrified by cold or fear (or both) and was unable to move up or down. Eventually the corporal gave instructions that the man should be pushed off the ladder, and he was never seen again. The corporal and many others were then able to climb up the ladder to safety'.[115] Of course, had he been the subject of a prosecution, a necessity debate would have been pleaded in his defence and a moral and highly publicised public debate would have ensued in which the competing claims of saving ten lives as against saving one life would have been considered. For many, no doubt, the army corporal was a hero (as was the fireman in Denning's hypothetical example in *Buckoke*),[116] acting swiftly and decisively in an *in extremis* situation. Yet, judges (following *Dudley and Stephens*, cited earlier) have decided that necessity can never be a defence to murder. But Smith (again), in commenting on the apparent resiling from this rule in the *Zeebrugge* case, asserts: '[W]e have breached the supposed rule that necessity can never be a defence to a murder charge'.[117]

The purpose and object of allowing a defence of necessity to succeed is to mitigate the harshness of the law. Clearly there is no consistent framework, making it impossible to say with any certainty whether the law will consider a lesser evils justification defence or best interests intervention.[118] What moral claims trump? Who is to say? Williams writes, 'In a manner of speaking the whole law is based on social necessity'.[119] Certainly, the claims of necessity are cogitated and conceded or rejected against a background of socially constructed exonerations that are shaped by culture, time and place as standards of public morality change and depend on the nature of the competing claims and the unruly horse of public policy.

Necessity Claims in Disguise: Battered Women, Wives, Mothers, and Children

Further instances of necessity claims entertained behind the legal framework of necessity include essentially necessity arguments run as other defences. Here, such cases, rather than being run as necessity defences, have been shochorned into existing defences as the law—in recognising its own normative gaps—tries to avoid injustice. But like the feet of the ugly sisters, defendants' necessity claims have not properly fitted the shoes of the legal categories into which they have been pressed.

Statistics on the death of female partners at the hands of male partners[120] suggest that women in violent relationships face a crisis situation, often only to be averted by victims themselves killing violent partners in self-preservation. Yet such women find themselves convicted of murder/manslaughter. In the US, in such circumstances clemency is considered for such women and certainly a class action of necessity might

---

111   As Stark notes, 'It must be assumed that other decisions about whether to institute prosecutions, and about how to argue cases have also impacted upon the ability of the courts to develop the law' (n 21).

112   JC Smith, *Justification and Excuse in the Criminal Law*, The Hamlyn Lectures (London Stevens 1989) 73.

113   Smith, ibid 77.

114   ibid (n 45) [2000] 4 All ER 961.

115   [2001] Fam 147, 229.

116   *Buckoke* (n 74).

117   Smith (n 113) 78.

118   Chan and Simester (n 19).

119   Williams (n 7) 217.

120   See Susan Edwards, 'Loss of Self-Control: When His Anger is Worth More Than Her Fear' in Bohlander and Reed (eds), *Loss of Control and Diminished Responsibility: Domestic, Comparative and International* (Ashgate 2011) 79–96.

be appropriate.[121] In the UK since the 1980s, counsel and judges, in avoiding injustice,[122] have stretched provocations' elements[123] in order to bring battered women within the defence. Arguably, battered women who killed violent spouses did so out of necessity for self-preservation, but the defence of self-defence, as framed, excluded them, as did provocation and duress, all of which embodied a masculinist framing of the elements founded on gendered notions of reasonableness and proportionality, and in the case of provocation, immediacy. Necessity's absolute exclusion of killing from its ambit, in my view, furthers this masculinism. The new defence of loss of self-control (fear) incorporates some understanding of the reasons why women might kill abusive spouses but falls short as it limits the plea to circumstances where the fear arises from '**D's fear of** *serious violence* from V against D or another identified person'.[124] From the defendant's experience and linguistic accounts, necessity has also been the driver where children have killed a violent parent. Accounts articulated by children who kill a violent father have been frequently couched in the language of necessity and the need for self-preservation, either of themselves and/or their mother. Again, as necessity is excluded from a defence to murder, such circumstances have also been shoehorned into provocation or diminished responsibility defences. In *R v Rose*, where a son believed his father was about to kill his mother, and so in preserving her life killed him, Lopes J said, 'homicide may be excusable … if the fatal blow inflicted was necessary for preservation of life'.[125]

Two sisters, Annette and Charlene Maw, killed a violent father of whom the mother, Beryl, had said that he had told her she should eat one meal a day like a dog. The wife said, 'The night he died I arrived home from work, he said he felt like punching me and he started drinking and then my youngest daughter came downstairs and tried to make some supper and he followed her into the kitchen and he started punching her and spitting in her face …'[126] Annette went on to stab him, having been given the knife by Charlene. Lord Lane CJ, Lord Justice Frederick Lawton, and Judge Leslie Boreham reduced Charlene's sentence to six months.[127] Lord Lane said the stabbing went beyond self-defence or actions committed in the 'agony of the moment'[128] and asked, '[W]hat should be the attitude of the law to those who unlawfully and with violence kill someone who has treated them badly? Can the law tolerate this kind of behaviour when there are ample remedies'.[129] In 1976, Noreen Winchester received a seven-year prison sentence for killing her father who had sexually abused her,[130] whilst William John Pearson killed a violent father who was abusive to his mother, and on appeal against a conviction for murder, a manslaughter/provocation verdict was substituted.[131] In *R v Tyler*,[132] the defendant had been convicted of killing a brutal and bullying father who had threatened her mother and her brother, called her mother and the defendant sluts, and asked the mother if she wanted a vinegar bottle put up her vagina. All these cases turn on necessity (in fact) and necessity is found in the linguistic accounts presented by the defendants, but following the *Dudley and Stephens* rule, no defence of necessity was available in law. Angela Browne,[133] concluding on the battered women, writes that their 'affective cognitive, and behavioural responses are likely to be distorted by their intense focus on survival' and are indeed necessity pleas 'to stop him from hurting me'.[134]

---

121   Michigan Project on Clemency, <https://www.legalmomentum.org/referral-directory/michigan-womens-justice-clemency-project>.

122   Lord Taylor in *Ahluwalia* [1992] 4 All ER 889; Lord Steyn in *Luc* [1996] 2 All ER 1033.

123   Lord Hoffman in *Smith* [2000] 1 AC 146; 4 All ER 289, said that the law on provocation 'has serious logical and moral flaws'.

124   Coroners and Justice Act 2009 s 55(3) [emphasis added].

125   *R v Rose* [1884] 15 Cox 540.

126   See <http://bufvc.ac.uk/tvandradio/lbc/index.php/segment/0014700491008> accessed 1 January 2014.

127   *R v Maw and another* [1980] Court of Appeal (Criminal Division) No 4795/R/80 (Transcript: Walsh, Cherer). See also *The Times* (18 November 1980).

128   *The Glasgow Herald* (4 December 1980) 5. Also reported in the US in *The Blade* (Toledo, Ohio, 4 December 1980) 16.

129   Cited in Susan Edwards, *Policing Domestic Violence* (Sage 1989) 179; *The Times* (London, 4 December 1980).

130   Susan Edwards, *Gender, Sex and the Law* (Croom Helm 1985) 141.

131   *R v Pearson* [1991] Court of Appeal (Criminal Division) (Transcript: Marten Walsh Cherer).

132   Edwards, ibid (n 130) 177–179.

133   Angela Browne, *When the Battered Woman Kills* (Springer 1987) 126.

134   ibid 160.

Necessity as a Challenge to State Secrecy

Necessity claims have also arisen in cases where defendants challenge state secrecy and rely on necessity arguments also evident in their intersubjective accounts explaining their actions. But legal necessity has never been acceded where an individual wishes to use it to challenge State power. Simon Gardner[135] is also interested in this question. Clive Ponting admitted revealing the secrets of the Belgrano affair and was charged with a criminal offence under Section 2 of the Official Secrets Act of 1911. His defence was that disclosure was in the public interest and disclosure to a Member of Parliament was protected. He was acquitted by the jury. The women of Greenham common certainly regarded their actions as not only necessary but a matter of conscience necessary to preserve the world and the future. Well before the *Jones* defendants[136] committed criminal damage at an RAF airbase, Greenham Common peace women were prosecuted regularly in the courts where they pleaded necessity and appealed to higher loyalties.[137] One woman charged with breach of the peace said: 'I challenge you now to show me this peace that you talk about. How can you say such/peace exists, when people are dying all over the world? If you ask me now to keep the peace, I shall say you are either blind or a fool'.[138] As Rebecca Johnson wrote in 1989:

> Our use of non violence is not synonymous with passive resistance, for in intervening to prevent violence, we challenge the militarists and those carrying out government orders, confronting then with their personal responsibility for what they are doing, whether they are planning for war, building silos, driving cruise missile launchers or policing the bases.[139]

There have been other claims couched in the language of necessity, for example Katharine Gun, a GCHQ employee, was acquitted in 2004 of leaking state secrets over the Iraq war. In her defence she was to have argued necessity. Yet, the case was dropped at the door of the court so we were not to hear it.[140] The defence of necessity clearly occupies a much more prominent place in legal defences than its case law reports. And like heretics, its challenge must be supressed or eschewed, for its presence casts a shadow over the sanctity of the law and its rules.

Necessity's Motives

Much of the academic legal debate on necessity has also considered whether necessity functions as a justification or an excuse. Why should it matter? The view is that the construction of necessity's ascribed motive may also intersect with whether the breach in question is accepted and, if accepted, how then is it dealt with? Adopting Fletcher's view, 'justifications confer 'privileges' to infringe the prohibitory norm'.[141] For Austin, '[i]n the one defence [justification], we accept responsibility but deny that it was bad: in the other [excuse], we admit that it was bad but don't accept full, or even any, responsibility'.[142] The broad argument is that justifications and excuses function differently in the criminal law and convey different meanings. When an excuse is invoked, the actor usually accepts that the conduct was wrong, both legally and morally, and that it was wrong to transgress the legal rule but was he unable because of some individual factor to conform. Diminished responsibility provides such an example of the functioning of an excuse in a recognition of rule

---

135   'Direct Action and the Defence of Necessity' [2005] Crim LR 371.

136   *Jones* [2006] UKHL 16, on appeal from [2004] EWCA Crim 1981 and [2005] EWHC 684 (Admin).

137   Susan Edwards, *Women on Trial* (Manchester University Press 1984) 162.

138   ibid 162; see also 'Greenham Women the Control of Protest' in C Dunhill (ed), The Boys in Blue (Virago 1989) 155.

139   ibid 155.

140   See <http://www.theguardiancom/world/2013/mar/03/katharine-gun-iraq-war-whistleblower> accessed 1 Jan 2014.

141   George P Fletcher, *Rethinking Criminal Law* (Reprint, Little Brown 2000) 562–566; George P Fletcher, 'The Right and the Reasonable' [1985] 98 Harvard L Rev 949, 978.

142   JL Austin, 'A Plea for Excuses' [1956–57] 57 Proc Aristotelian Soc 1. See JL Austin, *Philosophical Papers* (Clarendon Oxford 1960), JL Austin, *How to do Things With Words* (Harvard Cambridge 1975).

breaking whilst pleading illness and an inability to control himself. When a justification is invoked to explain conduct the actor may not accept that the action was morally wrong although recognises that it is legally wrong. His justification may range from a rejection of the law to a strident expression of its moral fallibility.[143] Provocation provided an instance of justification with its rhetoric, 'She deserved it' serving as an example in partner homicide cases. What is being done is variously justified, condemned, excused, or permitted, by and through the use of language and rhetoric which is performative,[144] that is, when a word is spoken or written it becomes a relational entity; where words are used to justify and condone a behaviour or action, or otherwise condemn. The words themselves have a force and signify and give permission for, or else prohibit, the action. I want to rethink the relationship of legal categories of excuses and justification in the criminal law and particularly to rethink these constructs within the paradigm of necessity and the consequences the 'motive label' or attribution, has for human agency has for permissions and development of the defence. Thinking outside the excuse/justification dualism in the context of necessity for a moment I want to examine and revert back to the dualism implicit in Schutz's[145] thought and examine his 'because of' and 'in order to' motives and their relevance for understanding necessity's claims and acceptances and rejections. The actor claiming necessity appeals to both 'because of' motives—because my conscience compelled me to do it and 'in order to' motives—a teleological prospective orientated action to achieve an ulterior future goal.

'Because of motives' notionally contain more of a duress or duress of circumstance motivator, whilst 'in order to' action involves being drawn towards the accomplishment of an ulterior purpose. Are these motives examples of justifications or excuses? I think that both types of motive 'because of' and 'in order to'and their relationship to the cause or precursor of action can be regarded as justificatory. The real issue here and throughout all the academic debates on motive in necessity lies in the quality and the nature of the action to be accomplished regardless of whether the motive drives or pulls. It is the moral/ethical/philosophical/ political imperative that really counts. Horder[146] states, and I agree: 'In necessity cases, the key issue is the m*oral imperative* to act: what matters is whether in the circumstances it was morally imperative to act, even if this might involve the commission of wrongdoing, in order to negate or avoid some other evil. In duress cases, the key issue is the *personal sacrifice* [the accused] is being asked to make: should [the accused] be expected to make the personal sacrifice involved in refusing to give in to a coercive threat, rather than avoid implementation of the coercive threat by doing wrong'? In expressing excuse it is usually the actor who is excused. In expressing justification it is the circumstances and herein we implicitly see a repudiation of law and a challenge to its figurative cage. Actors acting in justification may appeal to a variety of motives from an appeal to higher loyalties, altruism, preservation of others, or conscience.[147] Many actors convicted of criminal offences believe their actions were justified. However, in only limited circumstances is the law willing to accept justifications for conduct as functioning in mitigation. In fact it is here when justifications are mooted, either a change in the law is pressed for (as in the case of householder-self-defence), or else necessity occupies that moral/legal space and is provided for in statute. As Judge Stephen recognised, 'it is just possible to imagine cases in which expediency of breaking the law is so overwhelmingly great that people may be justified in breaking it'.[148]

But how important is this excuse/justification distinction to necessity? Chalmers and Leverick,[149] in their distinction, build on a considerable body of academic commentary. In teasing out the notion that necessity is really a defence where circumstances arise that call for the criminal law to be abandoned in favour of embracing the greater good, the term 'duress of circumstance' has evolved. This more clearly denotes that circumstances outside the individual intervene or supervene to make obedience to the criminal law blind

---

143   Clarkson (n 16) 82.
144   See JR Searle, *Speech Acts: An Essay in the Philosophy of Language* (Cambridge University Press 1969, 1999); Austin (n 138).
145   Schutz (n 14).
146   J Horder, 'Self-Defence, Necessity and Duress: Uunderstanding the Relationship' (1998) 11 Can JL & Jurisp 143.
147   Itzhak Kugler, 'Necessity as a Justification in Re A (Children)' (2004) 68 JCL 440–450.
148   J F Stephen, *Digest of the Criminal Law* (vol II, 1887) 108.
149   J Chalmers and F Leverick, 'Fair Labelling in Criminal Law' (2008) 71 Mod L Rev 217.

in the circumstances. Ashworth has argued that duress of circumstances has taken over necessity.[150] Into this framework for motives/excuses/justifications enters 'permission' which in effect places the power at least from a performative perspective back into the hands of the law presenting the law as a self-reflective arena. Ashworth and Horder avoid the language of both excuse and justification instead using the language of 'residual permissions'.[151] When medical necessity is discussed they momentarily move from a doctor giving permission slipping back to the language of 'is it ever justifiable for a doctor',[152] but quickly return to the use of the word 'permission'. They then go on to consider several examples where 'permissions' have been inserted into statute, citing, for example, Section 5(4) Misuse of Drugs Act 1971, which allows a defence where D's purpose is to prevent another from committing an offence, Section 87 of the Road Traffic Regulation Act 1984, which exempts an emergency vehicle from observing the speed limit.

Necessity Good and Harm—The Moral Mesh

Whatever the scheme is, either the one rationale à la Clarkson, or the four as for Chan and Simester, necessity as an excuse or justification, the question of which moral/ethical/philosophical argument in particular circumstances might trump legal arguments; nothing of any of this is fixed, all is negotiable. Outside the law there is considerable debate as to which moral goods or harms to be avoided trumps the harm of breaking which law. As Endicott has said in another context, we have the rule of judges and not the rule of law.[153] The defence of necessity clearly demonstrates that the law is not infallible and tries to provide a body of rules setting out when its veil of fallibility can be lifted. Necessity when it works outside the courtroom shows it is potentially a defence to all offences. Lawyers search for consistency and principle, but the Holy Grail search for the sense in necessity is elusive. It is the product of competing morals, which in 1520 resulted in Brooke J asserting, 'It is said that if I come into your land and kill a fox, a gray, or an otter, I shall not be punished for this entry, because they are beasts against the common profit'.[154] On some occasions it does provide a route of escape from the figurative and iron cage of law when higher values demand. Certainly defence lawyers will continue to advance necessity claims on behalf of their clients. In *R v S*,[155] the appellant (S) appealed against a decision dismissing her defence of necessity to a charge of removing a child from the jurisdiction where she feared that her daughter would be sexually abused since the child had made such allegations in the course of proceedings to decide contact. The court did not accept this as reasonable or proportionate or indeed the lesser of two evils. Perhaps a court of mothers whose children had been abused may have done so. It is impossible to discern a rationale; the law has developed on a case-by-case basis and should do so to mitigate the iron cage of the law. The courts have responded in accordance with public or government policy and the social construction of reasonableness, proportionality and the social construction of lesser evils. All these concepts are shaped by societal codes and conventions about behaviour, and persons and are informed by constructions of class, culture, power (private power and state power), rights and gender and other considerations of the day, and time and place. It would be foolish to pretend otherwise.

---

150   A Ashworth, *Principles of Criminal Law* (6th edn, OUP 2009) 206.
151   A Ashworth and J Horder, *Principles of Criminal Law* (2013 edn, OUP) 130.
152   ibid 132.
153   See <http://denning.law.ox.ac.uk/news/events_files/Proportionality_and_incommensurability.pdf>.
154   Williams (n 7) 220.
155   *R v S*, also known as *R v CS* [2012] EWCA Crim 389, [2012] 1 WLR 3081, [2012] 1 Cr App R 31, [2012] Crim LR 623; *The Times* (8 May 2012).

Chapter 7

Duress and Normative Moral Excuse: Comparative Standardisations and the Ambit of Affirmative Defences

Alan Reed

Law is ineffective in the deepest sense, indeed … it is hypocritical, if it imposes on the actor who has the misfortune to confront a dilemmatic choice, a standard that his judges are not prepared to affirm that they should and could comply with if their turn to face the problem should arise. Condemnation in such a case is bound to be an ineffective threat; what is, however, more significant is that it is divorced from any moral base and is unjust.[1]

Introduction

The defence of duress *per* minas (by threats), as identified above in the context of the Commentaries to the US Model Penal Code, is atypical within the taxonomy of general defences in criminal law.[2] A coerced actor evokes our compassion and empathy in the context of the dilemmatic choice that may be presented to either kill another or suffer dire personalised consequences[3] The anthropomorphic normal person is placed in an abnormal situation in that their will is subjugated by that of the duressor;[4] 'we find it impossible to separate him from ourselves; there, but for the grace of God or good fortune, go the rest of us'.[5] An odious Hobson's Choice may be applicable to the duressee in a setting whereby an 'intentional' killing is inter-twined with moral involuntariness, and couched in a 'Do this, or else' imperative.[6]

Consider a scenario where an individual, after many years of family heartache, is thrilled by the birth of a cherished daughter. The child is the centre of the actor's existence. One day, subsequently, when collecting their daughter from primary school, they enter the classroom where a gunman is present. A threat is uttered that their daughter will be killed unless D kills both the principal and deputy of the school. These intentional killings are carried out and the daughter survives as stated. How should the ambit of exculpation extend to this coerced individual in terms of culpability and blameworthiness? The intentional killings are not warranted

---

1 Model Penal Code and Commentaries s. 2.09 cmt (1985) at 374–75.

2 See Herbert Fingarette, 'Victimization: A Legalist Analysis of Coercion, Deception, Undue Influence, and Excusable Prison Escape' (1985) 42 Wash & Lee L Rev 65, 84–85, n 54 ('[T]he moral that has to be drawn seems to be that in the eye of the law there has consistently been something systematically significant, and more forceful, about a plea of [defence to] a criminal act motivated by a danger to the actor that was designedly created for that very purpose by a wrongful human threat … as contrasted with a defense based merely on the actor having faced a choice-of-evils dilemma').

3 See generally Steven J Mulroy, 'The Duress Defence's Uncharted Terrain: Applying it to Murder, Felony Murder, and the Mentally Retarded Defendant' (2006) 46 San Diego L Rev 159; Luis E. Chiesa, 'Duress, Demanding Heroism and Proportionality' (2008) 41 Vand J Transnat'l L 741; Joshua Dressler, 'Some Very Modest Reflections on Excusing Criminal Wrongdoers' (2009) 42 Tex Tech L Rev 247; and Russell Shankland, 'Duress and the Underlying Felony' (2009) 99 J Crim L & Criminology 1277.

4 See generally Monu Bedi, 'Excusing Behavior: Reclassifying the Federal Common Law Defenses of Duress and Necessity Relying on the Victim's Role' (2011) 101 J Crim L & Criminology 575.

5 Joshua Dressler, 'Reflections on Excusing Wrongdoers: Moral Theory, New Excuses and the Model Penal Code' (1988) 19 Rutgers LJ 671, 683.

6 See generally Daniel Gomez, 'Duress and the Ant Colony's Ethic: Reflections on Foundations of the Defense and its Limits' (2008) 11 New Crim L Rev 615.

on utilitarian or deontological grounds, but nonetheless it is hypocritical to expect selfless heroism and 'unacceptably Draconian' to demand infelicitous disattachment.

Normative judgements must apply about the personal responsibility of the duressee and the extent that we ought to be held responsible for our actions.[8] In the above postulation two individuals are killed to save the life of the child. Our view as to any personalised defence may differ if the demand, acceded to by D, had been to kill all twenty children in the classroom in order to save the life of her daughter. Societal expectations are invoked in this defence as a barometer of moral excuse, and proportionality requirements are elided appurtenant to standardisations of ordinary and reasonable steadfastness in presented exigencies.[9] The essence of duress as a defence is that the actor has committed an unjustified act, but one for which they ought to be excused when the individual is not morally blameworthy. This requires a particularised evaluation by the fact finders of the coercee's conduct, and asks whether only persons of 'special virtue could have done better'.[10] In this moral equation we should look to whether the circumstances of the offence indicate that it would be unfair to blame D for committing the wrongful act; and in some situations the, 'unique combination of a good motive operating in a penologically acceptable context'.[11]

The nature and ambit of duress as a defence to intentional killings is addressed in four particularised sections: the theoretical underpinnings of the defence are deconstructed and it is subsequently contended that it should be conceptually predicated on moral normative excuse; Anglo-American perspectives on duress as a defence to murder or otherwise are evaluated and the straitened boundaries of the ambit of the defence are criticised; juridical precepts and constraints of the duress defence in common law legal systems are comparatively extirpated and contrasted with more enlightened doctrinal practice in civil law jurisdictions and criminal codes; and judicial activism is propounded to reform substantive Anglo-American duress principles transmogrifying the spatial reach of this affirmative defence to all crimes including murder, with a balance of persuasion interposed on the individual coerced actor. A new optimal pathway is charted to reflect legitimate societal expectations and appropriate individual blameworthiness. This new standardised template is needed to identify the lineage of duress as a personalised concessionary excuse, but reflecting contemporary tenets of imputed proportionality, reasonable steadfastness, and the corrosive effect of fear attached to culpability thresholds.

The Personalised Affirmative Defence of Duress: A Conceptual Edifice of Moral Normative Excuse

The defences of duress and provocation (loss of control) can be analogised as concessions to human frailty. Both defences are predicated upon 'confession and avoidance'.[12] In each scenario, the defendants actually admit the completion of the *actus reus* element of the substantive offence with the attendant *mens rea* (confession) but seek to excuse their conduct to deny criminal liability (avoidance).[13] Essentially, both defences involve a concoction of excuse, moral involuntariness and human frailty.[14]

---

7   Andrew P Simester, John R Spencer, GR Sullivan, and Graham J Virgo, *Criminal Law: Theory and Doctrine* (5th edn, Hart 2013) 739.

8   See Kyron Huigens, 'Duress is Not a Justification' (2004) 2 Ohio St J Crim Law 303, 311: 'Duress as an excuse is premised on the idea that it is unfair to punish someone of ordinary fortitude who nevertheless did wrong, precisely because their fortitude is ordinary, even if inadequate; that is, because no one who would presume to punish this wrongdoer would have made a different choice under the same circumstances. The question of ordinary fortitude might be an empirical one, but the decision to punish for this reason of course a normative one'.

9   See Joshua Dressler, 'Exegis of the Law of Duress: Justifying the Excuse and Searching for its Proper Limits' (1989) 62 S Cal L Rev 1331, 1366: 'At its core, the defense of duress requires us to determine what conduct we, a society of individual members of the human race, may legitimately expect of our fellow threatened humans. Can society fairly expect the coerced actor to risk suffering the loss in question (or allow the loss to occur if the threat is to X)? Ultimately, society does not and should not expect the impossible; indeed, it should not always expect even the possible'.

10   ibid.

11   William Wilson, *Criminal Law: Doctrine and Theory* (4th edn, Longman 2011) 236.

12   See Jeremy Horder, 'Autonomy, Provocation and Duress' [1992] Crim LR 706, 706.

13   ibid.

14   ibid 707.

The duressee does not operate involuntarily in a fashion akin to automatism, but rather from conscious volitional control of their body, in that the muscular movements producing the criminal act can be ascribed to 'independent' will and choice.[15] The criminal conduct is not attendant to a reflex response or lack of willed muscular movement[16] and a 'calculated choice'[17] is established. The prosecution's case, consequently, does not fail because of a denial of the *actus reus* definitional component of unlawful killing, albeit that Fletcher in the different reduced choice context has embodied the coerced actor as operating in a sphere of 'moral or normative involuntariness'.[18] The compulsion threshold may only be marginally apart from physical involuntariness,[19] but the calculation ingredient renders them significantly divergent.[20] A constrained choice to act is made by D, that is a product of deliberation, 'of a different order from that involved in choosing, say, between a winter and summer holiday'.[21] A deliberate calculus results in a decision to kill another rather than suffer individuated defined consequences. A rational, albeit unpalatable conscious action has been made by D, controlled by the mind and not simply the brain and nonconscious impulses:[22] '[T]he claim is not so much that the actor had no will to do the relevant act; it is rather that he had no wish to do it'.[23]

The coerced actor who kills another is not exculpated via any denial of the fault element for murder. At the time of the killing D may be as 'cool as a cucumber'[24] in respect to immediate thought processes and decision-making attached to premeditated killing. *Mens rea* can be ascribed to the individual actor relationally to the intentional deliberate wrong committed irrespective of attributional coerced motives or desires. It is moral not mental involuntariness that remains in debate when pared to the definitional core.[25] A calculated choice, albeit of a disturbed nature, has been made by D, as cogently stated by Lord Kilbrandon in *Director of Public Prosecutions for Northern Ireland v Lynch*,[26] 'the decision of the threatened man whose constancy is overborne so that he yields to the threat, is a calculated decision to do what he knows to be wrong, and is therefore that of a man with . . . a guilty mind'.[27]

The duressee understands the nature and consequences of their consciously formulated actions, and intentional killings in such circumstances establish the constituent external and fault offence—nexus elements for murder. This has prompted Schopp to iterate that a byproduct of this analysis is that presumptively duress does not provide a legitimate excuse or justification for unlawful conduct where all definitional offence elements are self-contained;[28] and coercees 'act on action plans that include the acts exemplifying the objective offence elements as intended consequences'.[29] The influence of duress, consequently, would be confined to punishment exclusively, and not as a general defence, but limited to a mitigation factorisation. In this construct, Schopp identifies a constricted ambit for duress, allowing a special verdict to be available in defined circumstances, but only as 'a purely vindicating conviction'.[30] Any conviction, however, has a stigmatic censure and consequentialist branding. More fundamentally, a view of criminal law that is wholly punishment-driven fails to accord appropriate significance to actor blameworthiness and culpability, disavows moral evaluation of D's conduct, and thus downplays the central questions that attach to duress.[31]

---

15   See Andrew Ashworth, *Principles of Criminal Law* (6th edn, OUP 2009) 210.

16   See Ian Dennis, 'Duress, Murder and Criminal Responsibility' (1980) 96 LQR 208, 220–221.

17   See The Law Commission, *Murder, Manslaughter and Infanticide* (Law Com. No. 304, 2006) [6.39] (cmt provided by Professor David Ormerod).

18   George P Fletcher, *Rethinking Criminal Law* (1978) 803, adopted by Dickson J in the Supreme Court of Canada in *Perka v R* (1984) 13 DLR (4th).

19   Simester, Spencer, Sullivan and Virgo (n 7) 751.

20   Dennis (n 16) 221.

21   Simester, Spencer, Sullivan and Virgo (n 7) 751.

22   Joshua Dressler, 'Duress' in *The Oxford Handbook of Philosophy of Criminal Law* (OUP 2011) 273.

23   Dennis (n 16) 221.

24   Ashworth (n 15) 211.

25   Dennis (n 16) 221.

26   [1975] AC 653.

27   ibid 703 per Lord Kilbrandon.

28   Schopp, *Justification Defenses and Just Convictions* (Cambridge University Press 1998) 141.

29   ibid.

30   ibid.

31   See Simester, Spencer, Sullivan and Virgo (n 7) 753.

Duress should be viewed through a legal prism as a personalised affirmative defence with a concomitant that the balance of persuasion rests on the coerced actor to convince the fact-finders as arbiters[32] The conduct of the excused actor is *wrongful*, but nonetheless D may be acquitted as, 'the circumstances of the offence indicate that it would be wrong to blame her for committing the wrongful act'.[33] Duress does not exonerate on the premise of a strict proportionality nexus between threatened harm and the harm caused, but rather, 'exculpates actors who cause a net harm but who are blameless'.[34]

In terms of *blameworthiness*, the defence requires an evaluation of the duressee's conduct in consideration of the type of action legitimately expected of our fellow citizens who are threatened by dire consequences engaging catastrophic harm to themselves or others.[35] The wrongful coerced behaviour may be repugnant to the threatened individual and wholly contradictory to their previous code of conduct. Actors will not be excused in a vacuum and the course of conduct needs to be understandable in that wrongful action is viewed as a reasonable response to extreme danger[36] occurring at a time individuation when 'the rational will is deposed from the throne of action'.[37] Stoicism is demanded, but it is hypocritical to set a threshold level requirement of heroism. The evaluation that should occur of D's conduct is set against societal expectations and the standardisation of the ordinary person of reasonable firmness, and whether they would have exceeded the steadfast response of the coerced actor.[38] Individuated characteristics of the duressee that are not morally discreditable ought to be relevant to the gravity of the threatened harm in particularistic situations as part of a balanced exemption consideration. In this theatre of morality the jurors, as normative fact-finders, are best placed to make 'intractable decisions'[39] in all the circumstances in terms of culpability and blame subject to stringent requirements. The conundrum presented as to threshold gradations of understanding and responsibility should be left at their door.[40]

The parameters of the defence of duress in English law, and acknowledgment of extant perspectives on blameworthiness, due proportionality and the requirement of reasonable steadfastness, were established by the House of Lords in *Hasan*.[41] Lord Bingham, who provided the leading judgment, expressly acknowledged the excuse rather than justification operational predicate[42] but then adopted a traditional delimiting template whereby duress should be constrained in ambit and subject to very specific circumstances: (i) duress does not afford a defence to charges of murder, attempted murder and some forms of treason; (ii) to found a plea of duress the threat relied upon must be to cause death or serious injury;[43] (iii) the threat must be directed against D, his immediate family, someone close to him or, someone for whom D would reasonably regard himself as

---

32   Shankland (n 3) 1246.

33   Chiesa (n 3) 750; see also Stanford Kadish, 'Excusing Crime' (1987) 75 Cal L Rev 257, 264: 'To blame a person is to express a moral criticism, and if the person's action does not deserve criticism, blaming him is a kind of falsehood and is, to the extent the person is injured by being blamed, unjust to him'.

34   Paul H. Robinson, *Criminal Law Defences* (West 1984) 367–368.

35   See Dressler (n 9) 1372–1373: '[T]he real issue . . . is whether a coerced person who unjustifiably violates the moral principle *necessarily, unalterably and unfailingly* deserves to be punished as a murderer, as the common law insists. If a murderer were insane, involuntarily intoxicated, or especially young, society would not necessarily, unalterably, and unfailingly demand punishment'.

36   Kadish (n 33) 266: '[H]is action does not merit blame because it fails to distinguish him from the common run of human kind'.

37   See Alan Norrie, 'Free Will, Determinism and Criminal Justice' [1983] LS 60, 63.

38   Dennis (n 16) 232.

39   Simester, Spencer, Sullivan and Virgo (n 7) 753.

40   See Dressler (n 22) 286: 'The more apt question to ask in the duress context is whether the juror believes it is unfair to punish the person, given the threatening circumstances, for having chosen the wrong option'.

41   [2005] 4 All ER 685, 694–695.

42   ibid at [18] and [19] per Lord Bingham: 'Where duress is established it does not ordinarily operate to negative any legal ingredient of the crime which the defendant has committed. Nor is it now regarded as justifying the conduct of the defendant, as has in the past been suggested. . . . Duress is now properly to be regarded as a defence which, if established, excuses what would otherwise be criminal conduct'.

43   Note that the appellate court in *A (RJ)* [2012] EWCA Crim 434 and *CS* [2012] EWCA Crim 389 have determined that in principle a threat of rape could raise the defence of duress. In *Dao* [2012] EWCA Crim 1717, however, false imprisonment was viewed as insufficient to raise the gravamen of the serious threat requirement.

responsible;[44] (iv) the relevant tests pertaining to duress have been largely stated objectively, with reference to the reasonableness of the defendant's perceptions and conduct and not, as is usual in many other areas of the criminal law, with primary reference to his subjective perception;[45] (v) the criminal conduct which the defence is sought to excuse must be directly caused by the threats which are relied upon; (vi) D may excuse his criminal conduct on grounds of duress only if, placed as he was, there was no evasive action he could reasonably have expected to take; and (vii) the defendant may not rely on duress to which he has voluntarily laid himself open.[46]

The conceptual approach to duress, however, has not been heterologous and a number of academicians and courts have supported a justification rationale.[47] A justification defence operates to negate the wrongfulness of the individual actor's conduct.[48] The harm effected, where special justifying circumstances are operating, is counter-balanced by the requirement to promote a higher societal interest or avoidance of greater harm.[49] This utilitarian calculus, engaging a choice of evils in action, has been propounded by some as the essence of the theoretical basis for duress:

> [W]hether an actor has a choice of evils defence of justification are contextualised and take into account the normative relationships among the parties and the causal nature of resulting harms, and that by those reasons, actors are justified who choose either lesser evils or equal evils under the circumstances.[50]

The majority of commentators have viewed duress through the excuse kaleidoscope, and this is vitally important to the extended ambit argument subsequently presented herein.[51] The deed itself may be inherently wrongful at the highest level engaging the unlawful killing of others, but the duressee may be excused individually because conditions superimpose a lack of responsibility on their part.[52] This equates to moral involuntariness on the part of the coerced actor who in the particularised exigencies may not be blameworthy as no more could have been expected from the reasonable person in their situation. They lacked fair opportunity to conform to

---

44   See Simester, Spencer, Sullivan and Virgo (n 7) 753, arguing that the concessionary defence of duress is more limited than permissions granted within self-defence and necessity: 'Duress differs from self-defence in that the victim of any harmful act done by D will not be the duressor whereas self-defence is directed at the source of the danger (or a person who, inadvertently or otherwise, is assisting or impeding an effective response to the danger)'. For consideration of a suggested broader defence of necessary action, conjoining together duress, necessity and self-defence, see also Chris Clarkson, 'Necessary Action: A New Defence' [2004] Crim LR 81.

45   See *Hasan* [2005] 4 All ER 685, 714, where Baroness Hale, contrary to Lord Bingham, favoured a more subjective perspective: 'I accept that even the person with a knife at her back has a choice whether or not to do as the knifeman says. The question is whether she should have resisted the threat. But perhaps because I am a reasonable but comparatively weak and fearful grandmother, I do not understand why the defendant's beliefs and personal characteristics are not morally relevant to whether she could reasonably have been expected to resist'.

46   See generally William Wilson, 'The Structure of Criminal Law Defences' [2005] Crim LR 108.

47   See Peter Western and James Mangiafico, 'The Criminal Defense of Duress: A Justification, Not an Excuse – And Why It Matters' (2003) 6 Buff Crim L Rev 833; Arnold N. Enker, 'In Support of the Distinction Between Justification and Excuse' [2009] 42 Tex Tech L Rev 273; John Lawrence Hill, 'A Utilitarian Theory of Duress' (1999) 84 Iowa L Rev 275; and see below for discussion of justificatory conduct in the South African criminal justice system.

48   See Chiesa (n 3) 747; and see Paul H. Robinson, 'Criminal Law Defenses: A Systematic Analysis' (1982) 82 Columbia L Rev 199, 213: 'The harm caused by the justified behaviour remains a legally recognised harm which is to be avoided whenever possible. Under the special justifying circumstances, however that harm is outweighed by the need to avoid an even greater harm or to further a greater societal interest'.

49   See Clarkson (n 44) 81.

50   Western and Mangiafico (n 47) 949.

51   See generally Huigens (n 8); Dressler (n 3); Dressler (n 5); Mitchell N Berman, 'The Normative Function of Coercion Claims' (2002) 8 Legal Theory 45; and note that the drafters of the Model Penal Code also asserted that duress was an excuse and not a justification, see Model Penal Code and Commentaries, s 2.09 cmt 2 (1985): 'The problem of s. 2.09 (duress) then, reduces to the question of whether there are cases where the actor cannot justify his conduct under S. 3.02 (choice of evils), as when his choice involves an equal or greater evil than that threatened, but where he nonetheless should be excused because he was subjected to coercion'.

52   See Robinson (n 48) 222: 'The requirement of an excusing condition, then, is not an element independent of the actor's disability, but rather a requirement that the actor's disability cause a particular result, a particular exculpating mental condition in relation to the conduct constituting the offense'.

standardised behaviour, and should be exculpated because the admittedly unlawful act was not attributionally blameworthy[53] The bifurcation between justification and excuse in this regard has been pithily identified by Robinson in that, 'an actor's conduct is justified; an actor is excused'.[54]

The excusatory nature of duress as a defence, in contrast to a utilitarian choice of evils determination as applied to necessity, is exemplified by a classic illustration derived from the U.S. Model Penal Code principles[55] By way of postulation, consider a situation where D1 is driving a car under the command of D2 an escaping felon, who holds a gun to his head, and under D2's instruction D1 runs over and kills two drunks lying in the road. Duress *per minas* as an excuse in terms of lack of blameworthiness of D1 may exculpate on the predicate of moral involuntariness, but the act is not justified in terms of saving of lives, deontological reasoning, or lesser evil principles.[56] Duress may apply if the jury should find that a person of reasonable firmness in his situation would have been unable to resist the threat, and in this context ought to provide a defence to all crimes including intentional killings. Criminal fault is an aspect of criminal wrongdoing in this perspective, and requires a normative evaluation of ordinary fortitude expected of any coercee.[57]

In summary, the moral evaluation of the actor's conduct is related to fair opportunity within the purview of duress as a defence. It reflects a societal judgement about personal responsibility and the extent to which we are held accountable for deliberate albeit constrained actions.[58] Fundamental issues of justice and expediency in the administration of penal law are presented in stark contrast. The essence of duress is that the duressee may lack fair opportunity to prevent even unlawful killings, as presented in the primary school scenario in the introductory section of this chapter, and ought therefore to be excused in certain circumstances even for murder.[59] A successful defence plea may legitimately apply if D could not reasonably have prevented the threatened harm by declining to accede to undue coercion. Duress, as constructed, presents an excuse rather than a justification as a defence, and does not operate to abrogate the offence-nexus definitional elements of either fault or external constituents.[60] It is an affirmative defence and should be reviewed against a backdrop of comprehensible understanding, of fair deserts, and as part of individual blameworthiness for fact-finders determination.

Intentional Killing and the Ambit of the Duress Defence

Duress and Murder in English Law

The denial of duress as an excuse to murder reflects an unbroken tradition of legal writing dating back to Hale's *The History of the Pleas of the Crown*,[61] and repeated by Blackstone's *Commentaries on the Laws of England*.[62] Hale stated that as a matter of principle:

---

53   See Mulroy (n 3) 171; and see Wayne R LaFave, *Substantiare Criminal Law* (2d edn, West 2003) s. 9.7(a), 73–75: 'The rationale of the defense is not that the defendant, faced with the unnerving threat of harm unless he does an act which violates the literal language of the criminal law, somehow loses his mental capacity to commit the crime in question. Nor is it that the defendant has not engaged in a voluntary act. Rather it is that, even though he has done the act the crime requires and has the mental state which the crime requires, his conduct which violates the literal language of the criminal law is excused because he lacked a fair opportunity to avoid acting unlawfully'.

54   Paul H Robinson, *Fundamentals of Criminal Law* (1988) 664.

55   See Huigens (n 8) 304; Mulroy (n 3).

56   See Sharon Byrd, 'Wrongdoing and Attribution: Implications Beyond the Justification – Excuse Distinction' (1987) 33 Wayne L Rev 1289.

57   See Meir Dan-Cohen, 'Responsibility and the Boundaries of the Self' (1992) 105 Harvard L Rev 959, 997: '[T] he defense of duress does not suggest a total lack of choice. Instead, the defendant points to a severe limitation of choice caused by a serious threat made against him'.

58   See Dressler (n 9) 1343: '[T]he jury must make a moral judgment about the degree of moral firmness that can be expected of persons in the actor's circumstances'.

59   See Dressler (n 3) 247–249.

60   See generally Paul H Robinson, 'A System of Excuses: How Criminal Law's Excuse Defences Do and Don't Work Together to Exculpate Blameless (and Only Blameless) Offenders' (2009) 42 Tex Tech L Rev 259; and Madeline Engel, 'Unweaving the Dixon Blanket Rule: Flexible Treatment to Protect the Morally Innocent' (2008) Or L Rev 1327.

61   Matthew Hale, *The History of the Pleas of the Crown* (PR Glazebrook ed) (1971) 51.

62   William Blackstone, Commentaries on the Laws of England (1809) 30.

[I]f a man be desperately assaulted and in peril of death, and cannot otherwise escape, unless to satisfy his assailant's fury he will kill an innocent person then present, the fear and actual force will not acquit him of the crime and punishment of murder, if he commits the fact; for he ought rather to die himself, than kill an innocent. ...[63]

Despite the clear statement in legal writings denying duress as a defence to murder, no clear judicial authority was operative on this issue until relatively recently. A series of juridical precepts have appraised this matter over the course of the last three decades. An examination of these precedential authorities reveals the arbitrary and casuistic nature of developmental principles by reference to which the extant limitation has been determined.[64] Initial consideration, arose before the House of Lords in *DPP for Northern Ireland v Lynch*.[65] A police officer had been fatally wounded in Northern Ireland by the IRA. The appellant, Lynch, had not taken part in the actual shooting but had driven the terrorists to and from the garage where the murder took place. His participation in the murder was therefore as a secondary party, and he claimed that he had participated under duress. By a bare majority their Lordships held that the coerced actor could rely on the defence where charged with aiding and abetting an intentional killing. In *Abbott v The Queen*,[66] however, the decision in *Lynch* was distinguished by the Privy Council and the Judicial Committee held that the defence was not available to the principal in the first degree, the actual killer.

The binary divide between a principal and secondary offender may be exceedingly hard to draw, but on it could rest the difference between a conviction for murder and a complete acquittal. This was clearly an unsatisfactory state of affairs and the House of Lords took the opportunity to review the position in *Howe*,[67] and subsequently in *Hasan*.[68] In effect, their Lordships saw the decision lying between an extension of the defence to all murders or a complete withdrawal of the defence in murder cases, and no via media. While prepared to consider making the defence available to one who has played a minor role in the intentional killing of another, their Lordships in *Howe* could not see any practical and reliable manner to demarcate such duressees.[69] The previous attempt to do so by reference to principal and secondary offenders did not necessarily identify the importance of the various participatory engagements; a secondary party may well have played the major role. In the result the House of Lords in *Howe*, overruling its own decision in *Lynch*, decided that the general defence should not be available to anyone charged with murder whether as a principal or secondary party. The decision has simplified the law, but at the cost of injustice and undue constraint with attendant deleterious consequences creating unfortunate anomalies. It is regrettable that an analysis of the five main arguments advanced by their Lordships in *Howe*, and supported in *Hasan*, reveal that the propositions are built on a castle made out of sand.[70]

The primary argument advanced for denial of duress as a defence to murder relates to the special sanctity that the law attaches to human life and which denies to a man the right to take an innocent life—even at the price of his own or another's life.[71] Lord Hailsham's analysis was quite unrestricted on this issue, and according to his view, the law is neither: 'just [n]or humane which withdraws the protection of the criminal law from the innocent victim and casts the cloak of its protection upon the coward and the poltroon in the name of a concession to human frailty'.[72] This ordinary and reasonable man, apparently, rather than kill

---

63   Hale (n 61) 51.

64   See generally GL Peiris, 'Duress, Volition and Criminal Responsibility: Current Problems in English and Commonwealth Law' (1988) 17 Anglo-Am L Rev 182.

65   [1975] AC 653. Note in the notorious case of Kray [1970] 1 QB 125, it had been asserted, albeit obiter by Widgery LJ, that duress could be available as a defence even to an individual charged with being an accessory to murder.

66   [1977] AC 755.

67   See generally Helen P Milgate, 'Duress and the Criminal Law: Another About Turn by the House of Lords' (1988) 47 Cambridge LJ 61; and Ian H Dennis, 'Developments in Duress' (1987) 51 JCL 463.

68   [2005] 4 All ER 685.

69   [1987] AC 417, per Lord Griffiths, 439–440.

70   See Alan Reed, 'Duress and Provocation as Excuses to Murder: Salutary Lessons from Recent Anglo-American Jurisprudence' (1996) 6 J Transnat'l L & Policy 51, 55–58.

71   [1987] AC 417, 439 per Lord Griffiths.

72   ibid 432.

another, must be expected to sacrifice their own life.[73] Hard cases make bad law and this is no exception. The view propounded imposes a fundamentally false standard on criminal conduct: '[H]eroism is a quality to be praised but it does not follow that its absence is reason for censure'.[74] There is palpably no 'duty' of heroism in the criminal law; the standard is that of the reasonable person, not the reasonable hero. To suggest otherwise is absurd and this requirement makes obligatory a form of self-sacrifice which should be regarded as supererogatory, as above and beyond the call of duty.[75] The moral equation engaged is far more nuanced and principled than the blanket non-exemption criterion, and Mullender vividly asserts: 'Examination of this issue, bearing as it does on the relationship between law and morality, involves making a hazardous journey, to use Jhering's striking image, around the Cape Horn of jurisprudence'.[76]

It is inapt to demand heroism as a pre-requisite for exculpation. A point of radical departure from English law in this regard was identified by the drafters of the U.S. Model Penal Code. This is evaluated further below, but at this juncture is helpful to elaborate that, in light of entrenched U.S. perspectives, the MPC cogently states that the predicate for the exculpatory nature of the defence of duress is that it would be 'socially debilitating' to 'demand that heroism be the standard of legality'.[77] This more enlightened *raison d'etre* has been propounded by Dressler in a series of seminal articles in this arena,[78] suggesting that to demand self-sacrifice and heroism is hypocritical as it is outwith standardisations of reasonable moral firmness:

> I am afraid that such a rule, like Lord Hailsham's opinion, has the imprint of self-righteousness, which the law should avoid. The rule asks us to be virtuous; more accurately, it demands our virtual saintliness, which the law has no right to require. It is precisely in the case of kill-or-be-killed threats that the criminal law ought to be prepared in some cases to assuage the guilt feelings of the homicidal wrongdoer by excusing him – by reminding him that he acted no less valiantly than any person of reasonable moral strength would have done.[79]

A flagrant anomaly operates within the ambit of the duress defence in that it may provide exculpation for a defendant who intentionally causes grievous bodily harm, under Section 18 of the Offences Against the Person Act 1861.[80] The fault element for their non-fatal offence coalesces with that for murder itself, constructively based on an intention to cause grievous bodily harm. The consequence is that a duressee may be acquitted of intentionally causing grievous bodily harm based on the defence of duress, but if the victim dies subsequently then duress is inapplicable and a murder conviction is potentially operative. In each scenario, the culpability of the coerced criminal actor is identical, but liability is imposed depending on survival. This pernicious injustice is indefensible: '[L]iability goes from zero to the maximum, all depending on the victim's physiological powers of recovery. This should not be the result. The law should not be a crap shoot'.[81] It provides further succour for the urgent need to reform this substantive arena. The unfortunate stringency of the defence is exacerbated by its applicability in full force to the young offender, as in *Wilson*[82] where poignantly it applied to a 13-year-old threatened by his violent father.[83]

---

73   ibid.

74   Simester, Spencer, Sullivan and Virgo (n 7) 744.

75   See Reed (n 70) 55.

76   Richard Mullender, 'Murder, Attempted Murder and the Defence of Duress: Some Objections to the Present State of the Law' (1993) 25 Bracton LJ 15.

77   Model Penal Code and Commentaries, s 2.09 (1985).

78   See Dressler (n 3); Dressler (n 5); Dressler (n 9); and Dressler (n 22).

79   Dressler (n 9) 1372–1373; see also The Law Commission, *Legislating the Criminal Code: Offences Against the Person and General Principles* (Law Comm. No. 218, 1993) at para. 30–11: 'In our view, it is not only futile, but also wrong, for the criminal law to demand heroic behaviour. The attainment of a heroic standard of behaviour will always count for great merit; but failure to achieve that standard should not be met with punishment by the State. . . . [C]riminal punishment, as opposed to more exhortation, should not be used to try to achieve a standard of behaviour higher than that'.

80   See Reed (n 70) 63.

81   Mulroy (n 3) 177.

82   [2007] QB 960.

83   See also *Hampshire County Council v E* [2007] EWHC 2584 (Admin), where duress was denied where a mother failed to ensure the attendance of her 15 year old son at school (a strict liability offence). The son was a drug-taker and dealer who had threatened her with death and also serious injury.

Their Lordships in *Howe* also focused on the dangers of terrorism as a bulwark against extending the ambit of duress to murder, asserting the importance of standing firm against an increase in violence and terrorist threat.[84] The articulated concern was that terrorists via human tools, could kill many innocent victims if duress were embraced as a viable defence to murder. Lord Lane in the Court of Appeal in *Howe*, supported by Lords Bridge and Griffiths in the House of Lords, viewed duress as a:

> [H]ighly dangerous relaxation in the laws allowing a person who has deliberately killed, maybe a number of innocent people, to escape conviction and punishment altogether because of a fear that his own life or those of his family might be in danger if he did not.[85]

The presented danger, according to Lord Lane, was exacerbated because 'the defence was so easy to raise and may be so difficult for the prosecution to disprove beyond a reasonable doubt'.[86] The reality, as Lord Hailsham admits in *Howe*, is that juries have been commendably robust in rejecting duress where appropriate, as the verdicts in the trials of *Howe*, *Bannister*, and *Burke* clearly demonstrate.[87] The charter for terrorism argument has also lost much of its force as a result of more recent appellate jurisprudential authorities, which establish that where a defendant voluntarily joins a terrorist group or criminal gang, and is forced by pressure of violence to commit an offence for that group or gang, he cannot raise the defence of duress. If, when he joined the gang, he knew that it took part in violent crime or that violence might be used against him to take part in the gang's activities, then the defence is precluded.[88]

The terrorism argument needs to be reappraised *de novo*. Consider the following postulation[89]: A female army officer is driving her two young children to school when gunmen hijack the car and tell her that both children will be shot unless she drives the car back to the barracks where they intend to shoot a guard. The officer, constrained by the threat to her children and the imminent peril of their deaths, acts as an accomplice by driving the vehicle; the gunmen accomplish the unlawful plan and kill the guard. Since duress is inapplicable to murder under prevailing doctrine, the woman would be guilty of murder.[90] The logical corollary, however, must be that no criminal liability should be attached when individuals cannot reasonably be expected to behave other than the way they did. In such a scenario, no real choice exists because the actions involve moral involuntariness. Lord Morris in *Lynch* arguably provides the correct analysis:

> [I]t is proper that any rational system of law should take fully into account the standards of honest and reasonable men. By those standards it is fair that actions and reactions may be tested. If then someone is really threatened with death or serious injury unless he does what he is told to do is the law to pay no heed to the miserable, agonising plight of such a person? For the law to understand not only how the timid but also the stalwart may in a moment of crisis behave is not to make the law weak but to make it just. In the calm of the courtroom measures of fortitude or of heroic behaviour are surely not to be demanded when they could not in moments for decision reasonably have been expected even of the resolute and well disposed.[91]

It is eminently logical that extant juridical precepts do not make duress available to members of criminal or terrorist gangs. However, it is illogical to deny it to innocent tools of such groups, as in the earlier scenario. A corollary exists here with gross negligence manslaughter and societal expectations in that these matters ought to be left for jury determination, and there is no doubt that fact finders are commendably robust in rejecting

---

84 [1987] AC 417, 443–444 per Lord Griffiths (Lord Bridge concurring at 438): '[W]e face a rising tide of violence and terrorism against which the law must stand firm recognising that its highest duty is to protect the freedom and lives of those that live under it'.

85 [1986] QB 626, 641.

86 ibid.

87 [1987] AC 417, 434.

88 Milgate (n 67) 73.

89 See Reed (n 70) 62.

90 Of course, it may be possible through prosecutorial discretion for the individual not to be prosecuted; nonetheless, by strict analysis liability is incurred for murder.

91 [1975] AC 653, 670.

the defence where appropriate.[92] When the offence is more heinous and a greater number are killed, juries are best placed to determine the desert of punishment. Jurors are peculiarly well-suited to normatively determine society's legitimate expectations of moral courage, so they should be charged with applying duress to murder. A jury applying Lord Hailsham's demand of heroism would leave the current law unaltered; however, a less rigorous test, applying the reasonable man standard would be more humane and compassionate.[93]

The latter propositions in *Howe* on the ambit of the defence can be succinctly grouped together, and centred around executive discretion, a comparison with the necessity defence, and a legislative argument. Their Lordships recognised the extreme rigour attached to a complete denial of the defence, but argued that this could simply be ameliorated by the exercise of prosecutorial licence.[94] Flexibility could prevail by executive discretion not to prosecute or, alternatively, by the expeditious release by licence of an individual serving a life sentence for murder.[95] Such an argument is not convincing. Axiomatically, as Lord Wilberforce stated in *Lynch*, 'if the defence is excluded in law, much of the evidence which would prove the duress would be inadmissible at the trial, not brought out in court, and not tested by cross-examination'.[96] The discretion not to prosecute does not, in any event, ensure that the law is saved from irrationality; the accused was prosecuted in *Anderton v Ryan*[97] for an attempted handling offence on the basis of a factual scenario in which the Law Commission had predicted no prosecution would take place. There would be nothing to stop such a result occurring in duress.

A comparison was drawn in *Howe*[98] between the defences of duress and necessity, and the antediluvian decision in *Dudley and Stephens*[99] where arguably the House of Lords had determined that necessity could not present a defence to murder, whatever the degree of participation. According to the argument propounded by Lords Hailsham and Mackay in *Howe*, necessity and duress are analogous, and duress cannot be available on a murder charge whilst *Dudley and Stephens* remained part of the common law.[100] Although this is the strongest argument advanced in *Howe* it is not without weaknesses. The two defences of necessity and duress, although conceptually linked, are not identical and different rationales apply to justificatory and excusatory behaviour. Duress can be raised as a defence to theft; the thief cannot successfully rely on necessity.[101] The parallels drawn here are arguably no stronger than those between duress and loss of control; loss of control is a defence, albeit of a partial nature to murder, but duress is no defence at all. Indeed it can be argued that the individual who kills under duress, a morally involuntary actor, is less blameworthy than the provoked killer.[102] Reform is urgently needed to both the ambit and constituent elements of duress, but as subsequently highlighted, this should be expedited through judicial activism rather than await any legislative response as stated in *Howe*.[103]

Duress and Reasonable Steadfastness: The Constituent Elements

The constituent elements of the duress defence, as well as its overarching ambit, have also been constrained in English law.[104] A two-prong test, established in *Graham*[105] and followed in *Howe*,[106] provides that fact-finders must be satisfied on two questions: first, that the actual duressee was impelled to act because of a reasonable belief derived from the existence of good cause to fear death or serious injury; and second, that a sober

---

92   Even Lord Hailsham was prepared to accept that juries are commendably robust!
93   See Reed (n 70) 60–63.
94   [1987] AC 417, 433 per Lord Hailsham; see also 454 (Lord Griffiths concurring).
95   ibid.
96   [1975] AC 675, 685.
97   [1985] AC 560; see also Alan Reed and Ben Fitzpatrick, *Criminal Law* (4th edn, Sweet and Maxwell 2009) 295–297.
98   [1987] AC 417, 432.
99   (1884) 14 QBD 273.
100   Reed and Fitzpatrick (n 97) 236–237.
101   ibid.
102   See generally Kadish (n 33).
103   See Alan Reed, 'The Need for a New Anglo-American Approach to Duress' (1997) 61 JCL 209.
104   See KJM Smith, 'Duress and Steadfastness: In Pursuit of the Unintelligible' [1999] Crim LR 363, 364–365.
105   [1982] 1 All ER 801, 805–806 per Lord Lane.
106   [1987] AC 417.

person of reasonable firmness sharing the characteristics of the defendant, would have responded in a similar manner.[107] It is unfortunate that extant law does not recognise the defence for the weak or timorous accused who fails to meet the anthropomorphic 'reasonable steadfastness' standardisation, and judicial activism here would also be beneficial.[108] The adoption of a more subjectivist perspective would be a welcome reform, and should ask whether, considering all the circumstances including relevant personal characteristics, the coercee could reasonably have been expected to resist the threat.

An overt public policy constraint has been interposed to confine duress within narrow limits, but intractable problems have been created over admissible personal characteristics in establishing the standard of reasonable steadfastness.[109] Beyond age and sex of the individual defendant, precedential authorities have only accorded relevance to character traits that constitute severe mental illness or psychiatric disorder.[110] A wide exclusionary list has been created of irrelevant individual characteristics: alcoholism;[111] drug-taking;[112] low intelligence quotient;[113] unusual vulnerability;[114] grossly elevated neurotic states;[115] and even pliancy attributable to cumulative sexual abuse.[116]

There is a failure to accord due recognition to the requirements of justice in that duress as an personalised excuse operates as a concession to human frailty: 'if the defendant was a large, muscular boxer the jury would be entitled to expect a greater standard of fortitude than from an elderly, frail ex-teacher with a heart complaint'.[117] The defence should apply where fact-finders believe that the duressee is not blameworthy in acting in self-preservation as an understandable human response predicated, as in self-defence, on an honest belief as to the perceived threat.[118] This embraces a 'moral scrutiny' of the coercee's decision to accede to the threatened harm, and in such dilemmatic circumstances individuated characteristics should be relevant as part of the fair opportunity to conform to the law or otherwise.[119] A more enlightened perspective in this regard is adopted in the US Model Penal Code provisions which, albeit incorporating a 'reasonable firmness' criterion, is not constrained by a fixed universal level of threatened harm as a threshold gradation.[120] This facilitates a true proportionality inquiry in that normatively the fact-finders can juxtapose the inculcated threatened harm against the threshold of the seriousness of the offence effected by the duressee.[121]

Personalised characteristics are part of the moral barometer proportionality test for duress provided that they are not discreditable; pliancy created by cumulative sexual abuse and grossly evaluated neurotic states ought to be accessible for consideration by jurors, but not vulnerability created via drug-taking. This moral barometer standardisation[122] on relevant characteristics was appositely propounded for provocation by Lord

---

107 [1982] 1 All ER 801, 805–806.

108 KJM Smith (n 104) 372–373.

109 See generally Jeremy Horder, 'Pleading Involuntary Lack of Capacity' (1993) 52 Cambridge LJ 298.

110 See Alec Buchanan and Graeme Virgo, 'Duress and Mental Abnormality' [1999] Crim LR 517; and see Bowen [1996] 4 All ER 837, 844, categorising availability to individuals suffering from 'some mental illness, mental impairment, or a recognised psychiatric condition, provided persons generally suffering from such a condition may be more susceptible to pressure and threats'.

111 *Bowen* [1996] 4 All ER 837.

112 ibid.

113 ibid.

114 *Horne* [1994] Crim LR 584.

115 *Hegarty* [1994] Crim LR 353.

116 *Hirst* [1995] 1 Cr App R 82.

117 Wilson (n 11) 241.

118 See Jeremy Horder, 'Occupying the Moral High Ground? The Law Commission on Duress' [1994] CrimL Rev 334.

119 ibid 342.

120 Section 2.09 MPC; see also Model Penal Code and Commentaries (1985) 375–380.

121 KJM Smith (n 104) 375.

122 See Alan Reed and Nicola Wake, 'Anglo American Perspectives on Partial Defences: Something Old, Something Borrowed, and Something New' in Reed and Bohlander (eds), *Loss of Control and Diminished Responsibility: Domestic, Comparative and International Perspectives* (Ashgate 2011) 183, 198–200, evaluating moral barometer standardisations in the loss of control context.

Taylor in *Morhall*,[123] but jettisoned by the House of Lords[124] with consequential egregious impact for the future of the partial defence of provocation. It should apply to duress to contextualise that a defendant's response has been framed by earlier abuse, by neurosis or by vulnerability.[125]

The reality is that within duress, as a concession to human frailty, some individuals are more pliable than others with attendant individuated characteristics; 'the jury must still consider, in effect, whether the defendant's choice of self-preservation was morally acceptable bearing in mind his personal characteristics; in other words, in the jury's view did the defendant deserve to be excused?'[126] An extremely welcome and long overdue reform would be the adoption of the Law Commission's proposals in which the recommended template looks to whether, 'the threat is one which in all the circumstances (including any of his personal characteristics that affect its gravity) he cannot reasonably be expected to resist'.[127] Duress operates as a concession to human frailty, and, 'the frailer the person the greater perhaps should be the concession'.[128] By adopting a more subjective approach that focuses on the peculiarities of the individual, and renewed onus on jury determination replicating the excusing decision imposed on fact finders under the Model Penal Code in the U.S. set out below,[129] more logical and humane principles can be effected.[130]

The Development of Substantive Duress Principles in the US

The virtually unassailable position in Anglo-American common law has been that duress never excuses murder and that the threatened individual ought to die himself rather than escape by killing another human being.[131] As with English law, this constraint has been of venerable antiquity in the US, as identified in the nineteenth century jurisprudential authority of *Arp v State*.[132] Therein, the coerced perpetrator, acting under a threat to his own life by duressors who were present and armed with double-barrelled shotguns, took the life of an innocent third party. The co-adventurers, including the defendant, then stole money from the victim and the duressee followed the others making no effort to leave them.[133] The Alabama Supreme Court, invoking traditional common law doctrine, determined that a threatened defendant ought to die himself rather than escape by murdering an innocent victim.[134] The established precept was that duress was inapplicable as a defence to an intentional killing.

The prevailing orthodoxy at common law on both sides of the Atlantic presupposes that cogent and extensive arguments need to be iterated in support of any fundamental changes to the current position. It is not the case that all coercees who kill another deserve an excuse, but a preferential equipoise is illustrated within the American Law Institute's perspective in the Model Penal Code.[135] This should form part of our reflective considerations for optimal reform pathways in that it allows juries to excuse murder in exceptional

---

123   [1993] 4 All ER 888.

124   [1996] 1 AC 90, 98 per Lord Goff, suggesting that the 'reasonable person', in this context, was merely a yardstick to measure the conduct of the defendant taking into account all the relevant circumstances.

125   See Buchanan and Virgo (n 110) 530, drawing analogy with previous appellate decisions on provocation: 'all characteristics which affected the defendant's ability to exercise self-control are relevant'.

126   KJM Smith (n 104) 371.

127   See The Law Commission No 218 (n 79) cl 25. For a contrary perspective, mandating greater objective personification, see Horder (n 118) 340–341: '[T]he Commission falls prey to a species of crude behaviourism . . . permits defendants to indulge prejudice and act without proper regard for the interests of victims who are then harmed or killed by them'. This perspective is refuted in this chapter in aligning with the excusatory and concessionary nature of the defence of duress.

128   Wilson (n 11) 241.

129   See Mulroy (n 3) 203: 'According to the M.P.C., consideration of the stark, tangible factors of the defendant's situation under s. 2.09 can also include both age and health'.

130   See KJM Smith (n 104) 371: '[I]n making a moral judgment on the defendant's excusability it is permissible to draw in not only the defendant's particular circumstances and action, but also the wider sweep of current social and political realities as perceived by the jury'.

131   See Dressler (n 9) 1370.

132   12 So 301 (Ala 1893).

133   ibid 304.

134   ibid 302.

135   Model Penal Code ss 2.09(1)–(2) (1985).

situations and within defined elements.[136] The MPC vastly enhances the jury's role in the determination of the duress excuse, and proportionality applies between the threat-offence nexus.[137] In the MPC terminology, the fact-finders must consider 'whether the hypothetical 'person of reasonable firmness' would have resisted the threat'.[138] Within that choice is, in essence, a moral judgment regarding the ambit of fortitude of individuals constrained by prevailing circumstances; a fundamental dichotomy exists between the MPC standardisation and the limited role of jurors as an evaluate determiner of social norms at common law.[139] The material part of the MPC, adopted by a limited number of states,[140] defines the defence of duress as follows:

(1) It is an affirmative defense that the actor engaged in the conduct charged to constitute an offense because he was coerced to do so by the use of, or threat to use, unlawful force against his person or the person of another, that a person of reasonable firmness in his situation would have been unable to resist.

(2) The defense . . . is unavailable if the actor recklessly placed himself in a situation in which it was probable that he would be subjected to duress. The defence is also unavailable if he was negligent in placing himself in such a situation, whenever negligence suffices to establish culpability for the offense charged.[141]

The construct for duress adopted by the Model Penal Code significantly differs from current English practice, whereby the prevailing threat must be that of death or serious physical injury. The Model Penal Code template facilitates imputed proportionality of harm in the moral balanced equation in that it may suffice for exculpation for some offences that the threat is to cause a less serious physical injury to either the coerced actor or to a third party.[142] This engrained flexibility and wider articulation, acknowledging more broadly the potential involuntariness of the defendant, reflects a laudable approach and should be welcomed.

More recently, the US Supreme Court in *Dixon v United States*[143] have had opportunity to consider the constitutional parameters of duress at common law, and appropriate categorisation. The Court accepted the formulation of duress provided at district court level, under which it is incumbent upon a defendant to provide an affirmative defence that:

(1) [He] was under an unlawful and imminent threat . . . of death or serious bodily injury; (2) [He] had not recklessly or negligently placed [himself] in [this] situation; (3) [He] had no reasonable, legal alternative. ... And (4) That a direct causal relationship [existed] between the criminal act and the avoidance of the threatened harm.[144]

It was determined in *Dixon* that the defendant bears the burden of persuasion for the defence of duress and, as suggested below, this forms part of a preferred reformed model of duress in English law reflective of an appropriate via media ambit.[145] It is a concomitant and predeterminant of extending duress as a defence to all crimes, including intentional killings. Further support for an exemption defence is also provided by comparatively extirpating the doctrinal and theoretical underpinnings of other legal systems, including civil law constructs for duress.

---

136 See generally Reed (n 103).

137 See Mulroy (n 3) 166–169.

138 Section 2.09(1).

139 See Eugene R Milhizer, 'Justification and Excuse: What They Were, What They Are, and What They Ought to Be' (2004) 78 St. John's L Rev 725.

140 See, for example, Alaska Stat s. 11.81.440 (1995); NJ Stat s. 7C:2–9 (1995); and Utah Code Ann s. 76.2–302.

141 Model Penal Code ss 2.09 (1)–(2) (1985).

142 See Shankland (n 3) 1277–1280.

143 548 US 1 (2006).

144 ibid 5 (n 2); and see generally Bedi (n 4).

145 See generally Engel (n 60) 1327–1330.

A Comparative Extirpation of Alternative Legal Systems: A Schism Between Common and Civil Law Boundaries of Duress

A schism applies between common and civil law jurisdictions in their construction of the ambit of duress as a defence to murder.[146] A comparative extirpation of the prevailing common law legal systems reveals a general denial to extend excusatory concessions to human frailty into the sphere of intentional killings. The duressee is not exculpated for either murder or attempted murder in England, and federal courts in the US also adopt this exclusion. It is only in those limited number of US states that follow the MPC rationale that are unique in facilitating the potential for a defence to apply even to intentional killing of another. This applies to duress by threats but not to circumstantial duress as the drafters of the MPC identified that for duress *per minas* (unlike situational duress) an alternative prosecutorial option applies against the duressor who issued the threat and precipitated the criminal conduct of the coercee.[147] Guilt lies accordingly with that individual actor who is blameworthy. The MPC is also atypical in terms of the construct of the defence as the Code does not require the threatened harm to be imminent, nor does it require actual directed proportionality between the threats of harm and harm effected, but simply that a 'person of reasonable firmness in the actor's situation would not have yielded to the threat'.[148] The Code's template consequently extends to all crimes, even intentional homicide, committed by the duressee who bears the burden of persuasion for duress to apply as an affirmative defence.[149]

The overwhelming majority of common law jurisdictions have rejected the proposition that duress may provide a defence to murder, either by statutory delineation or through juridical precepts.[150] In Canada,[151] a statutory duress defence is applicable in Section 17 of the Canadian Criminal Code, but providing limited exemptions and, refuting application to those coercees who commit offences under duress as a principal offender, and explicitly excluding murder within this categorisation. A common law defence may be applied if the duressee was a party to the offence, and very recently in *Ryan*[152] the Supreme Court adopted a restricted contextual standardisation to the common law association defence, engaging: (i) a threat of future death or bodily harm to the accused or a third party; (ii) a reasonable belief that the threat will be carried out; (iii) no safe avenue of escape; (iv) close temporal connection between the threat and the death or serious injury anticipated; and (v) imputed proportionality between the threatened harm and offence nexus, embracing a 'general moral judgment regarding the accused's behaviour in the circumstances'.[153]

In Australia,[154] the defence of duress has a common law foundation that has been adapted now in statutory form by most jurisdictions to deny exculpatory excuse for intentional killings.[155] Exceptions apply within the legal systems of the Commonwealth jurisdiction, the ACT, Victoria, and Western Australia, where the coerced killer may theoretically be able to rely on duress, albeit the practical reality is that it has never been raised successfully.[156] In general terms, the common law constituents of this constrained defence and overarching foundational tenets derive from the principles established in *Hurley*:[157]

> Where the accused has been required to do the acts charged against him (i) under a threat that death or grievous bodily harm will be inflicted unlawfully upon a human being if the accused fails to do the act and (ii) the circumstances were such that a person of ordinary firmness would have been likely to yield to the threat in the

---

146 See generally Bedi (n 3); Mulroy (n 3); and Shankland (n 3).

147 See Rose Ehrenreich Brooks, 'Law in the Heart of Darkness: Atrocity and Duress' (2003) 43 Va J Int'l L 861, 861–864.

148 s 2.09(1); and see Mulroy (n 3) 176.

149 See Bedi (n 4) 576–578.

150 See Brooks (n 147) 867.

151 See generally Kent Roach, *Criminal Law* (5th edn, Irwin Law 2012).

152 (2013) SCC 3.

153 ibid [72].

154 See generally Ken J. Arenson, Mirko Bagaric and Peter Gillies, *Australian Criminal Law In The Common Law Jurisdictions* (3rd edn, OUP 2011) and Ken Arenson, 'The Paradox of Disallowing Duress as a Defence to Murder' (2014) 78 JCL 65.

155 ibid.

156 See Arenson (n 154) 68.

157 [1967] VR 526, 543 per Smith J.

way the accused did and (iii) the threat was present and continuing, imminent and impending (as previously described) and (iv) the accused reasonably apprehended that the threat would be carried out and (v) he was induced thereby to commit the crime charged and (vi) that the crime was not murder, nor any other crime so heinous as to be excepted from the doctrine and (vii) the accused did not, by fault on his part when free from the duress, expose himself to its application and (viii) he had no means, with safety to himself, or preventing the execution of the threat, then the accused, in such circumstances at least, has a defence of duress.

In a similar vein, a constrained approach to duress has also been prevalent before Dutch courts,[158] denying on proportionality grounds any defence to homicide and the prohibition on killing another to save the life of the coercee or immediate family member applies in a non-exempting manner. This restrictive perspective is replicated in New Zealand,[159] where the common law defence of duress by threats was statutorily replaced by a limited compulsion defence within section 24(1) of the Crimes Act 1961.[160] The reductionist defence of compulsion was delimited in *Teichelman*[161] by three mandatory prerequisites: (a) a threat to kill or cause grievous bodily harm which is to be executed immediately following a refusal to commit the offence; (b) the person making the threat is present during the commission of the offence; and (c) the accused committed the offence in the belief that otherwise the threat would be carried out.

By way of extrapolation, an alternative juristic concept of duress applies in South African law,[162] grounded in justificatory defence underpinnings. The foundational principles, however, remain embryonic in nature and subject to very limited judicial review. Duress can constitutionally provide a defence to even the killing of an innocent third party, but only in rare occurrences, and if applicable it provides a justification to unlawful actions contrary to contemporary standardisations in other common law legal systems.[163] The limited appellate review of the tenets of the defence mean that extant law, as a number of commentators have cogently stated, should be treated with caution.[164]

A more enlightened reform pathway for Anglo-American substantive duress principles is provided by the civil law legal systems of France and Germany, legitimately addressing hard choices on coercion, moral involuntariness and directed proportionality. The German Criminal Code[165] looks normatively at the choice made by the duressee to examine if it is 'comprehensible' in terms of appropriate societal expectations imposed on a coerced actor in order to provide an 'understanding' of culpability, and provide an exemption from liability within defined parameters.[166] The nexus created looks to potential absolution from blame as part of effective communitarian determinism and prevailing social mores.[167] A full exculpatory defence, even to intentional killings, may apply, but within a restricted and prescriptive juxtaposition of constituent duress elements. In accordance with Section 35(1) StGB, a 'person who, faced with an imminent danger to life, limb or freedom which cannot otherwise be averted, commits an unlawful act to avert the danger from himself, a relative or person close to him, acts without guilt'.[168] The threat of imminent danger must be, consequentially, directed at the coerced individual or a person close to him,[169] and it is only in those prescribed circumstances, excluding property threats, that an unlawful act becomes comprehensible and meets societal expectations, as Roxin has cogently adumbrated:

---

158 See generally J De Hullu, *Materieel Strafrecht – Over Algemene Leerstukken Van Stratrechtelijke Aansprakelijkheid Naar Netherlands* (5th edn, Kluwer 2011).

159 See generally Andrew P Simester and Warren J Brookbanks, *Principles Of Criminal Law* (4th edn, Thomson Reuters 2012).

160 See *Witika* (1992) 9 CRNZ 272.

161 [1981] 2 NZLR 64.

162 See generally Jonathan Burchell, *South African Criminal Law and Procedure* (4th edn, Juta 2011); CR Snyman, *Strafreg* (6th edn, Lexis Nexis 2012); and R. Louw, 'Principles of Criminal Law: Pathological and Non-Pathological Criminal Incapacity' in S Kalinski (ed), Psycholegal Assessment in South Africa (OUP 2006).

163 See *S v Goliath* 1972 (3) SA 1.

164 Burchell (n 162); Snyman (n 162).

165 See generally Michael Bohlander, *Principles of German Criminal Law* (Hart 2009); Kai Ambos, 'Toward a Universal System of Crime: Comments on George Fletcher's *Grammar of Criminal Law*' (2007) 28 Cardozo L Rev.

166 See Chiesa (n 3) 760–765.

167 See Dressler (n 5) 712.

168 See Michael Bohlander, *The German Criminal Code – A Modern English Translation* (Hart 2008) 45.

169 ibid.

The truth is that the [limitations set forth in s. 35 of the Penal Code] [are] explained by the fact that only in the cases that fall within the scope of the text of the provision does the wrongful act performed under duress find sufficient understanding amongst the public that the exculpation seems defensible.[170]

A choice of evils or balancing of harms is excluded from consideration in Germanic law, but rather the essential focal enquiry is directed at the culpability and blameworthiness of the actor not the act.[171] Duress is excluded as an excusatory defence if the defendant is culpable to the extent that they, 'could be expected . . . to accept the danger, in particular, because he himself had caused the danger, or was under a special obligation to do so', or in circumstances where the harm caused is clearly disproportionate to the harm sought to be avoided.[172]

The defence of duress in Section 35(1) StGB of the German Criminal Code mirrors the MPC perspective in the U.S. in that it legitimately encompasses intentional killings within its purview subject to strict constraints. The examination focuses on the blameworthiness of the individual actor not the act itself.[173] The standardisation looks to social mores and communitarian obligations in the normative question, excluding threats to property and other legally protected interests, and ultimately addresses whether the coercee acted in a manner that is comprehensible and understandable.[174] This broadened understanding of individual culpability or otherwise is adopted in French law,[175] focusing on lack of real choice in behaviour, and adoption of a defence of constraint akin to moral involuntariness. Constraint as a defence applies to all crimes, including murder, and threats of death or personal injury are not a proportional imperative where it is viewed that the defendant has no choice but to commit the offence: 'A person is not criminally liable who acted under the influence of a force or a constraint which they could not resist'.[176] The personalised defence in French law concentrates on whether the actor, given the unforeseeable constraint, could possibly have resisted committing the offence, including intentional killing of another. Lessons drawn from civil law code jurisdictions, notably in terms of comprehension and understanding of individual action, societal expectations,[177] and due constraint are developed further in the next section which concentrates on optimal reform pathways for duress in terms of culpability thresholds and offence specifications.

Duress and Murder: Judicial Activism and Optimal Reform Pathways

Extending the Ambit of Duress

[W]here the duress is so compelling that the defendant could not reasonably have been expected to resist it, perhaps being a threat not to the defendant himself but to an innocent hostage dear to him, it would be . . . unjust that the defendant should suffer the stigma of a conviction even for manslaughter. We do not think that any social purpose is served by requiring the law to prescribe such standards, of determination and heroism.[178]

---

170   Claus Roxin, *Derecho Penal Parte General* 909 (Luzon Pena tr, 2d edn, 2000).

171   ibid.

172   See Bohlander (n 168) 45.

173   In German criminal law, adopting communitarian obligations and societal expectations, high thresholds will consequently apply to certain individuals, such as police officers, in terms of exemption: see Hans Heinrich Jescheck and Thomas Weigend, *Tratado De Derecho Penal* 523: 'The [duty] to control the instinct of self-preservation is . . . required of those who have assumed the obligation to tolerate [threats] in light of their lives. [The reason for this is that] it is in precisely these circumstances when the community should be able to rely on them'; see also Chiesa (n 3) 764–767 for further detailed consideration.

174   See Larry Alexander, 'Self-Defense, Justification, and Excuse' (1993) 22 Phil & Pub Aff 53, 53, asserting that excuses represent 'understandable though regrettable human reaction(s)' to presented exigencies.

175   See *infra*, discussion by Catherine Elliott.

176   ibid.

177   See Laurie L Levenson, 'Change of Venue and the Role of the Criminal Jury' [1993] 66 So Cal L Rev 1533, 1555 (stating that 'the duress defense . . . . [e]ntails a standard that looks to the values and politics of the affected community'.

178   The Law Commission, *Report on Defences of General Application* (Law Com No 83) [2.43]; and cited with approval by the Commission in *Legislating the Criminal Code: Offences Against the Person and General Principles* (Law Com No 218) [30.17].

The Law Commission have consistently advocated that duress should be a defence to murder and attempted murder.[179] The arguments presented for denial in *Howe* have been deconstructed in this chapter, and reform is needed expeditiously to extend the exemption. The defence is not predicated on a justificatory lesser-harm or a 'deontological moral positive'[180] of choice of evil, but presents a normative moral excuse; and, 'in short the question is whether the coerced actor is a fair candidate for blame and punishment'.[181] Self-preservation inherent to all counsels against a non-exemption rule in all circumstances and legitimate societal expectations are at odds with hypocritical demands of heroism and fortitude. An orator of hard truths would ask in this regard whether it is 'better' to prevent the death of a stranger than to prevent the deaths of one's children?[182]

The sanctity of life argument is inapposite to the coerced 13 year old in *Wilson* or peripherally engaged aiders and abettors who become embroiled in unlawful joint ventures involving killing under duress.[183] If a jury is satisfied that a reasonable person, sharing relevant characteristics of the defendant as articulated earlier, might have acted in a way that the coercee did, then a defence ought reasonably to extend to murder.[184]

The defence presented is a normative moral excuse, operating as a concession to human frailty, and is centred around a denial of fair opportunity prevalent to the coerced actor: 'No person has a fair opportunity to comply with a law with which the highest judicial authorities admit that they, themselves, could not comply'.[185] The moral equation, as under extant Germanic law, relates to whether the defendant is blameworthy, or whether behaviour may be categorised as understandable and comprehensible in the circumstances examining the proportionality nexus between threatened harm and offence commission.[186] The practical reality is that for all crimes the jury as arbiters should form a judgement whether a reasonable person in the duressee's position might have committed intentional killing(s).[187] The quintessential debate is, thus, whether a juror believes it is unfair to punish and stigmatise an individual, in light of the threatening circumstances, for making a calculated choice that is wrongful.[188] As such, loss of control and diminished responsibility have weaker moral underpinnings as exculpatory defences for murder in that the duressee has, at least, striven to avoid death or serious injury to an innocent person set against prevailing exigencies, but the preserving of innocent life is outwith the loss of control/diminished responsibility partial defences.[189]

The duress defence is also different to other defences, notably self-defence, loss of control and diminished responsibility, in that an idiosyncratic temporal individuation nexus will apply between the threatened harm and an initial offence specification, and then intervening period until effectuation of the offence itself.[190] This sequence of events is contrary to other defences, where, typically, '[t]he evidence of circumstances founding the defence is part and parcel of the incident during which the offence is committed'.[191] The duressor is often not present at the time specificity of offence commission, and as the Law Commission have cogently stated, the duressee may be the sole source of the evidence that provides the foundation for the defence.[192] This difficulty was identified by Lord Bingham in *Hasan*, who asserted that the defence of duress is 'peculiarly difficult for the prosecution to investigate and disprove beyond reasonable doubt'.[193]

An optimal reform pathway, however, is presented in this regard by French law where the burden of proving the defence of constraint rests upon the individual defendant, and it is identified that the coercee is in a position to provide his or her own testimony as evidence.[194] This testimony will allow a focus on

179   ibid; see also Law Com No 304, 2006 (n 17) [6.65].
180   Dressler (n 22) 287.
181   ibid 288.
182   Law Com No 304 (n 17) [6.51].
183   ibid [6.46].
184   See Shankland (n 3) 1277–1279.
185   Dressler (n 22) 288.
186   Levenson (n 177) 1555–1556.
187   Dressler (n 9) 1345.
188   ibid 1374 where Dressler states, 'If criminal trials are morality plays, they are especially so when excuses are pleaded, and perhaps most of all when a claim of duress is raised. Juries should write the final act of such plays'.
189   See Law Com No 304 (n 17) [6.60].
190   ibid [6.79].
191   Law Com No 218, 1993 (n 178) [33.6].
192   Law Com No 304 (n 17) [6.10]4.
193   [2005] 2 AC 467 [20].
194   See generally Reed (n 103).

calculated choice processes within the temporal individuation spatial nexus, importantly in the threatened harm-offence commission timeframe.[195] The duressee can sequentially articulate their conduct and beliefs at the relevant period. A beneficial equipoise should be created between exemption for all crimes even murder, but concomitantly reversing the burden of proof to the defendant on a balance of probabilities perspective. This perspective received the endorsement of the US Supreme Court in *Dixon v US*, where Justice Kennedy stated:

> The claim of duress in most instances depends upon conduct that takes place before the criminal act; and, as the person who coerced the defendant is often unwilling to come forward and testify, the prosecution may be without practical means of disproving the defendant's allegation. There is good reason, then to maintain the usual rule of placing the burden or production and persuasion together on the party raising the issue.[196]

The practical argument is that, given that the coercee will have the superior access to the relevant proof, the burden of persuasion should rest accordingly.[197] It is submitted that a reverse burden in this regard will not unduly conflict with the presumption of innocence in Article 6(2) of the ECHR, which asserts that everyone charged with a criminal offence shall be presumed innocent until proved guilty according to law.[198] This, however, in accordance with the jurisprudence of the European Court of Human Rights and domestic case law, is not an absolute rule, and may be qualified where a reverse onus is imposed in pursuance of a legitimate aim and is proportionate to the achievement of that aim.[199] It is reasonably proportionate to reverse the burden for the exempting defence of duress to murder in that all definitional elements of the offence must still be proven by the prosecution beyond reasonable doubt; and, 'an onus to prove facts taking the defendant outside the rationale of the offence, meaning the danger with which the prohibited, morally blameworthy, conduct is intended to deal may be upheld'.[200] Practical reforms on reverse onus should be conjoined together with substantive extension of the exempting defence to place the fact-finders in a lead role as normative arbiters of the excuse question in this theatre of morality. Dressler has clearly identified the concessionary true ambit of duress:

> As long as jurors are not hypocritical – as long as they would demand as much of themselves as they demand of others – then the duress defence justly accords an excuse to wrongful-but-coerced actors while still treating them with respect as responsible moral agents.[201]

Judicial Activism and the Creation of New Defences

Practical reforms are needed to the defence of defence, and recent judicial developments providing a novel duress of circumstances, and recognising a defence of necessity, indicate that judicial activism can beneficially revolutionise contemporary exculpation mores.[202] Their Lordships in *Howe* were not prepared to proactively extend the ambit of duress to murder, noting that this imitative had been proposed 12 years earlier by the Law Commission but Parliament had failed to act in this regard.[203] Recent precepts have demonstrated a clear dichotomy between principles of *stare decisis* and judicial law-making, and the appropriate role of the legislature when legal reform is needed.[204] It is suggested that inculpatory conduct sits within the proper

---

195   ibid.

196   413 F 3rd 520 (2005); see generally Engel (n 60).

197   ibid, per Justice Breyer, and contrasting loss of control cases, wherein proving an absence of passion in murder, 'imposes no unique hardship on the prosecution'.

198   See Ian Dennis, 'Reverse Onuses and the Presumption of Innocence: In Search of Principle' [2005] Crim LR 901, 901–903.

199   ibid; see also *Sheldrake v DPP* [2004] UKHL 43; *Janosevic v Sweden* (2004) 38 EHRR 473; and *Lambert* [2002].

200   Dennis (n 198) 927.

201   Dressler (n 22) 286.

202   See Reed (n 70) 64–65.

203   [1987] AC 4.7, 437 (Lord Bridge) and 443 (Lord Griffiths).

204   Reed (n 70) 65.

sphere of legislative determination, but that for exculpatory defence standardisations reflective amendments via judicial law-making is appropriate and at times essential: 'it is possible to craft principled responses to the quiddity of a particular case without undermining the normative framework of the criminal law'.[205]

The contrasting views presented by Lord Salmon in *Abbott*[206] and Lord Wilberforce in *Lynch*,[207] restricting the ambit of the defence of duress in the former but fundamentally more permissive in the latter, vividly reflect the debate over the judiciary's role in determining exculpatory behaviour and the limits of societal expectations and blameworthiness. Lord Salmon in *Abbott* couched his judgment in restrictive parameters:

> Judges have no power to create new criminal offences; nor in their Lordships opinion ... have they the power to invent a new defence to murder which is entirely contrary to fundamental legal doctrine accepted for hundreds of years without question. If a policy charge of such a fundamental nature were to be made it could, in their Lordships view, be made only by Parliament. Whilst their Lordships strongly uphold the right and indeed the duty of the judges to adapt and develop the principles of the common law in an orderly fashion they are equally opposed to any usurpation by the courts of the functions of Parliament.[208]

Lord Wilberforce in *Lynch* cogently advocated for judicial activism to prospectively extend the ambit of the duress defence:

> We are here in the domain of the common law: our task is to fit what we can see as principle and authority to the facts before us, and it is no obstacle that these facts are new. The judges have always assumed responsibility for deciding questions of principle relating to criminal liability and guilt, and particularly for setting the standards by which the law expects normal men to act. . . . The House is not inventing a new defence: on the contrary it would not discharge its judicial duty if it failed to define the law's attitude to this particular defence in particular circumstances.[209]

Judicial law-making has operated to provide a cathartic panacea to areas of lacunae in substantive doctrine. Creativity has been promulgated to the defences of necessity and duress of circumstances,[210] but also in other constructs where extant law has proved egregiously out of kilter with societal mores and contemporary standardisations. A common law doctrine dating back to Hale and Blackstone, similar to duress in antediluvian nature, had denied rape convictions when marital partners co-habited together, albeit limited assault charges could be brought.[211] In *R v R*, however, this iniquity was abrogated by the House of Lords through judicial legitimacy: 'there was no longer a rule of law that a wife was deemed to have consented irrevocably to sexual intercourse with her husband; and that, therefore, a husband could be convicted of the rape or attempted rape of his wife where she had withdrawn her consent to sexual intercourse'.[212] More limited 'aids of navigation' were laid out by Lord Lowry on behalf of the appellate committee in *C (A Minor) v Director of Public Prosecutions*,[213] in rejecting the proposition that at common law the *doli incapax* presumption could be disregarded, whereby the prosecution had to also establish mischievous discretion on the part of children aged between ten and fourteen:

> (1) If the solution is doubtful, the judges should beware of imposing their own remedy (2) caution should prevail if Parliament has rejected opportunities of clearing up a known difficulty or has legislated, while leaving

---

205 Simester, Spencer, Sullivan and Virgo (n 7) 825.
206 [1977] AC 755.
207 [1975] AC 653.
208 [1977] AC 755, 767.
209 [1975] AC 653, 684–685.
210 Simester, Spencer, Sullivan and Virgo (n 7) 826.
211 Hale (n 61) 629: 'But the husband cannot be guilty of a rape committed by himself upon his lawful wife, for by their mutual matrimonial consent and contract the wife hath given up herself in this kind unto her husband, which she cannot retract'.
212 [1992] 1 AC 599, 600.
213 [1995] 2 WLR 383.

the difficulty untouched. (3) Disputed matters of social policy are less suitable areas for judicial intervention than purely legal problems. (4) Fundamental legal doctrines should not be lightly set aside. (5) Judges should not make a change unless they can achieve finality and certainty.[214]

The practical reality is that, on occasion, judicial law-making should disavow the norms of finality and certainty to give primordial effect to comprehensible excusatory behaviour. In the realm of exculpation it is important to judicially extend the ambit of general defences to reflect lack of blameworthiness or fair opportunity to correlate conduct with societal norms, and reflect moral understanding. The exemption of duress as a defence even to intentional killings, a widened perspective of relevant characteristics for normative fact-finder evaluation, and reverse burden should be facilitated by judicial response rather than accept legislative stultification and prevarication.

Conclusion

The introductory section of this chapter posited a scenario where a coerced parent killed others to save the life of their child. It is argued that duress should be extended to provide a defence to all crimes, including intentional killings, theoretically identified as a normative moral excuse not a justification, and proportionally linking together the threat–offence equation. A wider range of personalised characteristics of the defendant than extantly apply should be relevant for consideration by our moral arbiters. The reality is that excused conduct is wrongful, but because of the excusing condition fact-finders may in certain circumstances understand the dire predicament of the individual actor and can conclude that a judgment of blameworthiness is inapt. The nature of the threat may determine whether the duressee is fairly subject to inculpation.

A comparative examination of common and civil law legal systems reveal fundamentally different perspectives on the ambit of the duress exemption for murder. A more enlightened pathway is chartered by French and German precepts, extending the exemption where the constraint is comprehensible to the moral arbiters in terms of legitimate societal expectations and communitarian standardisations. The individuated affirmative nature of the defence supports a reverse burden of persuasion as within the constructs of the US Model Penal Code, and concentrating on explanatory conduct and beliefs of the duressee in the temporal specificity between threatened harm and commission of the offence. It is unjust to punish an individual who succumbed to a threat of harm to which normatively most members of society would have yielded, and hypocritical to indiscriminately punish for murder in such constrained circumstances.

---

214   ibid 402.

Chapter 8

Of Blurred Boundaries and Prior Fault: Insanity, Automatism and Intoxication

Arlie Loughnan and Nicola Wake[1]

Introduction

It is well known that, while a significant number of defendants facing criminal trials were inebriated at the time of committing the alleged offence, only a relatively small percentage of these defendants raise intoxication as part of their defence case.[2] That is in significant part a result of the criminal law on intoxicated offending, which, as is also well known, restricts the contexts in which intoxication can be used to cast doubt upon whether the Crown has proved the elements of the offence beyond a reasonable doubt. It is also in part a result of strategic decisions made by defendants and defence lawyers, decisions that are made in light of the multiple (and contradictory) moral–social meanings of intoxication. If these defendants raise a defence, it may be one of the general defences, such as insanity or automatism, considered below, or an alternative defence discussed in detail elsewhere in this edited collection. And when this occurs, factual intoxication, the law on intoxicated offending, and general criminal law defences are brought into interaction with each other.

Over recent decades, the legal treatment of this interaction has developed on the basis of a particular set of attitudes towards the 'problem' of intoxicated offending. These attitudes—epitomised by the House of Lords' decision of *Majewski*[3]—have given rise to a condemnatory approach to intoxicated offending.[4] This condemnatory approach has coalesced around a moral-evaluative notion of prior fault, which now sits at the heart of the law on intoxicated offending, and which, as we discuss in this chapter, is central to the recent Law Commission for England and Wales (the Commission) proposals concerning intoxication, insanity and automatism. At its core, the notion of prior fault conveys the idea that an individual should not be able to rely on a defence when he or she has culpably brought about the condition that forms the basis of that defence.[5] The significance of prior fault in the criminal law has affected the construction of the law on intoxicated offending—restricting the contexts in which intoxication may be raised by the defendant to suggest that he or she did not form the requisite *mens rea* for the offence[6]—and the relationship between intoxication and general defences—the ways in which factual intoxication relates to claims to exculpation advanced under other criminal law doctrines.

This situation, which was arguably always fragile, is now coming under increased pressure. The pressure arises from two main sources. The first of these is the rising profile of defendants intoxicated by what have been called non-dangerous drugs, individuals who appear not to be at fault, although they became intoxicated

---

1 The authors would like to thank Andrew Ashworth and Jesse Elvin for their comments on an earlier version of this chapter, and Alexandra Chappell for her assistance in the preparation of this chapter for publication.

2 See, for example, RJ Stevenson, L Bind and D Weatherburn, 'The Relationship Between Alcohol Sales and Assault in New South Wales, Australia' (1999) 94 Addiction 397–410; RDF Bromley and AL Nelson, 'Alcohol-Related Crime and Disorder Across Urban Space and Ttime: Evidence From a British City' (2002) Geoforum 239–254.

3 *DPP v Majewski* [1977] AC 443.

4 See Andrew Simester, 'Intoxication Is Never A Defence' [2009] Crim LR 3. See also herein, JJ Child, 37–50.

5 Law Commission for England and Wales, *Criminal Liability: Insanity and Automatism, A Discussion Paper*. Law Com DP, 2013 [6.1].

6 In this chapter, we refer to the doctrine of intoxication and the law on intoxicated offending, using these references interchangeably. See further Arlie Loughnan, 'Putting Mental Incapacity Together Again' (2012) 15 New Crim L Rev 1.

willingly or consciously.[7] These defendants may be intoxicated by prescription, soporific or sedative drugs, for instance, and are not assumed to have been aware of the consequences of consumption of the drug, at least in the same way as knowledge of the effects of alcohol is presumed to be generalised within the community.[8] These cases have generated a thin line of case law in which defendants, although not involuntarily intoxicated, are not as readily blameworthy as the quintessential intoxicated defendant, one who is intoxicated by voluntary consumption of alcohol or dangerous drugs. The second source of pressure on the current situation is the increasing attention given to the cases of mentally ill defendants who were also intoxicated at the time of the offence.[9] These defendants raise the spectre of co-morbidity, a medical term that denotes the co-existence of two or more psychiatric conditions, or the co-existence of mental illness and substance abuse.[10] In this chapter, we use the term in the latter sense. Co-morbid defendants are not generally viewed with the same degree of compassion as defendants intoxicated by non-dangerous drugs, and, indeed, have been the subject of significant concern regarding the relative importance of the intoxication and of the mental condition in the offending behaviour, and the appropriateness of using the insanity defence to accommodate such defendants.[11]

This complex and dynamic situation forms the starting point for our discussion of the relationship between intoxication and the insanity and automatism defences in this chapter. The central issue animating the legal relationship between intoxication and insanity/automatism is deceptively simple. As recently articulated by the Commission, the issue is accurately distinguishing 'between those who should be held criminally responsible for what they have done, and those who should not because of their condition'.[12] But this is easier to state than to achieve—it is difficult to neatly demarcate between defendants in this way. On the one hand, the spectre of co-morbidity means that certain defendants raising insanity may be thought to be culpable for their condition, challenging the assumption that insanity correlates with an absence of prior fault. On the other hand, while the *Majewski* approach to intoxication is predicated on the idea that (voluntarily) intoxicated defendants are culpable in some way, this is overly simplistic and those intoxicated by non-dangerous drugs subvert this idea. Here, we focus on the situation of the defendants who resist the neat categorisations of the criminal law, via a critical assessment of the inter-relation between intoxication and the general defences of insanity and automatism.[13] We suggest that the increasingly apparent difficulties associated with co-morbid defendants raising insanity, and the challenges of accommodating an increasingly differentiated group of defendants beneath the scope of the *Majewski* approach to intoxication, are putting pressure on the neat distinctions currently structuring this area of criminal law, and on the notion of prior fault that constitutes its centrepiece.

---

7   See *Quick* [1973] 3 All ER 347; *Bailey* [1983] EWCA Crim 2; and *Hardie* [1985] 1 WLR 64. In recent years, in the UK, controversy over the mismatch between drug policy and the relative harms of illicit and licit drugs has led to the creation of the Independent Scientific Committee on Drugs: <http://www.drugscience.org.uk/> accessed 16 January 2014. On the relative harms of illicit and licit drugs, see David J Nutt, Leslie A King and Lawrence D Phillips, 'Drug Harms in the UK: A Multicriteria Decision Analysis (2010) 376 The Lancet 1558–1565; and David J Nutt, Leslie A King, W Saulsbury, and C Blakemore, 'Development of a Rational Scale to Assess the Harm of Drugs of Potential Misuse' (2007) 369 The Lancet 1047–1053.

8   In relation to knowledge of intoxicants, see Arlie Loughnan, *Manifest Madness: Mental Incapacity in the Criminal Law* (OUP 2012) ch 7.

9   See, for example, Coley [2013] EWCA Crim 223; New South Wales Law Reform Commission, *People with Cognitive and Mental Health Impairments in the Criminal Justice System: Criminal Responsibility and Consequences* (NSWLRC No 138, 2013); Attorney-General's Department, South Australia (2013) *A Discussion Paper Considering the Operation of Part 8A of the* Criminal Law Consolidation Act 1935 (SA), July 2013 <http://www.agd.sa.gov.au/about-agd/what-we-do/services-government/sentencing-advisory-council-south-australia> accessed on 28 December 2013.

10   See generally on co-morbidity, Maree Teeson and Lucy Burns (eds), *National Drug Strategy and National Mental Health Strategy*, National Co-Morbidity Project, National Drug and Alcohol Research Centre (2001) <http://www.health.gov.au/internet/main/publishing.nsf/Content/health-pubhlth-publicat-document-metadata-comorbidity.htm> accessed 28 December 2013.

11   See, for example, *A Discussion Paper Considering the Operation of Part 8A of the Criminal Law Consolidation Act 1935 (SA)*, July 2013 (n 8).

12   Law Com DP, 2013 (n 4) [1.18] [6.3].

13   Challenges relating to intoxication also arise in the context of other defences such as self-defence and duress. See Ronnie Mackay, *Mental Condition Defences and the Criminal Law* (OUP 1995) 165–168..

Examination of the interaction of intoxication and insanity and automatism is timely, as it has recently received high profile legal attention.[14] In its latest assessment of insanity and automatism, the Commission dedicated an entire chapter of its Discussion Paper to 'The relationship to the law on prior fault and intoxication'.[15] The Commission acknowledges that the 'complex and heavily policy laden' *Majewski* approach has created difficulties, but explains that it was not possible to revisit the law on intoxication generally within its terms of reference.[16] As a result, the Commission's proposed 'recognised medical condition' defence (hereinafter 'RMC defence'), and substantially altered automatism defence, are designed to ameliorate the difficulties in the law whilst operating alongside the intoxication rules and existing principles on prior fault.[17] As we suggest below, it might be that it is not possible to 'fix' this area of the criminal law in the absence of reform to the law on intoxicated offending.

In our discussion of the approach taken to intoxication and insanity/automatism in England and Wales, we draw on the law, and law reform debates, in several Australian jurisdictions.[18] There are interesting differences between these two national contexts. For instance, while NSW has followed England and Wales in adopting the law on intoxication set out by the House of Lords in the decision of *Majewski* (albeit with some modifications in form rather than substance), Victoria has rejected the *Majewski* approach, and, in accordance with the Australian High Court decision of *O'Connor*,[19] permits evidence of intoxication to be adduced in relation to all criminal offences. Despite these differences in approach to intoxicated offending, each jurisdiction faces similar challenges in responding to defendants who fall on the fault lines between insanity, automatism and intoxication.

This chapter consists of three main parts. In Part 2, we demonstrate the centrality of prior fault in the current law via an overview of the law on intoxicated offending, and the insanity and automatism defences. In Part 3, we examine the impact of co-morbidity on the relationship between the *Majewski* approach and the insanity/automatism defences, and in Part 4, we explore the fragility of prior fault through a discussion of the treatment of defendants who become incapacitated by taking non-dangerous drugs or failing to comply with a prescribed medication regimen. In each of these parts, we also consider the Law Commission's proposals for changes to this area of the law and suggest that the recommendations may not provide the coherence and certainty trumpeted by the Commission.

The State of Play: The Role and Significance of Prior Fault

In this part of the chapter, we lay the ground for our subsequent discussion with a brief overview of the law on intoxication, insanity and automatism. This discussion shows the central role the defendant's perceived prior fault plays in the *Majewski* approach to intoxication, and, by its absence (a negative significance), in the law on insanity and automatism. This in turn allows us to reveal the challenge posed by defendants who fall on the fault lines between intoxication on the one hand and insanity or automatism on the other.

As mentioned above, intoxication is (merely) evidence that may be raised by the defence to cast doubt on whether the Crown has proved the elements of the offence to the beyond reasonable doubt standard.[20] The law on intoxicated offending is notoriously complex. In England and Wales, it is structured across two axes.

---

14   Law Com DP, 2013 (n 4). See also England and Wales Law Commission, *Insanity and Automatism: A Scoping Paper* (Law Com SP 2012) and England and Wales Law Commission, *Insanity and Automatism: Supplementary Material to the Scoping Paper* (Law Com SP/SM 2012).

15   Law Com DP, 2013 (n 4) ch 6.

16   ibid [1.16]–[1.17].

17   ibid [6.1].

18   There are 9 jurisdictions in Australia, of which NSW and Victoria are by far the most populous. Although Australia has a federal criminal jurisdiction (and a Commonwealth Criminal Code), reflecting the origins of the states as separate British colonies, most criminal law is state-based.

19   *O'Connor* (1980) 146 CLR 64.

20   Thus, contrary to popular understanding (and popular press), intoxication is not a defence. Intoxication is most accurately understood as a doctrine of imputation, whereby the missing mental element of the offence may be imputed to the defendant. See Simester (n 3). See also Paul H Robinson, *Structure and Function in Criminal Law* (Clarendon Press 1997) 57–59.

The first axis is the cause of the intoxication (voluntary or involuntary) and, if the intoxication is voluntary, the second axis, which comprises the type of offence with which the defendant is charged (a 'specific intent' or 'basic intent' offence), is enlivened, determining whether evidence of intoxication is admissible. Evidence of voluntary intoxication may only be raised when a defendant is alleged to have committed a 'specific intent' offence. By contrast, if intoxication is involuntary, it may be adduced to cast doubt on whether the prosecution has proved that the defendant formed the *mens rea* required for any offence.[21] Somewhat notoriously, the law of intoxication does not distinguish between intoxication by alcohol and intoxication by drugs, and, as we discuss below, has only relatively recently come to distinguish between intoxication by legal and illegal drugs.

This approach to the problem of intoxicated offending was set out by the House of Lords in *Majewski*, a decision that built on the earlier decision of *Beard*.[22] While there was some initial uncertainty about the import of the detail of the *Majewski* judgments, and how evidence of voluntary intoxication is to be treated where an individual is charged with a 'basic intent' offence, it was the approach to 'basic intent' offences as those for which recklessness will suffice for liability that became the settled interpretation of *Majewski* and approach to the law on intoxicated offending.[23] And it is on this basis that, in the years since *Majewski* was decided, a sizeable body of case law has evolved, categorising crimes as either offences of 'specific' or 'basic' intent. This interpretation of *Majewski* has been questioned, with the Court of Appeal in *Heard* commenting *obiter* that 'specific intent' is aligned to 'ulterior intent', and defining 'specific intent' offences as those which require 'proof of a state of mind addressing something beyond the prohibited act itself, namely its consequences'.[24] As these different interpretations suggest, the meaning of the terms 'specific intent' and 'basic intent' may not be as precise as is sometimes assumed. Indeed, the Commission has admitted that the terms 'specific intent' and 'basic intent' are 'ambiguous, misleading and confusing'.[25] However, it concluded nonetheless that, when properly understood, they refer to genuinely different mental or fault elements for criminal offences, and maintained that evidence of intoxication should only be able to be adduced in relation to some offences and not others.[26] We return to the criticisms of the 'specific intent'/'basic intent' distinction below.

The *Majewski* approach to intoxicated offending rests on the basis that a defendant should not be entitled to rely on a lack of capacity where that incapacity was self-induced.[27] This is the notion of prior fault and it encodes the policy rationale of the legal treatment of intoxicated defendants. Under the *Majewski* approach to intoxicated offending, the defendant's prior fault lies at the heart of the law. The Law Commission refers to prior fault as a 'supervening principle' in the criminal law.[28] As is widely recognised, prior fault provides the moral-evaluative backbone of the law on intoxicated offending, and also informs the dividing line between intoxication and defences such as insanity and automatism. As the judgments of the Law Lords in *Majewski* indicate, voluntarily intoxicated defendants are, either overtly or in effect, to be blamed for getting drunk in the first place.[29] By contrast, and as we discuss further below, the law on insanity and automatism is

---

21   Involuntary intoxication has been narrowly defined to cover only intoxication that is the result of subterfuge or trickery—merely underestimating the effects of alcohol will not constitute involuntary intoxication. Further, even when intoxication is involuntary, it will not necessarily assist the defendant in casting doubt on the Crown case. As the court indicated in the high-profile decision of *Kingston*, involuntary intoxication will only assist the defendant if he or she would not have formed the *mens rea* for the offence in any case. See *Kingston* [1994] 3 All ER 353. As the jury found that Kingston had formed the requisite *mens rea*, the fact that his behaviour was affected by a drug administered without his knowledge was no defence. See further Loughnan, *Manifest Madness* (n 7) ch 7.

22   *Beard* [1920] AC 479.

23   The Lords seem to have used the terms 'specific intent' and 'basic intent' in three different ways, and articulated three different approaches to the way in which evidence of voluntary intoxication is to be treated where an individual is charged with an offence of 'basic intent': see further Loughnan, *Manifest Madness* (n 7) 187–188.

24   *Heard* [2007] 3 WLR 475, 485. According to the *Heard* approach to *Majewski*, the distinction between 'basic intent' and 'specific intent' offences is a distinction between 'intention as applied to acts considered in relation to their purposes' ('specific intent') and 'intention as applied to acts apart from their purposes' ('basic intent') ([485]).

25   Law Commission for England and Wales, *Intoxication and Criminal Liability* (Law Com No 214, 2009) [2.22].

26   ibid Law Com No 214, 2009, [2.22].

27   Law Com DP, 2013 (n 4) [6.4]. See generally Paul H Robinson, 'Causing The Conditions Of One's Own Defense: A Study In The Limits Of Theory In Criminal Law Doctrine' [1985] 71 Va L Rev 1.

28   ibid, Law Com DP, 2013 (n 4) [1.116].

29   '[T]he cause of the punishment is the drunkenness which has led to the crime, rather than the crime itself'; *Beard* (n 21). As Simester (n 3) asks: '[D]oes D commit a crime on the basis of her intoxication?' Ashworth also asks: 'Is D to

structured around the absence (either assumed in the context of insanity or required in relation to automatism) of prior fault. The role of policy, and of prior fault, in *Majewski* made it controversial. The controversy arises because the law on intoxicated offending derogates from the principle of subjectivism, generally assumed to be cardinal in the criminal law.[30] As the Commission noted recently, what it called a strictly logical approach would mean that, where the requisite *mens rea* is absent as a result of intoxication, it would not be possible to establish criminal liability irrespective of the offence charged.[31] By contrast, what the Commission called an absolutist view would equate moral culpability associated with the deliberate ingestion of intoxicants with legal culpability for the offence charged—again, no matter what the offence.[32] The *Majewski* approach represents a compromise between these two positions, achieved via the imperfect categorisation of offences as either crimes of 'specific intent' or 'basic intent'. In relation to voluntarily intoxicated defendants charged with 'basic intent' offences, an ingredient of the fact scenario is disregarded when determining liability. The effect of the law on intoxicated offending is such that, for the majority of cases—which consists of voluntarily intoxicated defendants charged with 'basic intent' offences—evidence of intoxication will be inadmissible. Further, while evidence of voluntary intoxication is admissible in relation to 'specific intent' offences, there may be a 'basic intent' offence which can function as a backup should the defendant not be convicted.[33]

The problems with *Majewski* and prior fault were thoroughly documented by the Australian High Court when it considered whether to follow the House of Lords' decision. The High Court adopted an alternative approach to the law on intoxicated offending—one that bypassed the categorisation of offences as 'specific intent' or 'basic intent', and the issue of the defendant's prior fault in becoming intoxicated—in *O'Connor*, and this decision forms the basis of the law in Victoria.[34] In *O'Connor*, the High Court rejected the House of Lords' decision of *Majewski*. O'Connor had been charged with stealing and wounding with intent to resist arrest, but was acquitted and found guilty of the statutory alternative of unlawful wounding. Adopting the approach to 'specific intent' formulated by Lord Simon (as ulterior intent—the 'purposive nature of the proscribed act'[35]), the leading judgment, given by the then Chief Justice, concluded that 'the distinction between basic and specific intent is unhelpful as a basis for distinction of crimes by reference to *mens rea*',[36] and opted instead not to classify defences as one or the other, and not to distinguish between voluntary and involuntary intoxication. According to *O'Connor*, intoxication will be admissible to assist the defendant to cast doubt on the prosecution case that the defendant's acts were voluntary or whether the defendant had formed the *mens rea* required for the offence.[37]

---

blame for becoming intoxicated or for causing the proscribed harm?'; Andrew Ashworth, *Principles of Criminal Law* (OUP 2009) 202. Although cf *Heard* (n 23): 'there were . . . many difficulties in the proposition that voluntary intoxication actually supplies the *mens rea*, whether on the basis of recklessness as re-defined in *Caldwell* or on the basis of recklessness as now understood; if that were so the drunken man might be guilty simply by becoming drunk and whether or not the risk would be obvious to a sober person, himself or anyone else. That reinforces our opinion that the proposition being advanced was one of broadly equivalent culpability, rather than of drink by itself supplying the mens rea'.

30 See, generally, Alan Norrie, *Crime, Reason and History: A Critical Introduction to Criminal Law* (Cambridge University Press 2001).

31 *DPP v Morgan* [1976] AC 182, 214 (Lord Hailsham); Law Com DP 2013 (n 4) [6.3]. See Law Com No 214, 2009 (n 24) [1.49]–[1.55]; and see generally Stephen Gough, 'Intoxication and Criminal Liability: The Law Commission's Proposed Reforms' (1996) 112 LQR 335; and Ewan Paton, 'Reformulating The Intoxication Rules: The Law Commission's Report' [1995] Crim LR 382.

32 Law Com DP, 2013 (n 4) [6.3]. See generally Alan Reed and Nicola Wake, 'Potentiate Liability and Prevening Fault Attribution: The Intoxicated "Offender" and Anglo-American *Dépecage* Standardisations' [2014] John Marshall L Rev (forthcoming); John Child, 'Drink, Drugs And Law Reform: A Review Of The Law Commission Report No. 314' [2009] Crim LR 488, and Chester Mitchell, 'The Intoxicated Offender – Refuting The Legal And Medical Myths' (1988) 11 Int'l J Law & Psychiatry 77–103.

33 Law Com No 214, 2009 (n 24) ch 1 n 29.

34 After *O'Connor* (n 18), in 1995, NSW reverted to the approach outlined in Majewski, following the high-profile decision of *R v Paxman* (unreported, 21 June 1995, NSW District Court), in which a low sentence for the defendant's manslaughter conviction was blamed on the availability of intoxication as an excuse. See further Simon Bronitt and Bernadette McSherry, *Principles of Criminal Law* (3rd edn, Law Book Co 2010) 273.

35 *O'Connor* (n 18) 78 (Barwick CJ).

36 ibid 82 (Barwick CJ).

37 ibid 88 (Barwick CJ).

The Australian High Court's approach also entailed rejecting the notion of prior fault. In a compelling discussion that, in substance, amounts to an indictment of the notion, the Court identified two main problems with prior fault. First, the idea was considered to be problematic because it rests on a non-legal rather than legal conception of recklessness. According to the Court, taking 'alcohol or drugs with at least the risk of becoming intoxicated is in one sense a reckless thing to do, yet that variety of recklessness can scarce be carried forward and attributed as a substitute for actual intent to do the pro-scribed act'.[38] Second, the notion of prior fault was regarded as overly general. The court in *O'Connor* questioned whether the same kind of moral culpability (or perhaps we could say the degree of 'prior fault') pertained in all cases of 'self-induced intoxication'. Barwick CJ stated: 'It seems to me unsatisfactory to place all instances of intoxication as the result of a voluntary imbibing of alcohol or a voluntary administration of another drug in one undifferentiated classification as self-induced'.[39]

As the *O'Connor* analysis of prior fault suggests, it is a rather problematic notion.[40] While part of the controversy in this area arises because the law on intoxicated offending derogates from the principle of subjectivism, the problems with prior fault are both deeper and more pervasive than that. Although it plays a central role in the law on intoxicated offending, as discussed, it has subsisted as a more or less nebulous moral notion. In such a state, it has been able to serve as something of a talisman in the criminal law on intoxicated offending, but viewed up close, and as *O'Connor* indicates, its moral and conceptual coherence seems to fall away. Further, as we suggest in relation to the recent recommendations advanced by the Law Commission (discussed below), attempts to imbue this notion with doctrinal precision may not deliver the certainty and coherency promised. While it may have a strong moral pull, the use of prior fault in criminal law should be subject to both careful definition and close scrutiny. We return to particular problems with prior fault in the final part of this chapter.

By contrast with the law on intoxicated offending, the criminal law's approach to insanity is structured around the (assumed) absence of prior fault. As is well known, the *M'Naghten* Rules[41] provide that, in order to successfully raise insanity, the accused must prove, on the balance of probabilities, that 'at the time of committing the act, the party accused was labouring under such a defect of reason, from disease of the mind, as to not know the nature and quality of the act he was doing; or, if he did know it, that he did not know he was doing what was wrong'.[42] The 'disease of the mind' limb of *M'Naghten* has been interpreted broadly, around the apparently technical and precise idea of an 'internal' as opposed to 'external' cause, a distinction which has been informed by consideration of the likelihood of recurrence and the prospect of violence.[43] Although not always articulated in such terms, an 'internal' cause is assumed to be something over which the defendant had no control, and thus for which he/she was not at fault. This is evident in what is excluded from insanity. Neither the direct acute effects of voluntarily consumed intoxicants, nor a diabetic's injection of insulin,[44] nor a 'psychological blow' (to an ordinary person)[45] are able to constitute a 'disease of the mind' and form the basis for the insanity defence. Somewhat controversially, a 'blanket exclusion of fault' operates where the defendant does not take medication resulting in a state of insanity ('non-compliance').[46] The court does not question whether the defendant was at fault in such non-compliance since the respective incapacity has been interpreted to be a consequence of the 'disease of the mind' as opposed to the defendant's failure to act.[47] This

---

38   ibid 85 (Barwick CJ).

39   ibid 74 (Barwick CJ).

40   See further Gerald Orchard, 'Surviving Without Majewski – A View from Down Under' [1993] Crim LR 426; *R v McCullagh* [2002] VSCA 163.

41   (1843) 10 Cl & Fin 200. See also *Oye* [2013] EWCA Crim 1725.

42   *M'Naghten*, ibid 210.

43   *Bratty v Attorney-General for Northern Ireland* [1963] AC 386. Lord Denning stated in *Bratty* that 'any mental disorder which has manifested itself in violence and is prone to recur is a disease of the mind' (ibid 412). The consideration of likelihood of recurrence—which is a concern with dangerousness—exposes the policy aspect of the law on insanity. For critical discussion, see Law Com DP, 2013 (n 4) [5.37].

44   See *Quick* (n 6).

45   *R v Falconer* (1990) 171 CLR 30, 55.

46   Mackay, *Mental Condition Defences and the Criminal Law* (n 12) 165–168.

47   ibid.

exclusionary fault approach has polarised opinion, and the Commission has rejected it for the purposes of the proposed RMC defence, considered in more detail below.

In relation to automatism, the significance of the absence of prior fault is more evident than in insanity, as it is a requirement of the defence. Exculpation on the basis of automatism is available only to those individuals who are unconscious or acting involuntarily—their loss of voluntary control must be total (albeit temporary)—and whose automatistic condition arises from an external (as opposed to internal) factor.[48] The most important aspect of automatism is, however, its third component part—the no prior fault requirement.

> The no prior fault requirement for automatism is typically hidden in the definition of voluntariness. As only certain types of conduct (those for which the defendant is not at fault) will be regarded as 'involuntary', the descriptive aspect of automatism (was a defendant in a state of automatism?) obscures its moral-evaluative aspect (does he or she deserve to be held liable for the offence?).[49]

Unrestricted to incapacity arising from a particular set of causes (such as mental illness), automatism is the most overtly morally-evaluative part of the 'mental incapacity terrain'.[50] Here, prior fault circumscribes exculpatory involuntariness for the purposes of automatism along moral culpability lines—and also ensures the scope of the doctrine lies in judicial hands.[51] Although an intoxicated defendant may be in an automatistic state, because the intoxicated defendant is assumed to be at fault for his intoxication, he or she is dealt with via *Majewski*, as opposed to via the defence of automatism.[52] In terms of policy objectives, the test for automatism was designed to 'protect society against recurrence of the dangerous conduct',[53] and has meant that automatism is now a particularly narrow defence.[54] A successful automatism plea results in an outright acquittal (whereas a range of disposal options is available to the sentencing judge if the defendant is found to be insane[55]).

The contrasting legal position of intoxicated defendants and those defendants raising insanity or automatism was neatly articulated in the recent joint appellate court decision of *Coley, McGhee and Harris*.[56] Coley had been convicted of attempted murder and appealed his conviction. The appellant was a heavy user of cannabis and he played violent video games frequently. On the night of the alleged offence, after having smoked cannabis throughout the day, Coley entered his neighbour's home armed with a 'rambo' knife. He

---

48   *Smallshire* [2008] EWCA Crim 3217 [8].

49   Loughnan, *Manifest Madness* (n 7) 132.

50   ibid.

51   See further ibid ch 5.

52   *Coley* (n 8) [18]. The distinction between automatism and intoxication has been muddied by the use of the term automatism in a descriptive sense, to denote automatistic conduct or movement. On this basis, intoxication is sometimes called self-induced automatism. In this chapter, we refer to automatistic conduct and the defence of automatism, to distinguish between a description of behaviour and reference to the law. But see also Ronnie Mackay, 'Intoxication as a Factor in Automatism' [1982] Crim LR 146.

53   *Sullivan* [1983] 3 WLR 123; [1984] AC 156, 172 (Lord Diplock): 'It seems to us that if there is a danger of recurrence that may be an added reason for categorising the condition as a disease of the mind'; *Burgess* [1991] 2 All ER 769, [1991] 2 QB 92, 99. The validity of this distinction is questionable since it does not always follow that internal causes are likely to recur while external causes are not; Law Com DP, 2013 (n 4) [5.41]–[5.43]. See also *Harman* [2004] EWCA Crim 5217.

54   As Mackay has argued, the scope of the phrase 'disease of the mind' has ensured that most states of what can be described as automatistic behaviour (where the defendant is not in control of their actions) fall within the bounds of insanity (rather than the defence of automatism), and thus result in special verdicts/'not guilty by reason of mental incompetence' (as opposed to ordinary acquittals, which follow a successful automatism defence): see Mackay, *Mental Condition Defences in the Criminal Law* (n 12) 98.

55   Following the Criminal Procedure (Insanity and Unfitness to Plead) Act 1991 (as amended by the Domestic, Violence, Crimes and Victims Act 2004), the trial judge may issue a hospital order (with or without restriction), a supervision order or an absolute discharge.

56   *Coley* (n 8). For further discussion see Ronnie Mackay (note), 'R v Coley; R v McGhee; R v Harris: Insanity – Distinction Between Voluntary Intoxication and Disease of Mind Caused by Voluntary Intoxication' [2013] Crim LR 923; Sally Ramage (note), 'C v R, McGhee v R, Harris v R' (2013) Crim Lawyer 1; and Tony Storey, 'The Borderline Between Insanity and Intoxication' (2013) JCL 77, 194–201.

inflicted multiple stab wounds upon the victim, resulting in life-threatening injuries. In his evidence, Coley alleged that he had 'blacked out' and had no recollection of the events. Psychiatric reports indicated that, although Coley did not suffer from an underlying medical condition or personality disorder, it was possible that he had suffered a 'brief psychotic episode' triggered by his cannabis use, and that he may have been acting out the role of a character from a video game. The defence argued that a 'psychotic episode' is a 'defect of reason' attributable to a 'disease of the mind', which may have caused him to lose touch with reality, and thus, Coley might not have known the nature and quality of his act, or that what he was doing was wrong.[57] However, the trial judge ruled that this was a case of voluntary intoxication, rather than insanity or automatism and the Court of Appeal upheld the judge's decision, and Coley's conviction.[58] According to the Court, while the defendant might have suffered from a 'defect of reason', not every such defect is a 'disease of the mind' and, for 'pressing social reasons', 'direct acute effects on the mind of intoxicants, voluntarily taken, are not so classified'.[59] The defendant's condition could not give rise to an automatism defence because, as the Court of Appeal stated, 'quite apart from the fact that the evidence was of voluntary, if irrational action, the defence of automatism is not available to a defendant who has induced an acute state of involuntary behaviour by his own fault'.[60] For the Court of Appeal in *Coley*, there was a 'sharp distinction' between voluntary intoxication and automatism, with voluntary intoxication by alcohol or dangerous drugs representing an *a fortiori* case of culpable conduct, meaning that no further enquiry is needed into whether the defendant foresaw the potential consequences of consuming such intoxicants.[61]

As this case, and our discussion in this section, reveals, the idea of prior fault animates the law on intoxication, and structures the law on insanity and automatism by its absence. But, as we discuss below, some fractures are appearing in this edifice, and the neat distinctions and apparent clarity around prior fault that characterise the current law are under pressure.

Blurred Boundaries: The Challenges of Co-Morbidity

In this part of the chapter, we assess the approach to cases in which there is evidence that a defendant engaged in criminal conduct while he or she suffered from a 'disease of the mind', as required under the *M'Naghten* Rules, but also while intoxicated by drugs or alcohol. We suggest that these individuals challenge the sharp boundaries that currently structure this part of the criminal law. We then assess the Commission's recommendation that these defendants be dealt with by reference to that cause which was 'the most significant or prominent cause of the loss of capacity'. We suggest that, in some cases, the problems associated with discerning the 'predominant cause' of the defendant's incapacity will make it difficult to determine whether the new RMC defence or the *Majewski* approach is applicable. We also suggest that the Commission's assessment of co-morbid defendants masks a more pressing social concern; namely, that mentally impaired defendants who fail to meet the threshold for the RMC defence are at risk of being convicted of 'basic intent' offences in accordance with the prior fault principles. This issue cannot be resolved in the absence of reform to the law on intoxicated offending.

The starting point for this discussion is the evidence suggesting that co-morbidity is a significant issue for mentally ill and mentally impaired defendants facing criminal charges.[62] The data available on mental

---

57   '[T]o establish a defence on the ground of insanity, it must be clearly proved that, at the time of the committing of the act, the party accused was labouring under such a defect of reason, from disease of the mind, as not to know the nature and quality of his act he was doing; or, if he did know it, that he did not know he was doing what was wrong'. *M'Naghten* (n 41). The fact that the episode was transient is irrelevant for the purposes of the insanity defence: '[I]nsanity which is temporary is as much insanity as that which is long-lasting or permanent'. *Coley* (n 8) [14].

58   *Coley* ibid [13]. Coley voluntarily took the cannabis. Hughes LJ noted: '[E]xternal factors inducing a condition of the mind and internal factors which can properly be described as a disease can give rise to apparently strange results at the margin'. *Coley* ibid [20].

59   ibid [17]–[18].

60   ibid [24].

61   ibid [19].

62   A recent Case File Review undertaken by the Sentencing Advisory Council (SAC) in South Australia indicated that the primary psychiatric diagnosis of defendants successfully raising mental incompetence defences was schizophrenia

illness, substance abuse and criminality do suggest some connection between these things, although some of the studies done in this area have been subject to criticism.[63] Other studies suggest that the likelihood of offending by individuals who are mentally ill is greater among those who have a history of substance abuse.[64] It is important to note, however, that this is not the same as saying that mental illness or substance abuse or their combination *cause* criminal conduct. The relationships among these predisposing factors and criminal conduct are complex and the subject of ongoing scientific and other investigation.[65] The correlations among mental illness, drug and alcohol abuse and criminal conduct are nevertheless a significant cause for social concern.

In relation to the criminal law, there are two main areas of concern or uncertainty with respect to co-morbidity.[66] The first pertains to defendants who are alleged to have committed offences when both mentally ill and intoxicated. The mental illness could have been both known and established by prior diagnosis or it may have been latent and stimulated to florid expression by the defendant's state of intoxication. The second area of concern relates to those defendants whose criminal conduct occurs after a course of habitual or intensive taking of drugs or alcohol, where that consumption has resulted in a more or less persistent or ongoing state of mental impairment, but where the defendant is not actually intoxicated at the time of the offence. The Commission analyses these situations as concurrent and successive 'causes of incapacity', respectively,[67] and we adopt that terminology here.

The case law from England and Wales and the Australian jurisdictions furnishes several examples of the difficulties caused by concurrent 'causes of incapacity'. In *Meddings*, the Victorian Supreme Court heard an appeal from an individual convicted of a non-fatal violence offence.[68] There was evidence that the defendant, who was epileptic, was drunk at the time of the attack. He sought an unqualified acquittal on the grounds of automatism, arguing that the alcohol had triggered an epileptic state in which his conduct was unconscious and involuntary. The trial judge had held that the jury should consider, as an alternative to acquittal on the ground of automatism, a special verdict of not guilty by reason of insanity, which would result in an order for Meddings' indefinite detention. The trial judge acknowledged that 'mere transient causes such as alcohol alone or anger alone would not result in a mental impairment defence within the meaning of the *M'Naghten Rules*', but held that, if the defendant had a disease predisposing him to a particular condition then, for the purpose of the defence of mental impairment (as insanity is known in Victoria), it does not matter whether

---

(47%) followed by drug-induced psychosis (15%) and bipolar disorder (10%) (there were often multiple diagnoses for individuals); and 80% of all individuals indicated that drugs and/or alcohol had been a problem for them in the past; and 73% of all individuals had ingested drugs and/or significant amounts of alcohol in the weeks or days leading up to the commission of the offence. See *A Discussion Paper Considering the Operation of Part 8A of the* Criminal Law Consolidation Act 1935 (n 10) [2.127] and, more generally, Appendix B.

63   See Jenny Mouzos, 'Mental Disorder & Homicide in Australia' (1999) 133 *Trends & Issues in Crime and Criminal Justice* (Australian Institute of Criminology) <http://www.aic.gov.au/publications/current%20series/tandi/121–140/tandi133.aspx> accessed 31 December 2013; Paul E Mullen, 'A Review of the Relationship between Mental Disorders and Offending Behaviours and on the Management of Mentally Abnormal Offenders in the Health and Criminal Justice Services' (2001) *Criminology Research Council* <http://www.criminologyresearchcouncil.gov.au/reports/mullen.html> accessed 31 December 2013; PJ Taylor and J Gunn, 'Homicides by People with Mental Illness: Myth and Reality' (1999) 174 British J Psychiatry 9; Lubica Forsythe and Antonette Gaffney, 'Mental Disorder Prevalence at the Gateway to the Criminal Justice System, Australian Institute of Criminology' [2012] 438 Trends and Issues.

64   See, for example, Cameron Wallace, Paul Mullen, and Phillip Burgess, 'Criminal Offending in Schizophrenia Over a 25-Year Period Marked by Deinstitutionalisation and Increasing Prevalence of Comorbid Substance Abuse Disorders' (2004) 161 Am J Psychiatry 4, 716–27. See also Michelle Edgely, 'Common Law Sentencing of Mentally Impaired Offenders in Australian Courts: A Call for Consistency and Coherency' (2009) 16 Psychiatry, Psychology and Law 240, 241–244.

65   Cameron Wallace, Paul Mullen, and Phillip Burgess, ibid. For a critical assessment of the relationship between mental disorder and crime, see Jill Peay, *Mental Health and Crime* (Routledge 2011) ch 4.

66   See further Attorney-General's Department, South Australia (2013) *A Discussion Paper Considering the Operation of Part 8A of the Criminal Law Consolidation Act 1935* (SA), July 2013 [2.129].

67   Law Com DP 2013 (n 4) [6.81]–[6.90].

68   *Meddings* [1966] VR 306.

the trigger is a factor internal to the defendant or an external factor such as the consumption of alcohol.[69] The NSW Court of Criminal Appeal took a similar view in *Derbin*, in which it held that the defence of insanity was available to an individual with schizophrenia who committed an assault while in a psychotic state, where that state was triggered by a 'lethal cocktail of alcohol, cannabis and butane fume ingestion'.[70]

This type of approach has also been adopted by the House of Lords, in the context of the partial defence of diminished responsibility.[71] In *Dietschmann*,[72] the defendant was convicted of killing the victim by repeatedly kicking and punching him in the head. At the time of the offence, Dietschmann was heavily intoxicated, and there was also evidence that he was suffering from a depressed grief reaction following the death of his aunt. On appeal, Lord Hutton stated that in such cases fact-finders should be directed to focus exclusively upon the effects of the defendant's underlying medical condition and to ignore the effects of the voluntary intoxication.[73]

But it is not always the case that examples of co-morbidity will come down on the side of insanity or diminished responsibility. A controversial decision, adopting the opposing approach to co-morbidity, arose in South Australia, where the *M'Naghten* insanity defence has been reformulated as the defence of mental incompetence in the *Criminal Law Consolidation Act* 1935.[74] In *Police v Hellyer*, the defendant was charged with committing a burglary while intoxicated from the combined effects of alcohol and cannabis.[75] Medical evidence suggested that he was suffering either from a drug-induced psychosis or an evolving schizophrenic disorder at the time of his offence that may have been precipitated by his use of drugs and alcohol. Contrary to the decision of the magistrate, the appeal court judge concluded that the defence of mental incompetence was not open to Hellyer. According to the court, if the defendant suffered from mental disorder at the time of his offence, 'it was either directly induced by drugs or triggered by drugs'.[76]

As these cases suggest, because a successful insanity defence brings certain disposal options, courts may be inclined to extend the application of the insanity defence in order to avoid the risk that dangerous individuals might gain a complete acquittal via the law on intoxicated offending. But uncertainty about the law—and concerns about its policy purposes—has led to calls to clarify the boundary between intoxication and insanity. These calls have been advanced in Victoria, South Australia and NSW. In Victoria, it appears that drug induced psychoses is not capable of giving rise to an insanity defence.[77] In South Australia, intoxication is

---

69   ibid 310. See also *R v Carter* [1959] VR 105. See further the discussion by His Honour, Justice Millsteed, in 'Mental Competence', a paper presented to the law Society of South Australia, 21 March 2012 (SA Attorney General's Dept).

70   *R v Derbin* [2000] NSWCCA 361.

71   Homicide Act 1957, s 2. Recently, s 2 was amended by the Coroners and Justice Act 2009, s 52. See for discussion Loughnan, *Manifest Madness* (n 7) ch 9.

72   *Dietschmann* [2003] 1 AC 1209. See also *R v Wood* [2008] EWCA (Crim) 1305; [2008] 2 Cr App R 34, 507; *R v James Stewart* [2009] EWCA (Crim) 593; [2009] 2 Cr App R 30. These cases pre-date the amendments made to s 2 of the Homicide Act 1957 by s 52 of the Coroners and Justice Act 2009. However, the cases of *R v Dowds* [2012] EWCA Crim 281 and *R v Asmelash* [2013] EWCA Crim 157 (loss of control) imply that the approach adopted in *Dietschmann* will continue to apply.

73   '[I]f the defendant satisfies the jury that, notwithstanding the alcohol he had consumed and its effect on him, his abnormality of mind substantially impaired his mental responsibility for his acts in doing the killing, the jury should find him . . . guilty of manslaughter. I take this view because I think that in referring to substantial impairment of mental responsibility, the subsection does not require the abnormality of mind to be the sole cause of the defendant's acts in doing the killing. In my opinion, even if the defendant would not have killed if he had not taken drink, the causative effect of the drink does not necessarily prevent an abnormality of mind suffered by the defendant from substantially impairing his mental responsibility for his fatal acts'. *Dietschmann*, ibid 1216–1217.

74   See Section 269C *Criminal Law Consolidation Act* 1935 (SA).

75   *Police v Hellyer* [2002] SASC 61.

76   ibid [92]. The court concluded that Hellyer's mental state had to be characterised as intoxication, defined in the 1935 Act as 'a temporary disorder, abnormality or impairment of the mind' resulting from the consumption or administration of intoxicants, one that will pass on 'metabolism or elimination' of the intoxicants from the body. ibid [92].

77   See *Martin* (No. 1) (2005) 159 A Crim R 314, *Sebalj* [2006] VSCA 106 (2 May 2006), and *Whelan* [2006] VSC 319 (27 April 2006), Victorian Law Reform Commission Consultation Paper, *Review of the Crimes (Mental Impairment and Unfitness to be Tried) Act 1997* (VLRC CP 2013) para 5.50, and Victorian Law Reform Commission, *Defences to Homicide* (2004) para 5.42. In this Review, the Victorian Law Reform Commission considered whether to include a statutory definition of mental impairment in the *Crimes (Mental Impairment and Unfitness to be Tried) Act 1997* which governs the mental impairment defence in Victoria.

excluded from the definition of mental illness provided in the statute, and a new consultation paper published by the Attorney-General's Department seeks comment on whether to specifically exclude drug-induced incapacity from the scope of the defence of mental incompetence.[78] Recently, in NSW, the NSW Law Reform Commission recommended codification of the law on intoxicated offending in the context of the *M'Naghten* Rules.[79] This recommendation formed part of a raft of proposals centered upon a revised and updated version of *M'Naghten* insanity (known as the defence of mental impairment in NSW).[80] Currently, the position in NSW is that substance abuse disorders (addiction to substances), and the transient effects of the consumption of such substances, are incapable of satisfying the mental impairment defence.[81] The recommendations would amend the Mental Health (Forensic Provisions) Act 1990 (NSW) such that these conditions would be statutorily excluded from the mental illness defence.[82] The defendant's substance abuse would have to reach the level at which it has resulted in brain damage or induced an alternative mental impairment (for example, drug induced psychoses) (a 'substance induced mental disorder') before the defence would be available.[83] This is problematic since it places insanity beyond the reach of the defendant with a substance addiction, and in effect assumes that the alcohol or drug dependent defendant is responsible for his or her addiction – unless or until it has become so serious as to have caused brain damage or another mental disorder.

This punitive approach to alcohol dependent defendants was adopted in England and Wales[84] until it came under fire by the House of Lords in *Dietschmann* (which, as mentioned above, concerned the diminished responsibility defence, not the insanity defence).[85] Subsequently, the Court of Appeal in *Wood*,[86] and *Stewart*[87] held that it was unnecessary for habitual substance misuse to have resulted in brain damage or a secondary medical condition before the diminished responsibility could apply. In cases involving alcohol dependence syndrome, jurors should now be directed to 'focus exclusively on the effect of alcohol consumed by the defendant as a direct result of his illness or disease and ignore the effect of any alcohol consumed voluntarily'.[88] Although this approach represents a more 'empathetically valid' perspective than that which prevailed prior to *Dietschmann*, it requires potentially perplexed jurors to engage in the arguably impossible task of determining 'the degree of voluntariness and involuntariness in the defendant's drinking'.[89]

The case law similarly demonstrates that successive 'causes of incapacity' also challenges any neat distinction between the law of insanity and intoxicated offending. In the Queensland case of *Re Clough*, the court was presented with the problem of co-morbidity arising from the defendant's prior use of cannabis and methylamphetamine in combination with his pre-existing psychotic disorder.[90] The Mental Health Court concluded that the defendant was not intoxicated at the time of the offence. He killed his wife during a psychotic episode, which occurred one or two days after his last use of methylamphetamine, by when the drug had been metabolized or eliminated from his body. The Judge of the Mental Health Court found

---

78 See the Criminal Law Consolidation Act 1935 (SA) s 269A (defence of mental incompetence), and discussion in *A Discussion Paper Considering the Operation of Part 8A of the* Criminal Law Consolidation Act 1935 (SA), July 2013 (n 10) [2.126]–[2.152].

79 New South Wales Law Reform Commission, *People with Cognitive and Mental Health Impairments in the Criminal Justice System: Criminal Responsibility and Consequences* (NSWLRC No 138 2013) ch 4 <http://www.lawreform.lawlink.nsw.gov.au/agdbasev7wr/lrc/documents/pdf/report%20138.pdf> accessed 21 December 2013.

80 The revised version of *M'Naghten* would be incorporated into the *Mental Health (Forensic Provisions) Act 1990*. For assessment of the NSWLRC's proposals, see Arlie Loughnan, 'Reforming the Criminal Law on Mental Incapacity' (2013) 25 Current Issues in Crim Justice 703.

81 *Radford* (1985) 42 SASR 266, 274. See also *Falconer* (n 44) 53–54, 78, 85.

82 NSWLRC No 138, 2013 (n 74) [4.87].

83 ibid paras 3.82–3.85.

84 *R v Tandy* [1989] 1 WLR 350 (CA), (1988) 87 Cr App R 45 (CA).

85 *Dietschmann* (n 71).

86 *Wood* (n 71).

87 *Stewart* (n 71).

88 *Wood* (n 71) [41].

89 Alan Reed and Nicola Wake, 'Anglo-American Perspectives on Partial Defences' in A Reed and M Bohlander (eds), *Loss of Control and Diminished Responsibility: Domestic, Comparative and International Perspectives* (Ashgate 2011) 189; and Andrew Ashworth, 'Diminished Responsibility: Defendant Diagnosed as Suffering from Alcohol Dependency Syndrome but Having Sustained No Brian Damage as Result' [2008] Crim LR 976, 978.

90 *Re Clough* [2007] QMHC 002.

that 'intoxication' included the secondary effect of amphetamine consumption, described as a 'cerebral disturbance', from which Clough was suffering at the time of the killing. The trial judge was satisfied that Clough had intentionally caused himself to be intoxicated with methylamphetamine and therefore could not rely on either the defence of insanity or diminished responsibility as contained in the Queensland Criminal Code to deny criminal responsibility for the killing. On appeal, counsel for Clough argued that the first instance judge should have found that the mental impairment provisions did apply because the appellant was not intoxicated at the relevant times. The Court of Appeal rejected the argument. In a decision that evokes the South Australian approach in *Hellyer*, the Court held that the ordinary meaning of 'intoxication' was 'wide enough to encompass more than a comparatively short-term elation or stimulation', and that intoxication under the legislation included 'the secondary effect of amphetamine consumption from which the appellant was suffering at relevant times'.[91]

The issue of successive 'causes of incapacity' was also considered in the Court of Appeal case of *Coley*,[92] outlined above. In a way that is similar to *Meddings*, their Lordships distinguished between drunkenness *simpliciter* and the level of impairment required to satisfy the *M'Naghten* Rules. The Court, referring to the earlier cases of *Davis*[93] and *Beard*,[94] reiterated that in cases where intoxication results in a recognised mental impairment, for example, *delirium tremens*, the insanity defence ought to be left to the jury.[95] For the purposes of the defence, it is irrelevant whether the impairment is temporary. However, not all medical conditions will be capable of satisfying the 'disease of mind' requirement. LJ Hughes urged caution where expert testimony refers to 'psychosis' or 'psychotic' conditions which may be used to describe symptoms of the defendant's preexisting medical condition, as in the case of *Derbin*,[96] or alternatively, to denote a state of mind induced by drug abuse, as in the case of *Coley*.[97] In the latter case, it is the *Majewski* approach rather than the insanity defence that applies.

In relation to both successive and concurrent 'causes of incapacity', the overarching principles of criminal liability in this area appear to suggest that where the defendant's incapacity is induced by a mental disorder, the *M'Naghten* Rules or the insanity defence should apply. In contrast, where the defendant's incapacity was induced by voluntary intoxication the *Majewski* approach is applicable. But the apparent neutrality of this statement masks the differences in the ways in which the criminal law focuses on causes and effects of incapacity. When intoxication is a factor, the law focuses on the cause of the incapacity (voluntary or involuntary consumption, dangerous or non-dangerous drugs), while, except for dividing cases between insanity and automatism, cause is less of a preoccupation (perhaps we can say it has reduced moral salience) in relation to mental disorder.[98] But, arguably, the moral salience of causes of incapacity should either matter or not matter, but do so consistently. In our opinion, we should question whether causes of incapacity should be such a (variable or) prominent feature of the criminal law, as is the case in relation to intoxicated offending: given that the self-narrative of criminal law doctrines and practices is that they apply to autonomous and agentic individuals, it seems that what should matter is the individual's incapacity, with factors such as causes of incapacity perhaps best addressed at sentencing.

The problems with the current law of insanity and automatism in England and Wales have prompted the Commission's self-described 'radical' reform proposals.[99] According to the Commission's recommendations, the current common law rules on automatism and insanity would be replaced with two new statutory defences of 'not criminally responsible by reason of recognised medical condition', and a reformulated automatism defence.[100] The defendant seeking to rely on the RMC defence must adduce expert evidence on which, in the opinion of the court, a properly directed jury could conclude that at the time of the alleged offence the

---

91   *R v Clough* (No 2) [2010] QCA 120 [14].
92   *Coley* (n 8) [15]. It is worth noting here that the Law Commission identifies a second type of successive incapacity where insanity induces a state of intoxication; Law Com DP 2013 (n 4) [6.82]. See also *Kingston* (n 20).
93   *Davis* (1881) 14 Cox CC 563.
94   See *Beard* (n 21).
95   *Coley* (n 8) [15].
96   *Derbin* (n 69).
97   *Coley* (n 8) [16].
98   We are grateful to Andrew Ashworth for this point.
99   Law Com DP 2013 (n 4) [1.85].
100   ibid [5.123].

defendant wholly lacked the capacity: (i) to form a judgment about the relevant conduct or circumstances; (ii) to understand the wrongfulness of what he or she is charged with having done; or (iii) to control his or her physical acts in relation to the relevant conduct or circumstances as a result of a qualifying and recognised medical condition.[101] The burden of proof would be on the party raising the defence, and, if there was sufficient evidence to leave the defence to the jury, the prosecution's standard of disproof would be the criminal standard.[102] This is a significant (but arguably appropriate and positive) departure from the current law, which requires the defendant to prove insanity to the civil standard, and it casts doubt upon the sustainability of the reverse burden in diminished responsibility cases.[103]

In order to successfully plead the RMC defence, the defendant must suffer from a 'qualifying' as well as 'recognised' medical condition.[104] The trial judge is charged with considering whether the condition qualifies for the purposes of the affirmative defence.[105] As the Commission itself acknowledges, the multidimensional nature of mental incapacities renders it difficult to determine whether a particular condition has reached the level of a recognised medical condition, and divergence in syndrome and criterion levels in the world-leading DSM-V and ICD-10 manuals exacerbate this problem.[106] In light of these difficulties it is perhaps inevitable that the individual perception of the medical practitioner impacts upon diagnoses, which may result in conflicting expert testimony at trial. This problem is compounded by the fact that on grounds of public policy not all recognised medical conditions 'qualify' for the purposes of the new defence.[107] The new proposals exclude voluntary acute intoxication, and conditions manifested solely or principally by abnormally aggressive or seriously irresponsible behaviour, from satisfying the affirmative defence and the trial judge has the discretion to exclude other medical conditions on public policy grounds.[108] These recommendations reflect the general consensus that the 'recognised medical condition' requirement of the recently reformulated diminished responsibility plea ought to have been statutorily qualified to exclude voluntary acute intoxication, as is the case in relation to the substantial impairment by abnormality of mind defence in NSW.[109] It might be preferable for the proposals to stipulate that acute intoxication does not prevent the availability of the affirmative defence where the defendant suffers from an alternative medical condition that is capable of satisfying the remaining criteria of the plea.

If the defendant's condition 'qualifies' for the purposes of the new defence, expert evidence will be required to inform the fact-finders' determination as to whether that condition existed at the time of the alleged offence, and whether it could have caused a lack of the relevant capacity in relation to the charge.[110] The defendant must provide evidence that the condition is recognised by two medical experts, thereby circumventing the reverse burden of proof which currently applies in the context of the insanity defence.[111] In both cases where

---

101   ibid [4.160]. The wide ambit of the proposed RMC defence has resulted in recommendations for a narrower automatism defence (ibid [5.1]), which we discuss below.

102   ibid [4.163].

103   Andrew Ashworth, 'Insanity and Automatism: A Discussion Paper' [2013] Crim LR 787. See also *Foye* [2013] EWCA Crim 475, and Andrew Ashworth, '*R v Foye* (Lee Robert): Diminished Responsibility – Homicide Act 1957 s 2(2)' [2013] Crim LR 839.

104   Law Com DP, 2013 (n 4) [4.160].

105   ibid para 4.79.

106   Law Com DP, 2013 (n 4) [4.69] and [4.74] respectively.

107   ibid [4.158]–[4.161]. See also *Dowds* (n 71) [31].

108   ibid [4.158]–[4.161]. There is concern as to the manner in which the 'acute intoxication' and 'antisocial personality disorder' exclusionary clauses will be applied in practice. The Law Commission states that 'acute intoxication should not, of itself, constitute a qualifying medical condition'. ibid [4.93]. This statement is likely to refer to the fact that the acute intoxication exclusion is not designed to prevent the availability of the defence where another recognised medical condition is present, but it would be preferable to make this explicit in the proposals. This could be done by stating that the fact that at the time of the offence the defendant was (a) acutely intoxicated or (b) suffering from a condition manifested solely or principally by abnormally aggressive or seriously irresponsible behaviour, does not (i) constitute a recognised medical condition, or (ii) prevent such a condition from being established for the purposes of the RMC defence.

109   See Nicola Wake, 'Recognising Acute Intoxication As Diminished Responsibility? A Comparative Aanalysis' [2012] JCL 71–98. See also Nicola Wake (note), 'Diminished Responsibility: Raising the Bar?' [2012] JCL 76, 197–202; *R v Asmelash* (n 71).

110   Law Com DP, 2013 (n 4) [4.118]. The Court of Appeal recently reaffirmed the importance of expert evidence at such trials in the context of the diminished responsibility defence. *R v Bunch* [2013] EWCA Crim 2498.

111   Law Com DP, 2013 (n 4)[4.67]. See also Ashworth, 'Insanity and Automatism: A Discussion Paper' (n 102).

intoxication and a recognised medical condition arise in succession or concurrently, jurors would be directed to assess whether the intoxication or the mental illness is the most significant cause of the defendant's lack of capacity.[112] If the disorder is the most significant cause, the defendant would be found 'not criminally responsible by reason of recognised medical condition', assuming the remaining elements of the defence are satisfied. In contrast, where voluntary intoxication is the most significant or prominent cause of the incapacity, the *Majewski* approach will apply.[113]

The Commission's proposal that the 'predominant cause' approach should be adopted in *all* co-morbidity cases is deceptively simple. As the foregoing analysis demonstrates, in some cases determining the most significant cause of a defendant's incapacity will be difficult, particularly where the condition is one that is inextricably linked to the consumption of intoxicants.[114] The Commission's recommended approach is currently used in cases where both automatism and insanity are open on the facts, but it is not without its problems. In some cases, it might be difficult to discern the predominant cause of the respective incapacity. In the case of *Roach,* the defendant was charged with wounding with intent to do grievous bodily harm under Section 18 of the Offences Against the Person Act 1861.[115] Following an altercation, the defendant stabbed his supervisor in the neck and shoulder in what was described by one witness as a 'psycho-style' stabbing action. Expert testimony suggested that the defendant's incapacity was consequent upon the defendant's mixed personality disorder, long-standing sensitivity to humiliation and aggressive authority figures, and a mixture of non-dangerous drugs (Carbamazepine (Tegretol) and Paroxetine (Seroxat)) and alcohol.[116] The prosecution asserted that if the defendant was acting in a state of automatism it was 'Insane Automatism of the Psychogenic Type'.[117] The defence, in contrast, argued that the contributory effect of the alcohol and non-dangerous drugs combined with the defendant's pre-existing personality disorder indicated that the defendant was in a state of automatism at the time of the offence.[118] The trial judge refused to leave the issue of automatism to the jury and the defendant was subsequently convicted. The conviction was quashed on appeal on account of judicial errors, including, *inter alia*, the trial judge's failure to leave automatism to the jury where external factors operated on an underlying condition that might not have otherwise resulted in an automatistic state.[119] Thus, as stated in *Pooley,*[120] concurrent causes of incapacity permit automatism to be left to the jury 'even if one of the concurrent causes is self-induced'.[121]

Ultimately, the Commission's narrow terms of reference and its focus on the approach which ought to be adopted in this type of case detracts from the more pressing concern regarding the significant difference in outcome for defendants who satisfy the requirements of the new defence and those who do not. Defendants who are regarded as mentally ill are entitled to a defence and are more likely to receive treatment following a special verdict, whereas those who do not meet the threshold for the RMC defence (or, as it is currently, the insanity defence) may be convicted and sentenced in accordance with the *Majewski* approach.[122] In this regard, clarifying the approach which ought to be adopted in this type of case is desirable, but it does not resolve the fundamental problem that in many borderline cases where intoxication presents as a predominant cause of the defendant's incapacity he or she may be convicted in line with the prior fault principles, notwithstanding his or her mental abnormality. This problem cannot be resolved in the absence of reform to the law on intoxicated offending.

---

112   Law Com DP, 2013, ibid [4.160].
113   ibid [6.68].
114   ibid [6.87].
115   *Roach* [2001] EWCA Crim 2698, [2001] All ER (D) 98.
116   ibid [13].
117   ibid [16].
118   ibid [17].
119   Ibid [30].
120   *Pooley*, unreported, Jan 16 2007 Aylesbury Crown Court (cited in Law Com DP, 2013 (n 4) [5.62]).
121   Law Com DP, 2013 ibid [5.62].
122   The result is that this type of defendant is less likely to receive appropriate treatment, their condition may deteriorate and they may be more prone to recidivism. See generally The Bradley Report, *Lord Bradley's Review of People with Mental Health Problems or Learning Difficulties in the Criminal Justice System* (2009) <http://www.rcpsych.ac.uk/pdf/Bradley%20Report11.pdf> accessed 22 December 2013. It is worth noting that treatment may be provided to these defendants under the Mental Health Act 1983. We are grateful to Jesse Elvin for this point.

Prior Fault: Non-Dangerous Drugs and Non-Compliance with Medication

In this section, we critically assess the role of prior fault in the criminal law on intoxication, insanity and automatism. A rather fraught fault line exists between cases involving defendants who take non-dangerous drugs (e.g., prescription medication, sedative and soporific drugs) and those who deliberately fail to comply with a prescribed medication regimen. As mentioned above, while voluntarily intoxicated defendants have not been able to rely on the defence of automatism, on the basis that their automatistic condition is in some sense their own fault, it is not clear that all intoxicated defendants can be assumed to be culpable in this way. In this section, we suggest that re-inscribing the ostensibly bright-line divide between those who are at fault for their automatistic conduct and those who are not via the use of 'recognised medical condition' is not straightforward, and may not achieve the requisite clarity and certainty desired by the law reform process.

The starting point for this part of our discussion is the current prominence of intoxication by non-dangerous drugs (including prescription medication) in appellate level decisions concerning intoxicated defendants. As mentioned above, it has not been possible to make the same assumptions about knowledge of the effects of these drugs, and culpability for conduct taking place when intoxicated by them is not straightforward. As a result, the courts have come to consider whether the defendant was *reckless* in taking the drugs, and/or failing to eat where medication must be taken before/after/with food. In *Burns*,[123] the court was presented with the problem of incapacity arising from the defendant's clinical alcoholism, combined with his consumption of alcohol and a mixture of Mandrax tablets and other pills containing morphia or morphine. The defendant had rugby tackled the victim to the floor, where he lay on top of him trying to kiss him. Although the victim managed to break free, the defendant caught him and declared that he was aroused and would wait all night until the victim succumbed to his advances. Expert testimony suggested that the defendant may not have known what he was doing partly because of brain damage caused by the alcoholism and partly because of the drink and drugs. The trial judge directed the jury as follows:

> It is for the defence to satisfy you on a balance of probabilities that the appellant was unaware of what he was doing and that unawareness was caused by disease of the mind; if you consider, however, that there is evidence that his unawareness was caused at least partly by factors other than a disease of the mind, then it is for the prosecution to satisfy you beyond reasonable doubt that he knew what he was doing.[124]

It is difficult to align this approach with the *M'Naghten* Rules and the *Majewski* approach to intoxicated offending. It is unclear how the defendant would be entitled to a complete acquittal in this situation.[125] Mackay suggests that the case should have been interpreted as one involving non-dangerous drugs, alcohol, and insanity, and thus that the court should have considered whether the consumption of the non-dangerous drug was reckless.[126] Indeed, the Court of Appeal in *Roach* explained that the issue of automatism should have been considered as a separate issue from insanity, since the consumption of alcohol and non-dangerous drugs in a situation where the defendant does not appreciate the effects may be a basis for the defence,[127] with a successful plea resulting in a normal (outright) acquittal.

In *Bailey*,[128] a diabetic defendant struck the victim with a lead pipe during the course of a hypoglycaemic attack, which had been precipitated by the defendant's failure to take sufficient food after his earlier insulin injection. As Lord Justice Griffiths stated, the relevant consideration is the defendant's subjective recklessness:

> [I]t seems to us that there may be material distinctions between a man who consumes alcohol or takes dangerous drugs and one who fails to take sufficient food after insulin to avert hypoglycaemia. It is common knowledge that those who take alcohol or drugs to excess may become aggressive or do dangerous and unpredictable

---

123   *Burns* (1974) 58 Cr App R 364.

124   *Burns*, ibid 374–375.

125   See David Ormerod, *Smith and Hogan's Criminal Law* (OUP 2011) 327–330.

126   Mackay, *Mental Condition Defences in Criminal Law* (n 12) 158–159. See also Law Com DP, 2013 (n 4) [6.83]. See also *Hardie* (n 6).

127   *Roach* (n 114) [17].

128   *Bailey* (n 6).

things. But the same cannot be said without more of a man who fails to take food after an insulin injection. If he does appreciate the risk that such a failure may lead to aggressive, unpredictable and uncontrollable conduct and he nevertheless runs the risk or otherwise disregards it, this will amount to recklessness.[129]

Taking into account the defendant's subjective recklessness will mean that, as the Court of Appeal stated in *Quick*,[130] jurors must consider the defendant's fault in failing to follow the doctor's instructions, whether he or she was aware that he/she was entering into a hypoglycaemic state, and whether he/she could have prevented the incapacity.[131] By imputing liability on the basis of the defendant's responsibility to manage his own illness in such cases, the *Bailey* and *Quick* approaches may be viewed as an attempt to extend the controversial *Majewski* approach.

However, it has not proved possible to get recklessness to do all the sorting work required in these types of cases. In *Hardie*, Lord Justice Parker stated:

> It is true that Valium is a drug and it is true that it was taken deliberately and not taken on medical prescription, but the drug is, in our view, wholly different in kind from drugs which are liable to cause unpredictability or aggressiveness. It may well be that the taking of a sedative or soporific drug will, in certain circumstances, be no answer, for example in a case of reckless driving, but if the effect of a drug is merely soporific or sedative the taking of it, even in some excessive quantity, cannot in the ordinary way raise a conclusive presumption against the admission of proof of intoxication for the purpose of disproving *mens rea* in ordinary crimes, such as would be the case with alcoholic intoxication or incapacity or automatism resulting from the self-administration of dangerous drugs.[132]

As this extract suggests, *Hardie* may be contrasted with *Burns*, *Bailey*, and *Quick*. According to the Law Commission, the divergence in the legal treatment of defendant's taking non-dangerous drugs and those failing to comply with medication, and the 'illogical and inconsistent' verdicts that result, cannot be justified.[133]

In response to perceived problems exposed by the line of case law dealing with intoxication by non-dangerous drugs, the Commission initially proposed what may be considered a technical solution. In 2009, it recommended that intoxication by non-dangerous drugs be deemed to be cases of *involuntary* intoxication.[134] In its 2013 Discussion Paper, however, the Commission withdrew this idea. It has now proposed two related changes to the law. The first change is to the scope of the automatism defence, which will not be available to a defendant whose incapacity can be attributed to any kind of medical condition. The second change is to the boundary between involuntary intoxication and the new RMC defence. Under the Commission's proposals, the RMC defence would be available to the defendant who becomes (involuntarily) intoxicated through the proper use of non-dangerous drugs, and to the defendant who has a valid reason for failing to take prescribed medication ('non-compliance').[135] This second proposed change represents a significant departure from the Commission's 2009 position, and the exclusionary fault approach adopted in relation to the insanity defence, referred to above. The Commission's 2009 suggestions would have entitled individuals in the former category to an acquittal, should it not have been possible for the prosecution to prove beyond reasonable doubt that he or she formed the requisite *mens rea*. The latter category of defendant would have been entitled to plead insanity (irrespective of the reason for non-compliance) on the basis that it was his or her 'disease of the mind', rather than his or her omission, that caused the incapacity. We consider the first and second proposed changes in turn.

The first of the Commission's proposed changes is the redrawing of the boundary around automatism. Under the Commission's proposals, automatism would continue to be orientated around the absence of prior

---

129   ibid (n 6).

130   *Quick* (n 6).

131   ibid 923; see also Law Com DP, 2013 (n 4) [6.12]–[6.28].

132   *Hardie* (n 6) 70.

133   Law Com DP, 2013 (n 4) [1.41], [6.50], [6.77].

134   See Law Commission, *Intoxication and Criminal Liability* (Law Com No 314, 2009) [3.125(4)] and [3.128]–[3.136].

135   Law Com DP, 2013 (n 4) [6.42] and [6.46] respectively.

fault, but, in addition, the new defence would also require that a medical condition is not the source of the incapacity. The new automatism defence would be available where the defendant raises evidence that at the time of the alleged offence he or she wholly lacked the capacity to control his or her conduct, and the loss of capacity was not a result of a recognised medical condition (of any kind).[136] As this suggests, the defence would no longer require an 'external' rather than 'internal' cause, a distinction which the Commission labels 'incoherent' and 'overly-simplistic'.[137] This effectively moves all cases of automatistic behaviour following consumption of non-dangerous drugs out of the category of automatism, where the defendant has a 'recognised medical condition'. As the Commission acknowledges, the new defence would be 'much narrower' than the existing defence (perhaps limited to reflexes, spasms and convulsions, or what the Commission refers to as transient states and circumstances[138]), as the broad ambit of the proposed RMC defence restricts the scope of automatism.[139] The new automatism defence would only apply where the automatistic conduct resulted from something other than a recognised medical condition, or the voluntary consumption of intoxicants.[140] The Commission claims that the new automatism defence and the RMC defence are 'mutually exclusive', and that the circumstances 'in which automatism occurs together with a recognised medical condition or with intoxication, either in succession or concurrently, should occur rarely, if at all'.[141]

The second of the Law Commission's proposed changes concerns the boundary between intoxication and the new RMC defence: the Commission's proposed law reform would shift the boundary between intoxication and insanity to expand the former and shrink the latter. As it is at present, failure to take medication, as in the case of *Hennessy* (in which the defendant suffered from hyperglycaemia, having failed to take insulin), leaves it open to the defendant to raise insanity (on the basis that his or her incapacity is the result of an 'internal' cause, for example, diabetes).[142] The Commission proposes that in cases where the consumption of non-dangerous drugs results in an unforeseen incapacity, the defendant will be eligible to raise the RMC defence. This redraws the lines in this area of criminal law, meaning that a normal acquittal will not be available to this sort of intoxicated defendant, a change the Commission considers justified on the basis that the trial judge requires a number of disposal options for use in appropriate cases.[143] As this rationale suggests, the question of disposal is driving the substantive law. The absence of disposal powers following an automatism defence, for instance, has long been a source of concern,[144] and, as mentioned above, the availability of disposals

---

136   ibid [5.124] (Proposal 13).

137   ibid [5.70] and [5.71] respectively.

138   ibid [5.110].

139   ibid [6.30]. As a matter of practice, the defence would thus be available only to automatic reflex actions or transient states or circumstances. ibid [5.110].

140   ibid [5.106]. This would mean that a defendant who commits an assault and suffers from PTSD would no longer be able to raise automatism, assuming PTSD is accepted as a 'recognised medical condition'. ibid [5.67]. The exclusion of voluntarily consumed intoxicants is implicit in the Commission's exclusion of (qualifying or non-qualifying) recognised medical conditions for the purposes of the RMC defence. Acute intoxication arguably falls into the category of a non-qualifying medical condition. As with the RMC defence, it might be preferable for the Commission to explicitly exclude acute intoxication in the context of the proposed automatism defence.

141   ibid [5.119] and [6.84] respectively.

142   *Hennessy* [1990] 2 All ER 9, 292. Hennessy had argued that he had forgotten his medication due to stress, anxiety and depression, and claimed that he should be able to raise automatism. The Court of Appeal approved the trial judge's ruling that stress, anxiety and depression, separately or cumulatively, are incapable of producing a state of automatism. The court noted that barring the 'features of novelty or accident', such states of mind are 'prone to recur' and therefore the appropriate defence would be one of insanity. Similarly, in *Rabey* (1977) 37 CCC2d 461, the court ruled that rejection by a love interest is part of 'the ordinary stresses and disappointments of life which are the common lot of mankind'. Subsequently, in T [1990] Crim LR 256, the court was required to consider the case of a defendant who was suffering from post-traumatic stress disorder as a result of being raped three days prior to the commission of the alleged offence. The court concluded that post-traumatic stress disorder in a normal person arising from an act of violence is an external factor for the purposes of the automatism defence.

143   Law Com DP, 2013 (n 4) [6.48]. For example, Quick's incapacitated state was categorised as one of sane automatism, despite the fact that he had 'on 12 or more occasions ... been admitted to hospital either unconscious or semi-conscious due to *hypo*glycaemia'; (n 6), 350 [authors' emphasis added]. See generally Ronnie Mackay and Markus Reuber, 'Epilepsy and the Defence of Insanity: Time for Change?' [2007] Crim LR 782, 792.

144   Norrie (n 29) 182.

following a successful insanity plea has driven the courts' approach to co-morbidity in several common law jurisdictions.

This significant change is clearly articulated in Proposal 14 of the Commission's recommendations. The RMC defence would apply in cases where the defendant totally lacked the relevant capacity for an offence charged as a result of ingesting a properly authorised medicine for treatment of his/her recognised medical condition. The defendant must have ingested the medicine or drug in accordance with a prescription, advice given by a qualified practitioner and/or in accordance with the instructions accompanying over-the-counter medication. The defence will remain available where the defendant did not comply with the instructions, providing that his conduct was reasonable in the circumstances. Further, the defendant must have no reason to believe that the medication would induce an adverse reaction that could cause him/her to act in the way that he/she did.

The Commission also proposes to distinguish between those defendants who do not appreciate the risks of non-compliance and, therefore should not be held to be accountable for their incapacitated state, and those who knowingly disregard such risks.[145] Only those defendants who do not appreciate the risks of non-compliance would be eligible to raise the RMC defence. According to the Commission such defendants might include the anosognostic schizophrenic, the Alzheimer's sufferer who forgets to take medication at the correct times, and the person who leaves an aeroplane having forgotten to take hand luggage containing prescribed medication.[146] On the other side of the dividing line, according to the Commission's proposals, lie those defendants who knowingly disregard the risks of non-compliance, or turn to alcohol and dangerous drugs in a bid to self-medicate. The *Majewski* approach would apply to these individuals, providing that non-compliance with medication was a predominant cause of the defendant's incapacity and assuming that it was unreasonable for the defendant to omit to take the medication.[147] As this suggests, the Commission's proposed reform would align non-compliance with medication, where the defendant was aware of the likely consequences, with the defendant who knowingly overdoses in the same circumstances.[148] Although the law distinguishes between active and passive conduct in the context of acts and omissions,[149] the suggestion here is that there is no moral difference between a defendant who actively overdoses and a defendant who culpably fails to follow a prescribed medication regimen.[150]

But, it is not clear that such a sharp moral divide distinguishes these defendants from each other. In harnessing prior fault to the task of distinguishing between defendants intoxicated by non-dangerous drugs for different reasons, the Commission is bolstering the legal status of this moral-evaluative notion, and, in effect, advocating for it to play an even more significant role in the criminal law. The assumed absence of fault on the part of defendants raising insanity has been controversial, because it blocks an inquiry into what one commentator has called the defendant's meta-responsibility, his or her responsibility to be responsible, to take prescribed medication.[151] In the view of some commentators, the insanity defence improperly shields from conviction those who have culpably caused the conditions of their own defence from conviction in line with the *Majewski* approach. According to Robinson:

---

145   Law Com DP, 2013 (n 4) [6.42]–[6.44] and [6.76]–[6.77] respectively.

146   ibid [6.80] and ch 6 n 33.

147   See for discussion, Harry Kennedy, 'Limits of Psychiatric Evidence in Criminal Courts: Morals and Madness' [2005] Medico Legal Journal of Ireland 11, 1–17. Kennedy suggests that a not guilty verdict in such cases can have ethe anti-therapeutic effect of persuading the insanity acquitee that he does not need psychological treatments to change his attitudes and behaviour or to adhere to treatment in future.' See also ibid [6.76]–[6.78].

148   ibid [6.76].

149   See generally Andrew Ashworth, *Positive Obligations in Criminal Law* (Hart Publishing 2013).

150   Law Com DP, 2013 (n 4) [6.77]; Edward E Mitchell, 'Culpability for Inducing Mental States: The Insanity Defense of Dr Jekyll' [2004] J Am Acad Psychiatry & L 32, 63–69. See also Zachary D Torry and Kenneth J, 'Non-Compliance With Medication and Criminal Responsibility: Is the Insanity Defense Legitimate?' (2012) J Psychiatry & L 40, 233.

151   On meta-responsibility, see Edward W Mitchell, *Self-Made Madness: Rethinking Illness and Criminal Responsibility* (Ashgate Publishing 2003).

> Every jurisdiction considers an actor's causing his own defense for some defenses, and every jurisdiction thus acknowledges that such causing one's defense can be relevant to the actor's liability. If it is relevant when the actor causes one defense, why is it not equally relevant when he causes another.[152]

This approach mirrors the views of other academics, who argue that a defendant's 'madness' is regarded as being precipitated by his/her 'badness' both when a defendant actively overdoses and when he or she culpably fails to follow a prescribed medication regimen.[153] Medical advances that have resulted in the ability to control, or at least partially control, certain conditions arguably provide a medical basis for such an approach.[154] Thus, according to some commentators, the 'susceptibility of the condition to control and cure' should be considered when evaluating a defendant's individual responsibility.[155]

The points are not all on one side, however, and there are some concerns that may be raised regarding the Commission's proposals distinguishing between defendants intoxicated by non-dangerous drugs for different reasons. Here, we mention four concerns, one normative and three practical. The first concern relates to whether there is a clear moral distinction to be drawn between defendants on the basis of the reasons for their non-compliance with medication. In reality, there may be numerous reasons for non-compliance including, *inter alia*, the stigma attached to certain medications, religious beliefs, paranoia,[156] side effects, and depression.[157] Arguably, the notion that a defendant appreciates the risks associated with taking medication or fails to do so would require that the defendant had adequate notice of the consequences of his/her conduct or that it has happened before. Each of these reasons for non-compliance places a question mark over the extent to which the automatistic condition is genuinely attributable to the defendant's decision to take or omit to take medication in the way that he or she did.[158]

There are also three practical concerns with the Law Commission's proposals. First, bearing in mind that neither wholesale nor partial non-compliance with medication is atypical,[159] it is foreseeable that, in a number of cases, it might be difficult for jurors to evaluate whether either individual choice or will, or the medical condition itself, was a predominant factor in the defendant's non-compliance with his or her medication. As a matter of practice, drawing the dividing line between intoxicated defendants will entail an examination of the defendant's reasons for non-compliance,[160] i.e., whether there is an excusatory (for example, anosognosia) or a justificatory (for example, the side-effects outweigh the therapeutic benefits of treatment) basis for the defendant's omission.[161] Fact-finders would also be charged with evaluating whether the defendant foresaw that failure to take medication or to comply with a particular treatment regimen would result in a state of unpredictability or aggression.[162] This is an onerous task that would potentially require an assessment of the defendant's antecedent record, medical history, and the documentation provided to the individual regarding the medication regimen.[163] In some cases recurrence may be used as evidence to suggest an awareness of the likely consequences of non-compliance. Equally, however, a recurrent failure to take medication may be inextricably linked to the condition suffered by the defendant. In this respect, 'even if there is a strong enough

---

152   Robinson, 'Causing the Conditions of One's Own Defense: A Study In The Limits Of Theory In Criminal Law Doctrine' (n 26) 24. See also Mitchell, *Self-Made Madness: Rethinking Illness and Criminal Responsibility* (ibid); Stephen Yannoulidis, *Mental State Defences in Criminal Law* (Ashgate Publishing 2012); and Herbert Fingarette, 'Diminished Mental Capacity as a Criminal Law Defence' (1974) MLR 264. For other commentators, the insanity label is inappropriately attached to the ordinary person who forgets to take medication as a result of, *inter alia*, work-related stress, relationship breakdown, and/or depression. See William Wilson, Irshadd Ibrahim, Peter Fenwick, and Richard Marks, 'Violence, Sleepwalking, and the Criminal Law: Part 2 the Legal Aspects' [2005] Crim LR 614, 618.

153   See eg Mitchell, *Self-Made Madness: Rethinking Illness and Criminal Responsibility* ibid 37.

154   Torry and Weiss (n 149) 219.

155   Wilson, Ibrahim, Fenwick and Marks (n 151) 617.

156   Law Com DP, 2013 (n 4) [6.80].

157   Torry and Weiss (n 149) 231.

158   Kennedy (n 146) 1–17.

159   SR Mardner, 'Overview of Partial Compliance' (2003) J Clinical Psychiatry 64 (Supplement 16), 3–9.

160   Richard Sherlock, 'Compliance and Responsibility: New Issues for the Insanity Defense' (1983) J Psychiatry & L 12, 483–505.

161   Torry and Weiss (n 149) 231.

162   Sherlock (n 159) 483–505.

163   ibid.

moral argument for a suitably defined doctrine of prior fault it may be empirically difficult to tell whether a given condition is controllable by the defendant'.[164] As noted in Part 2, above, the test articulated in *Wood*[165] distinguishing between those who can resist the impulse to drink and those who cannot requires jurors to engage in mental gymnastics, and similar problems are likely to arise in this context should the Commission's recommendations be adopted. Jurors will be required to engage in similar gymnastics in order to determine whether the defendant was capable of controlling his/her condition via medication and further whether he/she was at fault in failing to comply with his/her prescription.

The second practical concern with the Commission's proposals relates to labelling. Commentators have voiced concern over attaching the RMC label to defendants who do comply with a prescribed medication regimen and/or those who have a valid reason for non-compliance. The labels attached to defences in this context are potentially susceptible to negative association,[166] and accordingly there is a possibility that the novel special verdict will become equally as 'unpalatable' as the current law (which, notoriously, categorises the diabetic as insane).[167] It is hoped, as Ashworth pointed out, that the new defence 'will be abbreviated to NCR or (as the Commission prefers) RMC', rather than something more stigmatic.[168]

The third and final practical concern relates to the policy impact of the proposals. In cases where the defendant was aware of the likely consequences of non-compliance, he or she will be convicted of any basic intent offence charged (assuming the remaining elements of the offence are satisfied) and sentenced accordingly. It is unlikely that the imposition of criminal liability in cases of this context will encourage individuals to take their medication, since, as previously noted, the decision not to comply is likely to be a consequence of a variety of factors unrelated to criminal offending. In such cases the defendant may not be thinking about the consequences of his/her failure to take medication and will not foresee the potential harm that may result. In this respect, the efficacy of imposing criminal liability in these cases is questionable.

Conclusion

The contrast in the legal treatment of intoxicated defendants and defendants making pleas of insanity and automatism has been clear since the first decades of the twentieth century.[169] Since then, and in particular, after the high point of the *Majewski* decision, the moral clarity that animates this contrast has been subject to significant challenges. On the one hand, greater recognition of the coincidence of mental illness and drug use has made it harder to neatly demarcate defendants within existing defence categories. On the other hand, the high profile of intoxication from so-called non-dangerous drugs has challenged the idea that all (voluntarily) intoxicated defendants are culpable for their condition in some way, which in turn has made it harder to utilise prior fault to bolster the coherence of and certainty in this area of criminal law. We suggested that these difficulties also infect the Law Commission's proposals to reform the law in this area, meaning that they may not enhance the coherency, or increase certainty, in this part of the criminal law.

---

164   We are grateful to Andrew Ashworth for this point.

165   *Wood* (n 71).

166   At Northumbria University's 'Mental Disorder and Criminal Justice' conference, Dr John Stanton-Ife commented that stigma is likely to attach to the defence irrespective of the form it takes. Dr John Stanton-Ife, 'Philosophical Foundations of the Insanity Defence' (2013) <http://www.numyspace.co.uk/~unn_mlif1/school_of_law/mdcjc/abstracts.html> accessed 14 November 2013.

167   Law Com DP, 2013 (n 4) [1.46], [6.47], [6.54]. See also Adam Jackson, Nicola Wake and Natalie Wortley, 'Insanity and Automatism: A Response to the Law Commission: Part 1' (2012) Crim L & Justice Weekly, 176, 50, 732.

168   Ashworth, 'Insanity and Automatism: A Discussion Paper' (n 110).

169   See *Beard* (n 21).

Chapter 9
Mistaken Private Defence:
The Case for Reform

Claire de Than and Jesse Elvin

Introduction

In this chapter, we will examine the complex and contradictory position of the current law on mistakes in relation to self-defence, defence of property and the similar statutory defences. We will argue that any mistaken belief in the need to use force in self-defence, defence of property and for related reasons should be based upon reasonable grounds, at least when it leads to lethal force or disabling injury, and that there is therefore a need for reform of English law in this respect. In addition, we will critically consider the Law Commission proposals from 2009 on intoxicated mistakes, particularly their recommendation that the rule from *O'Grady*,[1] now codified in Section 76 of the Criminal Justice and Immigration Act 2008, should remain in place.[2] We will further argue that reasonable mistakes about the existence of exculpatory factors should found a new general defence based on 'acting reasonably' regardless of voluntary intoxication, and assess the merits of the current subjective test under *Williams (Gladstone)* and statute.[3] We will also critically analyse the 2013 introduction of a 'grossly disproportionate' test in relation to householders who use force against intruders. The current law and potential reforms will be subjected to critical evaluation and testing through the use of hypothetical case studies. Furthermore, the approach of other jurisdictions and the impact of international law on these issues will be examined as part of the search for coherent and logical principles.

The Current Law on Private Defence

It is sensible to start by outlining very briefly the law on private defence. The relevant rules are an unnecessarily complicated mixture of three statutes and common law principles. The Criminal Law Act 1967 allows a person to 'use such force as is reasonable in the circumstances in the prevention of crime, or in effecting or assisting in the lawful arrest of offenders or suspected offenders or of persons unlawfully at large'.[4] The common law contains similar provisions. These provisions apply only where the Criminal Law Act 1967 is not relevant:[5] e.g., where a person uses to force to defend himself from someone who is legally insane or under the age of criminal responsibility, and thus not committing a crime while attacking another, 'or where no ... attack on D is being made but D mistakenly thinks there is'.[6] The common law allows a person to use such force as is reasonable in the circumstances to defend him or herself from attack, to rescue another person from attack, or to defend his or her property. In practice, it does not matter whether the common law or the Criminal Law Act 1967 applies, since it has long been clear that both sets of rules are governed by the concept of reasonable force.[7] The relevant law is now stated in the Criminal Justice and Immigration Act 2008, which codified the case law dealing with the issue.[8] The general rule is that '[t]he question whether the degree of force used by D

---

1 [1987] QB 995.
2 Law Commission, *Intoxication and Criminal Liability* (Law Com No 314, 2009) [3.53]–[3.65].
3 *Williams (Gladstone)* (1984) 78 Cr App R 276 and Criminal Justice and Immigration Act 2008, s 76(3)–(4).
4 s 3(1).
5 s 3(2).
6 Claire de Than and Russell Heaton, *Criminal Law* (4th edn, OUP 2013) 272.
7 See *McInnes* [1971] 3 All ER 295.
8 s 76.

was reasonable in the circumstances is to be decided by reference to the circumstances as D believed them to be'.[9] It has long been clear that 'a possibility that D could have retreated is to be considered (so far as relevant) as a factor to be taken into account, rather than as giving rise to a duty to retreat',[10] and that D is generally entitled to be judged on the circumstances as he or she believed them to be.[11] However, D's defence will fail where he or she relied 'on any mistaken belief attributable to intoxication that was voluntarily induced'.[12] Judges have continued to develop the principles post-codification: in *R v Oye (Seun)*, the Court of Appeal also stated that 'in self-defence cases the psychiatric characteristics of an accused cannot be brought into account on the issue of whether the degree of force used was reasonable in the circumstances'.[13] The central issue in this case was whether 'an insanely held delusion on the part of the appellant that he was being attacked or threatened, causing him violently to respond, entitle[d] him to an acquittal on the basis of reasonable self-defence'.[14] The Court of Appeal held that '[a]n insane person cannot set the standards of reasonableness as to the degree of force used by reference to his own insanity'.[15] However, this is a conflation of the two limbs in self-defence. The best interpretation of this case is that the Court decided that a defence of private defence will automatically fail where D used force as a result of an insane delusion, since the correct defence in such circumstances is insanity.

As a result of recent statutory amendment, there are now special provisions relating to 'householder cases'. The approach in a householder case is that 'the degree of force used by D is not to be regarded as having been reasonable in the circumstances as D believed them to be if it was grossly disproportionate in those circumstances'.[16] At least in principle, this is different from the rule in a non-householder case, where the 'degree of force used by D is not to be regarded as having been reasonable in the circumstances as D believed them to be if it was disproportionate in those circumstances'.[17] The Ministry of Justice claims that these special statutory provisions relating to householder 'go further than clarifying existing law; they strengthen the law in relation to householders who are defending themselves from intruders in their homes'.[18] The validity of this claim is discussed below. The Explanatory Notes relating to the relevant statutory amendment outline the scope of the householder provisions:

> The use of disproportionate force can be regarded as reasonable in the circumstances as the accused believed them to be when householders are acting to protect themselves or others from trespassers in their homes. The use of grossly disproportionate force would still not be permitted. The provisions also extend to people who live and work in the same premises and armed forces personnel who may live and work in buildings such as barracks for periods of time. The provisions will not cover other scenarios where the use of force might be required, for example when people are defending themselves from attack on the street, preventing crime or protecting property, but the current law on the use of reasonable force will continue to apply in these situations.[19]

As we shall explain below, it may matter little in practical terms whether D uses the householder provisions or the general provisions relating to the use of force, since D must always use reasonable force in the circumstances as D perceived them to be. However, this remains to be seen.

---

9   ibid s 76(3).

10   The law on this point is stated in s 76(6A) of the Criminal Justice and Immigration Act 2008. However, see previously *Bird* [1985] 2 All ER 513.

11   See Law Com No 314 (n 3) [2.51].

12   ibid s 76(5).

13   [2013] EWCA Crim 1725 [50].

14   ibid [2].

15   ibid [47]. However, D would by definition presumably be able to plead insanity.

16   Law Com No 314 (n 4), s 75(5A), as amended by s 43 of the Crime and Courts Act 2013.

17   ibid s 76(6).

18   Ministry of Justice, Circular No. 213/02 [8].

19   Explanatory Notes to the Crime and Courts Act 2013, [57]. The definition of a householder case is in the Criminal Justice and Immigration Act, ss 76(8A)–(8F), as amended by s 43 of the Crime and Courts Act 2013.

Issues in the Current Law on Mistaken Private Defence

For reasons of space, we will not try to examine every possible issue in the current law relating to mistaken private defence. Rather, we will focus upon three matters that are of particular importance, discussed below.

Unreasonable Mistakes About the Need for Force

As the Court of Appeal noted in *Oye (Seun)*, the general rule is that 'the assessment of the reasonableness of the force used is to be decided by reference to the circumstances as the defendant believed them to be'.[20] However, the Court added that policy demands that 'in self-defence cases the psychiatric characteristics of an accused cannot be brought into account on the issue of whether the degree of force used was reasonable in the circumstances'.[21] The Court was concerned that adopting the alternative approach could have detrimental consequences:

> It could mean that the more insanely deluded a person may be in using violence in purported self-defence the more likely that an entire acquittal may result. It could mean that such an individual who for his own benefit and protection may require hospital treatment or supervision gets none. It could mean that the public is exposed to possible further violence from an individual with a propensity for suffering insane delusions, without any intervening preventative remedies being available to the courts in the form of hospital or supervision orders. Thus, whatever the purist force in the argument, there are strong policy objections to the approach advocated on behalf of the appellant.[22]

It is easy to sympathise with the Court's position: the public deserve protection from those who might have a tendency to act violently when suffering delusions caused by psychiatric conditions. However, some of the policy considerations identified by the Court in *Oye (Seun)* could be applied to *any* unreasonable mistake made by D, at least where D's characteristics predispose him or to her to make unreasonable mistakes about the circumstances. By allowing D to rely upon an unreasonable mistake about the circumstances, the current law on private defence can be criticised on two grounds: first, it could mean that, in cases where insanity is not an issue, the more pre-disposed D is to assume unreasonably that he or she is being threatened or attacked the more likely it is that a complete acquittal will result. This could mean that the public is exposed to possible further violence from an individual with a propensity for mistaking unreasonable mistakes. Although there are philosophical arguments in favour of subjectivist approaches in criminal law,[23] where a person makes an unreasonable mistake they may be denied other defences, such as duress. Glanville Williams argued that '[i]f the defendant, believing that he has to act urgently in self-defence, kills or wounds a person who is completely innocent, this must be accounted a tragic accident, and it is pointless to punish for it'.[24] However, Andrew Simester claims in response:

> A defendant who relies upon a supervening defence knowingly commits a prima-facie offence. In the words of Lord Diplock, and unlike the case where he is unaware that he is committing the *actus reus* at all, '[t]here is nothing unreasonable in requiring a citizen to take reasonable care to ascertain the facts relevant to his avoiding doing a prohibited act'.[25]

---

20   See n 14 [42].

21   ibid [50].

22   ibid [45].

23   There is great debate about whether mistaken private defence is a justification and hence lawful, or an excuse and hence unlawful but exempt from liability. See J Gardner, *Offences and Defences* (OUP 2007) 108–113 and 269–276, and H Stewart, 'The Role of Reasonableness in Self-Defence' (2003) 14 Can JLaw & Juris 317, 320–323.

24   G Williams, *Textbook of Criminal Law* (1st edn, Stevens & Sons 1978) 452. For further argument in favour of a subjectivist position, see, e.g., R Singer, 'The Resurgence of *Mens Rea*: II – Honest but Unreasonable Mistake of Fact in Self Defense' (1986–1987) 28 BC L Rev 459, 510–518.

25   A Simester, 'Mistakes in Defence' (1992) 12 OJLS 295, 308–309 (citing *Sweet v Parsley* [1970] AC 132, 165).

If one accepts Simester's point, the current criminal law in this area is problematic. Since the general rule allows D to rely upon an unreasonable but genuine mistake about the circumstances, 'the defence of self-defence may have the result, for example, of allowing the defence to a racist who shoots a black man, after interpreting his request for money as a potentially lethal threat, based on the honest but unreasonable belief that this particular racial group are uncontrollably violent'.[26] Equally a successful defence could be available to a person whose sane but irrational fear of clowns leads her to believe that all such entertainers are about to attack her. Disallowing unreasonable mistakes about the need for the use of force could reduce inconsistency between cases, and guidance and model directions could be developed to assist juries in applying objective standards. Secondly, as Fiona Leverick has stated, a law which allows D to rely upon an unreasonable mistake about the circumstances is arguably inconsistent with Article 2 of the European Convention on Human Rights, the right to life.[27] Article 3 of the Convention is also particularly relevant here, since it secures freedom from torture and inhuman or degrading treatment and punishment. Both Articles include positive obligations on states to ensure that citizens' rights are upheld, and so require the criminal law to protect (*inter alia*) the lives and bodily integrity of citizens from unjustified attacks. States must have in place effective criminal law provisions, backed up by effective law enforcement machinery.[28] When D has made an unreasonable mistake about the circumstances and has caused the death of, or serious injury to V, the person he perceived to be an attacker, criminal law fails to uphold the Article 2 or 3 rights of V if it allows D a complete defence. Although action taken in actual self-defence is an implied exception to Article 3, this does not appear to extend to mistaken belief in the need for self-defence.[29] Further, in some cases there may also be a need to examine the impact of Article 14, which stipulates that '[t]he enjoyment of the rights and freedoms set forth in this Convention shall be secured without discrimination on any ground'. An unreasonable mistaken belief in private defence based on, for example, racism would hence raise human rights issues in multiple ways since the current law allows a complete acquittal even where death or disabling injury is caused.

The above difficulties are arguably compounded by the House of Lords' confirmation in *Ashley v Chief Constable of Sussex*[30] that civil and criminal law have diverged on several aspects of private defence. In a tort claim for battery, the burden of proof is on the defendant to show that the force used was in private defence. Further, no equivalent of the rulings in *Williams (Gladstone)* or *Beckford*[31] has occurred in civil cases;[32] a mistaken belief in private defence must be reasonable in tort. As explained by Lord Scott in *Ashley v Chief Constable of Sussex*,[33] the purposes of tort law concern the balancing of conflicting rights with the availability of appropriate compensation, in contrast to the purposes of the criminal law. With respect, both bodies of law must comply with human rights balancing tests; the rationale behind tort law has long been a matter of heated debate; the existence of private prosecutions and of compensation in criminal cases make Lord Scott's distinction much more difficult to justify; and the threat of incarceration may appear illusory in many criminal trials for non-fatal offences against the person.[34] But the House of Lords made this line of argument to reject a

---

26 F Leverick, 'Unreasonable Mistake in Self-Defence: *Lieser v HM Advocate*' (2009) 13 Edinburgh L Rev 100, 103 (arguing that Scots law correctly prevents D from relying upon an unreasonable mistake about the circumstances).

27 ibid; see also F Leverick, *Killing In Self-Defence* (OUP 2006) ch 10.

28 For positive obligations under Article 2 where the threat to life comes from private individuals, see, e.g., *LCB v United Kingdom*, judgment of 9.06.1998; *Osman v United Kingdom*, no. 14/1997/798/1001, judgment of 28.10.1998; *Angelova and Iliev v Bulgaria*, no. 55523/00, judgment of 26.07.2007. See also *A v United Kingdom* (1999) 27 E.H.R.R. 611 (regarding positive obligations under Article 3 where the defence of reasonable chastisement prevented punishment of a stepfather for beating his stepson), and generally C de Than, 'Positive Obligations Under the European Convention on Human Rights: Towards the Human Rights of Victims and Vulnerable Witnesses' [2003] 67 JCL 165.

29 See *Rivas v France*, Application No.59584/00, judgment of 1.4.2004.

30 [2008] UKHL 25.

31 *Beckford v R* [1987] 3 All ER 425 (holding that Williams (Gladstone) (n 4) had been correctly decided).

32 Indeed, there is a dearth of case law on private defence in tort.

33 *Ashley* (n 32) [17]–[18].

34 There are some issues with the comparison made by the House of Lords in *Ashley* between criminal law and tort, since several judges appear to have proceeded on the basis of their own honest mistake, i.e., that in criminal law an honest but unreasonable mistake about consent will still found a defence in sex offences, when that has not been the case since the Sexual Offences Act 2003. This diminishes the impact of the line of argument; and, in any case, consent in criminal law is perhaps not the best model, being a minefield of inconsistent principles and autonomy issues. See C Elliott and C de Than, 'The Case for a Rational Reconstruction of Consent in Criminal Law' (2007) 70 Mod L Rev 225.

suggestion that honest mistakes should found private defence in tort even if these mistakes are unreasonable, not to prevent reasonable mistakes founding private defence in criminal law. Even if the divergence in aims and outcomes between the two fields of law justifies more lenient rules in criminal law through allowing unreasonable mistakes to found private defence, it does not justify the criminalisation of those who make reasonable mistakes about the need to act in private defence and hence are not liable in tort.[35] A logical, humane and human rights-compliant legal system might well require those who cannot be convicted of a crime to pay civil compensation to a victim who has suffered harm as a result of their mistake, but not vice versa. Thirdly, the statutory codification of much of private defence applies only to criminal law, which leads to the possibility of further, as yet uncertain, divergence, such as what a civil court would do with a drunken or insane mistake relating to private defence. Although there may indeed be principled grounds why civil law and criminal law should have divergent rules for identical cases,[36] it would be much easier to justify the divergence if civil law operated as a 'safety-net' below the criminal law, allowing compensation for victims of attacks when the attacker fell below the threshold of the criminal law. However it may well be that it is easier to be guilty of a crime than a tort in this field (for example where a drunken mistake leads to the infliction of physical harm on a victim), and the lack of authority in tort is a cause for concern rather than complacency.[37]

Mistakes Induced by Voluntary Intoxication

The current law in this context can be traced back to Lord Lane's speech in *O'Grady*.[38] In this case, he identified two competing interests where D used force because of a mistake caused by voluntary intoxication:

> On the one hand the interest of the defendant who has only acted according to what he believed to be necessary to protect himself, and on the other hand that of the public in general and the victim in particular who, probably through no fault of his own, has been B injured or perhaps killed because of the defendant's drunken mistake. Reason recoils from the conclusion that in such circumstances a defendant is entitled to leave the Court without a stain on his character.[39]

The Court of Appeal followed this reasoning in both *Hatton* and *O'Connor*,[40] in spite of its evident inconsistency with general principles of criminal law defences,[41] and it is now codified in statute.[42] The view of the Court of Appeal in this line of cases appears to be that there is a general principle throughout criminal law that a mistake of fact brought about by self-induced intoxication is to be ignored and D judged on the facts as they actually were, not as he or she drunkenly perceived them to be. However, this rule has been criticised

---

35 Caroline Forell argues that American jurisdictions should allow reasonable mistakes in private defence in criminal law, but require compensation to the victim in tort. 'What's Reasonable?: Self-Defense and Mistake in Criminal and Tort Law' (2010) 17 Lewis & Clark L Rev 1402. Lord Scott in *Ashley* showed sympathy for this view, but was not able to adopt it since it had not been argued by the parties. *Ashley* (n 32) [20]. If any such reform were made in English law, our observations and concerns detailed above would not be affected by moving of the threshold for liability.

36 For judicial consideration of this issue, see *Ashley* (n 31) [3] (Lord Bingham), [17]–[18] (Lord Scott), [51]–[53] (Lord Rodger), [76] (Lord Carswell), and [87] (Lord Neuberger).

37 Lord Rodger identified one such area of uncertainty in the law of tort in *Ashley*: 'Arden LJ [2007] 1 WLR 398, 449, para 196, drew attention to the situation where D shoots V, in the reasonable belief that V is about to attack him, but that belief is based to a material extent, not on V's actions, but on something which D has been told previously by a third party. Like Arden LJ and Lord Scott, I should wish to leave the effect of a reasonable belief of that kind open for further consideration'. Ashley (n 31) [54]. This is an area where the source of the mistake would be irrelevant in criminal law (n 10).

38 [1987] 1 QB 995.

39 ibid 1000.

40 [1991] Crim LR 135 and [2005] EWCA Crim 2951 respectively.

41 E.g., the rulings in both Kimber, [1983] 1 WLR 118, and *Williams (Gladstone)* (n 4) that 'unlawful' is a definitional element of the offence, and the distinction between offences of specific and basic intent. See M Giles, 'Self-Defence and Mistake: A Way Forward' (1990) 52 Mod L Rev 187, 197.

42 Criminal Justice and Immigration Act 2008, s 76(5).

extensively,[43] and further objections may be raised on grounds of the principle and policy underlying this chapter; i.e. that English law should recognise that reasonable mistakes about private defence or other matters fall below the threshold of criminal liability, with a resulting reform proposal of a codified general defence of reasonable mistake. We will return to this suggested reform at the end of the chapter.

The 'Grossly Disproportionate' Test: Improving the Law?

It is hard to understand the rationale behind the introduction of the 'grossly disproportionate' test in relation to householders who use force against intruders. The Conservative Party pledged to change the law on private defence in their 2010 manifesto, stating: '[w]e will change the law so that anyone acting reasonably to stop a crime or apprehend a criminal is not arrested or prosecuted, and we will give householders greater legal protection if they have to defend themselves against intruders in their homes'.[44] This suggests that the Conservative Party wanted to make substantive changes to the law on using force to stop a crime, apprehend a criminal, or defend oneself against an intruder. However, the law already provided protection to those who used reasonable force for these purposes, at least where D did not make a mistake about the need for force due to voluntary intoxication. Indeed, the law even allowed D to rely upon an unreasonable mistaken belief about the circumstances, if this mistaken belief was not induced by voluntary intoxication (as we have outlined above, this is still the law today).

According to the Ministry of Justice, the 'grossly disproportionate' test introduced as a result of a 2013 reform is part of the Government's commitment to ensuring that it is clear that the law is balanced against intruders in the favour of householders:

> It is rare for householders to be confronted by intruders in their homes and even rarer for them to be arrested, prosecuted and convicted as a result of any force they used to protect themselves. When such cases do occur, the Government believes they can give rise to a public perception that the law is balanced in favour of the intruder. In response to these concerns the Coalition Agreement committed 'to ensure that people have the protection that they need when they defend themselves against intruders'.[45]

Given this stated goal, an obvious criticism of the introduction of the 'grossly disproportionate' test is that it has not changed the perception amongst some elements of the public and the media that the law is balanced in favour of the intruder. This lack of a change in perception is not surprising, since it is not clear how much, if at all, the law has really changed. The Ministry of Justice claim that '[t]he provision is designed to give householders greater latitude in terrifying or extreme situations where they may not be thinking clearly about the precise level of force that is necessary to deal with the threat faced'.[46] However, they contradictorily also suggest that there has been no substantive law reform in this respect in the sense that the level of force used must still be reasonable in the circumstances as D perceived them to be:

> The provision does **not** give householders free rein to use disproportionate force in every case they are confronted by an intruder. The new provision must be read in conjunction with the other elements of section 76 of the 2008 [Criminal Justice and Immigration] Act. The level of force used must still be reasonable in the circumstances as the householder believed them to be.[47]

A perceived lack of meaningful substantive reform in favour of the rights of householders has been the subject of much disapproval amongst those who supported an expansion of the right to use force to against intruders. *The Daily Mail*, a newspaper renowned for its general support of the Conservative Party, highlighted a number of limitations to the new law immediately after the 2013 amendment was passed, noting the view of campaigners

---

43   E.g., JC Smith [1987] Crim LR 706; F McAuley, 'The Intoxication Defence in Criminal Law' [1997] 32 Irish Jurist 243; JR Spencer, 'Drunken Defence' [2006] Cam L J 267; C de Than and R Heaton (n 7) at 8.4.7.1.

44   Conservative Party, 'Invitation to Join the Government: Conservative Party Manifesto 2010' 56.

45   Ministry of Justice, Circular No. 213/02.

46   ibid [11].

47   ibid [10.2].

who 'said that, as a result of the exceptions to the new law, there was still a chance that homeowners and small businesses would [face] possible prosecution if they lash out'.[48] *The Daily Mail* criticised the reforms, reporting them in an article headlined: '[y]ou can't bash a burglar after all: Government's tough rhetoric branded a farce as it's revealed homeowners are barred from fighting raiders in the garden or chasing them outside'![49] This headline is potentially seriously misleading in a number of respects: for example, there are no specific rules relating to homeowners, as opposed to householders. Similarly, householders do have a right to chase intruders: in the words of the Crown Prosecution Service and the Association of Chief Police Offers, '[t]his situation is different as you are no longer acting in self-defence and so the same degree of force may not be reasonable. However, you are still allowed to use reasonable force to recover your property and make a citizen's arrest'.[50] Nonetheless, this criticism of the amended law by *The Daily Mail* is significant because it suggests that the 2013 reform has not removed a perception among at least some elements of the public and the media that the law is biased against householders: indeed, it indicates that it may have reinforced it!

Lord Woolf objected to the proposed introduction of the 'grossly disproportionate' test during the related Parliamentary debate on the grounds that it would simply re-state the existing law in more complex terms. His point was that '[t]he position here is that nearly every word the Minister used in moving this amendment is the sort of remark that judges up and down the country would make to a jury when dealing with those very few cases in which a householder is prosecuted'.[51] His Lordship highlighted a disadvantage with trying to make the law too specific:

> You will always try to put into language the appropriate circumstances where you think a particular result is desired. However, there will be circumstances that are very similar to those circumstances, but where the language used does not apply. You cannot anticipate all the circumstances. One inevitable difficulty with this sort of amendment is that there will be amendment after amendment to the law, making it more and more complex and difficult to apply.[52]

Lord Woolf's concern was valid: the 'grossly disproportionate' amendment introduced needless complexity. It is hard to understand the logic behind the scope of the householder provisions. One limitation is that they only apply where 'the force concerned is force used by D while in or partly in a building, or part of a building, that is a dwelling or is forces accommodation (or is both)'.[53] Let us suppose that D sees an intruder climbing through an open window in D's home. D knows that his young children and partner are sleeping in his home, and believes that this intruder might attack them. The householder provisions would not apply in these circumstances if D, standing in the garden outside of his home, strikes a part of the intruder that is still in the garden rather than in D's house: D would not use force while in or partly in his dwelling. However, they would apply if D, standing in the garden, reaches through the open window from outside to strike a part of the intruder that is already inside D's house, since D would use the force concerned while partly in his dwelling. In both situations, D would be acting honestly and instinctively, using force to protect loved ones from an intruder who was attempting to enter D's home. In practice, it is hard to imagine a judge telling a jury to draw a sharp distinction between these two situations, since such a distinction would be unmerited on the facts. The example may be taken further: what if the householder mistakenly believes that the person climbing through the window is an intruder set upon attacking his family? The relevant law becomes even more complex: an honest but unreasonable mistake may acquit him of harm whether in or outside the house, but not if his mistake was caused by a few drinks in the comfort of his own home. Add in a mental health condition and the ability of even an extremely able lawyer to explain the relevant law to one of the parties may disappear,

---

48   J Slack, 'Now We CAN Bash a Burglar, But Not in Our Gardens' *The Daily Mail* (London, 29 April 2013).

49   M Beckford, 'You Can't Bash a Burglar After All: Government's Tough Rhetoric Branded a Farce as It's Revealed Homeowners are Barred from Fighting Raiders in the Garden or Chasing them Outside' *The Daily Mail* (London, 27 April 2013).

50   CPS, 'Householders and the Use of Force Against Intruders' <http://www.cps.gov.uk/publications/prosecution/householders.html> accessed 4 February 2014.

51   Hansard, 10 December 2012: Column 885.

52   ibid.

53   Criminal Justice and Immigration Act 2008 (n 4), s 76(8A)(b).

in which case there is a clear issue with legal certainty both at common law and under the general principles of the ECHR.[54]

Consider the following example: a student at drama school decides to pay a surprise visit to his parents during half term, accompanied by two of his classmates. He arrives at his parents' home to find that they are out. The student and his friends make themselves at home and, to pass the time, decide to rehearse some scenes from Julius Caesar, their play for that term. The parents arrive home a little later and, as they pull into their driveway, they are surprised to see a light on in the living room. The father walks quietly to the window and is shocked to see his son lying on the floor with two strange men standing over him, both holding knives. He bursts into the house and attacks the two 'assailants' with a handy golf club. At present, a householder is entitled to use disproportionate force, and the father's mistaken belief appears to be not only honest but reasonable, yet he may only use it to argue self-defence if it was not attributable to voluntary intoxication or an insane delusion. Should the events occur while the family is staying in a holiday cottage then less force may be justifiable under the current law. The disparity of potential outcomes depending on those variables is illogical and indefensible.

It might be objected that the purpose of the introduction of the 'grossly disproportionate' reform was to address a public perception that the law is balanced in favour of the intruder. However, any misconception about the law not allowing householders to use reasonable force to defend themselves could have been addressed more effectively in other ways: for example, by the Government trying to correct rather than reinforce it! Making a general point about criminal justice reform, John Spencer has observed:

> Legislating about criminal justice in the hope of pleasing public opinion as reflected in the popular press is a dangerous and foolish game to play, because on criminal justice matters, public opinion – as misled by the popular press – is seriously misinformed. . . . [I]t marks a grave deterioration in the standards of behaviour in public life that certain of our politicians . . . have been prepared to play the demagogue and legislate in criminal justice matters in response to this sort of misunderstanding, when they should be using their position to correct it.[55]

Spencer was not referring to the recent amendment to the law on private defence as it relates to householders. However, his point is particularly apt in this context. Explaining why he wanted to introduce a 'grossly disproportionate' test for householders, Chris Grayling, the Justice Secretary, used his position to reinforce misunderstanding about the law rather than correct it. He stated in November 2012:

> [N]ow the deal will be this: if you are confronted by a burglar in your own home and you fear for your safety, or the safety of others, and in the heat of the moment use force that is reasonable in the circumstances, but in the cold light of day seems disproportionate, you will not be deemed guilty of an offence.[56]

This statement by Grayling is misleading because, as Liberty have pointed out, the law has long been clear that the general rule is that householders are allowed to use a reasonable degree of force to defend themselves in the circumstances as they perceived them to be. Thus, as they stated in opposing Grayling's proposal, '[t]he repeated claims at the highest level of Government that this change to the law of self-defence is needed because the law is unclear are simply misleading. It is grim, headline chasing at its very worst'.[57] The overall picture in our view is that the law on private defence is rendered less clear, not clearer, by the reform.

---

54   See for example *Sunday Times v United Kingdom* (1979–80) 2 EHRR 245 under which all criminal laws should have 'sufficient precision to enable the citizen to regulate his conduct: he must be able – if need be with appropriate advice – to foresee to a degree that is reasonable in the circumstances, the consequences which any given action may entail'. There is also a potential issue under Article 7, which requires that 'the individual can know from the wording of the relevant provision and, if need be, with the assistance of the courts' interpretation of it, what acts and omissions will make him criminally liable'. *C and SW v United Kingdom* [1995] 21 EHRR 363 [33].

55   JR Spencer, 'The Drafting of Criminal Legislation – Need it be So Impenetrable?' [2008] Cam L J 585, 599.

56   C Grayling, 'How I'm Fulfilling My Promise on New Rights for Householders' *The Daily Telegraph* (London, 24 November 2012).

57   Liberty, *Liberty's Report stage briefing on the Crime and Courts Bill in the House of Commons* (2013) 10.

Liberty have expressed concern that the introduction of a statutory 'grossly disproportionate' test could encourage inappropriate vigilante action because it 'sends a message that the law will be on your side whatever action you take'.[58] This is a genuine danger.[59] However, it is reduced by the fact that the statutory provisions, official pronouncements and related newspaper coverage do not send a consistent message in this respect. The reality may be that the amendment concerning 'grossly disproportionate' force has little, if any, effect, except the pointless spending of public money on reform, legal interpretation and court time.

Law Reform Proposals

There has been much debate about the correct approach of the law to a defendant who used force in private defence because of a mistaken belief about the facts.[60] One issue here is how the law should deal with mistaken beliefs caused by voluntary intoxication. In their 2009 report on intoxication, the Law Commission recommended that legislation should 'provide a single rule for any situation where D wishes to rely on a general defence to which his or her state of mind is relevant, if D's state of mind was affected by voluntary intoxication'.[61] In relation to mistakes and general defences, they proposed: 'if D's intoxication was voluntary, D's actual belief is to be taken into account only if D would have held the same belief if not intoxicated'.[62] They argued that the rule derived from *O'Grady*,[63] now codified in Section 76 of the Criminal Justice and Immigration Act 2008, should be retained.[64] As the Commission explained in their 2009 report, under the current law D1 would be liable for murder where he or she intentionally kills V1 in the mistaken belief that V1 was about to attack him or her, where D1's mistake was caused by voluntary intoxication[65] (at least where the partial loss of control defence is not relevant).[66] In contrast, D2 would not be liable for murder where he drunkenly mistook another person, V2, for an ape, and killed V2 under that assumption. This is because 'it is [currently legally] permissible for D to rely on a mistake induced by voluntary intoxication insofar as it relates to the presence or absence of the intent to kill or cause grievous bodily harm to a person',[67] but D cannot rely upon voluntary intoxication 'to show that he or she was mistaken as to the factual circumstances relevant to the claim that D believed he or she faced an attack by the deceased'.[68] The Commission's view is that this distinction in terms of liability is justifiable:

> The difference is that, in the first situation, D is aware that he or she is inflicting harm against a *person* and therefore that his or her conduct requires a truly compelling justification or excuse. . . . By contrast, in the second situation D believes, albeit unreasonably, that he or she is killing an ape.[69]

It might be objected that this argument incorrectly assumes that it is acceptable to inflict harm against an ape without either a justification or excuse, apparently on the basis that an ape is 'only' an animal rather than a person, and that any such assumption about the infliction of harm on an ape is obviously incorrect: many species of ape are extremely rare and killing them would therefore be contrary to, say, the UK's biodiversity

---

58   ibid .

59   On this point, see S Miller, 'Grossly Disproportionate': Home Owners Legal License to Kill' [2013] JCL 299, 301–302.

60   See, e.g., the discussion of this issue in *B v DPP* [2000] AC 428, 461–463, per Lord Mackay.

61   ibid [3.24].

62   New Criminal Law (Intoxication) Bill, cl 5(3)(b).

63   See (n 3).

64   ibid [3.60].

65   ibid [3.61].

66   On the potential operation of this partial defence in relation to mistaken beliefs about the facts, see J Elvin, 'Killing in Response to Circumstances of an Extremely Grave Character' in A Reed and M Bohlander (eds), *Loss of Control and Diminished Responsibility: Domestic, Comparative, and International Perspectives* (Ashgate 2011) 134, 142–144.

67   See (n 3) [3.57].

68   ibid [3.56].

69   ibid [3.62].

strategy.[70] However, the Law Commission's central point here seems to be that, in the second situation, D2 does not form the *mens rea* for murder, and thus should not be liable for this offence. While we agree with this point and with the Law Commission's view that deliberately inflicting harm knowingly against a person requires a truly compelling justification or excuse, we do not share their conclusion that this means that, if D's intoxication was voluntary, D's actual belief should be taken into account only if D would have held the same belief if not intoxicated. Our view is that a mistake about circumstances is not unreasonable simply because it is induced by voluntary intoxication. In principle, it could be a mistake that a reasonable, sober person would have made. If so, it is not an unreasonable mistake just because the particular defendant would not have made it if not intoxicated. To say that all voluntarily intoxicated mistakes are unreasonable is to set standards according to each individual defendant. Focusing upon whether D would have held the same belief if not intoxicated introduces what can be called an undesirable personal equation, since it is purely dependent on what might be called 'the idiosyncrasies of the particular person whose conduct is in question'.[71] It is well established in criminal law that there is a significant distinction between a reasonable person approach and one that does not seek to impose an 'objective' standard of general application, even if there is often fierce debate as to what is meant by a 'reasonable' person.[72] As the criminal law on private defence and mistaken beliefs caused by voluntary intoxication currently stands, English criminal law does not purely adopt the standard of the reasonable person; rather, by stating that D's defence will fail where s/he relies 'on any mistaken belief attributable to intoxication that was voluntarily induced',[73] it allows D to set the standard in an important sense. This is potentially harsh on certain voluntarily intoxicated defendants: for example, those who are normally exceptionally able at ascertaining factual circumstances but less so when intoxicated, since they will be judged against what might be called their usual high standard rather than against the standard of the reasonable person if they make a mistake about the circumstances.

We argue that the focus should be upon whether D was acting reasonably: reasonable mistakes about the existence of exculpatory factors should found a general defence based on 'acting reasonably' regardless of voluntary intoxication. In contrast, unreasonable mistakes about the existence of exculpatory factors should not found a defence. English criminal law in this area is wrong to adopt what might be called the general 'honest belief' approach. Lord Lane CJ explained the rationale behind this 'honest belief' approach in *Williams (Gladstone)*:

> The reasonableness or unreasonableness of the defendant's belief is material to the question of whether the belief was held by the defendant at all. If the belief was in fact held, its unreasonableness, so far as guilt or innocence is concerned, is neither here nor there. It is irrelevant. Were it otherwise, the defendant would be convicted because he was negligent in failing to recognise that the victim was not consenting or that a crime was not being committed and so on.[74]

Lord Lane CJ's reference to the law on consent is now out of date, at least in so far as it could be taken as applying to the law on sexual offences: as a result of reforms introduced by the Sexual Offences Act 2003, it is now possible for D to be convicted for negligently failing to recognise that V was not consenting. However, it is Lord Lane CJ's 'honest belief' approach that currently holds sway in the English law on private defence. The logic underpinning it seems to be that 'the defendant's "fault" [in relation to an unreasonable belief] lies exclusively in falling short of an objective standard',[75] and that negligence generally should not be enough to create criminal liability in relation to mistaken beliefs about the circumstances.

---

70   On the issue of biodiversity, see Department for Environment, Food and Rural Affairs, 'Protecting Diversity and Eco-Systems at Home and Abroad' <https://www.gov.uk/government/policies/protecting-biodiversity-and-ecosystems-at-home-and-abroad/supporting-pages/protecting-biodiversity-abroad> accessed 4 February 2014.

71   *Glasgow Corporation v Muir* [1943] AC 448, 457, per Lord MacMillan (discussing the duty to take reasonable care in tort law rather than the criminal law relating to intoxicated mistakes).

72   See, e,g., *Attorney General for Jersey v Holley* [2005] UKPC 23, dealing with the now abolished provocation defence.

73   See (n 4) s 76(5).

74   See (n 4) 281.

75   See (n 62) 462.

In contrast to Lord Lane CJ, certain scholars have argued that D should only be allowed to rely upon a reasonable mistake about the circumstances when pleading mistaken force in private defence. Leverick claims that there is a compelling justification for requiring any mistaken belief about the circumstances to be reasonable where force is used in private defence against another person:

> In acting upon an unreasonable belief in an imminent attack, the accused displays a lack of respect and concern for the life or bodily integrity of another. He has killed or injured someone who, in reality, posed no threat whatsoever or gave any reason to suppose he was doing so.[76]

Leverick's view is that Scots law takes the correct approach in this respect: 'a person who claims that he acted in self-defence … because he believed that he was in imminent danger must have had reasonable grounds for his belief'.[77] Scots law adopts what might be called the 'reasonable belief' approach. Many other jurisdictions do the same: for example, the law in nearly every United States jurisdiction is that 'one can only use a certain degree of force in self-defense if one honestly and reasonably believes that a serious enough threat has been posed, and if one honestly and reasonably believes that the use of force in self-defense is necessary to prevent that threat'.[78]

We agree with the approach that these jurisdictions take to unreasonable mistakes about the need for private defence. As George Fletcher puts it, a defendant who relies upon a mistake is making an excuse: 'It follows that the conditions for excusing wrongful conduct must themselves be free of grounds for blaming the actor. Yet if his or her mistake reflects an unreasonable and irrational judgment of the facts, the conditions of the excuses are hardly fault-free'.[79] Fletcher's point is that mistaken perceptions of consent can lead to liability in rape cases, and that '[t]here is no less need to sanction thoughtless, negligent overreaction in cases of self defense'.[80] The negligent mistake is the grounds 'for blaming the person who claims his wrongdoing is excused'.[81] While we agree with this point, we believe that simply reforming the English law dealing with private defence to require any mistaken belief to be based upon reasonable grounds would not go far enough. We believe that English law should also recognise a general defence of reasonable mistake, and that a defendant who made a reasonable mistake about the existence of exculpatory factors should fall within the scope of this defence even if the mistake was attributable to matters such as voluntary intoxication and insanity. At present, a defence of 'acting reasonably' under Section 50 of the Serious Crime Act 2007 is available to charges of encouraging or assisting crime under that Act, and one of the circumstances to which it applies is where D acts on the basis of a reasonable mistaken belief about the circumstances; but there is no equivalent general defence for those charged with other offences. We do not propose that Section 50 should be extended to apply to all offences, nor that its reversed burden of proof and other intricacies should apply to the new general defence, since the wording and scope of Section 50 has been subjected to criticism,[82] and introducing more grounds for potential human rights challenges to this area of law would be far from ideal! The burden of proof should remain on the prosecution to disprove the new defence beyond reasonable doubt. Our proposed defence would apply to all criminal offences except where excluded by statute, and would set a base-line threshold for criminal liability. As we have seen, the result would be the removal of many of the issues with the current law which we have identified in this chapter.

---

76 See (n 28) 103.
77 *Lieser v HM Advocate* [2008] HCJAC 42, 2008 SLT 866 [7].
78 K Simons, 'Self-Defence: Reasonable Beliefs or Reasonable Self-Control?' (2008) 11 New Crim L Rev 51, 52–53.
79 G Fletcher, 'The Psychotic Aggressor – A Generation Later' (1993) 27 Israel L Rev 227, 240–241.
80 ibid 241.
81 ibid.
82 See, e.g., A Simester, G Sullivan, J Spencer, and G Virgo, *Simester and Sullivan's Criminal Law: Theory and Doctrine* (4th edn, Hart 2010) 298–299, and C de Than and R Heaton (n 7) 542.

Conclusion

Critics may find it difficult to believe that people make reasonable mistakes which lead them to act under mistaken private defence, and academic examples such as those we have used in this chapter may appear unlikely. However our examples are based on real events and hence there is evidence to support a general defence of reasonable mistake in this context; e.g., police in Harrogate were called to deal with an 'axe attack' which turned out to be a scene of a zombie film,[83] and the father of one of the present authors reasonably believed he was being shot at by a gunman on the steps of the British Museum, only realising that something strange was going on when a mummy staggered past him, trailing bandages.[84]

The current position in English law is indefensible: sometimes a defendant who makes a reasonable mistake cannot argue private defence, and in other cases a defendant who makes an unreasonable mistake is entitled to a complete acquittal. The law currently allows a staggering number of concessions for some defendants, going as far as householders being entitled to an acquittal for *pre-emptive* use of *excessive* force on the basis of what is an *unreasonable* mistake about the circumstances even when judged *in the heat of the moment*, where the perceived attacker poses no real threat whatsoever. The best way forward is a statutory reform to recognise a general defence of reasonable mistake, with similarities to Section 50 of the Serious Crime Act 2007, but available to those charged with full offences as well as assisting or encouraging crime. Such a defence would act as a safety net to ensure that reasonable behaviour is not criminalised, regardless of other attributes of the defendant such as legal insanity or intoxication. We should not be seeking to deny private defence to people merely to enable their detention or treatment, especially in the light of Article 5 of the European Convention on Human Rights[85] and the United Nations Convention on the Rights of Persons with Disabilities, in circumstances where a person without their mental characteristics would be acquitted. This would also create greater synergy between the relevant principles of criminal law and tort. Consideration should also be given to methods by which the remaining gaps in authority in tort in relation to private defence may be plugged, and it may be time for Parliament to think again about the wisdom of the householder provisions.

---

83   '999 Call Over "Axe Attack" Has Happy Ending' The Guardian (London, 3 January 2014).

84   It appears to be a de Than family trait to wander onto film sets, with resultant accidental cameo performances.

85   See *Winterwerp v Netherlands* [1979] 2 EHRR 387: the burden of proof rests on the authorities to show that the mental state of the individual is so serious that only compulsory confinement is the appropriate step to take in the circumstances. There is also a potential discrimination issue.

Chapter 10

Statutory Defences of Reasonableness: Inexcusable Uncertainty or Reasonable Pragmatism

Christopher J. Newman

There are a number of criminal offences within the legal system of England and Wales where the defendant can rely on the reasonableness of his actions to exculpate conduct which otherwise would have attracted criminal liability. Sitting outside of the usual discussions on general defences,[1] this chapter will examine the operation of those circumstances that are not applicable to the criminal law as a whole, but instead focus on the statutory provisions, where Parliament has seen fit to incorporate a specific reasonableness or reasonable excuse defence in respect of the parent offence. This discussion will examine the operation of these individually applicable, statutory defences through twin prisms. Offences regulating the unlawful possession of weapons and terrorist information will be juxtaposed against the operation of the reasonableness defence as it is found in low-level public order offences.

Whilst the scope of these offences covers very different activities and the selection may appear somewhat arbitrary, it is submitted that they have a degree of commonality in their nature and function in so far as they are strict liability offences augmented with a reasonable excuse defence. As well as employing traditional criminal doctrine, it is impossible to ignore the further effect to the rights enunciated in the ECHR[2] by means of the Human Rights Act 1998. The impact of Human Rights jurisprudence cannot be ignored in this context and will form a critical part of the examination of the operation of the defence of reasonableness.

It is hypothesized that the abdication of responsibility by the drafters of statutes that employ the 'reasonableness' defence places an undue interpretive burden upon the police and lower courts. In turn, the failure of the legislators to provide further clarity as to the contours of reasonableness has resulted in these bodies indulging in an ad-hoc limitation of acceptable excuses to the point where the integrity and meaning defence may well be being compromised. This chapter will therefore conduct an evaluation of a number of statutes which employ defences that require the defendant to establish that her actions were reasonable, and establish whether such requirements are a dereliction of duty by legislators, leaving citizens uncertain as to when their actions will be accepted as reasonable.

Classification Conundrum: Statutory Defences and Criminal Doctrine

Criminal law theorists have tended to focus on the operation and scope of reasonable excuse in those areas 'we often see as the core of criminal behaviour (intentional acts of murder, assault, rape, robbery, theft, etc.)'.[3] Whilst conviction for such an offence has severe consequences for the defendant, it is equally submitted that these areas are extremely well served by the panoply of writing on this subject.[4] In any event, general

---

1   See, for example, Paul H Robinson, 'Criminal Law Defenses: A Systematic Analysis' (1982) Colum L Rev 199; Glanville Williams, 'Offences and Defences' (1982) 2 LS 233; RA Duff, *Answering for Crime – Responsibility and Liability in the Criminal Law* (Hart Publishing 2007); John Gardner, *Offences and Defences* (OUP 2007).

2   European Convention for the Protection of Human Rights and Fundamental Freedoms (1953) (Cmd 8969), as given further effect by the Human Rights Act 1998.

3   Tatjana Hornle, 'Social Expectation in the Criminal Law: The Reasonable Person in a Comparative Perspective' (2008) 11 New Crim L Rev 1, 5.

4   In particular Robinson (n 1).

exculpatory and non-exculpatory defences cover these areas.[5] This inquiry will examine those provisions that ATH Smith would refer to as 'nuisances on the outer margins of criminality',[6] legislative provisions governing low-level public order and the carrying of offensive weapons. Such legislation potentially extends the tendrils of the criminal law into behaviour that is arbitrarily determined to be undesirable by the police and the lower courts. These concerns are compounded when taken alongside the large number of people affected by legislation that has the potential to be used in a capricious or arbitrary fashion.

The defences that operate within statutes 'impose a legal or persuasive burden on a defendant in criminal proceedings to prove the matters respectively specified in those subsections if he is to be exonerated from liability on the grounds there provided'.[7] Students of criminal doctrine will be familiar with the debate as to whether justification or excuse is inherent within the *actus reus* of the offence.[8] The antithetical view, that a criminal offence has three essential elements, the *actus reus*, *mens rea*, and the subsequent absence of a valid defence,[9] seems to fit nicely around the statutory model for a reasonableness defence. At this juncture, it is also helpful to consider the classification of defences as outlined by Professor Robinson.[10] According to this taxonomy, a reasonableness defence included in the statute would fall into the category of 'offence modification defences' that 'modifies or refines the criminalization decision embodied in the definition of a particular offence'.[11] A traditional, doctrinal discussion as to whether statutory defences are of an excusatory or a justificatory nature is therefore not wholly significant.

It is significant that the classification of the statutory defence must be considered alongside the criminal trial and the burden of proof. Where statutory defences are relied upon, the burden of proving any 'excuse' shall fall upon the defendant.[12] According to Lord Bingham, 'that means that [the defendant] must, to be exonerated, establish those matters on the balance of probabilities. If he fails to discharge that burden he will be convicted'[13] It was established in *Lambert*[14] that the Higher Courts have deliberately eschewed laying general principles in this respect in favour of deciding each individual case according to its merits.[15] The House of Lords in *Sheldrake* went further and considered the extent to which these reverse onus of proof provisions interfere with a defendant's right to be presumed innocent until proven guilty as provided for in Article 6(2) of the European Convention on Human Rights (ECHR). Their Lordships held that placing a legal burden on the accused does engage Article 6(2) of the Convention but does not necessarily mean that there will be a violation. Lord Bingham stated that this 'cannot be resolved by any rule of thumb, but on examination of all the facts and circumstances of the particular provision as applied in the particular case'.[16]

Compliance with the Convention does not liberate reverse onus provisions from criticism, especially when considering the lower-level offences under discussion. The court in *Sheldrake* identified three major factors which courts should be mindful of when considering the proportionality of reverse onus provisions: maximum penalty, danger of convicting the innocent and the ease of the prosecution proving the offence. The second consideration outlined by Lord Bingham, the conviction of a non-blameworthy defendant, will

---

5   Although the focus of this discussion is reasonableness, the general defences available within the criminal law with regard to capacity, such as insanity, automatism and infancy apply equally to low-level public order offences and possession offences as they do to the more serious counterparts. The situation applies equally to the so-called general defences in respect of necessity/duress, prevention of crime and self-defence. As with the capacity based offences, whilst there is a lack of case law on the doctrine of self-defence operating within low-level public order, it is almost inconceivable that these two issues have not overlapped. Like insanity, it is suggested that this lack of litigation is due to police and prosecutorial discretion.

6   ATH Smith, *Offences Against Public Order* (Sweet & Maxwell 1987) 1.

7   *Sheldrake v DPP* [2004] UKHL 43, 1.

8   Glanville Williams, *Textbook of Criminal Law* (2nd edn, Stevens & Sons 1983).

9   DJ Lanham, 'Larsonneur Revisited' [1976] Criml L Rev 276–281.

10   Robinson (n 1) 203.

11   ibid 203.

12   See Meredith Blake and Andrew Ashworth, 'The Presumption of Innocence in English Criminal Law' [1996] Crim LR 306.

13   *Sheldrake* (n 7) 1.

14   [2001] UKHL 37.

15   The ambiguity of this area is explored in Ian Dennis, 'Reverse Onuses and the Presumption of Innocence: In Search of Principle. [2005] Crim LR 901.

16   *Sheldrake* (n 7) 21.

be considered at length elsewhere. Suffice to say that in many cases, the evidence of the low-level offence may well be entirely based around statements of police officers.[17] In such cases, imposing a probative burden on the defendant is imbued with practical difficulties. Accordingly there is a close link with Lord Bingham's third factor: ease of prosecution. Professor Ashworth, in his commentary on *Sheldrake* questions the appropriateness of this consideration 'making a case easier for the prosecution to prove is not a major reason for upholding a reverse onus'.[18] The concern regarding the imposition of a reverse onus provision is even more prescient when considered against the aforementioned dependence of many low-level convictions entirely upon police-based evidence.

Perhaps most disturbing, is the notion in the first of these considerations; that the more severe the potential punishment, the more careful a court should be about imposing a reverse onus provision. At first glance, this would seem to be prudent; indeed, Ashworth states, 'It ought surely to be insisted that, where deprivation of liberty is a possible penalty, there is no place for a reversal of the burden of proof'.[19] The implication is that lower down the scale of criminality a disproportionate burden is somehow more acceptable is, seemingly, a recurring fault line within the criminal justice system. It is accepted that the consequences of conviction for low-level offences are not as serious as loss of liberty or even the threat of such through a suspended custodial sentence. The stigma of criminality, even for a low-level offence can be a serious punishment of itself. In addition, it is submitted the lower-level offences are ubiquitous; while the scale of the injustice may be smaller, the number of occurrences may be immeasurably higher.

Softening Strict Liability: Reasonableness and Regulation

An examination of the statutes that employ a reasonableness defence illustrates that a great many of them are strict liability offences,[20] whilst there is considerable disagreement amongst criminal theorists as to when criminal liability should be classified as 'strict',[21] for the purpose of this inquiry, the term refers to offences which have *actus reus*, but in relation to one or more elements of the *actus reus*, there is no corresponding *mens rea* element.[22] These statutes mollify their apparent regulatory harshness by the inclusion of the aforementioned reasonableness excuse.

To try and deal with every individual offence would be unworkable.[23] This inquiry will restrict itself to a particular subset of offences concerning possession of objects that the state does not wish an individual to possess such as information relating to terrorism,[24] firearms,[25] and offensive weapons.[26] These offences, sit on the boundary between criminality and regulation and the defence of reasonableness 'applies at the fulcrum of honest belief in prevailing circumstances. It ameliorates the harshness of liability without fault contrary to legislative intent',[27] and this is illustrated in a number of different circumstances.

---

17   Richard Card, *Public Order Law* (Jordans 2000) 142–143.

18   Andrew Ashworth, 'Burden of Proof: Whether Reverse Burden of Proof in Road Traffic and Terrorism Legislation Incompatible With the Presumption of Innocence in Art.6(2) of the European Convention on Human Rights: Case Comment' *Sheldrake v DPP* [2005] Crim LR 218, 219 (note).

19   Andrew Ashworth, 'Four Threats to the Presumption of Innocence' (2006) 10 Int'l J Evid & Proof 241, 262.

20   For a detailed discussion on the ambit of strict liability and the operation within the criminal law, see Jeremy Horder, 'Strict Liability, Statutory Construction and the Spirit of Liberty' (2002) 118 LQR 458; Douglas Husak, 'Varieties of Strict Liability' (1995) 8 Can J L & Juris 189.

21   Andrew Ashworth & Jeremy Horder, *Principles of Criminal Law* (7th edn, OUP 2013) 160. Indeed, Husak identifies at least seven different variants of strict liability offences. (n 20) 458.

22   The definition used here is taken from Andrew Simester, Robert Sullivan, John Spencer and Graham Virgo, *Criminal Law: Theory and Doctrine* (4th edn, Hart Publishing 2010) 173.

23   It has been identified that, within the English legal system there are a considerable number of offences that incorporate reasonable excuse, see Christopher J Newman & Ben Middleton, 'Any Excuse for Certainty: English Perspectives on the Defence of Reasonable Excuse' (2010) 74 JCL 472, 472.

24   Specifically, Terrorism Act, ss 38B 57 and 58.

25   Firearms Act 1968, s 19.

26   Prevention of Crime Act 1953, s 1.

27   Alan Reed, 'Strict Liability and Reasonable Excuse: Case Comment', *R v Unah* [2011] EWCA Crim 1837, (2012) 76 JCL 293, 297 (note).

Public safety provides the clearest rationale for the employment of pseudo-criminal, regulatory offences.[28] This is particularly germane with respect to the possession of firearms and offensive weapons. Whilst legislation regulating the control of firearms encompasses a range of different offences,[29] it is recognised by the courts that that legislative intention is to create offences of strict liability.[30] It has also been held that where the statute introduces a defence of reasonable excuse,[31] unless expressly provided for by that statute, that this defence will impose a legal (persuasive) burden rather than a mere evidential one.[32] The scope of excuses that have been permitted by courts in relation to possession of firearms has been narrowly construed. *Ross v Collins*[33] held that possession of a shotgun in a public place, even with a valid firearms certificate was not a lawful authority, and accordingly a mistaken belief in having a lawful authority did not provide the defendant with a reasonable excuse.

English court[34] have acknowledged that a relationship exists between reasonable excuse in terms of legislation seeking to control possession of firearms and provisions designed to control the proliferation of offensive weapons generally.[35] This helps broaden the visible contours of reasonable excuse in so far as they intersect with two distinct but synergistic strict liability offences. Recognising the apparent social utility of restricting possession of these items, Gage J was explicit about the approach of the courts in *Densu*,[36] stating: 'The cases where the defence of reasonable excuse will be available are restricted … (it) is not permissible is for a lack of knowledge to be coupled with an explanation for the use of the weapon so as in combination to provide a reasonable excuse'.[37] Indeed, a lack of knowledge of the nature of the weapon will not be a reasonable excuse to possessing it—to that extent there is unanimity in the case law and a rare, if valuable, thread that weaves throughout such cases.

Densu did not settle the matter unequivocally and the High Court was called in *Patterson*[38] to consider the reasonableness of possession of a butterfly knife because the defendant required it for his work of feeding and stabling horses. The defendant stated that he had intended to deposit it in a safe place during the day but had been unable to do so. Whilst considering *Densu*, Sibler J seemed to open the door for less restrictive interpretation of what constituted a reasonable excuse when stating 'if, as I consider to be the case, Parliament had intended to give the fact-finders a wide discretion to determine whether some matter was a "reasonable excuse", they would have used precisely the words that they had actually used'.[39] Collins J added a cautionary

---

28   Despite being an understandable rationale, the current construction of firearms legislation, specifically the use of strict liability offences and severe custodial sentences has been the subject of severe criticism from commentators. See Andrew Ashworth, 'Editorial: Firearms and Justice' [2013] Crim LR 447.

29   'As was stated in *Bewley* [2012] EWCA Crim 1457 the 1968 Act and the 1982 Act may be regarded as a single code. The 2006 Act (and ancillary Regulations) may itself also be regarded as part of the evolving intention of Parliament with regard to the ever present, and ever increasing, menace of firearms, imitation or otherwise'. *R v Williams (Orette)* [2012] EWCA Crim 2162 [17] (Davis LJ).

30   ibid *Williams (Orette)* 18.

31   For example, Firearms Act, s 19, which states, *inter alia*, that a person commits an offence if, without lawful authority or reasonable excuse (the proof whereof lies on him) he has a firearm with him in a public place.

32   In *R v McCalla* (1988) 87 Cr App R 372, this was expressed in the following terms: 'If the defendant himself proves that he had some lawful authority or reasonable excuse for having the offensive weapon with him, he is to be acquitted. I say if he proves it, because the Act of Parliament says that the proof of that particular lawful authority or reasonable excuse lies on him. It does not mean that he has to prove it as the prosecution have to prove, beyond reasonable doubt or so that you are sure. It means that he has to prove lawful authority or reasonable excuse on the balance of probabilities; in other words, it is more likely than not that facts exist which constitute lawful authority or reasonable excuse'. [375] (May LJ).

33   [1982] Crim LR 368 DC.

34   *R v Jones (Terence)* [1995] QB 235, 241.

35   Prevention of Crime Act 1953, s 1(4) defines an offensive weapon as any article made or adapted for use for causing injury to the person, or intended by the person having it with him for such use by him or by some other person.

36   *R v Densu* [1998] 1 Cr App R 400.

37   ibid [405] (Gage J).

38   *DPP v Patterson* [2004] EWHC 2744 (Admin).

39   ibid [17] Sibler J.

note, that whilst the wording of the statute meant it was open for the finders of fact to find a reasonable excuse, the appellant was fortunate that they had done so and that such a finding would be extremely rare.[40]

Reasonable Excuse and the Counter Terrorist Paradigm

Whilst heartening, there should be a limit as to how much one attaches to the apparent congruity of judicial reasoning in this area. Legislation regulating possession of firearms and offensive weapons are of the same genus. It is, perhaps understandable that reasonableness within that genus should have coherence. The question arises whether such structural integrity is maintained when the ambit is extended to cover possession of material within the corpus of counter-terrorism offences. Section 58 of the Terrorism Act 2000 provides that a person will commit an offence if he collects or makes a record of information of a kind likely to be useful to a person committing or preparing an act of terrorism and also of possessing a document or record.[41] As with the previous offences under discussion, the statute provides that it is a defence for a person charged with an offence under Section 58 to prove that he had a reasonable excuse for his collection or possession of the material.[42]

This offence provides a suitable analogue as it fulfils a broadly similar role to the legislation controlling firearms and offensive weapons. Of greatest significance, is that the provisions of Section 58 of the 2000 Act differ from the firearms and offensive weapons offences in that, as discussed in *R v G; R v J*, they: 'cover a multitude of records of everyday common or garden information, which might actually be useful to a person who was preparing to carry out an act of terrorism'.[43] The operation of the defence of reasonable excuse within a terrorism context has been the subject of extensive judicial discussion[44] and is worth considering in the context of this inquiry.[45]

The defendant, J, had possession of electronic files relating to jihad training and was charged, *inter alia,* under Section 58 of the 2000 Act. When interviewed, J stated that he had acquired the material as a result of searching for information about a military career in his home country of Gambia and also out of a desire to learn more about the Islamic faith. After initially pleading guilty, J vacated those guilty pleas following the decision of the Court of Appeal in *R v K*,[46] where Lord Phillips had stated:

> As for the nature of a 'reasonable excuse', it seems to us that this is simply an explanation that the document or record is possessed for a purpose other than to assist in the commission or preparation of an act of terrorism. It matters not that that other purpose may infringe some other provision of the criminal or civil law".[47]

---

40   'I entirely accept that it will be an exceedingly rare case in relation to an object which is an offensive weapon per se that, absent some sort of necessity or some immediate temporal connection between the possession of the object and the innocent purpose for which it is being carried, that the Tribunal of fact will be persuaded that there is a reasonable excuse. For my part I think that this respondent was exceedingly fortunate in the decision on the facts that the Justices reached However, I cannot say that it was a decision which they were unable, as a matter of law, to reach'. ibid [25, 26] (Collins J).

41   Terrorism Act 2000, s 58(1).

42   Terrorism Act 2000, s 58(3).

43   *R v G; R v J* [2009] UKHL 13 [42].

44   In *R v G; R v J*, the House of Lords considered two unrelated appeals which concerned the relationship between s 57 and s 58 of the 2000 Act. Much of the appeal focused on differentiating the purpose of the two provisions. According to Ormerod, 'Section 58 focuses on the nature of the information. Section 57 focuses on the circumstances in which D possesses the article … it is clear that the offences do overlap'. David Ormerod, 'Terrorism Act 2000 ss. 57 and 58 – scope of offences – defences under ss. 57(2) and 58(3): Case Comment' *R v G; R v J* [2009] UKHL 13, Crim LR 679, 683 (note). Accordingly, in order to avoid conflating the two offences, so far as it is possible, discussion will be restricted herein to the offence under s 58 of the 2000 Act.

45   Newman and Middleton (n 23) 477–480.

46   [2008] EWCA Crim 185.

47   ibid [15].

The Court of Appeal[48] allowed J to vacate his guilty plea and dismissed the Crown's appeal on the grounds that it was bound by the decision in *K*. The Crown appealed to the House of Lords asking, inter alia, to identify the scope of the defence contained in Section 58(3).[49]

Their Lordships first identified that for conviction under Section 58(1) it was not necessary for the defendant to have a terrorist purpose. What was needed for conviction was the defendant to be in control of a record, which contained information likely to provide practical assistance to a person preparing to or committing a terrorist act, for the defendant to know that he had that record and that he knew the kind of information that the record contained. If the prosecution establishes these three elements, then the defendant is liable to be convicted unless the defence of reasonable excuse can be established.[50]

J argued that Section 118(2) of the 2000 Act applied and that if a person adduces evidence, which is sufficient to raise an issue with respect to the matter the court or jury shall assume that the defence is satisfied unless the prosecution proves beyond reasonable doubt that it is not. The court referring back to the component elements of the offence under Section 58(1), stating that if Section 118(2) did apply, then the prosecution must prove beyond reasonable doubt that D's possession of the article was for a purpose connected with an act of terrorism. Their Lordships stated that doing this would be to misapply Section 118(2) and 'to mix up what the Crown has to prove in order to establish the offence and what the Crown has to prove in order to rebut the defence'.

When addressing the scope of the defence of reasonable excuse, the court made the following point that is worth considering in full:

> A defence in terms of reasonable excuse is to be found in a whole range of provisions under the 2000 Act. And it is, of course, a familiar feature of many other offences, such as possession of an offensive weapon under section 1(1) of the Prevention of Crime Act 1953 and section 47(1) of the Criminal Law (Consolidation) (Scotland) Act 1995, and failure to provide a specimen of blood or urine under section 7(6) of the Road Traffic 1988. The Court of Appeal's decision in R v K[2008] 2 WLR 1026, 1031, para 15, singles out this particular use of the defence in section 58(3) and imposes on it a construction which is utterly different from the construction which has been put on the equivalent defence in other statutes.[51]

The court then goes on to give numerous examples as to what may, or may not be a reasonable excuse. Gratifyingly, the judgment explicitly stated that an unlawful excuse for possessing the information, such as possessing plans of a politicians dwelling for the purpose of burglary rather than terrorism, could not be 'reasonable' in all of the circumstances.[52]

The case of *G* provides some much needed and well directed judicial discourse on the operation of reasonable excuse defences. This did not prevent the appeal in *AY*,[53] a case that once again involved a lower court requiring clarification on the ambit of the reasonable excuse defence found in Section 58(3) of the 2000 Act.[54] The defendant had been charged with four counts of possessing documents which, when judged objectively, are likely to be of practical use to terrorists. The defendant stated, *inter alia*, that he believed the information might be useful in defending those people who supported the Islamic Courts Union (ICU) in Somalia. It was claimed that these people were the victims of unlawful force and he believed that the

---

48   [2008] EWCA Crim 1161.

49   *R v G* (n 43) [37].

50   ibid [50].

51   ibid (n 49) [76].

52   'Of course, if accepted, the explanation would show that the accused's purpose was not to commit an act of terrorism. But that is not the issue under section 58. Under section 58(1), the mere fact that the defendant's purpose was not to commit an act of terrorism is neutral. What he has to show is that he had an objectively reasonable excuse for possessing something which Parliament has made it, prima facie, a crime for him to possess because of its potential utility to a terrorist. An intention to use information in connection with a bank robbery may well be an explanation of why the defendant had the information, but it cannot be a 'reasonable' excuse for having it. So the accused would be guilty of the section 58(1) offence'. ibid (n 49) [79].

53   *R v AY* [2010] EWCA Crim 762.

54   In this case, it was an interlocutory appeal brought by the Crown concerning the ruling of law made by the trial judge at a preparatory hearing prior to the retrial of the defendant.

information would be able to be used in self-defence and resisting the unlawful occupation.[55] The defendant furthermore added that at the time of his arrest, he no longer had any intention to use the information. The Crown had argued that the bounds of reasonable excuse did not extend to the purpose for which the defendant held the material (the purpose argument) and that the reasonable excuse should be limited to the possession of the material rather than the use that the defendant was intending to make of the material (the deployment argument).[56]

The Court of Appeal dismissed the appeal by the Crown. Professor Walker, in his commentary on the case highlighted that a defendant's purpose remains relevant to a defence of reasonable excuse and this was acknowledged by the judgment of Hughes LJ.[57] In respect of the way in which the information might be deployed, the use of violence against any foreign state and whether this can ever been considered a reasonable excuse has been considered a number of times. Walker indicates that the preceding case law[58] suggested that such an excuse would not be accepted.[59] The Court of Appeal in this case did not go so far as to legitimise this excuse, what Hughes LJ did affirm was that the defence could only be removed from the consideration of the jury only if the excuse is one which is incapable of being held by the jury to be a reasonable excuse. Their Lordships decided that as the Crown had accepted that:

> self-defence might be relevant in the case of an act which would be within the definition of an act of terrorism or in that of a terrorist offence, the proposed element of the defence could not be withdrawn only on the ground that it involved the proposition that the information might be used "in the field"[60]

Both *G* and *AY* acknowledge that 'there are outer limits where the courts will declare that patently unlawful actions can never be accepted as reasonable'.[61] Whilst there is no explicit reference made in either case, this approach can be seen as part of a thread running through the possessory offences, as they relate to both terrorism and firearms/offensive weapons, which can be traced back at least as far as *Ross v Collins*. This serves to place only the broadest parameters by which reasonable excuse can be discerned. This would appear to be of only peripheral utility to the thousands of cases where reasonable excuse is used by defendants in summary trials and is a recurring theme when considering the operation of reasonableness as a specific defence within English statute-based criminal law.

The question of reasonableness does not end with regulatory offences. Within low-level public order law, there is still a regulatory element, even without considering rights based discourse, any examination of the reasonableness of prohibited behaviour becomes an inherently subjective decision on the part of the police and the finder of fact. In order to establish the different contours of reasonableness within this field it will be necessary to examine the operative statutory provisions in some detail. Significantly, the definition of the term 'public order' itself is somewhat elusive.[62] There does appear to be consensus in respect of the broad statements of behaviour that low-level public order law seeks to prohibit.[63] If the wider criminal law is employed to protect members of society from 'harm', Smith states:

> The interests protected by public order law are diffuse and indeterminate. Public order law ranges in its extent from the preservation of mere peace and tranquility as between rowing neighbour or preventing unreasonable street exhibitionism – nuisances on the outer margins of criminality ... to serious outbreaks of disorder amounting to riot (whereby) the constitutional stability of the country seems threatened. [64]

---

55   ibid (n 53) [5].
56   ibid (n 53) [15].
57   Clive Walker, '*R. v AY*: Terrorism – Possessing Document or Record Containing Information Likely to be Useful to Person Committing or Preparing Act of Terrorism: Case Comment' [2010] Crim LR 882, 884 (note).
58   See, for example, *R v Jones* [2006] UKHL 16, *R v Rowe* [2007] EWCA Crim 635, *R v F* [2007] EWCA Crim 243.
59   *Walker* (n 57) 885.
60   *AY* (n 53) [26].
61   *Walker* (n 57) 884.
62   See, for example, the discussion in Card (n 17) 1–7.
63   Card (n 17) 1.
64   Smith (n 6) 1.

Commentators on criminal doctrine have acknowledged the ambiguity inherent within offences that punish behaviour on the margins of criminality simply because it causes offence:

> With conduct that is supposedly offensive one must ... ask: why does the actor deserve censure? If the essence of the offence is merely that conduct displeases many people, then it is not clear the wrongdoing has occurred at all. "I don't like it" should never suffice as a basis for criminalization regardless of the numbers who say it. [65]

The operative statutory provision under consideration, and one which is used primarily to deal with the lowest level public order offences within England and Wales, is to be found under Section 5 of the Public Order Act 1986. This, *inter alia*, provides that a person is guilty of an offence if he uses threatening or abusive[66] words or behaviour or disorderly behaviour, or displays any writing, sign or other visible representation which is threatening or abusive within sight or hearing of a person likely to be caused harassment alarm or distress.[67]

The *actus reus* of Section 5 is that the conduct[68] of the accused must be within the sight or hearing of someone likely to be caused harassment, alarm or distress.[69] There is no need for the conduct to be directed at any particular victim but (unlike other more serious offences under the 1986 Act[70]) the person who is likely to be caused harassment, alarm or distress must actually witness the conduct, even if it is by CCTV[71] or on the Internet.[72] The *mens rea*, found in Section 6(4) of the 1986 Act, is that the accused must either intend his words or behaviour to be threatening, abusive or insulting or intend his conduct to be disorderly or be aware that it may be.[73]

The range of conduct that is prohibited includes disorderly behaviour. In *Chambers & Edwards*,[74] it was held that whether the conduct was disorderly was a question of fact to be determined by the court depending on the circumstances of the case. It is assumed, in reaching this decision, the word disorderly is to be given its natural meaning.[75] The *mens rea* of Section 5 requires proof either that the defendant intended his conduct to be threatening, abusive or insulting or disorderly or that he was aware that it might be so.[76] Professor Ormerod asserts that, at its lowest, this requires proof of an awareness of a possibility.[77]

Section 5 of the 1986 Act integrates specific defences within the various low-level provisions. These defences, as with the previous offences under discussion, mandate that the defendant acknowledges (or at least does not dispute) the commission of the *actus reus* with the appropriate *mens rea* but then seeks to assert one of the following: either he had no reason to believe that his conduct was within the sight or hearing of a person who might be caused harassment, alarm or distress,[78] or that the accused was in a dwelling and had no reason to believe that his conduct could be heard or seen by anyone outside that or any other dwelling.[79]

The most controversial of the specific defences, and the one which of most significance to this inquiry, is to be found under Section 5(3)(c) of the 1986 Act. This provides that it is a defence for the accused to prove that his conduct was reasonable.[80] It can be stated, in broad terms,[81] that as with the other defences under

---

65   Simester (n 22) 646.

66   The previous requirement that behaviour be 'threatening, abusive or insulting' was modified by Crime and Courts Act 2013, s 57(2), where the requirement for the behaviour was amended to 'threatening or abusive'.

67   Public Order Act 1986, s 5(1).

68   Either the words or behaviour or disorderly behaviour according to s 5(1).

69   For further exploration of these concepts, see Peter Thornton, The Law of Public Order and Protest (OUP 2010) 36–49.

70   See, for example, the requirement under Public Order Act 1986 s 3(2).

71   *Rogers v DPP* (1999), unreported 22 July DC as cited in David Ormerod, *Smith & Hogan's Criminal Law* (13th edn, OUP 2011) 1075.

72   *S v Crown Prosecution Service* [2008] EWHC 438 (Admin) 2008 WL 924.

73   *DPP v Clarke* (1991) 94 Cr App R 359.

74   [1995] Crim LR 896.

75   Ormerod (n 71) 1074.

76   Public Order Act 1986, s 6(3).

77   Ormerod (n 71) 1075.

78   Public Order Act 1986, s 5 (3)(a).

79   Public Order Act 1986, s 5 (3)(b).

80   Public Order Act, s 5 (3)(c).

81   Card (n 17) 140.

discussion, this is intended to provide an exemption for the commission of the offence where a criminal conviction is inappropriate. As with the other reasonableness provisions under consideration, the defence under Section 5(3)(c) of the 1986 Act is a reverse onus provision. In this case, proof of reasonable conduct requires the accused to adduce and prove evidence of the circumstances that relied on at the time. He then has to prove, on the balance of probabilities, that in those proven circumstances, his conduct was reasonable.[82]

As can be seen from the description of the elements of the offence above, once a police officer decides that it necessary to arrest an individual under Section 5, the court will then make a decision as to whether the defendant's behaviour was *in fact* threatening or abusive. Once that determination is made, all that is left for the prosecution to show is that the conduct occurred within the within the sight or hearing[83] of a person who might be caused harassment, alarm or distress. Should the defendant wish to claim that his conduct was reasonable, he would have to prove this on the balance of probabilities. As has been previously identified, where the accused imports a sufficiency of circumstance or even sufficiency of motive, which is accepted by the finders of fact, despite the ingredients of the offence being made out, the defendant will be acquitted.[84]

The nature of the reverse onus provision and the nature of the assertion being made[85] see the courts make use of an objective test to determine the nature of the conduct.[86] This, potentially harsh test, is mitigated by the finding of the court in *DPP v Clarke*.[87] Nolan LJ stated, in respect of the required mental element, that

> the question whether the defendant had the intention or awareness which is required as a condition of guilt under section 6(4) can only be answered subjectively by reference to the state of mind of that defendant. The state of mind of a defendant must be judged in the light of the whole of the evidence (including, most particularly, the evidence of the defendant himself, if he chooses to give it) concerning his words and behaviour and the surrounding circumstances. [88]

Unsurprisingly, given the approaches adopted in respect of the firearms and terrorism offences outlined above, the Public Order Act offers no guidance as to what is considered to be reasonable conduct, leaving the determination to be a finding of fact. As one would expect from the attitude of the court in *G*, the case law provides individual examples of when conduct will be reasonable but little by way of general principles that a legal adviser could extrapolate for a client. It is with such practical considerations in mind that it becomes germane to consider the reach of these low-level offences. Some statistics are available from the first decade of the twenty first century,[89] which show 196,687 convictions under Section 5 between 2000 and 2009. This indicates a widespread usage of Section 5 of the 1986 Act by the police. It should also be noted that these figures only speak of convictions. There is no mention as regards the number of arrests, nor of the other disposals such as cautions, penalty notice for disorder and decisions to take no further police action.

Such widespread usage serves to emphasise the aforementioned ubiquity of these low-level offences and reinforce the extent to which large numbers of people are liable for criminal conviction based on little more than the capricious whim of either the police or the finders of fact. Given these figures, the reasonableness defence needs to provide a crucial buttress against arbitrary criminalization of low-level behaviour. Unfortunately an examination of the case law would suggest that the interpretation of reasonableness of conduct by the courts is far from consistent.

In *Poku*,[90] the defendant had been selling ice creams from his van without a street licence. A police officer stated that he would be reported for unlicensed street trading and that the local authority was empowered

---

82   Card (n 17) 142.

83   The prosecution does not have to show that the words or disorderly conduct was actually seen or heard but there must be a potential victim rather than a hypothetical one. See Thornton (n 69) 39.

84   Newman & Middleton (n 23) 476.

85   *Le Vine v DPP* [2010] EWHC 1128 Admin.

86   *Brutus v Cozens* [1973] AC 854.

87   (1992) 94 Cr App R 359.

88   ibid [12].

89   Taken from written statements and answers 20 December 2010, written question by Dominic Raab (Esher & Walton) Cons <http://www.theyworkforyou.com/wrans/?id=2010–12–20b.30917.h>.

90   *Poku (Kwasi) v DPP* [1993] Crim LR 705.

to seize the van as evidence of the unlawful trading. The defendant pushed the police officer away, saying: 'You're not taking my fucking van'. With the prosecution having proved the elements of the offence, the defendant put forward that, given the fact that his van was being taken unlawfully, his language and conduct to try and prevent this had been reasonable. The Queens Bench Division Divisional Court accepted that the response to a false threat by the police in the circumstances was reasonable.

What is significant about *Poku* is its rarity within the body of case law in that the defendant was relying completely on an objective assessment of the reasonableness of his actions. Since the coming into force of the Human Rights Act 1998, the issue of reasonableness has almost exclusively been intertwined with Art 10 and 11 of the ECHR. Accordingly prosecutions under Section 5, especially those involving protestors, have been disputed on the grounds that the words or conduct were part of a protest.[91] The accused protestor(s) base the reasonableness of their conduct on the guaranteed rights to freedom of expression[92] and freedom of assembly.[93] Significantly, it has been stated that there have been a number of cases in which the offence under s.5 has been challenged in the courts as being incompatible with Article 10 of the ECHR.[94] This is not necessarily the case. The challenges in the courts have been targeted at the appropriateness of the individual conviction not at the underlying offence itself.

Reasonableness from Rights: A Developing Discourse

Thus far, the inquiry has attempted to divine principles of reasonableness from within the individual facts of the case whilst drawing through the criminal doctrine that interacts with reasonableness. Since the enactment of the Human Rights Act, the articles of the ECHR have added an additional ingredient for finders of fact to consider when examining the matrix of factors that contribute to reasonableness. Counter-terrorism law has been at the vanguard of the development of human rights jurisprudence in many areas.[95] In respect of reasonableness, there has been little by way of human rights driving changes in the attitude of the courts. The case law that does exist is illustrative of a cautious approach on behalf of the courts. It is necessary to first consider the operative Article of the ECHR that protesters tend to rely on before examining how the courts have read this right in conjunction with the reasonableness defence.

1) Everyone has the right to freedom of expression. This right shall include freedom to hold opinions and to receive and impart information and ideas without interference by public authority and regardless of frontiers … [96]
2) The exercise of these freedoms, since it carries with it duties and responsibilities, may be subject to such formalities, conditions, restrictions or penalties as are prescribed by law and are necessary in a democratic society, in the interests of national security, territorial integrity or public safety for the prevention of disorder or crime, for the protection of the reputation or rights of others … [97]

When discussing the human rights framework and Article 10 considerations, issues of reasonableness are not necessarily confined to low-level protest offences. In *R v Brown (Terence Roy)*[98] the appellant had, *inter alia*, been convicted under Section 58(1) of the 2000 Act of collecting information likely to be useful to a person committing or preparing a terrorist act when selling copies of the 'Anarchists Cookbook' through his own internet site. At the Court of Appeal, it was argued that the prosecution interfered with his right to free

---

91   See, for example, *Hammond v DPP* [2004] EWHC 69, [2004] Crim LR 851.
92   The right to freedom of expression can be found Article 10 of the ECHR.
93   Freedom of Association and Assembly found under Article 11 of the ECHR.
94   Ormerod (n 71) 1076.
95   For the latest discussion, see Aniceto Masferrer and Clive Walker (eds), *Counter-Terrorism, Human Rights and the Rule of Law: Crossing Legal Boundaries in Defence of the State* (Edward Elgar 2013).
96   Art 10(1) goes on to state: 'This Article shall not prevent States from requiring the licensing of broadcasting, television or cinema enterprises'.
97   Art 10(2) goes on to provide that States can further limit the right under Art 10(1): 'for preventing the disclosure of information received in confidence, or for maintaining the authority and impartiality of the judiciary'.
98   [2011] EWCA Crim 2751.

expression under Article 10 of the ECHR and additionally, that the law had been so uncertain when he carried out his activities that a reasonable citizen could not have known whether they constituted a breach of the criminal law and accordingly violated Article 7 of the ECHR.

The court swiftly dismissed both of these assertions. In relation to the Article 10 claim it was stated that the provisions of Section 58, whilst protecting the right to impart information, may be subject to restrictions prescribed by law and necessary in a democratic society in the interests of, among other things, national security and that the proportionate interference with this right was legitimate. 'The question whether the excuse is reasonable on the basis of the exercise of the right to freedom of speech or freedom of expression may be left to the jury to be decided as a question of fact in the individual case'.[99] The court was equally unequivocal that, whilst Section 58 had been the subject of judicial reinterpretation, the ingredients of the offence was clear, it could not be committed inadvertently and the motivation behind the offence was not relevant to liability.[100]

Rights-based concerns also pervade consideration of Section 38B Terrorism Act 2000. This creates the offence of failing to disclose information, which the defendant knows or believes, might be of material assistance in preventing the commission of an act of terrorism or of securing the apprehension, prosecution or conviction of someone involved in terrorism. Within the statute there is a defence, if a person charged under this provision, that he had a reasonable excuse for not making the disclosure.[101] Professor Walker has criticized this offence extensively[102] on a number of grounds, and specifically highlights four discrete reasonable excuses that will engage the ECHR.

The first excuse that Walker suggests may arise under Section 38B of the 2000 Act is where the information in question relates to a close personal relationship.[103] Disclosure of such information would invoke sinister undertones of Nazi Germany. Walker gives the example of husband and wife, but such an excuse extends to other close family relationships such as parent and child.[104] The existing case law should also be considered alongside the Home Office guidance for this offence, which states, 'Having a legal or familial relationship with someone does not constitute immunity from the obligation to disclose information'.[105] The other potential excuses—the legal advisor who becomes aware of material information,[106] the disclosure of information that may lead to the self-incrimination of the individual possessing the information,[107] and material information received during the course of journalism[108]—follow well-trodden legal paths in respect of ECHR issues. Suffice to say that, as was seen in *Brown,* none of these *per se* would appear to furnish the defendant with a reasonable excuse.

Public Order, Protest and Reasonableness

The principal issue regarding reasonableness of conduct in the arena of low-level public order is the defence under Section 5(3)(c) and the inter-relationship this has with specific articles of the ECHR. A defendant engaged in protest would seek to use Article 10 of the ECHR to support the contention that her conduct was reasonable:

---

99   ibid [22].

100   ibid (n 98) [31–32].

101   Terrorism Act 2000, s 38B(4).

102   Clive Walker, 'Conscripting the Public in Terrorism Policing: Towards Safer Communities or a Police State?' [2010] Crim LR 441.

103   ibid 445–446.

104   R v Girma [2009] EWCA Crim 912 concerns the wife and sister-in-law of July 21st bomber.

105   Home Office Circ. 7/2002, p 5, cited in Walker (n 102) 446.

106   'It is proper for a lawyer to advise a client on how to stay within the law and avoid committing a crime, or to warn a client that proposed actions could attract prosecution, and such advice will be protected by privilege.' Anti-Terrorism Practice Note 8. See further *Bullivant v Attorney-General of Victoria* [1901] AC 196 HL; *Butler v Board of Trade* [1971] Ch. 680 Ch D, cited in Walker (n 102) 447.

107   Walker (n 102) 447–449.

108   Walker (n 102) 449–450.

> The specific reasonable conduct defence under both Sections 4A and 5 ought to mean greater protection for peaceful protest. Surely it must always be 'reasonable' conduct peacefully to exercise a Convention right?[109]

In attempting to answer the question posed by Professor Mead, an examination of the case law surrounding protest illustrates the inconsistency of reasoning and the lack of certainty by a defendant seeking to rely on Section 5(3)(c) of the 1986 Act. The defence of reasonable conduct, under Section 5(3)(c) needs to be considered alongside the revivified interpretive duty imposed on the Courts by the Human Rights Act 1998.[110]

In the case of *Percy*,[111] a peace campaigner objecting to American military policy defaced the flag of America in sight of American service personnel. Convicted at first instance, she appealed that insufficient account had been taken of her Article 10 right to express her beliefs. Although her defence was based around Section 5(3)(c) and that her conduct was reasonable because she was peacefully exercising her Article 10 Convention right, the Divisional Court instead 'conflated the reasonableness defence in the immediate, individual case with the balancing exercise required by Art.10 ECHR ... and approached the case as a rights review'.[112]

Often viewed alongside *Percy*, the case of *Hammond*[113] provides an indication of the unpredictability of the operation of reasonable excuse as they collide with Convention rights. The facts in the two cases are similar to the extent they are both engaged in protest. In *Hammond*, the accused was a lay preacher protesting about homosexuality. He did this by means of carrying a sign through a pedestrianized part of Bournemouth. His protest attracted a crowd of around 40 people, some of whom were scuffling with him and trying to disrupt his protest. He was arrested and charged under Section 5. At trial he claimed that his conduct was reasonable in that he was peacefully exercising his convention rights and that it was the audience who were hostile. He was convicted by magistrates at first instance and appealed. The High Court decided that it was open to Magistrates to conclude that H's conduct was not reasonable because of the pressing need to show tolerance to all sections of society and the fact that the defendant's conduct was provoking violence and disorder and interfered with others' rights.

It has been pointed out[114] that the construction of the reasonable conduct defence, as interpreted by the Divisional Court in *Hammond*, means that when it comes to an appeal against conviction, the appellate court merely has to satisfy itself that rejection of the defence was not unreasonable with reference to *Wednesbury* criteria.[115] This phenomenon was seen in the previously discussed case of *Patterson*,[116] and in that instance, unlike *Hammond*, it worked to the advantage of the appellant. Bestowing such latitude on the lower courts, given the already articulated confusion about the scope and operation of the defence, does lend weight to those arguing for reform of the provision.[117]

In *Abdul*,[118] the protestors were engaging in a highly controversial protest that was always likely to provoke an outraged response. They were attending a homecoming parade for British soldiers protesting about their involvement in Afghanistan and Iraq. The defendants had co-operated with police directions and had tried to facilitate peaceful protest. The protesters were not arrested at the time of the protest but they were arrested 5 months later. The protestors were convicted of an offence under Section 5 of the 1986 Act. At trial, the District Judge held, 'the method they chose to convey an otherwise legitimate belief ... was so unreasonable and disproportionately expressed so as to deprive them of the protection of article 10'.[119]

---

109 David Mead, *The New Law of Peaceful Protest* (Hart Publishing 2010) 223.

110 Human Rights Act, s 3 provides that primary and secondary legislation must, so far as is possible, be read and given effect to in a way which is compatible with the Convention rights, and this means even if there is contrary authority on the question.

111 *Percy v DPP* (2001) EWHC 1125.

112 Andrew Geddis, 'Free Speech Martyrs or Unreasonable Threats to Social Peace? – "Insulting" Expression and Section 5 of the Public Order Act 1986' [2004] Pub L 853, 860–861.

113 [2004] EWHC 69 (Admin).

114 Geddis (n 112) 865.

115 *Associated Provincial Picture Houses Ltd v Wednesbury Corporation* [1947] 2 All ER 680 CA.

116 [2004] EWHC 2744 (Admin).

117 See Thornton (n 69) 42.

118 *Abdul and Others v DPP* [2011] EWHC 247 (Admin).

119 ibid [32].

The Divisional Court dismissed the appeal against conviction. Whilst much of the discussion concerned the proportionality of the prosecution, the court did make mention of the defence under Section 5(3)(c):

> It follows that, in a factual context of a kind where the right of freedom of expression is being asserted, whether a prosecution and conviction under section 5 of the Act is justified and proportionate has to be assessed on the facts and circumstances of the individual case. To an extent, that is imparted by s.5 (3) (c) of the Act, albeit it is for the defendant under that sub-section to prove that his conduct was "reasonable".[120]

Given the facts of *Abdul*, despite the finding of the court that the defendants had overstepped the boundaries of legitimate protest, it is difficult to project a way in which the defendants could ever make their point at that particular parade without infringing Section 5 even taking into account Article 10 of the ECHR and the defence of reasonable conduct under Section 5(3)(c).

When discussing these from the perspective of Article 10, Professor Barendt has stated that the broad scope of Section 5 of the 1986 Act has serious implications for freedom of speech and it is now necessary for the courts to read Section 5, and especially Section 5(3)(c), in the context of Article 10.[121] Such an analysis would involve determining whether the defendant had shown on the balance of probabilities that the conduct was reasonable given all of the circumstances. This would include the defendant's illustrating her own appreciation of the circumstances and an acknowledgment of the rights guaranteed. Instead of doing this, courts have largely forsaken discussion of the reasonableness defence and its relationship with Article 10. Moreover, the case law seems to indicate that courts actually engage in an unpredictable and ad-hoc balancing of competing rights and public policy.

Conclusion: Reasonable Reform?

In attempting to discern the contours of reasonableness as it operates within a statutory context, there are a number of conclusions that become apparent. One of the key issues faced by those who seek to rely on the defence of reasonableness is that Parliament consistently declines to provide any statutory explanation of what will, or indeed what will not, constitute a reasonable excuse in respect of any of the offences under consideration. Whilst the case of *G* articulated why this might be desirable, it is asserted that the statutory ambiguity inherent in construction of the 'reasonable excuse' defence has serious ramifications for those whose prosecution never leaves the lower courts, especially those prosecuted for low-level public order offences. As has been seen from the various cases under discussion, in such instances courts are invited to indulge in an ad-hoc limitation of acceptable excuses to the point where a legal adviser trying to communicate the essence of the defence to a defendant will be poorly placed to advise whether such a defence will be accepted.[122]

The picture is a little more settled, if less encouraging, for those who seek to rely on reasonable excuse to defend the possession of a firearm. Clearly, Parliament and the judiciary are of the same mind, insofar as limiting the scope of reasonable excuse to a narrow range of responses, and even reiterating the requirement of a legal burden rather than an evidential one being imposed on the defendant.[123] It is difficult to escape the conclusion offered by Professor Ashworth, that the current judicial approach to reasonableness of excuse is driven by a desire to ease of conviction for prosecutors rather than in the interests of justice.[124]

It has been suggested that an objective assessment of reasonableness is not within the defendant's knowledge and that it would be more logical to have the prosecution prove unreasonableness beyond reasonable doubt in all of the circumstances.[125] Whilst this was said in the special circumstances surrounding public order law, it is not irreconcilable with any of the offences that have been discussed within this inquiry.

---

120   ibid [56].

121   Eric Barendt, *Freedom of Speech* (2nd edn, OUP 2008) 300.

122   For discussion on the notion of ad hoc balancing in an international context see Adrienne Stone, 'The Limits of Constitutional Text and Structure' (1999) 23 Melbourne U L Rev 668.

123   *R v Williams* (Orette) (n 29).

124   Ashworth (n 28) 448.

125   Thornton (n 69) 42.

In seeking to offer solutions, it is difficult to see how the reasonableness of conduct is not part of the prevailing circumstances in which the offences under consideration are committed. It is not beyond the bounds of logic to suggest that reasonableness should, in fact, be regarded as central element of the offence: a finding of reasonableness by the court means that there is no criminal sanction attached to the conduct.[126]

If reasonableness is determinative of conviction and the reasonableness of the conduct is a central element of the offence then irrespective of the seriousness of the sentence, or of any public policy it seems disproportionate to make this a reverse onus provision[127] simply as a device to make prosecution easier. Similarly, the lack of statutory guidance for courts serves only to add to the muddled analysis that has characterized much of the case law in both terrorism and public order cases. This is a state of affairs that should not continue. Given the ubiquity of many of these offences, the current lack of clarity around reasonableness leaves accused individuals facing unacceptable ambiguity. Indeed, one might almost say, it is unreasonable.

---

126   Thornton (n 69) 42.
127   *Sheldrake* (n 7) 266.

Chapter 11

How Do They Do That?
Automatism, Coercion, Necessity, and *Mens Rea* in Scots Criminal Law

Claire McDiarmid

Introduction

The provision of defences in the criminal law is perhaps the first and most basic requirement of equality of arms. The criminal justice system (in both Scotland and England and Wales) is set up so that, initially, the state applies its resources to prove that the accused carried out the proscribed conduct with the requisite mental attitude. There is then an opportunity for the defendant to present to the court exculpatory evidence. General defences formalise this second process, creating defined mechanisms in terms of which the accused may put forward 'good' or legally recognised reasons for his/her conduct which, in law, will render him/her criminally blameless. This chapter will consider the defences of automatism, coercion, and necessity as these are defined in Scots law. It will examine particularly the way in which these defences operate in relation to the negation of *mens rea* looking at whether this is the central basis of the exculpation which they offer.

The Structure of the Criminal Law following *Drury*

The role of defences, and the way in which they function to provide exoneration in Scots law, was put under scrutiny by the decision of a five-judge bench in an appeal to the High Court of Justiciary in the case of *Drury v HM Advocate*.[1] At his trial, Stuart Drury had pled the partial defence of provocation to a charge of murdering his former partner. He was, nonetheless, convicted of murder and appealed on the basis that the test of provocation, where the provoking act was the discovery of sexual infidelity, had been wrongly explained to the jury as one of proportionality.[2] In principle, then, all that the appeal court was required to determine was this limited issue: the test for provocation in these circumstances. In fact, it effected a change to the *mens rea* of murder itself doing so in a manner which, 'threaten[ed] to turn the Scottish law of criminal defences upside down'.[3]

Prior to *Drury*, two alternative *mentes reae* for murder existed. These can be summarised as 'intention to kill' and 'wicked recklessness'.[4] In the case, from the outset of his *dicta* on the first form (intention to kill), Lord Justice-General Rodger seemed to envisage a coming together of mental element and defence. He said:

> [A]s it stands, the definition [i.e., in summary, intention to kill] … is at best incomplete and, to that extent, inaccurate. Most obviously, someone who is subject to a murderous attack may defend himself by intentionally

---

1   [2001] SLT 1013.

2   Only two provoking acts are recognised in Scots law: an initial attack by the ultimate deceased (see *Gillon v HM Advocate* [2007] JC 24 and the discovery of sexual infidelity the test for which was clarified in *Drury* (n 1)). For a critique of the law, see Claire McDiarmid, 'Don't Look Back in Anger: The Partial Defence of Provocation in Scots Criminal Law' in James Chalmers, Fiona Leverick and Lindsay Farmer (eds), *Essays in Criminal Law in Honour of Sir Gerald Gordon* (Edinburgh University Press 2010) 195–217.

3   James Chalmers, 'Collapsing the Structure of Criminal Law' [2001] SLT 241, 242.

4   The 'classic' definition is that provided by JHA Macdonald in his *Practical Treatise on the Criminal Law of Scotland* (5th edn, James Walker, DJ Stevenson, W Green eds 1948) 89.

killing his assailant. … But, of course, a person who intentionally kills in self defence is not guilty of murder or indeed of any other crime.[5]

Accordingly, he went on to argue that the first form (intention to kill) was incorrect: 'The definition of murder in the direction is somewhat elliptical because it does not describe the relevant intention. In truth, just as the recklessness has to be wicked so also must the intention be wicked'.[6] An intention to kill, then, had ceased to be sufficient for murder. 'Wickedness' of that intention also had to be established. Further on, Lord Justice-General Rodger explained that provocation did not 'reduce' murder to culpable homicide but was 'simply one of the factors which the jury should take into account in performing their general task of determining the accused's state of mind at the time when he killed his victim'.[7] In short, if the accused had been provoked, then, while s/he would still have intended to kill, that intention would be shorn of its wickedness. A conviction for culpable homicide would still be apposite but the *mens rea* of murder (which now required a '*wicked* intention') would not have been made out.

Thus, as a number of commentators pointed out,[8] the all but mathematical equation which had previously been applied in Scottish criminal procedure (*actus reus* + *mens rea* = crime **unless** there is a defence) seemed to have been displaced. On Lord Rodger's definition, *mens rea* could not be made out without consideration of any defence which might negate it. *Mens rea* and defences appeared to be collapsing into each other.

Of course, this state of affairs applied directly only to murder but murder is something of a figurehead or motif for the rest of the criminal law—partly by virtue of its symbolic status as the most serious crime, partly, perhaps, because it is one of few crimes where the **degree** of culpability may be considered at the stage of determining guilt (in the possibility of the return of a culpable homicide verdict instead) and not only at sentence. As Chloe Kennedy has noted, 'judicial decisions on the *mens rea* of homicide have genuine influence over the rest of the law, rather than being confined to that sphere'.[9] Rather more graphically, Gordon has stated that:

> There is no doubt that the law of murder still lives in the shadow of the gallows, or that discussions of mens rea in general tend to be influenced by cases of murder, if only because most of the cases on mens rea were murder cases.[10]

Arguably, in relation to murder, a common sense view has prevailed that the *mens rea* of wicked intention to kill is established where the accused intended to kill **and** no recognised defence applies.[11] In stating, '[w]e reject any suggestion that the question of the wickedness of an intention to kill is at large for the jury in every case, or that the determination of that question is not constrained by any legal limits',[12] the case of *Elsherkisi v HM Advocate* reined in some of the uncertainty arising from *Drury*. *Elsherkisi* did not, however, lay bare the underlying structural issue as to the relationship between *mens rea* and defences.[13] Given the way in which murder permeates the legal landscape, then, this may still be of importance in relation to other general defences. Even if this is not the case, their own relationship to *mens rea* (and, indeed, *actus reus*) is

---

5   *Drury* (n 1) [10].

6   ibid [11].

7   ibid [17]. This view was shared by Lord Nimmo Smith in his judgment, ibid [3].

8   This was done most explicitly by Chalmers (n 3). In a commentary to the case, Gerald Gordon stated: 'It seems that what the court has done has been to incorporate the defences to the crime of murder into the definition of the crime by using the word 'wicked' as a shorthand for all of them. … I remain uneasy, however, about the concept of 'wicked intention' in the context of a modern system of law … And this is apart from the fact that it is, I think, analytically helpful to distinguish between the definition of a crime, and matters which can constitute defences to the crime'. Commentary to *Drury* (n 1) [2001] SCCR 583 at 618–619. See also Michael GA Christie, 'The Coherence of Scots Criminal Law: Some Aspects of *Drury v HM Advocate*' [2002] JR 273, especially 281–284.

9   'Criminal Law and the Scottish Moral Tradition' (PhD thesis, University of Edinburgh, 2013).

10   Commentary to *Petto v HM Advocate* [2011] SCCR 519, 534. See also Pamela R Ferguson and Claire McDiarmid, *Scots Criminal Law: A Critical Analysis* (Dundee University Press 2009) [9.2.1].

11   See *Elsherkisi v HM Advocate* [2011] HCJAC 100, 2011 SCCR 735; 2012 SCL 181 [11]–[13].

12   ibid [12] (Lord Hardie).

13   ibid, especially [12].

highlighted as worthy of consideration by the way in which the matter was dissected by *Drury*'s five-judge bench. Accordingly, this chapter will now turn its attention to automatism, coercion and necessity in Scots law.

The Operation of Automatism

Automatism is an interesting defence for a number of reasons, including that its appearance in the Scottish case reports is so patchy, with a successful plea in 1925 in *HM Advocate v Ritchie*[14] (though the defence was not so called in the report) followed by a barren period until 1991[15] when success in *Ross v HM Advocate*[16] brought a (small!) glut—in all of which cases the defence ultimately failed.[17] Another interesting side-issue is that the interpretation of the facts of *Ritchie* which, to an extent, underpinned the decision in *Ross* may not have been entirely correct.[18] Finally, in terms of its theoretical basis,[19] while automatism could not justify the accused's conduct, it might operate either as an excuse—'what the accused did was wrong but automatism provides a good reason why s/he is not blameworthy'—or as an exemption or capacity defence in that its essence is the absence of rationality on the accused's part. In *Ross*, the statement of the principles of automatism drew closely on the then definition of insanity in Scots law ('absolute alienation of reason')[20] but that defence (now known as 'mental disorder') has been changed in its recent passage into legislation.[21]

For present purposes, interest is directed towards automatism's actual operation in terms of the way in which the courts apply it to elide blameworthiness. There appears to have been no significant case since *Drury*. Thus, there has been no occasion to challenge automatism's status as a free-standing defence coming into play after establishment of *actus reus* and *mens rea*. We may therefore accept that it is correct to characterise it as working solely to demonstrate the accused's lack of culpability where, *prima facie*, there is clear evidence that s/he is the medium by which the proscribed harm constituting the gravamen of the charge has been brought about. In his judgment in *Ross*, Lord McCluskey made no bones about this. He said: 'I know of no exceptions, other than statutory ones, to the rule that the Crown must prove *mens rea* beyond reasonable doubt. ... If there were to be no such evidence at all the proper verdict even in such a case would be a simple verdict of 'not guilty".[22]

Ross, then, falls back on what may be regarded as the logical order of the criminal law (*mens rea* (delineated narrowly as the specific, proscribed mental state in the offence definition) + *actus reus*) = crime **unless** automatism applies. In other words, proof of the absence of automatism is not required to establish the *mens rea* of the crime charged. The defence is a separate and subsequent issue. Unlike *Drury*'s conception of provocation as 'just' one of several sources of evidence on the accused's mental state, automatism is a general defence with clear rules of engagement. Nonetheless, these relate so closely to the presence or absence of *mens rea* (and/or *actus reus*) that it serves as much to disprove the Crown's case as separately to elide the accused's culpability. Indeed, automatism has been categorised as a 'failure of proof' defence being an

---

14   [1926] JC 45.

15   Though accused persons did occasionally seek to use the plea in this period. See, for example, *Stevenson v Beatson* [1965] SLT (Sh Ct) 11.

16   [1991] JC 210.

17   *Sorley v HM Advocate* [1992] JC 102; *Cardle v Mulrainey* [1992] SLT 1152; *Ebsworth v HM Advocate* [1992] SLT 1161.

18   See Jenifer M Ross, 'A Long Motor Run on a Dark Night: Reconstructing *HM Advocate v Ritchie*' (2010) 14 Edinburgh L Rev 193. The accused was adversely affected by 'toxic exhaustive factors'. This phrase had been taken to mean toxic car exhaust fumes (a factor external to the accused). Ross's research into the original evidence presented in the trial uncovered that, in fact, it referred to a medical condition arising from injuries sustained in the First World War (which might have been characterised as an internal factor).

19   See, for example, Celia Wells and Oliver Quick, *Lacey, Wells & Quick Reconstructing Criminal Law: Text and Materials* (4th edn, Cambridge University Press 2010) 119–123.

20   Baron David Hume, *Commentaries on the Law of Scotland, Respecting Crimes* (vol I, 4th edn, The Law Society of Scotland 1986, reprint 1844) 37.

21   Criminal Procedure (Scotland) Act 1995, s 51A.

22   *Ross* (n 16) 228.

'instance [...] where the prosecution, because of the 'defence', are unable to prove all of the required elements of the offence'.[23] How, then, does automatism work?

We may deal with its principles in short compass. First there must be 'some external factor which was outwith the accused's control and which he was not bound to foresee'.[24] The (*Ross*) case offers some examples of external factors for this purpose including 'the consumption of drink or drugs' or 'toxic exhaust fumes',[25] 'a blow on the head causing concussion' or 'the administering of an anaesthetic for therapeutic purposes'.[26] The external factor must also 'have resulted in a total alienation of reason amounting to a complete absence of self-control'.[27] The facts of *Ross* provide a clear illustration. The accused had been drinking lager from a can into which, *without his knowledge*, had been put, five or six Temazepam tablets and an unspecified quantity of LSD which he then ingested with the lager. Together, these drugs constituted the 'external factor'. Shortly after ingestion, Ross started to scream and to lunge with a knife, attacking a number of people such that he was eventually charged with seven counts of attempted murder (among other offences). Ross was convicted at trial and appealed. The defence argued that the drugs had adversely affected his ability to exercise self-control and to formulate *mens rea*.

Essentially, automatism goes to the very roots of the capacity-based approach to the attribution of criminal responsibility which requires that individuals exercise freewill and understanding in making the choice to commit crime **and** that the circumstances are such that they would have had a fair chance to do otherwise.[28] If avoidance of the criminal behaviour was impossible in an individual case then, no liability should attach. At the risk of oversimplification, to be subject to the norms of the criminal law, conduct must be voluntary. Automatism is often discussed as 'involuntariness' whether in relation to the ingestion or application of the external factor or the subsequent 'criminal' activity, or both.[29]

In *Ross*, the appeal court characterised the matter as an inability on the accused's part to formulate *mens rea*.[30] If the issue is one of involuntariness, however, then this compels us to consider firstly whether, in fact, the accused acted at all. In other words, there may be a case that it is the *actus reus* with which automatism engages and which it operates to negate, without any need to consider at all its role in *mens rea*.[31] At one level, this is compelling. Involuntariness equates, or is certainly taken to equate, to the negation of criminality *tout court*. Indeed, in summarising the Crown submissions, Lord Justice-General Hope noted, 'I understood [the Solicitor General] to accept that there was evidence that the appellant had no control over his actions with the result that they were involuntary'.[32]

In practice, however, it would appear that there are degrees of voluntariness (of acting) all of which are on a continuum towards the mental element of strongly intending. On this analysis then, the *actus reus* and the *mens rea* of any crime cannot be *completely* separated from each other. Gordon explains: 'To be classed as automatic, behaviour must be wholly unconscious, and a person who acts when his consciousness is reduced, impaired or merely clouded is not acting automatically'.[33]

Scots law has recognised the absence (which may be different from the negation) of the *actus reus* in the case of *Hogg v Macpherson*[34] where a strong gust of wind blew over the accused's horse-drawn furniture van and it, in turn, knocked a municipal lamp standard to the ground, breaking the bulb. It was held that the

---

23   James Chalmers and Fiona Leverick, *Criminal Defences and Pleas in Bar of Trial* (W Green ed, 2006) [1.06].

24   *Ross* (n 16) 218 (LJ-G Hope).

25   ibid 214 (LJ-G Hope).

26   ibid 216 (LJ-G Hope, quoting Lord Diplock in *R v Sullivan* [1984] AC 156, 172).

27   ibid 218 (LJ-G Hope).

28   This is famously iterated by HLA Hart in *Punishment and Responsibility: Essays in the Philosophy of Law* (Clarendon Press 1968), especially ch 1.

29   See, for example Gerald H Gordon, *The Criminal Law of Scotland* (vol I, 3rd edn, Michael GA Christie, W Green eds, 2000) para 3.16; TH Jones & MGA Christie, *Criminal Law* (5th edn, W Green ed, 2012) from [4-11].

30   *Ross* (n 16) 213–214 (LJ-G Hope).

31   This argument has been advanced by, among others, Pamela Ferguson. See 'The Limits of the Automatism Defence' (1991) 36 JLSS 446.

32   *Ross* (n 16) 214.

33   Gordon (n 29) [3.16].

34   [1928] JC 15.

'breaking of the lamp was not the appellant's act at all, either negligent or accidental'.[35] It was the wind. In automatism cases, on the other hand, a proscribed act will have occurred 'through' the accused. Ross, for example, stabbed a number of people. It is unclear whether it is this proximity to mediating the wrongful behaviour which has left the *actus reus* in place in automatism cases or whether it is that the definition of the offence using 'insanity' terminology simply serves to direct inquiry to the accused's mental state. Certainly, it has been suggested that no criminal liability would attach to a 'real' reflex act.[36] Nonetheless, while automatism has been pled to a strict liability charge, with no apparent difficulty, though, equally, with no specific discussion,[37] the High Court's approach has been to concentrate on its effect in relation to *mens rea*.

The real issue in *Ross* was whether a mental condition which did not meet the legal definition of insanity could offer exculpation. This was not in terms of the actual mental state in which Ross committed the offences—no one seems to have doubted that it amounted to a 'total alienation of reason'. It was to do with its cause. At the time, insanity required that that mental state should arise 'as the result of mental illness, mental disease or defect or unsoundness of mind'.[38] Ross's mental state arose from the ingestion of drugs. Ross was not at fault for this however. The ingestion was involuntary.[39] At one level, then, all that *Ross* determined was that, in these circumstances a defence (automatism) was available. All of the judges characterised it as the absence of *mens rea*[40] but, clearly, if the Crown is unable to prove *mens rea* in *any* case, the accused must be acquitted. The case's real innovation was its affirmation that that particular reason for the absence of *mens rea*—an external factor neither self-induced nor foreseeable—was acceptable in law. It is as a formal mechanism by which the accused may bring to the court's attention that his/her reason was alienated blamelessly that automatism operates as a defence.[41]

Mens rea must be completely absent. Automatism is not comparable, in that sense, to diminished responsibility where the accused may retain *some* ability to rationalise thought and behaviour.[42] This was clarified in the case of *Cardle v Mulrainey*,[43] where Lord Justice-General Hope stated:

> Where ... the accused knew what he was doing and was aware of the nature and quality of his acts and that what he was doing was wrong, he cannot be said to be suffering from some total alienation of reason in regard to the crime with which he is charged which the defence requires. ... [An] inability to exert self control, which the [first instance judge] has described as an inability to complete the reasoning process, must be distinguished from the essential requirement that there should be a total alienation of the accused's mental faculties of reasoning and of understanding what he is doing. As in the case of provocation, which provides another example of a stimulus resulting in a loss of self control at the time of the act, this may mitigate the offence but it cannot be held to justify an acquittal on the ground that there is an absence of mens rea.[44]

In this case, the accused had ingested amphetamine which had been introduced, without his knowledge, into a can of lager from which he had been drinking. He was aware that what he was doing (he committed a number of motoring offences) was wrong but claimed that the effect of the external factor (the amphetamine) was that he was unable to stop himself doing so.

---

35 ibid 17 (LJ-G Clyde).

36 See *Jessop v Johnstone* [1991] SCCR 238, 240 (LJ-C Ross).

37 See *Mulrainey* (n 17), where the accused was charged with a number of road traffic offences, some of which were of strict liability. See also Ferguson and McDiarmid (n 10) from [20.20.2].

38 *Brennan v HM Advocate* [1977] JC 38, 45 (LJ-G Emslie).

39 No matter its effect on actual mental state, voluntary intoxication is not a defence in Scots law. Hume (n 20) 45; *Brennan* (ibid) 46; *Ross* (n 16) 214 (LJ-G Hope).

40 *Ross* (n 16) 213–214 (LJ-G Hope); 223 (Lord Allanbridge); 229 (Lord McCluskey); 232 (Lord Brand). Lord Weir did not specifically refer to the absence of *mens rea* but stated at 232: 'the state of mind of the accused is at the heart of the issue'.

41 It is recognised as a defence in terms of the Criminal Procedure (Scotland) Act 1995, s 78(2).

42 The legal test in Scotland is one of substantial impairment of the ability to determine or control conduct by reason of abnormality of mind: ibid s 51B(1).

43 *Mulrainey* (n 17).

44 ibid 1160.

The reference to provocation is perhaps unhelpful here in that automatism, even if pled to murder, would not constitute a partial defence. It operates on an all-or-nothing basis. The accused in *Cardle v Mulrainey* was charged, *inter alia*, with attempted theft, the *mens rea* of which is an intention to deprive the owner of his/her property. His automatism plea was based on volition—indeed, it was an almost textbook one of 'inability to resist an impulse' or to control action. While this is a key component of criminal capacity on the Hartian definition espoused above, it was not specifically considered. For those offences for which it was necessary, bearing in mind that a number of the charges against Mulrainey related to strict liability crimes, the accused was held to have *mens rea*. The court must be deemed to have considered that this rested on criminal capacity, defined, presumably in a restricted fashion to include only understanding of the nature of the behaviour.[45] Perhaps the argument is that, if *some* rationality is retained, no impulse is, in fact, irresistible. The conceptual difficulty (in relation to the strict liability offences) of holding that automatism operates in relation to *mens rea* was similarly not addressed.

If it can be accepted, then, that automatism works by setting up, in law, as a good reason for a complete loss of rationality, the application to the accused of an external factor, one further question remains: why should a factor *internal* to the accused but having the same effect not also serve the same exculpatory function? The basic answer to this, arising from the doctrine of precedent, is found in the case of *Cunningham v HM Advocate*[46] in which the line of defence put forward (to a number of motoring offences) was that the accused had committed these whilst in the throes of an 'epileptic fugue'.[47] Lord Justice-General Clyde said: 'Any mental or pathological condition short of insanity – any question of diminished responsibility owing to any cause, which does not involve insanity – is relevant only to the question of mitigating circumstances and sentence'.[48] *Ross* expressly overruled this principle in relation to *external* factors. Scots law has accepted (at sheriff court level only but subsequent to *Ross*) that hypoglycaemia caused by diabetes could constitute an external factor[49] but only where it was a first attack. If the accused knew that s/he suffered from diabetes, the foreseeability strand of the *Ross* test could not be satisfied. The underlying justification is public safety in that conditions of this nature might recur.[50] The application of an external factor (the spiking of a drink etc.) is, by its nature, a one-off.

Some aspects of automatism do remain somewhat obscure. Its definition of the mental state required for exculpation is based on an old formulation of the insanity defence which no longer applies in Scotland. There is no indication of whether this might, or, indeed, should, change in line with the shift to inability to appreciate the nature or wrongfulness of the conduct which is now the basis of the defence of mental disorder.[51] Automatism's engagement with conditions like epilepsy and diabetes, which may be *difficult* to control,[52] is still rudimentary and may not properly capture blameworthiness. Overall, however, where an accused has, without fault, lost all rational control of his/her actions, criminal liability is inappropriate and automatism recognises this where the cause is an unforeseeable external factor which was not self-induced. While the effect of the defence on the foundational elements of the crime charged is, necessarily, direct, these elements remain intact. Automatism does not affect the boundary between offence and defence. It is necessary now to consider this issue in relation to coercion.

---

45   For a full discussion of one possible view of the relationship between mens rea and criminal capacity, see Claire McDiarmid, *Childhood and Crime* (Dundee University Press 2007) ch 3.

46   [1963] JC 80.

47   ibid 83.

48   ibid 84.

49   *MacLeod v Mathieson* [1993] SCCR 488.

50   *Ross* (n 18) 203.

51   Criminal Procedure (Scotland) Act 1995, s 51A(1).

52   For a discussion of certain aspects of the English position, see J Rumbold and M Wasik, 'Diabetic Drivers, Hypoglycaemic Unawareness and Automatism' [2011] Crim LR 863.

Coercion

Introduction

Coercion has been recognised in Scots law since the time of Baron David Hume[53] and, indeed, the modern law (in which there are few cases) rests on his exposition.[54] Developments in the defence of necessity[55] have brought some overlap however the two defences have not been collapsed into a generalised form of duress and, for that reason, they will be discussed separately. The essence of coercion is that the accused was forced, by threats made against him/her by a third party, to commit a crime. It is in the way in which the law characterises the accused's response to such threats that the defence's relationship to the *mens rea* for the crime is most clearly discernible. There is both a factual and a normative element to that characterisation.

Key Principles

According to Hume, coercion could be established where there was 'an immediate danger of death or great bodily harm [and] an inability to resist the violence'.[56] The implicit emphasis on the effect on the accused of the fear thus generated is discernible in some attempts to explain the modern law. In his charge to the jury in *HM Advocate v Raiker*,[57] for example, Lord McCluskey stated:

> [T]he law is that where a person has a real, a genuine, a justifiable fear that if he does not act in accordance with the orders of another person, that other person will use life-threatening violence against him or cause it to be used, and if as a result of that fear and for no other reason he carries out acts which have all the typical external characteristics of criminal acts like assault or theft, then in that situation he cannot be said to have the evil intention which the law says is a necessary ingredient in the carrying out of a crime. In other words, he lacks the criminal state of mind that is a necessary ingredient of any crime, he lacks the evil intention which I have sought to describe earlier and which is part of my description or definition of assault.[58]

This explanation, given for the use of the lay members of the jury, seems straightforwardly to indicate that coercion operates to elide *mens rea*. There is no issue in relation to the *actus reus*: the accused acted in a way which was willed. We see again, here, however, the existence of the continuum mentioned above in relation to automatism between acting voluntarily[59] and directly intending an outcome. The essence of coercion, on this explanation, is that the accused was so frightened by the threat made against him/her that s/he acted in a way in which s/he would not otherwise have done. It is not entirely clear from this charge (and the matter was not tested on appeal) whether Lord McCluskey's view is that the accused simply does not have *mens rea* ('s/he did not intend at all') or whether he is falling back on the old concept of *dole*. This was defined by Baron Hume as:

> that corrupt and evil intention, which is essential (so the light of nature teaches, and so all authorities have said) to the guilt of any crime … [For *dole* to be established] the act must be attended with such circumstances as indicate a corrupt and malignant disposition, a heart contemptuous of order and regardless of social duty.[60]

---

53   The first edition of his Commentaries was published in 1797, with the fourth and final version issued in 1844 (n 20).

54   ibid 53.

55   See *Moss v Howdle* [1997] JC 123.

56   Hume (n 20) 53. He also required (ibid) 'a backward and inferior part in the perpetration; and a disclosure of the fact, as well as restitution of the spoil, on the first safe and convenient occasion'. In *Thomson v HM Advocate* [1983] JC 69, these were considered not to be conditions of the use of the defence but rather merely 'measures of the accused's credibility and reliability on the issue of the defence'. ibid 78 (LJ-C Wheatley).

57   [1989] SCCR 149.

58   ibid 154.

59   The matter was touched on in the trial judge's report to the appeal court in *Thomson* (n 56), where Lord Hunter said: 'I leave out of account situations where evil intent is manifestly absent – for example, if a person has been compelled by sheer physical force to place his hand on a weapon with which others have inflicted a wound on a victim'. ibid 72.

60   Hume (n 20) 21, 22.

In other words, it is not obvious, examining this *dictum* from *Raiker*, whether the jury was to understand that coercion elides the intention itself or merely its 'evil' quality. (The co-accused in the case were charged, with, *inter alia*, a number of assaults arising from a prison riot and hostage-taking.) The former, more straightforward interpretation is more likely, given that the case occurred prior to *Drury* so that the issue of negation of an evaluative moral component (the 'evil' of 'evil intent' which is the *mens rea* of assault) had not, in 1989, been canvassed in Scots law. The idea that extreme fear would, or could, paralyse the exercise of moral and rational constraint seems to be taken for granted.

In charging the jury in the earlier case of *Thomson*, the trial judge had used a similar formulation. That case was appealed but the appeal court's judgment expressly endorsed the 'essence [of] the view of the law taken and applied by the trial judge'.[61] As part of his charge he (Lord Hunter) had said: 'if a defence of this sort as a complete defence leading to an acquittal is to succeed the will and resolution of the accused must, in fact, have been overborne and overcome by the threats and the danger'.[62] The use of the term 'will' is not entirely helpful in determining whether the matter relates to mind or act. Nonetheless, both juries (in *Raiker* and in *Thomson*) would have understood that, for coercion to succeed, the fear generated must have been so strong that it interacted with (indeed overrode) the accused's ability to determine his/her own actions. On this explanation, then, the relationship between the defence and, certainly, the *mens rea*, is particularly close. As with automatism, if there is no *mens rea* then the Crown has not proved its case. It is hard to see, conceptually, how it is possible to say that *mens rea* has been established but, subsequently considering the defence of coercion, in fact, the extreme fear meant that the mental element was not made out. Either the accused has *mens rea* or s/he does not.

Ultimately, however, on appeal, *Thomson*[63] fell back on a straightforwardly factual interpretation of coercion,[64] which served to reinforce its separation from *mens rea*. The key point was that not only must the threats themselves be made contemporaneously with the commission of the crime but the (irresistible) danger which will result from non-compliance must also be bearing down on the accused.[65] The 'gun to the head' scenario is, therefore, the classic example. Coercion then, on this analysis, would sit clearly within the traditional *actus reus* + *mens rea* = offence equation, with the defence itself falling to be considered once the commission of the offence has, *prima facie*, been established.

This analysis of its operation was affirmed in the case of *Cochrane v HM Advocate*,[66] which moved even further away from the direct effect of the threat and the fear it generates on the accused's ability personally to decide to commit the crime. *Cochrane*, where a candlestick was used as a weapon in a robbery, arose from relatively non-specific (and probably future) threats[67] made against an accused who was, on a formal psychological assessment, 'highly compliant'[68] and therefore much more likely than members of the general population to be persuaded—and terrified—by such intimidation. The appeal court held, faced with these facts, that the test for coercion was primarily objective, stating it to be 'whether an ordinary sober person of reasonable firmness, sharing the characteristics of the accused, would have responded as the accused did'.[69] It elucidated the matter further as follows:

> Therefore, in a case where the accused lacks reasonable firmness, the jury must disregard that particular characteristic but have regard to his other characteristics. At the same time I bear firmly in mind that the judge is entitled to have regard to all the accused's characteristics in determining what punishment, if any, is appropriate in the particular circumstances.[70]

---

61   *Thomson* (n 56) 80 (LJ-C Wheatley).

62   ibid 75 (LJ-C Wheatley quoting Lord Hunter). See also Chalmers and Leverick (n 23) [5.04], where they argue that coercion does not operate to negate *mens rea*.

63   ibid.

64   ibid 77–80.

65   Some elements of the threat on which the accused sought to rely related to future events. ibid 76.

66   [2001] SCCR 655.

67   In the accused's own words, the alleged coercer had said: 'If you don't [carry out the robbery], I'll hammer you and blow your house up'. ibid [6].

68   ibid [7] (LJ-G Rodger).

69   ibid [29] (LJ-G Rodger).

70   ibid [30] (LJ-G Rodger).

By definition, objective tests focus attention away from the effect of exculpatory factors on the accused him or herself. The concern is, primarily, on hypothesising as to how such factors would have affected an individual regarded as representative of the general population—an 'average' person or, in coercion, an 'ordinary' one who is 'sober' and 'of reasonable firmness'. In other words, '[h]eroic qualities are not required by the law in this context, nor is allowance made for excessive cowardice or timidity'.[71]

The jury's task is complicated by the fact that the relevant ordinary person *also* shares the characteristics of the accused. Since it is logically impossible for an individual to be simultaneously 'of reasonable firmness' and 'highly compliant', individual characteristics relating specifically to levels of bravery are to be disregarded for the purpose of coercion.

The insistence on objectivism does assist, however, in clarifying the relationship between *actus reus*, *mens rea*, and coercion and the operation of the defence on the elements of the crime. If the concern is specifically *not* with the effect **on the accused** of the threats and the resultant fear but rather on what would have been their effect on the defined representative of the general population, then the defence is clearly detached from the prior question of whether the elements of the crime have been proved beyond reasonable doubt. The Crown must prove that the accused, individually, carried out the proscribed act and that s/he did this with the proscribed mental attitude. The defence is only slightly concerned with whether the threat operated to elide either element. Rather, it is focused more on the acceptability generally of such a claim in the context created by the circumstances of the case. It is here that we can identify the normative component: in the 'ordinary, sober person of reasonable firmness', the law is setting out the basic standard of stoicism or courage which all citizens should meet.

It is submitted, therefore, that the objective approach brings into the spotlight the **reasons** for permitting a defence of coercion both generally and in the individual case. In *Cochrane*, for example, the psychological evidence was that

> the appellant had 'most certainly not' wanted to behave in the manner that he did at the time of the offence. [The expert psychological witness] added that he believed that the appellant had believed that he would be assaulted and that his house would be blown up. The appellant had been of the belief that he would be quite severely assaulted if he did not behave in the manner he was instructed to.[72]

Whether this extreme fear had, in fact, negated Cochrane's *mens rea* is debatable, but the matter was not at issue. Coercion weighs the quality of the threat and the nature of the fear which are generated in their own right. Only if these stand up to scrutiny, detached from the accused's own response to them, will the defence be made out. There is no direct effect on presence or absence of the core elements of the crime. Coercion stands alone to be determined subsequently. The only overlap (or collapse of *mens rea* and coercion into each other) might arise if the accused claimed that s/he did not have the relevant mental element at all. In most cases, however, absent a claim of hypnotic control or the equivalent, this is unlikely to be successful because the accused will have taken a decision to carry out the crime (albeit in preference to succumbing to the danger threatened). These issues—of danger, choice and objectivism—are also prominent in the defence of necessity which will now be considered.

Necessity

Until the case of *Moss v Howdle*[73] in 1997, necessity was ill-defined in Scots law. Compared to international, historical cases involving tales of cannibalism[74] and shipwreck,[75] *Moss*'s facts (speeding on the M74 motorway) are prosaic. Nonetheless, it brought some precision to the law, confirming, at its outset, that the defence is available, in appropriate circumstances, for *all* crimes. It did this by rejecting the possible interpretation of

---

71 *Thomson* (n 56) 72 (Lord Hunter – trial judge's report).
72 *Cochrane* (n 66) [7].
73 *Moss* (n 55).
74 *R v Dudley & Stephens* (1884) 14 QBD 273.
75 *United States v Holmes* (1842)

Thomson[76] that a defence based in any form of duress was available only for 'atrocious crimes'.[77] The charge in *Moss* related to an offence of strict liability[78] and the court had no difficulty in determining that necessity could be pled. It can be inferred from this that necessity cannot operate to negate *mens rea*—or, at least, that this could not be its only function—since, by definition, strict liability offences are established by commission of a criminal act only. Coercion, as has been discussed, arises when the accused is faced with life-threatening violence. Necessity can be pled in a broader range of circumstances. The severity of the threat must be as desperate,[79] but it may arise from 'some contingency such as a natural disaster or illness rather than from the deliberate threats of another'.[80] It is regarded as 'consistent with the ethos of [the Scottish] system'[81] that the defence should be capable of use where the actions were to save a third party rather than the accused him or herself. Finally, if any alternative course of action existed which would have been lawful, the defence will not succeed.[82]

Necessity builds, in some respects, on the principles of coercion as set down in *Thomson*[83] however it is fair to say that the nature of the fear generated by the extreme danger is likely to be slightly different, since the accused's own life need not be endangered – altruistic action is equally acceptable. Also, the range of possible responses to the danger is likely to be broader. In coercion, the coercer seeks to force the commission of a particular crime. In necessity, the accused may have a number of alternative courses of action available and, given that the defence fails if any of these would have been legal, there is a greater element of choice and greater rationality is expected. This can be seen in the case of *Dawson v Dickson*,[84] where Lord Sutherland stated:

> [T]he defence of necessity only arises when there is a conscious dilemma faced by a person who has to decide between saving life or avoiding serious body harm on the one hand and breaking the law on the other hand. If, in the circumstances of the case, he elects to break the law rather than risk life, the defence of necessity may well be open to him.[85]

This demonstrates the separation between *mens rea* and necessity. There is no suggestion that fear overrode the accused's ability to decide to commit the crime. Rather, this 'elect[ion]' is central. The possible courses of action available for avoiding the danger are recognised to be limited but the accused still has choice and control over which of these to choose. *Dawson* turned on this element of choice. In fact, the accused's commission of the crime (careless driving under the influence of alcohol) was *not* because the danger was so pressing that offending was his only option. He had not, in fact, thought about the danger (which, nonetheless, did exist) at all and would have driven regardless. The absence of a (personal) dilemma was fatal to the use of the defence.

The clear distinction between the offence elements and necessity is also accentuated in the *Lord Advocate's Reference (No 1 of 2000)*[86] which adopted an objective approach, similar to that of *Cochrane* in relation to the effect which the danger had to have. The case related to a charge of malicious mischief where nuclear protestors had boarded a naval ship berthed in Loch Goil and, *inter alia*, thrown equipment overboard. They argued that they had had to do so to prevent another crime: the use of nuclear weapons by the United Kingdom which, they asserted, would have been contrary to customary international law.

According to Lord Prosser, 'the defence will only be available if a sober person of reasonable firmness, sharing the characteristics of the actor, would have responded as he did'[87] showing the law's recognition that

---

76   *Thomson* (n 56).
77   ibid 78. See *Moss* (n 55) 126 (LJ-G Rodger).
78   Motorways Traffic (Speed Limit) Regulations 1974, SI 1974/502, reg 3.
79   According to Lord Justice-General Rodger, 'the minimum requirement of any defence of this kind is that the accused acted in the face of an immediate danger of death or great bodily harm'. *Moss* (n 55) 126.
80   ibid 128 (LJ-G Rodger).
81   ibid 128 (LJ-G Rodger).
82   ibid 129–30.
83   *Thomson* (n 56).
84   [1999] JC 315.
85   ibid 318.
86   [2001] JC 143.
87   ibid [42].

'different people respond to danger in different ways'.[88] In the same way as for coercion, then, this objective approach affirms the separation between the elements of any offence and the defence of necessity.

Overall, necessity, having been adapted from the (historical) principles of coercion is possibly more stringent than it needs to be, given that individuals may be faced with dangers which are not in any way life-threatening but which might still reasonably be countered with minor breaches of the criminal law.[89] Equally, if the (criminal) course of action is reasonable in all the circumstances, it is harsh that it will not exculpate if *any* other legal way of proceeding could be identified.[90] Nonetheless, there is no doubt that this strict and objective formulation leaves intact the separation between the elements of the offence and the defence of necessity. Commenting on the *Lord Advocate's Reference (No 1 of 2000)*, Chalmers said:

> [I]n [this case which was] the first major criminal appeal decision since *Drury*, ... the traditional tripartite analysis of criminal offences was reaffirmed. ... [T]he court was adamant that a defence of necessity would *not* affect the mens rea of malicious mischief. Instead, it operates as a freestanding defence. The mens rea of malicious mischief is simply intention or recklessness. There is no question, it seems, of malicious mischief requiring "malicious intent", which can then be rendered non-malicious if the accused believed that his actions were justified. That, it is submitted, is the correct approach – but at the same time, it is entirely inconsistent with the *Drury* analysis.[91]

Conclusion

The approach taken by *Drury*[92] to the offence/defence structure in Scots criminal law is not replicated in relation to other defences. Automatism, coercion and necessity each provide good reasons for exculpating an accused person. In the latter two, the objectivism of the defence definition actually serves to spotlight the importance of having such reasons. Where the defence is not concerned with the accused's own response to extreme danger but rather with that of an 'ordinary' person any connection between the *actus reus* and the *mens rea* on the one hand, and the defence on the other is, necessarily, attenuated. This brings about a more detached focus on whether the reasons for allowing exoneration are actually good ones. Coercion and necessity both exculpate a criminal response to extreme danger. Both are restrictive. The reported cases show few successful pleas. In coercion, the outstanding question is whether a more subjective response could still strike an appropriate balance between the rights of the accused and the public interest. In necessity, calls for a relaxation of the stringency of the tests where the danger (and the response) are not of death or great bodily harm should be considered. Automatism, rightly, recognises the unfairness of convicting an accused where s/he has been unable to exercise rational control over his/her actions through no fault attributable to him/her. It would benefit from greater clarity in relation to the internal/external factor distinction.

In general, *Drury*, while an interesting examination of the criminal law of homicide in its historical context, did little to clarify or elucidate the principles of general defences in the criminal law of Scotland. It did, however, serve to focus attention on their operation, at least in homicide, a worthwhile exercise which has been carried forward here. Ultimately, automatism, coercion and necessity accord with the traditional structure of criminal law and procedure which postpones consideration of any defence until the offence elements (*actus reus* and *mens rea*) have, at least *prima facie*, been made out by the prosecution. While the relationship to *mens rea* may sometimes be close and direct, the view taken here is that the separation of defences is most conducive to fairness in the administration of justice.

---

88   ibid [43].

89   See Gerald Gordon's commentary on Moss (n 70), [1997] SCCR 215, 224. See also *Ruxton v Lang* [1998] SCCR 1 and *D v Donnelly* [2009] SLT 476, in both of which cases the appeal court ruled that the danger had passed so that the defence of necessity was no longer available though, in each, the accused's subjective perspective may have been that she was not (yet) safe.

90   See Victor Tadros, 'The Structure of Defences in Scots Criminal Law' (2003) 7 Edinburgh L Rev 60, 68.

91   Chalmers (n 3) 242–243.

92   *Drury* (n 1).

Chapter 12
In a Spirit of Compromise:
The Irish Doctrine of Excessive Defence

John E Stannard

Lawyers love a compromise. Most cases are settled out of court; the metaphor of striking a balance is well engrained in the judicial consciousness, and the traditional figure of Justice would not be complete without her scales. Indeed, according to Robert Louis Stevenson compromise is the best and cheapest lawyer of all.[1]

Be that as it may, the notion of compromise does not sit so well in the context of the adversarial criminal justice system in general, or in the context of defences in particular. For the most part, a defence either applies or it does not; there is no half way house, and the more subtle gradations of culpability have to be dealt with either before the case comes to trial (in the form of plea bargaining) or at the sentencing stage. For the jury or magistrate faced with giving a verdict, there are only two choices; guilty or not guilty. A defendant cannot be found partly guilty.

However, the position is different when it comes to mitigating defences which reduce murder to manslaughter. A person who kills while suffering from a mental abnormality can raise the defence of diminished responsibility, and one who kills in hot blood may be able to rely on provocation or loss of control. The same result is reached by a different route in the case of the intoxicated killer, who may be able to escape a murder conviction on the basis of his or her lack of specific intent, but will still be guilty of manslaughter. In these cases the jury has not two choices of verdict but three; guilty of murder, guilty of manslaughter, and not guilty.

To what extent does this apply in the context of private and public defence? In most jurisdictions it does not: in the words of Lord Morris, the defence either succeeds so as to result in an acquittal or it is disproved, in which case as a defence it is rejected.[2] However, the so-called doctrine of 'excessive defence' is an exception to this. Broadly speaking, this doctrine reduces murder to manslaughter in cases where the defendant was entitled to use a certain degree of force, but goes beyond what was necessary and justified and kills as a result.[3] Though the doctrine has been rejected in England and Wales[4] and in Northern Ireland,[5] it still forms part of Irish law,[6] and there have from time to time been calls for it to be extended to other parts of the British Isles.[7] In this chapter we shall look at the history and development of the excessive defence doctrine before examining its constituent elements in more detail. After that, we shall look at some of the problems to which it gives rise before asking to what extent it would form a useful part of the criminal law.

---

1   Cited from <http://omegaquote.com/quote.php?id=342> accessed 28 October 2013.

2   *Palmer* [1971] AC 814 at 832. In this context, Lord Morris refers in particular to self-defence, but the same applies equally to force used in the prevention of crime and in effecting a lawful arrest.

3   See further below (nn 22–30).

4   *Palmer* (n 2); *Shannon* (1980) 71 Cr App R 192..

5   *Clegg* [1995] 1 AC 482.

6   *People (A-G) v Dwyer* [1972] IR 416.

7   Most notably by the Northern Ireland Court of Appeal in Clegg, and by Lord Lloyd of Berwick giving the opinion of the House of Lords in the case; [1995] 1 AC 482, 491–492 and 498–499; see also Criminal Law Revision Committee, *Fourteenth Report, Offences Against the Person* (Cmnd 7844 1980) para 73; Law Commission, *Criminal Law: A Criminal Code for England and Wales* (Law Com No 177 1989) para 59; *House of Select Committee on Murder and Life Imprisonment* (House of Lords Papers, Session 1988–89, 78) HMSO, London, 1989, Vol III, 542 (Viscount Colville); see also Alec Samuels, 'Excessive Self-Defence – A Missed Opportunity' (1971) 121 New LJ 669; Sean Doran, 'The Doctrine of Excessive Defence' (1985) 36 N Ire LQ314.

Development of the Doctrine

The doctrine of excessive defence has been traced back as far as the seventeenth century,[8] but a good starting point for the present discussion is the decision of the Victoria Court of Criminal Appeal in *McKay*.[9] In this case, the defendant shot and killed the victim, whom he had caught stealing chickens from his father's farm. Evidence was given that the farm had been subjected to a spate of such thefts, and that the defendant had tried in vain to prevent them. In his statement to the police he declared that he considered himself entitled to wound a person who was stealing fowls from his property, all the more so given that there were notices up saying that trespassers would be prosecuted.[10] The issues in the case were somewhat complicated by the uncertainty as to whether the defendant intended to kill or do serious harm to his victim, but during the course of his judgement Lowe J stated that if the occasion warranted action in self-defence or for the prevention of felony or the apprehension of the felon, but the person taking action acted beyond the necessity of the occasion and killed the offender, the crime was manslaughter and not murder.[11]

As we shall see, the precise ambit of this principle is not clear, but it was considered further by the High Court of Australia in *Howe*.[12] Here the defendant shot his victim dead with a rifle, claiming that he had been subjected to homosexual advances on his part.[13] Once again there was some uncertainty both as to the degree of harm threatened by the victim, and to that intended by the defendant,[14] but in his judgement Dixon CJ stated the key issue in the following terms:[15]

> [W]hether, where on an indictment of murder the accused relies on self-defence as a plea and all the elements of that defence are made out except that which relates to the proportion of the force used to the degree of danger threatened or reasonably apprehended, the verdict against the accused should be, or at all events may be, manslaughter and not murder. The assumption made for the purpose of this question is that a man actually defending himself from the real or apprehended violence of the deceased has used more force than was justified by the occasion and that death has ensued from this use of excessive force. In all other respects, so it is assumed, the elements of a plea of self-defence existed. That is to say it is assumed that an attack of a violent and felonious nature, or at least of an unlawful nature, was made or threatened so that the person under attack or threat of attack reasonably feared for his life or the safety of his person from injury, violation or indecent and insulting usage … . There is no clear and definite judicial decision providing an answer to this question but it seems reasonable in principle to regard such a homicide as reduced to manslaughter, and that view has the support of not a few judicial statements to be found in the reports.

Despite the uncertainties to which this formulation gives rise,[16] the doctrine was subsequently followed in a number of American and Commonwealth jurisdictions,[17] and was adopted by the Irish Supreme Court in *People (Attorney-General) v Dwyer*.[18] Here the defendant was convicted of murder after stabbing an unarmed man to death during the course of a street fight, evidence being given that he mistakenly believed his life to

---

8   Colin Howard, 'An Australian Letter – Excessive Defence' [1964] Crim LR 448; M Sornarajah, 'Excessive Defence in Commonwealth Law' (1972) 21 Int'l &CompLQ 758.

9   [1957] VR 560; Norval Morris, 'The Slain Chicken Thief' (1958) 2 Syd LRev 414.

10   ibid 416.

11   [1957] VLR 560, 561.

12   (1958) 100 CLR 448.

13   The defence of provocation was raised by the defendant in this connection, but it was rejected by the jury. [1957] VR 448 at 459 (Dixon CJ).

14   According to Fullagar J, all that could be said is that there was some evidence of an attack on the defendant, and that it might be possible to perceive some evidence that in shooting the deceased he believed that the action was necessary for his protection: [1957] VR 448, 465.

15   ibid 460–461.

16   See further below (nn 31–62).

17   In this connection, James refers to 'a Tanganikan burglar, a Nebraskan rapist, a Trinidadian drunk, a Guyanese duck marksman and a small-time Jamaican ganja-dealer': see Charles James, 'The Queensbury Rules of Self-Defence' (1972) 21 Int'l &CompLQ 357. A similar defence also appears in Section 300 of the Indian Penal Code. M Sornarajah (n 8).

18   [1972] IR 416.

be under threat. The question for the Supreme Court was whether the judge should have left to the jury the option of a manslaughter verdict on the basis of *Howe*, or whether the court should follow the lead of the Privy Council[19] and of the English Court of Appeal[20] in rejecting the doctrine. The court held that the requirement of subjective intent for murder in section 4 of the Criminal Justice Act 1964 prevented a person being convicted of murder when his or her primary intent was one of self-defence, using no more force than was honestly believed to be necessary. In the words of Butler J:[21]

> A person is entitled to defend himself from unlawful attack. If in doing so he uses no more force than is reasonably necessary, he is acting lawfully and commits no crime even though he kill his assailant. If he uses more force than may objectively be considered necessary, his act is unlawful and, if he kills, the killing is unlawful. His intention, however, falls to be treated subjectively, and if it would appear logical to conclude that, if his intention in doing the unlawful act was primarily to defend himself, he should not be held to have the necessary intention to kill or cause serious injury. The result of this view would be that the killing, though unlawful, would be manslaughter only.

Elements of the Doctrine

So what are the elements of the doctrine, or as one might say the requirements that have to be met to found a plea of excessive defence? Though the matter is not entirely clear, there seem to be four of these.[22]

The first is that the case must be one of homicide. Since the effect of the doctrine is to reduce murder to manslaughter,[23] it cannot apply in cases involving non-fatal harm. In such cases the fact that the defendant has in good faith used an excessive degree of force can only go to the issue of sentencing.

The second is that the defendant must have been legally entitled to use a certain degree of force in the first place. In the words of Lowe J, the occasion must warrant action in self-defence or for the prevention of felony or for the apprehension of the felon; in the words of Dixon CJ, the defendant must be actually defending himself; in the words of Butler J, he must be defending himself from unlawful attack.[24] What is less clear is the *degree* of force that must be warranted to trigger the application of the doctrine. In his formulation in *Howe*, as we have seen, Dixon CJ lists a wide range of possibilities: there must be 'an attack of a violent and felonious nature' or 'at least of an unlawful nature'; the attack must be 'made' or at least 'threatened'; the person under attack of the threat of attack must 'reasonably fear for his life', or 'or the safety of his person from injury', or 'violation' or 'indecent and insulting usage'. According to the Supreme Court of Victoria in *Tikos (No 2)*, there had to be an attack of such a degree as to warrant the accused 'acting with the intent to do grievous bodily harm at the least',[25] but not only is this inconsistent with the approach taken in *McKay*, and, indeed, in *Howe*,[26] but it also reduces the significance of the doctrine to vanishing point, since a person who is entitled to do grievous bodily harm in response to an attack will normally be acquitted altogether.[27] Given

---

19   *Palmer* [1971] AC 814.

20   *McInnes* [1971] 1 WLR 1600.

21   [1972] IR 416, 429.

22   See further the formulation of the Supreme Court of South Australia in Howe (1958) 100 CLR 448, 456; Doran (n 7) 318.

23   Whether it is a mitigating defence in the strict sense is a moot point: see below (n 48–54). For this and other reasons Howard suggests that the defence need not necessarily be confined to cases of homicide, but unless it is to be regarded as a complete defence it is hard to see how this would work: Colin Howard, 'Two Problems in Excessive Defence' (1968) 84 LQ Rev 343, 352.

24   This also seems to be the Irish approach. See *People (Attorney-General) v Dwyer* [1972] IR 416, 424 (Walsh J).

25   [1963] VR 306 at 313; Howard (n 8).

26   In the former case the victim was merely stealing chickens, and in the latter there was no evidence to suggest a threat of physical harm as opposed to indecent assault. Howard(n 23) 347 and 350.

27   Howard (n 23) 347–348; Ian D Elliott, 'Excessive Self-Defence in Commonwealth Law: A Comment' (1973) 22 Int'l &CompLQ 727, 734.

that as we shall see the excessive defence doctrine has now been rejected in its entirety in the country of its origin,[28] the point is unlikely to be clarified now.

The third is that the force used by the defendant must, objectively speaking, be shown to be excessive in the circumstances. Were it not so, he or she would obviously be entitled to a full acquittal.

Finally, the defendant must have honestly believed the force to be warranted; that is to say, there must have been an honest mistake on his or her part as to the degree of force called for in the circumstances. Though the cases do not make this explicit, there are clearly two different types of mistake that can be made here.[29] In most of the cases from *Howe* onwards, including *Dwyer*, the defendant appears to have misjudged the factual situation and responded to a threat that was not present, believing that his or her life was at risk. The case of *McKay*, in contrast, demonstrates a mistake of a totally different kind. Here the defendant was under no misapprehension as to the facts; on the contrary, he knew full well that the victim was merely stealing his chickens. His mistake was as to the degree of force that the law allowed him to use in such circumstances; as he himself said, he considered himself fully entitled to shoot a person who was stealing his property. As we shall see, these two types of mistake give rise to completely different policy considerations,[30] and one of the weaknesses of the doctrine is the way it lumps them together under the broad heading of 'excessive force'.

Problems of Analysis

Be that as it may, there are a number of analytical uncertainties with regard to the doctrine and its scope. Five issues in particular deserve mention in this regard.

Private and Public Defence

The first issue concerns the extent to which the doctrine is applicable to cases of public as opposed to private defence—that is, cases involving force used in the prevention of crime and in effecting a lawful arrest. All of the leading cases on the subject, as we have seen, involve an attack of some sort on the defendant or at least on his or her property,[31] and several of the judges confine their remarks to this type of case.[32] Others, however, specifically include cases of public defence,[33] and it has been argued that there is no reason in principle to distinguish between the two in this connection.[34] As against that, it has been said that different policy considerations apply to public defence,[35] and this view has a lot to commend it. Say, for instance, an armed police constable was to shoot someone dead who was spraying graffiti on the wall, or an escaping shoplifter. Should the constable in question be entitled to argue, on the lines of *McKay*, that he or she thought that the use of lethal force in such circumstances was justified?[36]

Excessive Defence and the Principle in Beckford

Another tricky problem is the relationship of the excessive defence doctrine to the principle in *Beckford v R*,[37] whereby a defendant who relies on private or public defence is judged on the facts as he or she honestly perceived them to exist, regardless of whether that belief was reasonable or not. As has been pointed out, the

---

28   See nn 98–102.

29   Doran (n 7) 317–318.

30   See nn 55–62.

31   Howard (n 8) 449.

32   *Howe* (1958) 100 CLR 448, 465 (Supreme Court of South Australia), 460 (Dixon CJ) and 471 (Menzies J); Selemani [1963] EA 442, 446. In the same way, the relevant provisions of the Indian Penal Code confine themselves to private defence of the person and of property. Elliott (n 27) 738–740.

33   This was certainly the position taken by Lowe J in McKay [1957] VR 560 at 563; Sornarajah (n 8) 766.

34   Doran (n 7) 314.

35   Howard (n 23) 343.

36   This would be a particularly sore point in Northern Ireland; see Doran(n 7) 335–340.

37   [1988] AC 130.

doctrine of excessive defence presupposes a largely objective approach to the main defence,[38] and the more that approach is watered down the less need there is for the doctrine.[39] Indeed, the approach in *Beckford* cannot really be reconciled with a doctrine of excessive defence at all except by restricting the latter to mistakes of law,[40] or by treating it as a species of involuntary manslaughter on the basis that the defendant has made a grossly negligent mistake as to the facts.[41] Both of these issues will be examined in more detail below.[42]

Relationship with Provocation

There is a clear overlap between cases of excessive defence and cases of provocation, or what would now be the statutory defence of loss of control.[43] Indeed, the two doctrines have been shown to share a common historical root,[44] and the sort of facts which give rise to the first will often also give rise to the second.[45] This has given rise to the suggestion that the law does not need both doctrines, and that one of them would suffice.[46] However, there is a clear difference between them, in that provocation and its successors, unlike excessive defence, require evidence of a loss of control on the part of the defendant.[47] Whilst many defendants who kill in an excessive defence situation will be able to claim a loss of self-control, the excessive defence doctrine is not based on loss of control but on the need to make allowance for the fact that the defendant was entitled to use *some* degree of force in the circumstances, albeit not lethal force.

Voluntary or Involuntary Manslaughter?

Another issue is whether excessive defence is to be classified as a case of voluntary or involuntary manslaughter. In all of the cases so far discussed, the issue has been argued in mitigation of what would otherwise be a case of murder, and in the light of this the doctrine has been seen as a species of voluntary manslaughter;[48] the defendant intends to kill or do grievous bodily harm, but the fact that this was done in defence—albeit going beyond what a reasonable person would consider necessary, prevents him or her being convicted of murder.[49] However, some have argued that excessive defence would better be regarded as a species of involuntary manslaughter.[50] Thus it could be said that the act of the defendant leading to death is clearly dangerous, and derives its unlawfulness from the very fact of its being excessive.[51] Alternatively, as we have seen, liability for manslaughter can be predicated on the basis that the defendant, though honestly acting in self-defence, has made a grossly negligent mistake as to the facts.[52] While both of these approaches are undoubtedly sound as far as they go, they do not explain why the defendant is spared from a murder conviction in these cases. In particular, the mere fact that a killing can be classified as involuntary manslaughter does not prevent it from being murder unless it can be argued that the defendant lacks the necessary intention to kill or do serious injury. As we have seen, this is precisely the line of reasoning adopted by Butler J in the *Dwyer* case,[53] but as will be

---

38 Sornarajah (n 8) 760.
39 This tendency could be seen in some of the cases even before *Beckford*; see, for instance,*Brown v US*, 256 US 335 (1920); *R v Bohan* (1979) 5 NIJB; *R v Shannon* (n 4).
40 As in *McKay* (nn 9–11).
41 As was suggested in *Foxford* [1974] NI 181, 188 (Kelly J).
42 See nn 48–54 and 55–62.
43 Coroners and Justice Act 2009 s 54.
44 Sornarajah (n 8) 762–763.
45 As in *Howe* itself (nn 12–15), where the defence of provocation was relied on at trial but rejected by the jury. No appeal was pursued on the provocation issue (1958) 100 CLR 448, 459 (Dixon CJ),
46 See, for instance, John E Stannard, 'Shooting to Kill and the Manslaughter Option' (1992) 2 Irish CrimLJ 19.
47 Elliott (n 27) 729–731; Doran (n 7) 326–327.
48 Sornarajah (n 8) 761.
49 *Dwyer* (n 6) 423 (Walsh J).
50 ibid 422–423 (Walsh J); Howard (n 23) 357–359.
51 Doran (n 7) 331.
52 Howard (n 23) 358–359; *Foxford* (n 41).
53 *Dwyer* (n 6).

argued below, this can only be supported on the basis of a very narrow meaning of intention.[54] This being so, the voluntary manslaughter analysis would appear at the end of the day to be the more convincing one.

Mistakes of Fact or Law?

There is also some uncertainty as to the kind of mistake encompassed by the doctrine. The notion of reasonable force has traditionally been held to comprise two elements.[55] The first is that of necessity, namely that the accused could not have achieved the relevant end, be it self-defence, prevention of the crime or the effecting of the lawful arrest in question, without the degree of force in fact used.[56] The second is that of justification, namely that the harm done by the use of that force was not out of proportion to the harm prevented.[57] Most of the cases on excessive defence involve mistakes of the first kind; the reason why the force was excessive was that the accused misjudged the situation and perceived that a certain degree of threat existed when in fact it did not.[58] Clearly the law can and should make allowances for this situation, the only question being whether it should do so by means of a mitigating defence (as with the doctrine under discussion) or by allowing the accused to be judged on the basis of the facts as he or she honestly perceived them to exist (as in the *Beckford* principle). Some cases however, most notably *McKay*,[59] suggest a mistake of a different sort, namely a mistake as to the degree of force allowable in response to the given threat; here the accused knew full well that the threat was only to his property, but thought that the law allowed him to use lethal force in response to that threat. In these cases, as Elliott says, the force used is 'instrumentally necessary' but 'morally and legally disproportionate'.[60] Such cases are not covered by the *Beckford* principle, so here the doctrine under discussion is all that stands between the accused and a murder conviction. Whether the law should, again in Elliott's words, make allowances for one who acts in full knowledge of the facts but 'out of a misguided sense of the righteousness of his cause'[61] is a moot point; many would argue that it is for the law to set the standards here, not the accused,[62] but perhaps this should not be carried so far as to convict him or her of murder in this situation.

Rationale of the Doctrine

Another challenge is to identify the rationale behind the doctrine. In particular, is its purpose to provide a concession to a defendant who would otherwise be convicted of manslaughter, or is it to impose liability on one who would otherwise be entitled to a complete acquittal?[63] All in all no less than four different justifications can be discerned for the existence of the doctrine.

The first is that a defendant who uses excessive force in this situation does not have the necessary specific intent for murder. Thus in *Howe* it was argued by the defendant that an intention to kill and an intention to defend oneself were in two different categories of thought,[64] and this was accepted by the Supreme Court of South Australia[65] and also by Taylor J in the High Court,[66] who said that if it appeared that what the accused did was done primarily for the purpose of defending himself against an aggressor, the jury should be told that

---

54   See nn 64–73.

55   Doran (n 7) 315; John E Stannard, 'Excessive Defence in Northern Ireland' (1992) 43 N Ire LQ 147.

56   D Ormerod, *Smith and Hogan's Criminal Law* (13th edn, 2011) 387.

57   ibid.

58   Doran (n 7) 315. *Dwyer* itself is a good example of this, his mistake being as to whether the use of lethal force was 'reasonably necessary'. [1972] IR 416, 424 (Walsh J).

59   See nn 9–12.

60   Elliott (n 27) 735.

61   ibid 731.

62   Doran (n 7) 315; Stannard (n 46) 198.

63   Elliott (n 27) 728.

64   (1958) 100 CLR 448 at 453. Compare the reasoning of the House of Lords in *DPP v Morgan* [1976] AC 182 (belief that victim consenting sufficient to negative intent to have sexual intercourse with non-consenting victim).

65   (1958) 100 CLR 448 at 465.

66   ibid 468.

unless satisfied beyond reasonable doubt that this was not so a verdict of manslaughter should be returned. As we have already seen, the same line of reasoning lies at the heart of the decision of the Irish Supreme Court in *Dwyer*,[67] where the key factor relied on by the court in recognising the doctrine was section 4 of the Criminal Justice Act 1964, which was (and is) in the following terms:

1) Where a person kills unlawfully the killing shall not be murder unless the accused person intended to kill, or cause serious injury to some person, whether the person actually killed or not.
2) The accused person shall be presumed to have intended the natural and probable consequences of his conduct, but that presumption may be rebutted.

Since the 'primary intent' of the accused in these cases is to defend himself or herself rather than to kill or do serious injury to the deceased, there can according to the Supreme Court be no conviction of murder in these circumstances.[68] The difficulty with this approach is that it presupposes an extremely narrow meaning of intent,[69] for after all it can surely be said in some of these cases that though the primary aim of the accused was indeed self-defence, he or she may have set out to achieve that aim by means of killing the deceased,[70] or at least knew that it was virtually certain that this would be the result.[71] For this reason a weaker version of this approach has been formulated, whereby the intention to kill or do serious harm is admitted, but the motive of the accused in defending himself or herself against the attack is regarded as a mitigating factor sufficient to reduce the crime to manslaughter,[72] but given that the criminal law does not generally recognise defences based on motive this leaves open the question why it should do so in this case. This aspect of the matter will be considered more fully below.[73]

The second rationale seen in the cases is the futility of expecting a person under attack to measure with precision what degree of force might be appropriate in the circumstances. As Taylor J put it in *Howe*:[74]

[A]ction in self-defence is instinctive and does not wait upon the precise appreciation of the exigencies of the occasion or upon the formation of a belief concerning the precise measures which are necessary.

In the same way, it has been said that the Indian courts have rationalised the doctrine on the ground that someone subject to a physical attack cannot be expected to measure to any degree of precision the extent of violence he should use to protect himself.[75] While this approach has a lot to commend it, it has now largely been outflanked, at least in English law, by the so-called 'jeweller's scales' principle, under which a defendant is entitled to a *complete acquittal* if in the heat of the moment he or she has used more force than is strictly justified. As Lord Morris put it in *Palmer v R*:[76]

If there has been attack so that defence is reasonably necessary it will be recognised that a person defending himself cannot weigh to a nicety the exact measure of his necessary defensive action. If a jury thought that in a moment of unexpected anguish a person attacked had only done what he honestly and instinctively thought was necessary that would be most potent evidence that only reasonable defensive action had been taken.

---

67   [1972] IR 416; discussed above (n 18–21).
68   Ibid., 424 (Walsh J) and 429 (Butler J).
69   See generally John E Stannard, 'Murder and the Ruthless Risk Taker' (2008) 8 OUCLJ 137; and compare *Ahlers* [1915] 1 KB 616 and *Steane* [1947] KB 997.
70   Compare *Cunliffe v Goodman* [1950] 2 KB 237, 253 (Asquith LJ) with *R v Mohan* [1976] QB 1, 11 (James LJ).
71   According to *R v Woollin* [1999] 1 AC 82, 96, the jury is at the very least entitled to find intent in such cases.
72   James (n 17) 361.
73   See nn 73–82.
74   (1958) 100 CLR 448, 468.
75   Sornarajah (n 8) 767–768.
76   [1971] AC 814, 832.

On the basis of this rationale the doctrine of excessive defence, where it applies, is not so much a concession to the accused as a recognition that even in extreme situations the law must set the appropriate standards of conduct. Again this is a matter to which we shall return in due course.[77]

A third rationale for the doctrine, though not one explicit in the cases, is that to a certain extent a person has an absolute right to bodily integrity, and that there are limits to which he or she can be expected to submit tamely when that integrity is threatened.[78] To take an example given by Howard, say that someone is threatened with a sexual assault which can only be prevented by the use of lethal force?[79] The traditional principle of proportionality would say that in such a situation the defendant must submit to the assault in question rather than resort to a disproportionate use of force, but should the law insist on this principle to the extent of labelling the defendant as a murderer if he or she refuses to do so?[80] Whilst there is force in this argument, it must again be subject to some qualifications. In particular, the argument is not as convincing when taken outside the field of self-defence, as in cases such as *McKay*, where the attack was on the defendant's property rather than his or her person.[81] And it has even less to commend it in the context of public defence, as where a police constable has resorted to the use of lethal force in order to prevent some trivial crime. Here again, it must surely be for the law to set the appropriate standard of conduct, and not the defendant.

A broader and less focussed justification is the need for flexibility, and the inherent inconvenience of having no intermediate step available between a conviction of murder and a complete acquittal.[82] This was well expressed by the Indian Penal Code Commissioners in the following words:[83]

> [T]hat a man should be merely exercising a right by fracturing the skull and knocking out the eye of the assailant, and should be guilty of the highest crime in the code if he kills the same assailant, that there should be only a single step between perfect innocence and murder, between perfect impunity and liability of capital punishment, seems unreasonable. In a case in which the law itself empowers an individual to inflict any harm short of death, it ought hardly, we think, to visit him with the highest punishment if he inflicts death.

The difficulty with this is that it proves too much; the problem of the 'single step' between complete acquittal and liability for murder arises in other contexts too,[84] which then gives rise to the question why the intermediate step should be made available in cases of excessive defence in particular. Perhaps the answer is to recognise a general mitigating principle in cases of murder based on diminished culpability, but whilst this would obviate the need for a doctrine of excessive defence there is, as has been conceded, little support for it in the law as it stands.[85]

---

77   See n 113.

78   See Sornarajah (n 8) 765 (defence of chastity), and compare Fletcher's 'third model of necessary defense' based on 'violation of autonomy'. George P Fletcher, *Rethinking Criminal Law* (Little Brown 1978) [10.5.3].

79   Howard (n 23) 352–353.

80   ibid.

81   James (n 17) 360. However, traces of it can be found in the so-called 'castle doctrine' whereby a person can use lethal force in the protection of his or her home. See *R v Hussey* (1924) 18 Cr App R 160.

82   Howard (n 23) 360; Samuels (n 7) 669; Doran (n 7) 314–315. Doran also makes the point that some flexibility would have been particularly desirable in the Northern Ireland context given the reluctance of judges under the Diplock court system to bring in a murder conviction against members of the security forces. Doran (n 7) 337–338.

83   *The Introductory Report of the Indian Law Commission on the Indian Penal Code*, Note M, 147, cited by Sornarajah (n 8) 767.

84   In cases of mental abnormality an intermediate verdict is possible on the basis of diminished responsibility, and a similar result can be reached in cases of intoxication where the defendant lacks the specific intent for murder, but in cases of duress and necessity either the defence applies or it does not. Indeed, with duress murder is the one crime where the defence is not available, giving rise to the anomaly that the defendant acting under duress who sets out to do grievous bodily harm is completely acquitted if the victim lives but is guilty of murder if the victim dies. See *R v Howe* [1987] AC 147.

85   Doran (n 7) 321; Smith and Hogan (n 56) 398 n437.

A Response to Emotion?

Given these uncertainties, it is worth asking if light can be cast on the doctrine by the study of law and emotion. This discipline has come to the fore in recent years, and has sought to examine the relationship of law and emotion from a variety of perspectives, most notably the ways in which the law reacts to emotion, the ways in which the law seeks to create emotion, and the ways in which emotion can pervade the practice of the law.[86] With regard to excessive defence this gives rise to two questions: one relating to the emotions of the accused and the other relating to the emotions of the jury (or other finder of fact) in applying the doctrine.

Emotions of the Accused

As we have seen, one obvious rationale for the excessive defence doctrine is that, in the words of Oliver Wendell Holmes, detached reflection cannot be demanded in the presence of an uplifted knife.[87] Why not? From a psychological standpoint, two reasons can be given. The first relates to the nature of the decision-making process in this sort of situation; as Burrows has argued in relation to the use of firearms by police officers, it is not a case of the defendant taking time to assess what is happening and *then* deciding what to do in response—rather, the processes of assessment, decision making and reaction all occur more or less simultaneously.[88] The other relevant factor in the equation is the cognitive distortion caused by stress; thus as Bernstein and others indicate,[89] overarousal created by stressors can lead to cognitive distortions of various kinds, including a narrowing of attention, making it harder to scan the full range of possible solutions to complex problems.[90] In the same way, stress can impair judgement and decision making in responding to these problems.[91] All of this suggests that the law is right to make *some* allowance for these factors, though whether this should be by means of a complete defence (as in the *Beckford* and 'jeweller's scales' principles described above)[92] or as a mitigating factor (as in the doctrine under discussion) must obviously depend on wider policy issues.

Emotions of the Jury

An equally interesting question is the extent to which the provision of an intermediate choice (in this case a manslaughter verdict) in addition to the stark alternatives of conviction and acquittal affects the decision making processes of the jury or other finder of fact.[93] There is evidence to show that juries are more inclined to bring in a conviction in cases of homicide when presented with the intermediate option of a manslaughter verdict rather than being asked to choose between the stark alternatives of a murder conviction and a complete

---

86   There is now a vast literature on law and emotion, but for a good starting point see Terry Maroney, 'Law and Emotion: A Proposed Taxonomy of an Emerging Field' (2006) 30 L&HumBehav 119; Jennifer Schweppe, and John E Stannard, 'What's So Special About Law and Emotion?' (2013) 64 NIreLQ 1.

87   *Brown v US*, 256 US 335, 343 (1921).

88   Colin Burrows, 'Critical Decision Making by Police Firearms Officers: A Review of Officer Perception, Response and Reaction' (2007) 1 Policing 273. Reference has often been made in this context to a 'shoot-to-kill' policy, but this is a red herring in so far as it suggests that one can shoot to disable rather than kill; the real question is whether the police should have opened fire in the first place: see P Squires and P Kennison, *Shooting to Kill* (Wiley-Blackwell 2010) 90.

89   Douglas A Bernstein et al., *Psychology* (8th edn, 2008) 526.

90   Thus we have the phenomenon of 'tunnel vision', whereby a person confronted with a knife or a gun—or what is thought to be a knife or a gun—is likely to concentrate the attention on the weapon or supposed weapon to the exclusion of all else. See Burrows (n 88) 281 and the sources cited therein. In the same way, it has been argued that people are more motivated to detect weapons than innocuous objects because threat has a central role in surviving. See LP Luiniand FS Marucci, 'Effect of Emotions on Cognitive Processes' in H Chaudet et al. (eds), *Proceedings of the 11th International Conference on Naturalistic Decision-Making* (2013) 87, 92.

91   Bernstein (n 89).

92   See nn 37 and 74–77.

93   This reference to other finders of fact is significant, as it has been argued that judges trying cases without a jury in Northern Ireland under the emergency legislation were markedly reluctant to bring in murder convictions against members of the security forces. See Doran (n 7) 335–340.

acquittal,[94] and this chimes in with the sentiments of those who argue that the law should allow for a middle way in cases of this type.[95] It has been argued that allowing for a manslaughter verdict allows juries an easy way of decision avoidance, but this is an option that must be left to them if there is evidence to support it,[96] and it has been said that there is no direct evidence to support the hypothesis that third options function as decision-avoidant alternatives to conviction or acquittal.[97]

The Present Position

Given what has just been said, it is perhaps significant that the doctrine of excessive defence has its origin in the days of the death penalty, where the consequences of an unjust murder conviction were much more stark. In a context where the distinction between a murder and a manslaughter conviction are largely symbolic, the need for the doctrine is less marked. Indeed, it has now been abandoned in the place of its origin, where, following the decision in *Palmer*,[98] the state courts began to apply the law as set out by the Privy Council in that case rather than *Howe*.[99] In *Viro*[100] the High Court of Australia decided, albeit with some reluctance, that *Howe* should continue to apply, but that decision was subsequently reversed by a majority of the same court in *Zecevic v DPP*.[101] Here it was confirmed that where a person charged with homicide went beyond what he believed to be necessary to defend himself, or where he had no reasonable grounds for such a belief, self-defence was not made out, and that in these circumstances—assuming the necessary intent to be present— he should be convicted of murder. The reason for this *volte face* seems to have been not so much that the approach in *Howe* was felt to be unsound, rather that it was unduly difficult to present to juries. In the words of Mason CJ:[102]

> I still believe that the doctrine enunciated in *Howe* and *Viro* expresses a concept of self-defence which best accords with acceptable standards of culpability, so that an accused whose only error is that he lacks reasonable grounds for his belief that the degree of force used was necessary for his self-defence is guilty of manslaughter, not murder. But in the light of experience since *Viro* … I recognize that the doctrine imposes an onerous burden on trial judges and juries. For this reason there is a serious risk that the doctrine will not achieve its desired goal.

In the light of this, he concluded that from now on the courts in Australia should follow the law as set out in *Palmer*.

---

94   Neil Vidmar, 'Effect of Decision Alternatives on the Verdicts and Social Perceptions of Simulated Jurors' (1972) 22 JPersonality & Social Psych 211; Allison Orr Larsen, 'Bargaining Inside the Black Box' (2010), available at http:// works.bepress.com/allisonorr_larsen/1 <accessed 30 October 2013>. This tendency is especially marked where the penalty for the greater offence is felt to be excessively severe: Bernard Grofman, 'The Effect of Restricted and Unrestricted Verdict Options on Juror Choice' (1985) 14 SocSci Research195; Reid K Hester and Ronald E Smith, 'Effects of a Mandatory Death Penalty on the Decisions of Simulated Jurors as a Function of the Heinousness of Crime' (1973) 1 J Crim Just 319. But this does not apply to situations where the middle option has the same effect as a complete acquittal, as in cases of a 'not proven' verdict. Michael Smithsonet al., 'Guilty, Not Guilty or … ? Multiple Options in Jury Verdict Choices' (2007) 20 J Decision Making 481; Lorraine Hope et al., 'A Third Verdict Option: Exploring the Impact of the Not Proven Verdict on Mock Juror Decision Making' (2008) 32 L& Hum Behav 241. Nor does it apply to the same extent where the jury are given a careful direction on the meaning of 'reasonable doubt': Chantal M Koch and Dennis J Devine, 'Effects of Reasonable Doubt Definition and Inclusion of a Lesser Charge on Jury Verdicts' (1999) 23 L& Hum Behav 653.

95   See nn 82–83.

96   Doran (n 7) 332–333; see also *Roberts* [1942] 1 All ER 187, 192 (Humphreys J).

97   Smithson et al. (n 94); Larsen (n 94).

98   [1971] AC 814; see also (n 19).

99   [1958] 100 CLR 448; see also (nn 12–15). The reason for this was the rule that State courts, at least in non-federal matters, were bound by decisions of the Privy Council rather than those of the High Court. This rule ceased to apply following the abolition of appeals to the Privy Council in the Privy Council (Appeals from the High Court) Act 1975: *Zecevic v DPP (Victoria)* (1987) 162 CLR 645, 650 (Mason CJ).

100   (1978) 141 CLR 88.

101   (1987)162 CLR 645 (Mason CJ, Wilson, Brennan, Dawson and Toohey JJ, Deane and Gaudron JJ dissenting).

102   ibid 661–662.

In Ireland, by contrast, the doctrine of excessive defence continues to apply to this day.[103] The doctrine has been applied in recent years by the Court of Criminal Appeal,[104] and the Law Reform Commission have recommended that it be retained.[105] This has to be seen in the context of the more general reforms proposed for the use of lethal force in self-defence, which incorporate a threshold requirement involving a threat of death, serious injury, rape or aggravated sexual assault, or false imprisonment involving the use of force,[106] together with a requirement that the force used be in proportion to the threat.[107] In deciding whether the requirement of proportionality is met, the court is to have regard to all the circumstances, including the circumstances as the defendant reasonably believed them to be.[108] However, the Commission went on to recommend that this be subject to the excessive defence doctrine as set out in *Dwyer*, saying:[109]

> The continued use of the 'half way' house approach in recent cases indicates to the Commission that, where the circumstances give rise to a finding that, although the force used was disproportionate from an objective, reasonable, perspective, it is appropriate that while the death cannot be justified, a court or juries may consider that the defendant's honest (but unreasonable) belief that lethal force was required should be given some weight, even if only to reduce a charge of murder to manslaughter.

And this is duly provided for in clause 2(8) of the Draft Bill appended to the Report.

The Way Forward

It is clear that, for some jurisdictions at least, the doctrine of excessive defence is thought to serve a useful function. It is equally clear, however, that there are problems in determining both the rationale of the doctrine and the way in which it should be applied. All in all, there seem to be three possible approaches here.

The first is to follow the approach of the Irish Law Reform Commission in retaining an objective approach to self-defence whilst mitigating it in cases of homicide by a doctrine of excessive defence. Whilst few would cavil at making allowance for the person whose only error, in the words of Mason CJ, is that he lacks reasonable grounds for his belief as to the necessity of the force used, this is a comparatively harsh approach[110] compared to the position in England and Wales where, as we have seen, the accused is judged on the basis of the facts as he or she honestly believed them to be, without any requirement that the belief be held on reasonable grounds.[111] However, the subjective approach may be felt by some to be too generous to the accused, and certainly the Irish approach is more in accordance with Article 2 of the European Convention on Human Rights, which requires that the force used be 'absolutely necessary'[112] in the circumstances.

The second is to combine the approaches in *McKay* and in *Beckford* by applying a subjective test to mistakes of fact, leaving the doctrine of excessive defence to take care of mistakes of law.[113] On this approach the accused would be judged, as at present in English law, on the basis of the facts as he or she honestly believed them to exist. Even where the use of lethal force could not be justified on the basis of those facts, the accused would still have a defence if he or she honestly thought that it was. The difficulty with this is that while it certainly succeeds in accommodating the excessive defence doctrine within the present English

---

103   Conor Hanly, *An Introduction to Irish Criminal Law* (2nd edn, 2006) 131.
104   *People (DPP) v Nally* [2006] IECCA 128, [2007] 4 IR 145; *People (DPP) v Barnes* [2006] IECCA 165, [2007] 3 IR 130.
105   Law Reform Commission Report: Defences in Criminal Law (LRC95–2009) para 2.215.
106   ibid para 2.56.
107   ibid para 2.207.
108   ibid para 2.205. In this respect there is a marked difference from Section 18 of the Non-Fatal Offences against the Person Act 1997, which only requires that the use of the force be reasonable 'in the circumstances as he or she believes them to be'.
109   Law Reform Commission Report (n 105) para 2.214.
110   All the more so given the strict threshold requirement recommended at para 2.56 of the Report. See n 108.
111   See n 37.
112   ECHR, Article 2(2); Fiona Leverick, *Killing in Self-Defence* (OUP 2006) ch 10.
113   See nn 55–62.

framework, it goes contrary to the principle that it is for the law rather than the accused to set standards of conduct in this situation. After all, why should a person who uses lethal force knowing full well that his or her victim poses no threat to life or limb be spared a murder conviction simply because he or she made a mistake as to the law?

The third possibility would be to leave the precise relationship between the *Beckford* principle and the doctrine of excessive defence undefined, and to allow it to be used as a kind of safety valve for cases where neither a murder conviction nor a complete acquittal was thought to be justified. Whilst lack of precision in the legal context is often seen as the unforgiveable sin, this has been open to challenge; thus for instance it has been argued that in certain contexts such as contract and international law the constructive use of ambiguity might help to sustain important relationships that otherwise would not survive.[114] Whilst the use of ambiguity and vagueness in the definition of criminal conduct would be intolerable, the same arguments may not apply in the field of mitigating defences, the sole function of which is to give the judge a sentencing discretion which otherwise he or she would not possess. In this context, is there not something to be said for flexibility?

Conclusion

The doctrine of excessive defence is like one of those pictures that are best viewed from a distance. The basic idea behind the doctrine—that a person who was entitled to use some degree of force, but overreacts and kills as a result should be convicted of manslaughter rather than murder—seems sound enough at first sight, but gets one into difficulties once one tries to unpack it in detail. But that need not necessarily be an insuperable disadvantage. Sometimes it is hard to see the wood for the trees, and where this is the case, is there not something to be said for forgetting about the trees and concentrating on the wood?

---

114   Philip Thomas, 'Legal Skills and the Use of Ambiguity' (1991) 42 N Ire LQ 14.

PART II

Chapter 13
Australia

Mirko Bagaric

General Issues

Justificatory and Excusatory Defences—Distinction and Seat in the Offence Structure

Each of the nine Australian jurisdictions—the six states (New South Wales, Queensland, South Australia, Tasmania, Victoria and Western Australia); the two territories (the Australian Capital Territory and the Northern Territory); and the federal jurisdiction—has its own criminal law.

The common law, derived from England, is the main source of criminal law in the three largest jurisdictions, Victoria, New South Wales, and in South Australia.[1] The criminal law in the other jurisdictions is almost exclusively based in statute,[2] and for this reason they are referred to as 'Code jurisdictions'. The Codes in Queensland and Western Australia are similar. The Code in the Australian Capital Territory is modelled on the Commonwealth Code, and the Northern Territory Code also contains aspects of the Commonwealth Code.

Despite the different sources of law, there is a considerable convergence regarding criminal offences and defences throughout Australia. This chapter focuses on the core defences and explains the major disparities that exist between the jurisdictions.

Some commentators divide criminal defences into two broad categories: justificatory and excusatory defences.[3] Excusatory defences are typically referred to as those where the accused admits committing a criminal act but denies responsibility on the basis that the necessary mental state is absent. Defences falling into this category include intoxication, insanity, and mistake. Justification defences are those where the criminal act has occurred but the act is justified by the exigencies of the situation. The main justification defences are self-defence, provocation, necessity, and duress. This chapter analyses both forms of defence.

Criminal offences are relatively clearly demarcated and can be broken down into a number of elements. In order for an accused to be guilty of a crime, every element must be established by the prosecution beyond a reasonable doubt. Most offences contain a combination of mental elements (known as the *mens rea*) and physical elements (known as the *actus reus*).[4]

The manner in which an offence is structured has an important impact on the availability and application of a defence. There is no coherent process for demarcating the distinction between an element of an offence and the operation of a defence.

For example, the offence of assault at common law requires the following *three* elements to be established:

1) The offender intentionally or recklessly;
2) Applies force or threatens;
3) Another person.

---

1 The criminal law in each of these jurisdictions is supplemented by various statutory provisions, with the main statutes being the *Crimes Act* 1900 (NSW); *Criminal Law Consolidation Act* 1935 (SA); and the *Crimes Act* 1958 (Vic).

2 See the *Criminal Code Act 1995* (Cth); *Criminal Code 2002* (ACT); *Criminal Code Act 1983* (NT); *Criminal Code Act 1899* (Qld); *Criminal Code Act 1924* (Tas); *Criminal Code Act Compilation Act 1913* (WA).

3 See Victorian Law Reform Commission, *Report 9: Duress, Necessity and Coercion* (1980) 9. The distinction between 'justification' and 'excuse' defences, however, is not settled and has no formal legal significance. *Mamote-Kulang v The Queen* (1964) 111 CLR 62, 78; *Zecevic v Director of Public Prosecutions (Vic)* (1987) 162 CLR 645, 658.

4 As is discussed below, 'strict liability offences' do not contain a mental element and are normally confined to non-serious offences.

A defence to the assault is consent of the victim to the application of force or the threat. In principle, there is no reason that the absence of consent could not be an element of the defence. If this was the case, consent would not be a defence in the strict sense, however, whether or not the offence was constituted would still require analysis of the existence of consent but in the context of whether this was established as an element of the offence. Thus, in order to fully understand the parameters and availability of a defence, it is necessary to first commence with an analysis of the precise elements of the offence in question.

Whether a requirement of an offence is embedded into the elements of the offence, or is dealt with at the defence stage, is also relevant for evidentiary purposes. Where the accused raises a defence, it will succeed unless the prosecution can rebut it beyond reasonable doubt. However, in order for this burden to be imposed on the prosecution, the accused must satisfy the evidential burden in relation to the defence. Thus, he or she must adduce some evidence in support of the defence.[5] By contrast, in relation to the elements of the offence, the evidential burden sits with the prosecution. Thus, doctrinally, it is easier for an accused to establish an excusatory defence, than a justificatory defence.

Conceptual Foundations

Criminal liability is the greatest form of legal condemnation and can result in harsh sanctions. As a result of the moral dimensions of the criminal law, the focus is not solely on what the offenders do, but also on their objectives and, in particular, their intentions. It is generally regarded as being unfair to make individuals criminally liable for harmful acts, which they did not want to bring about. Accordingly, most offences require the offender to have a culpable mental state which involves wanting to commit the physical elements of the offence. This element is subjective and usually consists of an 'intention' to commit the crime, or at least being 'reckless' as to whether it occurs.

Given that the mental element of an offence is usually subjective, it follows that where the defence consists of a denial of such an element, then the defence is also subjective in nature—there is no additional objective dimension associated with the defence. The situation is different with justificatory defences. In most cases, these have both a subjective and objective component. The rationale for this is to limit the availability of the defence. Given that the criminal law generally aims to prevent harmful conduct, there is a public policy rationale for confining to the operation of defences to as limited range of circumstances of possible. The disadvantage of too tightly confining the operation of the defences is that some accused who lack subjective culpability will be found guilty of a crime. However, as we shall see in the discussion below, this has not resulted in a move to liberalise the operation of criminal defences.

Cumulation/Cumulative or Alternative Pleading of Defences

The criminal justice process in Australia is adversarial. As noted above, in order for an accused to be found guilty of a crime, the prosecution must establish all elements of the offence beyond reasonable doubt and negate all relevant defences to the same standard.[6]

In order for the prosecution to be required to negate a defence, the accused must raise a defence (and adduce evidence which satisfies the evidential burden in support of the defence). However, for this obligation to fall on the prosecution, there is no need for the accused to expressly raise a defence. The prosecution must rebut all defences emerging from the evidence, irrespective of whether the evidence is adduced from a prosecution or defence witness. Thus, defences do not need to be expressly or formally pleaded.

Moreover, there is a limit to the number of defences that an accused can raise. Each defence that emerges from the evidence needs to be rebutted by the prosecution. Hence defences operate in a cumulative manner.

---

5   *Queen v Getachew* [2012] HCA 10.

6   The only exception to this is the defence of insanity, which, as is discussed below, must be established by the accused on the balance of probabilities.

Provocation of Defence Situation

In Australia, defences are still available to individuals who initiate the situation that gives rise to relevant exigency. Thus, if an accused provokes or even attacks another person who then assaults the accused, the accused can in certain circumstances still invoke the defence of self-defence (or other defences that may arise, such as necessity). This reflects the view that personal responsibility and culpability are matters of degree and that a degree of wrongdoing does not justify subjecting an individual to a disproportionate level of blame or punishment.

The main common law authority dealing with the availability of the self-defence is the High Court decision of *Zecevic v Director of Public Prosecutions (Vic)*.[7] In defining the scope of self-defence, the court did not preclude the operation of the defence from individuals who are the initial aggressors or who provoke an assault. In such cases, self-defence can apply so long as the initial aggression or provocation had ceased. In these circumstances, there is no need for initial aggressor to retreat before using force to negate the attack. However, if the initial aggressor does not attempt to retreat, as a matter of fact this may make it difficult for him or her establish that he or she genuinely believed that force was necessary to negate the attack.[8]

In Queensland, the availability of self-defence to a person who provokes an assault or commits an assault is more limited. In such circumstances, the initiator can only use defensive force if there is a reasonable likelihood that they may be killed or subjected to grievous bodily harm. Further, the accused cannot use defensive force unless he or she had not initially attempted to kill or cause grievous bodily harm to the other person unless the accused ceased further hostility and retreated before he or she attached.

Mistakes of Fact and Defences

There is no separate jurisprudence regarding the operation of a defence where the accused mistakenly believes in the existence of a fact that is relevant to the applicability of the defence. Instead this scenario is dealt with under the general principles relating to the relevance of mistaken beliefs held by an accused charged with criminal offences. As noted above, there is a connectedness between the elements of an offence and the elements of a defence. In relation to both constructs, the individual elements can be either subjective or objective.

Where the relevant element is purely subjective, an honest belief in the existence of a state of affairs, which, if true, would satisfy that element is sufficient. Thus, in the context of an element of an offence a mistake of fact negate the existence of the *mens rea* of an offence where the *mens rea* is totally subjective. Thus, for example, if a person mistakes a human being for a kangaroo and shoots and kills a person, or pulls the trigger of a gun wrongly believing that the gun is not loaded,[9] there is no liability for homicide. Likewise, a wrongful belief that a person is consenting to sexual intercourse will exculpate an accused from rape.[10]

The defence of mistake at common law has statutory recognition in a number of jurisdictions.[11] Typical of this is the Criminal Code 1995 (Cth), which states:

9.1 Mistake or ignorance of fact (fault elements other than negligence)
(1) A person is not criminally responsible for an offence that has a physical element for which there is a fault element other than negligence if:
(a) at the time of the conduct constituting the physical element, the person is under a mistaken belief about, or is ignorant of, facts; and
(b) the existence of that mistaken belief or ignorance negates any fault element applying to that physical element.

---

7   (1987) 162 CLR 645. This is discussed further below.
8   See, for example, *Massey v R* [2013] ACTSC 5 [98]–[108].
9   *R v Lamb* [1967] 2 All ER 1282.
10   *DPP v Morgan* [1976] AC 182.
11   Sections 9.2 and 9.3 of the *Criminal Code* (Cth), ss 35 and 36 of the *Criminal Code 2002* (ACT), s 32 of the *Criminal Code* (NT), s 24 of the *Criminal Code* (Qld), s 14 of the *Criminal Code* (Tas) and s 24 of the *Criminal Code* (WA).

(2) In determining whether a person was under a mistaken belief about, or was ignorant of, facts, the tribunal of fact may consider whether the mistaken belief or ignorance was reasonable in the circumstances.

Where the mistake relates not to the existence of an element of an offence, but rather to a defence, the same principle applies—the mistake need only be honest not reasonable, so long as the relevant defence is only subjective. Thus, if an accused wrongly believes that an attacker is pointing a loaded gun at him or her, but which transpires to be a stick, the accused would be entitled to use force commensurate with the perceived level of threat.[12]

It is important to emphasise that in order for a mistake to prove exculpatory in these circumstances, the mistake need only be honest; it does not need to also have a reasonable foundation.[13] However, if the mistake is objectively unreasonable this will, as a pragmatic matter, make it more difficult for the accused to convince the judge or jury of the existence of the mistake.[14]

Transferred Defences/Collateral Damage Defences

In Australia, the notion of transferred malice operates. Thus, if an accused intends to shoot person A, but instead the bullet strikes and kills person B, the accused is liable for the murder of B. The doctrine of transferred malice provides that when an accused acts with the requisite *mens rea* to commit an offence against a particular person or property and instead succeeds in causing the same type of harm to another person or property, the law regards the *mens rea* as being transferred from the intended person or property to that which is actually harmed.[15]

However, the doctrine only applies if the accused achieves the same offence that he or she intended. Thus, if the accused throws a rock intending to break a window but instead it strikes a person, he or she is not responsible for the assault, unless the accused was reckless regarding that consequence.

Individual Defences

Self-Defence and Excessive Self-Defence

Self-defence is a fundamental right. It is a universally recognised defence. It is available in relation to all crimes, including murder, and is the main limitation on the right to life. The defence is so well entrenched that it is the perhaps the only absolute right recognised in most moral and legal codes. It is not tenable to suggest that humans do not have the right to self-defence and no legal system has attempted to fully negate this right— given the human instinct for survival, this would arguably be futile in any event.

Self-defence applies in relation to all forms of attack to the person, and to ward off serious attack, even lethal force can be used. Self-defence is not confined to cases where there is danger of death or serious injury.[16] It also applies to the defence of property, although the level of force that can be invoked to protect property is normally considerably less than can be applied to protect the person.[17]

Despite the importance of self-defence, the parameters of the defence are relatively narrow in Australia. In most jurisdictions, the defence contains both a subjective and objective component. The leading common law decision on self-defence is *Zecevic v Director of Public Prosecutions (Vic)*,[18] where the High Court of

---

12   *R v Gladstone Williams* (1984) 78 Cr App R 276. However, as is discussed below, in most Australian jurisdictions self-defence now also has an objective requirement.

13   *Re A-G (WA) Reference (No 1 of 1977)* [1979] WAR 45.

14   See *R v Saragozza* [1984] VR 187.

15   See *R v Newman* [1948] VLR 61; *R v Bacash* [1981] VR 923.

16   *R v Walden* (1986) 19 A Crim R 444.

17   *Zecevic* (n 3).

18   (1987) 162 CLR 645.

Australia stated that the test for the defence of self-defence 'is whether the accused believed upon reasonable grounds that it was necessary in self-defence to do what he did'.[19]

The brevity and seeming simplicity of this test, glosses over the fact that there are in fact four elements to the test. The accused must actually believe that it is necessary to (i) use force and (ii) to the extent to which it was used. The third and fourth requirements are that there must be reasonable grounds for both of these beliefs. The parameters of the defence are slightly broadened by the fact that the point of reference for the 'reasonableness' requirement is not the beliefs that a hypothetical reasonable person would have formed, but what the accused might reasonably have believed in the relevant circumstances.[20] Thus, if the accused has particular knowledge of the assailant, this can be factored into the test for the existence of the defence.

The *Zecevic* test operates in Victoria and has influenced the development of the test in the other jurisdictions. In the Australian Capital Territory, New South Wales, the Northern Territory, South Australia, and Tasmania, the test is similar to *Zecevic*; however, the 'necessity' element of self-defence is solely subjective, while the 'proportionality' requirement has both a subjective and objective requirement. Thus, in these jurisdictions the right to self-defence is applied more broadly and can excuse defensive action that the accused wrongly believed was necessary, so long as the response was not disproportionate to the harm or threat perceived by the accused.

The most controversial aspect of the right to self-defence is when defensive action is justified, but is excessive, relative to the level of the threat. The proportionality requirement is an essential ingredient of the defence; otherwise, gratuitous violence and harm could be used. On the other hand, those accused who over-react to a threat are not as culpable as those who initiate harm to others. The law balances these competing considerations by negating the use of the defence where it is excessive. However, in relation to murder where the accused uses excessive self-defence, the offence is reduced to manslaughter in New South Wales, South Australia, Western Australia, and Victoria.[21]

Thus, while the test in Australia in not uniform, it applies relatively broadly in that it can justify (proportionate) lethal force; it applies to the defence of property and also to the defence of other persons. The scope of the defence is limited by objective requirements in relation to either the necessity requirement or the extent of the response (or both).

Doctrinal equivocation regarding the justification for the objective elements is evidenced by the fact that some jurisdictions do not require it as part of the 'necessity' limb and in some jurisdictions when the 'proportionality' aspect of the test is not objectively established, the defence operates in a partial manner to reduce the offence from murder to manslaughter. From the perspective of legal coherence, the least sound aspect of this approach is that excessive self-defence can be a partial defence to murder, and only murder. If excessive self-defence ought to operate as a partial defence, this mitigating outcome should not be confined to the offence (murder) which results in the most serious offence known to our system of law and which causes the greatest level of harm.

Necessity

Necessity, like self-defence, is a defence with near universal application. It is the defence with the most overtly utilitarian foundation. The main distinction with self-defence is that in the case of necessity the emergency or the peril does not need to stem from an aggressor, but can emanate from any cause, including natural events. Necessity operates in all Australian jurisdictions and the defence is based on the definition at common law. In *R v Loughnan*,[22] the Full Court of the Supreme Court of Victoria held that the defence has the following *three* elements:

- The criminal act must have been done solely for the purpose of preventing certain and irreparable harm from being inflicted upon the accused or someone he or she was legally obliged to protect;

---

19   *Zecevic* (n 3).
20   *Viro v The Queen* (1978) 141 CLR 88.
21   *Crimes Act 1900* (NSW) s 421; *Criminal Law Consolidation Act 1935* (SA) s 15(2); *Crimes Act 1958* (Vic) s 9AC; *Criminal Code* (WA) s 248(3).
22   [1981] VR 443.

- The accused must have honestly believed on reasonable grounds that s/he (or someone s/he was bound to protect) was placed in a position of imminent peril; and
- The acts undertaken must have been no greater than was reasonably necessary to avert the peril.

The defence is recognition of the fact that people in rare circumstances are placed in difficult predicaments and that committing what would otherwise be a criminal act causes less bad consequences than an alternative course of conduct. The bias that the law has for promoting observance of the general legal standards is manifested in the requirement that there must be reasonable grounds for the assumption that a situation of peril exists. Perhaps the most common scenario in which this defence applies is where a person exceeds the speed limit to rush a sick person to hospital.

A more extreme case in which the defence applied were the facts underpinning the decision in in *Re A (Children)*,[23] where the English Court of Appeal was confronted with what it understandably termed the truly agonising dilemma of what ought to be done in the case of conjoined twins, Mary and Jodie. They each had their own brain, heart, lungs, and other vital organs, and they each had arms and legs; they were joined at the lower abdomen and could be separated. But the operation would kill the weaker twin, Mary. That is because her lungs and heart were too deficient to oxygenate and pump blood through her body. Had she been born a singleton, she would not have been viable and resuscitation would have been abandoned. She would have died shortly after her birth. She was alive only because a common artery enabled her sister, who was stronger, to circulate life-sustaining oxygenated blood for both of them. Separation would require the clamping and then the severing of that common artery. Within minutes of so doing Mary would die. Yet if the operation did not take place, both would die within three to six months, or perhaps a little longer, because Jodie's heart would eventually fail. The Court of Appeal held that the operation could occur.

Brooke LJ grounded his decision in the necessity doctrine and, in doing so, held that the disinclination of previous courts to extend this defence to deliberate killing was not an absolute bar. He noted that there were two main policy reasons that historically had been given for not extending this defence to intentional killing. First, no person was in a position to judge the comparative value of life. Secondly, that to condone intentional killing would be to constitute a separation of law and morality. He stated that neither of these reasons was a powerful consideration in this case, given the uniqueness of the situation.

Ward LJ took a similar approach to that of Brooke LJ in finding in that in some circumstances the law should recognise the right to choose that one innocent person should be killed rather than another. He stated that the doctors who were to perform the operation would not be guilty of murder because doctors, like the court, should be permitted to choose the lesser of two evils. He also believed that the killing of Mary could be regarded as an act of quasi self-defence to save Jodie. This is because Mary could be viewed as killing Jodie by using Jodie's heart and lungs to receive and use Jodie's oxygenated blood, which would eventually cause Jodie's heart to fail.

Several Australian jurisdictions have codified the defence into a statutory form and in some cases the defence is termed 'sudden and extraordinary' emergency. The elements of the defence remain similar to those at common law.[24] In these jurisdictions, it is clear that the defence can apply to intentional killing.

Duress by Threats/Circumstances

Duress, like necessity, has a utilitarian underpinning but applies in a much more limited range of circumstances. Effectively, it is also a lesser of two evils defence, but its key restriction stems from the fact that the accused must have been commanded to commit the offence by the wrongdoer. Wrongdoers rarely co-opt innocent agents to commit crimes for them; this induces an additional layer of complexity and increases the potential for detection and hence the defence has only been successfully pleaded in a small number of circumstances.

---

23   [2001] Fam 147.
24   *Criminal Code* (Cth) s 10.3; *Criminal Code 2002* (ACT) s 41; *Criminal Code* (NT) s 33; *Criminal Code* (Qld) s 25; *Criminal Code* (WA) s 25; *Crimes Act 1958* (Vic) s 9AI(3).

The rarity of the defence is matched by the strictness of the elements that must be established in order for it to operate. The defence has a common law foundation in Australia. The scope of the defence is set out by Smith J in *R v Hurley*:

> Where the accused has been required to do the act charged against him (i) under a threat that death or grievous bodily harm will be inflicted unlawfully upon a human being if the accused fails to do the act and (ii) the circumstances were such that a person of ordinary firmness would have been likely to yield to the threat in the way the accused did and (iii) the threat was present and continuing, imminent and impending (as previously described) and (iv) the accused reasonably apprehended that the threat would be carried out and (v) he was induced thereby to commit the crime charged and (vi) that the crime was not murder, nor any other crime so heinous as to be excepted from the doctrine and (vii) the accused did not, by fault on his part when free from the duress, expose himself to its application and (viii) he had no means, with safety to himself, of preventing the execution of the threat, then the accused, in such circumstances at least, has a defence of duress.[25]

As with self-defence and necessity, the defence has both subjective and objective elements. The threat need not in reality exist, but the accused must actually believe in the existence of the threat based on a concrete factual foundation.[26] There must also be proportionality between the severity of the threat and the crime committed.[27] Another limitation is that the defence does not apply to accused who voluntarily join criminal enterprises which engage in violent and coercive conduct.[28]

The defence has a statutory foundation in most Australian jurisdictions, which, with minor adaptions, mirror the common law position.[29] A departure from the common law that applies in the Commonwealth jurisdiction, the ACT, Victorian and Western Australia is that the defence can also include intentional killing— although the defence has never been successfully raised in such circumstances.

General Mental Condition Defences

Insanity

Underpinning the notion of criminal liability is personal responsibility. This requires the cognitive capacity to make rational decisions and an awareness of the consequences of one's actions. People with certain types and degrees of mental illness lack this capacity and hence are excused from criminal liability. This defence has a common law foundation basis and is known as 'insanity'. It now has a statutory basis in all Australian jurisdictions and is most widely termed 'mental impairment'.[30]

The relevant point of reference for determining the mental state of the accused is at the time of offence, not at the time of trial. Mental impairment at the time of the trial is relevant to the issue of whether the accused is fit to plead. At common law, the test to be applied in relation to an accused's fitness to stand trial is 'whether the accused, because of mental defect, fails to come up to certain minimum standards which he needs to equal

---

25   [1967] VR 526, 543.

26   *R v Graham* [1982] 1 WLR 294.

27   *R v Abusafiah* [1991] 24 NSWLR 531.

28   *R v Palazoff* [1986] 43 SASR 99. The statutory versions of the defence normally have a narrower exclusion, requiring the accused to have been threatened by a person with whom the accused associated for the express purpose of carrying out conduct of the kind that was actually carried out.

29   See *Criminal Code* (Cth) s 10.2; *Criminal Code* 2002 (ACT) s 40; *Criminal Code* (NT) s 40; *Criminal Code* (Qld) ss 31(1)(c), (d); *Criminal Code* (Tas) s 20(1); *Crimes Act 1958* (Vic) s 9AG; *Criminal Code* (WA) s 32(2).

30   The term 'insanity' continues to be used in Tasmania. *Criminal Code* (Tas) s 381. 'Mental illness' is the phrase used in New South Wales. *Crimes Act 1900* (NSW) s 428N; *Mental Health Criminal Procedure Act 1900* (NSW) s 38. In Queensland and Western Australia, the relevant terminology is 'mental incompetence' and 'unsoundness of the mind', respectively. *Criminal Code* (Qld) s 647; *Criminal Code* (WA) s 653. In the Commonwealth jurisdiction, the ACT, the Northern Territory, South Australia, and Victoria, the defence has been labelled as 'mental impairment'. *Criminal Code* (Cth) s 7.3; *Criminal Code* (ACT) s 27; *Criminal Code* (NT) s 43C; *Criminal Law Consolidation Act 1935* (SA) s 269C; *Crimes (Mental Impairment and Unfitness to be Tried) Act 1997* (Vic) s 20(2).

before he can be tried without unfairness or injustice to him'.[31] If an accused is unfit to stand trial, in most Australian jurisdictions he or she is placed in custody. If the accused recovers, the trial may then take place.

The defence of insanity applies in relation to all offences. However, it is rarely pleaded. This is because an acquittal on the basis of insanity will often lead to the confinement of the accused in an institution for an indefinite period of time. In some cases, the period of detention can exceed the period of incarceration that the accused would have been likely to have received had s/he been adjudicated guilty of the relevant offence. In New South Wales, for example, acquittal on the grounds of insanity results in an order of indefinite detention.[32] The timing of release is a matter for the government. In Victoria, the regime is less harsh. A successful plea of insanity will result in the accused being placed on a supervision order, the maximum duration of which is the maximum term of imprisonment for the offence with which the accused was charged.[33]

There is a presumption that an accused is sane at the time of the offence. This presumption is rebuttable, although it is the accused who bears the proof on the insanity defence. The relevant standard of proof is on the balance of probabilities. Insanity is one of the few defences where the burden of proof rests on the accused. The reason for this is that the factual information relevant to this is peculiarly within the knowledge of the accused. It would impose an unrealistic burden on the prosecution for it to be required to positively establish that the accused was not insane.

The origin of the insanity defence stems from *M'Naghten's* case[34] where the *M'Naghten* Rules, which spell out the scope and content of the defence, were formulated. These *Rules* are still influential in informing the content of the current statutory insanity defences. In order to establish the defence of insanity at common law, the accused must prove the following elements:

(i) the accused was suffering from a disease of the mind;
(ii) the disease of the mind caused such a defect of reasoning that the accused was not aware of the nature and quality of his or her act or, alternatively, that the accused was not aware that his or her act was wrong.[35]

There is no requirement for the 'disease of the mind' to be permanent. It can be a periodic. However, in order to constitute a disease of the mind, a 'defect of reason' must result from an underlying pathological infirmity of the mind.[36]

The *nature and quality* of an act refers to the essence of the conduct and its outcome. It is explained by Dixon J in *R v Porter* as follows:

> In a case where a man intentionally destroys life he may have so little capacity for understanding the nature of life and the destruction of life, that to him it is no more than breaking a twig or destroying an inanimate object. In such a case he would not know the physical nature of what he was doing. He would not know the implications and what it really amounted to.[37]

The meaning of 'wrong' is also explained by Dixon J in *R v Porter*:

> What is meant by 'wrong' is wrong having regard to the everyday standards of reasonable people. If you think that at the time when he administered the poison to the child he had such a mental disorder or disturbance or derangement that he was incapable of reasoning about the right or wrongness, according to ordinary standards, of the thing which he was doing, not that he reasoned wrongly ... but that he was quite incapable of taking

---

31 *R v Presser* [1958] VR 45, 48.
32 *Mental Health (Criminal Procedure) Act 1990* (NSW) s 39.
33 *Crimes (Mental Impairment and Unfitness to be Tried) Act 1997* (Vic) s 27.
34 See *M'Naghten's Case* (1843–1869), All ER Rep 229 at 223–234.
35 *R v Porter* (1936) 55 CLR 182
36 *R v Falconer* (1990) 171 CLR 30.
37 (1933) 55 CLR 182 at 188 .

into account the considerations which go to make right or wrong, then you should find him not guilty upon the ground that he was insane at the time he committed the acts charged.[38]

In the Commonwealth jurisdiction, the test is slightly broader in that it also applies to situation where the accused could not control the conduct. Section 7.3 of the Criminal Code 1995 (Cth) states:

(1) A person is not criminally responsible for an offence if, at the time of carrying out the conduct constituting the offence, the person was suffering from a mental impairment that had the effect that:

(a) the person did not know the nature and quality of the conduct; or
(b) the person did not know that the conduct was wrong (that is, the person could not reason with a moderate degree of sense and composure about whether the conduct, as perceived by reasonable people, was wrong); or
(c) the person was unable to control the conduct …

…   .

(3) A person is presumed not to have been suffering from such a mental impairment. The presumption is only displaced if it is proved on the balance of probabilities (by the prosecution or the defence) that the person was suffering from such a mental impairment …

…

(8) In this Code:

'mental impairment' includes senility, intellectual disability, mental illness, brain damage, and severe personality disorder.

(9) The reference in subsection (8) to mental illness is a reference to an underlying pathological infirmity of the mind, whether of long or short duration and whether permanent or temporary, but does not include a condition that results from the reaction of a healthy mind to extraordinary external stimuli. However, such a condition may be evidence of a mental illness if it involves some abnormality and is prone to recur.[39]

Intoxication
Intoxication is also a defence in all Australian jurisdictions. It derives from the common law. The leading common law case is *R v O'Connor*,[40] where the High Court set out the contours and scope of the defence. The Court noted that the defence may operate in two ways. It can either negate the voluntariness element of the *actus reus* or the *mens rea* (or both). The Court also noted that the defence may apply for involuntary, as well as self-induced, intoxication.

The Court abolished the distinction between offences of basic intent and specific intent for the purposes of the defence and held that that intoxication applies for both types of offences. A *basic intention* is an intention to perform the physical act of a crime that lacks a particular purpose, for example shooting a gun. A *specific intention* is an intention to perform the physical act of a crime that has a specific objective, such as to cause injury. The distinction remains relevant in a number of jurisdictions, such that intoxication can be used to only rebut basic intent elements.

In order to negate the *actus reus*, it needs to be effectively established that the accused was not acting voluntarily. This requires a high degree of intoxication. In *R v Cottle*, it was stated:

---

38   (1933) 55 CLR 182 at 190.
39   In South Australia, the defence of insanity has an even wider scope. Even where an accused knows that his or her act is wrong (in accordance with the meaning stipulated above), he or she s/he will not incur criminal liability if the act is a result of an irresistible impulse. *Criminal Law Consolidation Act 1935* (SA) s 269C(c).
40   (1980) 146 CLR 64.

> [A]utomatism which strictly means action without conscious volition, has been adopted … to denote conduct of which the doer is not conscious – in short doing something without knowledge of it … a temporary lapse of consciousness that nevertheless leaves the person so affected able to exercise bodily movements. In such a case, the action is one which the mind in its normal functioning does not control.[41]

The defence of intoxication is most often used to challenge the *mens rea* component of an offence. Here, the level of intoxication that the defendant must establish is less than that required in respect of voluntariness. Thus, the accused may submit that while he or she may have been acting voluntarily, the level of intoxication was such as to result in him or her failing to advert to the possible or probable consequences of his conduct.

While intoxication derives from the common law, all jurisdictions except Victoria have codified this defence in statute. The statutes setting out the intoxication defence narrow its availability compared to that at common law. A key distinction that is adopted is between self-induced and involuntary intoxication. In jurisdictions where the common law does not apply, evidence of self-induced intoxication cannot be used to deny an element of basic intent.[42] Intoxication, whether self-induced or involuntary, cannot be used to deny an element of specific intent.[43] Further, in relation to denying the *actus reus* of an offence, self-induced intoxication can only be invoked in relation to offences of specific intention, but not basic intention.[44]

Thus, the defence of intoxication applies differently throughout Australia. The broadest and most doctrinally clear expression of the defence is as developed at common law. Legislative forms of the defence limit its scope. This is understandable given community disquiet regarding alcohol fuelled crime and the link between alcohol and crime, especially violent crime. However, the attempt to confine the defence has introduced a level of complexity that undermines the transparency and clarity of the law. Distinctions between self-induced and involuntary intoxication and crimes of basic and specific intent are obscure and arguably illusory. The desirability of the statutory forms of the defence are questionable given that the common law version of the defence has not resulted in documented instances of abuse of the defence and the common law defence in unavailable in instances where an accused consumes alcohol to garner the 'courage' to commit the offence or is aware that intoxication may result in him or her engaging in criminal conduct.

Mistake of Law

In all Australian jurisdictions a mistake of law, relating to either the scope of an offence or the availability of a defence, is not an excuse. In *Ostrowski v Palmer*,[45] Gleeson CJ and Kirby J stated:

> Professor Glanville Williams said that almost the only knowledge of law that many people possess is the knowledge that ignorance of the law is no excuse when a person is charged with an offence. This does not mean that people are presumed to know the law. Such a presumption would be absurd. Rather, it means that, if a person is alleged to have committed an offence, it is both necessary and sufficient for the prosecution to prove the elements of the offence, and it is irrelevant to the question of guilt that the accused person was not aware that those elements constituted an offence.

> [2] For present purposes, we use the expression "elements of the offence" to embrace matters of exculpation, and without regard to any special consideration as to onus of proof that might exist in relation to particular offences. Ignorance of the legal consequences that flow from the existence of the facts that constitute an offence

---

41   [1958] NZLR 999 at 1007. See also *Barker v Burke* [1970] VR 884.

42   *Criminal Code* (Cth) s 8.2, *Criminal Code 2002* (ACT) s 31(1); *Crimes Act 1900* (NSW) s 428D(a); *Criminal Code* (NT) s 43AS; *Criminal Law Consolidation Act 1935* (SA) s 268(2); *Criminal Code* (Qld) s 28; *Criminal Code* (WA) s 28; *Criminal Code* (Tas) s 17.

43   *Criminal Code* (Cth) s 8.2(2); *Criminal Code 2002* (ACT) s 30(1); *Crimes Act 1900* (NSW) s 428C(1); *Criminal Code* (NT) s 43AS(1); *Criminal Law Consolidation Act 1935* (SA) ss 268(2), (3); *Criminal Code* (Tas) s 17(2); *Criminal Code* (Qld) s 28; *Criminal Code* (WA) s 28(3).

44   *Criminal Code* (Qld) s 23; *Criminal Code* (WA) ss 23, 23A; *Criminal Code 2002* (ACT) s 30(1); *Crimes Act 1900* (NSW) s 428G; *Criminal Code* (NT) s 43AS(1); *Criminal Law Consolidation Act 1935* (SA) s 268(2), (3); *Criminal Code* (Tas) s 17(2).

45   [2004] HCA 30.

is ordinarily not a matter of exculpation, although it may be a matter of mitigation, and in some circumstances it may enliven a discretion not to prosecute.[46]

However, the distinction between a mistake of fact and mistake of law is often obscure. In theory, a mistake of fact occurs where an individual has a wrong impression about the existence of a state of affairs, such as whether a gun is loaded. A mistake of law occurs where a person is wrong about the legal consequences or significance relating to a fact. The fine, often illusory, distinction between the two forms of mistake has emerged in a number of cases.

In *Iannella v French*,[47] the accused landlord increased the rent payable by his tenants in excess of amounts that were regulated by statute. The accused did this because he wrongly believed (pursuant to a newspaper story) that the statutory limits applying to rent controls had been abolished. In overturning his conviction, two members of the High Court (Barwick CJ and Windeyer J) stated that the mistake was one of fact not law. The rent limits had been abolished in relation to some, but not all properties (including those owned by accused) and to identify which properties the rent limits applied to was characterised by them as a mistake of fact given that the issue could only be resolved after evidence of facts was adduced. Taylor and Owen JJ, however, held that the mistake was one of law, given that the accused was mistaken about the existence and operation of a statute. In reality, the mistake could be characterised as either fact or law, as is the case with most false beliefs that have a legal aspect.[48]

Mistake of law operates as a defence in only one situation. This is where an individual honestly believes that he is entitled to deal with property (for example, taking, destroying or appropriating it) in a certain way. This defence is known as a claim of right. To apply, the accused's belief need only be honest it does not also need to be reasonable.[49] The defence arises because the offence of theft in a number of Australian jurisdictions expressly requires that an accused act in a dishonest manner, which is negated if the accused believes that in law he or she is entitled to act in the way that he or she acted.[50]

Residual Catch-All Defences/Existence and Ambit of Statutory Defences

The commentary above explains the key criminal defences in Australia in terms of those which have been subject to the most judicial and legal analysis and which have are more regularly invoked. There are also several other defences, some of which are now briefly considered.

As noted above, criminal liability involves personal culpability. Thus, young children cannot be found guilty of a criminal offence. The minimum age at which a person is deemed capable of committing a crime is now ten.[51] There is a rebuttable presumption that children who are age ten and under the age of fourteen are incapable of committing a crime. In these instances, the prosecutor must establish that reasonable doubt that the child knew that the acts were seriously wrong.[52]

There is also a defence of martial coercion in some Australian jurisdictions, which applies where a husband forces his wife through threats into committing a criminal act.[53] The defence does not apply to murder or treason. As a practical reality the defence is rarely pleaded given the access that all Australians have to police protection.

The defence of mistake was considered above. This is a defence to all crimes except for strict liability offences, which are a common feature of the Australian criminal law landscape. Strict liability offences are offences that do not require *mens rea*. Generally speaking, they are less serious offences and are often referred

---

46   [2004] HCA 30, [2].

47   (1968) 119 CLR 84.

48   In *Thomas v R* (1937) 59 CLR 279 it was held that an accused's mistake about his marriage status was a mistake of a fact.

49   *R v Langham* (1984) 36 SASR 48.

50   See, for example, *Crimes Act 1900* (ACT) s 96; *Crimes Act 1958* (Vic) s 37.

51   See, for example, *Children (Criminal Proceedings) Act 1987* (NSW) s 5; *Young Offenders Act 1993* (SA) s 5; and *Children, Youth and Families Act 2005* (Vic) s 344.

52   *R v ALH* (2003) 6 VR 276; [2003] VSCA 129.

53   *Criminal Law Consolidation Act 1935* (SA) s 328A; *Crimes Act 1958* (Vic) s 336(2).

to as regulatory offences. Most statutory offences do not expressly indicate whether or not they contain a *mens rea* and it is a matter of interpretation to determine if they are strict liability offences.

There is a statutory presumption that all offences have *mens rea*, but considerations that incline an offence to be interpreted as of one strict liability are:

1) The omission of words denoting mens rea (such as 'intends') from the particular legislative provision that creates the offence;
2) A low maximum penalty, especially if the sanction does not include imprisonment;
3) There is considerable utility in making the offence strict liability because it is likely to result in greater compliance with the law; and[54]
4) Moral opprobrium does not attach to the offence.[55]

If all of these considerations are powerfully slanted in favour of strict liability, then the offence may even be one of absolute liability—in which cases the offence is complete on the commission of the prohibited behaviour and there are no mental state defences. While mistake is not a defence for strict liability offences, there is a defence of 'honest and reasonable' mistake. In order for this defence to apply, the following *four* elements need to be satisfied:

1) The mistaken belief must be genuinely and reasonably held;
2) There must be an actual mistake and not mere ignorance;
3) The mistake must be of fact and not law; and
4) The mistaken belief must relate to the existence of facts which, if true, would have made the accused's conduct lawful.[56]

Conclusion

There are considerable jurisdictional differences in Australia relating to defences that are available to criminal acts. The nature of these differences is generally at the margins. There are core defences that operate in all jurisdictions. These defences stem from the nature of criminal liability in Australian jurisprudence and, in particular, the fact that the default position is that criminal liability requires a wrongful act that has harmful consequences and a culpable mind.

Circumstances that negate either of these requirements provide a defence to criminal conduct. Hence automatism, insanity, intoxication, and mistake constitute criminal defences because they negate individual culpability. In addition to this, it is accepted that, in rare instances, circumstances occur such that a criminal act is justified by more pressing matters and hence self-defence, necessity and duress are established criminal defences.

Thus, although there is some variation in the precise nature and scope of criminal defences, the core defences are similar. The defences are generally morally sound and legally coherent given that most of them (with the possible exception of provocation, superior orders and marital coercion) derive from the fundamental principle that a crime consists of a harmful act and culpable state of mind.

---

54 *Chin Aik v R* [1963] AC 160.

55 Thus, matters of broad public safety, health, and welfare are less likely to require a *mens rea*. See *Proudman v Dayman* (1941) 67 CLR 536.

56 *Proudman v Dayman* (1941) 67 CLR 536; *Ostrowski v Palmer* (2004) 78 ALJR 957.

Chapter 14
Canada

Kent Roach

This chapter will provide an overview of a range of defences in Canadian criminal law. Although the courts recognise distinctions between justifications and excuses and reject necessity and duress as justifications, it will be seen that the conceptual distinction between the two forms of defences has been blurred. For example, Canadian courts require proportionality between the act threatened and the act avoided for the so-called excuses of duress and necessity, but the legislature does not require proportionality for the justification of self-defence.

Canadian defences should be of interest to those who study comparative criminal law because the courts have partially constitutionalized some aspects of defences. For example, the Supreme Court of Canada has held that the conviction of people for morally involuntary conduct would violate the principles of fundamental justice and with that Canada's constitutional bill of rights. It has applied this principle to strike down restrictive statutory requirements that duress only applies if the accused is threatened with immediate death or bodily harm from a person who is present.[1] Canadian jurisprudence also no longer follows English law in limiting the intoxication defences to more serious specific intent offences. In 1994, the Canadian court created a new defence of extreme intoxication producing involuntary behaviour.[2] In 1995, the Canadian Parliament purported to abolish this controversial extreme intoxication defence as it applies to violent offences such as assault, sexual assault and manslaughter.[3] The Supreme Court has yet to rule on the constitutionality of this legislative restriction on the defence.

General Issues

Justificatory and Excusatory Defences—Distinction and Seat in the Offence Structure

Canadian criminal law recognizes the distinction between defences that excuse and justify crime. The Supreme Court of Canada has explained that excuses rest 'on a realistic assessment of human weakness, recognizing that a liberal and humane criminal law cannot hold people to the strict obedience of laws in emergency situations where normal human instincts, whether of self-preservation or altruism, overwhelmingly impel disobedience'.[4] In contrast, a defence that acts as a justification 'challenges the wrongfulness of an action which technically constitutes a crime'. The accused is not punished because, in the circumstances, 'the values of society, indeed of the criminal law itself, are better promoted by disobeying a given statute than by observing it'.[5] The Court has elaborated that 'excuses absolve the accused of personal accountability by focussing, not on the wrongful act, but on the circumstances of the act and the accused's personal capacity to avoid it'. Because the accused has no realistic choice but to commit the crime, 'criminal attribution points not to the accused but to the exigent circumstances facing him'.[6]

---

1   *R v. Ruzic*, [2001] 1 S.C.R. 687. All Supreme Court decisions are available at: <http://scc.lexum.org/decisia-scc-csc/scc-csc/en/nav.do> (accessed 13 November 2013).

2   *R v. Daviault*, [1994] 3 S.C.R. 63.

3   Criminal Code §§ 33.1–33.3. The Criminal Code of Canada is available at: <http://laws.justice.gc.ca/eng/acts/C-46/index.html> (accessed 13 November 2013).

4   *R v. Perka*, [1984] 14 C.C.C. (3d) 385, 398 (S.C.C.).

5   Ibid. 396–97.

6   *Ruzic* (n 1) at 40, 46.

The distinction between excuses and justification has done much work in Canadian criminal law because the Supreme Court has only recognized the common law defence of necessity when it operates as an excuse but not as a justification for illegal activity. The Supreme Court has even constitutionalized some elements of excuse by holding that parts of a restrictive statutory duress defence violated constitutional principles of fundamental justice to the extent that they would punish a person for committing crimes in circumstances where no reasonable person could resist committing the crime. The Supreme Court has accepted the idea that a conviction of a person who committed a crime in a morally involuntary manner because the circumstances were so exigent that there was no realistic choice but to commit the crime would offend Section 7 of the Charter, which provides that no one should be deprived of life, liberty or security of the person except in accordance with the principles of fundamental justice. The Court's attraction to the concept of an excuse as both a defining feature of the defence of necessity and as a principle of fundamental justice can be explained by the self-defining and self-limiting nature of the juristic category of an excuse.

Canadian courts frequently use distinctions between justifications and excuses, but not always in a consistent or principled manner. Canadian courts conceptualize and limit both necessity and duress as an excuse, but also require that there be proportionality between the threatened harm and the crime committed by the accused even though proportionality is theoretically associated with justifications. Conversely, the courts have not insisted on strict proportionality requirements with respect to the justification of self-defence, especially with respect to claims of self-defence by battered women. A new self-defence law enacted by the Canadian Parliament in 2012 makes no reference to self-defence being a justification or an excuse. It also considers the proportionality between the crime and the threat simply as one of a non-exhaustive list of factors that may be relevant to determining whether self-defence is reasonable.[7] Contrary to most understandings of the distinctions between excuses and justifications, proportionality between the threats and the act done is required for the 'excuses' of duress and necessity but is not required for the 'justification' of self-defence in Canadian criminal law.

In a recent case, the Court relied on the distinction between self-defence as a justification and duress as an excuse in deciding that a woman who attempted to hire an undercover police officer to kill her abusive husband must rely on self-defence and not duress as a defence. The Court explained that with respect to self-defence 'less emphasis is placed on the particular circumstances and concessions to human frailty and more importance is attached to the action itself and the reason why the accused was justified in meeting force with force'.[8] This statement is consistent with the theoretical nature of a justification as an act that challenges the wrongfulness of a crime, but it is also in some tension with the Court's long standing willingness to factor in the circumstances that battered women face when administering self-defence.[9] The distinction between excuses and justifications is more easily maintained in theory than in practice. In particular, self-defence cases involving battered women tend to focus more on the excusing conditions faced by the accused than the proportionality or rightfulness of their actions despite the idea that self-defence is a justification and not an excuse.

The Court has very tentatively also suggested that the mental disorder defence might be conceptualized as an excuse for involuntary conduct that is constitutionally protected under Section 7 of the Charter.[10] The idea that Parliament could not constitutionally abolish the mental disorder defence is attractive, but the Court has not explained how the defence can be fitted into the juristic category of excuses given the centrality of a reasonable person's reactions to outside threats in the concept of an excuse. Finally, the classification of a defence as an excuse or a justification does not affect the disposition of the accused as they would both result in an acquittal to either a criminal or regulatory offence.

---

7   Criminal Code § 34(2) (as amended by S.C. 2012 c. 9).

8   *R v. Ryan*, [2013] S.C.C. 3 [24].

9   *R v. Lavallee*, [1990] 55 C.C.C.(3d) 97 (S.C.C.).

10   *R v. Bouchard-Lebrun*, [2011] 3 S.C.R. 575 [51].

Conceptual Foundations

Self-defence, duress, and necessity as defences all have subjective and objective requirements. There is less clarity with respect to the role of subjective and objective requirements with respect to the mental disorder defence. The focus in that defence is generally on the accused's subjective capacity for rational thought though objective factors play a role most notably in the requirement that for the defence to apply, the mental disorder must render the accused incapable of knowing that society or a reasonable person would recognize actions as wrongful. The Court has consistently rejected the idea that the mental disorder defence should apply if a mental disorder has prevented the accused subjectively from thinking that his or her actions were wrong or from having the appropriate subjective emotional responses to the crime. In all of these areas, objective requirements in defences limit the availability of the defence for reasons of social protection.

In order to qualify for the defences of self-defence, necessity, or common law duress, the accused must not only subjectively and honestly perceive the need to respond to the relevant external pressures or threats, but the accused must also act reasonably. The Supreme Court has explained that it is 'society's concern that reasonable and non-violent behaviour be encouraged that prompts the law to endorse the objective standard'.[11] This restriction makes sense when it is recognized that an accused who qualifies for these defences will nevertheless have committed a crime (frequently an offence involving violence) with the required fault element.

The use of objective standards raises the challenge of ensuring that an accused with particular characteristics and experiences can fairly be expected to conform to the objective standard required by the law. Canadian courts have since the 1990's responded to this dilemma by applying objective standards in a contextual manner. For example, the Court has recognized that evidence of past battering and expert evidence concerning how battered women respond to cycles of violence is relevant in assessing the reasonableness of claims of self-defence.[12] Such contextual evidence may also be relevant with respect to duress and necessity. The emphasis is on how the context affects the accused's perceptions and responses, not the level of self-control that the law expects. The distinction[13] between modifying the objective standard in order to place the events in context and individualizing it in a manner that lowers the standard of reasonable conduct expected can be difficult to maintain in practice, but is a critical concept in the administration of objective elements in Canadian criminal defences.

Cumulation/Cumulative or Alternative Pleading of Defences

There are no statutory rules that prohibit pleading defences cumulatively or alternatively. For example, an accused could argue a lack of *mens rea* or duress defence and then plead the mental disorder defence as an alternative. The alternative or cumulative pleading of defences does not mean that the courts will blur distinct defences. The Supreme Court has held that self-induced states produced by alcohol or drugs are excluded from the insanity or mental disorder defence and applied this principle to hold that a person with toxic psychosis caused by the consumption of drugs could only plead the intoxication and not the mental disorder defence.[14] In another recent case, the Supreme Court held that a woman charged with counselling the death of her husband could not plead the duress defence, but should be limited to self-defence. The Court reasoned that 'self-defence is an attempt to stop the victim's threats or assaults by meeting force with force; duress is succumbing to the threats by committing an offence'.[15] The Court also suggested that self-defence should be more readily available than duress which as an excuse only applies if there is no legal way out of

---

11   *R v Hill*, [1986] 25 C.C.C. (3d) 322 at 330 (S.C.C.).

12   *Lavallee* (n 9); *Malott*, [1997] 121 C.C.C. (3d) 457 (S.C.C.) .

13   In *R v. Tran*, [2010] 3 S.C.R. 350 [35], the Court warned 'there is an important distinction between contextualizing the objective standard, which is necessary and proper, and individualizing it, which only serves to defeat its purpose' in encouraging reasonable behaviour.

14   *Bouchard-Lebrun* (n 10).

15   *Ryan* (n 8) at [20].

a difficult situation.[16] New self-defence provisions enacted by Parliament in 2012[17] (which contemplate that self-defence can be a defence to any offence and can apply when the accused responds to even a threat of force against a third party), may result in self-defence being pled in cases of threats that might ordinarily be thought to produce duress situations. Self-defence is emerging as a defence that can be pled in the alternative to duress, but duress will not be pled in the absence of evidence of threats from a third party.

Provocation of Defence Situation

Following the logic of excuses, the necessity or duress defence should not be excluded simply because the accused engaged in illegal behaviour at the time that the dire circumstances arose. Thus one of the leading cases on necessity applied the defence to a sinking boat that was importing large amounts of illegal drugs.[18] At the same time, the courts will reject the necessity defence if the accused clearly could have foreseen that the dire circumstances would arise. Thus, the court held that necessity was not available to an accused who made a decision to live in the wild because he reasonably could have foreseen that he might have to break into a dwelling to obtain food and water.[19] This limitation of the necessity defence seems designed for social protection, but if extended too far can be in tension with the logic of excuses which focus on whether a reasonable person could resist threats and pressures at the time that he or she committed the crime.

Until 1994, Canadian courts applied the traditional common law restriction on the intoxication defence which precluded the defence for 'general intent' offences such as assault on the basis that the accused was at fault for becoming intoxicated even if he or she was too intoxicated to have the necessary *mens rea* at the time that the actual act was committed. In 1994, a majority of the Canadian Supreme Court held that the substitution of the prior fault of becoming intoxicated for the fault of a general intent offence would violate both the presumption of innocence and the principles of fundamental justice.[20] This ruling was consistent with criminal law principles that determine the existence of both fault and defences at the time that the act was committed, but it was controversial. As examined below, Parliament responded to this ruling with new legislation[21] deeming that the fault of becoming extremely intoxicated was sufficient and should be substituted for any absence of fault or voluntary behaviour at the time when the accused committed a violent general intent offence such as assault or sexual assault.

The Criminal Code formerly contained complex and cumbersome rules that attempted to limit self-defence claims when the accused provoked or initiated a fight. These provisions were replaced in 2012 by the more flexible notion that the trier of fact may consider the accused's 'role in the incident' in determining whether the act that was committed was reasonable in the circumstances.[22] Now the fact that accused provoked the situation that made their self-defence necessary will only be one factor in determining whether the acts were reasonable in the circumstances.

Provoked or self-induced defences can also take place with respect to provocation which is a special defence that reduces murder to manslaughter. There is no absolute or special rule that an accused who manufactures or initiates a confrontation should be deprived of a defence. Nevertheless, the accused's actions should be considered in determining whether the relevant subjective and objective requirements of the defence are satisfied. In one case, the Court held that an accused who confronted a person who was extorting him could not claim provocation because the threats that the deceased made against the accused were familiar to him and could not have resulted in subjective and sudden provocation.[23] In another case, the accused's actions in threatening the deceased with a gun in an attempt to ensure that the deceased did not continue to abuse his partner (who was the accused's cousin) had the predictable result that the deceased provoked the accused with a verbal insult. Even if the accused was subjectively and suddenly provoked by the deceased's verbal insults,

---

16   Ibid. at [31].
17   Criminal Code § 34.
18   *Perka* (n 4).
19   *R v. Nelson*, [2007] 228 C.C.C.(3d) 302.
20   *Daviault* (n 2).
21   Criminal Code §§ 33.1–33.3.
22   Criminal Code § 34(2)(c).
23   *R v. Pappas*, [2013] S.C.C. 56.

an ordinary person would not be so provoked. The accused's provocation or inducement of the defence was relevant to the objective arm of the defence and provocation should not have been left to the jury.[24]

Mistake of Fact and Defences

Mistake of fact issues are resolved in accordance with the dual subjective and objective requirements of self-defence, duress and necessity. In other words, the accused can be acquitted on the basis on a mistaken perception of events provided that accused's mistaken belief was both honestly held and reasonable in the circumstances.[25] Although prior self-defence provisions seemed to require that an accused must be unlawfully assaulted before claiming the defence, the Supreme Court held that a reasonable mistake about the existence of an assault would be sufficient to ensure that the accused was given a benefit of a reasonable doubt about guilt.[26] Parliament has now codified this approach so that in order to claim a defence an accused need only believe on reasonable grounds that force or the threat of force is being used against them or another person.[27]

Transferred Defences/Collateral Damage Defences

A person who is threatened or attacked by one person, but mistakenly responds with force against another would have a defence if the mistake made was reasonable in the circumstances. In self-defence, for example, the person would not only have to act for the subjective purpose of self-defence, but have a belief on reasonable grounds that he is using force against the person that is threatening him. Mistakes can be made, but they must be reasonable.[28]

Individual Defences

As a preliminary matter, self-defence,[29] mental disorder (insanity),[30] and duress as applied to principal offenders[31] are codified in Canada's Criminal Code. In contrast, necessity or duress by circumstances and duress as applied to secondary parties and intoxication are common law defences. As will be seen, the statutory defence of duress has historically been more restrictive than the common law defence, though this gap has been narrowed considerably by rulings that part of the statutory defence was unconstitutional and by recent judicial interpretation of both defences.

Self-Defence and Excessive Self-Defence

In 2012, Parliament replaced self-defence provisions in the Criminal Code that had long been criticised for their complexity with a much simpler defence. The new defence will be easier to administer and explain to the jury, but also less predictable as it focuses on whether the act of self-defence was reasonable in light of a non-exhaustive list of factors. The new self-defence provisions are less demanding of the accused than the defences of necessity and duress, which explicitly require proportionality between the harm inflicted and the harm caused and that there be no legal way out. The new provisions instead simply require that the acts of self-defence be reasonable in the circumstances. As suggested above, the strictness of the excuses of necessity and duress compared to the justification of self-defence is in tension with the nature of excuses and justifications,

---

24   *R v. Cairney*, [2013] S.C.C. 55.
25   *R v. Reilly*, [1984] 15 C.C.C.(3d) 1 (S.C.C.).
26   *R v. Pétel*, [1994] 87 C.C.C.(3d) 97 (S.C.C.).
27   Criminal Code § 34(1)(a).
28   *Reilly* (n 25).
29   Criminal Code § 34.
30   Criminal Code § 16.
31   Criminal Code § 17.

but perhaps can be explained by perceptions that acts done in self-defence will usually harm a guilty person,[32] whereas acts done under duress and necessity will harm 'innocent' victims.

Before the 2012 amendments, the courts took the position that Parliament had comprehensively codified self-defence and refused to recognize any residual defence in cases where the accused subjectively acted in self-defence but his or her actions were excessive and unreasonable.[33] There is no reason to think that the 2012 amendments have changed this state of affairs. The result makes self-defence, especially when the accused has the intent required for murder, an all or nothing proposition. The options are either to acquit on the basis of self-defence or to convict the accused of the most serious offence with its mandatory penalty of life imprisonment. Concern about the ultimate disposition of an accused may have influenced the development of the law of self-defence to factor in the difficult circumstances faced by battered women. The all-or-nothing nature of self-defence also places significant pressure on the accused to accept a plea bargain to manslaughter should one be offered.

The first requirement for self-defence in Section 34(1)(a) is that the accused believe on reasonable grounds that force or the threat of force is being used against them or another person. As under the old law, the jury can be guided by the accused's subjective beliefs 'so long as there exists an objectively verifiable basis for his perception'.[34] A mistake by the accused as to the existence of force or threat of force is not fatal to a self-defence claim, but the mistake must be reasonable. The new Section 34(1)(a) expands the old law of self-defence by including threats of force as well as actual force and by providing that a person can claim self-defence when any third party is exposed to force or threat of force.

The new concept of a threat of force is consistent with the Supreme Court's landmark ruling in *Lavallee* decided under the old self-defence provisions.[35] In that case, the Court held that there was no legal requirement that the accused wait until she faced an imminent attack from the deceased. In doing so, the Court upheld the acquittal of a woman who had shot her abusive partner in the back of the head after he had threatened that she would be harmed after guests had left their house. The Court stated that expert testimony about the effects of battering on women can cast doubt on the view expressed in a previous case that it was 'inherently unreasonable to apprehend death or grievous bodily harm unless and until the physical assault is actually in progress'.[36] Expert evidence could suggest that 'it may in fact be possible for a battered spouse to accurately predict the onset of violence before the first blow is struck, even if an outsider to the relationship cannot'.[37] Justice Wilson stressed for the Court:

> [t]he issue is not, however, what an outsider would have reasonably perceived but what the accused reasonably perceived, given her situation and her experience ... I do not think it is an unwarranted generalization to say that due to their size, strength, socialization and lack of training, women are typically no match for men in hand-to-hand combat. The requirement ... that a battered woman wait until the physical assault is 'underway' before her apprehensions can be validated in law would ... be tantamount to sentencing her to 'murder by installment'.[38]

In the context of spousal battering, 'the definition of what is reasonable must be adapted to circumstances which are, by and large, foreign to the world inhabited by the hypothetical 'reasonable man'.[39]

In subsequent cases, the Supreme Court affirmed that evidence of prior threats and beatings would be relevant to the determination of whether the accused could perceive danger from an abuser.[40] The accused's

---

32   An act of self-defence against an 'innocent victim' could be justified if the accused made a reasonable mistake that he or she was being threatened by the person but are less common than crimes committed under duress or necessity against victims who have no fault in the matter.

33   *R v. Faid*, [1983] 2 C.C.C.(3d) 513, 518 (S.C.C.).

34   *Reilly* (n 25) at 7.

35   *Lavallee* (n 9).

36   Ibid. 116 (citing *R v. Whynot*, (1983) 9 C.C.C. (3d) 449 (N.S.C.A.)).

37   *Lavallee* (n 9) at 130

38   Ibid. at 120.

39   Ibid. at 114.

40   *Pétel* (n 26); *Malott* (n 12).

knowledge of the complainant's propensity for violence is also relevant.[41] Although the history of the relationship between the parties to the incident is only mentioned explicitly in the new Section 34(2)(f.1) as a factor to be considered in determining whether the act of self-defence was reasonable in the circumstances, it should also be relevant in determining whether the accused believed on reasonable grounds that he or she faced force or a threat of force.

Although the imminence of the force is likewise only mentioned in Section 34(2)(b) as a factor in determining the reasonableness of the act and there is no legal requirement of an imminent attack, the presence or absence of an imminent threat is a factor that can be considered in determining whether the accused had a reasonable belief of force or threat of force. In one case decided under the old self-defence provisions, the Supreme Court denied self-defence claims when an accused shot his accomplices in the back of the head because he feared they were planning to kill him later that night.[42] The new statutory concept of a threat of force extends the law of self-defence, but only so far.

The second requirement for self-defence is the requirement in Section 34(1)(b) of the Code that that those claiming self-defence have the subjective purpose of defending themselves or others. In most cases, this subjective inquiry will be the least challenging requirement for the accused of the three elements of self-defence. It will, however, exclude those accused who do not subjectively intend to defend themselves or others but rather desire to seek vengeance, punishment, or vindicate honour against someone who has used force against them or threatened to do so. As with the other two elements of self-defence, the prosecution must prove beyond a reasonable doubt that this element of self-defence does not exist to ensure that the accused is given the benefit of a reasonable doubt about the existence of the defence and guilt.

The third and final requirement for self-defence is the requirement under Section 34(1)(c) of the Code that the act must be reasonable in the circumstances. In most cases, this will be the most contested and important factor. Section 34(2) provides that the 'court shall consider the relevant circumstances of the person, the other parties and the act, including, but not limited to' nine specified factors. The specified factors are:

(a)   the nature of the force or threat;

(b)   the extent to which the use of force was imminent and whether there were other means available to respond to the potential use of force;

(c)   the person's role in the incident;

(d)   whether any party to the incident used or threatened to use a weapon;

(e)   the size, age, gender and physical capabilities of the parties to the incident;

(f)   the nature, duration and history of any relationship between the parties to the incident, including any prior use or threat of force and the nature of that force or threat;

(f.1)   any history of interaction or communication between the parties to the incident;

(g)   the nature and proportionality of the person's response to the use or threat of force; and

(h)   whether the act committed was in response to a use or threat of force that the person knew was lawful.[43]

The reference to the reasonableness of the accused's response in section 34(1)(c) should be read in light of the Court's use of the contextual objective standard since *Lavallee*. The contextual objective standard articulated in *Lavallee* is not limited to issues of gender and spousal abuse. In *Nelson*,[44] the Ontario Court of Appeal held that an accused's diminished intelligence should be considered in determining whether he had a self-defence claim. The Court of Appeal stated that an accused with an intellectual impairment relating to his or her ability

---

41   *R v. Pintar*, (1996), 110 C.C.C.(3d) 402, 435 (Ont.C.A.).

42   *Cinous*, [2002] 2 S.C.R. 3.

43   Section 34(3) addresses self-defence in the context of legally authorized actions and provides:

     3)   Subsection (1) does not apply if the force is used or threatened by another person for the purpose of doing something that they are required by law to do in the administration or enforcement of the law, unless the person who commits the act that constitutes the offence believes on reasonable grounds that the other person is acting unlawfully.

44   *R v. Nelson* (1992), 71 C.C.C.(3d) 449 (Ont. C.A.).

to perceive and react to an assault 'may be in a position similar to that of the accused in *Lavallee* in that his or her apprehension and belief could not be fairly measured against the perceptions of an "ordinary man"'. [45]

The specifically enumerated factors in Section 34(2) must be considered. They include the reference in Section 34(2)(e) to the 'size, age gender and physical capabilities of the parties to the incident'; in Section 34(2)(f) to 'the nature, duration and history of any relationship between the parties to the incident, including any prior use or threat of force and the nature of that force or threat'; and in Section 34(2)(f.1) to 'any history of interaction or communication between the parties to the incident'. It could be argued that the specific reference to size, age, physical capabilities, and gender is exhaustive of the contextual objective standard, but this would be a mistake given both the specifically non-exhaustive nature of the Section 34(2) factors and the development of the modified objective standard to incorporate other factors that the accused cannot control such as mental disabilities.

The reference in Section 34(2)(f) and (f.1) to the relationship between the parties including the use of force and threats between the parties and the history of their interaction and communication reflects a series of cases involving claims of self-defence by battered women. As mentioned above, the Supreme Court held in *Lavallee* that evidence of battering and expert evidence on the effects of battering was relevant in determining the reasonableness of the response.[46] In *Pétel*, the Supreme Court affirmed that the prior assaults suffered by the accused and her daughter would be relevant to determining the reasonableness of her 'belief that she could not extricate herself otherwise than by killing the attacker'.[47] In *Malott*,[48] the Court again affirmed that evidence with respect to past battering may be relevant in determining the reasonableness of the accused's response.

One characteristic of the particular accused that should not be considered is intoxication. In *Reilly*,[49] the Supreme Court held that the accused's intoxication could not be considered because 'a reasonable man is a man in full possession of his faculties. In contrast, a drunken man is one whose ability to reason and to perceive are diminished by the alcohol he has consumed'. The Court left open the possibility that an intoxicated accused could have a valid self-defence claim provided that he or she still had reasonable grounds for his or her beliefs. Although Section 34(2) allows a non-exhaustive use of factors to be considered, intoxication is simply not relevant to determining whether an act of self-defence is reasonable in the circumstances.

The reference to particular characteristics and past circumstances in Sections 34(2) (e) and (f) is not limited to those of the accused but extend to those of all parties to the incident. As in *Lavallee*, it is relevant that the victim is a larger male with a past history of beating and threatening the female accused. At the same time, Sections 34(2) (d) and (e) suggest that the old age or small size of a victim and whether a weapon was used or threatened could also be relevant to whether the accused responded reasonably to force or a threat of force. At the end of the day, however, the focus should be on the accused and the accused should be given the benefit of the doubt about whether he or she acted in self-defence.

In determining the reasonableness of the act done in self-defence, the trier of fact should also consider a number of specifically enumerated factors. These factors include 'the nature of the force or threat' to be avoided;[50] whether the force 'was imminent and whether there were other means available to respond to it;[51] whether weapons were used or threatened;[52] and 'the nature and proportionality of the person's response to the use or threat of force'.[53] These factors can all be grouped under the general heading of the proportionality and relative harm of the force resisted or threatened and the force used by the accused. At the same time, the only absolute requirement in Section 34(1)(c) is that the act done must be reasonable in the circumstances. There is no requirement that the force or threat faced by the accused must be imminent or even that the accused's response must be proportionate, though these are factors must be considered in determining the

---

45   Ibid. 467.
46   Ibid. 125.
47   *Pétel* (n 26) at 104.
48   *Malott* (n 12).
49   *Reilly* (n 25) at 8.
50   Criminal Code § 34(2)(1).
51   Criminal Code § 34(2)(b).
52   Criminal Code § 34(2)(d).
53   Criminal Code § 34(3)(h).

reasonableness of the act done. Similarly there is no requirement that the accused must retreat in all cases. This is consistent with the historical tendency of Canadian courts not to demand that all self-defence be strictly proportional or that the accused take all possible routes of retreat.[54]

In conclusion, the accused must both subjectively act in self-defence or defence of others and act reasonably to have a valid claim to self-defence. Self-defence is classified as a justification but it does not have a strict proportionality requirement and the objective standards are administered in a contextual manner that factors in the accused's past experiences and capabilities.

Necessity

Necessity was rejected by Canadian courts as late as the 1970's as an 'ill-defined and elusive' defence.[55] The Supreme Court finally recognized necessity as a common law defence in *Perka*,[56] which involved smugglers of large amounts of illegal drugs who were forced to come ashore in Canada because of dangerous seas. At the same time, the Court was cautious in defining necessity as only an excuse and not a justification and in requiring that there be proportionality between the crime and the harm avoided.

The Supreme Court in *Latimer*[57] articulated the three requirements of the necessity defence. The first requirement is that there must be an imminent peril or danger. The Court explained that 'disaster must be imminent, or harm unavoidable and near. It is not enough that the peril is foreseeable or likely; it must be on the verge of transpiring and virtually certain to occur'.[58] On the facts of the case, the Court concluded that there was no imminent harm when the accused killed his daughter because the daughter's 'ongoing pain did not constitute an emergency in this case' but was rather 'an obstinate and long-standing state of affairs' and that the proposed surgery 'did not pose an imminent threat to her life, nor did her medical condition'.[59] There is a danger that a restrictive approach to imminent danger might run afoul of Canadian constitutional norms which prohibit punishing a person for morally involuntary behaviour that no reasonable person in similar circumstances could resist.[60] In order to ensure compliance with this constitutional principle, and also to make necessity consistent with self-defence[61] and duress,[62] the requirement of an imminent peril should not be reduced to a requirement of an immediate threat and it should be applied in a contextual manner that is sensitive to any prior knowledge or experience of the accused.

The second requirement is that the accused must have a reasonable belief that there is no legal way out or safe avenue of escape. In *Perka*, the Court suggested that 'if there is a reasonable legal alternative to disobeying the law, then the decision to disobey becomes a voluntary one, imperilled by some consideration beyond the dictates of 'necessity' and human instincts'.[63] In that case, there was no legal way out because the accused faced disaster and drowning at sea if they did not put ashore with their large cargo of drugs.

In *Latimer*,[64] the Court affirmed that 'if there was a reasonable legal alternative to breaking the law, there is no necessity'. It indicated that legal alternatives must be pursued even though they may be 'demanding', 'sad', 'unappealing'.[65] On the facts, the Court concluded that allowing the victim Tracy Latimer to go through a required operation and inserting a feeding tube to assist with pain management were reasonable legal alternatives that the accused should have pursued. The determination of no reasonable legal alternative should be determined on a modified objective standard so that any past experiences that the accused had with the victim's pain, pain management, and surgeries should have been relevant in determining the reasonableness of legal alternatives.

---

54 *R v. Kong*, [2006] S.C.C. 40.
55 *R v. Morgentaler* (No. 5) (1975), 20 C.C.C. (2d) 449 at 497 (S.C.C.).
56 *Perka* (n 4).
57 *R v. Latimer* (2001), 150 C.C.C.(3d) 129 (S.C.C.).
58 Ibid. [29].
59 Ibid. [38].
60 *Ruzic* (n 1).
61 *Lavallee* (n 9).
62 *Ruzic* (n 1).
63 *Perka* (n 4) at 401.
64 *Latimer* (n 57) at 30.
65 Ibid. [38].

The third and final requirement is proportionality between the crime and the harm avoided. The Supreme Court has justified this requirement on the basis that 'No rational criminal justice system, no matter how humane or liberal, could excuse the infliction of a greater harm to allow the actor to avert a lesser evil'.[66] In *Latimer*,[67] the Court affirmed the importance of the proportionality requirement and held that killing a person was 'completely disproportionate' to 'non-life-threatening suffering' should Tracy Latimer have had the proposed operation. It was not necessary that the harm avoided 'clearly outweigh' the harm inflicted, but only that the two harms be 'of a comparable gravity'.[68] In this vein, the Court declined to create an absolute rule that murder would be categorically excluded from the necessity defence as a disproportionate response to all possible perils. At the same time, the case stands for the proposition that killing is disproportionate to relieving non–life-threatening suffering. Proportionality is determined on a purely objective standard that factors in the rights of the vulnerable.

Duress by Threats/Circumstances

Duress by circumstances would be decided in Canada according to the necessity defence discussed above. Duress by threats, however, would be decided under the expanded self-defence provisions which as examined above apply to the commission of a wide of range of crimes and include reasonable responses to threats of force against the accused or third parties done for the purpose of defending or protecting the accused or the third party. In addition, two different duress defences could apply depending on the circumstances. A codified duress defence in Section 17 of the Canadian Criminal Code could apply to those who commit offences under duress as a principal offender. Canadian courts have long read this restrictive statutory duress defence down to not apply to those who commit offences as a party to the offence and these parties could benefit from a more flexible common law defence of duress.[69] This act of judicial creativity mitigated the harshness of the statutory restrictions on the duress defence which still categorically excludes duress as a possible defence for a long list of offences including some that only involve property damage or minor physical harm. At the same time it complicated the law and in some cases requires the jury to be instructed about two different duress defences, the Section 17 defence that would be applied if the accused acted as a principal offender and a less restrictive common law defence that would be applied if the accused was a party to the offence.[70]

There has been a recent trend to convergence between the Section 17 and common law duress defences. The main factor has been the Court's decision that some but not all of the restrictive features of the Section 17 defence are constitutionally invalid because they would punish morally involuntary behaviour that should be excused.[71] More recently, the Court has restricted the common law defence by borrowing the reference in Section 17 to the defence not being available if the accused is 'a party to a conspiracy or association whereby the person is subject to compulsion'. It will be suggested below that this latter innovation is in potential tension with the Court's underlying conceptualization of duress as an excuse-based defence. Another questionable innovation with respect to duress is the Court's decision that a different and perhaps more lenient proportionality requirement should apply to the common law duress defence than is applied to the common law necessity defence.

Section 17 of the Criminal Code provides that the defence of duress is available only when an accused 'commits an offence under compulsion by threats of immediate death or bodily harm from a person who is present when the offence is committed'. The Supreme Court held in *Ruzic* that the requirements of immediacy and presence violated Section 7 of the Charter because they could result in the punishment of a person who committed a crime in a morally involuntary manner. The Court held:

> It is a principle of fundamental justice that only voluntary conduct – behaviour that is the product of a free will and controlled body, unhindered by external constraints – should attract the penalty and stigma of criminal

---

66   *Perka* (n 4) at 400–401.
67   *Latimer* (n 57) at 41.
68   Ibid. [31].
69   *R v. Paquette*, [1977] 2 S.C.R. 189.
70   *R v. Mena* (1987) 34 C.C.C.(3d) 304 (Ont.C.A.).
71   *Ruzic* (n 1).

liability. Depriving a person of liberty and branding her with the stigma of criminal liability would infringe the principles of fundamental justice if the accused did not have any realistic choice.[72]

On the facts of the case, the accused was charged with importing heroin after a person had threatened to kill her mother who lived in a foreign country, if she did not import the drugs. The threats produced morally involuntary behaviour even though they were not of immediate death from a person present with the accused. The Court clarified that threats of death or bodily harm against third parties such as the accused's family may be considered under Section 17 of the Criminal Code.[73] This seems appropriate as threats to one's family or loved ones may be just as compelling as threats to oneself, and Parliament has not clearly excluded threats to third parties from Section 17. At the same time, the Court has recently highlighted that any gaps left by the striking out of the immediacy and presence requirements from Section 17 should be filled by common law requirements that: 1) there be a close temporal connection between threats and the accused's response; 2) there is no safe avenue of escape; 3) the defendant reasonably believed that the threats would be carried out; and 4) there exists proportionality between the harm threatened and the harm inflicted by the accused.[74] Although these requirements are not specifically enumerated in Section 17, the courts will now read them into the defence achieving considerable convergence with the common law defence.

The major difference between the Section 17 and the common law defence is the long list of offences ranging from murder to arson that are categorically excluded from the statutory but not the common law duress defence. The excluded offences will have to be measured against the constitutional principle that it violates the principles of fundamental justice to convict a person who commits a crime in a morally involuntary manner on a case by case basis in subsequent cases. Although it can be argued that an accused should not be able to commit a crime such as murder that is clearly disproportionate to a threat of bodily harm, it is also doubtful that the exclusion of offences such as arson can be justified under Section 7 of the Charter when the accused or a third party has been threatened with death or even bodily harm. Subsequent to *Ruzic*, one court has held that the exclusion of robbery in Section 17 of the Code violated the principle that no one should be convicted for a morally involuntary crime.[75]

It is not clear that even the exclusion of the most serious crimes such as murder and attempted murder from the Section 17 defence can be justified in cases where the accused is threatened with death and commits the crime in a morally involuntary manner. The categorical exclusion of offences from the defence is a blunt and potentially overbroad means of ensuring social protection compared to the more proportionate approach of requiring true moral involuntariness as measured by the common law requirements of proportionality and no legal way out before a defence of duress is recognized for the commission of any crime.

Another restriction is that a person cannot benefit from the Section 17 defence of duress if they are 'a party to a conspiracy or association whereby the person is subject to compulsion'. Like the excluded offences, this categorical restriction could be found to violate Section 7 of the Charter when applied to those who commit a crime under circumstances of true moral involuntariness. The Court may have recently restricted the exclusion, however, by indicating that it should only apply if the accused subjectively knows that he or she will be threatened as a result of a conspiracy or association with others.[76] In any event, the principled focus should be on whether the accused had any realistic choice but to commit the offence at the time it was committed and not on accused's prior crime or unwise associations. This is consistent with the general principle that the accused's fault and lack of fault as manifested by the presence of a defence should be determined at the time that the prohibited act occurs. As will be seen, the Court also seems prepared to apply this restriction from Section 17 to the common law defence of duress.

The common law defence of duress that applies to parties to an offence has the same juridical basis as the common law defence of necessity.[77] Both common law defences are characterized by the general requirement that the accused respond reasonably and in a morally involuntary manner to threats of imminent death or

---

72   *Ruzic* (n 1) at [47].
73   *Ruzic* (n 1) at [54].
74   *Ryan* (n 8) at [49]–[54].
75   *R v. Fraser* (2002), 6 C.R.(5th) 308 (N.S. Prov. Ct.).
76   *Ryan* (n 8) at 79–80.
77   *Hibbert*, [1995] 2 S.C.R. 973.

harm when there is no safe avenue of escape or legal way out. Canadian courts have been cautious in applying both defences and in addition require proportionality between the harm avoided and the harm inflicted. As discussed above, the concept of proportionality is normally associated with justifications such as self-defence that are based on a judgment that breaking the law can be correct in some cases as opposed to excuses which are a concession to human frailty that excuses wrongful conduct in extenuating circumstances.

A further complication is that the proportionality requirements in the common law defences of necessity and duress are strangely different. The *Latimer*[78] case discussed above stands for the proposition that proportionality between the harm threatened and committed in necessity must be judged on a purely objective basis. In contrast, the Supreme Court in the recent *Ryan* case has indicated that proportionality in the common law defence of duress should be evaluated according to a different and potentially more lenient contextual objective standard that makes some allowance for the personal characteristics of the accused.[79] The Court provided no persuasive explanation for this distinction.[80] It is unfortunate that the Court has created the complexity of two different proportionality tests given the similar excuse-based juristic basis of the two defences.

In *Ryan*,[81] the Supreme Court articulated the common law defence of duress as requiring: 1) a threat of future death or bodily harm to the accused or a third party; 2) a reasonable belief that the threat will be carried out; 3) no safe avenue of escape; 4) close temporal connection between the threat and the death or bodily harm threatened; and 5) proportionality between the harm threatened and the harm inflicted including ' general moral judgment regarding the accused's behaviour in the circumstances'.[82] All but the first requirement is judged on the basis on a modified objective standard of a reasonable person similarly situated as the accused.

The Court in *Ryan* also read in the exclusion of threats produced through the accused's prior conspiracy or associations found in Section 17 into the common law defence. The Court justified this abnormal import of restrictive statutory concepts into a common law defence on the basis that accused would not be acting in a morally involuntary manner if they made voluntary choices to conspire or associate with those that subsequently threatened them. Both under Section 17 and the common law, the Court restricted this exclusion of the duress defence by requiring that the accused must know that they will be threatened as a result of entering into a prior conspiracy or association.[83] Nevertheless, there is still a danger here that accused could be punished for responding to threats in a morally involuntary manner simply because of their prior conspiracies or associations. For example, the fact that a person associated and even conspired with robbers does not take away from the power of threats of death and bodily harm over an accused when that person refuses to participate in the robbery or additional crimes committed by the group. A conviction in such circumstances could be contrary to the logic of excuses and the principles of fundamental justice which prohibit the punishment of morally involuntary behaviour.

General Mental Condition Defences

Insanity

Canada's insanity defence is based on the 1843 decision of the House of Lords in *M'Naghten's Case*[84] but with some significant modifications. In 1992, the insanity defence was re-named the mental disorder defence. The first requirement is the existence of a mental disorder. Mental disorder, defined in Section 2 of the Criminal Code as a 'disease of the mind;, has been interpreted by the courts broadly to include 'any illness, disorder or abnormal condition which impairs the human mind and its functioning, excluding however, self-induced

---

78   *Latimer* (n 57).
79   *Ryan* (n 8) at [74].
80   The Court did note that necessity only applies to imminent harms whereas duress applies to future harms. *Ryan* (n 8) at [74]. This could, however, just as well justify a more demanding proportionality test for duress as a less demanding one.
81   *Ryan* (n 8).
82   *Ryan* (n 8) at [72].
83   Ibid. [79]–[80].
84   8 E.R. 718 (H.L. 1843).

states caused by alcohol or drugs, as well as transitory mental states such as hysteria or concussion'.[85] Subject to these exclusions, a disease of the mind includes a wide and expanding range of mental disorders. For example, newly diagnosed diseases such as the brain damage caused by foetal alcohol spectrum disorder have been recognised by Canadian courts as a disease of the mind. At the same time, the Supreme Court has recently held that toxic psychosis was not a mental disorder when it was produced by the voluntary consumption of drugs.[86] In such a case, the accused can only plead intoxication and not mental disorder.

Some conditions that might not constitute mental disorders in a medical sense may nevertheless for reasons of social protection be classified as diseases of the mind. A classification of a condition producing involuntary behaviour as a mental disorder will mean that the accused who satisfies the second or third requirements of the mental disorder defence (discussed below) will not receive an outright acquittal but will if judged dangerous be subject to indeterminate detention or conditions as a person held not criminally responsible by reason of mental disorder. In 1999, the Supreme Court for social protection reasons decided that there would be a presumption that automatic states where the accused acted in a physically uncontrolled and involuntary manner would be presumed to be caused by a disease of the mind.[87] Since that decision, courts have departed from prior precedents holding that sleepwalking was not a disease of the mind and could be the basis for an acquittal[88] to hold that sleepwalking was a disease of the mind.[89] The practical result of these changes means that an accused who committed crimes while sleepwalking or in another unconscious state will not receive an acquittal but be found not criminally responsible by reason of mental disorder. As such, they will be subject to potential further control by the state if determined to be a significant threat to public safety.[90]

Even if the courts find there is a mental disorder, it must under Section 16 of the Criminal Code be so extreme as to render the accused incapable of knowing that the actions were wrong or of appreciating the nature and quality of the act. Canadian courts have stressed that Section 16 of the Criminal Code refers to an inability to *appreciate* the nature and quality of acts, as opposed to the *M'Naghten* rules, which refer to an inability to *know* the nature and quality of the act. The ability to appreciate the nature and quality of an act involves more than knowledge or cognition that the act is being committed. Specifically, it includes the capacity to measure and foresee the consequences of the conduct. In *Cooper*, Dickson J stated:

> The requirement, unique to Canada, is that of perception, an ability to perceive the consequences, impact, and results of a physical act. An accused may be aware of the physical character of his action (i.e., in choking) without necessarily having the capacity to appreciate that, in nature and quality, the act will result in the death of a human being.[91]

The courts have not expanded the defence to apply to those who, because of mental disorder, were unable emotionally to appreciate the effect of their actions on the victim.[92] Thus, an inability to appreciate that a victim may die can result in a mental disorder defence. An inability to have appropriate emotions about the death of another person, however, does not result in a mental disorder defence, even if it is an indication of a mental disorder such as a psychopathic personality. The courts have also held that an inability to appreciate the penal consequences of an act does not render an accused incapable of appreciating the physical consequences of the act as required under Section 16.[93]

An alternative basis for the mental disorder defence is an inability because of a mental disorder to know that the act is wrong. After having initially restricted the meaning of wrong to legal wrong, the Court in 1990

85   *R v. Cooper* (1979), 51 C.C.C. (2d) 129 at 144 (S.C.C.).
86   *Bouchard-Lebrun* (n 10).
87   *R v. Stone*, [1999] 2 S.C.R. 290.
88   *R v. Parks*, [1992] 2 S.C.R. 871.
89   *R v. Luedecke*, [2008] O.N.C.A. 716.
90   Criminal Code § 672.54. This determination has to be made by the court or a mental health review board on the basis of evidence about the individual. *Winko v. British Columbia (Forensic Psychiatric Institute)*, [1999] 2 S.C.R. 626.
91   *Cooper* (n 85) at 147.
92   *R v. Simpson* (1977) 35 C.C.C.(2d) 337 at 355 (Ont.C.A.).
93   *R v. Abbey* (1982), 68 C.C.C.(2d) 394 at 405–406 (S.C.C.).

expanded it to include inability to know that the act was morally wrong.[94] The mental disorder defence has been applied to a person acting under the delusion that he was God killing Satan[95] but not to a person who despite delusions that killing would save the world still knew that killing was morally wrong.[96] The mental disorder defence will not apply to a 'psychopath or a person following a deviant moral code' if such a person 'is capable of knowing that his or her acts are wrong in the eyes of society, and despite such knowledge, chooses to commit them'.[97] The focus is on the accused's capacity for rational choice about the particular criminal act at the time the act was committed, not his or her general intellectual ability to know right from wrong.[98]

The Supreme Court of Canada has recently indicated that those with a valid mental disorder defence act in a morally involuntary manner. In other words, the acts are 'not actually the product of his or her free will', and the refusal to convict such persons is 'therefore consistent with the principles of fundamental justice' under Section 7 of the Charter[99] that, as examined above, prevent the conviction of those who act in a morally involuntary manner. These underdeveloped dicta would appear to make a legislative attempt to abolish the mental disorder defence unconstitutional. Although courts are willing to entertain a broad range of newly discovered mental disorder under the Canadian mental disorder defence, the mental disorder defence will only exempt an accused from criminal responsibility if it is so extreme as to prevent the accused from appreciating the physical nature and quality of the act or from knowing that society and reasonable people consider the act to be wrong.

Intoxication

Canada followed the general pattern of English common law with respect to the intoxication defence,[100] but important modifications have made to the treatment of intoxication under the influence of the Canadian Charter of Rights and Freedoms.

The simplest and most traditional intoxication defence applies only to offences that are classified as specific intent offences that involve acts to achieve some ulterior purpose. Murder and robbery are specific intent offences because they involve doing acts for ulterior purposes while manslaughter and assault are general intent offences that only require a more minimal intent to do the immediate act.[101] If the offence is classified as specific intent, the accused will be acquitted if the evidence of intoxication raises a reasonable doubt about the intent to commit the offence. The Supreme Court has held that the traditional focus of the common law on whether the intoxication raises a reasonable doubt about the accused's capacity to have a specific intent violated the Charter: the proper issue, consistent with *mens rea* theory, is whether intoxication raises a reasonable doubt about the accused's actual intent.[102] This recognizes that an intoxicated accused may still have the capacity to form the requisite specific intent but nevertheless not have formed that intent.

Canadian courts traditionally followed the English common law in holding that intoxication could not be a defence for offences classified as general intent.[103] In the 1994 case of *Daviault*,[104] however, the Supreme Court decided that extreme intoxication could in rare cases be a defence to general intent offences such as assault or sexual assault. The Court concluded that application of the common law rule that substituted the intent of voluntarily becoming intoxicated for the intent of the general intent offence violated the principles of fundamental justice and the presumption of innocence as protected under the Charter. It did so by punishing the accused for involuntary conduct and by substituting the fault of becoming extremely intoxicated for the fault of the particular offence. The new extreme intoxication defence would focus on the accused's capacity

---

94   Ibid. 232–233.
95   *R v. Landry*, [1991] 1 S.C.R. 99.
96   *R v. Baker*, [2010] 1 S.C.R. 329.
97   *Oommen*, (1994) 91 C.C.C.(3d) 8 [19] (S.C.C.).
98   Ibid. [18].
99   *Bouchard-Lebrun* (n 10) at 51.
100   *DPP v. Beard*, [1920] A.C. 479 (H.L.).
101   *R v. George*, [1960] S.C.R. 871.
102   *R v. Robinson* (1996), 105 C.C.C. (3d) 97 (S.C.C.); R v. Daley, [2007] 3 S.C.R. 523.
103   *R v. Leary* (1977) 33 C.C.C. (2d) 473 (S.C.C.).
104   *Daviault* (n 2).

for voluntary action. It would have to be proven by the accused on a balance of probabilities and with expert evidence. It was intended to be a rare defence.

Parliament was not satisfied with any possibility that an accused would be acquitted for intoxicated acts of violence. In 1995, it enacted Sections 33.1–33.3 of the Criminal Code, which essentially repealed the extreme intoxication defence for violent general intent offences. The new law reaffirmed the common law's substitution of the fault of becoming extremely intoxicated for the fault of the general intent offence. This provision only applies to offences that interfere with bodily integrity leaving the new extreme intoxication defence available for non-violent general intent offences.[105]

The Supreme Court has not ruled on the constitutionality of Parliament's partial repeal of an extreme intoxication defence. It has, however, applied Section 33.1 to convict a person of the general intent offence of aggravated assault even though the person was acting in an involuntary manner and without intent as a result of a toxic psychosis produced by his voluntary consumption of a drug, The Court stressed that Section 33.1 applies even to 'toxic psychosis' produced by drugs that would render the accused incapable of knowing that his or her acts were wrong. The Court explained that Section 33.1 'applies where three conditions are met: (1) the accused was intoxicated at the material time; (2) the intoxication was self-induced; and (3) the accused departed from the standard of reasonable care generally recognized in Canadian society by interfering or threatening to interfere with the bodily integrity of another person. Where these three things are proved, it is not a defence that the accused lacked the general intent or the voluntariness required to commit the offence'.[106]

There is still no definitive ruling of the constitutionality of Section 33.1 almost 20 years after its enactment. This may be a product of the rarity of the defence. The trend in lower courts has been to uphold Section 33.1 usually as a reasonable limit on the accused's constitutional rights. Section 33.1 likely violates the principles of fundamental justice and the presumption of innocence under Sections 7 and 11(d) of the Charter by convicting a person for involuntary behaviour and by substituting the fault of becoming intoxicated for the fault of the violent crime. At the same time, it may be possible to uphold Section 33.1 as a reasonable and proportionate limit on these rights because it is limited to violent offences. In addition, the courts may also be influenced by Parliament's expression of its special concern about intoxicated violence against women and children and its conclusion that there is no scientific evidence supporting the idea that intoxication produces involuntary behaviour.

Finally, the courts apply different rules for involuntary intoxication. An accused has been acquitted of impaired driving after being giving a drug at the dentist without proper warnings.[107] An accused will not benefit from the involuntary intoxication defence if he should have reasonably been expected to know that a drug was impairing.[108] An accused will not be subject to the restrictions in Section 33.1 on the extreme intoxication defence if the intoxication was involuntary on the basis that the fault for becoming intoxicated is not present and cannot be substituted for the fault and voluntary conduct that is absent when the accused is extremely intoxicated.[109]

Mistake of Law

Section 19 of the Criminal Code provides that ignorance of the law is not an excuse. The Court has interpreted this as making it 'a principle of our criminal law that an honest but mistaken belief in respect of the legal consequences of one's deliberate actions does not furnish a defence to a criminal charge, even when the mistake cannot be attributed to the negligence of the accused'.[110] There are a few limited incursions on this harsh principle. Some offences such as theft and fraud provide the accused with a colour of right defence that may partially be based on a mistaken belief of legal entitlement.[111] In one regulatory offence case, the Supreme Court has held that because the accused's only possible defence was precluded by the ignorance

105   *R. v. Bouchard-Lebrun*, [2011] 3 S.C.R. 575 35.
106   Ibid. 89.
107   *R v. King* (1962) 133 CCC 1 (S.C.C.).
108   Ibid.; *R v. Chauk* (2007) 223 C.C.C.(3d) 174 (N.S.C.A.).
109   *R v. Vickberg* (1998) 16 C.R. (5th) 164 (B.C.S.C.).
110   *R. v. Forster* (1992) 70 C.C.C. (3d) 59 [64] (S.C.C.).
111   *R v. Lilly* [1983] 1 SCR 794, 798–799.

of the law is not an excuse principle that the offence was a no fault absolute liability offence for which it is unconstitutional to imprison violators.[112]

More recently, the Supreme Court has recognized a defence of officially induced error for all criminal and regulatory offences. The Court affirmed its commitment to the principle that ignorance of the law is not an excuse, but recognized that an inflexible approach to this rule could cause injustice 'where the error in law of the accused arises out of an error of an authorized representative of the state'.[113] The accused must establish the defence of officially induced error on a balance of probabilities and it results in a stay of proceedings. The defence applies to errors of law or mixed law and fact where the accused 'considered the legal consequences of his or her actions' and obtained erroneous legal advice 'from an appropriate official' and 'relied on the advice in committing the act'.[114] Both the advice received from an appropriate official and the accused's reliance on the advice must be reasonable. The defence did not apply in the case because the accused relied on an 'administrative practice' that they would receive a renewal notice when their licences expired and they did not obtain specific legal advice from an appropriate official.[115] This novel defence responds to the injustice of the state with one hand approving of conduct and on the other hand prosecuting the approved conduct. It is, however, a limited exception to the basic principle that mistake of law is not a valid defence.

Residual Catch-All Defences/Existence and Ambit of Statutory Defences Related to Distinct Offences

The Supreme Court has interpreted Section 8(3) of the Criminal Code, which preserves common law defences to the extent that they are not inconsistent with the Criminal Code or other federal statutes, as allowing it to create and apply retroactively new common law defences. It has used this jurisdiction to recognize a range of common law defences including the officially induced error, common law duress and necessity defences examined above. It has also recognized a defence of due diligence to regulatory offences[116] that is constitutionally required when the accused can be imprisoned for violation of the offence.[117] The Court has been asked to recognize a *de minimus* defence for acts that are only minor violations of statutory offences but has so far declined to do so in the context of Criminal Code offences[118] while recognizing it for more minor regulatory offences.[119]

Even if Parliament attempted to abolish the ability of courts to create new common law defences in response to new circumstances, the courts might achieve similar results by ruling that a conviction without the new defence would deprive a person of liberty in a manner not in accordance with the principles of fundamental justice under Section 7 of the Charter. As seen above, the Supreme Court of Canada has done just this in ruling that Section 7 requires a new defence of extreme intoxication to general intent offences,[120] that it is violated by an overly restrictive statutory duress defence,[121] and that it would be violated by the abolition of the mental disorder defence.[122] Indeed, these cases constitutionalizing some criminal defences are some of the most significant and interesting Canadian decisions about defences from a comparative perspective.

---

112   *R v. Pontes* [1995] 3 S.C.R. 44.
113   *Lévis (City) v. Tetreault*, [2006] 1 S.C.R. 420 [26]–[27] .
114   *Lévis (City) v. Tetreault*, [2006] 1 S.C.R. 420 [26]–[27], following the approach taken by Lamer CJ in *Jorgensen*, [1995] 4 S.C.R. 55 [28]–[35].
115   Ibid. *Jorgensen* [34].
116   *R v. Sault Ste Marie*, [1978] 2 S.C.R. 1299.
117   *Re B.C. Motor Vehicles*, [1985] 2 S.C.R. 486.
118   *R v. Hinchley*, [1996] 3 S.C.R. 1128 ¶ 69; R v. J.A., [2011] 2 S.C.R. 440 [63].
119   *Ontario v. Canadian Pacific*, [1995] 2 S.C.R. 1031 [65].
120   *Daviault* (n 2).
121   *Ruzic* (n 1).
122   *Bouchard-Lebrun* (n 10).

Chapter 15
France

Catherine Elliott

General Issues

Conceptual Foundations

After the French Revolution, the criminal law was codified in the French Criminal Code of 1810. This was subsequently replaced by a new Criminal Code, which was brought into force in 1994. The defences can be found in Articles 122–1 to 122–8, which together form a single chapter of the Code. The most senior appellate court that hears criminal cases is the *Cour de cassation*.

Justificatory and Excusatory Defences—Distinction and Seat in the Offence Structure

Defences can be categorised as either providing an excuse or a justification. An excuse focuses on the defendants themselves: their personalities and their mental health. A justification is concerned with the surrounding circumstances in which the offence was committed, with the external circumstances providing a justification for the criminal conduct, which ceases to be viewed as anti-social. Thus excuses are subjective defences, while justifications are objective defences. This distinction is drawn by French academics but is not expressly referred to by the French Criminal Code, though the distinction appears to have influenced the order in which the defences are listed in the Code. There are four justifications: order of law, superior orders, legitimate defence and necessity.[1] There are also four excuses: mental illness, the defence of being a minor, constraint and mistake of law.[2] The limits of this analysis can be seen with the defence of constraint. This is generally viewed as a subjective defence because it focuses on the fact that the victim's free will has been repressed, but the constraint normally stems from circumstances that are external to the defendant (like self-defence and necessity). So the boundary between subjective and objective defences is not always straightforward.

Objective defences, unlike subjective defences, remove civil liability as well as criminal liability. This is because with subjective defences the offence still exists, the defence simply removes liability for its commission from the individual. As a result, secondary parties can be liable for the offence even where the principal offender has avoided liability by relying on the subjective defence.

The duress of constraint removes not only criminal responsibility but also civil responsibility (with the doctrine of force majeure) which makes it different from the subjective causes of irresponsibility and brings it closer to the objective causes of irresponsibility.

Cumulation/Cumulative or Alternative Pleading of Defences

The defendant can present to the court multiple defences even where these are mutually exclusive. Thus, they can present the court with different possible scenarios on the basis that if one defence is rejected another could be considered in the alternative. For example, a defendant may argue that she did not commit the offence, but if she had committed the offence she should benefit from a defence on the basis of her mental health problems. If the defences are contradictory, they may undermine each other in practice.

---

1 Articles 122-1, 122-2, 122-3 and 122-8.
2 Articles 122-4, 122-5, 122-6 and 122-7.

Provocation of the Defence Situation

The issue of defendants themselves provoking the defensive situation has been considered by the French courts. Organisations fighting racism have sought to show the existence of discriminatory conduct amounting to a criminal offence under Article 225–2 of the Criminal Code. For example, several different groups of people were asked to try to enter a nightclub to show that the club's admissions policy was discriminating against the group containing people of North African descent who were refused entry when the white French group were allowed in. While the trial judges treated this evidence as unfair and inadmissible, the *Cour de cassation* allowed the proceedings on the basis of this evidence, relying on their case law that under the rules on criminal procedure everyone has the right to prove their case.[3] The validity of this type of evidence in the specific context of the fight against discrimination has been confirmed by the Act of the 31 March 2006 For Equality of Chances which added Article 225-3-1 to the Criminal Code. It lays down that the offences of discrimination are committed even if the victims solicited the property, acts, services or contracts 'with the aim of demonstrating the existence of the discriminatory conduct', as long as the proof of this conduct is established.

   On the other hand, the provocation of a third party can never amount to the defence of constraint, and the person doing the provoking might be found liable as an accomplice. This issue has arisen in the context of police provocations (particularly involving drug trafficking), when the police pretend to be drug users buying drugs.[4]

Mistakes of Fact and Defences

Where defendants mistakenly believe they are about to be attacked they will be able to rely on the defence of legitimate defence (similar to the English defence of self-defence) if that mistake was reasonable.[5] Where there are no good reasons for the defendant to make the mistake, the defence will not be available, though defendants may be acquitted if they lack *mens rea*. For example, a police officer had come across two individuals trying to steal some property in the middle of the night. He was hit by one of them while the other, armed with a crowbar, had disappeared. He mistakenly believed that this person might return at any moment and shot the remaining defendant to defend himself. As his mistaken belief was reasonable he successfully relied on the defence of legitimate defence.[6] In another case, a father had a defence when he shot a third party who appeared to be threatening his son with a gun, though in fact it had only been a game.[7] Sometimes the judges will not allow the defence if they consider the mistake to be inexcusable. Thus, the defence was rejected when a father killed his son who had gone down to the kitchen in the middle of the night and been mistaken by his father for a burglar.[8]

Transferred Defences/Collateral Damage Defences

If the defendant killed A, having mistaken A for B, then the defendant is guilty of murder as this mistake is irrelevant, there is still an intention to kill.[9] The same is true when an individual misses their target. One case concerned the sending of a booby-trapped parcel, opened by people for whom it was not destined.[10] The courts take into account the circumstances of the planned offence to determine the extent of liability: if the defendant was in a state of legitimate defence *vis-à-vis* A, he will be found not liable for the offence committed against B.[11]

---

3   Crim 11 juin 2002, B no 131.
4   Crim 16 mars 1972, B, no 108.
5   Crim 21 fév 1996, B 84, obs Bouloc, RSC, 1996, p 849.
6   Paris, 9 oct 1979, JCP, 1979.II.19232, note Bouzat.
7   Crim 5 juin 1984, B, 209.
8   Crim 21 déc 1954, B, 423, RSC, 1956, 311, obs Legal.
9   Crim 31 janv 1835, S, 1835, I, 564.
10   Crim 4 janv 1978, B no 5.
11   Crim 18 fév 1922, I, 239, note Roux.

Individual Defences

Self-Defence and Excessive Self-Defence

Article 122-5 of the Criminal Code lays down the parameters of self-defence, called 'legitimate defence'[12] in France. This states:

> A person who, faced with an unjustified attack against himself or another, carries out at that time an act required by the necessity of the legitimate defence of himself or another is not criminally liable, except if there is a disproportion between the means of defence used and the gravity of the attack.

> A person who, in order to prevent the commission of a serious or major offence against property, carries out an act of defence, other than voluntary homicide, when this act is strictly necessary for the goal sought, is not criminally liable when the means used are proportionate to the gravity of the offence.[13]

The traditional concept of self-defence thus falls within this defence, though its parameters are wider than this. The attack that gave rise to the response must be in breach of the law,[14] there must be an actual or imminent attack[15] and the defendant's response must bear some relation to the intensity of the attack.[16]

The attack that gave rise to the response must be in breach of the law; though it need not pose a threat to a person's life.[17] The defence will not, therefore, be available to prevent a lawful arrest. An attack on a person's honour will not ground the defence,[18] though an attack on a person's morals can be sufficient, particularly where the morals of a minor are concerned. In one case, the defence was available where a mother hit a young girl with loose morals who was corrupting her sixteen-year-old son.[19]

Article 122-5 requires that the defence be carried out at the same time as the attack. For the defence to be available there must be an actual or imminent attack. If a person is threatened, but the aggressor is held back by others present at the scene, the person threatened cannot lash out violently at their aggressor and then rely on their legitimate defence, as the attack was no longer actual or imminent.[20] If the threat is not actual or imminent, an immediate response is not necessary and people are expected to seek the protection of the authorities. If there is a time lapse between the attack and the response, the defendant's conduct amounts to revenge and falls outside the defence.[21] There is no defence if a person shoots the aggressor when they are running away.[22]

The defence will cease to exist where the threat has come to an end, such as where an aggressor has seen the defendant's gun and put his hands up in the air.[23] Nor can the defence be relied on where, in order to prevent a possible future attack, a person has attacked first.[24] While a person cannot attack first, they can take precautions to prevent a possible attack. But the means of defence prepared in advance must not be susceptible to produce a disproportionate response compared with the actual attack eventually suffered. This problem has

---

12 *La légitime défense.*

13 Article 122-5:

> *N'est pas pénalement responsable la personne qui, devant une atteinte injustifiée envers elle-même ou autrui, accomplit, dans le même temps, un acte commandé par la nécessité de la légitime défense d'elle-même ou d'autrui, sauf s'il y a disproportion entre les moyens de défense employés et la gravité de l'atteinte.*

> *N'est pas pénalement responsable la personne qui, pour interrompre l'exécution d'un crime ou d'un délit contre un bien, accomplit un acte de défense, autre qu'un homicide volontaire, lorsque cet acte est strictement nécessaire au but poursuivi dès lors que les moyens employés sont proportionnés à la gravité de l'infraction.*

14 Crim 14 avr 1956, Rec dr pén 1956, 191.

15 Crim 28 mai 1937, GP 1937.2.336.

16 Crim 4 aôut 1949, RSC, 1950, 47, observations Magnoil.

17 Crim 14 avr 1956, Rec dr pén, 1956.191.

18 Crim 24 nov 1899, D 1901, I, 373.

19 Trib Pol Valence, 19 mai 1960, S, 1960.271, note L Hugueney; obs Légal, RSC, 1962.321.

20 Crim 28 mai 1937, GP, 1937.2.336.

21 Crim 4 juill 1907, B, 243; Crim 28 mai 1937, GP 1937.2.336; Crim 16 oct 1979, D, 1980, IR, 522.

22 Crim 7 déc 1999, B, no 292.

23 Crim 20 oct 1993, Dr Pén 1993, 34.

24 Crim 27 juin 1927, S, 1929.I.356.

arisen in relation to property owners who, in an attempt to protect their property, leave booby traps, which explode automatically on contact.[25] The approach of the courts to such devices will depend on the facts of each particular case. In one case, a farmer had suffered several thefts, and had installed a trap gun in his chicken shed, which had injured a thief. The farmer was convicted of an intentional offence against the person.[26]

The response must be proportionate to the intensity of the attack. It is the means of defence used, and not the result of these means, which must be proportionate to the gravity of the attack.[27] The issue of proportionality is left to the judges of fact.[28] The defence was available to a person who shot a burglar in the behind who was scaling the outside of an inhabited house at night.[29] In another case, some people had just climbed over a boundary wall and the property owner had tried to frighten them away by shooting without visibility into the darkness. One of the intruders was hit and injured. The defence was not available to the property owner as he had carelessly used excessive force.[30] In another prosecution, the defendant had been grabbed by her collar and, in response, she had hit her aggressor with her high heeled shoe causing a lesion to the optic nerve of the victim's left eye. This response was considered to be disproportionate by the *Cour de cassation*.[31]

By definition, the defendant will have responded to the attack by the commission of a crime. The legitimate defence can apply to any crime, though it is primarily concerned with offences against the person. The traditional view is that the nature of involuntary offences means that legitimate defence will not be available: an act of defence is by its nature voluntary. Thus the *Cour de cassation* rejected the defence for an involuntary crime on the basis that the defence requires a deliberate response to the attack.[32] But this exception has been thrown into doubt by the broad wording of the new Code.

Defence of property was not expressly mentioned by the old Criminal Code but had been developed by the courts since 1902. In that year, a defence had been allowed in civil proceedings where a poacher had lost a leg after being injured by a trap placed in a pond by the property owner, M. Fraville.[33] The National Assembly hesitated about including this form of the defence in the new Code as it was worried about encouraging vigilante activity but, having reached a compromise with the Senate, it is now expressly provided for in the second paragraph of Article 122-5. It is therefore possible to use force against a thief. The criteria for the defence of property are more rigorous than those for the defence of the person. Article 122-5 states that the response must have been 'strictly' necessary to prevent the attack; this adverb is not used in relation to the prevention of an offence against the person. The defendant should normally have given the victim a warning before using violence. On the issue of proportionality, a voluntary homicide cannot be committed in order to protect property. The defence can only be exercised in relation to serious and major offences against property and not minor offences.

Normally the defendant has to prove that the conditions of the defence have been satisfied. On the issue of proportionality, where the threat was to the person, the burden of proof is on the prosecution to show that the response was disproportionate, while with threats to property it is on the defendant.

More significantly, the legislator has sought to strengthen the protection of individuals in particularly dangerous situations by reversing the burden of proof. Article 122–6 of the Criminal Code states:

> A person is presumed to have acted in a state of legitimate defence when they carry out the act:
> 1) To repel, at night, an entrance by force, violence or fraud into inhabited premises;
> 2) To defend themselves against the authors of theft or looting executed with force.[34]

---

25   Levasseur, 'Les pièges à feux' (RSC 1979) 329; Romerio, 'Les pièges à voleurs et le droit' (JCP 1979) I.2939; Pradel, 'La défense automatique des biens' (Mélanges Bouzat 1980) 217.

26   T Corr Toulouse, 8 oct 1969, D, 1970, 315, note Cédié.

27   Crim 21 févr 1996, B, no 84; D, 1997, p 234, note Chr. Paulin.

28   Crim 4 août 1949, B. no 274; 21 févr 1996, Dr pén, 1996, comm 98; JCP, 1996 éd GI 3959, notes M Véron.

29   Crim 11 oct 1994, Dr pén, 1995, comm no 37.

30   T Corr Mayenne, 6 mars 1957, D, 1957, p 458, note Pageaud.

31   Crim 6 déc 1995, Dr Pén, 1996, comm 98.

32   Crim 16 fév 1967 (JCP,1967) II.15034, note Combaldieu. This decision has been strongly criticised by some authors. See, for example, Légal (RSC 1967) 854; Levasseu (RSC 1967) 659.

33   Req, 25 mars 1902, S, 1903.I.5, note Lyon-Caen, D, 1902.I.356, affaire de Fraville.

34   Article 122-6:

>   *Est présumé avoir agi en état de légitime défense celui qui accomplit l'acte: 1. Pour repousser, de nuit, l'entrée par effraction, violence ou ruse dans un lieu habité; 2. Pour se défendre contre les auteurs de vols ou de pillages exécutés avec violence.*

In such circumstances, it would be up to the prosecution to prove that the individual was not acting in a state of legitimate defence. For a long time this presumption was thought to be irrebuttable. Thus, on several occasions an individual had entered a house for an amorous rendezvous with a woman inside. Her husband was aware of his intentions and, having armed himself for his arrival, killed or injured him with a gun. In such cases, the conditions of legitimate defence were not satisfied, but the prosecution could not rebut the presumption that the defence applied.[35] In 1959 the *Cour de cassation* reversed its position on the matter, ruling that the presumption was rebuttable[36] and this is the approach adopted by the new Code.

Necessity

The old Criminal Code did not lay down a general defence of necessity, but there were certain offences that could not be committed where the person acted through necessity, such as obstructing the highway[37] or having an abortion.[38] During the nineteenth century, the courts were reluctant to recognise openly a general defence of necessity, preferring to treat such cases as falling within the defence of constraint.[39] Thus, in the famous case of *Ménard*,[40] the mother of a family who had stolen some bread to feed her children was acquitted. In another trial, some Jews were acquitted of using false administrative documents that they had used to escape a police search under German occupation, by relying on the defence of constraint.[41] Alternatively the courts would avoid imposing liability on the grounds that the defendant lacked the requisite intention to commit the offence.[42] But both approaches were artificial, as the defence of constraint suggests the defendant could not make a free choice, but actually the defendant acting under necessity has made a positive choice. This is also why the defendant in reality had the *mens rea* of the offence and to pretend otherwise is to confuse *mens rea* with motive.

It was in the 1950s that a court of first instance recognized the defence of necessity. The court acquitted the accused of the charge of building without a permit as he was trying to provide decent living conditions for his family who had been living in slum accommodation.[43] Soon afterwards the *Cour de cassation* formally recognized the defence of necessity.[44]

The defence of necessity is now expressly provided for in Article 122-7 of the Criminal Code, which states:

> A person is not criminally liable who, faced with an existing or imminent danger which threatens themselves, another or property, carries out a necessary act to safeguard the person or property, except if there is disproportion between the means used and the gravity of the threat.[45]

The defence of necessity is available to all types of offences, but three conditions must be satisfied in order for it to be applied: there must be an existing or imminent danger, this danger must have necessitated the commission of the offence, and the offence must have been proportionate to the danger. These conditions are very similar to those for the legitimate defence because the latter is really just a special case of the former, always requiring that the danger to which the defendant was responding be a criminal offence. Each of these requirements will now be considered in turn.

---

35   Crim 11 juill 1844, S 1844.I.777.
36   Crim 19 fév 1959, D, 1959.161, note MRMP, JCP, 1959.II.1112, note Bouzat.
37   '*encombrement de la voie publique*': art R 38, old Criminal Code.
38   Act of 17 January 1975.
39   Crim 15 nov 1856, B, no 358; 14 aôut 1863, DP, 64.I.399.
40   Amiens, 22 avr 1898, S, 1899.2.1, note Roux.
41   Paris, 6 oct 1944 and 5 janv 1945, S 1945.2.81.
42   Amiens, 22 avr 1898, S, 1899.2.1, note Roux.
43   Tribunal Correctionnel Colmar, 27 avril 1956, D, 1956, 500.
44   Crim 25 juin 1958, Lesage, JCP, 1959.II.10941, note J Larguier, D 1958, 693, note Marcel Rousselet and Maurice Patin.
45   Article 122-7:
    N'est pas pénalement responsable la personne qui, face à un danger actuel ou imminent qui menace elle-même, autrui ou un bien, accomplit un acte nécessaire à la sauvegarde de la personne ou du bien, sauf s'il y a disproportion entre les moyens employés et la gravité de la menace.

As with legitimate defence, the defence of necessity is only available when there is an existing or imminent danger. The danger can be to the defendant, a third party or to property, and the nature of the danger does not matter. In one case, the defence was allowed where the danger was to a family's wellbeing: a tenant had destroyed a fence which had been built by the landlord to stop the tenant's family from having access to the water, gas and electricity meters and to the toilet facilities.[46] Where squatters have broken into property and argued it was in order to have shelter during a housing crisis, the courts have not been prepared to accept that the danger existed or was imminent.[47]

The danger must not be imposed by the law. For example, a soldier cannot flee combat as he has an obligation to fight when ordered to do so. The defence is also not available if the defendant had created the danger through his own fault, though this condition has been criticised by some academic writers.[48] Thus, a lorry driver could not rely on the defence when he had been forced to knock down the barrier of a level crossing, onto which he had unwisely driven, to avoid being crushed by a train.[49]

The danger must have truly necessitated the offence—if offenders had other means of safeguarding their threatened interests, they will be convicted,[50] unless this was the best course of action.[51] In one case, a defendant had taken some meat from a shop to improve the diet of his children. But his bank account was in credit and he had stolen more than £100 worth of meat, so the defence of necessity was rejected.[52]

The offence must be proportionate to the danger. The offence will only be justified if it protected an interest of superior or equivalent value to the one sacrificed. Thus, the hungry vagabond cannot kill the baker who refuses to give him food. In practice, comparing the relative values of different interests can often prove difficult. The burden of proof is on the prosecution to show the offence was not proportionate to the original danger.

Duress by Threats/Circumstances

Criminal liability will only be imposed if defendants acted of their own free will. The French defence of constraint is very similar to the English defence of duress, particularly now that the English defence of duress has been extended to include duress of circumstances as well as duress of threats. However, the French defence remains more broadly defined, as there is no requirement that there be a threat of death or serious personal injury—other types of threat can suffice.

The defence of constraint applies when the defendant had no choice but to commit the offence. Article 122-2 of the new Criminal Code states:

> A person is not criminally liable who acted under the influence of a force or a constraint which they could not resist.[53]

While the legislation appears to draw a distinction between 'force' and 'constraint' that distinction was not drawn by the old Code, and force is really just a specific example of a constraint. To benefit from the defence, it must have been absolutely impossible for the defendant to resist the constraint[54] and the constraint must have been unforeseeable.[55]

---

46   Crim 4 janv 1956, D, 1956, S, 130; obs Légal, RSC, 1956, p 831.

47   Tribunal Correctionnel Nantes, 12 nov 1956, D, 1957.30; T Corr Brest, 20 déc 1956, D, 1957.348; Tribunal Correctionnel Avesnes-sur-Helpe, 19 nov 1958, JCP 59, II, 366; Angers 11 juil 1957 D 1958.357.

48   Cf Bouzat, note in S, 1954.2.185.

49   Rennes, 12 avril 1954 S 1954, II, 185.

50   Crim 25 juin 1958, D, 1958.693, note MRMP; JCP, 1959.II.10941, note Larguier.

51   Paris, 6 oct 1944 and 5 janv 1945, S 1945.2.81.

52   Poitiers 11 avril 1997, D 1997.512, note A. Waxin, JCP, 1997, 1997.II.22933, note A Olive.

53   '*N'est pas pénalement responsable la personne qui a agi sous l'empire d'une force ou d'une contrainte à laquelle elle n'a pu résister*'.

54   '*L'impossibilité absolue de se conformer à la loi*': Crim 8 févr 1936, D, 1936.I.44, note Donnedieu de Vabres; Crim 28 déc 1900, D, 1901.I.81, note Le Poittevin.

55   Crim 29 janv 1921, S, 1922.I.185, note Roux; Crim 15 nov 1934, D, 1935.I.11, note Donnedieu de Vabres.

The different types of possible constraint can be distinguished according to their form (physical or psychological), or according to their origin (external or internal). Physical constraints have an impact on the defendant's body, while psychological constraints have an impact on their mind.

The constraint normally stems from an external force. The external force can be due to the forces of nature such as a storm, an earthquake, a flood, or a fire. Where torrential rain caused a wall to collapse, the defendant had a defence to a charge of obstructing the highway.[56] Alternatively, the external force can be due to acts of third parties such as wars, riots and strikes. A theatre owner had a defence where his customers had stopped him being able to close his establishment at the time required by his licence.[57]

Internal physical constraints take the form of illnesses. The *Cour de cassation* has ruled that a prostitute was not liable for failing to attend a compulsory health visit as she had been ill;[58] a defendant was not liable for abandoning his family when he was unable to work due to a serious heart problem;[59] and a passenger was not liable for travelling without a valid ticket when he fell asleep on a train and went past his station.[60]

An internal psychological constraint might be the result of passion, impulsiveness or emotion, but these will not provide a defence. Thus, parents whose child died when they failed to seek medical treatment due to their beliefs in the doctrine of a religious sect were successfully prosecuted for not assisting a person in danger.[61] In another case, a woman had an irresistible impulse to write an offensive letter to a government minister because her husband was a civil servant threatened with early retirement. The defence of constraint was not available to her.[62]

An external psychological constraint exists, for example, when the offence is committed through fear induced by a threat made by a third party. The threat could be against the defendant or someone for whom the defendant feels responsible. There are only a few case law examples of this form of constraint.[63] One concerned an Algerian who, during the War for Independence of 1956, had provided shelter to 40 armed rebels who had threatened to kill him.[64] This form of the defence can overlap with the defence of necessity and the law is more demanding for this form of the defence to succeed.

It must have been absolutely impossible for the defendant to resist the constraint.[65] This condition is logical as if the defendant had the possibility of following another course of conduct and failed to do so, their acts are the expression of their own will, and there is then no reason why they should not answer for this before a criminal court. The courts have taken a strict approach to this matter. For example, the defence was not allowed where a lorry carrying fresh produce had broken down and its load had been added to that of a second lorry so that the produce would not perish while the vehicle was repaired. The offence of taking a vehicle on a road in excess of the permitted weight was committed.[66]

It is not sufficient that the defendant would have found it very difficult to abide by the law, it must have been impossible to abide by the law. Thus, where passengers on a boat were carrying contraband products in their luggage, the boat's owner could not avoid liability for smuggling on the basis that he could have checked everybody's luggage.[67]

In applying this provision, the courts first apply an objective test and determine whether an ordinary person would have been able to resist committing the offence. The circumstances of the individual defendant are not taken into account. The *Cour de cassation* therefore considered the defence could not be applied to individuals who had failed to leave the country after they had been ordered to do so. The stateless people had argued they had been turned away by all the neighbouring countries of France, and so were unable to leave

---

56 Crim 6 mai 1887, D, 88.I.332.
57 Crim 8 août 1840, S, 1841.I.549.
58 Crim 3 mars 1865, D, 66.5.394.
59 Crim 24 avr 1937, DH, 1937.429.
60 Crim 19 oct 1922, DP, 1922.I.233.
61 Crim 29 juill 1967, JCP, 1968.II.15377 note J Pradel.
62 Crim 11 avril 1908 DP, 1908.1.261.
63 T Corr Versailles, 27 fév 1963, D, 1963, S, 110.
64 Crim 26 nov 1959, D, 1959.301, B, 139.
65 '*l'impossibilité absolue de se conformer à la loi*'. Crim 8 fév 1936, DP, 1936.I.44, note Donnedieu de Vabres; Crim 28 déc 1900, DP, 1901.I.81, note Le Poittevin.
66 Crim 10 fév 1960, B 79.
67 Crim 30 déc 1953, B, 360, obs Légal, RSC, 1954, p 753.

the French territory. But the Court took the view they could have tried to enter countries that did not share a border with France, without looking at whether the defendants could have afforded to fly or sail to these more distant destinations.[68] The constraint is considered objectively, in abstract, when it might be fairer to appreciate it subjectively, taking into account the defendants themselves, including perhaps their financial means, in considering whether the particular defendant could have resisted.

Defendants will be treated as having been at fault if they fail to foresee a foreseeable constraint that they could have then acted to prevent. The classic example is the sailor found guilty of desertion when he was unable to regain his ship at the required time—he had got himself drunk on land and was arrested for being found drunk and disorderly in a public place.[69] The courts have also considered that a breakdown does not excuse the parking of a vehicle in a no-parking zone, because the driver should have foreseen it by a preliminary verification of the condition of the vehicle before commencing the journey.[70] The defence was not available when a driver with a serious heart condition who had only slept for 3 hours, drove and caused an accident.[71] On the other hand the defence was successful when a person fell unconscious for the first time causing an accident.[72] This approach has been heavily criticised by academics as it is essentially imposing criminal liability for a prior fault. The requirement that the constraint was unforeseeable is not expressly mentioned by the new Code (nor the old Code) and some academics hope that future case law will consider it no longer applies.

General Mental Condition Defences

Insanity
Article 64 of the 1810 Criminal Code stated:

> There is neither a serious nor major crime when the suspect was in a state of dementia at the time of his actions.[73]

There were significant weaknesses in the drafting of the old Criminal Code. The notion of dementia was too narrow, as in medicine it refers to a particular type of mental illness taking the form of a progressive and irreversible deterioration in the mental faculties. This often affects old people (senile dementia) but it can also affect young people (precocious dementia). In law, the court gave the concept a much wider meaning to include any person suffering from mental delusions. The definition was also misleading in suggesting that no offence was committed, while in fact the defence simply removed the individual's personal responsibility, but their accomplices could still be liable. Article 64 did not assist people suffering from a mental problem which was insufficiently grave to be qualified as a state of dementia, but of a nature to influence their conduct and thus to reduce their free will. In practice, these people were declared criminally liable, but would have mitigating circumstances when the court chose the appropriate sentence.

Some of these problems have been removed by the new Criminal Code, which states at Article 122-1:

> A person is not criminally liable who was affected at the time of the facts, by a psychological or neuro-psychological problem which had removed his discernment or his control over his acts.[74]

While at the time of its introduction the media described this provision as a legal revolution, it in fact merely adopts much of the earlier case law and clarifies the legislation on the subject, rather than making any radical changes. The three main changes to the old law are that it abandons the notion of dementia and replaces it with psychological or neuropsychological problems; it specifies that, as a defence, the mental problem removes the

---

68   Crim 8 fév 1936, DP, 1936.I.44, note Donnedieu de Vabres; Crim 21 mai 1941, GP, 1941.2.132.
69   Crim 29 janv 1921, S 1922.I.185, note Roux; Crim 15 nov 1934, DP, 1935.I.11, note Donnedieu de Vabres.
70   Crim 4 déc 1958, D, 1959.36.
71   Crim 11 mai 2004, B No 115.
72   Douai, 24 oct 2000, JCP 2002.II.10012.
73   '*Il n'y a ni crime ni délit lorsque le prévenu était en état de démence au temps de l'action*'.
74   '*N'est pas pénalement responsable la personne qui était atteinte au moment des faits, d'un trouble psychique ou neuropsychique ayant aboli son discernement ou le contrôle de ses actes*'.

punishment for any crime, including minor offences, but does not prevent the crime from existing; finally, it distinguishes more clearly between mental health problems which remove discernment altogether and those which simply reduce a person's discernment.

The courts start with a presumption that the person is sane and the burden of proof is on the defendants to prove they fall within the defence. Three conditions must be satisfied: the defendants must have been suffering from a mental health problem, this must have removed their discernment or their control over their acts and, lastly, the mental health problem must have existed at the time of the commission of the offence. Those people with a mental health problem, but who are at least partially capable of discerning their wrongdoing or of controlling their conduct, fall outside the defence.

The new Code has replaced the concept of dementia by 'psychological or neuro-psychological problems' as this reflects more closely existing medical knowledge. The circular of the Minister of Justice dated 14 May 1993, which provides a commentary of the Code, states that:

> The new provisions, by abolishing the notion of dementia, highlight that the criminal defence flows from the loss of free will, whatever the nature of the mental health problem that has caused this.[75]

Thus, these terms seek to cover all forms of mental health problems, whatever their origin or nature. The expression 'psychological or neuro-psychological' takes into account the current scientific knowledge and extends to illnesses stemming from a psychological trauma, congenital conditions, illnesses resulting from accidents, and non-pathological problems, such as naturally occurring sleep walking, epilepsy,[76] or hypnotism. In all of these hypotheses, the mental problem only constitutes a defence if it is sufficiently serious.

The central issue for the courts is whether defendants have been deprived of their discernment or control over their acts due to a mental health problem. This requirement really means the defendants were not acting as free agents. There is an absence of discernment when people have lost the capacity to understand the nature of their acts. This could be the case if a person suffered from hallucinations, became delirious or had an epileptic fit.

Defendants must have either lost the capacity to understand (in other words, of interpreting their acts in reality); or they must have lost the capacity to will (in other words, to control) their acts. Mental health problems which only alter the defendants' discernment or limit their control over their acts, without totally supressing their free will, do not give rise to this defence, though in practice the border between these two situations is sometimes difficult to establish.

The distinction between the conscience (capacity to understand) and the will (capacity to will) is fundamental, even if it is sometimes not clearly drawn by the courts. There is a defence if one of these two elements is lacking, even if the other exists. The *Cour de cassation* has thus censored for contradiction of reasoning a decision which declared the defendant liable while stating he 'remained conscious, that his intellectual or cognitive faculties remained', even if his faculties of judgement were 'diminished', while considering that 'he had carried out inconsiderate acts which he was incapable of mastering' and 'he was subjected to impulses which he could not master': if the conscience remained, the will had disappeared.[77]

The mental illness must exist at the time of the commission of the offence. Prior mental illness will only be taken into account when determining the appropriate sentence. Later mental illness will lead to the suspension of the prosecution, but the judicial investigation will continue. While investigatory procedures directly linked to the mentally ill person (such as questioning the suspect) cannot take place, other aspects of the investigation will proceed, including the gathering of witness statements, questioning accomplices and collecting expert evidence. If the suspect recovers from the mental illness the prosecution can recommence.

The timing of the mental health problem implies a causal aspect to the offence: the mental health problem must have some bearing on the offence. Thus a paranoid individual suffering from a delirium of persecution

---

75   'Les dispositions nouvelles, en supprimant la notion de démence, mettant en évidence que l'irresponsabilité découle de la perte du libre arbitre, quelle que soit la nature du trouble mental qui en est à l'origine'.

76   Orléans, 22 juin 1886, D, 1887.V.213; Crim 14 déc 1982, GP, 1983.I.doctr.178.

77   Crim 21 janv 1992, Dr pén, 1992, comm no 196.

(which might perhaps lead him to kill the person who is the object of his delirium) is criminally liable if he commits a theft that has no bearing on his madness.

The existence of a mental health problem constituting a defence is never presumed, it must be proved. This is a question of pure fact that falls within the sole appreciation of the judges of fact of first instance, and over which the *Cour de cassation* exercises no control, except if there is a contradiction in the reasoning of the court.[78] In practice, the criminal court that is looking at the mental faculties of the defendant orders an expert psychiatric report. This is usually requested by the investigating judge and is compulsory for serious criminal matters. The conclusions of the expert are not legally binding on the judge,[79] though they are clearly very persuasive.

Before 2008, a finding that the defendant was suffering from a mental health problem, could lead to a decision to terminate the case by the prosecutor, the investigating judge or the trial judge. The decision to terminate a case before it reached a trial court was particularly controversial as this decision was taken unilaterally behind closed doors. The procedure was therefore changed by the Act of 25 February 2008. This Act has inserted Articles 706-119 to 706-140 into the Code of Criminal Procedure. Where the case is dropped, the courts will now issue a declaration that the defendant is not responsible due to mental health problems (rather than simply dismissing the case). Thus, there is an acknowledgement that an offence has been committed. If the investigating judge intends to terminate the prosecution in this way, the parties (including the prosecutor) can request that the investigating judge passes the case to the investigating chamber to decide the issue. There will then be a public hearing and witnesses and experts will give evidence and the accused will be present if he is well enough. Following the 2008 Act, defendants can be ordered to attend a hospital when they have been found not guilty by reason of a mental health problem.[80] In addition, security measures can be imposed, such as a ban on meeting the victim, or frequenting certain places.[81]

Those people who have a mental health problem but who are at least partially capable of discerning their wrongdoing or of controlling their conduct, fall outside the defence of insanity. They are sometimes described as the 'mentally abnormal',[82] as opposed to those who fall within the defence of insanity who are sometimes described as the 'alienated'.[83] People of extremely low intelligence may have no free choice and fall within the defence of insanity. Those who are of low intelligence, but not extremely low intelligence, might be found to have diminished capacity but not the defence of insanity. Those who know they are doing wrong but cannot control their impulses could fall into the category of people with diminished capacity, for example, kleptomaniacs, sexual perverts, pyromaniacs, and psychopaths.

In the past, a famous ministerial circular of 12 December 1905—the Chaumié circular (named after a senior prosecutor)—regulated the approach of the courts to such individuals. This circular invited psychiatric experts to look into how far these mentally abnormal people could have their criminal responsibility reduced. In the light of this circular, it became established practice for this category of offender to benefit from mitigating circumstances at the time of sentencing in proportion to the gravity of their mental illness. The circular filled a legislative gap, but was criticised as encouraging an artificial mathematical equation—could one consider a person to be half or two-thirds mad in order to give them half or two-thirds of a sentence? A person suffering from such a mental illness was in many ways more dangerous but received less punishment than a person with no mental illness. From a medical perspective, a therapeutic treatment might be more effective than a prison sentence. Despite these criticisms, this approach continued to be followed even after the circular was repealed by Article C. 345 of the Code of Criminal Procedure of 1959.

The partially responsible are now covered by Article 122-1, Paragraph 2 of the Criminal Code, which keeps the earlier approach. It states:

---

78   Crim 21 janv 1992, Dr pén, 1992, comm no 196.
79   Crim 6 juin 1979, B, no 194.
80   Art. 706-135 Code of Criminal Procedure.
81   Art. 706-125 [4], 706-133 [4], 706-136 to 706-139 of the Code of Criminal Procedure.
82   *Les anormaux mentaux.*
83   *Les aliénés.*

> A person suffering, at the time of the facts, from a psychological or neuro-psychological problem which altered his discernment or impeded his control over his acts remains punishable; however, the case law takes account of this circumstance when it determines the length and mode of punishment.[84]

People falling within this provision remain criminally responsible for their acts, but their responsibility may be reduced. A reduction in sentence is not automatic and the sentence may, where appropriate, even be increased.

Intoxication

There is no general defence of intoxication in French criminal law. Until 1957, the *Cour de cassation* took the view that intoxication could never give rise to a defence. In 1957 the Court abandoned this dogmatic approach and decided that the influence of drink on criminal responsibility was a question of fact that could only be resolved on the facts of each case.[85] Intoxication through the consumption of drink or drugs can exceptionally fall within the defence of diminished capacity. If intoxication has led to a total loss of control it could in theory give rise to a total loss of responsibility under the defence of insanity, as Article 122-1 does not distinguish according to the origin of the mental health problem, provided the intoxication leads to complete disappearance of a person's free will. However, the Act of the 5 March 2007 on the Prevention of Delinquency has laid down that where violent and sexual offences have been committed under the obvious influence of drink or drugs, this will be treated as an aggravating factor.[86] Thus, increasingly intoxication is likely to be viewed as an aggravating factor rather than giving rise to a defence or mitigation.

Mistake of Law

Under the old Criminal Code there was no defence of mistake of law;[87] this is a completely new defence created by the Criminal Code of 1994 and was one of the major changes introduced by the new Code. Article 122-3 of the Criminal Code states:

> A person is not criminally liable who proves that he believed, because of a mistake of law which he was not in a position to avoid, that he could legitimately carry out the act.[88]

This is a very narrow definition that has been restrictively interpreted by the courts so the defence is of only limited application. Everyone is still presumed to know the law[89] and the burden of proof to displace this presumption lies on the defendant. The defence of mistake of law will only reverse this presumption in very limited circumstances. The presumption has been justified on the basis that it is necessary in order to maintain social discipline, but it is a legal fiction as in reality it is impossible to know all the laws in force.

When the old law applied, a case arose where a horticulturalist had asked the town hall on several occasions whether he needed planning permission to build some greenhouses. He was told he did not and went ahead with the building. He was subsequently convicted of building without the necessary construction permit.[90] If the same facts occurred today the horticulturalist would be able to avail himself of the new defence of mistake of law. The *Cour de cassation* does, however, seem to be taking a strict view of this defence. In one of its first cases on the subject,[91] it quashed a decision of the Court of Appeal that had allowed the defence, because the suspects had not themselves sought to rely on the provisions of Article 122-3, instead the issue

---

84 Article 122-1:

   La personne qui était atteinte, au moment des faits, d'un trouble psychique ou neuropsychique ayant altéré son discernement ou entravé le contrôle de ses actes demeure punissable; toutefois, la juridiction tient compte de cette circonstance lorsqu'elle détermine la peine et en fixe le régime.

85 Crim 5 févr 1957, B, 112, observations Ligal, RSC, 1958, 93.

86 Art 222-12, 222-13, 222-24, 222-28, 222-30, and 227-26 of the new Criminal Code.

87 Crim 24 juill 1903, D 1903.I.490; Crim 16 mars 1972, B no 110.

88 '*N'est pas pénalement responsable la personne qui justifie avoir cru, par une erreur sur le droit qu'elle n'était pas en mesure d'éviter, pouvoir légitimement accomplir l'acte*'.

89 '*nul n'est censé ignorer la loi*'. Crim 24 fév 1820, B no 33.

90 Crim 26 fév 1964, B no 71.

91 Crim 15 nov 1995, Dr pén 1996, comm 56; JCP 1996, éd G, IV 440; JCP 1996, éd G I, 3950, M Véron.

had been raised on the initiative of the judge. According to the Criminal Division, 'only the person prosecuted has the capacity to invoke a mistake of law within the terms of this text'.[92]

Three conditions must be satisfied for the defence to succeed: the mistake must have been one of law and not fact, defendants must not have been in a position to avoid the mistake and they must have thought their conduct was legal. Each of these will be considered in turn.

There are no limits on the type of law that can be the subject of the mistake: it can thus be criminal or civil, a regulation or an Act of Parliament. The defence will normally be invoked in the more technical areas of the law, such as environmental law and company law.

Mistakes of fact may mean the *mens rea* of an intentional offence is absent. Thus, the person who takes an object belonging to another thinking she is the owner does not commit a theft. For the same reason, the head of a business, who irregularly employs a foreign worker believing the employee to be a French national, is not liable.[93] If the intention remains because the mistake related to a secondary element of the offence, then the defendant will still be liable. For example, if defendants take jewels believing them to be made with precious stones when in fact the jewels are made of glass, they will still be liable for theft; or if defendants kill one person thinking they are killing another, they have no defence.[94]

Mistakes of fact for non-intentional offences will not constitute a defence, and may actually amount to carelessness sufficient to form the *mens rea* of the offence. The offence of involuntary homicide is therefore committed if a person accidentally kills a friend when cleaning a gun thinking it was unloaded.

Only two examples of unavoidable mistakes were given during the course of the parliamentary debates on Article 122-3 of the type of mistake that would justify the defence: wrong information provided by the administration inducing the mistake and the failure of the administration to publicise a normative text. The latter situation is of very limited practical importance as Acts and regulations only come into force once they have been published in the *Journal Officiel*. Following the parliamentary debates during the passing of the relevant legislation, it seemed that false information emanating from a private person, including professionals (for example, a lawyer) could not constitute an unavoidable mistake. However, one of the first decisions of the *Cour de cassation* on Article 122-3 appeared to accept the possibility that a mistake could be induced by the advice of a lawyer, though on the facts the mistake had not been unavoidable.[95] A couple had been going through a divorce and a court order had awarded the family home to the wife. The husband had sought professional advice from a lawyer on the meaning of the court order. It seems the lawyer had advised the husband in writing that he had the right to enter the family home. While the wife was on holiday, he entered the house and changed the locks, so that the wife and his children were forced to stay in a hotel when they returned. The husband was prosecuted for entering the home without authority. The Court of Appeal in Versailles accepted the defence of mistake; however, this decision was quashed by the Criminal Division, which considered that the mistake was not unavoidable, as a request to a court for the order to be interpreted could have been made.[96]

In another case, a lorry driver from abroad had driven in excess of the speed limit. It was held that he could not rely on the defence of mistake of law as his attention had been drawn to the speed limit by signs along the roadside.[97]

The mistake of law can only be allowed if it caused defendants to believe their conduct was legal. Employers in particular have benefited from this defence, arguing they had made a mistake on a technical issue of employment law. So a mistake about the amount of hours a person could work has been allowed.[98]

---

92   '*seule la personne poursuivie est fondée à invoquer une erreur de droit au sens de ce texte*'.

93   Crim 1 oct 1987 B no 327.

94   Crim 31 janv 1835 S 1835.I.564.

95   CA Versailles, 24 juin 1994; Gaz Pal 26/30 août 1994, p 6; Crim 11 oct 1995, Dr Pén 1996, comm 56; JCP 1996, éd G, I, 3950, commentaires critiques de M Véron; D 1996, p 469, note M Muller.

96   Under art 461 of the Code of Civil Procedure.

97   Douai, 26 oct 1994, GP 8 déc 1994.

98   Crim 24 nov 1998.

Residual Catch-All Defences/Existence and Ambit of Statutory Defences

The second paragraph of Article 122-4 of the Criminal Code contains the defence of superior orders. It states:

> A person who carries out an act ordered by a legitimate authority is not criminally liable, except if this act is obviously illegal.[99]

In determining the applicability of the defence, the courts need to consider whether the order came from a legitimate authority and if it was obviously illegal.

The authority must be a public authority (either civil or military), not a private authority. Thus the authority cannot be the head of a family ordering his children,[100] a husband ordering his wife,[101] or an employer ordering his employee.[102] The person obeying the order must have been the subordinate of the authority issuing it. The authority must have had the competence to issue the order, which is particularly problematic where a person has, in good faith, carried out orders from an incompetent authority that appeared to be competent.

Where an order was obviously illegal, people who carried it out have no defence on the grounds of superior orders, though they may be able to argue they acted under a constraint. A police officer who carries out an arrest under a mandate issued by an investigating judge, which is subsequently declared to be illegal, would have a defence if the illegality was not obvious. But if the police officer knew the order was illegal then no defence would be available. The more serious the conduct the more likely a court will conclude it was obviously illegal. Article 213-4 of the Criminal Code expressly states that a person who commits a crime against humanity cannot rely on this defence, such an argument only being available as a cause of mitigation when the court is determining what sentence to impose. If it can be shown that the subordinate knew the order was illegal, even though this illegality was not obvious, then the courts are not likely to allow this defence.

Where a person appears to have committed an offence, they may have a defence if their conduct was authorised by another piece of legislation. The Criminal Code states in the first paragraph of Article 122-4:

> A person is not criminally liable who carries out an act ordered or authorized by legislative or regulatory provisions.[103]

Problems have arisen when the professional obligation of secrecy comes into conflict with the crime of failing to report an offence against a minor. The new Criminal Code has resolved this problem by providing that the offence of failing to report cannot be committed by a person subjected to a requirement of secrecy.[104] This does not mean people can remain totally passive when they know of bad treatment, because they can still be liable for the offence of failing to assist a person in danger.[105] But their actions can take other forms than reporting the offence (for example, taking the badly treated child to hospital) though reporting the offence is expressly authorised by Article 226-14 of the Criminal Code.

Article 122-8 of the Criminal Code states:

> Minors capable of knowing right from wrong are criminally responsible for serious, major or minor offences for which they have been found guilty, and can be subjected to measures of protection, assistance, supervision and education in accordance with conditions fixed by a special law.

---

99 '*N'est pas pénalement responsable la personne qui accomplit un acte commandé par l'autorité légitime, sauf si cet acte est manifestement illégal*'.

100 Crim 4 mai 1837, B, 143 (an offence committed by a son on the order of his father).

101 Crim 25 sept 1818, *Ancien Rép. Dalloz, Vo. Peine*, no 418 (theft).

102 Crim 20 nov 1834, B 380 (tax offence).

103 '*N'est pas pénalement responsable la personne qui accomplit un acte prescrit ou autorisé par des dispositions législatives ou réglementaires*'.

104 Art 434-1 and 434-3.

105 Art 223-5 of the Criminal Code.

This law also determines the educative sanctions which can be imposed on minors aged ten to eighteen as well as the punishments which can be handed down to minors aged thirteen to eighteen, while taking into account their reduced responsibility due to their age.[106]

Young offenders under 13 can never receive a criminal sanction. They can, instead, be subjected in appropriate cases to educative measures. This can include them being ordered to receive professional training, being removed from their parents into the care of the social services, or being placed under supervision.

Minors aged 13 to 18 can be punished for committing an offence, though the level of the punishment should take into account the fact they were only minors at the time of the offending.[107]

Following the Act of 9 September 2002, amending Article 122-8 of the Criminal Code, minors capable of discernment are criminally responsible. Educative measures are available to all minors, educative sanctions are available to minors aged at least 10 years old who are capable of discernment, while punishments are only applicable to minors aged over 13. Educative sanctions include confiscating an item used in the commission of the offence, being banned for up to a year from the place where the offence was committed, and being banned from meeting the victim or their accomplices for up to a year, being ordered to commit an act of reparation and being required to undertake a training programme for up to a month. Breach of one of these educative sanctions is not a crime, but can give rise to the child being sent to an educative establishment.

---

106   Article 122-8:
Les mineurs capables de discernement sont pénalement responsables des crimes, délits ou contraventions dont ils ont été reconnus coupables, dans des conditions fixées par une loi particulière qui détermine les mesures de protection, d'assistance, de surveillance et d'éducation dont ils peuvent faire l'objet.

Cette loi détermine également les sanctions éducatives qui peuvent être prononcées à l'encontre des mineurs de dix à dix-huit ans ainsi que les peines auxquelles peuvent être condamnés les mineurs de treize à dix-huit ans, en tenant compte de l'atténuation de responsabilité dont ils bénéficient en raison de leur âge.

107   Philippe Bonfils, '*Les dispositions relatives au droit pénal des mineurs délinquants dans la loi prévention de la délinquance*', *Le Dalloz*, 12 avril 2007, n° 15, 1027–1034.

Chapter 16
Germany

Kai Ambos and Stefanie Bock

General Issues

Justificatory and Excusatory Defences—Distinction and Seat in the Offence Structure

German Criminal Law is based on a tripartite structure of crime distinguishing between offence definition (*Tatbestand*), general wrongfulness (*Rechtswidrigkeit*), and culpability in a normative sense.[1] In such a system, the distinction between justifications and excuses is mandatory, since the former negate the (act-related) wrongdoing while the latter exclude the actor's culpability.[2]

A justification bars a person from criminal responsibility for an act which fulfils the elements of the offence definition (*actus reus*) but is regarded as lawful because the actor acted on the basis of a permissive norm which negates the effect of the *actus reus*.[3] The most important justifications in German Criminal Law are self-defence, necessity, citizen's arrest, and (presumed) consent. Excuses, by contrast, do not render the act lawful. Rather, the individual wrongdoer is not blamed for having carried it out since he was unable to recognize the unlawfulness of his conduct or he could not be expected to act lawfully.[4] German Criminal Law recognises, *inter alia*, mistake of law, duress, excessive self-defence, and insanity as valid excuses.

Conceptual Foundations

As counterparts of the offence definition, consisting of the objective elements of the offence and the respective *mens rea* requirements, justificatory defences are also composed of objective and subjective elements.[5] On the objective level, justifications presuppose the existence of a defence situation (*Rechtfertigungslage*) and the performance of a permissible action (*Rechtfertigungshandlung*).[6] Regarding the subjective requirements, it is a contentious issue if awareness of the defence situation is sufficient or if the agent must have acted with the desire to exercise the defence, for example, with the will to defend himself.[7] The prevailing opinion in

---

1   George P Fletcher, *Basic Concepts of Criminal Law* (OUP 1998) 101; Claus Roxin, *Strafrecht Allgemeiner Teil, Band I, Grundlagen. Der Aufbau der Verbrechenslehre* (4th edn, CH Beck 2006) s 10 marginal note [hereinafter: mn] 13–26; Kai Ambos, 'Toward a Universal System of Crime: Comments on George Fletcher's *Grammar of Criminal Law*' (2007) 28 Cardozo Law Review 2647, 2650–2652; see also Michael Bohlander, *Principles of German Criminal Law* (Hart 2009) 16–18.

2   George P Fletcher, 'The Influence of the Common Law and Civil Law Traditions on International Criminal Law' in Antonio Cassese (ed), *The Oxford Companion to International Criminal Justice* (OUP 2009) 104, 105; Bernd Heinrich, *Strafrecht – Allgemeiner Teil* (3rd edn, Kohlhammer 2012) mn 317; Kai Ambos, *Treatise on International Criminal Law – Volume I: Foundations and General Part* (OUP 2013) 304.

3   Ambos (n 2) 304–305; see also Bohlander (n 1) 78; Roxin (n 1) s 14 rn 1, 3; Thomas Weigend, 'Germany' in Kevin Jon Heller and Markus D Dubber (eds), *The Handbook of Comparative Criminal Law* (Stanford University Press 2011) 252, 269.

4   Ambos (n 2) 305; see also Kent Greenawalt, 'The Perplexing Borders of Justification and Excuse' [1984] 84 Columbia L Rev 1897, 1900; Bohlander (n 1) 78; Weigend (n 3) 269.

5   Rudolf Rengier, *Strafrecht Allgemeiner Teil* (5th edn, CH Beck 2013) s 17 mn 9; Johannes Wessels, Werner Beulke and Helmut Satzger, *Strafrecht Allgemeiner Teil* (43nd edn, CF Müller 2013) mn 275–276; Heinrich (n 2) mn 323.

6   Rengier (n 5) s 17 mn 10; Heinrich (n 2) mn 323a-324.

7   For more detail on this issue, see Volker Krey and Robert Esser, *Deutsches Strafrecht Allgemeiner Teil* (5th edn, Kohlhammer 2012) mn 454–464.

German case law and doctrine prefers the latter,[8] but is increasingly criticised for being incompatible with the subjective elements of the offence which only require that the defendant acts with intent; possible motives, that is, the reasons why he performed the act, are irrelevant.[9] If the subjective elements of a justificatory defence are missing, the respective conduct is wrongful since the defendant acted only on the occasion of a defence situation. In most cases, the Federal Supreme Court deemed this sufficient to establish full criminal liability.[10] The opposite view, to the contrary, qualifies such situations as mere attempts arguing that the act is at least half-lawful: while the wrongful act (*Handlungs-* or *Verhaltensunwert*) continues to exist, the wrongful result (*Erfolgsunrecht*) of the offence (the prohibitive norm) is negated by the objective defence situation (the permissive norm).[11]

With regard to excusatory defences, German criminal law distinguishes between circumstances which affect the criminal capability of the agent (*Schuldausschließungsgründe*), for example, insanity, and grounds which under certain pressing circumstances negate the personal blameworthiness of the actor (*Entschuldigungsgründe*), for example, duress.[12] Only the latter require a subjective element, that is, at least awareness of the defence situation. However, since these defences are concessions to human frailty in exceptional conflict-situations it is more commonly expected than in the context of justifications that the agent acts with the actual will to exercise the defence.[13] If these subjective requirements are not fulfilled, the actor is blameworthy and thus fully liable.[14]

Cumulation/Cumulative or Alternative Pleading of Defences

German criminal courts are under legal obligation to establish the truth and to extend the taking of evidence on their own motion to all facts and means of proof relevant to the decision.[15] This includes the duty to take into account possible defences even if not raised by the defendant.[16] Although a pleading of defences is therefore *de jure* not necessary, it may be nevertheless advisable from a tactical point of view to direct the court's attention to exonerating circumstances. In case of a cumulation of defences, German law does not provide for a strict hierarchy of defences.[17] However, it follows from the tripartite structure of offences that justifications enjoy 'a natural priority over questions of excuse'.[18] A person who acts under a justification acts in accordance with the law, that is, there is nothing, from a legal perspective, which he can be blamed for.[19] If D, for example, kills V in justified self-defence, this does not mean that D is not insane or that he has not simultaneously acted under duress, but this is plainly irrelevant.[20] Within the justificatory defences, self-defence takes precedence since it grants the defendant the most extensive rights. Necessity, to the contrary, may be regarded as a fall-back provision which only comes into play if the more specific grounds for justification are not applicable.[21]

---

8   Bundesgerichtshof (Federal Supreme Court) [hereinafter BGH], Neue Zeitschrift für Strafrecht [hereinafter NStZ] 2000, 365; BGHSt (Entscheidungen des Bundesgerichtshofes in Strafsachen) 56, 11, 26; Wessels, Beulke and Satzger (n 5) mn 277; Rengier (n 5) s 17 mn 12; Heinrich (n 2) mn 325, all with further references.

9   See Roxin (n 1) s 14 mn 97–103.

10   BGHSt 2, 111, 114; BGH NStZ 2005, 332, 334; but see also BGHSt 38, 144, 155.

11   Roxin (n 1) s 14 mn 104; Rengier (n 5) s 17 mn 18; Wessels, Beulke and Satzger (n 5) mn 279. This approach was also adopted in BGHSt 38, 144, 155.

12   Uwe Murmann, *Grundkurs Strafrecht* (2nd edn, CH Beck 2013) s 16 mn 10–11; Kristian Kühl, *Strafrecht – Allgemeiner Teil* (7th edn, Vahlen 2012) s 12 mn 9.

13   See Murmann (n 12) s 26 mn 65; Helmut Frister, *Strafrecht Allgemeiner Teil* (6th edn, CH Beck 2013) 273; for a different view, see Günther Jakobs, *Strafrecht Allgemeiner Teil* (2nd edn, Walter de Gruyter 1991) 572.

14   Günter Stratenwerth and Lothar Kuhlen, *Strafrecht Allgemeiner Teil* (6th edn, Vahlen 2011) s 10 mn 116.

15   s 244(2) of the German Code of Criminal Procedure (*Strafprozessordnung – StPO*), English translation available at <http://www.gesetze-im-internet.de/englisch_stpo/englisch_stpo.html#p1626> accessed 26 August 2014.

16   Weigend (n 3) 268; see also Michael Bohlander, *Principles of German Criminal Procedure* (Hart 2012) 27–28.

17   See Heinrich (n 2) mn 332; Rengier (n 5) s 17 mn 6–7; Bohlander (n 1) 79.

18   Greenawalt (n 4) 1899.

19   Krey and Esser (n 7) mn 264; see also Roxin (n 1) s 7 mn 8.

20   Ambos (n 3) 310.

21   Rengier (n 5) s 17 mn 6; Heinrich (n 2) mn 332.

Provocation of Defence Situation

It is generally accepted that provocation of a defence situation might under certain circumstances lead to a limitation or even a total exclusion of a defence. The details depend, however, on the scope and nature of the respective defence. We will therefore come back to this point in the context of the individual defences.[22]

Mistakes of Fact and Defences

As regards the defence situation, German criminal law opts for an objective *ex ante* test, which means that the situation must exist objectively and not only in the actor's mind. However, this does not mean that mistakes concerning the factual basis[23] of a recognized justificatory defence (*Erlaubnistatbestandsirrtum*) are always irrelevant. In a case decided recently by the Federal Supreme Court, D, a member of the violent Hells Angels Motorcycle Club, shot and killed V, who was about to enter his flat. D believed V to be a member of the enemy Motorcycle Club Banditos who had been ordered to kill him. In fact V was a police officer wanting to arrest D.[24] Due to the lack of an unlawful, imminent attack the killing of V was not justified by self-defence, as per s 32 StGB. If, however, the facts had been as D believed them to be, his counter-strike would have been a legitimate means to avert the attempt on his life. Thus, D did not intentionally commit a wrong. He did not want to break the law but rather believed he is acting in accordance with the law. Therefore, the majority opinion in German case law[25] and doctrine takes the view that in analogous application of s 16(1) StGB on mistake of fact[26] D is not liable for intentional murder (s 212 StGB), but—as the case may be—for negligent manslaughter (s 222 StGB) if his factual misconception was avoidable. The details, however, are very controversial.[27]

With regard to mistakes concerning the factual basis of a recognized excusatory defence (*Entschuldigungstatbestandsirrtum*), s 35(2) StGB on duress provides that 'if at the time of the commission of the act a person mistakenly assumes that circumstances exist which would excuse him under subsection (1) above, he will only be liable if the mistake was avoidable'.[28] This avoidability test is applied analogously to factual mistakes concerning other excusatory defences which also presuppose the existence of a pressing situation (*Entschuldigungsgründe*).[29]

Transferred Defences/Collateral Damage Defences

If and under which circumstances a defence allows for the infringement of rights of uninvolved third parties depends on the respective defence. German law does not recognise a general doctrine of transferred defence which transfers any defence the offender may have had *vis-à-vis* his intended victim to the actual (accidentally harmed) victim.[30] We will come back to this point in the context of self-defence.[31]

---

22   See below (n 69) (self-defence), (n 77) (excessive self-defence), (n 101) (necessity), (n 123) (duress), and accompanying texts.

23   As to mistakes of law concerning the existence or reach of a defence, see below (n 151) and accompanying text.

24   BGH NStZ 2012, 272.

25   BGH NStZ 2012, 272, 275.

26   s 16(1) StGB reads: 'Whosoever at the time of the commission of the offence is unaware of a fact which is a statutory element of the offence shall be deemed to lack intention. Any liability for negligence remains unaffected' (translation according to Michael Bohlander, *The German Criminal Code – A Modern English Translation* (Hart 2008) 41).

27   See the overview on the discussion by Hans-Heinrich Jescheck and Thomas Weigend, *Lehrbuch des Strafrechts Allgemeiner Teil* (5th edn, Duncker & Humblot 1996) 462–467; Krey and Esser (n 7) mn 731–745; Urs Kindhäuser, *Strafrecht Allgemeiner Teil* (6th edn, Nomos 2013) s 29 mn 11–26.

28   Translation according to Bohlander (n 26) 45.

29   Kühl (n 12) s 13 mn 84; Stratenwerth and Kuhlen (n 14) s 10 mn 123.

30   On this doctrine in more detail, see Michael Bohlander, 'Problems of Transferred Malice in Multiple-Actor Scenarios' [2010] 74 JCL 145.

31   See below (n 49) and accompanying text.

Individual Defences

Self-Defence and Excessive Self-Defence

The right to self-defence is codified in s 32 StGB:[32]

1) A person who commits an act in self-defence does not act unlawfully.
2) Self-defence means any defensive action that is necessary to avert an imminent unlawful attack on oneself or another.

First, s 32 StGB requires the existence of a defence situation, that is, an imminent unlawful attack. Attack means any threat to a legally protected interest through human behaviour.[33] Protected by s 32 StGB are all legal values of individuals, in particular life, physical integrity or property, but not the interests of the community as a whole, like for example traffic safety or environmental conversation.[34] If an interest of an individual is affected, s 32 StGB equalizes the right to self-defence with the right to defend others.[35] The latter, however, ceases to exist if the victim of the attack does not want protection.[36] Attacks of animals do not fall within the scope of s 32 StGB, but may give rise to necessity.[37] However, it qualifies as an attack through human behaviour if a person orders an animal to attack and thus uses it as a weapon.[38] In principle, an attack may also be committed by omission—for example, by starving the victim—provided that the defendant is under a legal duty to act.[39] The details, however, are very controversial.[40]

An attack is imminent if it is immediately antecedent, presently exercised or still enduring.[41] A pre-emptive strike against a feared attack is thus excluded, as is retaliation against a successful attack.[42] A battered woman, for example, who kills her husband while he is asleep, cannot rely on self-defence because there is no *immediate* attack on her right to physical integrity.[43] The attack must further be unlawful. In other words, there is no right to defend oneself against someone who is acting lawfully.[44] This brings us back to the differentiation between justifications and excuses.[45] Since the latter do not affect the unlawfulness of the action, but only the blameworthiness of the actor, self-defence against insane or intoxicated persons[46] etc. is readily possible. Section 32 StGB, to the contrary, is excluded if the attack is justified und thus rendered lawful.[47] In any case, the unlawfulness requirement does not necessarily presuppose criminal behaviour, but refers to any conduct which is inconsistent with the legal order.[48]

Second, if there exists a defence situation, the defence must in itself be permissible. This means first and foremost that the defence must be directed at the attacker. Section 32 StGB does not allow for any infringement of the rights of uninvolved third parties.[49] Collateral damages may be covered by other defences, in particular by necessity. In the classical textbook example, which is based on a decision of the Supreme

---

32 Translation according to Bohlander (n 26) 44.
33 Bohlander (n 1) 100; Wessels, Beulke and Satzger (n 5) mn 325.
34 Rengier (n 5) s 18 mn 10; Heinrich (n 2) mn 344; Krey and Esser (n 7) mn 475.
35 Weigend (n 3) 270; Murmann (n 12) s 25 mn 69.
36 BGHSt 5, 245, 247–248.
37 See, in particular to s 228 of the Civil Code, below (n 84) and accompanying text.
38 Krey and Esser (n 7) mn 474; Rengier (n 5) s 18 mn 7.
39 Bohlander (n 1) 100; Jescheck and Weigend (n 27) 339; Wessels, Beulke and Satzger (n 5) mn 326.
40 See the overview on the discussion by Roxin (n 1) s 15 mn 11–13.
41 Kai Ambos, 'May a State Torture Suspects to Save the Life of Innocents' [2008] 6 J Int'l Crim Just 261, 273; Rengier (n 5) s 18 mn 19.
42 Rengier (n 5) s 18 mn 22–27; Roxin (n 1) s 15 mn 22–29; Krey and Esser (n 7) mn 486–498.
43 BGHSt 48, 255, 257; on these so-called 'domestic tyrant' cases, see also below (n 103) and accompanying text.
44 Bohlander (n 1) 102; Wessels, Beulke and Satzger (n 5) mn 331; Heinrich (n 2) mn 350.
45 See (n 2) and accompanying text.
46 For a different view, see Jakobs (n 13) 387.
47 Krey and Esser (n 7) mn 477–479; Rengier (n 5) s 18 mn 28; see also Ambos (n 2) 339–340.
48 Heinrich (n 2) mn 350; Bohlander (n 1) 102.
49 BGHSt 5, 248; Rengier (n 5) s 18 mn 31; Kühl (n 12) s 7 mn 84; Roxin (n 1) s 15 mn 124.

Court of the German Reich,[50] V attacks D in a bar. D defends himself using a beer mug belonging to the host which gets broken. The causing of bodily harm to V is justified by self-defence. Section 32 StGB, however, does not allow D to damage an object belonging to the uninvolved host (criminal offence according to s 303 StGB). He can rely (merely) on necessity with its more strict requirements.[51] The same applies if the defendant unintentionally harms another person than intended. If, for example, D wants to knock a burglar down, but accidently hits his wife, the causing of bodily harm to his wife by negligence[52] can only be justified by necessity, not by self-defence.[53]

In addition, the defence must be necessary, that is, the defence must create only such harm to the aggressor as is absolutely necessary to prevent or avert the attack, and the means must not be inept or inefficient.[54] In other words, the countermeasure must be a minimally severe,[55] but equally effective means to repel the attack.[56] It follows from the latter, that the defendant need not take the risk of uncertain measures which might not be sufficient to avert the attack reliably and permanently.[57] Moreover, s 32 StGB does not demand from the attacked person to retreat—not even if a retreat had prevented harm from both the attacked person and the attacker. This is a consequence from the twofold rationale of the right to self-defence: s 32 StGB is based not only on the protection of the individual interests at stake (*Individualschutz*) but also on the reaffirmation of the law as such (*Rechtsbewährung*) against the unlawful attacker. Since 'right need never yield to wrong' (*Das Recht braucht dem Unrecht nicht zu weichen*), the attacked person always has the right to fight back.[58]

Notably, the necessity test refers to the defensive conduct, not to its results. Accordingly, a person who exercises his right to self-defence in a legitimate manner is also relieved from criminal responsibility for any unintended infringement upon the rights of the attacker.[59] If, for example, D permissibly repels V's attack with a hard strike, D is justified if V tumbles, hits the ground with his head and dies.[60]

As a rule, s 32 StGB does not require the defence to be proportional, so that a balancing of the conflicting interests between the agent and the aggressor is not necessary.[61] This means in particular, that s 32 StGB even allows the use of deadly force for the protection of property if not other less intrusive defensive means are available.[62] The strength of the right to self-defence follows from the idea that the attacked person also defends the legal order as such (*Rechtsbewährungsprinzip*) and with it a superior interest.[63] Under certain circumstances, however, the right to self-defence is limited for socio-ethical reasons[64] and, thus, arguably, there are proportionality limits. Depending on the circumstances of the case, the defendant may be obliged to retreat, to restrict himself to defensive means instead of initiating a counter-strike, or to accept minor

---

50   RGSt (Entscheidungen des Reichsgerichts in Strafsachen) 23, 116.

51   Kühl (n 12) s 7 mn 86; Roxin (n 1) s 15 mn 125; Kindhäuser (n 27) s 16 mn 26; see also *infra* n 87 and accompanying text.

52   German doctrine distinguishes between a pure mistake about the identity of the victim (*error in persona*), which leaves the mental element intact, and a so-called *aberratio ictus*, that is, a situation where the act goes amiss. If a defendant misses the selected and targeted object and hits another by accident, the prevailing opinion in German case law and doctrine takes the view that he is only liable for negligence; in more detail Kai Ambos and Stefanie Bock, 'Germany' in Alan Reed and Michael Bohlander (eds), *Participation in Crime* (Ashgate 2013) 323, 336.

53   Roxin (n 1) s 15 mn 125; for further examples see Kühl (n 12) s 7 mn 86.

54   See Heinrich (n 2) mn 354–355; Krey and Esser (n 7) mn 503; also Ambos (n 2) 341.

55   Bohlander (n 1) 104; Heinrich (n 2) mn 355; Wessels, Beulke and Satzger (n 5) mn 335.

56   Wessels, Beulke and Satzger (n 5) mn 335; Kühl (n 12) s 7 mn 89; see also Ambos (n 2) 341.

57   See only BGH NStZ 2006, 152, 153; BGH NStZ 2012, 272; Krey and Esser (n 7) mn 508; Weigend (n 3) 270.

58   Ambos (n 41) 274–275; Weigend (n 3) 270; Rengier (n 5) s 24 mn 38; see also BGH *Neue Juristische Wochenschrift* (hereinafter: NJW) 1980, 2263.

59   BGHSt 27, 313; Bohlander (n 1) 103; Kühl (n 12) s 17 mn 112–113.

60   See also Wessels, Beulke and Satzger (n 5) mn 336; for further examples see Kühl (n 12) s 17 mn 112.

61   BGH NStZ 1996, 29; Bohlander (n 1) 104; Heinrich (n 2) mn 335.

62   Heinrich (n 2) mn 335; Rengier (n 5) s 18 mn 38; Wessels, Beulke and Satzger (n 5) mn 340; see also BGH NJW 2003, 1955, 1957.

63   See also Ambos (n 41) 275; Weigend (n 3) 270; Kindhäuser (n 27) s 16 mn 28; Heinrich (n 2) mn 337.

64   As to the contested question if these restrictions can be reconciled with the principle of legality, see Roxin (n 1) s 15 mn 56–57; Krey and Esser (n 7) mn 566.

infringement of his rights.[65] Such restrictions upon the right to self-defence apply in particular[66] in the following type of cases:[67]

- There is a gross and inacceptable discrepancy between the harm caused and the harm sought to be avoided, for example, the defendant kills a person to prevent him from stealing an apple.
- The attacker acts without guilt, for example, he is insane or below the minimum age of criminal capacity.[68]
- The attacker and defender have a special (close) relationship, for example, they are married, and are thus under the legal duty of mutual consideration.

Under certain circumstances, provocation of the attack may also bar self-defence. If D intentionally provokes the attack in order to harm or kill V in the course of his counter-strike (intentional provocation—*Absichtsprovokation*), the majority opinion regards the invocation of self-defence as an abuse of rights, which means that D has forfeited his right to self-defence.[69] Critics of this view argue that V—despite the provocation—decided on his own responsibility to unlawfully attack D. Therefore, it is deemed unjust to categorically deny D the right to defend himself, in particular, if he cannot retreat.[70] In cases, in which the agent merely negligently provokes the attack, it is unanimously accepted that an absolute exclusion of the right to self-defence would be inappropriate. D, however, is expected to retreat or to limit himself to purely defensive means, if possible.[71]

A person, who exceeds the limits of legitimate self-defence, acts unlawfully. He may, however, be excused pursuant to s 33 StGB (excessive self-defence) if he acts out of confusion, fear or terror. According to German case law, s 33 StGB is limited to so-called intensive excesses, that is, cases in which the defence went beyond what was necessary to avert the attack or in which the defendant violates the socio-ethical restrictions on his right to self-defence. If, to the contrary, the attack is not yet or no longer imminent, so-called extensive excess, s 33 StGB is deemed inapplicable.[72] Factual misconceptions about the very existence of an attack (putative self-defence) are no form of excessive self-defence, but may qualify as a mistake regarding the factual basis of a recognized justificatory defence.[73]

Section 33 StGB requires that the defendant acts in an asthenic state of fear, terror or confusion. A person who exceeds the limits of self-defence out of rage, hate, indignation or any other sthenic affect is not relieved from criminal responsibility.[74] However, the asthenic state need not to be the only or the predominant cause for the excess. It is sufficient that the defendant's actions were also motivated by fear, terror or confusion.[75] If this is the case, s 33 StGB applies also to defendants who are—despite their asthenic state—able to realize that their defence goes beyond the limits of s 32 StGB.[76] Even in cases of provocation an invocation of excessive self-defence is not excluded as long as the provocateur has retained the primary right to self-defence.[77]

---

65   Rengier (n 5) s 18 mn 56.
66   In detail on the socio-ethical restriction of self-defence in torture cases/ticking bomb scenarios, see Ambos (n 41) 267–269.
67   See in more detail Roxin (n 1) s 15 mn 55 et seq; see also Bohlander (n 1) 104–105.
68   According to s 19 StGB, children under 14 years of age lack criminal capacity.
69   BGH Neue Zeitschrift für Strafrecht – Rechtsprechungsreport [hereinafter NStZ-RR] 2011, 305; Roxin (n 1) s 15 mn 65; Krey and Esser (n 7) mn 555.
70   Jescheck and Weigend (n 27) 346–347; see also the overview on the discussion by Roxin (n 1) s 15 mn 66–68.
71   Stratenwerth and Kuhlen (n 14) s 9 mn 88; Krey and Esser (n 7) mn 558–559.
72   BGH NStZ 1987, 20; BGH NStZ 2002, 141. For a different view see for example, Roxin (n 1) s 22 mn 90 (full application of s 33 StGB to extensive excesses) and Rengier (n 5) s 27 mn 19 (application of s 33 StGB to extensive excesses if the attack is no longer imminent but not to cases of preventive self-defence).
73   Bohlander (n 1) 121; Wessels, Beulke and Satzger (n 5) mn 448; on the treatment of such mistakes see above (n 24) and accompanying text.
74   Rengier (n 5) s 27 mn 22; Kühl (n 12) s 12 mn 146.
75   BGH NStZ-RR 1999, 264; BGH NJW 2001, 3200, 3202.
76   BGHSt 39, 133, 139; Kühl (n 12) s 12 mn 148; Wessels, Beulke and Satzger (n 5) mn 446.
77   BGHSt 39, 133, 139. The BGH, however, argues for an absolute exclusion of s 33 StGB if the provocateur has intentionally engaged in the violent argument and deliberately decided not to call the police but to avert the attack on his own, ibid 140; cf Roxin (n 1) s 22 mn 93, Murmann (n 12) s 26 mn 89.

Necessity

Necessity is a classical lesser evil defence[78] which can be combined with the idea of solidarity: In precarious situations, everyone is expected to tolerate infringements upon his rights if this is necessary to avert greater harm from others.[79] The justificatory effect of necessity is recognised in s 34 StGB but also in ss 228 and 904 of the Civil Code (BGB). That the latter also exclude criminal responsibility follows from the principle of the unity of the legal order:[80] a conduct, which is allowed by private law, cannot be forbidden and penalized by criminal law.[81] The three provisions on necessity read as follows:[82]

§ 34 StGB

A person who, faced with an imminent danger to life, limb, freedom, honour, property or another legal interest which cannot otherwise be averted, commits an act to avert the danger from himself or another, does not act unlawfully, if, upon weighing the conflicting interests, in particular the affected legal interests and the degree of the danger facing them, the protected interest substantially outweighs the one interfered with. This shall apply only if and to the extent that the act committed is an adequate means to avert the danger.

§ 228 BGB

A person who damages or destroys on object belonging to another in order to avert from himself or from another a danger arising from the object does not act unlawfully if the damage or destruction is necessary to avert the danger and the damage is not out of proportion to the danger. If the person acting in this manner caused the danger, he is obliged to pay damages.

§ 904 BGB

The owner of an object is not entitled to refuse another to interfere with the object if the interference is necessary to avert an imminent danger and if the impending damage is disproportionately high if compared to the damage caused to the owner by the interference. The owner may claim damages for the damage caused to him.

Sections 228 and 904 BGB justify only infringements of property rights, that is, damaging or destroying of objects belonging to another person. Due to this limitation, both provisions are *lex specials* in relation to the general and broader s 34 StGB.[83] Section 228 BGB on the so-called defensive necessity (*Defensivnotstand*) applies in cases in which the actor defends himself against the source of the danger. If, for example, D kills a dog which is going to bite him, this destruction of an object in terms of s 303 StGB is justified pursuant to s 228 BGB.[84] The fact, that s 228 StGB presupposes that the danger arises from the respective object, brings it close to self-defence.[85] This is reflected in the balancing test: While s 904 BGB and s 34 StGB require that the protected interest substantially outweighs the one interfered with, s 228 StGB is only excluded if the caused harm is disproportionally greater than the one sought to avoid. Thus, s 228 BGB permits the killing of an expensive pedigree dog to prevent him from chewing trousers, but not to defend a chocolate bar.[86]

In contrast, s 904 BGB covers cases of aggressive necessity (*Aggressivnotstand*) and permits the damage of objects which present no danger. Take, for example, our pub brawl case.[87] The destruction of the beer mug belonging to the host as an uninvolved third party is not covered by self-defence. Section 904 BGB, however, obliged the host to accept the use of the beer mug as a defensive means und its resulting destruction, because this was necessary to avert the danger caused by V's attack and to protect a substantially higher good, namely

---

78   Ambos (n 41) 280; Rengier (n 5) s 19 mn 1; Wessels, Beulke and Satzger (n 5) mn 298.
79   Weigend (n 3) 270; Krey and Esser (n 7) mn 580.
80   Bohlander (n 1) 106; Murmann (n 12) s 15 mn 4; Krey and Esser (n 7) mn 449.
81   Roxin (n 1) s 14 mn 32; Krey and Esser (n 7) mn 450; Rengier (n 5) s 17 mn 3.
82   Translation according to Bohlander (n 26) 45; Bohlander (n 1) 107.
83   Rengier (n 5) s 20 mn 1; Heinrich (n 2) mn 482, 489; Kühl (n 12) s 9 mn 13.
84   Heinrich (n 2) mn 482; Krey and Esser (n 7) mn 579.
85   Krey and Esser (n 7) mn 578; Kühl (n 12) s 9 mn 16.
86   Kühl (n 12) s 9 mn 16; see also Roxin (n 1) s 16 mn 111.
87   See (n 50) and accompanying text.

D's right to physical integrity. Apart from these characteristics, s 228 and s 908 BGB follow the same rules as s 34 StGB.[88]

Section 34 StGB requires first of all the existence of a necessity situation, that is, an imminent danger to a protected interest. In contrast to self-defence,[89] necessity allows not only for the protection of individual but also of public interests.[90] If, for example, D causes bodily injury to V to keep him from driving drunk and thus to endanger traffic safety, he—depending upon the circumstances of the case—may be justified under s 34 StGB.[91] Moreover, s 34 StGB also applies to cases of altruistic necessity for the benefit of third persons without requiring a special relationship between the endangered person and the actor.[92] The origin of the danger is also irrelevant: it may be caused by human behaviour, natural phenomena or accident.[93] In any case, however, the danger must be imminent. This requirement must be understood more broadly than in the context of self-defence, since necessity does not presuppose a focused attack, but merely a (broad) danger.[94] In particular, s 34 StGB may also be applied in cases of preventive self-defence (not covered by s 32 StGB)[95] or permanent dangers that can realize at any time.[96] Nevertheless, even in case of necessity, the realization of the danger must not lie too far in the future. The crucial question is if immediate action is required, that is, later countermeasure would not be possible any more or only under much greater risks.[97]

The defensive action must be necessary, i.e., the suitable and least severe, but equally effective means to avert the danger.[98] In contrast to self-defence, however, s 34 StGB requires the defendant to retreat from the danger or to call the police or other authorities for help if possible.[99] The core element of s 34 StGB is its proportionality test. The commission of an act is only justified if the protected interest substantially outweighs the one interfered with. In conducting this balancing exercise one has to take into account, *inter alia*, the:[100]

- abstract value of the respective interests (the right to life and physical integrity, for example, is—generally speaking—more important than property rights);
- intensity of the danger and the degree of harm caused or threatened to the respective interests;
- individual meaning of the respective interests to the persons concerned;
- chances of saving the respective interests;
- causation of/voluntary exposure to the danger by the actor[101] or the victim; and
- special duties to take on dangers inherent in the actor's profession (e.g., soldiers, firemen).

What can be seen from this is that whether or not the protected interest substantially outweighs the one interfered with cannot be answered in the abstract, but depends on the circumstances of the case. Nevertheless, it is a fundamental principle of the German legal order that all lives are of equal value and no life prevails over another. Therefore, a balancing of life against life is not possible—be it in quantitative (one life against hundreds) or qualitative (the life of an old and frail man against the life of a newborn child) regard.[102] However,

---

88   Rengier (n 5) s 20 mn 1–2; see also Heinrich (n 2) mn 479 et seq.

89   See (n 34) and accompanying text.

90   Roxin (n 1) s 16 mn 13; Krey and Esser (n 7) mn 588; Rengier (n 5) s 19 mn 8.

91   OLG Frankfurt NStZ-RR 1996, 136.

92   This is an important difference between necessity as a justification (s 34 StGB) and as an excuse (s 35 StGB); see below (n 119) and accompanying text.

93   Bohlander (n 1) 110; Roxin (n 1) s 16 mn 19; Rengier (n 5) s 19 mn 13. If, however, the danger arises from an object, for example an animal, s 228 BGB takes precedence. As to 'duress of threats' cases, see (n 107) and accompanying text.

94   Ambos (n 41) 281; see also Wessels, Beulke and Satzger (n 5) mn 307; Kühl (n 12) s 8 mn 67.

95   Kühl (n 12) s 8 mn 71; Krey and Esser (n 7) mn 624; Kindhäuser (n 27) s 17 mn 20.

96   Bohlander (n 1) 111; Roxin (n 1) s 16 mn 21; Murmann (n 12) s 25 mn 47.

97   Ambos (n 41) 281; Bohlander (n 1) 111; Roxin (n 1) s 16 mn 20.

98   Wessels, Beulke and Satzger (n 5) mn 308; Heinrich (n 2) mn 416–418; Roxin (n 1) s 16 mn 23.

99   Heinrich (n 2) mn 420; Kühl (n 12) s 8 mn 76–77.

100   In detail Roxin (n 1) s 16 mn 26–88; Kühl (n 12) s 8 mn 107–165.

101   Differently from the case of self-defence, even the intentional causation of a danger does not lead to an automatic exclusion of the necessity defence, but has to be taken into account in the balancing test; in more detail, Roxin (n 1) s 16 mn 60–64.

102   Roxin (n 1) s 16 mn 33–34; Frister (n 13) 237; Rengier (n 5) s 19 mn 32.

under certain circumstances some authors feel the need to moderate this strict approach. In particular in battered women cases it is sometimes argued that ss 34 StGB, 228 BGB may even allow the use of deadly force. As previously noted, if D, who is frequently beaten by her husband V, kills him while he is asleep, she cannot rely on self-defence for lack of an imminent attack.[103] She lives, however, under the permanent threat of being harmed so that s 34 StGB might be applicable.[104] As a rule, however, D can be expected to file for divorce or to call the police instead of killing V. Only in exceptional cases, for example, if D fears for her life if she leaves V and if the police cannot guarantee her safety, the use of deadly force might be necessary in terms of s 34 StGB. According to the majority view, the killing of V nevertheless cannot be justified because D's right to physical integrity and—as the case may be—life does not substantially outweigh V's right to life.[105] D may only be excused according to s 35 StGB. Some authors, however, stress that V has caused the danger. In analogy to s 228 BGB it is therefore deemed sufficient that the caused harm is not disproportionally greater than the one sought to be avoided.[106]

Another controversy relates to the applicability of s 34 StGB to cases of 'duress by threats'. Imagine that A threatens to kill D if he does not falsely take an oath before a court. If D gives in to the threat and commits the crime of perjury (s 154 StGB), he—according to one view—may rely on necessity because he defended a superior good, namely his right to physical integrity.[107] The contrary view argues that D deliberately takes side with the wrong and thus cannot be justified but only excused.[108]

According to s 34 sent 2, the defensive act must be an *adequate* means to avert the danger. The scope of this clause is rather limited: an act which prevents greater harm is in most cases adequate.[109] Nevertheless, it constitutes an additional normative threshold which encompasses all considerations derived from constitutional and human rights law.[110] In particular, s 34 StGB can never justify the use of torture or comparable violations of the human dignity.[111]

Closely related to duress is the (unwritten) justification[112] of a collision of duties, which might become relevant in the field of offences by omission. If the agent is under two conflicting duties to act and if the exercise of one duty necessarily results in the breach of the other, he cannot be held criminally responsible for not having complied with both of them. Any other result would be incompatible with the ancient maxim *impossibilium nulla obligato est*—nobody has any obligation to do the impossible.[113] A justification, however, requires that both duties to act are of equal value. If this is not the case, the defendant must comply with the superior duty. Imagine, for example, that D sees that his two sons, S_1 and S_2 are drowning in a sea. It is impossible for him to safe both and he decides to rescue S_1. The two conflicting duties—the duty to save S_1 and the duty to save S_2—are equal in value. Thus, D cannot be held responsible for not having rescued S_2. If, in contrast, D has to decide whether to save his son S or his son's friend F, he has to opt for S. His close personal relationship to S generates a special duty of care (*Garantenpflicht*) which is superior to the general duty of averting damage from other persons to whom he is not closely connected.[114]

Duress by Threats/Circumstances

According to s 35(1) StGB, a 'person who, faced with an imminent danger to life, limb or freedom which cannot otherwise be averted, commits an unlawful act to avert the danger from himself, a relative or person

---

103   See (n 43) and accompanying text.

104   As to the applicability of s 34 StGB to permanent dangers, see (n 96) and accompanying text.

105   BGHSt 48, 255, 257; Heinrich (n 2) mn 421; Rengier (n 5) s 19 mn 41; Wessels, Beulke and Satzger (n 5) mn 316.

106   Krey and Esser (n 7) mn 629; see also Roxin (n 1) s 16 mn 78; Kühl (n 12) s 8 mn 138.

107   Frister (n 13) 238-239; Stratenwerth and Kuhlen (n 14) s 9 mn 105.

108   Kühl (n 12) s 8 mn 132; Wessels, Beulke and Satzger(n 5) mn 443; differentiating according to the value of the harmed interest Rengier (n 5) s 19 mn 54; in a similar vein Roxin (n 1) s 16 mn 68.

109   Heinrich (n 2) mn 427.

110   Ambos (n 41) 285; see also Murmann (n 12) s 25 mn 61.

111   Ambos (n 41) 285; Roxin (n 1) s 16 mn 99; for more examples see Kühl (n 12) s 8 mn 169–182.

112   Murmann (n 12) s 25 mn 65; Krey and Esser (n 7) mn 633.

113   Heinrich (n 2) mn 513; Murmann (n 12) s 25 mn 65; see also Krey and Esser (n 7) mn 633.

114   Case based on Heinrich (n 2) mn 513–514; see also Roxin (n 1) s 16 mn 125.

close to him, acts without guilt'.[115] Compared to necessity, duress as an excuse has a very limited scope.[116] The enumeration of the protected interests—life, limb and freedom—is exhaustive. An analogous application of s 35(1) StGB to, for example, dangers to property is not possible.[117] Moreover, the imminent danger[118] must be directed at the actor or a person close to him, because only then is the commission of a legal wrong understandable and socially tolerable.[119] If these conditions are fulfilled, s 35(1) StGB relieves the actor from criminal responsibility provided that his conduct is necessary to avert the danger.[120] Contrary to necessity, the duress defence, which only negates the actor's blameworthiness and not the wrongfulness of his conduct, does not require a balancing between the affected interests.[121] This means in particular, that a person may even kill several innocents to safe his own life.[122] However, duress is excluded if and to the extent that the defendant 'could be expected … to accept the danger, in particular, because he himself had caused the danger, or was under a special legal obligation to do so'[123] or the harm caused is clearly disproportionate to the harm sought to be avoided.[124]

General Mental Condition Defences

Insanity
According to s 20 StGB on insanity:

> any person who at the time of the commission of the offence is incapable of appreciating the unlawfulness of their actions or of acting in accordance with any such appreciation due to a pathological mental disorder, a profound consciousness disorder, debility or any other serious mental abnormality, shall be deemed to act without guilt.[125]

Thus, the insanity defence has two requirements: First, the defendant must suffer from one of the four mentioned psychological disorders. Second, because of this mental defect the defendant must be unable to appreciate the wrongfulness of his conduct or to act accordingly.[126] The latter requirement provides for an equal treatment of cognitive ('appreciating') and volitional ('acting accordingly') incapacity.[127] In both instances the defendant has no freedom to act[128] and thus cannot be blamed for having violated the law. In any case, s 20 StGB requires a complete destruction of the defendant's (cognitive or volitional) capacities.[129] Mental disorders falling short of this threshold may result in a mitigation of punishment pursuant to s 21 StGB (partial defence of diminished responsibility).[130] Even if s 20 StGB stands in the way of a criminal conviction, the courts may adopt preventive measures like a mental hospital order (s 63 StGB) provided that the defendant presents a danger to the general public.

---

115   Translation according to Bohlander (n 26) 45.
116   With regard to cases not falling within the limited scope of s 35(1) StGB, some authors recognise under certain circumstances the unwritten defence of supra-legal duress (übergesetzlicher Notstand) which relieves the actor from criminal responsibility whenever he cannot fairly be expected to act in accordance with the law, in more detail Bohlander (n 1) 129–130; Roxin (n 1) s 22 mn 142–145; Krey and Esser (n 7) mn 772–778.
117   Rengier (n 5) s 26 mn 6; Roxin (n 1) s 22 mn 23.
118   As to the term 'imminent danger' see (n 93) and accompanying text.
119   Weigend (n 3) 274; Heinrich (n 2) mn 567; Roxin (n 1) s 22 mn 30.
120   As to the meaning of 'necessary' see (n 98) and accompanying text.
121   Weigend (n 3) 274; Rengier (n 5) s 26 mn 10; Heinrich (n 2) mn 571.
122   BGH NJW 1964, 730.
123   Translation of the relevant parts of s 35(1) StGB according to Bohlander (n 26) 45.
124   Weigend (n 3) 274; Roxin (n 1) s 22 mn 53; see also Heinrich (n 2) mn 571; Bohlander (n 1) 129.
125   Translation according to Bohlander (n 26) 42.
126   Roxin (n 1) s 20 mn 1; Wessels, Beulke and Satzger (n 5) mn 410; Weigend (n 3) 273; see also Krey and Esser (n 19) mn 695.
127   Walter Perron and Bettina Weißer, '§ 20' in Adolf Schönke and Horst Schröder (eds), *Strafgesetzbuch – Kommentar* (29th edn, CH Beck 2014) mn 25; Heinrich (n 2) mn 539.
128   See Roxin (n 1) s 19 mn 56.
129   See Rengier (n 5) s 24 mn 7; Frister (n 13) 248.
130   Rengier (n 5) s 24 mn 7; see also Wessels, Beulke and Satzger (n 5) mn 413; Weigend (n 3) 273.

Intoxication

German criminal law does not treat intoxication as a discrete defence, but as a special form of insanity.[131] When intoxication amounts to a temporary mental disease[132] depends on the circumstances of the case, in particular on the physical condition of the defendant and—for example—his adaptation to alcohol or drugs effects.[133] If the threshold of s 20 StGB is met, the defendant, as a rule, is relieved from criminal responsibility even if he was voluntarily intoxicated.[134] This is the logical consequence of the principle of coincidence (Koinzidenzprinzip)[135] which requires the defendant's blameworthiness 'at the time of the commission of the act' (s 20 StGB). To avoid inacceptable loopholes, s 323a StGB penalizes the voluntary causation of complete intoxication. According to this provision, a person who 'intentionally or negligently puts himself into a drunken state by consuming alcoholic beverages or other intoxicants shall be liable ... if he commits an unlawful act while in this state and may not be punished because of it because he was insane due to the intoxication or if this cannot be excluded'.[136] Note, however, that s 323a StGB does not establish criminal responsibility for an act committed in a state of temporary insanity, but criminalises the act of intoxication itself.[137] The commission of a crime in a state of intoxication is a mere objective requirement for criminal liability (*objektive Bedingung der Strafbarkeit*), which means that it is not even necessary that the defendant could have foreseen his intoxication resulting in a criminal conduct.[138]

The recourse to s 323a StGB, with its rather low range of punishment (imprisonment not exceeding five years or a fine), may lead to unsatisfying results if the defendant becomes intentionally intoxicated with the preconceived intent to commit a grave crime, for example murder, in the resulting state of incapacity in order to then invoke insanity as a defence.[139] In such cases, German case law[140] and part of the literature[141] revert under certain limiting circumstances[142] to the *actio libera in causa* (alic) doctrine according to which the actor is punished for the crime committed as if he had committed it with full responsibility since he was free and fully responsible when he set the cause ('*in causa*') and thus is to be blamed for the intentional and attributable '*actio libera*' bringing about the state of non-responsibility.[143] It is, however, highly doubtful if and how this approach, which *de facto* undermines s 20 StGB and the principle of coincidence, can be reconciled with the principle of legality.[144]

Mistake of Law

German criminal doctrine regards (potential) consciousness of the legal wrong as a pre-requisite for the actor's personal blameworthiness: A person, who was not able to realize that he is committing a wrong, cannot

---

131 Bohlander (n 1) 132; Weigend (n 3) 273.

132 It is a contested issue whether a severe intoxication should be classified as a pathological mental disorder or a profound consciousness disorder, see Franz Streng, '§ 20' in Wolfgang Joecks and Klaus Miebach (eds), *Münchener Kommentar zum Strafgesetzbuch Band 1, §§ 1–37 StGB* (2nd edn, CH Beck 2011) mn 32, 36 with further references. In either way, the result stays the same: intoxication is a form of insanity.

133 BGH NStZ 1997, 591; BGH NStZ 2005, 329; Rengier (n 5) s 24 mn 8; Frister (n 13) 254.

134 Bohlander (n 1) 132; Weigend (n 3) 273; see also Perron and Weißer (n 127) mn 42.

135 Heinrich (n 2) mn 597; see also Roxin (n 1) s 20 mn 58; Krey and Esser (n 19) mn 695.

136 Translation according to Bohlander (n 26) 200.

137 Weigend (n 3) 274; see also Detlev Sternberg-Lieben and Bernd Hecker, '§ 323a' in Adolf Schönke and Horst Schröder (eds), *Strafgesetzbuch – Kommentar* (29th edn, CH Beck 2014) mn 1, 12; Rudolf Rengier, *Strafrecht Besonderer Teil II* (15th edn, CH Beck 2014) s 41 mn 6.

138 Sternberg-Lieben and Hecker (n 137) mn 12; Rengier (n 137) s 41 mn 18a.

139 See Heinrich (n 2) mn 598; Krey and Esser (n 19) mn 704.

140 BGHSt 34, 29, 33; BGH NStZ 2000, 584; BGH NStZ 2002, 28.

141 See only Roxin (n 1) s 20 mn 59–67; Rengier (n 5) s 25 mn 15; Wessels, Beulke and Satzger (n 5) mn 415; Krey and Esser (n 19) mn 704–710.

142 Most notably, the *alic* doctrine is not applicable to offences which require a particular conduct like 'driving a vehicle', BGHSt 42, 235; see also Weigend (n 3) 273–274; Krey and Esser (n 19) mn 706.

143 Rengier (n 5) s 25 mn 1; Wessels, Beulke and Satzger (n 5) mn 415; Ambos (n 3) 329.

144 Kai Ambos, '*Der Anfang vom Ende der actio libera in causa*' in [1997] NJW 2296 with further references; see also the overview on the discussion by Heinrich (n 2) mn 602–607

be motivated by the criminal norm and thus cannot be blamed for having violated it.[145] Accordingly, s 17 StGB provides that a person who at the time of the commission of the offence 'lacks the awareness that he is acting unlawfully' is 'deemed to have acted without guilt if the mistake was unavoidable'.[146] Section 17 StGB thus presupposes that the defendant does not realize that his conduct is forbidden by law. Mere ignorance of the *criminal* prohibition, however, does not exclude consciousness of the legal wrong.[147]

A mistake of law may relate to the existence of a prohibition as such (direct mistake of law). Imagine, for example, that the defendant has a sexual relationship with an insane person without knowing that this is prohibited (and criminalized) by s 179(1) StGB.[148] Moreover, the ignorance of the law may be the result of an incorrect evaluation of the respective norm (mistaken subsumption—*Subsumtionsirrtum*).[149] If D lets the air out of V's bicycle tyres believing that this is not legally forbidden because he does not damage the tyres' substance, he lacks the awareness of causing criminally relevant damage within the meaning of s 303 StGB.[150] Section 17 StGB is equally applicable if the defendant is mistaken about the existence or reach of a *justificatory* defence (indirect mistake of law).[151] A defendant who, for example, kills another person to prevent him from stealing an apple in the mistaken belief that he is exercising his right to self-defence in a legitimate way[152] does not realise that he is committing a legal wrong.[153] Note, however, that a defendant who is mistaken about the existence or reach of an *excusatory* defence knows that he is acting unlawfully. He merely believes that he will not be blamed for his conduct. Such a mistake is plainly irrelevant.[154]

In any case, s 17 StGB relieves the defendant from criminal responsibility only if the mistake was unavoidable. This is a relatively high threshold which aims to ensure that only those defendants benefit from s 17 StGB who cannot be blamed for their ignorance. According to the Federal Supreme Court, everyone is expected to reflect on the legality of his actions. In cases of doubts, one has to search one's conscience and/or to consult with legal experts on the lawfulness of the intended conduct.[155] In light of this, the recognition of an unavoidable mistake of law is the exception rather than the rule. However, s 17 StGB might be invoked successfully if the legal situation is ambiguous[156] or if the defendant relied on a wrong advice of an appropriate expert.[157]

Residual Catch-All Defences/Existence and Ambit of Statutory Defences Related to Distinct Offences[158]

Section 127(1) StPO grants everyone the *right to arrest a person* provisionally without an arrest warrant, if that person 'is caught in the act of committing an offence or is being pursued thereafter and if there is a danger that he will abscond or that his identity cannot be immediately ascertained' (citizens' arrest).[159] In doing so, s 127(1) StPO empowers any private person[160] to act as a representative of the (absent) law enforcement

145 In more detail Roxin (n 1) s 21 mn 1–10; see also BGHSt 2, 194, 200; Rengier (n 5) s 31 mn 1; Wessels, Beulke and Satzger (n 5) mn 461.
146 Translation according to Bohlander (n 26) 41.
147 BGHSt 2, 194, 202; Frister (n 13) 261; Roxin (n 1) s 21 mn 13.
148 BGH Juristische Rundschau 1954, 188.
149 Kühl (n 12) s 13 mn 56–57; Roxin (n 1) s 21 mn 23–24.
150 Example based on Kühl (n 12) s 13 mn 57.
151 BGH NStZ 2003, 596; Krey and Esser (n 7) mn 718.
152 See (n 67) and accompanying text.
153 See also Wessels, Beulke and Satzger (n 5) mn 482.
154 Heinrich (n 2) mn 1156–1158; Wessels, Beulke and Satzger (n 5) mn 490; for a different view, see Frister (n 13) 274 (analogous application of s 17 StGB).
155 BGHSt 2, 194, 209; see also Bohlander (n 1) 120; critically, as to the 'search of conscience' component, see Roxin (n 1) s 21 mn 46; Kühl (n 12) s 13 mn 61 (avoidability merely through intellectual reflection and consultation).
156 See LG Köln [2012] NJW 2128, 2129, which for the first time convicted a doctor for causing bodily injury by conducting a circumcision; an up to then contested but widely accepted practice.
157 BGH NJW 1995, 204, 205; Rengier (n 5) s 31 mn 22; Frister (n 13) 264.
158 The defences of consent and presumed consent will be treated in a separate volume.
159 Translation according to Bohlander (n 1) 98.
160 Ulrich Schultheis, '§ 127' in Rolf Hannich (ed), *Karlsruher Kommentar zur Strafprozessordnung* (7th edn, CH Beck 2013) mn 6; Heinrich (n 2) mn 499.

authorities and thus to assist the state in enforcing its right to inflict punishment.[161] On an objective level, a citizens' arrest presupposes that the suspect is caught or pursued *in flagranti delicto*,[162] that is, during or immediately after the commission of an offence at the crime scene or in striking distance thereof (arrest situation).[163] According to the presumably prevailing opinion in German jurisprudence and doctrine, it is not necessary that the suspect has indeed committed an offence. Rather, a high degree of suspicion is deemed sufficient.[164] In addition to the arrest situation, the defendant must have a legitimate reason for arrest, namely risk of flight or unknown identity of the suspect. Moreover, and notwithstanding the general discussion on the content of the subjective defence element,[165] the defendant must not only be aware of the arrest situation but must also act with the intent to surrender the suspect to the law enforcement authorities.[166] The reason for this increased subjective requirement lies in the *ratio* of s 127(1) StPO, according to which the defendant is justified, because, and only if, he acts in a public interest.[167] If all these preconditions are fulfilled, s 127(1) StPO allows for an arrest, that is infringements on the right to liberty, and a minimum amount of bodily harm necessary to enforce the arrest, but (as a rule)[168] not for the use of firearms.[169]

German criminal law also recognises several distinct defences which apply only to certain offences. Libel and slander (ss 185–188 StGB), for example, may be justified, if the critical opinion in question was made in order to exercise or protect rights or to safeguard legitimate interests, as per s 193 StGB. A person is relieved from criminal responsibility for abortion, if the termination of pregnancy is medically necessary (s 218a[2] StGB—medical indication) or if the pregnancy was probably caused by a sex offence (s 218a[3] StGB—criminological indication). In the context of environmental offences, the defence of official authorisation plays an important role. Section 3 of the German Criminal Code of Crimes against International Law (*Völkerstrafgesetzbuch*) introduces the special excuse of superior orders according to which the perpetrator is not blameworthy if he commits a war crime pursuant to a military or comparable order provided that he does not realize that the order is unlawful and that the order is not manifestly unlawful.

Similar in effect to justifications and excuses are the so-called *Straffreistellungsgründe*, which do not touch upon the wrongfulness of the act or the blameworthiness of the actor, but exclude the punishability of the perpetrator for policy reasons.[170] Section 258 (5) and (6) StGB, to give but one example,[171] exempts a person from criminal liability for assistance in avoiding prosecution or punishment if he wants to avoid his own punishment or the punishment of a close relative.

---

161   Schultheis (n 160) mn 6; Rengier (n 5) s 22 mn 1; see also Roxin (n 1) s 17 mn 22; Krey and Esser (n 7) mn 640.
162   Bohlander (n 1) 98.
163   Schultheis (n 160) mn 7–8; Rengier (n 5) s 22 mn 6.
164   BGH NJW 1981, 745; Schultheis (n 160) mn 9; Rengier (n 5) s 22 mn 10; Roxin (n 1) s 17 mn 24; for a different view (no arrest of an innocent by a private person) Wessels, Beulke and Satzger (n 5) mn 354; Krey and Esser (n 7) mn 646–647; detailed overview on the discussion by Heinrich (n 2) mn 506–508.
165   See supra (n 7) and accompanying text.
166   Bohlander (n 1) 98; Krey and Esser (n 7) mn 654; Kindhäuser (n 27) s 20 mn 10.
167   Rengier (n 5) s 22 mn 1.
168   For possible exceptions see Schultheis (n 160) mn 28.
169   Krey and Esser (n 7) mn 651–652; Roxin (n 1) s 17 mn 28; Kindhäuser (n 27) s 20 mn 8.
170   Weigend (n 3) 269; see also Frister (n 13) 280; Stratenwerth and Kuhlen (n 14) s 7 mn 30.
171   For more examples see Roxin (n 1) s 23 mn 4.

Chapter 17
Islamic Law

Mohammad M Hedayati-Kakhki

General Issues

Justificatory and Excusatory Defences—Distinction and Seat in the Offence Structure

Defences within Islamic criminal law generally deal with situations where the existence of a particular circumstance or factor will either remove all criminal liability, thus acting as a complete defence, or will establish that criminal responsibility should be reduced to a certain extent, thus acting as a partial defence. It is accepted by all schools of thought within *Shari'a* that fairness to all parties is a must within criminal proceedings and as such it is necessary to consider all defences and mitigating factors, before deciding upon guilt.[1] An important point to note is that in certain Islamic jurisdictions mitigating factors can be included for consideration in the assessment of guilt as well as during the sentencing process and a judge is free to accept or reject such mitigation at any stage.

It is also vital to understand that when dealing with jurisdictions that follow *Shari'a*, whilst societal values are open to change, that which is deemed religiously ordained by God remains the same. Any divergence is only acceptable where the primary sources of Islamic law allow for interpretive scope. This is especially crucial when considering the impact of *hadd*[2] crimes and the manner in which general defences are relied upon in an attempt to avoid the heavy sanctions prescribed by *Shari'a*, which cannot normally be overridden given its divine basis.

Conceptual Foundations

Generally, Islamic criminal law follows the tripartite structure by which three elements must be satisfied in order to complete the requirements of an offence, although its implementation can depend on each respective Islamic jurisdiction. The three components involve, first, an act or omission which has been completed with the necessary intention. Second, the act must be considered unlawful, whether wrongful in terms of societal values or indeed sinful as per Islamic law, with no justifications in terms of defences. The last category requires the establishment of blame or guilt with no excuses available which may mitigate the other elements.

A striking feature of Islamic criminal law is its emphasis on the subjective elements of a crime, that is, the defendant's intentions and understanding when committing an act; and the first stage would be to make an assessment from a subjective perspective. Where an individual for example, is of the belief that he has caught his wife in the act of committing adultery and kills her, he is entitled to a defence irrespective of the fact that his belief was mistaken and his wife was actually being raped. This is even so if in the same overall circumstances, another individual would have realised that she was being raped. However, it is important to note that even when the assessment is made by looking at the act subjectively, the overriding Islamic concepts are still taken into consideration. Thus, the actions of the husband in the above example must have been Islamically ordained.

Moreover, certain defences include assessment from an objective element by which the defendant's acts will be judged in accordance with what a Muslim[3] would do should they bear the Islamic principles as

---

1 Qur'an [5:8].
2 In Islamic law, a hadd crime refers to the class of punishments that are fixed for certain offences that are considered to be Divine rights or claims of God.
3 I.e., a 'good Muslim'.

ordained in mind. For example, the defence of duress is not available in murder cases due to the belief that the lives of all Muslims are equal and therefore a Muslim should not favour their life over that of another. This is irrespective of the fact that perhaps in reality, by virtue of human nature, every Muslim regardless of how devout they are would follow the same steps in the circumstances faced. Therefore, whilst defences are generally judged subjectively, it is the 'Islamic subjective' by which the actions are judged in accordance with Islamic principles. Where Islamically ordained, an individual's actions will be accepted even if no other individual would do the same; whilst if not in accordance with Islamic principles there is no defence even if in reality all individuals would react in the same manner.[4]

Judges and law makers in Islamic jurisdictions have a difficult task of finding a balance between restricting the requirements of defences, so as to ensure that they are not too wide, whilst at the same time trying to ensure they are not too narrow either as the latter may mean harsher sentences for defendants. As a result, general discretion is afforded to judges so that they can assess the subjective principles in light of individual autonomy whilst simultaneously considering the need for individuals to be viewed as part of an Islamic society, particularly in more modernised countries such as Turkey.

The general defences available in Islamic criminal law can be justificatory or excusatory and depending on the circumstances, it could be both. Defences that are justificatory are controversial in the sense that they suggest the defendant's actions were appropriate, even though the offence is complete. The exercise of such a defence can even go as far as to place blame on the victim, such as in Iran in cases of honour killing by the husband where the victim is accused of adultery.[5] On the other hand, defences which are excusatory suggest that whilst the actions of the defendant are unacceptable, there are additional factors by which the defendant should not be blamed or alternatively could be pardoned.

As Islam generally favours mercy, with ample principles in the *Qur'an* commenting on this,[6] the defences available tend to be more excusatory; and even where it is a justification-based defence narratives of a case would discuss it in an excusatory manner. This may also be partly due to the fact that Islam teaches to not speak ill of the dead, or by extension those affected, and therefore excuse-based defences are preferred as it achieves the aims of granting mercy and not unnecessarily punishing an individual, whilst at the same time giving due respects to the victim.[7] It is for this reason that it is suggested that a defence can be both justificatory and excusatory as it can be considered as such by Islamic judges when deciding upon conviction and sentencing. In reality, there is no particular need to decide upon whether a defence is deemed justification-based or excuse-based in practical terms in Islamic jurisdictions as the consequences of its reliance is of paramount importance. Naturally, for these reasons, an accumulation of defences as well as alternative pleadings of defences are allowed in Islamic criminal law, with procedures being prescribed by each individual Islamic jurisdiction in order to consider the totality of the circumstances and thus reach a determination regarding guilt. Therefore, a party may plead as many separate claims, or invoke as many defences as they deem appropriate, regardless of the consistency of the respective pleadings or the grounds upon which they are based. Due to the fact that the principle of fairness underscores the approach of Islamic judges when considering the defences, the merits of all pleadings will be considered equally under Islamic law. The effect of making cumulative pleadings will have a bearing on the burden of proof, in that the onus shifts to the defence to establish the existence of circumstances giving rise to the particular defences plead.

---

4 Evidentially individuals are being judged in light of a 'good Muslim' who may or may not in fact exist.

5 According to Article 630 of the Iranian Penal Code, 'If a man finds his wife in adulterous position with a strange man and has knowledge that the woman is willing he can kill both of them in that situation. If the woman is reluctant he can only kill the man. The same rules apply to beating and injury as it does to killing'. In fact, Iran recently solidified this defence even further through adding wording in Article 300 of the Penal Code which stresses the husband's exemption from retaliation (qisas) where the wife and lover are caught in the act. It must however be noted that not all countries following Islamic law have such provisions in relation to honour killings. Pakistan has for example a law by which honour killings are punishable by a prison term of seven years, or even the death penalty in extreme cases.

6 Qur'an [7:199].

7 Fiqh Us-Sunnah, vol 4: Burial 76; Sahih Bukhari recorded the Prophet saying: 'do not speak ill of the dead for they have reached the deeds that they have put forth'.

Transferred Defences/Collateral Damage Defences

Islamic criminal law is also unique in the sense it is one which in fact recognises the doctrine of transferred defences in certain circumstances. Thus, for example, in Iranian law a husband is entitled to kill a male who is trying to rape his wife, in an act defending his honour. If in the course of attempting to kill the male with a gun, with intent, he accidentally shoots his wife and kills her, not only will the intent to kill be transferred but so will the defence to kill. That is, as he was justified in law to kill the male who was attacking his honour, this justification can be transferred to the killing of the unintended victim. Similarly, Article 296 of the Iranian Penal Code states:

> [I]n cases where a person intends to shoot an object or an animal or another person but the bullet hits another person, his/her actions will be considered to be a simple mistake.

Therefore, provided that the initial intention was justified, any defences that were available such as provocation or self-defence will be transferred accordingly irrespective of the mistake that occurred.

Provocation of the Defence Situation

The defence of provocation is controversial in the sense it places the blame on the victim, and removes the stage of wrongfulness from the tripartite structure of Islamic criminal law. What is further interesting is where the provoker tries to defend themselves against the actions of the provoked. It is vital to remember that the Islamic basis of the defence is that the act in response to provocation occurred in the 'course of justice'[8] thus making it a justificatory defence; a term used varyingly across different Islamic jurisdictions. In general therefore, if an individual has initially provoked a situation there is no defence available in the face of a provoked attack.

However, this is dependent on the defence of provocation being available in the first place. The primary sources of *Shari'a* do not set out the boundaries by which provocation is to be made available; therefore each individual Islamic jurisdiction has discretion to decide the extent to which the defence is applicable. In many jurisdictions, the act of provocation is often considered to be an act which defies honour and in turn the defence is viewed in a particularly subjective manner, albeit this attack on honour must be considered in light of applicable Islamic morality standards. Thus, for example, a husband whose wife has committed adultery would be able to rely on the defence; whilst the brother whose sister gives evidence against him in court would not,[9] as with the latter example her actions are not one which would be viewed as having defied family honour from an Islamic perspective. In turn, the wife cannot defend herself against any attack but the sister can. Moreover, where the husband attempts to kill his wife believing he has caught her with her lover in the act of adultery but in fact it was against her will, his wife will be able to protect herself against her husband's 'provoked attack' as she had done no wrong. This is irrespective of the fact that should her husband kill her in his mistaken belief, he would still be able to rely on the defence of provocation.

The ability for the alleged provoker to put forward such a defence however will depend on each individual jurisdiction; a state which readily allows use of the defence is less likely to allow defence mechanisms to a victim. In Iran the defence of provocation is available where the victim insulted Prophet Muhammad.[10] Nigeria on the other hand has rejected such a defence in similar circumstances, stating that:

---

8   Qur'an [17:33]: 'You shall not kill any person – for GOD has made life sacred – except in the course of justice. If one is killed unjustly, then we give his heir authority to enforce justice. Thus, he shall not exceed the limits in avenging the murder; he will be helped'.

9   Abubakar *Dan Shalla v The State* (2007) Supreme Court of Nigeria SC 245/2004.

10   Article 513 of Iranian Penal Code states anyone who insults Holy Islam or the Prophet or any Imam, as well as the Prophet Mohammed's daughter, will be punished by death if the insult is so radical so as to amount to blasphemy; Article 226 of the same code states: 'Committing murder will result in retaliation provided the murdered person did not deserve to die in accordance with Islamic jurisprudence'.

Islamic religion is not a primitive religion that allows its adherents to take the law into their own hands and to commit jungle justice ... Although it is true that there is a provision in *Risala*[11] which prescribes punishment of death on any Muslim who insults the Holy Prophet such punishment can only be imposed by the appropriate authority (i.e. the court) rather than by any member of the society whether a Muslim or otherwise.[12]

Whether an alleged provoker is able to defend themselves from attack is thus dependent on an assessment of the provocation itself and whether the provoked defendant's response was justified, and depending on the jurisdiction, whether it was proportionate.

Mistakes of Fact and Defences

Mistakes, or *Shubha*, becomes a recurring theme when discussing general defences available under Islamic criminal law, not only as a general defence whether in fact or in law, but also in terms of transferring defences and forming a part of another available defence such as self-defence or provocation. Indeed as Islamic criminal law places great emphasis on assessing a defendant's intentions from a subjective point of view, the possibility of a mistake of fact having been made by the defendant is very relevant when considering the availability of general defences. Thus as previously stated, where a husband is of the mistaken belief he has caught his wife committing adultery he is able to rely on the defence of provocation when in reality she was unwilling.

However, the key consideration is that the defence would have been available had the mistaken facts been true; that is, the husband would have been entitled to rely on the defence of provocation if he had in fact caught his wife committing adultery. Accordingly, section 79 of the Singaporean Penal Code states:

[N]othing is an offence which is done by any person who is justified by law, or who by reason of a mistake of fact and not by reason of a mistake of law in good faith believes himself to be justified by law, in doing it.

This provision makes it clear that no offence has occurred where an individual believes themselves to be justified in their actions due to a mistake of fact of the situation; whether the existence of the mistake of fact was justified in the first place will depend not only on evidence available but also on socio-cultural factors prevalent in each Islamic jurisdiction.

An exception to this requirement however is the defence of intoxication; there is general consensus amongst Muslim jurists that where an individual drinks alcohol in the mistaken belief that it is water, he is exonerated of any blameworthiness given his mistake in fact on the realities of the situation.[13] The mistake of fact in having consumed alcohol does not mean that the resulting actions of the defendant were justified unlike other defences but rather a chain of causation is followed to the original mistake of fact which led to the actions. Where an individual was voluntarily intoxicated, no such consideration would occur. Such alcohol-related offences are of further interest as there may be an additional objective element involved in the sense that it would be thought that a 'good Muslim' may not be able to differentiate between alcohol and other beverages. Therefore, when dealing with the defence it may require greater emphasis on the personal character of the defendant.

Mistake of Law

Muslim jurists are generally reluctant to allow ignorance of law as a defence to subjects of an Islamic state. It is believed that every Muslim in an Islamic state is under a duty to acquire legal knowledge and in particular acquaint themselves with legal prohibitions as ordained in *Shari'a*.[14] To plead ignorance of the law

---

11   Risala or Resaleh is the reference book written by the Shi'a Jurists/Mojtahed for their followers. It contains a compilation of practical rulings applicable to all aspects of daily Muslim life. Every Shi'a Muslim must follow a Mojtahed, and live in accordance with his Risala.

12   *Shalla v The State*.

13   Abd al Qadir Udah,'Tashri'al-Jinai al-Islami' I: 439, cited in Tahir Mahmood (ed), *Criminal Law in Islam and the Muslim World* (1934) 130.

14   Asian-African Legal Consultative Organisation, *Human Rights in Islam* (2005) 31.

is indicative of ignorance of the Islamic religion itself which, in turn, evidences a lack of piety; being a 'bad Muslim' cannot be a defence. To allow such a defence would defeat the objectives of an Islamic state where teachings of *Shari'a* are of high importance. It is perhaps for such reasons that some jurisdictions make it clear that where mistake is available as a defence it is based on a mistake of fact even if the circumstances may overlap with a mistake of law. Article 79 of the Pakistan Penal Code states:

> [N]othing is an offence which is done by any person who is justified by law, or who by reason of a mistake
> of fact and not by reason of a mistake of law in good faith, believes himself to be justified by law, in doing it.

Thus, where a defendant's actions were not justified in law but he believed them to be justified due to a mistake of fact, the provisions allow for a defence of mistake of fact which led to a mistake of law. In a sense, defences are being accumulated together in order to reduce the blameworthiness of the defendant, and therefore ease the process.

However, in limited circumstances, mistake of law can be available as a defence to certain criminal acts, and may be accepted as a lawful excuse for illegal behaviour.[15] For instance, Article 198 of the Iranian Penal Code requires that for the act of theft to have been committed the defendant must be aware that stealing is religiously prohibited.[16] Whilst not directly allowing ignorance of law as a defence, the provision allows for it to be advanced as a defence which may be given due consideration in assessment of the overall circumstances. There is also general consensus on the point that mistake of law should be accepted where a defendant was unaware of a newly enacted law. This is especially relevant in Islamic jurisdictions which observe and give credibility to *fatwas* as a secondary source of law.

It is noteworthy that, despite the general reluctance to accept the defence as part of Islamic criminal law, approaches and understandings may vary between the different schools of thought. The *Hanafi* school of thought, for example, permits equitable consideration of cases involving an alleged mistake of law, especially by a recent convert, unless constructive knowledge can be implied.[17] In this regard, reliance can be played on the '*hadith* of lifted liability', which provides a presumption of innocence for, and removes criminal liability from, a defendant in a number of circumstances, including those of ignorance and mistake; it is thus suggested that the judge should perform an assessment of the extent to which the mistake is genuine or reasonable. Sheikh Ansari argued for an expansion on the traditionalist view; all sources should be read in conjunction to provide a complete picture of the law, and the law is illustrated by the prohibitions contained therein. Agreeing with the general Sunni and Shi'a position, Ansari accepts the lack of culpability of mistake of law, as well as fact, where the defendant is ignorant of the law and therefore any transgression he may have committed.[18] Interestingly, ample reputable *hadiths* are available which allow for possible acceptance of the doctrine of ignorance of law and it is questionable whether the reasons for limiting its availability is about upholding Islamic principles or really about state sovereignty.[19]

Mistakes can also arise from the definitions and interpretations of offences; drinking wine is specifically and explicitly prohibited under Islamic law, however, there is no mention of beer. Most Muslims extend the specified 'wine' to all alcoholic drinks; however, there is scope for misinterpretation and misunderstanding where the texts do not provide comprehensive and exhaustive guidance.

In this regard it is necessary to consider the impact of the availability of the defence to ethnic minorities of different sects of Islam who may fall foul of the legal provisions of an Islamic state despite the fact that their actions may be in line with the Islamic principles as followed within their own school of thought.

---

15   There is disparity between the various Islamic schools in the manner in which criminal defences such as the doctrine of mistake can be employed. Full discussion is beyond the scope of this chapter; therefore, the particular school of thought will be identified, where appropriate.

16   For example, the accused may have thought it was permissible under Shari'a to steal from a non-believer.

17   Intisar A Rabb, *The Benefit of Doubt in Islamic Law* (Cambridge University Press 2014) 211–212.

18   Ansari, Rasa'il 154–163.

19   Sahih Muslim, Hadith 1579: 'Once a man gave to the Prophet Pbuh a flask of wine as a gift. The Prophet Pbuh asked the man: Do you know that Allah has prohibited this? The man replied that he did not know of its prohibition. The man had not yet come to know what wine had been prohibited so he was not blamed or rebuked'; see also <http://xeniagreekmuslimah.wordpress.com/2011/03/30/when-ignorance-is-an-excuse/> accessed 10 October 2013.

Thus, for example, a defendant may find themselves guilty of adultery in Tunisia, which prohibits polygamy despite the fact that that it is held permissible within the primary sources themselves. Similarly, the concept of *Mu'tah*, or temporary marriage, is not generally observable by Sunni Muslims whilst it is by Shi'a Muslims. Furthermore, in some jurisdictions such as Iran a divorced woman is expected to observe a period of *Oudeh*[20] before she is able to remarry; but as this is not a unified approach between the different schools of thought in terms of the duration of *Oudeh*, she may find herself guilty of the offence of adultery. In a case in Sudan, a woman believed she was divorced because her husband had uttered the words and as per *Shari'a* this constitutes a divorce[21]. She went on to remarry to later find out that she was still legally married under the law. These examples are controversial in the sense that the reasons for the defence not being available is that they are expected to be aware of what has been ordained under *Shari'a*, and have in fact acted in accordance with a particular interpretation of it.

Individual Defences

Necessity

The defences of necessity, self-defence, and duress are derived from the same principles under Islamic criminal law, with the former acting as an underlying basis for the latter. Therefore it would more appropriate to commence discussion with the defence of necessity to allow better understanding of the other two defences.

Necessity (*Darurah*) is another general defence which is subject to varying approaches by the different schools of thought due to the need to balance the interests of society, whilst at the same time taking account of the specific circumstances of the defendant which led to criminality. Interestingly, there has been substantial discussion on the subject with alternative terms such as removing hardship (*Raf al-haraj*), need (*Hajah*), force majeure (*Ja'ihah*), and compulsion (*Ikrah*) being used interchangeably when considering the defence of necessity. As a result, the defence of necessity can overlap in discussions with self-defence and the defence of duress.

In general, Islamic criminal law approaches necessity in a particularly equitable light given it is permitted in the primary sources of *Shari'a*; it is stated in the *Qur'an*:

> He hath only forbidden you dead meat, and blood, and flesh of swine, and that on which any other name hath been invoked besides that of God. But if one is forced by necessity, without wilful obedience, nor transgressing due limits, then one is guiltless. For God is Oft-forgiving Most Merciful.[22]

Similarly, a number of *hadiths* are available which comment on the issue of necessity and its availability: '[T]he Apostle of Allah was asked about hanging fruit. He replied: If a needy person takes some and does not take a supply away in his garment, he is not to be blamed. . . .'[23] The direct application of these principles of Islamic law can be seen very quickly when analysing the provisions in different jurisdictions. Thus, in Yemen, it was decided that the sale by the mother of a property belonging to her child who was under 15 years of age was valid if the family was starving.[24] Similarly, Article 198 of the Iranian Penal Code states that the offence of theft is only complete where 'the thief is not destitute' as well as that 'the theft is not committed in a famine year' thus highlighting the specific need to take hunger and poverty into consideration.

Incidentally, despite the majority of sources referring to situations involving hunger and poverty, Muslim jurists have not attempted to limit the availability of the defence in this regard irrespective of the general desire to narrow the scope. General consensus seems to be that the defence of necessity should not be entirely limited to only situations as mentioned in the primary sources, but how far the ambit should be stretched remains debatable.

---

20 Alternatively pronounced Iddeh.
21 *Sudan Government v Adam Elrayah Elzaki & Another* AC/Maj Ct 1184/74.
22 Qur'an [2:173].
23 Sahih Bukhari, narrated by Abdullah Ibn Amr Ibn Al-As, Book 18, Number 1706.
24 Yemeni High Court of Cassation – Personal Status Division [1999] Judgment No 401/1420 AH.

Generally, the defence of necessity consists of the following elements: a compelling situation; a genuine fear of death or of severe injury; such injury should be directed to one of the five fundamentals (preservation of religion, preservation of life, preservation of mind, preservation of offspring, preservation of material wealth); committing an illegal act is the only way out of such a situation.[25]

In many Islamic jurisdictions, the act of necessity does not need to be against oneself but may be to protect another person. Article 61 of the Egyptian Penal Code sets out the elements of a necessity defence stating that there will be no punishment 'for an act performed out of necessity (*daruratan*) to prevent the actor or another from imminent and grievous harm, as long as the actor did not create the circumstances that engendered the necessity and had no other means of preventing the harm'. Under Egyptian law, therefore, necessity, once successfully established, is a complete and justificatory defence.[26] Article 95 of the Afghan Penal Code provides 'a person who for the sake of saving his own soul or good or the soul or good of someone else comes to face great and immediate danger, such as to be able to ward it off without committing an act of crime, shall not be considered responsible provided that the person has not deliberately caused the said danger and that the damage to be avoided should be greater than the damage from the act of crime'. Article 55 of the Iranian Penal Code goes even further by explicitly extending it to property as well.

It is also of note that in Iran, an individual would be able to argue that their actions were necessary to save the honour or property of another, albeit in such circumstances the defence available is that of self-defence rather than necessity irrespective of the fact that the individual is protecting a third person and not themselves. This may be due to the fact that a defendant who protects their honour or that of another is viewed as having been justified in their actions but there is a reluctance to categorise necessity as a justificatory defence. The defence relies on the notion that it was necessary to break an Islamic principle; to suggest that breaking a principle was justified sits uncomfortably with many who would rather consider it an excusatory defence by which the mercy of God can be invoked. Moreover, to consider it a justification would suggest that necessity will make a prohibited act legal which is not the case; the act remains prohibited but the state of necessity reduces culpability. It is perhaps due to such concerns that there is no consensus on the point.

In summary, the defence of necessity requires four conditions to be met:

> [F]irst, a great danger to the life or property of the perpetrator or another person, such as a fire or a flood, must exist; second, the commission of the crime must be necessary to avert danger; third, the perpetrator must not have intentionally caused the danger; and finally, the crime committed in order to avert the danger must have been proportionate to the danger.[27]

Thus, despite allowing application of the defence in various circumstances, there are still limits on its ambit. Indeed, general consensus suggests that the aim or object of the act of necessity should be of a higher value than that of the law to be broken. For example, a theft of milk to save the life of a child would outweigh the theft itself. It is for this reason that the defence of necessity is not available in murder cases as according to Islam the life of all Muslims is equal and therefore the killing of one to save another cannot be considered an act of necessity.

Self-Defence and Excessive Self-Defence

Unlike necessity, self-defence does not have such limits, and where it is accepted as a defence it allows complete exoneration of blameworthiness. Apart from the *Hanbali* school of thought, there is general consensus that it is obligatory to defend life against attacks even if this is at the expense of the life of the attacker. This is because a distinction is drawn between the victim in cases of necessity and in self-defence whereby in the latter situation the victim's actions justify such force to be used. In essence therefore the balancing exercise by which the act of necessity should be of a higher value is still relevant, but in circumstances of self-defence

---

25   Azhar Javed, *Intoxication & Self Defence: A Comparative Study of Principles of English Law and Shari'ah* (Leeds University 2004) 92.

26   Sadiq Reza, ch 5, 14.

27   Kevin Heller & Markus Dubber (eds), *The Handbook of Comparative Criminal Law* (Stanford University Press 2010) 333.

the victim's actions tip the scale in favour of the defendant. The 'defence of one's life is also a valid defence if a person, while being on the point of starvation, kills the owner of food necessary to save his life, after the latter's refusal to give it to him; for in that case the victim acted unlawfully against the killer'.[28] On one understanding it may be that the blame is shifted to the victim in this regard, who did not act as a 'good Muslim' should when faced with another who was starving given the emphasis of charity within Islam. This is controversial when considering the principles of individual autonomy, although it does seem that limits are placed; therefore the defendant will need to have been starving to death with no other recourse and even in the situation of a famine the defendant is not allowed to kill in order to eat the victim's flesh and it remains prohibited at all times.[29]

The *Qur'an* states: '[A]nd spend in the way of Allah and cast not yourselves to perdition with your own hands, and do good (to others); surely Allah loves the doers of good',[30] and this is interpreted as having decreed a duty on Muslims to save themselves where they are able to or more widely, pursue retaliation where it is just. For some this has extended even further to situations of war and other defensive measures with suggestions that those killed when attempting to defend in such a manner will be classed as martyrs. It is therefore from such considerations of self-defence that the concept of *Jihad* can be drawn. In fact, by stretching such principles further, the collateral damage which naturally arises out of such situations is defended on the basis of necessity and self-defence. This also demonstrates how defences can be accumulated together in Islamic criminal law so as to allow assessment in totality.

Of further relevance is the extension of the concept of self-defence in Islamic criminal law to not only protecting yourself, your family, property or honour but also that of others, thus including steps taken to stop a crime in progress from occurring. Support from the encompassment of halting a crime within self-defence may derive from a *hadith*; Anas Ibn Malik reported the Prophet stating, 'help your brother, whether he is an oppressor or is being oppressed' and on being asked how the oppressor can be helped the response given was, 'by seizing his hand'.[31] This in essence puts forward the 'good Muslim' dichotomy once again where an individual's actions are judged from within an Islamically objective perspective.

The defence is only available, however, when the actions of the defendant are considered proportionate and it is generally agreed that the acts must not exceed the level of violence necessary to defend oneself against the aggressor. Such requirements are certainly embodied in various legal provisions of different Islamic jurisdictions; Article 49 of the Indonesian Penal Code states that:

> [N]ot punishable shall be the person who commits an act necessitated by the defence of his own or another one's body, chastity or property against direct or immediate threatening unlawful assault. Not punishable shall be the overstepping of the bounds of necessary defence, if it has been the immediate result of a severe emotion caused by the assault.

Article 61 of the Iranian Penal Code, for example, states that the actions must be proportionate to the danger or aggression and not excessive; whilst Article 60 of the Afghan Penal Code requires proportionality as well as the acts to be the only way of removing the danger; Article 99 of the Pakistan Penal Code states 'the right of private defence in no case extends to the inflicting of more harm than it is necessary to inflict for the purpose of defence'. In each Code, the defence is unavailable where time was available to seek help from the police and public authorities thus highlighting the need for imminent threat and no alternative means by which to protect oneself.

It is interesting to note that Islamic jurisdictions require proportionality in assessing the availability of the defence, whereby suggestions have been made (above) that a starving individual killing an owner for food after being refused would be justified. It appears that whilst self-defence, *prima facie*, has a wide ambit and can encompass various situations, it is limited by an assessment of the circumstances of the particular case and therefore requires assessment from an objective perspective. Perhaps a parent who kills to save his or

---

28   Rudolph Peters, *Crime and Punishment in Islamic Law, Theory and Practice from the Sixteenth to the Twenty-First Centuries* (Cambridge University Press 2005) 25.

29   ibid.

30   *Qur'an* [2:195].

31   Sahih Bukhari, Book 85, Number 84.

her children will be more likely to be afforded the defence than one who kills only for him- or herself. It is also questionable how saving oneself or another from starvation is to be classified as self-defence rather than necessity; in fact to classify it as necessity would be more appropriate so as to not justify killing another in such situations. Alternatively, it may be that such a school of thought is now redundant given that at today's date it is unlikely that there is only one source from where food can be acquired.

A discrepancy is further uncovered when noting that an individual also has the right to self-defence in aid of property, whether that of your own or of another. Therefore what of the situation where a starving individual and the owner of the food both rely on self-defence with the former defending their life and the latter their property? More important perhaps is the consideration that defence of property allows use of excessive force, including death, which is demonstrated in a *fatwa* by a nineteenth century Malikite *Mufti* from Egypt, in which the death during a fight over ownership of a calf was justified.[32] In any event, provisions of law in various Islamic jurisdictions continue to require a proportionate response in such circumstances, and it may in fact be the case that the balancing act of values required when assessing the defence of necessity forms a part of the assessment when deciding upon self-defence over life or property.

On the other hand, whilst acceptability of excessive self-defence to the point of killing in cases of starvation is questionable, it appears to be clear where protecting honour is the focus. In fact self-defence may be put forward as a double shield for defendants as they are not only protecting their honour by killing another but also halting a crime from occurring. This would be the case in particular for a woman who, due to cultural reasons, would be expected to defend herself with all her might and stop an aggressor who is attacking her honour so as to prove her lack of consent.[33] In such circumstances the concepts of proportionality would be reduced to a lower burden of proof, given honour would be placed at a higher standing for a woman, perhaps even above life under *Shari'a*.

Duress by Threats/Circumstances

The defence of duress has a direct impact on a core aspect of the completion of an offence; the intent. Whilst in cases of self-defence and necessity the defendant committed both the act and had the correlating intention to do so, with duress this latter aspect is not available and therefore acts as a complete defence. Intent (*Niyah*)[34] is especially important in Islamic criminal law as it is an independent component without which an individual is deemed innocent and should not be punished. Indeed primary sources of *Shari'a* stress the point of forgiving acts made through duress very clearly[35] which are applied to various areas including criminal and family law. Interestingly it has been suggested that coercion does not only excuse the act but avoids illegality altogether 'in cases of eating carrion or drinking wine. In these acts, only the rights of God are involved and not the rights of men, therefore doing them without evil intent makes them perfectly legal'.[36]

Islamic jurisdictions make provisions for the defence of duress. For instance, Article 95 of the Afghan Penal Code states: '[A] person who commits a crime under the influence of a moral or material force, repulsion of which is not possible otherwise, shall not be considered responsible'. Similarly, Article 54 of the Iranian Penal Code holds that:

> [I]f the offence is subject to the *Ta'zir* and deterrent punishment and it was committed under duress or unbearable force, the offender will not be punished. In such a case the person who has forced the offender to commit the offence will be regarded as the actual offender.

However, Islamic criminal law still places limits on the availability of duress in line with the principles of *Shari'a*. In fact, Iranian law does not recognise duress as a defence to murder because, as stated in relation to the defence of necessity, as all lives of Muslims are sacred, one cannot choose their own life over that of

---

32 Rudolph Peters (n 28) 26.

33 ibid.

34 Alternatively, Niyat.

35 Al-Baihaqi and others, narrated by Ibn Abbas, the Prophet said, 'truly Allah has for my sake pardoned the mistakes and forgetfulness of my community, and for what they have done under force or duress'.

36 David F Forte, 'Islamic Law and the Crime of Theft' 34 Cleveland L Rev 57.

another. Therefore, whilst self-defence and to a certain extent even the defence of necessity can be classified as justificatory defences, the defence of duress remains only excusatory and is available only in limited circumstances.

The defence of duress of circumstance has a noticeable overlap with other defences, especially necessity. Indeed it may be argued that duress of circumstances does not in fact exist under Islamic criminal law as it is encompassed within the concept of necessity. Alternatively, duress of circumstances does not exist in its own right but rather exists as a combination with duress by threats. Thus for example, in the case of Zafran Bibi in Pakistan, she was acquitted after it was revealed that she had been pressurised into accusing another person of *zina-bil-jabr* in order to protect the younger brother of her husband who had also previously committed *zina-bil-jabr* with her.[37] This was due to the combined reasons of threats and circumstances given the cultural influences involved.

The compulsion must be actual and not merely conjectural, with the defendant only being considered coerced where they have been beaten, wounded, imprisoned or a threat is made against their life or bodily integrity.[38] Under both Iranian and Afghani law, the threat must be imminent and obvious with no alternative recourse such as the ability to seek help from the authorities. It is further stated that:

> [A] mere beating is not enough: it must instil a fear for one's life or limbs. Consequently, a single blow or a single day's imprisonment is insufficient to constitute duress, unless the victim is of high rank whose dignity would be harmed and impaired by lesser blows than would be necessary for a common person.[39]

This may seem unfair, however, when considering the cultural circumstances that individuals may find themselves in particular jurisdictions across the world. In the case of Zafran Bibi, for example, her duress arose out of the fact that she was pressurised into protecting her brother in law which is understandable given the time, place and context of her life and yet generally such circumstances will not be given due consideration. It is noteworthy that Zafran Bibi was in fact only acquitted as a result of public outrage and wide support for her, rather than purely on the defence advanced.

General Mental Condition Defences

Insanity
Insanity under Islamic law can be defined as an 'impairment of the power which distinguishes between fair and foul [good and evil] and conceives the consequences of those things. This power is no longer in evidence or it cannot do its function', or 'the impairment of the power in which the conception of the whole is achieved'.[40]

The defence of insanity involves significant questions regarding the mental capacity, and therefore intent, of the accused; under Islamic law there is no duty or punishment for the insane. The highest degree of legal capacity is that of the free Muslim who is sane ('*aqil*) and of age (*baligh)* and is therefore considered fully responsible (*mukallaf*). The *mukallaf* has the capacity to contract and to dispose (*tasarruf*), is bound to fulfil religious duties, and is fully subject to criminal law, being capable of deliberate intent ('*amd*).[41] Under Islamic criminal law, without full mental capacity it is a miscarriage of justice and against equitable principles to treat a defendant in an identical manner to an offender who was fully aware of their actions, and the consequences. The considerations are therefore similar to the defence of duress and in turn the defence of insanity would be classed as excusatory. Interestingly, it is noteworthy that in passing judgment Islamic judges should be wary of terming it as excusatory or even as a defence as to do so would still suggest wrongdoing and the *Qur'an*ic principles are clear that the insane should not be apportioned any.

An example of the application of insanity as a defence can be found at Section 84 of the Malaysian Penal Code (Act 574), demonstrating the inherent link between insanity and the lack of *mens rea* at the time of committing a crime. It states:

---

37   *Mst. Zafran Bibi v The State* [2002] PLD FSC 1.
38   Forte (n 36) 57.
39   ibid.
40   Kutaiba S Chaleby, *Forensic Psychiatry in Islamic Jurisprudence* (The International Institute of Islamic Thought) 20.
41   Azyumardi Azra and Wayne Hudson, *Islam Beyond Conflict* (Ashgate Publishing 2008) 158.

[N]othing is an offence which is done by a person who, at the time of doing it, by reason of unsoundness of mind, is incapable of knowing the nature of the act, or that he is doing what is either wrong or contrary to law.

Shari'a recognises three types of insanity: absolute (continuous/permanent), intermittent, and partial. If affected by continuous insanity the accused is entirely unable to reason properly; those afflicted by intermittent insanity will sometimes be capable of reasonable cognitive thought and, at others, suffer a total loss of mental faculties; and the accused suffering from partial insanity will have some perception, cognitive ability and awareness of actions and consequences in some circumstances, but lacks these abilities in other situations or environments and may experience periods of absolute insanity. The sufferer of absolute insanity is not held criminally responsible under Islamic law; sufferers of partial or intermittent insanity will be held criminally responsible for acts committed whilst cognisant of actions and with the capability of reasoning.

The ambit of insanity as a defence in Islamic criminal law has been broadened by some scholars with the inclusion of two additional mental conditions beyond that of a mental disorder characterised by disturbed reasoning. The sudden and temporary loss of reason due to alarm, terror, bewilderment or consternation is recognised as 'sudden perplexity', or *dahish*; *dahish* is considered similar to insanity in respect of criminal responsibility by the Hanafi school of thought. This is akin to the concept of automatism applied in Western jurisdictions. Interestingly, however, automatism is not limited to just the insanity defence and can be used collectively with other defences.[42]

In contrast, there is consensus that mental retardation, or '*atah*', is distinguishable from insanity; although an accused person suffering from mental retardation will be treated in the same manner to an insane individual, if the condition is severe, for the purposes of criminal responsibility. Mental retardation is seen as a diminished ability of the mind to reason effectively, therefore to appreciate the nature and consequences of actions, and can include sufferers of other 'diminished reasoning' conditions such as Alzheimer's. In milder cases of retardation where mental development is limited to that of a child who has some ability to distinguish between 'right and wrong', but certainly not an adult's competence and capacity for such, it is argued that the reasoning applied to the 'rational youth' (*al-sabi al-mummayiz*) recognised in Islamic Jurisprudence should also apply by analogy. The rational youth is ascribed partial culpability for his actions, as he can appreciate that some behaviours are right and some are wrong and therefore has some (not full) mental capacity.[43] It may be concerning that those of ill health, such as dementia sufferers, are categorized in such a manner; however, this is because of the need to focus on the mental elements in line with Islamic principles rather than in order to demean or victimize the defendant.

Islamic law also recognises that any offence committed whilst unconscious is lacking in intent, and therefore an offender who was unconscious at the time of his offence will not be culpable for his actions; '[t] he pen is lifted from three people: [a] person sleeping until he wakes up; an insane person until he regains sanity; and a child until he reaches the age of puberty'.[44] Offences committed by an individual who has a documented sleep disorder (such as night terrors, sleepwalking, etc.), whilst asleep and therefore susceptible to the effect of the disorder, can fall under the defence of insanity, due to lack of intent at the time the offence was committed.

A defendant who is deemed insane (at the time of the commission of the offence) is not held fully accountable for his or her actions; however, this does not necessarily mean the offender will escape punishment. Financial liability in murder cases, for example, remains applicable. This is because consideration is given to the victim's family who are also blameless; however, this does cause a contradiction whereby even a full defence does not fully exonerate a defendant. An insanity defence may also prove ineffective if the accused has committed an offence for which intent does not form part of the definition.

---

42   Chaleby (n 40) 21.

43   ibid.

44   Sunan Ibn Majah, *Book of Divorce*, Hadith No. 2042.

Intoxication

In Islam, intoxication is seen as a state in which mental capacity has been suspended until return to sobriety; its use as a defence therefore raises the question of *mens rea* and an individual's level of self-control over their actions during commission of a crime whilst intoxicated.

Intoxication as a result of duress, mistake or necessity does not attract criminal liability; that is, where circumstances bring about the forced consumption of intoxicants on an unwitting or unwilling Muslim, the defendant will not be liable for any illegal acts committed whilst suffering an unintentional temporary absence of mental capacity. This analysis is similar to those discussed under duress in that the individual did not have the intention, or *niyah*, to carry out the act and without this essential component the offence is not complete. Islam treats intoxicated persons as lacking in mental capacity for the duration of their intoxicated state, suggesting that such an individual is incapable of forming intent. Similarly, medical treatments that may cause intoxication are permissible under the exemption for necessity thus highlighting an accumulation of defences once more.

It is not a complete defence however, and an individual who, whilst intoxicated, inflicts damage upon another person or property is liable to pay compensation to the victim given that the victim is similarly not to blame. This is consistent with the treatment in terms of the defence of self-defence where the victim is to blame and also with the defence of duress where although the victim may be blameless the third party who threatened the defendant will be held responsible. However, the defendant will not face any corporal punishment where involuntary intoxication is accepted. In this regard it is viewed as an excusatory defence arising out of involuntary circumstances.

Under Malaysian Law, intoxication does not constitute a defence unless; the person charged at the time of the act or omission did not know that such act or omission was wrong or did not know what he was doing; and the state of intoxication was caused without his consent by the malicious or negligent act of another person; or the person charged was by reason of intoxication insane, temporarily or otherwise, at the time of such act or omission.[45]

Intoxication, where voluntary, is a notorious defence to be relied upon given the direct opposition of intoxication to the principles of *Shari'a*; the *Qur'an* provides: '[T]hey ask you about intoxicating drinks and games of chance. Say: 'In both there is great evil, though some use for people, but their evil is greater than their usefulness'.[46] At the same time, despite the disinclination to accept this as a defence, the differing schools of thought have not entirely dismissed it either. It is also important to remember that voluntary intoxication is in itself a crime and therefore to raise the defence against one offence will automatically make an individual liable for another.

The Hanafi school of thought considers that those who have become intoxicated voluntarily should be held to the same standard of conduct as a sober individual thus dismissing the effect of the intoxication altogether. It is therefore not recognised as a defence. There are several notable exceptions to this rule including apostasy, confession of a *hudud* offence or any statements made contradicting a previous deposition.[47] Due to the lack of mental capacity of an intoxicated individual, the requisite intention for apostasy cannot be accurately evidenced. Similarly, in relation to statements and confessions, benefit of doubt is afforded to the defendant that in an intoxicated condition the individual was unable to comprehend what was being said and its consequences.

However, the Hanafi school limits the ability to retract a confession secured in certain situations where despite the confession evidential burdens can be satisfied. For example, where an amount of damage can be easily quantified, such as in a theft case, liability in damages may arise despite any retraction of the confession once sober, especially if the circumstances of the theft can be verified as correct. Similarly, a confession to other categories of offences may still attract liability once sober, even when the accused retracts it. If the intoxicated individual confesses to a crime which has violated an exclusive right of man (for example, an offence punishable by *qisas*) this confession cannot later be retracted; he will be punished, according to the law, once sober.

---

45   Malaysian Penal Code, act 574, sec 85.
46   *Qur'an* [2:219].
47   Ibn Jujaym, *Al-Ashbah Wa Al-Nazair* (Moa'ssasa Al-Halbi Linnasher wa a-Touzih 1968) 310.

In the Hanbali school of thought, the voluntarily intoxicated individual is liable for any crime committed whilst in that condition. It is considered that intellectual capacity has not been destroyed but has rather been 'hidden' behind the effects of the intoxicating substance. Once again, intoxication is itself a crime, and therefore cannot be used as a defence against crimes committed whilst under the influence. A further similarity with the Hanafite position occurs with regards to confessions of the voluntarily intoxicated individual; he knows not what he says and therefore cannot be held to any confession made during the course of intoxication.[48]

Essentially, therefore there is general consensus that, save for in exceptional circumstances which are more to do with satisfying the burdens of evidence, voluntary intoxication is not available as a defence in Islamic criminal law. There is an element of public policy to this stance, preventing the use of voluntary intoxication as a defence to criminal acts is a deterrent against a wave of crime committed by intoxicated persons to which no liability could attach. Moreover, the religious and moral demands of Islam require continued adherence to religious law and piety and intoxication causes a loss of inhibitions and self-control which could threaten this structure.

It is possible that this forms the basis for why, intoxication, as a defence is not prescribed in the Criminal Codes of all Islamic jurisdictions, for example, the Egyptian Penal Code contains no Articles specifically providing a defence of intoxication. However, Article 62 effectively establishes a form of defence (excusatory) for involuntary intoxication by including acts committed under the influence of drugs ingested unknowingly or by force. The Court of Cassation has expanded on the Code provision by stating that intoxication, whether voluntary or involuntary, can negate specific intent as a general matter and particularly in the case of intentional homicide.[49]

Residual Catch-All Defences/Existence and Ambit of Statutory Defences

Given the individualities of each Islamic jurisdiction, naturally defences available under provisions of law vary in their ambit depending on the approaches by respective countries. It has already been discussed, for example, how the availability of the defence of duress was limited where help could be sought from the authorities. However, Islamic criminal law does allow catch-all defences which can be applied in all circumstances; age-related capacity and the legal duty to intervene are two such examples. It must be noted that for some schools of thought insanity would also be considered a catch-all defence; the level of assessment involved as well as the fact financial liability may remain applicable.

A *Hadith* of the Prophet Mohammad states: '[T]hree persons are not accountable: a child until he or she reaches the age of puberty, a person in sleep until awake and an insane person until he becomes normal'. The capacity to understand the consequences and effects of an illegal act has been discussed elsewhere in this chapter; however, it is significant when considering the defence of a minor accused of criminal conduct. Under Islamic law, minors reach the age of criminal responsibility on reaching puberty (*balig wa rashid*) whereby they are considered adults with full understanding.[50] Different countries integrate the Islamic age of criminal responsibility in different ways, for example Egypt sets the minimum age as 12 years old, as does Turkey. In contrast, Iran differentiates between the rate of female and male maturity, and according to Article 1210 of the Civil Code a female reaches the age of criminal responsibility at 9 lunar years of age (8 years 9 months), and a male at 15 lunar years (14 years 7 months). Article 49 of the Iranian Criminal Code provides an exemption from criminal liability for children; however, it must be considered that the definition of a child in Islamic law terms is a pre-pubescent minor/as per the definitions provided by the Civil Code. Moreover, other Articles provide for offenders who are 'minors', such as Article 50; a strong indication that the definition of a 'minor' in the Penal Code of Iran is an individual under 18 but over the statutory-defined age of criminal responsibility.

The severity of punishment meted out to child offenders also varies depending on the territory; current consensus on the new Iranian Penal Code agrees that the death penalty remains in place for those who are

---

48   ibid.
49   Reza (n 26).
50   Islam divides stages of childhood development between *sabiy ghar mumayiz* (a child incapable of understanding, generally under seven years old), *sabiyy mummayyiz* (a child with weak understanding, generally age 7 to 15) and *balig wa rashid*, discussed above.

balig wa Rashid, although punishment may be delayed until they reach the age of 18. In contrast, Egyptian 12-to-15-year-olds usually receive social punishments, and for those aged 15 to 18 a scaled down version of an adult sentence is imposed; Egypt does not sentence children to death.

Using age-related capacity as a defence under Islamic law is therefore subject to jurisdictional variances; the applicable guidelines in one state can be very different to another, and therefore the availability of the defence is highly dependent on the particular interpretation or definition of adulthood. As can be seen, the *Hadith* of the Prophet Muhammad defines adulthood as puberty, yet States may choose to introduce legislation assigning an adult level of criminal responsibility to a child on the basis of age, rather than sexual maturity.

Certain Islamic states have introduced a positive duty to intervene to (and to assist in effecting a) rescue.[51] Consequently, those abiding by that duty are protected from unintended consequences arising from the exercise of said duty; especially where the consequences for the victim would have been worse was it not for the individual intervening on their behalf. The legal duty to intervene often runs in parallel with a moral duty to intervene; religious values assist in the definition of moral values and, in an Islamic system, therefore legal requirements. This is, once again, an application of the 'good Muslim' dichotomy which can be used widely and varyingly.

Under Section 88 of the Singaporean Penal Code, 'nothing, which is not intended to cause death, is an offence by reason of any harm which it may cause, or be intended by the doer to cause, or be known by the doer to be likely to cause, to any person for whose benefit it is done in good faith, and who has given a consent, whether express or implied, to suffer that harm, or to take the risk of that harm'. Those intervening to effect a rescue in Singapore are therefore legally protected from any unintended consequences afflicting the victim and flowing from the rescue attempt.

Conclusion

In Islamic jurisdictions, there is great emphasis upon any available general defences within criminal proceedings in line with the principles of *Shari'a*, especially given the harsh sentences that may be decreed. It is for such reasons that focus is placed on subjective elements; the need to ensure guilt of the defendant, however, may be at the expense of the victim. It is also apparent that objective elements are still applied in order to ensure compatibility of actions with *Shari'a*; thus the 'good Muslim' ideal is in operation. This assessment from the 'good Muslim' perspective can cause uncertainty when considering the variations between different sects and schools of thought. The need to ensure compatibility of actions with principles of *Shari'a* also leads to interesting discussions as to the classification of general defences as excusatory or justificatory. In any event however, whilst the basis of general defences remains rooted in primary sources of *Shari'a*, application depends on the jurisdictional and cultural variations of each individual Islamic State.

---

51   Law Reform Commission, *Report on the Civil Liability of Good Samaritans and Volunteers* (LRC 93 2009) 19.

Chapter 18

The Netherlands

Erik Gritter

General Issues

Justificatory and Excusatory Defences—Distinction and Seat in the Offence Structure

The Dutch system of general defences consists of a written part, laid down in the general part of the Dutch Penal Code (DPC), and a collection of unwritten defences, accepted in the case law of the Dutch Supreme Court (Hoge Raad). This system stands next to a diverse system of (written) *special* defences that are linked to particular offences. Both the written and the unwritten general defences have evolved gradually over the years, leading to a 'dynamic system' of various exceptional circumstances.[1] All Dutch general defences are applicable to *any* offence, including, therefore, offences like murder and voluntary homicide.[2] The defences, if accepted, work as full or complete defences.[3]

The offence structure in Dutch criminal law is basically tripartite in nature, and the system of general defences can be understood accordingly. The first stage to be examined[4] is that of the offence description as can be found in the DPC or (for the greater part) in separate laws. As for felonies (*misdrijven*), the offence description ideally consists of an *actus reus* or conduct part (either a positive act, an omission or a state of affairs) and *mens rea* or a subjective element (for instance intention). As far as misdemeanours (*overtredingen*) are concerned, the subjective element might be absent. Apart from the influence of general defences in a concrete case, proof of the *actus reus* can be sufficient for a conviction when a defendant is charged with an *overtreding*.[5]

Normally, when the offence description is fulfilled, the act committed is presumed to be unlawful (second stage of examination), and the offender is presumed to be blameworthy (third stage of examination); unlawfulness (*wederrechtelijkheid*) and blameworthiness or culpability (*verwijtbaarheid*) act as general (albeit presumed) conditions for criminal liability. The presumption of unlawfulness might be negated by the existence of a ground for justification; blameworthiness is absent if a ground for excuse exists.

Grounds of justification are necessity or a conflict of duties (*overmacht-noodtoestand*, art 40 DPC), self-defence (art 41(1) DPC), acting in the exercise of legal provisions (art 42 DPC), acting in the exercise of a lawful civil order (art 43(1) DPC) and absence of substantive unlawfulness (case law). The latter may be said to include miscellaneous justificatory circumstances like consent and acting in a professional (medical) capacity, as will be discussed later on. Grounds for excuse are: absence of accountability (*ontoerekeningsvatbaarheid*, art 39 DPC), duress or mental pressure (*psychische overmacht*, art 40 DPC), excessive self-defence (art

---

1 J de Hullu, *Materieel strafrecht – Over algemene leerstukken van strafrechtelijke aansprakelijkheid naar Nederlands recht* (5th edn, Uitgeverij Kluwer BV 2011) 369 ff.

2 Murder (*moord*, art 289 DPC) in Dutch criminal law is described as any intentional and premeditated killing of another person. It may be punished with a temporary prison sentence up to 30 years or imprisonment for life. Voluntary homicide (doodslag, art 287 DPC) is defined as any intentional killing of another person (the maximum sentence is 15 years imprisonment).

3 If a general defence is not accepted, the circumstances that constituted the defence might work as (non-statutory) extenuating circumstances that can influence the sentence.

4 See Michael Bohlander, *Principles of German Criminal Law* (Hart Publishing 2009) 16, who talks of 'three stages of examination' in the tripartite structure of offences.

5 Dutch criminal evidence law not only requires sufficient evidence for the proof of a charge, but also that the court, upon this evidence, is 'convinced' that the defendant has committed the alleged offence. See art 338 Dutch Code of Criminal Procedure (DCCP).

41(2) DPC), acting upon an unlawful civil order (art 43(2) DPC) and lack of all culpability (case law). The existence of a ground for justification or excuse will lead to a 'discharge'; according to Dutch procedural law terminology, a discharge is possible if the defendant cannot be punished for a *proven* act, due to either a justification or an excuse. If the act itself cannot be proved, the defendant will be 'acquitted'.[6]

When the DPC came into force (1886), the division of defences in grounds for justification and grounds for excuse was still evolving in Dutch doctrine. The legislator had divided the general defences along other lines. This was a division between internal and external grounds for 'absence of liability'. This division was gradually replaced by a distinction between grounds of justification and grounds for excuse.[7]

Not every offence in Dutch criminal law follows the tripartite structure. With some offences, unlawfulness and/or culpability is a constituent element already of the offence description. In those cases, the general defences—related to either unlawfulness or culpability—will in fact act as absence of proof defences. If, for example, a defence of necessity (art 40 DPC) is raised and accepted in case of an unlawful violation of someone's property (art 350 DPC), the defendant will be 'acquitted' (and not 'discharged') because the unlawfulness of the violation—an essential written element of the offence—cannot be proved. According to the Supreme Court of the Netherlands (*Hoge Raad der Nederlanden* (HR)), unlawfulness generally has the broad meaning of 'violation of the law'.[8] Therefore, all defences aimed to attack unlawfulness will normally be 'examined' at the first stage, if unlawfulness is part of the offence description. In crimes of (gross) negligence, both unlawfulness and culpability are part of the offence description. The defence of excusable mistake of fact for instance, in Dutch law a variation of the unwritten excusatory defence of lack of all culpability, will in these cases—if accepted—lead to an acquittal.

Conceptual Foundations

An important issue in the examination of a general defence is the question of which viewpoint should be taken. With regard to self-defence and excessive self-defence, De Hullu discusses three possible viewpoints of relevance[9]: 1) an objective test 'afterwards', in which circumstances may be of relevance that became known after the commission of the offence; 2) an objective test at the time of the commission of the offence, which takes the viewpoint of an objective observer at that time; and 3) the subjective viewpoint of the perpetrator at the time of the commission of the offence.[10] According to De Hullu, a 'more or less' objective test seems to be generally accepted in Dutch criminal law.[11] The fact that this viewpoint is not entirely objective, is related to the fact that it concerns an *ex ante* test, while personal aspects in relation to the perpetrator may be considered.[12] This leaves the question, according to De Hullu, whether there is room for 'putative defences', now that mistakes that are purely subjective do not seem to be of relevance. In case of a 'putative defence', the perpetrator has (objectively) misjudged the situation, and mistakenly believed that a defence was available. If the observer would have made the same mistake (in case of self-defence for example, he would have also evaluated the situation as 'immediately threatening'), then one can talk of actual self-defence instead of putative self-defence.[13] But if the objective observer would *not* have made the same mistake as the defendant, the defence must be denied.[14] This leaves the conclusion, that there is not much room for putative defences in Dutch criminal law.

---

6   I use 'acquittal' for the verdict of *vrijspraak*, when there is no proof for the charge; the term 'discharge' will be used for the verdict of *ontslag van alle rechtsvervolging*, attached to the existence of a general defence (when the offence is proven, and seen as a punishable offence). A 'discharge' may also follow, if a proven act cannot be seen as a 'punishable' act.

7   De Hullu has put the distinction into perspective, and he takes the viewpoint that it is more important to look at the inner value of the different grounds, than at their classification. De Hullu (n 1) 282 ff.

8   De Hullu (n. 1) 187; DH de Jong & G Knigge, *Ons Strafrecht deel 1 – Het materiële strafrecht* (14th edn, Deventer, Kluwer 2003) 94.

9   De Hullu (n 1) 320 ff.

10   De Hullu (n 1) 320. The distinction is derived from the case note of N. Keijzer on HR 23 October 1984, NJ 1986, 56.

11   De Hullu (n 1) 321.

12   Case note Keijzer on 23 October 1984, NJ 1986, 56.

13   De Hullu (n 1) 321. According to Keijzer, putative self-defence presupposes a wrong decision (which decision requires an objective test). But he acknowledges that it is sometimes hard to distinguish between the different situations (case note on HR 23 October 1984, NJ 1986, 56).

14   De Hullu (n 1) 321.

Cumulation/Cumulative or Alternative Pleading of Defences

Dutch criminal procedure is in essence inquisitorial of nature, with some distinct adversarial features. Dutch criminal courts actively investigate the merits of the charge. Therefore, in Dutch criminal law one cannot speak of a 'burden of proof' with regard to the pleading or acceptance of a general defence. If a general defence has been raised[15] in court by the defendant, it is for the court to investigate the claim and decide whether it should be accepted. The standard of acceptance is the 'likelihood' (*aannemelijkheid*) of the claimed circumstances[16]; this is a lower standard than the standard of proof when elements of the offence are concerned.[17,18]

A ground for excuse logically denies blame for an *unlawful* act. Therefore, in its verdict, a court will firstly discuss any claims of justification if grounds for excuse have also been raised. Only if in such a situation a defence of justification is denied, the court will turn to an assessment of any exculpating claims. Within a defence category, a defendant might plead alternative or subsidiary grounds for justification or excuse. There are no strict rules governing the order in which alternatives within a defence category ought to be examined; each defence can be said to have its own characteristics, and sometimes defences overlap.[19] Nevertheless, Dutch literature offers some guidance as to the order of discussion. According to De Hullu, any special defences (related to specific offences) should be examined before any general defences; written defences should be examined before unwritten defences (stemming from case law), and 'external' causes for absence of criminal liability should be examined before any 'internal' grounds.[20]

Provocation of Defence Situation

Under the heading 'culpa in causa', Dutch doctrine deals with cases wherein the person who claims a defence can be 'blamed' himself for the 'defence situation' to arise.[21] If this is the case, the defence will not succeed. Nowadays, according to the case law of the Supreme Court, 'culpa in causa' can stand in the way of accepting self-defence for example, although it can be established that there was actually a necessary and required defence.[22] Whether or not 'culpa in causa' can be established in a given case, is highly factual; only through a thorough comparison of cases, some light can be shed on the matter. In case of excessive self-defence for example, the mere fact that the defendant arms himself (illegally) with a gun—which gun is used in a self-defence situation, wherein the limits of justificatory self-defence were exceeded—will not automatically stand in the way of the general defence.[23] In the Dutch *Bijlmer* case,[24] the defendant stood waiting in an elevator hall at night to return to her apartment, when she was confronted by two persons who tried to rob her.

---

15   When a defence has not been raised, but the case gives rise to serious questions regarding the existence of a ground for justification or excuse, the court may not ignore these questions and should *ex officio* investigate whether the defendant should be discharged; in the same sense a court cannot in principle ignore general defences, put forward in writing to the court, although art. 358(3) DCCP requires that the defence was stated in court. GJM Corstens, *Het Nederlands strafprocesrecht* (7th edn, MJ Borgers (ed), Deventer, Kluwer 2011) 761.

16   Corstens/Borgers (n 15) 761.

17   This standard can be described as 'showing that there is no reasonable doubt concerning the correctness of the fact the defendant is charged with'. Corstens/Borgers (n 15) 674.

18   If the claim is denied by the court, the court is obliged to give a reasoned decision on this point. See art 358(3) and 359(2) DCCP. The obligation to give a reasoned decision presumes that the defendant (or his councilor, see art 331 DCCP) has 'explicitly' claimed a ground for justification or excuse in court. If a general defence is actually an absence of proof defence to an element of unlawfulness or excuse, art 359(2) of the Dutch Code of Criminal Procedure demands a reasoned decision from the court if it denies the defence, but only if the claim that has been raised can be regarded as an 'explicitly substantiated point of view'.

19   A partial overlap may occur, for example, between necessity and self-defence.

20   De Hullu (n 1) 366, with references. The last mentioned category might structure an alternative pleading of duress (external mental pressure; art 40 DPC) and absence of accountability (art 39 DPC, by reason of insanity for instance).

21   For 'provoked defence situations', see Hein D. Wolswijk, 'Provocation and Diminished Responsibility in Dutch Homicide Law' in Alan Reed & Michael Bohlander (eds), *Loss of Control and Diminished Responsibility: Domestic, Comparative and International Perspectives* (Ashgate Publishing 2011) 332 ff.

22   HR 28 March 2006, NJ 2006, 509, among other cases.

23   De Hullu (n 1) 318.

24   HR 23 October 1984, NJ 1986, 56.

She was held by one of them while the other, armed with a knife, tried to take her bag. She was able to pull an armed handgun out of her bag, which she always carried to defend herself if necessary. She fired a warning shot, but the armed robber did not recoil. She feared being stabbed, and shot him in the upper body. Both men walked away, but the non-armed robber returned to the defendant, who had fallen on the floor. The man tried to grab her coat; the defendant, who feared for her life, shot the man in his right shoulder. The armed robber survived, and the defendant was charged with attempted voluntary homicide. The other man died, which led to a charge of voluntary homicide. She was convicted for these offences in first instance, but discharged by the Amsterdam Court of Appeal. The Court ruled that there had been an attack on her bag, and an immediate threat of her life. But the way she had defended herself, had exceeded the limits of self-defence. The defendant had much experience with handguns, the court established, and should have been able to direct at less vital body parts; nevertheless, her excessive way of defence was excused because the defence had taken place in a situation of panic and fear. The fact that the defendant had possessed an illegal handgun did not stand in the way of accepting the defence. In cassation, the Supreme Court ruled in clear terms that the illegal possession of the handgun did not restrain the Court of Appeal from accepting the defence of excessive self-defence.[25] However, regarding 'own fault in the cause' of an attack, there is sometimes a thin line between defence situations and cases in which the defendant, claiming self-defence, had actually made use of the situation and looked for a confrontation; a clear provocation of an unlawful attack will lead to a denial of the claim of self-defence.[26]

Mistakes of Fact and Defences

According to De Hullu, aspects of (excusatory) mistakes of fact in relation to general defences are mainly of interest with regard to justificatory defences.[27] In Dutch criminal law, the claim of a mistake of facts in relation to a general defence is a variation (or a subcategory) of the non-statutory defence of 'lack of all culpability', which has evolved in the case law of the Supreme Court of the Netherlands. Cases of mistake of facts in relation to defences are usually characterized by defendants who at the time of their (re)action *assumed* they acted under a general defence, for example because—in cases of self-defence—they mistook an innocent move for an attack. In case of self-defence for example, a defendant might claim that at the time of his 'defence' he acted under the assumption that he was attacked unlawfully. An example concerns the case of a defendant who had stabbed four members of a motorcycle club, and feared retaliation.[28] Three days later, he was chased by two cars, forced to the kerb and one of the attackers tried to pull the defendant out of his car. The defendant believed that he was allowed to defend himself, and a shooting started between the defendant and his attackers. Afterwards it became clear, that he had been followed and grabbed by plain-clothed policemen, who wanted to arrest him. The defendant's excusable mistake of facts (regarding the unlawfulness of the attack) was accepted, and he was discharged accordingly. When a mistake of fact is concerned regarding an aspect of the defence, the actual defence (of self-defence for example) can never be raised successfully; the defendant can only claim a 'putative' defence, in this case putative self-defence.

In the case of *Williams (Gladstone)*,[29] the defendant had rushed to defend a person who was the victim of an assault; the violence was committed by a person who said that he had seen the victim robbing an older woman, and that he was trying to arrest the person. The defendant did not believe this, and turned upon the person who claimed to perform an arrest. For a defence of mistake of fact to succeed, a court has to establish circumstances that could have reasonably led to a 'mistake'. The viewpoint that will be taken, as has already been mentioned, seems to be the 'more or less objective viewer' at the time of the supposed

---

25   In first instance and by the Court of Appeal, the defendant had been convicted for the illegal possession of a fire arm.

26   De Hullu (n 1) 319, with reference to HR 1 July 1996, NJ 1996, 753. J Remmelink, *Mr. D. Hazewinkel-Suringa's Inleiding tot de studie van het Nederlandse strafrecht* (15th edn, Arnhem 1995) 323, talks of 'abuse of the right to defend oneself' if the defender had actually sought confrontation.

27   De Hullu (n 1) 353.

28   Court of Appeal The Hague 28 February 1997, NJ 1997, 373. The case report does not make clear with what offence the defendant was charged.

29   *R v Gladstone Williams* (1984) Cr App R 276.

mistake, leaving some room for personal considerations. The defence will only succeed, if the mistake had been 'excusable' (*verschoonbaar*). This requires a normative approach, leading to questions—as the case may be —like whether or not due care had been exercised to avoid the error. If the objective observer would not have made the same mistake, there seems to be little room—as has already been discussed—for acceptance of the defence.

In the English case of *Dadson*,[30] a policeman was convicted for shooting at a person (with intent to do grievous bodily harm) who had stolen wood, in order to secure an arrest. The arrest could only have been made in a lawful manner, if the offence committed concerned a felony, which could only be the case if the stealing of wood could be qualified as a felony: if the thief had been convicted for the offence twice. The thief in question turned out to be a felon indeed, but it was also established that the fact that the thief had actually committed a felony, was not known to the policeman. In the end, the policeman was convicted for the shooting of the thief; the use of force in the arrest was not justified, because the arrest had been unlawful.

How will a case like *Dadson* be solved in Dutch criminal law? Due to the specific 'technicalities', it is not easy to find a solution. A possible approach, however, might be to start with the finding that the policeman may be said to have lacked reasonable suspicion for an 'arrestable offence'. At the time of the arrest, the policeman did not know nor had reason to believe that the thief had actually committed a felony (although in fact he had). In such a case, a Dutch court would probably rule that the arrest had been unlawful, and that the policeman was not allowed to use force because such use of force is only justified if the policeman acted in the 'lawful exercise of his duties'.[31] This line of reasoning can be illustrated by a Dutch case concerning 'a colored person' who was seen running from the direction of a café, which was known as a place where drug dealers met.[32] The man was arrested and searched by policemen for the possession of drugs, and they found an amount of heroine. The man had resisted the arrest, and was charged with the offence of 'resisting a policeman in the lawful exercise of his duties'. The Court of Appeal found that the policeman had not acted lawfully, because at the time of the arrest the policemen could not be said to have had a reasonable suspicion of possession of drugs. The fact that they actually found drugs, and so were right after all, did not make this different.[33]

Transferred Defences/Collateral Damage Defences

With regard to transferred defences, at least in the field of self-defence situations, it is of importance to notice that the Dutch definition of self-defence does not limit this defence to offences that are committed *against the attacker*. According to art 41(1) DPC, criminal liability will be absent if the commission of the defence was *required* for the *necessary* defence of one of the protected legal interests; art 41(1) presupposes a *situation* of self-defence, in which an offence has been committed. If, in a self-defence situation, an innocent victim is hurt or goods belonging to an innocent third party are damaged, the question will be whether the defender can successfully claim self-defence in relation to the offence that was committed in the self-defence situation against the innocent victim. In case of an innocent victim, art 41(1) DPC will require an examination of the proportionality and the subsidiarity of the defence. Looking at the interests of the victim, the subsidiarity test will be of great importance: was the commission of an offence against the victim required?

With regard to transferred defences, Machielse discusses the use of 'instruments' belonging to an innocent third party, which instruments are used by the attacker and damaged by the defender in the course of a self-defence.[34] His opinion seems to be, that the damaging is justified because it occurred in a situation of self-defence.[35] The fact that the instrument did not belong to the attacker should not be a circumstance for the defender to consider. According to Machielse, a difference in circumstances occurs if the *defender* uses an

---

30   *R v George Dadson* [1850] 175 ER 499.

31   Art. 7 Police Act 2012.

32   Court of Appeal Amsterdam 3 June 1977, NJ 1978, 601.

33   In some cases, courts are willing to find (*ex post*) that there had been a lawful ground for an arrest, although the policeman had based the arrest (and suspicion) on another ground which was found to be insufficient. The difference is, that in these cases there had (*ex ante*) been a lawful ground for the arrest after all (based on what was known at the time of the arrest). See, for example, Court of Appeal Den Bosch 18 February 2009, LJN: BH3551.

34   AJM Machielse, *Noodweer in het strafrecht* (Amsterdam 1986) 632.

35   Machielse (n 34) 632.

instrument, belonging to another. In that case, the defender will usually know that the instrument belongs to another person. Nevertheless, this should not stand in the way of self-defence.

Looking at 'collateral damage defences', it is important to note that in the Dutch system of criminal law there are no *a priori* restrictions in raising general defences; provided they are relevant in the given case, defences like duress or necessity can be raised to *any* offence, including murder. In cases where 'collateral damage' has occurred—cases wherein innocent people are sacrificed in order to protect a greater group of innocent persons[36]—the defence of self-defence seems to be a possible framework for decisions on the lawfulness of the conduct. Self-defence in Dutch criminal law justifies the defence of *other* persons against an immediate, unlawful attack; this attack also covers cases where there is immediate fear of an attack. But is it justified to sacrifice one group of humans for the welfare of another? On this point, self-defence seems to overlap with the justificatory ground of *necessity*. Necessity requires a balancing exercise between two conflicting duties, whereby the 'right'—though not necessarily the best—choice has been made. In balancing the interests—the protection of a large group of innocent human beings against the duty not to commit offences against the smaller group—the principles of subsidiarity and proportionality play an important role. If the larger group of persons can *only* be saved by sacrificing the smaller group—so in case there are no other (reasonable) options to avoid the damage, as of importance in the subsidiarity test—the weighing of the defence ultimately comes down to a proportionality test.[37]

Individual Defences

Self-Defence and Excessive Self-Defence

Before the Dutch Penal Code came into force, the defence of self-defence could only be raised in case of specific offences (including murder[38]). Since 1886, the defence applies to any offence. It is described as follows in art 41(1) DPC:

> A person who commits an offence is not criminally liable where this is required for the necessary defence of his person or the person of another, or his or another person's integrity or property, against an immediate, unlawful attack.[39, 40]

If someone is charged with an offence that was committed in self-defence under the conditions set out in art 41(1) DPC, the offender will be discharged because the commission of the offence was not unlawful. If the defence is denied, a discharge may still possible if the perpetrator's unlawful conduct falls under excusatory 'excessive self-defence', as described in art 41(2) DPC:

> A person exceeding the limits of a necessary defence is not criminally liable, where such excess directly resulted from a strong emotion brought about by the attack.

Both self-defence and excessive self-defence require a situation in which self-defence was necessary. Only if the limits of a necessary defence are exceeded, excessive self-defence comes in sight.

Self-defence may only justify the commission of an offence if it was aimed at the protection of one of the interests in art 41(1) DPC. 'Integrity' in this respect, means only sexual (physical) integrity. The protection

---

36   These are the dilemmas as described by Bohlander (n 4) 108 ff, and Michael Bohlander, 'In Extremis – Hijacked Airplanes, "Collateral Damage" and the Limits of Criminal Law' (2006) Crim LR 579 ff.

37   The group that will be saved will not survive *at the cost* of sacrificing the other group, according to MM Dolman, *Overmacht in het stelsel van strafuitsluitingsgronden* (Nijmegen 2006) 240; the life of both groups is threatened, and taking no action at all will definitely cost the lives of *everybody*.

38   This was for instance the case in the 'predecessor' of the DPC, the French Code Pénal.

39   All translations of the Dutch articles are by the author.

40   This translation differs from the one used by Wolswijk (n 21) 333, who uses the words 'where this is necessary to defend' instead of 'where this is required for the necessary defence'. Although the contraction Wolswijk uses seems to be preferred, Dutch legal doctrine tends to separate aspects of the defence being required (*geboden*) from the necessity of the attack (*noodzakelijkheid van de verdediging*).

of one's good reputation or honour is therefore not covered by the Dutch law of self-defence, with the consequence that for example a violent reaction to an insult can never result in a discharge based on art 41 DPC. Another interest not covered by Dutch self-defence law concerns the 'domestic peace'. The mere fact that someone has entered another person's home—without threatening that person, the house as such or any goods—can never justify a self-defence (or excuse excessive self-defence). The trespasser may be removed, though, but if this action is accompanied by violence, this will not be justified.[41]

The Supreme Court of the Netherlands ruled in 2010 that self-defence concerns the defence of certain interests against an unlawful attack.[42] This means, according to the Supreme Court, that a claim of self-defence must be denied if the perpetrator's conduct cannot be said to be 'defensive'—based on either his purpose or the appearance of his conduct—but in essence as aggressive (*aanvallend*) of nature: for example, aimed at a confrontation or the partaking in a fight. The defendant in this case had a row with a girl on the streets, and on some point the later victim went over with his bike. He held the front wheel up, and said that the defendant should back off. The defendant at first recoiled, but then turned aggressive and started beating the victim. Under these circumstances, the Supreme Court held, the defendant's conduct did not show any will for self-defense, but rather the will to start a counter-attack instead. Dutch criminal law can thus be said to require a 'will to defend', which in many cases will probably be presumed as long as the circumstances (either the appearance of the conduct of the defender, or his clear purpose) do not give rise to a denial.[43]

Self-defence requires an immediate, unlawful[44] attack. The Supreme Court does not require an actual physical attack. An 'immediate threat' of an attack is also an attack in the sense of art 41 DPC.[45] In order to avoid actual harm, the defence will as far as this point is concerned be lawful. If, however, the 'defender' only *feared* an attack, the defence of self-defence will be denied. In the standard case where this was decided, the defendant was in his neighbour's yard with an axe.[46] In court, he stated that he had taken the axe to open the gate to his own yard so he could freely leave it. It was clear, that both men lived in disagreement with each other. The neighbour had walked to the defendant at the gate in a threatening manner, holding a sledge hammer and an iron rod. It was accepted that the defendant could not flee. Because he feared that his neighbour would attack him, the defendant hit his neighbour on the head, with the blunt end of the axe. The Court of Appeal, following the judge in first instance, had denied his claim of self-defence, ruling that defending oneself by attacking another who merely threatened to attack, can never amount to self-defence. The Supreme Court ruled that mere fear to be attacked by someone who takes a threatening posture can never justify a pre-emptive strike, knowing that this fear might be imaginary while a real threat might not be followed by an attack.

Self-defence does not apply in a situation where the violation of an interest was lawful; this means for instance, that violent resistance against a lawful police arrest (which in itself may be accompanied by proportionate us of force) cannot be justified. The condition of unlawfulness of the attack also has the consequence, that 'self-defence' against someone who acts in self-defence can never be justified.[47] Self-defence against someone who attacks in excessive self-defence seems possible; such an 'excessive attack' is excusable, but unlawful.[48]

According to art 41(1) DPC, the self-defence must be 'necessary': in case (effective) alternative actions could have been taken, whereby the commission of an offence and further harm could be avoided—for example calling a nearby policeman—the defence reaction will not be seen as 'necessary' and the self-defence claim will be denied. The principle of subsidiarity can thus be coupled to the 'necessity' of the defence. An interesting question is, whether the (mere) possibility of fleeing from the attack can deny the necessity of

---

41 Remmelink (n 26) 315. Further on this subject: De Hullu (n 1) 324.

42 HR 8 June 2010, NJ 2010, 339.

43 See, for example, HR 10 February 1987, NJ 1987, 950 (defendant's conduct was aimed at partaking in a fight); HR 16 November 2004, NJ 2007, 467 (clear intention of confrontation).

44 This unlawful attack does not have to be a criminal offence in itself; an attempt to inflict bodily harm might be an (immediate threat of an) attack in the sense of art 41 DPC, although such an attempt in itself is not punishable (art 300(5) DPC). On this matter, see, e.g., De Hullu (n 1) 308, with references.

45 HR 30 March 1976, NJ 1976, 322 and HR 23 October 1984, NJ 1986, 56, among other cases.

46 HR 8 February 1932, NJ 1932, 617.

47 Remmelink (n 26) 319; HR 27 May 1986, NJ 1987, 8.

48 De Jong & Knigge (n 8) 171.

the defence. According to Dutch criminal law, it is not only important whether the defender *could* have fled, but also whether he *should* have fled.[49] In some cases, fleeing is not required of a defendant, although it is a real possibility. A situation may be so threatening to the defender, due to nearby aggressors, that fleeing is not required; the Supreme Court demands that a court gives sufficient reasons if a claim that fleeing was not required, is denied.[50] An example of a situation in which a court ruled that fleeing was not required, though it was a real possibility, concerns a policeman who was charged with inflicting serious bodily harm (art 302 DPC) through shooting in the victim's leg.[51] Together with another policeman the defendant had stopped a car, to see whether the driver was under the influence of alcohol. After a breath test, it was clear that the driver had drunk too much. The policemen ordered the driver to step out of the car, and come with them to the police station. Suddenly, a man appeared who turned out to be a friend of the driver's. He said that he would pay the fine, but that the policemen should leave the driver alone. The man became more and more aggressive and did not respond to orders to leave. The policemen used pepper spray and a truncheon to hold the man back, but these had no effect. Then the defendant, who had felt very threatened, ran away some twenty meters, and turned around. He saw that the man had run after him. The defendant then shot the man through the leg. The court ruled that there had been a self-defence situation, created by a man who had not responded to the use of force, and who was possibly under the influence of alcohol. Self-defence had been necessary, according to the court, knowing that means of defence other than the gun had been ineffective. Other ways of dealing with the situation were not suitable, the court ruled; running away had not been an option, according to the court, because it could not be required from a policeman that he flees if a confrontation is to be expected. Moreover, if the defendant had fled, he would have left his colleague alone with the aggressive man. The court ultimately discharged the policeman.

According to art 41(1) DPC, the commission of the offence must not only have been necessary, but also 'required'. According to the legislator, the word 'required' in the definition of self-defence was needed to confirm that the self-defence must have been *proportionate* in relation to the attack.[52] This requires an assessment of the means of defence (with or without a weapon, for example) and the intensity of the means used. The approach in Dutch criminal law seems to be to strike a reasonable balance between the interest at stake, and the means and the intensity of the defence. As De Hullu writes, the aim in court is not to discover the single *best* way to defend oneself.[53]

Dutch criminal law offers, as a ground for excuse, the defence of excessive self-defence if the limits of self-defence are exceeded. The examination of a claim of excessive self-defence will firstly concentrate on the question of whether the defendant had been in a situation where self-defence would have been available: there must have been an immediate, unlawful attack of one of the protected interests which made self-defence 'necessary'.[54] If this is not the case, the claim of excessive self-defence will be denied. This will happen, for instance, if the defence had not been necessary because the defendant could have fled, and should have fled.

Dutch case law recognizes two forms of excessive self-defence.[55] The first form covers cases in which the defendant acted *disproportionately*. Dutch case law provides several examples. One case is about a defendant who acts to defend his girlfriend, whose hair is pulled and who is beaten by several men.[56] The defendant runs to the kitchen and returns with a large meat knife, and starts stabbing at the victims. The regional court ruled that the defence had been necessary, but that the means used were disproportionate; instead, it ruled, the defendant could have merely threatened the attackers with the knife. However, the defendant's defence

---

49   HR 15 November 2011, NJ 2011, 542, among other cases. This aspect is discussed by De Hullu (n 1) 313 ff.
50   HR 6 October 2010, NJ 2010, 301.
51   Regional Court Middelburg, 23 February 2012, NJFS 2012, 107.
52   HJ Smidt, *Gechiedenis van het Wetboek van Strafrecht* part I (Smidt I; collection of parliamentary documents) (2nd edn, Haarlem 1891) 407.
53   De Hullu (n 1) 314.
54   The requirement of a *necessary* defence seems to limit the defence of excessive self-defence to *disproportionate* self-defence only (as long as the necessity of the defence (in the sense of art 41(1)) is coupled to the element of proportionality). The words 'required' and 'necessary' may, however, be read as expressing aspects of *subsidiarity* as well (De Jong & Knigge (n 8) 172). A solution is to accept that the elements of proportionality and subsidiarity can partly overlap (the use of a heavy stick might be deemed disproportionate, showing that another way of reacting should have been chosen).
55   Explicitly: HR 18 May 1993, NJ 1993, 691.
56   Regional Court East-Brabant 24 April 2013, LJN: BZ8312.

of excessive self-defence succeeded. The other form of excessive self-defence is covered under the heading of 'extensive excess', and concerns cases where the defendant exercised his defence for too long (he kept on beating his attacker, for example) or (even) wherein the defendant 'defended' himself after the attack was already over.[57]

Excessive self-defence may only be excused if the condition of double causation, as described in art 42(2) DPC, is met: the excessive action—the defendant for example kept on beating the attacker—must have been caused by a strong emotion brought about by the attack. In Dutch case law it is accepted, however, that the attack does not have to be the sole cause of the strong emotion that resulted in the excess. This means that the existence of strong emotions, stemming from an earlier attack for instance, does not have to stand in the way of the excuse. The Supreme Court struck a balance by ruling that the strong emotion, resulting from the attack, must have been the *decisive* cause of the excessive reaction.[58]

According to the Supreme Court, a defence of self-defence cannot be denied *a priori* if a defendant has aimed his defence at a third person, who had not initially attacked the defendant.[59] In the Supreme Court's ruling, examples were given of situations in which the defence could apply: the defendant's victim had 'a part' in the actual attack, or it can be found that there were 'other acts' by the victim, of which it could reasonable be said that they caused the defendant to retaliate against the victim. The ruling raises several questions, especially on the nature of the 'other acts' and the possible overlapping with other defences such as putative excessive self-defence.[60]

Necessity

Dutch criminal law recognizes three separate grounds of justification, in which aspects of necessity can be recognized. In this paragraph, the first defence that will be discussed is actual necessity, or a conflict of duties (art 40 DPC). The two variations of necessity—justification stemming from a conflict of *statutory* duties (art 42 DPC) and acting in the exercise of a civil order (art 43(1) DPC)—will be discussed briefly.

The defence of 'conflict of duties' is part of the Dutch general defence of *force majeure* ('overmacht'), the other part being duress (mental pressure). Unlike self-defence and excessive self-defence, the legal description of *force majeure* is remarkably short:

> Not criminally liable is the person who commits an offence as a result of an irresistible force.

The difference between duress and necessity within *force majeure* is usually found in the idea that duress influences the freedom of will or choice, while necessity normally consists of a well-considered decision, resulting in the commission of a criminal offence.

Initially, art 40 DPC only covered cases of duress whereby the defendant had been overborne by mental pressure. This pressure had to be acute, while any other way of acting in that situation could not be required from the defendant. The Supreme Court used a rather high standard for acceptance. Long term poverty, for instance, could never lead to acceptance of the defence, if for instance food had been stolen.[61] Situations of *Nothstand*, including compelling cases of life and death, were also said to be covered by art 40 DPC.[62] According to the legislator, *force majeure* was not limited to force or pressure that was exercised by another person.[63]

Gradually, however, less compelling situations were also covered by art 40 DPC, including cases in which an overwhelming *acute mental pressure* was absent. As far as necessity is concerned, the 'Optician case'

---

57 See, for an example, HR 18 October 1988, NJ 1989, 511 (The defendant was attacked by someone who tried to kick him between the legs. The later victim missed, and the defendant then reacted by hitting him).

58 HR 13 June 2006, NJ 2006, 343, among other cases.

59 HR 11 January 2011, NJ 2011, 339.

60 For a further discussion of this aspect, see Erik Gritter, 'Excessive Self-Defence: Third Party Problems' (2012) 76 JCL 456 ff.

61 De Jong & Knigge (n 8) 158 ff.

62 Smidt I (n 52) 404, 405.

63 Smidt I (n 52) 404.

from 1923[64] is usually seen as the turning point; since then, it is said, art. 40 DPC covers cases of 'extended' justificatory necessity, characterized by a conflict of duties: a conflict between the duty not to commit an offence (that might even be a homicide offence), and the duty to act upon a higher norm. This 'variation' of *force majeure* came to stand next to (excusatory) duress within the framework of art 40 DPC. The facts of the Optician case were rather straightforward. The defendant, an optician, was charged with having his shop open to the public at a time that was not allowed. His only customer was a man who needed new glasses. The court of first instance had discharged him, apparently on grounds of *force majeure*, finding that it was certain that the defendant's customer could not see without glasses, and that the customer was in a dangerous situation, or at least in a situation in which help was required. The court found that it had been a social duty for the shop owner to help the man; this duty had caused such a pressure that the optician should be discharged of the offence. In his advice to the Supreme Court, the Advocate-General argued that the optician should not have been discharged. According to the evidence, the customer had himself driven his car to the optician, and it had not been shown that there had been an acute pressure on the optician that had eliminated his free will. According to the Supreme Court, however, the court had correctly applied the concept of *force majeure*, which—according to the legislator—also covered situations of necessity (*nood*).

In more recent years, necessity became the framework for cases of euthanasia and assisted suicide. Euthanasia and assistance in a suicide, performed in a situation of unbearable and hopeless suffering, cannot be justified on mere medical grounds, according to the Supreme Court.[65] Necessity, however, could under circumstances lead to a discharge. According to the Supreme Court, especially medical doctors may be confronted with the necessity to choose between the duty to preserve life on the one hand, and the duty to relieve his patient from unbearable and hopeless suffering.[66] Nowadays, medical assistance in a suicide or euthanasia are covered by strict (complete) special defences.[67]

Dutch criminal law requires that the defendant who claims a conflict of duties, leading to the commission of the offence, has made the *right* choice between two 'evils'. The Supreme Court has ruled that a conflict of duties can only justify the commission of an offence in exceptional circumstances, whereby it is of relevance that, in a situation where it was necessary to choose between conflicting duties or interests, the perpetrator let the most substantial one prevail.[68] This is seen as an objective test, wherein the interest that weighs the most must be found by the court. However, the courts will not look into the question whether the perpetrator has made the *best* possible choice, but whether the perpetrator has made a reasonable choice, which allows for an appreciation by the courts.[69, 70]

The 'execution of a statutory duty' hardly plays a part in Dutch case law.[71] The defence is described as follows:

A person who commits an offence in the execution of a legal provision is not criminally liable.

This ground for justification is sometimes called a conflict of statutory duties; a conflict between the duty not to commit an offence, and the 'duty' to execute a legal provision. Strictly speaking, as De Hullu points out, the defence is superfluous.[72] After the DPC came into force, the defence of necessity (a conflict of duties) was accepted as a variation of *force majeure*. This conflict of duties might encompass a conflict of *statutory* duties, as meant in art 42 DPC.

---

64   HR 15 October 1923, NJ 1923, p. 1329 ff.
65   HR 27 November 1984, NJ 1985, 106, extensively discussed by De Hullu (n 1) 298 ff.
66   ibid.
67   The defences are laid down in arts 293(2) DPC and 294(2) DPC (the latter refers to art 293 DPC).
68   HR 12 July 2011, NJ 2011, 578.
69   De Hullu (n 1) 296.
70   Sometimes, other principles are also used in the assessment (usually: the denial) of a defence of necessity. If a perpetrator claims to have committed the offence to serve a higher goal, a court may look into the question of 'adequateness': was the commission of the offence an adequate means to serve this higher goal? See De Hullu (n 1) 297, with reference to HR 15 December 1987, NJ 1988, 811, concerning a medical doctor who had performed euthanasia, and had passed a forged statement on the natural cause of death of the patient.
71   De Hullu (n 1) 329.
72   De Hullu (n 1) 330; more strict on this point, requiring a duty to act: De Jong & Knigge (n 8) 177.

The nature of the legal provision, upon which the defendant had acted, is of interest. If it is a provision that only *allows* for a certain action, without any form of compulsion, it will be difficult to make a successful claim. The legal provision that was executed must have 'a certain compulsory' character.[73] Furthermore, the perpetrator must objectively have made the 'right' choice. As with necessity, based on art 40 DPC, the choice had to be right from a reasonable point of view; the principles of subsidiarity and proportionality play an important part.[74] If the statutory duty could reasonable have been performed without committing an offence, the defence will be denied; if the commission of the offence is disproportionate in relation to the execution of the provision, the defence will also be denied.

Art 43(1) DPC provides a ground for justification in the situation that a perpetrator has committed an offence in the execution of an official 'civil order':

> A person who commits an offence in the execution of a civil order, given by an empowered authority, is not criminally liable.

The order must have been given on administrative or state power (in Dutch: *ambtelijk bevel*); if such an order leads to the commission of an offence, the perpetrator will not be criminally liable. Being another variation of necessity, this general defence is also covered by the principles of subsidiarity and proportionality.

The commission of an offence in the execution of an 'unauthorized civil order' will in principle lead to criminal liability, unless the perpetrator acted in good faith regarding the authorized nature of the order. Art 43(2) DPC states as a ground for excuse:

> An unauthorized civil order cannot deny criminal liability, unless the subordinate who received the order considered in good faith that the order was lawful, while the execution of the order lay within the scope of his subordinacy.

This ground of excuse can be seen as a written defence of mistake of fact.[75]

Duress by Threats/Circumstances

Duress is, as was noted earlier, a variation of the Dutch defence of *force majeure* (*overmacht*). Cases of duress are characterized by situations in which the perpetrator was faced with an external mental pressure or an external 'force'. A central question in the examination of a claim of duress is whether the perpetrator *could have* and *should have* resisted the force; only an irresistible force may excuse the commission of an offence.[76]

Initially, Dutch criminal law emphasized the acuteness of the external force; an acute, compelling pressure had to be present at the time of the commission of the offence. Nowadays, the acuteness plays a 'milder' part. The effect is that in cases wherein one can speak of a more or less permanent pressure, eventually leading to the commission of an offence, an excuse may be accepted. Nevertheless, part of the examination of the question whether the perpetrator should have resisted the pressure, is whether there were other means than the commission of the offence to deal with the pressure. If 'a way out' had been open to the defendant, or, in cases wherein the perpetrator was under a long term pressure, help could have been sought, the principle of subsidiarity will deny the offence. A striking example of compelling circumstances not leading to an acceptance of the claim of duress concerns a woman who had for a long time been threatened and humiliated by her partner.[77] One night, she was raped by him, while he threatened to do the same to her daughter and to kill the woman the next day. That night, when the man lay asleep, she killed him. Her claim of duress in relation to the charge of voluntary homicide (art 287 DPC) was denied by the Court of Appeal; the Court recognized that she had acted under strong emotions, but not under a pressure that she could not have resisted. According to the Court of Appeal, the ban on killing another person is of a very fundamental nature, and the defendant must have known that her act was forbidden. Other options to escape the victim's power had been

---

73   De Hullu (n 1) 328.
74   De Hullu (n 1) 329.
75   De Hullu (n 1) 353.
76   De Jong & Knigge (n 8) 158.
77   HR 26 May 1992, NJ 1992, 681, also discussed by De Hullu (n 1) 290.

available, while there had not been a moment in which a choice had to be made between her own life and that of her victim. Of importance was, according to the Court of Appeal, that the killing took place several hours after the fight, while the victim lay asleep. The woman was convicted, and sentenced to two years imprisonment. The Supreme Court accepted the Court of Appeal's reasoning, with the result that the woman's conviction for voluntary homicide was not quashed.[78] Clearly, the case shows the application of two important principles of the limitations of duress as a defence, also of importance in a 'battered woman' context: the condition of acuteness (related to the principle of subsidiarity) and the principle of proportionality. If the threat is less acute, more can be expected of the defendant in terms of seeking help or escaping the situation, while the offence itself, allegedly committed in duress, should be proportionate in relation to the nature of the external pressure.

A defence of duress may be denied if the stressing situation wherein the defendant was, resulted from his 'own fault' (culpa in causa). This aspect, still evolving in Dutch law, has a high 'case law character'. The 'own fault' doctrine does not seem to lead to a (too) strict approach of the defence of duress, according to De Hullu.[79] Looking at the case law of the Supreme Court, it seems that if the defendant's own share in the cause of the situation of duress was merely 'blameworthy', this is not enough to deny a defence of duress. On the other hand, if the 'own fault' may be labelled in terms of intention, the defence will almost certainly be denied. In a case concerning resistance in a lawful police arrest,[80] the defendant had raised a defence of duress, but the Court of Appeal had failed to respond. According to the Supreme Court, however, this failure could not lead to cassation, because the Court could only have denied the defence. From the evidence, used by the Court of Appeal, it followed that the defendant had voluntarily taken part in a political demonstration, during which he had made himself guilty of 'public violence' against policemen and the State Secretary of Justice. In the following arrest, the defendant had resisted violently. According to the Supreme Court, the defendant had knowingly and willingly entered a situation where the police actions would cause strong emotions, which he could not resist. As a consequence, the defence of duress failed.

General Mental Condition Defences

Art 39 DPC describes the defence of 'absence of accountability', of relevance in cases wherein the defendant claims to be 'insane' or mentally disordered at the time of the commission of the offence:

> He who commits an offence for which he cannot be held accountable by reason of a mental defect or mental disease, is not criminally liable.

Aspects of drunkenness and other forms of intoxication may, under certain circumstances, be examined under this excuse.

The scope of art 39 DPC is limited to, as the provision describes, *mental disorders* leading to the commission of an offence. Examples (among many) include psychotic disorders, leading to hallucinations and delusions,[81] paranoid psychosis,[82] and schizophrenia.[83] The commission of an offence out of rage or fear, for instance, might generally speaking be of importance to the establishment of criminal liability, but if these emotions cannot be linked to a mental disorder at the time of the commission of the offence, only duress or excessive self-defence may be a relevant basis for an excuse.[84] The Dutch legislator explicitly refrained from a specification of defects or diseases that might be of relevance; it seemed wise not to do so, because in this way the courts or expert witnesses are not (too much) restricted in their examination and advice.[85]

---

78   See, for a more recent case: Regional Court Almelo 13 maart 2012, LJN: BV8659.
79   De Hullu (n 1) 302 ff.
80   HR 10 October 1995, NJ 1996, 356. The case concerns art 180 DPC (in this case in conjunction with art 181 sr, aggravating circumstances).
81   Regional Court Zutphen 12 January 2012, LJN: BV0733.
82   Regional Court Assen 4 July 2006, LJN: AY2608.
83   Court of Appeal Den Bosch 22 February 2012, LJN: BV7333.
84   De Hullu (n 1) 334, with reference.
85   De Hullu (n 1) 334, 335. See also HR 18 December 2012, NJ 2013, 466 (with a case note by BF Keulen), in which the Supreme Court ruled that if a psychiatric disorder is not described in the psychiatric classification of DSM-IV-TR, the

Following the description of art 39 DPC, the examination of a claim of insanity follows three stages.[86] The first question is whether, at the time of the commission of the offence, there was a mental disorder as meant in art 39 DPC. On this question, the court will seek the advice of an expert. The next question deals with *causality*: is there a causal relationship between the mental disorder and the commission of the offence? The last stage of the examination concerns the question whether the influence of the disorder on the commission of the offence is a reason for not holding the defendant accountable (or responsible) for the offence. This normative question, leaving room for an appreciation by the courts, requires reflecting on the person of the defendant, given the causal relationship of the disorder and the commission of the offence; could the defendant have acted otherwise, and should he have acted otherwise? It is possible that the offence was committed as a result of a mental disorder, while at the same time the perpetrator is accountable (liable) for the commission of the offence. An example can be found in a case regarding a grandson who had killed his grandmother with a knife. It was established by the Court that at the time of the commission of the offence the grandson had acted in a state of paranoid psychosis, caused by the use of a large amount of cocaine shortly before the offence.[87] Despite the existence of the mental disorder at the time of the offence, and a causal relation between the disorder and the commission of the offence, the Court of Appeal had convicted the grandson. Of relevance in its decision was that the grandson—due to previous experiences—had been aware of the disturbing effects that the taking of cocaine could cause. This meant that the grandson was himself to blame for the mental disorder. The Supreme Court found the court's reasoning sufficient.[88]

Within the tripartite structure, the acceptance of the defence of insanity will lead to a discharge.[89] In practice, however, insanity rarely leads to a discharge. Usually the courts find some culpability left, which makes a conviction possible.[90] In those cases, it is possible to convict the defendant to both a prison sentence and a hospital order. On the other hand, the existence of a mental (causal) disorder at the time of the commission of the offence may in extreme cases lead to an *acquittal* if the defendant cannot be said to have acted intentionally. In such cases, a hospital order is not possible. Cases like these are restricted to defendants who lack 'any insight in the effects and consequences' of their behaviour.[91] As long as a court is able to find that not *every* insight in the consequences of his behaviour was absent, the construction of (conditional intent) might be possible, leading to either a discharge (instead of an acquittal) or a conviction.[92]

The question whether voluntary (alcoholic) intoxication might lead to a discharge in relation to art 39 DPC has led to some discussions in the preparation stage of the Dutch Penal Code.[93] Was a drunken perpetrator able to form a free will, and was he thus able to act intentionally? If intention could be proved, should he then be held accountable for the commission of the offence? The discussions were triggered by the fact that in the draft version of the DPC, art 39 DPC also provided for a discharge in case an offence had been committed in a state of *unconsciousness* at the time of the offence. Examples of unconsciousness were sleep and narcosis. The Minister of Justice suggested that a condition of drunkenness might also be labelled as a state of unconsciousness. It was said that unconsciousness, caused by alcoholic intoxication, was a rare situation, but if it had existed, the perpetrator should not be criminally responsible.[94] Later, the opinion was expressed that only a total lack of consciousness might excuse a defendant.[95] The result of the debate was that unconsciousness as a ground for absence of accountability was taken out of art 39 DPC, because the total

---

disorder may still be found to be a mental disorder in law (required, e.g., for a hospital order), while at the same time the classification of a disorder does not mean that there is a mental disorder in law.

86   De Hullu (n 1) 335; De Jong & Knigge (n 8) 149.

87   HR 9 June 1981, NJ 1983, 412. The case is also discussed by De Hullu (n 1) 337.

88   The case can be seen as an example in which 'own fault' in the cause can be of relevance with regard to mental disorder defences.

89   In that case, the court has the power to order placement in a psychiatric hospital (art 37 DPC), or give a 'hospital order' with or without 'compulsory treatment' (arts 37a ff DPC).

90   De Jong & Knigge (n 8) 151.

91   Among other cases: HR 9 June 1981, NJ 1983, 412 and HR 14 December 2004, NJ 2006, 448. On this matter: De Hullu (n 1) 223ff.

92   De Hullu (n 1) 340.

93   Smidt I (n 52) 364 ff; Remmelink (n 26) 277–278.

94   Smidt I (n 52) 365; De Jong & Knigge (n 8) 152.

95   Smidt I (n 52) 377.

absence of consciousness fundamentally denied the existence of a will beforehand; an excuse in law was thus not needed.

Under current law, the question of whether drunkenness might lead to an absence of accountability is no longer seen as problematic. In extreme cases, as with insanity, the intoxication might have had the effect that the defendant cannot be said to have acted intentionally. But, as with insanity, usually some ground can be found for proving (conditional) intent. As for art 39 DPC in relation to intoxication, the correction principle of *culpa in causa* (own fault in the cause) can also come into play: at the time he started drinking, the perpetrator knew what he did, while the consequences of his prior actions were known to him.[96] Questions of 'own fault' seem to fall perfectly in the three-stage examination of 'insanity' and other disorders; despite the disorder, criminal liability is possible. An example, related to cocaine intoxication, was already described in paragraph 4.2. The case also indicates that the remarks on drunkenness are also relevant to (disorders caused by) drugs.

In theory it is also possible, nowadays, that a state of intoxication is of relevance in relation to the defence of absence of all culpability; one of the grounds for a discharge following this defence is, as will be discussed later on, 'excusable incapacity' (*verontschuldigbare onmacht*). The question then shifts to whether a given 'incapacity' due to intoxication could have been avoided. The taking of large amounts of alcohol (or drugs) will normally have effects that can be said to be known to the perpetrator.

For both insanity and 'excusable incapacity' it may be argued that if the taking of substances had been *involuntary*, the perpetrator cannot be said to have an 'own fault' in the cause. If the taking of substances had been unavoidable, the perpetrator can be excused.

Mistake of Law

Questions of excusatory mistake of law regarding the *existence* of a defence or the *reach* of a defence will in Dutch criminal law be solved under the general (unwritten) excusatory defence of *lack of all culpability*. Mistakes of law in relation to aspects of general defences fall under the same 'heading' as excusatory mistakes of law concerning (parts of) the offence description. Dutch law hardly provides examples of mistake of law in relation to defences. For one part this can be explained by the fact that mistakes of law are sometimes difficult to separate from mistakes of fact; a defendant might claim that he believed on reasonable grounds that he was under attack and was allowed to react proportionally, while in reality he had mistaken the move of the 'attacker'.[97] On the other hand it will be clear that in many cases mistakes of law can be said to be inexcusable, because the defendant should have had better knowledge of the law of self-defence. If the defendant would claim that he thought it was allowed to react on a gentle push with the stabbing of a knife, a discharge will be denied.

Residual Catch-All Defences/Existence and Ambit of Statutory Defences (Rrelated to Distinct Offences)

When the Dutch Penal Code came into force, the Dutch system of general defences consisted of *written* exceptions, as described in arts 39–43 of the Code. This changed at the beginning of the twentieth century. In 1916, the Supreme Court had to rule in a case wherein an employer was charged with the offence of supplying diluted milk through an innocent agent.[98] The milk was actually supplied by an employee, who had no knowledge of the fact that he had delivered diluted milk. According to the employer, he could not be convicted for supplying milk through an innocent agent because the employee had not been 'innocent'. The offence was a misdemeanour, and did not require proof of a subjective element; furthermore, there were no relevant written excuses available in law that the employee could raise. Although the concept of excusable mistake of fact was known at the time, this concept probably only applied—and still applies—as an absence of proof defence to serious offences, where it can negate intention.[99] Hence, in law, the employee was not an innocent agent, so the employer could not be convicted. The Supreme Court ruled, however, that the principle

---

96 On this matter: De Jong & Knigge (n 8) 154.
97 De Hullu (n 1) 320 ff and 353.
98 HR 14 February 1916, NJ 1916, 681 ff.
99 Smidt I (n 52) 82.

'no punishment without guilt' required that if all guilt was absent—although the written defences could not be applied—the defendant should be discharged anyway.

At first the case could be read as only recognizing an unwritten defence of mistake of fact with regard to minor offences. Later on it became clear, that the Supreme Court had actually developed a general, unwritten excusatory defence: the defence of lack of all culpability. Since 1916, Dutch case law gradually showed an expansion of the defence through the recognition of several different *grounds* for absence of 'all' culpability, among which 'mistake of fact' was the first. Dutch literature finally concluded that the Supreme Court had in 1916 actually recognized blameworthiness or culpability as a general condition for criminal liability[100]; thus, the ruling was actually of great importance to the development of the Dutch structure of offences.[101]

The Dutch defence of lack of all culpability is, nowadays, a distinct feature of Dutch criminal law. It usually works as a 'residual' defence category, supplementing the system of written defences. The words 'absence of all culpability' do not restrict the defence to situations in which literally *every* guilt is absent; in the end it can be successfully raised in situations in which all criminally 'relevant' guilt, needed as a basis for a conviction, is absent. The defence can be raised *vis-à-vis* any charge; whether it will be successful depends among other things on the specific ground that is raised and its specific conditions and the importance of what is at stake.

Through the years, the Supreme Court has recognized several sets of circumstances that might lead to a discharge based on absence of all guilt. Dutch literature usually categorizes these circumstances in four different groups, each a separate ground for the defence of lack of all culpability[102]: 1) mistake of fact, 2) mistake of law, 3) 'excusable incapacity' (*verontschuldigbare onmacht*), and 4) maximum care or due diligence (*maximale zorg/zorgvuldig gedrag*). These grounds will be discussed briefly in the following paragraphs.

Mistake of Fact

The defence of excusable mistake of fact is mainly of relevance for misdemeanours that do not require proof of a subjective element, and parts of descriptions of felonies that are not covered by such an element.[103] A mistake of fact relating to one or more elements of a charged offence might lead to a discharge only if the mistake was excusable. Whether or not this is the case requires an appreciation of the facts by the court. An example concerns a defendant who had been charged with the offence of driving a car that had not been properly maintained: three of the tire treads had almost worn out, and one had completely worn out.[104] In court, the defendant claimed that—until the fault was discovered—he had not known that his car was not equipped with tires that had the right profile. He declared that he had no knowledge of the technicalities of a car, and that he had trusted on the advice of his garage keeper who had said that he could make several journeys with the car. The regional court discharged the car owner; in cassation, the Supreme Court was of the opinion that the court—upon the delivered evidence—could have reached the decision that the car owner could have reasonably trusted the garage keeper.

Mistake of Law

Until 1949, it was uncertain whether Dutch criminal law recognized a defence of reasonable mistake of law. During the preparations of the Dutch Penal Code, the legislator was of the opinion that mistake of law could never lead to a discharge.[105] The emergence of the defence of absence of all culpability made room for such a defence, however, leading eventually to recognition in case law. In the case where it was accepted, the

---

100   De Hullu (n 1) 204–205; De Jong & Knigge (n 8) 43 ff; Remmelink (n 26) 376 ff.

101   It is questionable, though, whether this common opinion is entirely true. Another way of looking at the development is that the Supreme Court, upon the recognition of the general condition of culpability that could already be found in Dutch criminal law, 'only' gradually expanded the possible *range* of the general (excusatory) defences.

102   See, e.g., De Jong & Knigge (n 8) 180 ff; De Hullu (n 1) 352 ff.

103   An example of the second category concerns certain sexual crimes, wherein the age of the victim is not 'covered' by intention. The standard of acceptance of a defence of mistake of fact is, however, very high because of the protection of youngsters. See HR 20 January 1959, NJ 1959, 102 & 103, and E Gritter, *Effectiviteit en aansprakelijkheid in het economisch ordeningsrecht* (2003) 147 ff.

104   HR 13 February 1962, NJ 1962, 430.

105   Smidt I (n 52) 82; De Hullu (n 1) 354.

defendant, before going on the road with his new motorcycle, showed his papers to a policeman and asked whether he was in possession of all the required official papers.[106] The policeman assured him that such was the case, and the defendant went on the road. Later that day another policeman asked for his papers, and found that one required certificate was missing, for which the defendant was charged. The court discharged him, because he had excusably not known that his conduct was illegal. The Supreme Court accepted this outcome.

In many cases wherein the defence is raised, the act of seeking relevant (concrete) advice beforehand (which advice turns out to be wrong) is important. The person who has been asked for advice should be an independent and unbiased expert; it must be someone on whose advice the defendant might have relied. The individual character of the advice, however, is not a condition for a defence to succeed; under circumstances, trust might be based on a general leaflet, in the relevant case information issued by the Ministry of Justice on firearms.[107] More generally, the Supreme Court has ruled that cases of mistake of law are characterized by an 'excusable inadvertence regarding the illegitimacy of the blamed conduct'.[108]

Incapacity

The ground of 'excusable incapacity' can be relevant in cases wherein a defendant had taken medicine or other substances, of which the effects were not known to the defendant, when he ought to have known them either.[109] It has also been accepted in a case wherein the defendant suffered from a sudden diabetes attack, leading to a car accident.[110] Another case concerns a defendant, whose car had come on the wrong lane, causing a fatal accident.[111] He was charged with causing death by incautious driving (a felony), and dangerous driving (a misdemeanour).[112] The defendant claimed that, shortly before the accident, he had suffered from a sudden and ongoing coughing fit; he saw black, and regained consciousness only after he had hit the victim. He had suffered from such coughing fits before, though not in traffic situations, and he had received medication to suppress the fits. He was not warned that he should not drive a car. The regional court of Den Bosch ultimately acquitted the defendant for causing death by incautious driving, and he was discharged for dangerous driving, both on the ground of excusable incapacity; the defendant had sought medical treatment, and did not know— nor should have known, according to the court—that there was a risk of losing consciousness while driving a car. In a case of a truck driver who had caused a fatal accident after a blackout, the defence of excusable incapacity was not accepted; shortly before the accident, the driver was informed that she probably suffered from a local form of epilepsy, which might have consequences for her driving abilities.[113]

Maximum Care

The last category of lack of all culpability concerns the taking of maximum care (to avoid the commission of the offence). An example concerns a company that stood trial for selling peanuts that contained more than the allowed maximum of aflatoxin, contrary to the Dutch food legislation.[114] The court of first instance had convicted the company without sentencing to a penalty, although it had found that the company had taken maximum care in avoiding aflatoxin in the peanuts that were sold by taking (sufficient) random checks. The court ruled that peanut traders like the company on trial could never guarantee that 'pure products' were sold. According to the court, no one who partakes in such a 'problem area' can ever raise a defence of lack of all culpability. Ultimately, the Supreme Court ruled, upon the facts established by the court, that the company had taken maximum care to prevent the existence of too much aflatoxin in its products. The consequence was that the company could not be blamed for selling peanuts containing too much aflatoxin, so the company should have been discharged because it was not to blame.

---

106   HR 22 November 1949, NJ 1950, 180.
107   HR 23 May 1995, NJ 1995, 631.
108   ibid.
109   De Hullu (n 1) 358.
110   HR 24 November 1964, NJ 1965, 142 (discussed by De Hullu (n 1) 358).
111   Regional Court Den Bosch 5 December 2008, LJN: BG6091.
112   See arts 6 and 5 of the Dutch Traffic Act 1994.
113   Court of Appeal Amsterdam 14 February 2012, LJN: BV8205. As such, the defence seems to resemble (aspects of) the defence of automatism in English criminal law.
114   HR 2 februari 1993, NJ 1993, 476.

The recognition of the defence of lack of all culpability can be valued as the ultimate completion of the Dutch system of excusatory defences. New, 'unexpected' grounds for excuse will eventually find its place in the current system, either in one (or more) of the developing written defences, or in the defence of lack of all culpability. The presumed general condition of blameworthiness is thus secured. The question is whether Dutch criminal law has a similar approach towards justification of alleged criminal conduct.[115] Is there a general (unwritten) justificatory defence that covers cases of lawful conduct that cannot be 'solved' by applying the written justificatory defences?

It seemed that in 1933 the Supreme Court had indeed recognized such a defence. In this case, a veterinarian had mixed healthy cattle with cattle that suffered from foot-and-mouth disease, instead of injecting the healthy cows against the disease.[116] According to the veterinarian, the healthy cows would only suffer mildly, and in the end the effect would be the same. Dutch legislation at the time, however, prohibited this action, and the veterinarian was charged with the offence of 'bringing cattle in suspicious circumstances'. The Supreme Court accepted that the veterinarian's conduct had been lawful, under the condition that he had acted according to accepted academic, veterinarian standards covering the protection of cattle. In more general terms, the Supreme Court ruled that the unlawfulness of an act may be absent, although unlawfulness as such is not an element of the offence and there are no defences available.[117] The defence that seemed to have been accepted in this case became known as the defence of 'absence of substantial unlawfulness'; under this defence, the commission of the offence may be justified although the perpetrator had acted unlawfully in a 'formal' way (he had acted in violation of the written law, while written defences did not apply).[118]

The existence of a non-statutory *general* defence of absence of substantial unlawfulness is nowadays highly doubtful.[119] There have been no cases since in which the Supreme Court may be said to have accepted the defence. It has been argued, that such a general defence should not be accepted at all, because it denies the law as stated by the legislator.[120] It has also been said that the veterinarian case actually concerned a defence related to justified 'acting in a medical profession', an unwritten defence that in theory also plays a role to argue the lawfulness of—for example—causing a patient's death in or after risky surgery, which surgery was performed according to professional, academic medical standards.[121] In retrospect, another way of looking at the veterinarian case is that the dilemma that needed solving will nowadays fall under (extended) necessity (conflict of duties).[122]

De Hullu has argued that the defence of absence of substantial unlawfulness may actually be seen as a defence, encompassing several 'special' unwritten grounds for justification, which grounds are always related to specific offences and the special circumstances under which they have been committed.[123] According to this line of thought, several potential justificatory circumstances, like acting in a professional medical capacity or consent (for example in sports situations), can thus be categorized and understood as examples of exceptional circumstances, leading to 'substantial' unlawfulness. But this also means that the existence of a *general* defence of substantial unlawfulness lacks added value.[124]

Dutch criminal law recognizes several specific statutory defences that are explicitly related to specific offences or groups of specific offences. The category of special defences is rather diverse: several defences under this heading are actually defences that deny the *existence* of an offence or deny the possibility of prosecution.[125] In the first mentioned cases, proof of a charge may exist, but the defendant will be discharged because the proven act is not a 'punishable act' according to the law. An example of such a defence can be

---

115 De Hullu (n 1) 341–342.
116 HR 29 February 1933, NJ 1933, 918.
117 The Supreme Court probably referred to written defences.
118 De Hullu (n 1) 343.
119 De Hullu (n 1) 344; De Jong & Knigge (n 8) 184.
120 De Jong & Knigge (. 8) 184; Remmelink (n 26) 346.
121 Remmelink (n 26) 344–345; De Hullu (n 1) 345.
122 De Jong & Knigge (n 8) 185; De Hullu (n 1) 344. The defence of 'maximum care' will not be available because the act of the veterinarian was not aimed at taking the appropriate measures to avoid the commission of an offence.
123 De Hullu (n 1) 345 ff.
124 De Hullu (n 1) 348.
125 See, for an example of the last mentioned 'category' of defences, art 316 DPC: if the perpetrator is the husband or wife of the person who's good has been stolen, prosecution of the perpetrator is not possible.

found in art 293 DPC (euthanasia). According to art 293(1) DPC, it is an offence if a person takes the life of another person on his explicit and serious wish. Art 293(2) provides a ground for a discharge. It says that the conduct mentioned in subsection 1 is not 'punishable' if it has been committed by a medical doctor who has acted according to statutory euthanasia standards, and who has informed the authorised coroner. An example of a 'real' specific defence can be found in art 103a DPC. This defence relates to the offences, described in de arts 102 and 103 DPC: aiding the enemy or 'disadvantaging' the State towards the enemy in times of war (102) or conspiracy to commit these offences (art 103). Art 103a DPC states: 'Not criminally liable is he who has committed one of the offences mentioned in arts. 102 and 103 in the reasonable belief that he did not damage the interests of the Netherlands'.

Chapter 19

New Zealand

Julia Tolmie

General Issues

Justificatory and Excusatory Defences

In the Supreme Court of Canada in *Perka v R*[1] it was said that a '"justification" challenges the wrongfulness of an action which technically constitutes a crime'. In contrast, an '"excuse" concedes the wrongfulness of the action but asserts that the circumstances under which it was done are such that it ought not to be attributed to the actor'.

In New Zealand, the general defences traversed in this chapter—with the exception of necessity—are codified in the Crimes Act 1961 (NZ), which describes some defences as 'justifying' behaviour that would otherwise be an offence, and in other instances indicates that the defence results in the accused being 'protected from criminal responsibility', suggesting that it is more in the nature of an excuse. For example, self-defence is expressly described as a justification in section 48, as are the defences set out in sections 52, 55, and 56 in respect of the defence of property against a trespasser or burglar. On the other hand, section 24, which sets out the defence of compulsion (and is the statutory codification in New Zealand of the defence of duress by threats), provides that the accused 'is protected from criminal responsibility', as does the defence of property in the exercise of a claim of right against someone who is not a wrong doer in section 53. Section 23, setting out the defence of insanity, provides that no person who meets the criteria of the defence 'shall be convicted of an offence', but in section 23(4) parties can still be guilty of the offence (suggesting that a wrong-doing has taken place but the primary offender is excused from liability). Whilst the defence of necessity is still a common law defence of uncertain parameters,[2] the Court of Appeal in *R v Neho*[3] made it clear that the defence operates to 'protect or excuse' conduct that would otherwise be criminal.

In spite of the clarity of the classifications in New Zealand, there is not a strongly developed common law jurisprudence around the justification/excuse distinction, and it is rarely used to explain the interpretation of statute or shaping of common law doctrine. One possible explanation for this is that most of the general defences are legislated and the New Zealand courts tend to take a uniformly restrictive approach to the interpretation of all the defences.

Conceptual Foundations

Self-defence, compulsion and necessity each provide a complete acquittal for instances in which the defendant has committed a crime in order to avoid serious harm to themselves or another. The primary rationale for all three defences in New Zealand appears to be 'moral' or 'normative involuntariness'. The defences represent acknowledgement that, in their offending, the accused had their free will circumscribed by the unpalatable

---

1   [1984] 2 SCR 232, 246, 248–249.
2   Interestingly, where the defence has been codified in relation to the avoidance of particular harms it is generally described as a justification. See s 40 (preventing escape); s 41 (preventing suicide or crimes likely to cause immediate injury to person or property); s 42 (preventing breaches of the peace); s 42 (suppressing a riot); s 187A (performing an abortion to prevent serious danger to the mother's life or physical or mental health). Cf s 182(2) in respect of killing an unborn child.
3   [2009] NZCA 299 [9].

choices their circumstances presented them with.[4] All three defences require an assessment of the circumstances the defendant was facing, along with their response to those circumstances, with different weightings being given to their personal perceptions depending on whether the assessment for the particular legal requirements uses a test that is subjective, subjective/objective or objective. As noted below, self-defence gives the greatest weighting to the accused's perceptions because the assessment of whether the force that they employed was reasonable in self-defence is made in the context of their subjective appraisal of the circumstances that they were facing.

A serious gap in the development of the 'preservation defences' in New Zealand is the degree to which judges have required the normative involuntariness that underlies all three defences to be found in the *immediate* circumstances surrounding the offending. They have done so by requiring that the defendant be responding to an 'immediate' threat for self-defence[5] and necessity,[6] and taking a strict interpretation of the requirements of imminence and presence for the defence of compulsion.[7] Beyond the immediate circumstances, the courts typically use language of choice—for example, the assumption is that calling the police will always be an effective means of defusing a threat where the accused has advance notice that harm is impending. The result is that the legal requirements that give shape to these defences in New Zealand do not accommodate the entrapment which is inherent in some people's broader life circumstances—for example, intimate relationships or social milieu that are dangerous and complex and that may, in turn, make going to the police to avoid a future threat useless, as well as escalating the danger and/or attracting punitive consequences from the police towards the person who is under threat.[8]

To a lesser extent the legal requirements for the three 'preservation defences' reflect a balancing of evils rationale: the crime that the accused committed is judged less serious than the harm that they hoped to avoid.[9] Proportionality is a direct requirement of the defence of necessity[10] and finds expression as a mutable principle in relation to self-defence.[11] It also operates in respect of the defences of compulsion and necessity by making the defences unavailable for the more serious crimes. Necessity is not available for murder or attempted murder,[12] whilst section 24(2) of the Crimes Act 1961 (NZ) sets out an extensive list of serious offences (including murder and attempted murder) for which the defence of compulsion is not available. Both defences also cannot be raised in respect of threats less than serious injury or death, unlike self-defence.

Duress and necessity are more tightly circumscribed than self-defence in their legal requirements, because they involve criminal offending against an innocent victim. By way of contrast, in self-defence the defendant is responding to unjustified aggression from the victim, who can therefore be considered to have forfeited, to some degree at least, his or her own right to bodily integrity relative to the defendant. In the New Zealand context it is worth noting, however, that because of the high weighting given to the accused's perception of their circumstances in the test for self-defence that defence is available even where the victim is not an unjustified aggressor but the defendant mistakenly, even if unreasonably, thinks that he is.

By way of contrast, the general mental condition defences do not assess the nature of the circumstances the accused was in and their response to those circumstances, but are, instead, enquiries into the accused's personal capacity. The model of responsibility underpinning criminal liability predicated on establishing *mens rea* assumes a person with the capacity to make rational moral choices. The insanity defence excuses those who do not have the mental capacity to reason in this manner and is analogous to infancy as an instance of legal incapacity. Intoxication, on the other hand, is not so much a defence as an evidentiary strategy supporting a claim that the accused did not, on the facts, possess the mental processes required to establish criminal liability.

---

4   For a discussion of the concept of 'normative involuntariness' see *R v Perka* (n 1); *R v Ryan* [2011] NSCA 30; [2013] SCC 3.

5   *R v Wang* (1989) 4 CRNZ 674.

6   *R v Hutchinson* [2004] NZAR 303.

7   Crimes Act 1961, section 24; *R v Neho* (n 3).

8   See *R v Neho* (n 3); *Police v Kawiti* [2000] 1 NZLR 117.

9   *R v Teichelman* [1981] 2 NZLR 64, 66.

10   *R v Hutchinson* (n 6).

11   *R v Hill* [2009] NZCA 42.

12   *R v Martin* [2003] (HC, 24 March).

Cumulative or Alternative Pleading of the Defences

In New Zealand self-defence, compulsion and necessity require distinct facts and are therefore only available in the alternative. Thus, if the victim is also the aggressor then self-defence is the only available defence; if the human aggressor is not the victim then compulsion (although limited in scope) is the only available defence; whereas if the threat comes from a non-human source the defence of necessity is available.

Evidence of intoxication can, on the other hand, support the establishment of those aspects of the preservation defences that require a subjective belief on the part of the defendant. For example, in relation to self-defence, 'if an accused's subjective perception is clouded by alcohol, this is a matter that is able to be taken into account'[13] when determining what kind of threat they honestly believed that they were facing at the time. Their defensive force is then judged as reasonable or otherwise on the assumption that they were, in fact, facing a threat of that nature.

For beliefs requiring reasonable grounds or facts which must be objectively established, on the other hand, the accused's intoxication will be irrelevant to whether the necessary fact existed or whether there were reasonable grounds for the accused's belief that it did. It follows that in respect of the defence of compulsion set out in Section 24, the defendant's intoxication is irrelevant to the issue of whether they were under a threat of immediate death or grievous bodily harm from a person who was present when the offence was committed.[14] However, the defendant's intoxication is relevant in determining whether they believed that the threats would be carried out and committed the crime because of that belief.

Mental disorders short of insanity (such as depressive illnesses or post-traumatic stress disorders) are capable of affecting the defendant's subjective appraisal of their circumstances and their personal reactions to those circumstances for the purposes of establishing the subjective components of the preservation defences.[15] Yet to be resolved is whether, as a matter of policy, insane beliefs can similarly support the preservation defences.[16] For example, in *R v Bridger*[17] the Court of Appeal left open the question whether, as a matter of policy, the phrase 'the circumstances as he believes them to be' in the section 48 test for self-defence applies to sane beliefs only. How this issue is resolved in the future will determine whether an insane defendant, acting to defend themselves or another on the basis of an understanding of their circumstances which is distorted by insanity, can be acquitted on the basis of self-defence or whether they are confined to a verdict of not guilty by reason of insanity.

Of course, when defences built on incapacity (such as intoxication or insanity) are run in support of, or alternatively to, defences which necessitate a decision that the defendant responded reasonably or had reasonable grounds for their understanding of their situation, there is always a risk of undercutting the strength of those defences on the facts by suggesting that the defendant's responses were irrational.[18]

A disease of the mind is more than a transitory mental state caused by the effects of drugs or alcohol, even in cases of extreme intoxication.[19] Whilst alcohol or drug abuse can over time produce a disease of the mind in the form of delirium tremens or brain damage,[20] where intoxication triggers or aggravates a latent or pre-existing mental illness, the case law is mixed on whether an insanity defence is available on the facts.[21]

---

13 *Simpson v R* [2010] NZCA 140 [68].

14 *R v Sharma* [2009] NZCA 540 [32].

15 *R v Oakley* [2006] (CA, 22 September); *R v Ghabachi* [2007] NZCA 285; *R v Wang* (n 5).

16 Insanity and the automatism 'defence' are also viewed as alternative defences and raise tricky issues of demarcation which are beyond the scope of this paper. The defences have different burdens and standards of proof and different outcomes and yet overlap on some facts.

17 See text (n 31).

18 See *R v Nicholson* [1998] (CA, 8 October) 6.

19 *R v Dixon* [2008] 2 NZLR 617 [39]; H Fingarette, 'Alcoholism: Can Honest Mistake About One's Capacity for Self-Control be an Excuse?' (1990) 13 Int'l JL & Psych 77, 78.

20 *R v Davis* (1881) 14 Cov CC 563; *R v Kina* [1996] (NSWSC, 23 May).

21 *R v Dixon* (n 19 [39]–[40]); *DPP (Vic) v Whelan* [2006] 177 A Crim R 449 (Vic). Cf *R v Clough* [2010] 200 A Crim R 140, 146.

Provocation of the Defence

In 1981 the distinction between provoked and unprovoked self-defence was abolished in New Zealand. The result is that one can be the original aggressor in a confrontation and still be acting in self-defence at a later time. However, being an aggressor is clearly something that (along with other facts) is influential in determining whether the defendant was actually acting defensively at the time or was motivated by another agenda.[22] For example, in *Aoake v Police*[23] the court was not impressed by the fact that the defendant got out of his vehicle with a weapon before any verbal exchange had taken place with the complainant. It determined that he

> was not deploying the weapon in self-defence against the use or apprehended use of force. Instead he was using it to obtain a degree of ascendancy and control, and redress the imbalance which Mr Gardiner had created.[24]

Mistakes of Fact and the Defences

Because the focus of the insanity defence is on whether the defendant was able to understand the physical or moral character of their actions the defence is excusatory in the pure sense and, unlike the preservation defences, does not involve any normative appraisal by the court of the circumstances in which the defendant found themselves or their reactions to those circumstances. It follows that mistakes of fact on the part of the defendant are only relevant as evidence that might provide further insight into the defendant's mental capacity at the time of their offending.

Genuine mistakes of fact, however, will support self-defence, necessity and compulsion to the extent that the defendant's subjective belief is relevant in establishing a particular legal requirement. For example, as noted above, in relation to self-defence, if the accused mistakenly, even if unreasonably, believes that they were under a serious and lethal attack the reasonableness of their defensive force must be assessed as though their mistake was correct. However, it would seem from the manner in which self-defence is framed in section 48, although the issue has not been tested in the case law, that the defendant would be unable to benefit from objective circumstances they were unaware of that made their situation *more* threatening than they perceived it as being.

The defendant's mistaken belief that the defensive force they used was only what was 'reasonable' is, on the other hand, irrelevant to the courts normative evaluation of this issue for the purposes of self-defence. A trickier question, and one currently not resolved, is how any factual mistake the defendant made about the force they were using affects this normative judgment. In other words, is the assessment of reasonableness made on the basis of the force actually used or the force that the accused honestly, or honestly and reasonably, thought they were using?

In *R v Sharma*,[25] the Court of Appeal held that whether there is a relevant threat under section 24 sufficient to raise the defence of compulsion is simply a matter of fact; '[t]hat is, a mistaken belief in the existence of a threat is not sufficient, even if reasonable – there must be a threat in fact'.[26] If this is an objective question of fact and the defendant's belief, even if reasonable, is irrelevant to assessing whether such a threat is present, then if follows that the defendant should be entitled to the benefit of a threat that existed but of which they were not aware at the time. Having said this, the defendant's lack of awareness as to the true nature of the threat that they were facing is likely to prevent them from proving the subjective requirements of cause and effect that follow on from the threat being established. In other words, it is unlikely that they only committed the crime because they thought that otherwise the threat would be carried out.

22   See *R v Seu* [2005] (CA, 8 December); *Brown v Police* [2012] NZHC 1516.
23   [2009] (HC, 11 December).
24   ibid [21].
25   *Sharma* (n 14).
26   ibid [32].

Transferred Defences/Collateral Damage Defences

Self-defence, as set out in section 48, has been held to be limited to behaviours that are deliberate—even if there are unintended or accidental consequences that follow on from those actions.[27] It would seem to follow on from this, although the point has not been decided in the case law, that if the accused performs a deliberate act of self-defence that has the unintended consequence of killing someone other than their intended victim, self-defence should be available. It is not an express requirement of self-defence that the defensive action be targeted at the aggressor. On the other hand the defence will not be available if the accused accidently does something that kills either the person threatening them or a third party.

Whilst the distinction between actions and consequences might be easy to state in theory it is difficult to apply on the facts. For example, in the Australian case of *R v Mackenzie*[28] the accused tried to leave the house but needed to pass her abusive husband who was sitting outside the door. She took his gun in order to threaten him so she could exit, but tripped instead and accidently shot him in the back of the head. Were her actions best characterised as threatening someone with a firearm[29] (in which case the gun accidentally discharging and killing her husband was arguably an unintended consequence) or was her action, as was assumed by the court, tripping and discharging the gun (in which case it was accidental and not encompassed by self-defence even though she was acting defensively at the time she had the accident)? The case was complicated by the fact that she believed wrongly that the firearm was unloaded and therefore had made a mistake of fact that meant that her actions were more dangerous than she realised at the time.

Unlike self-defence, there is currently no authority limiting compulsion to deliberate, as opposed to accidental, actions by the defendant. Arguably, so long as the defendant was acting under the normative pressure provided by the threat they were under when they committed the crime, the defence will be available to them. Whether there is an additional requirement to the effect that the accused has to be acting within the parameters of what the person threatening them has demanded, or, alternatively, what they honestly or honestly and reasonably believed those demands to have been, is currently unresolved.

Individual Defences

Self-Defence

Self-defence as set out in section 48 of the Crimes Act 1961 is typically reduced to three jury questions:[30]

1) What were the circumstances as the defendant honestly believed them to be?
2) In those circumstances was the defendant acting in defence of self or other?
3) Was the force used reasonable in those circumstances?

New Zealand does not have a defence of excessive self-defence.[31] That the defendant was genuinely acting in self-defence but used more force than was objectively necessary will be taken into account at sentencing. However this consideration alone is unlikely to overturn the presumption in favour of life imprisonment if there has been a murder conviction.[32]

---

27 *R v Reihana* [2003] (CA, 26 July); *R v Tahana* [2000] (CA, 6 March); *Harris v R* [2011] NZCA 611; *Fairburn v R* [2010] NZSC 159.

28 [2000] QCA 324.

29 Note that an expansive interpretation of the actus reus of shooting, similar to this, has been taken in other contexts: *Ryan v R* [1961] 121 CLR 205; *R v Wickcliffe* [1987] 1 NZLR 55.

30 *R v Li* [2000] (CA, 28 June); *R v Bridger* [2003] 1 NZLR 636 (CA); *Fairburn v R* (n 27).

31 New Zealand has no partial defences to murder since the repeal of the defence of provocation in 2009.

32 *R v Keoghan* [2007] NZCA 109; *R v Goodlet* [2011] NZCA 357.

As a result of a literal reading of section 48, self-defence can only be raised in respect of offences that involve the use of 'force'. Whilst verbal threats of physical contact qualify,[33] insulting words,[34] damage to property,[35] and passive actions, such as obstruction,[36] or states, such as being in possession of a weapon,[37] do not. Having said this, self-defence might indirectly provide a defence to a status offence. For example, an intention only to use a weapon in self-defence might provide a defence to having an offensive weapon in a public place under section 202A(4)(a) by providing the defendant with a 'lawful authority or reasonable excuse'.[38]

What were the circumstances as the accused honestly believed them to be? A relevant threat for the purposes of section 48 will be a threat of bodily harm (which can be less than serious harm),[39] including psychiatric injury.[40]

This limb is subjective. An honest belief that the defendant has about the circumstances they were responding to is treated as if it were fact for the purposes of assessing the reasonableness of the defensive force used, no matter how mistaken or unreasonable the belief was.[41] By way of example, in *Mckay v Police*[42] self-defence was put the jury even though the defendant's attacker was on the ground with a broken jaw and was, in fact, clutching onto the defendant's leg to pull himself up, rather than to continue the attack. The court held that if the circumstances had been as the defendant believed them to be the fight had not come to an end and it was not unreasonable to continue defending himself.

The threat must be imminent. On the face of section 48, there is no legal rule that the defendant has to be facing an attack that is actually in progress before they are justified in using self-defence. However, *R v Wang*[43] required that the defendant be responding to an 'imminent harm' as an application of the rule that self-defence must not exceed what is reasonable in the circumstances. This is because a 'threat which does not involve a present danger can normally be answered by retreating or some other method of avoiding the future danger'.[44] In *R v Richardson*[45] the court added an additional gloss: the threat has to be 'specific'.

The need for a specific and imminent threat is a problematic feature of the law on self-defence for battered women who kill their violent partners and face homicide charges. Very few women will take a dangerous man on in hand-to-hand combat, which is required by the need to wait for an imminent threat. Furthermore, the need for a specific threat rules out the notion that the threat a battered woman faces might exist in her *ongoing* relationship with her violent partner (on the basis that domestic violence is better understood as a pattern of behaviour that has a cumulative impact on the victim, than a series of one off incidents).[46] In Australia and Canada the courts have begun to relax the requirement of imminence in cases in which a woman is in a violent relationship that poses an ongoing physical threat and from which she is unable to extricate herself.[47]

In *R v Wang*[48] the Court of Appeal concluded that the defendant believed that she and her family were under serious threat at some point in the future from her violent husband, but it was not reasonable defensive force in those circumstances for her to stab and suffocate him whilst he was unconscious. The court said:

---

33 *R v Hutchinson* (n 6); *AG v Leason* [2011] (HC, 31 August).
34 *Colman v Police* [2009] (HC, 22 December).
35 *R v Hutchinson* (n 6).
36 *Bayer v Police* [1994] 2 NZLR 48 (CA).
37 *R v Busby* [2001] (CA, 26 September); *R v Ahmed* [2009] 24 CRNZ 477.
38 *Thompson v Police* [1996] (HC, 26 April).
39 *R v Terewi* [1985] 1 CRNZ 623.
40 *R v Kneale* [1997] 15 CRNZ 392.
41 *R v Thomas* [1991] 3 NZLR 141; *R v Sarich* [2005] (CA, 16 May); *R v Christiansen* [2001] (CA, 24 October).
42 [1997] 3 NZLR 199.
43 *Wang* (n 5) 680.
44 *Wang* (n 5) 680, 683.
45 [2003] (CA, 19 March).
46 Evan Stark, *Coercive Control: How Men Entrap Women in Personal Life* (OUP 2007).
47 See *Secretary* [1996] 5 NTLR 96; *Lavallee v R* [1990] 76 CR (3d) 329; *R v Falls* [2010] (QSC, 2–3 June).
48 *Wang* (n 5).

[A]lternative courses were open to her. Her sister and her friend Susan were both in the house. She could have woken them and sought their help and advice. She could have left the house taking her sister with her in the car which was available. She could have gone to acquaintances in Christchurch or to the police.[49]

Fran Wright[50] criticises the court for not taking into account Wang's own perception of what assistance was available and effective to deal with the threat her husband posed. She argues that 'the circumstances as he believes them to be' include not only what kind of threat the accused believed they were facing but also what assistance they thought was available. Consequently the court in *Wang* incorrectly interpreted the availability of assistance as an objective matter for the court to decide, as opposed to an issue that the defendant could be honestly mistaken about.

Given that self-defence is about defending against an anticipated attack, it is clear that retaliation in respect of an attack that has taken place or to a person perceived to be an aggressor because of anger or frustration will not amount to self-defence.[51]

The defensive force used must be 'reasonable' in self-defence, as judged within the circumstances as the defendant perceived them to be. The principles of necessity and proportionality assist in assessing reasonableness. Force will be 'necessary' in self-defence when the threat could not have been prevented by less violent means.[52] Proportionality suggests that the defensive force should have some relationship to the level of the threat faced. Proportionality is, however, balanced by other considerations. In *R v Hill*[53] the Court of Appeal made it clear that the emergency faced by the defendant and the lack of an opportunity to make rational choices, or the lack of available means to defuse the threat, might render disproportionate defensive force reasonable in the circumstances. In other words, normative involuntariness, rather than a balancing of evils, is the primary rationale underlying this defence.

Whilst there is no formal duty to retreat in New Zealand, 'a threat which does not involve a present danger can normally be answered by retreating or adopting some other method of avoiding the present danger'.[54] However, retreat will not invariably be considered reasonable—much will depend on the circumstances, including how easy it was to escape.

Compulsion (Duress)

Section 24(1) of the Crimes Act 1961 sets out the defence of compulsion which replaces the common law defence of duress by threats.[55] The defence was distilled in *R v Teichelman*[56] into the following requirements:

1) A threat to kill or cause grievous bodily harm which is to be executed *immediately* following a refusal to commit the offence;
2) The person making the threat is present during the commission of the offence; and
3) The accused committed the offence in the belief that otherwise the threat would be carried out.

The defence has rarely been successful and, as a consequence, remains in a relatively undeveloped state. It appears from the limited case law currently available that the courts have interpreted the first two of these requirements as facts to be objectively determined by the court as existing or not. Accordingly, the defendant's mistaken belief that these facts exist, even if such belief is reasonable, may be irrelevant. This interpretation, if correct, sits awkwardly with the common law formulation of necessity (outlined below) in which an honest and reasonable belief by the defendant in an imminent threat is sufficient to meet the requirements of that defence. It also sits awkwardly with a conception of criminal liability based on moral fault in that if the

---

49   ibid 679.
50   'The Circumstances As She Believed Them to Be: A Reappraisal of Section 48 of the Crimes Act 1961' [1998] 7 Waikato L Rev 109.
51   *Johnston v Police* [2009] (HC, 30 September); *R v De May* [2004] (CA, 17 December).
52   *Wallace v Abbott* (2002) 19 CRNZ 585.
53   *Hill* (n 11).
54   *R v Savage* [1991] 3 NZLR 155; R v Terewi (n 39).
55   *Kapi v MOT* (1991) 8 CRNZ 49; R v Witika [1992] 9 CRNZ 272.
56   *Teichelman* (n 9).

defendant honestly and reasonably believed that facts existed giving rise to the defence then they cannot be personally faulted for the choices that they made. The final requirement, by way of contrast, is clearly expressed in subjective terms and is therefore dependent on the accused's actual beliefs and motivations.

The requirement that the threat be of 'immediate' death or serious harm has been interpreted to mean that the threat must be to the effect that the harm will take place 'there and then' if the accused refuses to commit the crime.[57]

The threat the accused is responding to may be express or implied, however the cases do insist on a *specific* threat to the accused, coupled with a demand. It will not be enough for the accused to comply with a request from someone because they are afraid of what that person will do to them if they do not, even if they have good reasons for being afraid.[58]

It is not clear whether only threats to the defendant satisfy the requirements of section 24 or whether threats to third parties also qualify. There seems little reason in logic or principle for allowing a defence of compulsion in respect of the former but not the latter. Nonetheless, New Zealand lacks an authoritative case dealing with the subject.[59]

Despite the fact that the Crimes Act 1961 (NZ) replaced the previous words 'actually present' with the word 'present'—suggesting that constructive presence might be contemplated by the new wording—in *R v Joyce*[60] the court limited the meaning of 'present' to physical presence only and interpreted that very strictly to mean immediate proximity at all times. *Joyce*[61] remains authoritative even after a number of unsuccessful attempts to widen the concept of presence to allow temporary absences in circumstances where offending is ongoing (for example, in respect of crimes founded on a failure to protect or possession) and where those being threatened are living 'entrapped lives' so that the threat is not easily avoided. The majority of these unsuccessful attempts have involved battered defendants.[62]

In *R v Neho*,[63] however, the Court of Appeal accepted that it was possible for a threat originally made by one person to be reinforced by their associates who *are* physically present when the offence is committed, thereby satisfying the presence requirements set out in section 24.

In New Zealand the defendant must commit the offence in the subjective belief that otherwise the threat will be carried out. There is no requirement that the threat must be one that a person of reasonable firmness of character could not have been expected to resist.[64] However, there is the need for the defendant to personally have his or her will overborn so that they commit the offence because of the defendant's threats.[65]

It is not a legal requirement that the defendant must avail himself or herself of any opportunity that was reasonably open to render the threat ineffective. However, if the accused recognizes that there is a viable escape route but does not take it then they do not believe in a continuing threat sufficient to qualify as compulsion.[66]

One could be critical of the courts for often failing to inquire into the defendant's subjective appraisal of their options for dealing with the violence and using language suggesting that this issue is to be assessed as an objective question of fact. For example, the courts often seem to assume that if members of the public or police officers are present this will prevent the execution of the threat and results in the defence being unavailable on the facts.[67] In *R v Neho*[68] the Court of Appeal stated:

---

57   *R v Neho* (n 3); *R v Joyce* [1968] NZLR 1070 (CA).
58   *R v Raroa* [1987] 2 NZLR 486; *R v Teichelman* (n 9).
59   *R v Sowman* [2007] NZCA 309 [34]; *R v Vickery* [2004] (HC, 6 May).
60   *Joyce* (n 58).
61   ibid.
62   See *Rihari v Department of Social Welfare* [1991] 7 CRNZ 586; *R v Witika* (n 55); *R v Richards* [1998] (CA, 15 October); *Accident Rehabilitation and Compensation Insurance Corporation v Tua* [1998] (DC, 18 February). See also *R v Sowman* (n 59) [34].
63   *Neho* (n 3).
64   *R v Raroa* [1987] (HC, 29 June), per Hardie Boys J, 24–25.
65   *R v Raroa*, ibid; *R v Sowman* (n 59) [34].
66   *R v Raroa* (n 64).
67   *R v Maurirere* [2000] (CA, 2 March).
68   *Neho* (n 3). See also *R v Sowman* (n 59).

It has been recognised as implicit in the defence of compulsion that the offender must have no realistic choice other than to break the law. If there is a reasonably available opportunity for the offender to seek help or protection or to escape the defence will not ordinarily be available.[69]

It is possible that this statement, which does not sit with the express wording of section 24, is incorrect.

Under section 24, the defendant is not able to access the defence if he is a 'party to any association or conspiracy whereby he is subject to compulsion'. It is thought that, in contrast to self-defence, the victim has usually done nothing to create the situation that the defendant is responding to and it is reasonable to expect the defendant to be similarly morally innocent.[70] The exception also avoids the possibility that unlawful associations might be able to confer criminal immunity on their members.

In *R v Joyce*[71] it was said that the limitation only operates when it is proved that

the very nature of the association was such that the offender, as a reasonable man, should have been able to foresee that the association was of a kind which at least rendered it possible that at a later stage he might be made subject to compulsion.[72]

Although this suggests the compulsion must be reasonably foreseeable, as opposed to being personally foreseen by the defendant, these comments were in obiter and the point has yet to be conclusively determined.[73]

Necessity

Section 20(1) of the Crimes Act 1961(NZ) provides that the common law defences survive 'except so far as they are altered by or are inconsistent with this Act ...' A general common law defence of necessity is preserved by this provision, but the scope and underlying rationale of the defence remains somewhat indeterminate. The defence has been successfully raised in only a handful of cases, generally involving low level offending.[74] The defence has four requirements:[75]

1) The defendant has a genuine belief, on reasonable grounds, of the imminent peril of death or serious injury;
2) The circumstances are such that there is no realistic choice but to break the law;
3) The breach of the law is proportionate to the peril involved; and
4) There is a nexus between the imminent peril of death or serious injury and the decision to respond to the threat by unlawful means, in the sense that the defendant commits the crime because in the agony of the moment their will is overborne.[76]

It appears that the first and fourth requirements depend on the defendant having a particular subjective state of mind, with the first additionally requiring reasonable grounds for the defendant's belief. It is possible that the second and third requirements, on the other hand, involve questions of fact to be objectively determined by

---

69 *Neho* (n 3) [13].
70 *R v Fitzpatrick* [1977] NI 20.
71 *Joyce* (n 57).
72 ibid 1076.
73 AP Simester and WJ Brookbanks, *Principles of Criminal Law* (4th edn, Thomson Reuters 2012) 417.
74 *Police v Coll* [2007] (DC, 15 January); *Police v Anthoni* [1997] DCR 1034; *U v R* [2011] NZCA 241; *Police v Robinson* [2008] (DC, 5 March).
75 *Police v Kawiti* (n 8); *Kapi v MOT* (n 55); *Cooke v Police* [2002] (HC, 7 November); *Hocking v Police* [2012] NZHC 3192; *Friend v Police* (2006) 23 CRNZ 319; *R v Hutchinson* (n 6). As noted above, *R v Martin* (n 12) held that necessity is not available for murder or attempted murder. However, the court in *Martin* was considering the defence outlined here and based on duress of circumstances, rather than the defence of necessity as applied by Brooke LJ in *Re A (Children)* [2000] 4 All ER.
76 *R v Hutchinson* (n 6).

the court and about which the accused's mistaken beliefs, even if reasonable, are irrelevant.[77] This was implied in *AG v Leason*,[78] where it was said:

> A key aspect of the defence is that it will not be available if the defendant has a realistic law abiding alternative available to him or her. In my view, the concepts of imminence and immediacy merely add to that objective analysis.[79]

This point has not been conclusively decided, however. Consistently with the first requirement, it could be that a belief on reasonable grounds is sufficient to establish a lack of realistic law-abiding alternatives. Whilst, as noted above, Wright argues that this issue necessitates an inquiry into the accused's subjective beliefs for the purposes of self-defence, necessity, by way of contrast, is excuse based and therefore legitimately requires reasonable grounds before the accused can benefit from their errors of fact.

In *Police v Kawiti*,[80] the court cited Simester and Brookbanks[81] as suggesting that proportionality is decided by asking whether 'a sober person of reasonable firmness sharing certain characteristics of the defendant, would have responded in like manner'. The better view, however, may be that the requirement of proportionality is not concerned with the overbearing of the defendant's will—which is already addressed when considering the nexus between the peril and the offending in the fourth requirement—but, instead, with the balancing of harms, and requires that the criminal offending be no more harmful than the threat that was being avoided.[82]

There are two forms of necessity at common law.[83] Duress of circumstances deals with situations in which the defendant's will is overborn by the need to escape death or serious injury in emergency circumstances. This defence has parallels with duress by threats, except that the defendant responds 'to the threat by committing a crime of his own choosing'.[84] Necessity, on the other hand, covers situations where the defendant commits a crime because it represents causing lesser harm than the alternative. This may involve a rational choice in circumstances other than emergency. The requirements of the common law defence of necessity in New Zealand, outlined above, with the exception of the proportionality requirement, appear to be primarily informed by the notion of normative involuntariness, and the defence may therefore owe its origins to 'duress by circumstances' rather than necessity. Consequently there is an argument for the survival of a broader common law defence of necessity, not subject to the limitations described here.

In *Kapi v Ministry of Transport*[85] the Court of Appeal held that:

> When section 24 provides a defence of compulsion (or duress) where the criminal act is done under threat of death or grievous bodily harm from a person who is present when the offence is committed, we do not consider that section 20 can be said to preserve a common law defence of duress by threat or fear of death or grievous bodily harm from a person not present.[86]

The result is an additional limitation on the common law defence of necessity—if the threat comes from a person the defence is not available. This interpretation leaves those caught up in emergency situations created by other people, but who are not in standover situations, in a hiatus—without access to either the common law

---

77   Whilst the accused's beliefs are justifiably irrelevant to the application of normative assessments to the facts it does not follow that they should be irrelevant to factual requirements of this nature.

78   *Leason* (n 33).

79   See also *Friend v Police* (n 75).

80   *Kawiti* (n 8).

81   Simester and Brookbanks (n 73).

82   See Wilson J in *Perka v R* (n 1). This interpretation is supported by *Friend v Police* (n 75); *Police v Coll* (n 74); *Kapi v MOT* (n 55) 57.

83   *AG v Leason* (n 33).

84   AP Simester, JR Spencer, GR Sullivan and GJ Virgo, *Simester and Sullivan's Criminal Law: Theory and Doctrine* (4th edn, Hart 2010) 734.

85   *Kapi* (n 55).

86   ibid 54–55.

defence of necessity or the defence of compulsion set out in section 24.[87] Ironically it means that, rather than attempting to escape the person threatening them, they would be better to retaliate with violence against this person because self-defence may then be available.

The position taken in *Kapi*[88] is not an obvious one. A principled distinction could have been drawn between the defence of duress by threats (stand-over situations) and the defence of necessity and/or duress by circumstances (emergency situations). It could have been concluded that section 24 codifies the former but not the latter—regardless of whether the origin of the emergency was human agency or not. The distinction that was made instead, between human and non-human sources of threat, is not supported by common law authority.[89] Nonetheless, in *Akulue v R*[90] the New Zealand Supreme Court refused to overturn this 'settled interpretation'.

General Mental Condition Defences

Insanity
Section 23(2) provides:

> No person shall be convicted of an offence by reason of an act done or omitted by him when labouring under natural imbecility or disease of the mind to such an extent as to render him incapable of understanding the nature and quality of the act or omission; or of knowing that the act or omission was morally wrong, having regard to the commonly accepted standards of right and wrong.

If the prosecution, defence and judge are all satisfied that the defendant was insane at the time of the offending then the judge can now record an insanity verdict—not guilty by reason of insanity—thus avoiding or terminating the trial process.[91]

'Natural imbecility' is an arrested or retarded development of the mind[92] and might allow an insanity defence not as a claim of 'global' incapacity but as a contextualized claim in relation to a particular offence on a particular set of facts. This could happen where a person's 'imbecility' means that they do not have the capacity to know facts relevant to a complainant's capacity, for example to consent, and thereby do not know that their acts were wrong.[93]

A 'disease of the mind' is an illness, disorder or abnormal condition that has the effect of impairing the faculties of reasoning, memory and understanding.[94] It is trite law that insanity is concerned with the 'mind', rather than any organic deterioration of the brain.[95]

A disease of the mind must originate in a source internal, rather than external, to the defendant. In *R v Yesler*,[96] it was held that whilst a psychological blow can be an external cause, if the emotional shock would not have been enough to cause an ordinary person in the defendant's circumstances to disassociate, then the cause of the dissociative state the defendant was triggered into was their own internal makeup and therefore a disease of the mind.

Although section 23 requires proof that the defendant was 'incapable' of understanding what he was doing was wrong, the court in *R v Dixon*[97] held that the issue is whether or not the defendant *actually knew* that what he was doing was wrong, not whether he lacked the complete capacity to know what was wrong.[98]

---

87   That this hiatus is particularly a problem for battered women is illustrated by *Police v Kawiti* (n 8).
88   *Kapi* (n 55).
89   *R v Miller* (1986) 83 Cr App R (CA); *R v Conway* [1989] QB 290 (CA). See Simester, Spencer, Sullivan and Virgo (n 84) 734.
90   [2013] NZSC 88.
91   Criminal Procedure (Mentally Impaired Persons Act) 2003 (NZ), section 20(2).
92   *Cooper v R* (1978) 40 CCC (2d) 145; R v Rolph [1962] Qd R 262, 271.
93   Simester and Brookbanks (n 73) 331.
94   *R v Porter* [1933] 55 CLR 182, 188; *R v Cottle* [1958] NZLR 999 (CA).
95   *R v Porter* ibid, 189.
96   [2007] 1 NZLR 240. Following *R v Rabey* [1980] 2 SCR 513; *R v Stone* [1999] 2 SCR 290.
97   *Dixon* (n 19).
98   Following *R v MacMillan* [1966] NZLR 616.

In *R v Hamblyn*[99] the defendant committed crimes whilst she was in a dissociative state—meaning that her mind was occupied and her actions were controlled by several 'alter' personalities. Her 'host personality'— the personality that she was born with and identified with in the world—was unaware of the commission of the crimes and therefore did not know what was physically happening at the time she offended. However, her knowledge was taken to be the state of consciousness that she had at the time of committing the crimes (the alter personalities) and this consciousness included awareness of what she was doing and knowledge that it was wrong. The result was that she had a disease of the mind but she was not insane.

The 'nature and quality of the act or omission' refers exclusively to the physical character of the act or omission performed by the defendant.[100] In other words, the defendant must be either not conscious of what s/he is doing at all or having some kind of delusional process so that they do not know the physical character of the act they are doing to satisfy this requirement.

In *R v MacMillan*[101] the Court of Appeal held that the test for knowledge of moral wrongfulness is based on a *subjective* not an *objective* standard. The test is whether the defendant knew the act was morally wrong for him/her to perform and not whether they know the act was wrong for others or 'morally wrong in the eyes of other people'. The court came to this conclusion because otherwise the test would exclude from the operation of the defence of insanity a substantial class of persons clinically demonstrable as persons of unsound mind.

Intoxication

New Zealand takes a liberal position on the relevance of intoxication to criminal liability, refusing to impose constructive liability on those who are intoxicated regardless of whether they were voluntarily or involuntarily so.[102] The law is simply stated—intoxication is an altered state of mind that must be considered, in so far as it is relevant, in deciding whether the accused voluntarily performed the *actus reus*, whilst possessing the appropriate *mens rea*, and had one of the defences available to him/her.[103] The issue is not what state of mind the defendant had the capacity to form but rather what state of mind they *actually had* because of the influence of intoxication.[104]

Intoxication is a subjective state of mind and therefore is only relevant to subjective *mens rea* concepts, such as intention, knowledge or recklessness. Having said this, alcohol is widely understood as removing normal restraints and inhibitions, impairing judgements about right and wrong and producing aggression—all of which are consistent with the presence of a drunken intent.[105] Juries are therefore typically directed that 'a drunken intent is still an intent'.[106]

Intoxication is not relevant to objective states of mind because the reasonable person is always sober, and reasonable grounds are always judged from a position of sobriety.[107] It is also generally not relevant to crimes that have no *mens rea* standards: such as crimes of strict or absolute liability. However, for offences of strict liability the accused has the defence of absence of fault available to them. Involuntary intoxication may be relevant in establishing this defence, but will not succeed if the defendant knew or ought to have known that they were affected by alcohol.[108]

---

99   [1997] 15 CRNZ 58 (CA).

100   *R v Codere* [1916] 12 Cr App R 21.

101   *MacMillan* (n 98).

102   However, it takes a restrictive view on the relevance of voluntary intoxication at sentencing. See section 9(3) of the Sentencing Act 2002.

103   *R v Kamipeli* [1975] 2 NZLR 610; *Steinberg v Police* [1983] 1 CRNZ 129; *R v Storer* [2006] (CA, 2 May) [26]; *R v Tihi* [1990] 1 NZLR 540.

104   *Steinberg v Police* ibid.

105   *R v Craig* [2002] (CA, 11 December) [41].

106   *R v Nicholson* [1998] (CA, 8 October); *R v O'Brien* [2003] (CA, 16 October); *McGowan v R* [2008] (CA, 1 July); *Hui v R* [2006] (CA, 28 Sept); *Cottle v R* [2004] (CA, 2 November).

107   *R v Clarke* [1992] 1 NZLR 147.

108   See *Keech v Pratt* [1994] 1 NZLR 65; *O'Neill v MOT* [1985] 2 NZLR 513.

Intoxication can also theoretically (but in practice rarely) operate to disprove the *actus reus* of an offence.[109] In other words, if it can be established that the accused was so drunk that they were acting involuntarily then the outcome would be an acquittal.[110]

As documented above, whether or not intoxication is relevant to a particular defence depends on the way that the defence is constructed in principle. If the defence uses subjective standards for assessing a particular issue then intoxication is relevant in assessing the defendant's actual state of mind on that issue.

Mistake of Law

Section 25 of the Crimes Act 1961 provides that '[t]he fact that an offender is ignorant of the law is not an excuse for any offence committed by him'. Whilst this would seem to negate the use of a mistake of law as a foundation for excusatory defences only, the provision has been interpreted more generally to mean that mistakes of law, whether reasonable or not, cannot be used to found an argument that the accused lacked *mens rea* or provide a foundation for any of the defences—whether justificatory or excusatory.[111] Underlying this position is the need to uphold the rule of law.

Whilst there are some authorities suggesting that, if a mistake of law on the part of the defendant means that the Crown cannot establish the required *mens rea* for offending, then the accused is entitled to an acquittal,[112] these decisions are out of line with the general trend of New Zealand authority.[113]

By way of contrast, mistakes of fact, where they are relevant, will negate *mens rea* and, as noted in specific instances above, will support the various defences where the defendant's belief is relevant to a particular legal requirement. Whether the mistake has to be reasonable or simply honestly held will depend on whether the element in question involves a subjective or objective standard.

In *Keung v Police*[114] the court held:

> [A]ll human mistakes will, to a greater or lesser extent, have factual elements. The difference between mistakes of law and mistakes of fact is often a fine one, and unfortunately the case law provides no definitive touchstone or guiding principle.[115]

There is a smorgasbord of sometimes contradictory decisions in New Zealand classifying mistakes as either law or fact. If the accused understands all of the relevant facts correctly but simply does not grasp their legal significance then it is easy to characterise the mistake as one of law.[116] On the other hand, mixed mistakes of fact and law, in which the accused is mistaken about their legal rights but only because they have made an underlying factual error, tend to be characterised as mistakes of fact.[117]

There are several exceptions to the rule that a mistake of law will not form the basis for arguing a lack of criminal liability. These are where the accused is asserting a claim of right in relation to a property offence and the doctrine of officially induced error.

---

109   *R v Hart* [1986] 2 NZLR 408 [50].

110   One interesting issue is whether automatism based on intoxication could be argued in relation to drink driving offences. In New Zealand automatism in these circumstances is treated as one way of proving lack of fault in relation to a strict liability offence: See *Keech v Pratt* (n 108); *O'Neill v MOT* (n 108). However, *Keech v Pratt* made it clear that intoxication is extremely unlikely to found a case of automatism because of the nature of driving requires complicated physical movements that suggest voluntary action.

111   *Skelton v Police* [1998] NZFLR 102; *Alofaki v Police* [2007] (HC, 19 March); *Labour Department v Green* [1973] 1 NZLR 412; *Fastlane Autos Ltd v Commerce Commission* [2004] 3 NZLR 513; *R v Leolahi* [2001] 1 NZLR 562; *Oosterman v Police* [2007] NZAR 147; *Breen v Police* (1989) 5 CRNZ 238; *Clarke v Police* [2000] (CA, 22 May).

112   *Booth v MOT* [1988] 2 NZLR 217; *Police v C* 15 FRNZ 269.

113   Simester and Brookbanks, (n 73) 487, argue that the only kinds of mistakes capable of negating mens rea are misunderstandings about civil rights as opposed to penal provisions.

114   [2009] (HC, 5 November).

115   ibid [19].

116   *R v Foox* [2000] 1 NZLR 64; *R v Cave* [2011] NZAR 498.

117   *Keung v Police* (n 114); *Police v Shadbolt* [1976] 2 NZLR 409.

A number of property offences in the Crimes Act 1961 require that the accused be acting without a 'claim of right'.[118] A claim of right is defined in section 2 to mean:

> [A] belief at the time of the act in a proprietary or possessory right in property in relation to which the offence
> is alleged to have been committed, although that belief may be based on ignorance or mistake of fact or of any
> matter of law other than the enactment against which the offence is alleged to have been committed.

The belief does not have to reasonable grounds so long as it is honestly held.[119]

The definition of 'claim of right' has only just recently been confined to a belief in a 'proprietary or possessory right in property'. The definition was amended to reverse *R v Murnane*.[120] In this case three men damaged a satellite dome in order to prevent the New Zealand government relaying information to the United States for use in the war in Iraq and the consequent murder of innocent civilians. They wrongly believed that they had a defence to their criminal actions on the basis of self-defence or necessity, or under international human right conventions, and their mistake was held to be a claim of right.

The defence of 'officially induced error of law' has been accepted in obiter as part of the law in New Zealand,[121] but has yet to be applied in practice.[122] Instead, the doctrine has been used on several occasions to support a discharge without conviction under section 106 of the Sentencing Act.[123] It has been suggested that it could also be used to stay proceedings for an abuse of process.[124]

The exact parameters of the doctrine have yet to be determined. It appears necessary that the defendant reasonably relied on the erroneous advice of an official responsible for the administration of the law in question.[125] The idea is that the citizen has behaved appropriately in relying on the advice of those whom the state has permitted to speak on its behalf and 'political decency demands that when the state choose to advise its citizens about the law, it should do so accurately'.[126]

Residual Defences

There are some additional defences that are generally available in relation to certain classes of offences. For example, the defence of absence of fault is available in relation to all offences classified as being offences of 'strict', as opposed to 'absolute', liability. For these types of offences the Crown has the burden of establishing the *actus reus* only on the facts. At that point the defence has the option of establishing, if they are able to do so, that they were not at fault. In *Civil Aviation Dept v MacKenzie*[127] it was held that an honest and *reasonable* belief in facts that if true would make the accused's act innocent will establish an absence of fault.[128]

Another example of this type of defence is the defence of 'parental control' contained in section 59 of the Crimes Act 1961. This justifies the use of physical force that might otherwise constitute one of the interpersonal violence offences. To satisfy the requirements of the section, the parent (or person in place of a parent) must use the force against a child either to prevent or minimise harm or offensive or disruptive behaviour, or to perform 'the normal daily tasks that are incidental to good care and parenting'. The force must not be for the purpose of 'correction', and must be 'reasonable in the circumstances'.

Sections 52–56 of the Crimes Act 1961 permit a limited use of force to protect property. The original laws criminalising property transgression were directed at preventing breaches of the peace rather than protecting

---

118   For example, theft (Crimes Act 1961, section 219) and dishonestly taking or using a document (Crimes Act 1961, section 228).

119   *R v Hayes* [2008] 2 NZLR 321 [35].

120   [2010] (DC, 16 March).

121   *Wilson v Auckland City Council* (No 1) [2007] NZAR 705.

122   *Crafar v Waikato Regional Council* [2010] (HC, 13 September).

123   *Tipple v Police* [1994] 2 NZLR 362; *Diriye v Police* [2009] NZAR 717.

124   *Ministry of Fisheries v New Zealand Wholesale Seafoods* [2001] DCR 85.

125   *R v Jorgensen* [1995] 4 SCR 55; Cardin Laurant Ltd v Commerce Commission [1990] 3 NZLR 563.

126   See Briggs, 'Officially Induced Error of Law' (1995) 16 NZ U L Rev 403 and *Diriye v Police* (n 123).

127   [1983] NZLR 78.

128   *Police v Creedon* [1976] 1 NZLR 571; *MOT v Burnetts Motors Ltd* [1980] 1 NZLR 51. Mistakes of law are excluded: *Kirkby v Mihinui* [1987] (HC, 20 October); *Waaka v Police* [1997] 1 NZLR 754, 759.

private property per se. Sections 52 and 53 (which create a defence in respect of moveable things) and sections 55 and 56 (which create a defence in respect of dwelling houses) accordingly still require that the person seeking to raise the defence was in 'possession' (there is an exception in section 52 if the property has just been taken by a trespasser). The law also prioritises human life and safety, even for a wrong doer, over the possession of property. Accordingly, force in protecting property is limited to what is necessary to protect that property and generally excludes striking or causing physical harm to another (except under section 55 when defending a dwelling house against a forcible breaking and entering).

In addition to these more general defences, criminal legislation in New Zealand is peppered with examples of particular defences tailored and attached to specific offences. For example, section 134A creates a specific defence to charges under section 134 for sexual conduct with a young person. The defence has the onus of establishing that reasonable steps were taken to find out whether the young person was of or over the age of 16, they believed on reasonable grounds that the person was of or over the age of 16, and the young person consented. Some of these specific defences represent areas in which the more general defences have been codified for particular contexts. For example, sections 182(2) and 187A provide a defence of necessity tailored to the abortion offences and necessity is codified in relation to trespass in section 3(2) of the Trespass Act 1980. The sheer number and diversity of these particular defences makes further summary impossible.

As will have become obvious in this chapter, many of the general defences in New Zealand are still in very embryonic stages of development. Even in respect of self-defence and insanity, which have a more fulsome body of case law explicating their legal requirements, there is much that still remains conceptually unresolved. Part of the reason for this may be a strong adherence to legal positivism in judicial law making, and therefore an approach that Ted Thomas has described as 'muddling along',[129] as opposed to a more principle-orientated approach.

---

129   See EW Thomas, *The Judicial Process: Realism, Pragmatism, Practical Reasoning and Principles* (Cambridge University Press 2005) 24.

Chapter 20
South Africa

Gerhard Kemp

General Issues

Justificatory and Excusatory Defences—Distinction and Seat in the Offence Structure

There are a number of general defences that exclude the unlawfulness element. Some authors emphasise the notion that unlawfulness actually entails a negative; it means the absence of any justification for the apparently unlawful act.[1] The conceptual foundations are more fully explained below.

The most important general defences are the following: private defence (also known as self-defence); necessity; impossibility to comply with the law (*lex non cogit ad impossibilia*); superior orders; moderate corporal chastisement; consent; and public authority. These defences or justifications are assessed objectively.[2] An accused who subjectively and 'genuinely believes that the requisite foundation [for a defence] exists will escape liability on the basis of lack of fault (*mens rea*) in the form of intention. If his belief is also reasonable, he will escape liability for negligence'.[3] The subjective forms of defences can be described as *putative* defences.

Conceptual Foundations

The conceptual foundations of general defences in South African criminal law can be found in the structure of general principles of criminal liability. The element of unlawfulness is relevant here. 'Unlawfulness' ('*wederregtelikheid*' in Afrikaans) literally means 'against the law' or the opposite of 'lawful'. In terms of criminal liability the literal concept of 'unlawful' is not very helpful. To kill someone is, on the face of it, unlawful. But it is not necessarily a crime. If the killing was justified, then the conduct will not be regarded as criminal conduct. This much is trite in many legal systems, including South Africa. The problem with the term 'unlawful' ('*wederregtelik*') is the fact that the term can lead to the erroneous equation between conduct that is in conflict with some or other law or prohibition and 'unlawfulness'. Unlawfulness is, of course, something more, namely 'unlawful' conduct that can also not be justified with reference to some or other defence or justification. Despite the above criticism, the terms 'unlawfulness' and '*wederregtelikheid*' are firmly established in South African criminal law literature and jurisprudence. Snyman therefore suggests the following approach:

> An act or conduct that satisfies the definition of a crime is prima facie or provisionally unlawful. The conduct will be regarded as unlawful if it can be determined that the (provisionally unlawful) conduct could not be justified.[4]

The term 'excused' (in the context of unlawfulness) is noticeably absent from most South African criminal law literature and case law.

---

1   CR Snyman, *Strafreg* (6th edn, LexisNexis 2012) 101.
2   Jonathan Burchell, *Principles of Criminal Law* (3rd edn, Juta 2005) 227.
3   Burchell ibid 227.
4   Snyman (n 1) 100–101.

Cumulation/Cumulative or Alternative Pleading of Defences

The general procedural principle is that the state must prove the absence of any defence raised by the accused. A notable exception is the defence of mental illness (see discussion under 4 below). The burden of proof is therefore on the accused should he raise the defence of mental illness. For the purpose of all other defences, whether raised cumulatively or alternatively, the duty to raise such defences rest on the accused, and the state bears the onus to disprove any such defence or defences.[5]

Provocation of Defence Situation

Consider the following scenario: A provoked B, who in turn retaliates against A in a violent way. The question is whether and to what extent A can still defend himself against B's provoked attack. Assuming that A can indeed defend himself against B's attack, the further question is whether A's right to self-defence is in any way restricted due to his (A's) act of provocation.

In principle, the person who relies on self-defence *must know that he or she is acting in self-defence*. The implication is that a person who provoked an attack cannot then abuse self-defence as a guise to use force against the provoked person.[6] Thus, in principle, A (in our scenario) would not be able to rely on self-defence as a justification for the use of force against B.

It is, however, also important to note that public policy demands that insofar as B would use excessive force (disproportionate to the provocation) then B's conduct will also be regarded as unlawful.[7] One can imagine a scenario where A mildly taunts B and B then reacts in an extremely violent way. A's defensive acts in this scenario will probably be regarded as legitimate self-defence.

Mistakes of Fact and Defences

In the English case of *R v Williams (Gladstone)*,[8] the court put forward the principle that where a person mistakenly believes that it is necessary to defend himself (or another person), *he must be judged against the fact or facts as he believes them to be*. Thus, mistake of fact in this context is a subjective test, because the court further held that such a mistake can be the basis for a defence, even where the mistake is unreasonable. The position in South Africa is that, in principle, the test for defences like self-defence/private defence is objective. Where an accused subjectively (but wrongly) believes that it is necessary to defend himself or another person, the situation is known as *putative* self-defence. Of course, the courts are sensitive to the fact that real people in real situations may not always act according to the standards of an abstract notion. The Supreme Court of Appeal put it as follows:

> In applying these formulations to flesh and blood facts, the Courts adopt a robust attitude, not seeking to measure with nice intellectual callipers the precise bounds of legitimate self-defence. ... [9]

However, if one finds that any given mistake of fact would amount to a situation of putative self-defence, the accused might still escape liability because of lack of intent. The facts as the accused (subjectively) believes them to be will be the determinant issue affecting intent.[10]

---

5   *S v Kok* [1998] (1) SACR 532 (N); PJ Schwikkard & SE van der Merwe, *Principles of Evidence* (3rd edn, Juta 2009) 563–564.

6   Snyman (n 1) 115–116 (with reference to various South African, Dutch, and German authors).

7   Snyman (n 1) 117.

8   *R v Williams (Gladstone)* (1984) 78 Cr App R 276 (CA).

9   *S v Ntuli* [1975] (1) SA 429 (a) 437.

10   Snyman (n 1) 198.

Transferred Defences/Collateral Damage Defences

Aberratio ictus—or, 'going astray of the blow'—is the situation where force or violence is meant for a particular person but accidentally goes astray and injures or kills the wrong (unintended) person. In South Africa, the majority of court cases seem to favour the concrete intent approach. Thus, when confronted with an *aberratio ictus* scenario, a court will normally enquire whether, despite the fact that the accused did not have *dolus directus* in respect of the unintended third party's death ('the collateral damage'), he nevertheless had *dolus* in one of the other accepted forms, for instance *dolus eventualis*. Insofar as the accused foresaw the possibility that he might cause the death of another person in the same position, class or category or place of the deceased, and in substantially the same manner as he did in fact cause the death, the accused can be held liable and the death of the third party will not be excusable. The accused will not be able to raise a successful defence excluding intent.[11]

Individual Defences

Self-Defence and Excessive Self-Defence

Self-defence forms part of the category of defences called 'private defence'. This category includes self-defence, defence of other persons and defence of property. Under South African law private-defence refers to the situation in which a *private* individual (as opposed to a public official, for instance a police officer) uses force to defend himself or another person.[12]

For purposes of this discussion, 'self-defence' can be viewed as the narrower concept, while 'private defence' is broad enough to include defence of a third party. The discussion is divided into three parts, namely:

- Requirements for the attack or threat;
- Requirements for the defender's response; and
- The use of excessive force.

In terms of the requirements for the attack or threat, three basic requirements can be identified. First, there must be an unlawful attack or threat of attack. This first requirement concerns a real, actual or threatened attack. It should be noted that a subjective fear of an attack will not normally qualify. The attack must be unlawful, which means that a person will not be able to use self-defence against a lawful invasion of his interests (for instance in the case of a lawful arrest or deprivation of liberty).[13] It is of course not required that the attack be criminal in the full sense of the word. Thus, if an insane person or a child (under the age of criminal capacity) attacks a person, the latter will be able to use legitimate self-defence even though the attack was performed by someone who could legally not be held accountable. Second, the attack must threaten some legally protected interest.

Under common law the interests of human life, physical integrity, sexual integrity and personal freedom were recognised as worthy of protection. South Africa's Bill of Rights gave further meaning and importance to these protected interests. The Constitutional Court, in arguably the most important decision in South Africa on the right to life, held in *S v Makwanyane* that the law may legitimately allow killing in self-defence.[14] While the Constitutional Court's decision on the limitation of the right to life in cases of self-defence appears to be a confirmation of the common law principle, there also seems to have been a more than subtle change in the traditional test for reasonableness of force in cases of self-defence. In *Ntamo v Minister of Safety and Security*,[15] for instance, the court held that the legal convictions of the community on the common law of self-defence are informed by constitutionally protected rights such as the right to life. Indeed, the court seemed

---

11 Kemp (n 6) 229; *S v Nkombani* [1963] (4) SA 877 (A).
12 Kemp (n 6) 77.
13 Kemp (n 6) 78.
14 *S v Makwanyane* [1995] (3) SA 391 (CC) [138].
15 *Ntamo v Minister of Safety and Security* [2001] (1) SA 830 (Tk).

to favour a strict approach and held that self-defence could not succeed where the threatened harm could be avoided *without* the use of force.

To the extent that force is necessary, it has to be proportional to the harm. The notion that, under the influence of the Bill of Rights, the test to determine whether an attacked person's defensive conduct was reasonable is now more onerous than under common law, was also followed in *S v Dougherty*.[16] This line of thought was criticised by some. The objection is that it is wrong to say that the Bill of Rights requires 'that the attacker must now be treated more leniently in that the person invoking private defence now has a "higher hurdle" to overcome before a court can find that he acted in private defence'.[17]

The third requirement for the attack is that the attack must be in progress, or imminent. This requirement is not always easy to ascertain. 'Imminent threat' is a matter of fact and there are most certainly grey areas. The principle in South African law has been for some time, and still is, that the attacked person is not obliged to wait for his attacker to strike the first blow. However, a preemptive attack is also not allowed where the future attack is unlikely or remote or might occur at some indefinite time in the future.[18]

The second set of requirements that we need to consider are the requirements for the defender's response. Firstly, the use of force must be necessary. As we have seen above, with reference to the influence of the Bill of Rights, the defensive use of force must now be evaluated in light of the rather strict test in terms of which the use of force will almost always be regarded as the last resort. The implication is that the law expects a person to rather flee an attack or retreat, where possible, rather than to use force. The Supreme Court of Appeal qualified this and held that a person is not expected to flee if doing so would expose him to more danger, or where it was not practical.[19] There does not appear to be a principle of stand your ground in South Africa, and the common law principles, as influenced by the Bill of Rights, put the emphasis on the use of force as a last resort.

The second requirement for the defender's response is that the force used must be reasonable and proportional. Again, the impact of the Bill of Rights, as briefly discussed above, must be noted. Equivalence of force, as under common law, is no longer applicable. The test now is whether there was a 'reasonable relationship between the attack and the defensive act'. Factors such as the relationship between the parties; the respective ages, gender and physical strength of the parties; the location of the incident; the nature, severity and persistence of the attack; the nature of any weapon used in the attack; the nature and severity of any injury or harm likely to be sustained in the attack; the means available to avert the attack; the nature of the means used to offer defence; and the nature and extent of the harm likely to be caused by the defence, can be taken into account.[20]

Flowing from the requirement that the force used must be reasonable and proportional, is the issue of the use of *excessive force*. 'Excessive force' in this context is the use of more force than is reasonably necessary. The test is objective.[21]

Necessity

The defence of necessity under South African common law arises when a person must choose between breaking the law and suffering a more serious fate.[22] The legal convictions of the community, and public policy, demand that the circumstances in which a person will be allowed to rely on the defence of necessity, are limited and the test is strict.

First, it is necessary to look at the *requirements for the threat or danger*. The first requirement here is that there must be some or other legal interest at stake. Protected interests include (human) life and bodily

---

16   *S v Dougherty* [2003] (2) SACR 36 (W).

17   CR Snyman, 'Private Defence in Criminal Law – An Unwarranted Raising of the Test of Unreasonableness' [2004] 67 *Tydskrif vir Hedendaags Romeins-Hollandse Reg* 325, 330.

18   *R v Hope* [1917] NPD 145; Kemp (n 6) 79.

19   *S v Steyn* [2010] (1) SACR 411 (SCA).

20   *S v Steyn* [2010] (1) SACR 411 (SCA); *S v Trainor* [2003] (1) SACR 35 (SCA); Kemp (n 6) 80.

21   *S v Ntuli* [1975] (1) SA 429 (A); Kemp (n 6) 81.

22   Kemp (n 6) 88.

integrity or property (one's own or another person's).[23] The second requirement is that the danger must have commenced or be imminent. This requirement corresponds with that of self-defence. However, it can certainly be argued that it will be in line with public policy for the accused to have acted in order to avert danger—and in this context the borders of 'imminence' might be flexible enough in order to encourage prudent behaviour.[24] The third requirement is that the danger must not have arisen through the accused's own fault. Public policy dictates, and the common law indeed provides, that 'a person may not profit from his own wrongdoing'.[25] This general principle is not very helpful if stated in such broad terms. Some commentators and judgments take a more nuanced view. Thus, the rule that an accused cannot act out of necessity if he caused the original danger through prior conduct, should only apply where the accused was actually aware the he was creating such a risk.[26] To this one must also add that if the danger is only the indirect result of the accused's conduct, the accused should, in principle, still be able to benefit from the necessity defence, where applicable.[27]

There are two *requirements for the response*: First, the act must be necessary. In popular parlance, conduct is sometimes described as an 'absolute' necessity. From a legal point of view, this type of description is not very helpful. It is submitted that the requirement of necessity in this context is that the conduct must be necessary (and reasonable) in order to avert the threatened harm or danger. The test is not cast in absolutist terms. Rather, the test is whether there was no other 'practical way of averting the threatened harm or danger'. To put it differently, the test is whether the threatened harm would 'probably have followed had the accused not acted as he did'.[28] The second requirement, as already mentioned, is that the conduct must be reasonable. Generally speaking, one can say that this objective requirement entails that the accused should not do more harm than was necessary to avert the danger, and if there is a choice between more or less harm, the accused should choose the latter.[29]

Duress by Threats/Circumstances

The Supreme Court of Appeal accepted that compulsion, or duress, can be a complete defence under South African criminal law. While the defence is available even in situations where the killing of an innocent third person is made necessary by duress, it is a defence that will not be accepted lightly.[30] This is especially true since the introduction of the Bill of Rights. Innocent third persons can certainly claim that their rights to equality, human dignity and the right to life cannot be regarded as of lesser value than the person who claims to act under duress due to a threat to his own life. South African criminal law doctrine as it currently stands does not provide a satisfactory answer to this moral and constitutional conundrum. Under the current law, the defence of duress is presented as a justification that excludes unlawfulness. It would be better to view (unlawful) acts done under duress as excusable. The conduct is therefore still unlawful, but excusable. This could either affect sentencing, or could, in appropriate circumstances, exclude culpability entirely.[31]

General Mental Condition Defences

Insanity
In South Africa the so-called 'insanity' defence, or, the defence of pathological criminal incapacity, first developed from English law, but later became the subject of major legislative reform. Although South African common law is the result of Roman-Dutch and English law influences, the defence of pathological criminal

---

23   Kemp (n 6) 88.
24   *S v Moller* [1971] (4) SA 327 (T) 329–330.
25   Kemp (n 6) 89.
26   *S v Bradbury* [1967] (1) SA 387 (A); *S v Lungile and another* [1999] (2) SACR 597 (SCA); Kemp (n 6) 89; Snyman (n 1) 119–120.
27   Burchell (n 2) 264; Kemp (n 6) 89.
28   Burchell (n 2) 265; Kemp (n 6) 89.
29   Kemp (n 6) 90.
30   S v Goliath [1972] (3) SA 1 (A); Kemp (n 6) 91.
31   J Burchell, *South African Criminal Law & Procedure Vol I* (4th edn, Juta 2011) 169; Kemp (n 6) 91.

incapacity in South African criminal law, was to a large extent based on the *M'Naghten* rules, laid down by the English courts. These rules in essence provided as follows:

- Every person is presumed to be sane and to have sufficient powers of reason to be held responsible for his crimes, until the contrary is proved;
- To establish a defence on the ground of insanity, it must be clearly proved that at the time of committing the act, the accused was labouring under such a defect of reason, from disease of the mind, as not to know the nature and quality of the act he was doing, or, if he did know it, he did not know that what he was doing was wrong.[32]

Early South African cases exposed an important deficiency in the *M'Naghten* rules. The problem was that the *M'Naghten* rules only focussed on the state of an accused's cognitive functions. The implication was that, as long as an accused had the necessary knowledge of the wrongfulness of his conduct, he could be held criminally responsible, regardless of the fact that he might not have had the conative functions to control his conduct and to act in accordance with the knowledge of wrongfulness. In *R v Hay*,[33] Chief Justice De Villiers accepted that mentally ill persons might (intellectually) be able to distinguish between right and wrong, but nevertheless be unable to control or direct an impulse to do wrong. The Chief Justice thus accepted the two components of the insanity defence, namely the cognitive and the conative components. The judgment in *Hay* was later followed by *R v Smit*,[34] where the then-Chief Justice Innes, formulated the defence of mental illness as follows:

> The first rule is this – that every man is presumed to be sane, and able to control his actions, and to be responsible for the consequences of his actions until it is proved that he is not.
>
> The second rule is that if a man is proved to have committed an act which in ordinary circumstances would be criminal, but owing to mental disease he did not know at the time what he was doing was wrong, then he is not criminally liable.
>
> [The third rule is] that though a man may have committed an act which, if an ordinary man had done it, would have entailed criminal consequences, yet if the jury are satisfied that by reason of mental disease he could not resist the impulse under which he acted, then he is not criminally liable.

The dramatic assassination of the South African Prime Minister HF Verwoerd in 1966 by a presumably mentally ill person prompted a commission of inquiry to conduct an extensive investigation into the facts surrounding the assassination. This commission of inquiry recommended a more systematic investigation into the criminal law consequences of mental illness. The Commission of Inquiry into the Responsibility of Mentally Deranged Individuals and Related Matters (chaired by Judge Rumpff) was established. The findings[35] of the Rumpff Commission of Inquiry resulted in the enactment of Chapter 13 of the Criminal Procedure Act 51 of 1977.[36]

Chapter 13 of the Criminal Procedure Act consists of three important provisions dealing with substantive and procedural matters concerning mental illness and the criminal justice system. Section 77 of the Act deals with an accused's fitness to stand trial; section 78 deals with the defence of mental illness and with diminished responsibility as a result of mental illness; and Section 79 deals with the procedure for inquiring into an accused's mental state for purposes of the preceding Sections 77 and 78.

Section 78(1), (1A) and (1B) of the Criminal Procedure Act, which deals with the defence of mental illness, provides as follows:

---

32 Kemp (n 6) 137.
33 *R v Hay* (1899) 9 CTR 292.
34 *R v Smit* [1906] TS 783.
35 *Government Gazette RP* 69/1967 (1967).
36 For detailed commentary, see E du Toit and others, *Commentary on the Criminal Procedure Act* (Revision Service 50, Juta 2013) 13-12–13-32.

(1) A person who commits an act or makes an omission which constitutes an offence and who at the time of such commission or omission suffers from a mental illness or mental defect which makes him or her incapable-

(a) of appreciating the wrongfulness of his or her act or omission; or

(b) of acting in accordance with an appreciation of the wrongfulness of his or her act or omission, shall not be criminally responsible for such act or omission.

(1A) Every person is presumed not to suffer from a mental illness or mental defect so as not to be criminally responsible in terms of s 78(1), until the contrary is proved on a balance of probabilities.

(1B) Whenever the criminal responsibility of an accused with reference to the commission of an act or an omission which constitutes an offence is in issue, the burden of proof with reference to the criminal responsibility of the accused shall be on the party who raises the issue.

It should be noted that, for purposes of a preliminary inquiry in terms of the Child Justice Act 75 of 2008, to determine the *criminal capacity of a child*, any such preliminary investigation may be postponed for a period determined by the inquiry magistrate in the case where the child has been referred for a decision relating to mental illness or defect in terms of Section 78 of the Criminal Procedure Act.

The earlier application and development of the *M'Naghten* rules by South African courts are no longer applied. Section 78 of the Criminal Procedure Act is the source of law on mental illness as a defence under South African criminal law. The test for the defence of mental illness can be described in terms of a three-stage enquiry:

- *First*, it is necessary to determine if the accused committed an unlawful act or omission;
- *Second*, if the accused did in fact commit an unlawful act, the next question is whether the accused was suffering from a mental illness or mental defect at the time of the unlawful act or omission;
- *Third*, if the accused was suffering from a mental illness or defect, the question is whether it was of such a nature or degree as to render the accused unable, either (a) to appreciate the wrongfulness of that unlawful act or omission, or (b) to act in accordance with that appreciation.[37]

A curious feature of Section 78 is the lack of a definition of 'mental illness' or 'mental defect'. It is submitted that other legislation might provide some assistance in this regard. The Mental Health Care Act 17 of 2002 defines 'mental illness' as follows:

A positive diagnosis of a mental health related illness in terms of accepted diagnostic criteria made by a mental health care practitioner authorised to make such diagnosis.

It thus refers to diagnostic criteria as applied by an expert. Courts also attempted to define mental illness, or at least to provide some judicial criteria for purposes of this defence. In *S v Stellmacher*,[38] the court held that a mental illness is 'a pathological disturbance of the accused's mental capacity and not a mere temporary mental confusion which is not attributable to a mental abnormality but rather attributable to external stimuli such as alcohol, drugs or provocation'. Thus, the *Stellmacher* approach holds that the mental illness must be a pathological condition. It must impair the cognitive, conative and/or affective functions of the accused. It must furthermore not be the result of external stimuli (such as alcohol) and must be endogenous (internal to the accused).[39]

Not all pathological conditions that affect the functioning of the brain are regarded as mental illnesses. Epilepsy, for instance, is regarded as a physical illness. This categorisation is not without controversy.[40] Ultimately, however, the responsibility rests with the courts to decide, on the basis of the relevant statutory

---

37   Kemp (n 6) 142–143.

38   [1983] (2) SA 181 (SWA) 187.

39   Kemp (n 6) 144; R Louw, 'Principles of Criminal Law: Pathological and Non-Pathological Criminal Incapacity' in S Kaliski (ed), *Psycholegal Assessment in South Africa* (OUP 2006) 47.

40   Blackbeard, 'Epilepsy and Criminal Liability' (1996) 9 So Af J Crim Just 191.

framework as well as other legal sources, common sense and medical opinion, whether a condition would qualify as a mental illness for purposes of a defence under Section 78 of the Criminal Procedure Act.

Intoxication

Mental illness (in the form of *delirium tremens*) can be caused by long-term chronic abuse of alcohol. This condition will fall within the meaning of mental illness for purposes of Section 78 of the Criminal Procedure Act (discussed above).[41] The question to be addressed here is what impact *short-term intoxication* (that leads to a malfunction of the mind) has on criminal responsibility, and if it can in any way serve as a defence.

In terms of the clinical and medico-legal effects of intoxication, one can identify the following symptoms:[42]

- Impairment of the cognitive functions: Intoxication can reduce a person's ability to think and reason clearly, and to form rational judgments. It can also impacts on the ability of a person to foresee the consequences of his conduct. Severe intoxication may even lead to total unconsciousness.
- Impairment of the conative functions: Intoxication may reduce a person's ability to withstand temptation or provocation. It can also alter a person's inhibitions.
- Impact on the affective functions: Intoxication can lead to changes in a person's mood and emotions, and in more severe cases it can lead to anti-social behaviour.

The question is to what extent voluntary intoxication can serve as a defence under South African criminal law, if at all. Historically, voluntary intoxication was not always recognised as a defence. Roman–Dutch law, and initially English law (as applied in South Africa), took the approach that voluntary intoxication cannot serve as a defence, but at best as a mitigating factor for purposes of punishment. In the early twentieth century the courts in South Africa adopted the position that voluntary intoxication can be a partial defence, since it could negate the specific intent required for certain crimes (for instance conviction for culpable homicide instead of murder).[43]

For the better part of the twentieth century South African courts followed the partial defence effect of voluntary intoxication. However, in 1981 the Supreme Court of Appeal,[44] in the case of *S v Chretien*, rejected the notion that voluntary intoxication can only serve as a partial defence, at best. The court took a purest position and held that voluntary intoxication can be a complete defence, since it can (depending on the level of intoxication) negate voluntary conduct, criminal capacity or *dolus*.

It can be said that the decision by the Supreme Court of Appeal in *Chretien* represented a return to strict legal principle: Voluntary intoxication can be a complete defence.[45] However, the decision proved to be unpalatable from a public policy point of view. The fear was raised in public discourse that the decision would lead to impunity for people who committed crimes under the influence of alcohol. The issue was taken up by Parliament. In 1988, in terms of the Criminal Law Amendment Act 1 of 1988, a new statutory offence was created.[46] Section 1(1) of the Act provides:

> Where a person who consumes or uses any substance which impairs his or her faculties to appreciate the wrongfulness of his or her acts, or to act in accordance with that appreciation, while knowing that such substance has that effect, and who while such faculties are thus impaired commits any act prohibited by law

---

41   Du Toit (n 36) 13–16.

42   Kemp (n 6) 163–164; S v Stellmacher [1983] (2) SA 181 (SWA); A le Roux, 'Medico-Legal Aspects Regarding Drunk Driving' [2007] 2 So Af J Crim Just 220, 221–229.

43   *Fowlie v Rex* [1906] TS 505; Kemp (n 6) 165.

44   *S v Chretien* [1981] (1) SA 1097 (A). In this case, the accused drove a motor vehicle into a crowd of people. One person was killed and several others were injured. The accused, who was 'somewhat intoxicated' at the time of the incident, was charged with one count of murder and five counts of attempted murder. The trial court accepted his defence, namely that he did not have the necessary intent to kill or injure anyone and that he thought the people would move out of his way. The Supreme Court of Appeal (Appellate Division of the High Court, as it was then) agreed with the trial court and confirmed that the defence of voluntary intoxication is, in principle, available as a complete defence in South African criminal law. For further comment, see A Paizes, 'Intoxication Through the Looking-Glass' (1988) 105 So Af LJ 776.

45   Kemp (n 6) 166.

46   For a critique of Act 1 of 1988, see Burchell (n 2) 406–418.

under any penalty, but is not criminally liable because his or her faculties were impaired as aforesaid, shall be guilty of an offence and shall be liable on conviction to the penalty which may be imposed in respect of the commission of that act.

Any contravention of section 1(1) of Act 1 of 1988 is a crime in its own right.[47] It would be wrong to argue that whenever an accused is acquitted of an offence on account of the defence of voluntary intoxication, that he will automatically be convicted of contravention of section 1(1) of Act 1 of 1988. The State still needs to prove all the elements of the statutory offence beyond reasonable doubt. The essential elements of the statutory offence can be summarised as follows:

- The accused must have voluntarily consumed or used an intoxicating substance (such as alcohol);
- The accused must have known that it was an intoxicating substance when consuming or using it. It is, however, not necessary for the accused to know the exact extent to which the substance will impair his faculties. A general realisation or awareness of the effect of the substance in question, will suffice[48];
- The accused's faculties of insight and/or self-control must, in fact, have been impaired by the intoxicating substance to such an extent that he lacked criminal capacity;
- The unlawful act must have been committed by the accused while he was lacking criminal capacity as a result of the intoxication;
- The accused must have been found to be lacking in criminal capacity because of the voluntary intoxication.[49]

Mistake of Law

The legal fiction that every person is presumed to know the law was rejected by the Supreme Court of Appeal in *S v De Blom*.[50] The court stated as follows:

> At this stage of our legal development it must be accepted that the cliché that 'every person is presumed to know the law' has no ground for its existence and that the view that 'ignorance of the law is no excuse' is not legally applicable in the light of the present-day concept of *mens rea* in our law.[51]

As a consequence of the judgment in *De Blom*, 'genuine ignorance or mistake of law invariably negatives *mens rea* in respect of the unlawfulness element and hence excludes liability'.[52] Knowledge of unlawfulness includes knowledge about any applicable defences. Mistake about the existence of a defence (putative defence) will be evaluated with reference to the type of defence (is it a well-known common law defence?) as well as the knowledge and experience of the accused (for instance, does the accused work in a particular sphere of activity?). The legal consequences of a putative defence can be summarised as follows:

> Where the accused genuinely believes that a defence excluding unlawfulness exists, whereas it does not, or that he or she is acting within the bounds of a legitimate defence, whereas he or she is exceeding these bounds, then he or she lacks fault (*mens rea*) in the form of intention. If the mistake is reasonable as well as genuine, the accused will not be negligent either.[53]

It is quite possible that an accused is justified and correct in his belief that a particular defence exists and is applicable to his situation. However, the accused can be mistaken about the reach or bounds of the particular defence. A classic example is the accused who acts in self-defence. The court might even agree that the accused was justified in his belief that he could act in self-defence. However, objectively speaking, the defensive steps

---

47 Kemp (n 6) 166; *S v Vika* [2010] (2) SACR 444 (ECG).
48 *S v Ingram* [1999] (2) SACR 127 (W).
49 Kemp (n 6) 167.
50 *S v De Blom* [1977] (3) SA 513 (A).
51 ibid 529H (tr).
52 Burchell (n 31) 396.
53 Burchell (n 31) 416.

exceeded what was under the circumstances necessary to repel the attack. The result is that the defence will fail and the defensive acts will be regarded as unlawful. It is important to note that, since intent is required for a charge of murder, the accused will still lack the requisite *mens rea* for murder since he did not intend his actions to be unlawful. Of course, if the accused mistakenly believed that his actions was covered by a lawful defence, but in reality, and objectively speaking, his actions exceeded the bounds of the defence, then the accused can still be convicted of a crime of negligence (for instance culpable homicide).[54]

Residual Catch-All Defences/Existence and Ambit of Statutory Defences Related to Distinct Offences

Some commentators have argued that there should not be a closed list of defences, but rather a general ground of justification (based on the 'crystallised' legal convictions of the community).[55] The accused can then simply raise the general defence that his conduct was 'reasonable for a person in the same circumstances and that it was therefore justified'.[56]

Some statutes contain specific provisions on defences related to distinct statutory offences. Defences are sometimes explicitly excluded. The Prevention and Combating of Corrupt Activities Act 12 of 2004, for instance, contains a provision which excludes certain defences that accused persons in certain positions might want to raise. With reference to the general crime of corruption, and specific crimes in respect of corrupt activities relating to specific persons, Section 25 of the Act provides:

> Whenever an accused person is charged with an offence under Part 1, 2, 3 or 4, or section 20 or 21 (in so far as it relates to the aforementioned offences) of Chapter 2, it is not a valid defence for that accused person to contend that he or she-
>
> (a) did not have the power, right or opportunity to perform or not to perform the act in relation to which the gratification was given, accepted or offered;
>
> (b) accepted or agreed or offered to accept, or gave or agreed or offered to give the gratification without intending to perform or not to perform the act in relation to which the gratification was given, accepted or offered; or
>
> (c) failed to perform or not to perform the act in relation to which the gratification was given, accepted or offered.

Some statutes provide for defences linked to official capacity, authority or duties. For instance, the Prevention of Organised Crime Act 121 of 1998 provides for crimes like racketeering and money laundering. Section 7A of the Prevention of Organised Crime Act provides for certain defences:

> (1) If a person is charged with committing an offence under section 2(1) (a) or (b) [racketeering], 4, 5 or 6 [money laundering], that person may raise as a defence the fact that he or she had reported a knowledge or suspicion in terms of section 29 of the Financial Intelligence Centre Act, 2001.
>
> (2) If a person who is an employee of an accountable institution as defined in the Financial Intelligence Centre Act, 2001, is charged with committing an offence under section 2(1)(a) or (b), 4, 5 or 6, that person may also raise as a defence that fact that he or she had-

---

54   *S v Mkosana* [2003] (2) SACR 63 (BCH); *S v Ngomane* [1979] (3) SA 859 (A); Burchell (n 31) 417–418.

55   CR Snyman, *Criminal Law* (5th edn, LexisNexis 2008) 97–98. See also *S v Engelbrecht* [2005] (2) SACR 41 (W), where the possibility of a general defence of reasonableness was raised. The court declined to make a decision on this point, but the possibility was left open. The notion of a general ground of justification is therefor still open for further debate in South African jurisprudence. See further Kemp (n 6) 76–77.

56   Kemp (n 6) 76.

(a) complied with the applicable obligations in terms of the internal rules relating to the reporting of information of the accountable institution; or

(b) reported the matter to the person charged with the responsibility of ensuring compliance by the accountable institution with its duties under that Act; or

(c) reported a suspicion to his or her superior, if any, if-

(i) the accountable institution had not appointed such a person or establish such rules;

(ii) the accountable institution had not complied with its obligations in section 42 (3) of that Act in respect of that person; or

(iii) those rules were not applicable to that person.

Chapter 21
Sweden

Petter Asp and Magnus Ulväng

General Issues

Justificatory and Excusatory Defences—Distinction and Seat in the Offence Structure

Swedish law makes a distinction between justificatory (justification) and excusatory defences (excuse) and the two types of defence form important components of the structure of an offence.[1] Under Swedish law, an offence is divided into four different parts:

A. An unlawful act

I. Criminalised act (or omission); the perpetrator must have performed an act which falls within the definition of an offence described in law; this may be either:

a) an act which corresponds to a specific offence (for example murder, assault, theft etc.);
b) an act that amounts to criminalised attempt, preparation, conspiracy etc.; or,
c) an act of complicity.

II. The act must not be justified; a justificatory defence that makes the act lawful (for example self-defence, necessity, consent etc.) cannot be applicable.

B. Personal responsibility for the unlawful act

III. Fault element: the perpetrator must have committed the act intentionally or, in cases where negligence is explicitly criminalised, in a negligent manner according to the relevant description.

IV. The person should not have an excusatory defence (for example an excusable mistake of law).[2]

The distinction between justification and excuse (and the distinction between the requirement for an unlawful act on the one hand and the requirement of personal responsibility on the other) is of importance in two (interrelated) respects.

First, the distinction reflects a difference in the message sent by a judgment in a criminal case. If an act is justified it is not wrongful. Thus, the message to the person concerned (and society at large) is that it was legally acceptable to perform the act, given the specific circumstances of the case (and thus, if the same situation was to arise again, he or she could take the same action). If the act is not justified, but the actor is excused, the message is very different. Basically the message is that it was *not* acceptable to perform the act, but that the actor cannot, given the circumstances, be blamed for acting as he or she did. A typical example of such a situation is when a person has used too much violence in a difficult self-defence situation. In such a situation the courts will at times find that the person has acted excessively (i.e., that the act was wrong), but that he or she cannot be blamed for taking the wrong decision in a very dangerous and stressful situation.

---

1   See, for example, Jareborg, *Essays in Criminal Law* (Iustus förlag 1988) ch 1.
2   See Petter Asp, Magnus Ulväng and Nils Jareborg, *Kriminalrättens grunder* (Iustus förlag 2013) 58 ff.

Second, the distinction between justification and excuse is of vital importance for the Swedish law concerning complicity. Participation always presupposes that an unlawful act has been committed. An unlawful act occurs when someone commits a criminalised act (or omission) in a situation where such an act is *not justified*. Thus, justification as regards the main act excludes responsibility for participation in the act, while excuses are always irrelevant with regard to responsibility for persons other than the person to whom the excuse applies.

Conceptual Foundations

Swedish law makes a distinction between an unlawful act (the first two levels of the concept of an offence) and personal responsibility (the last two levels of the concept of an offence). Justifications belong conceptually to the requirement for an unlawful act while excuses belong to the requirements for personal responsibility.

As regards justification, the assessment of the defence is based solely on what has actually happened (objectively), or rather, on that version of reality which, according to the rules on burden of proof, should be accepted by the court. Thus, when assessing whether an act is justified with reference to self-defence, the question is whether the defending person was actually subject to a criminal attack of the kind described in law (and not what the defendant thought about the situation).

Thus, as regards justification, there is no subjective requirement whatsoever. Also a person who is unaware of the presence of justifying circumstances at the time of his or her act may invoke such circumstances at a later point (and even if they are not invoked by the defendant, such circumstances should be considered by the prosecutor if the preliminary investigation shows that such circumstances may have applied). For example, if A throws a stone at a window in an act of vandalism and thereby happens to rescue B who is on the other side of the window and just about to be poisoned by a gas leak in the room, then A's act can (or rather will) be justified with reference to the rules on necessity (see below).[3]

The reason for accepting that justification exists in such cases has nothing to do with A acting for the right reason (in above example it is obvious that A was not acting for the right reason). The idea is rather that if there is a justification (in reality, objectively) then there is insufficient reason for the state to invoke the criminal justice system. The harm or the negative value brought about by the act is, on balance, not such as is required to trigger criminal law. In a sense one can more or less say that the presence of a justification is on the same footing as the absence of a prerequisite required under the relevant specific offence description.

It is a matter for discussion whether it would, at least at times, be possible to convict the person for an attempt in these cases. The answer is arguably no, since it seems inconsistent to say (i) that the criminalised act, which was actually consummated and which was brought about intentionally, was justified having regard to the circumstances, and (ii) that the attempt to commit the act which was actually committed is not justified. This question has not, however, been dealt with in case law.

Although justifications can also apply in cases where the actor is unaware of the justifying circumstances, the awareness of the actor is relevant when applying the rule on excess. Since excess is an excuse, the basis for the defence is that the person cannot be blamed for having acted wrongly and the basis for such an assessment is that the defendant found him- or herself in a difficult situation in which he or she cannot be blamed for not thinking clearly, etc. In cases where the actor is unaware of the difficult situation the rule on excess cannot normally be used as a reason of excuse.

Cumulation/Cumulative or Alternative Pleading of Defences

Defences can be invoked cumulatively and/or alternatively. There are neither substantive nor procedural impediments against this.

From a substantive perspective it is clear that several defences can apply at the same time. Practically this means that the most generous provision will apply. For example, if a person has the right to use violence when arresting someone (either when acting as a citizen or as a police officer) he or she might, at the same time, have the right of self-defence (for example if attacked by the person being arrested). In such a situation the

---

3   Asp, Ulväng and Jareborg (n 2) 215.

assessment will be made in accordance with the section on self-defence since this section is more generous towards the defendant (as it allows acts which are not clearly unjustifiable while the rules on arrest only allow for acts which are defensible).

From a procedural perspective there are no rules that exclude a cumulative or alternative invocation of a defence. A person may, for example, invoke self-defence while at the same time claiming that he or she was given consent by the victim and that he or she acted in an excusable mistake of law. Of course such an argument may affect the credibility of the defendant and the plausibility of his or her story, but that is another matter entirely.

Provocation of Defence Situation

The main rule under Swedish law is that the fact that the person has brought about the defence situation, for example by provoking someone to attack him or her or by creating a state of necessity by starting a fire is irrelevant. If the conditions for the defence exist in the situation brought about then the defence does apply and the situation must be assessed accordingly.[4]

It is arguable, however, that the assessment of defensibility may be affected at least as regards the section on necessity. Furthermore, as regards consent, the fact that the consent has been 'brought about' by the defendant may imply that the consent is not voluntarily given in the way presupposed by the section on consent. However it is unclear where the borders of voluntariness are drawn.

Mistakes of Fact and Defences

As indicated above, justifications are fundamentally assessed on the basis of what has actually happened (i.e., objectively).If no justifying circumstances exist (i.e., in reality or objectively), but the person believes that the circumstances are such that his or her act would be justified had the circumstances been such as he or she believes them to be, the person should then be acquitted due to *lack of intent*. The intent requirement is such that responsibility presupposes that the intent of the perpetrator covers the *absence of a justification* (this is often referred to as *putative justification*).[5] A two-step assessment should be performed in order to determine whether or not a person should be acquitted due to lack of intent in relation to the absence of a justification:

I)   First it has to be settled that the person actually believed that the circumstances was such that the person would act in a self-defence situation, a necessity situation etc. if the circumstances would have been such as the he or she believes them to be.

II) Second it has to be assessed whether the person would be justified to act in this way had the circumstances been such as he or she believes them to be. That is, the act performed in wrongful belief must stay within the limits provided by the justification in question (i.e. if the person acts in wrongful belief of a need for self-defence, the act must not be clearly unjustifiable, while if the person acts in wrongful belief of necessity or consent, the act must not be indefensible etc.).

If the outcome of these assessments is that the person is not acquitted, it will, in addition, have to be assessed whether the person should be acquitted with reference to the rules on excess in defences. Thus, the rules on excessive self-defence, excessive necessity, etc. also apply in situations of putative self-defence or necessity, etc. This means that a person can be excused for acting excessively (rules on excess) in a difficult situation which did not exist. However, since the person believed that a difficult situation was at hand, it is reasonable that the rule on excess in self-defence etc. applies.[6]

---

4   See, for example, Asp, Ulväng and Jareborg (n 2) 218.
5   See Asp, Ulväng and Jareborg (n 2) 343 ff.
6   Until 1994 the rules on excess were applied by analogy in putative cases; nowadays the wording of the section has been changed for the purpose of including putative cases.

With regard to exoneration, it is not necessary for it to be reasonable for the actor to mistakenly believe that justifying circumstances are present. The court shall consider the case based on the actor's actual belief at the time.

However, if negligence is criminalised, making an unreasonable mistake might suffice the requirement of culpability. Thus, whenever a court (or a prosecutor) finds that a person should not be held responsible for an intentional offence in accordance with the rules just described, the question should be asked whether the person should be convicted for an offence of negligence. This is possible if the wrongful belief that forms the basis of the putative justification (i.e., the wrongful belief that the circumstances are such that he or she is in a self-defence situation, etc.) is negligent. Thus one must ask whether the person was negligent in his or her wrongful belief (i.e. whether he or she ought to have understood that a situation of self-defence or necessity etc. did not exist).

Transferred Defences/Collateral Damage Defences

The issue of transferred defences does not really occur in Swedish law due to the fact that the defence act that should be assessed is the act consciously performed and controlled by the defending person. For example, if A acts in self-defence and as an act of defence pushes B (and B as a consequence falls down a stair and breaks a leg), the act to be assessed is 'pushing B (in a certain context)', not 'breaking B's leg'.[7] If this line of thought is transferred to a situation where harm is caused to a third party the problem disappears. For example, if A is attacked by B and defends him- or herself by firing a gun, but where the bullet misses B and hits C, the act to be assessed is the attempt to shoot at B. When assessing the act of 'shooting at B' it is necessary to take account of the fact that A's act put others at risk (the problem does not occur in most defences simply due to the fact that the defence does not require the defence act to be directed towards a specific person. The exceptions are cases of self-defence where the defence act must be directed towards the aggressor and certain types of exercise of public authority, for example violence in connection with the arrest of a specific person).

Individual Defences

Self-Defence and Excessive Self-Defence

The rule on self-defence is found in Chapter 24 Section 1 of the Swedish Criminal Code. Under Swedish law, self-defence is a justification as opposed to an excuse.[8] Section 1 states:

> An act committed by a person in self-defence constitutes a crime only if, having regard to the nature of the aggression, the importance of its object and the circumstances in general, it is clearly unjustifiable.

> A right to act in self-defence exists against,

> 1. an initiated or imminent criminal attack on a person or property,

> 2. a person who violently or by the threat of violence or in some other way obstructs the repossession of property when caught in the act,

> 3. a person who has unlawfully forced or is attempting to force entry into a room, house, yard or vessel, or

> 4. a person who refuses to leave a dwelling when ordered to do so. (Law 1994:458)

The preconditions for justification under this section are:

---

7   Asp, Ulväng and Jareborg (n 2) 219.

8   See above under justificatory and excusatory defences.

- that the person acts in a situation of self-defence (these situations are described in Chapter 24 section 1 paragraph 2 of the Swedish Criminal Code), and
- that the act performed in self-defence is not manifestly unjustifiable.[9]

The first, and most important, situation which gives rise to a right to act in self-defence is when a person is subject to an initiated or imminent criminal attack on person or property, as per Chapter 24 Section 1 Paragraph 2 Point 1.

The attack must be at least imminent. This means that preventive self-defence (i.e. when a person believes that he or she will be attacked and therefore approaches the presumptive attacker and attacks him or her) is not accepted. However, in a situation where an attack is imminent one does not have to wait until the aggressor has actually initiated the attack.

An attack on property normally presupposes an intrusion against someone else's possession (to misuse or defend an existing possession is not an attack) or that damage is caused on the property. An attack can, as a matter of principle, be committed by omission. For example, an owner of a dog can commit an attack by not intervening when his or her dog attacks another person. Only criminal attacks give rise to a self-defence situation under Chapter 24 Section 1 Paragraph 2 Point 1. This means that the attack must fulfil all requirements for an offence, i.e., the act must be criminalised, there must be no justification, the actor must fulfil the requirement of intent (or negligence if this is criminalised) and the actor must not be completely excused. Under Swedish law, both mentally disabled persons and children can commit crimes (even though mentally disabled persons normally cannot be sentenced to imprisonment and children cannot be prosecuted), which means that they can also bring about a self-defence situation in accordance with Chapter 24 Section 1 Paragraph 2 Point 1. The fact that an attack is brought about by, for example, a child may, however, affect the assessment of whether the defence act is manifestly unjustified or not.

The section on self-defence is also applicable when a criminal attack is brought about in connection with the exercise of public authority (for example by a police officer). However, it seems clear that the assessment of justifiability will be much less generous. It has even been suggested that a right to self-defence would exist only when the attack is manifestly unlawful. Such a position is, however, hard to accept given the wording of Chapter 24 Section 1 Paragraph 2.

When two people engage in a fight, both may be acting in self-defence and this may exclude both from responsibility. Self-defence may be invoked against accessories, but this presupposes that the act performed by the accessory can be considered to constitute an attack.

A self-defence situation only exists as long as the attack is on-going. Thus, acts committed against the aggressor after the attack has been concluded cannot be justified with reference to self-defence. However, the Supreme Court of Sweden has held that one can, under certain circumstances, view a series of events as a unit in cases where a person (according to a more formal point of view) has the right to self-defence in the first phase and some other right (for example, the right to use violence for the purpose of arresting a person) in the latter phase.[10]

The second situation which gives rise to a right of self-defence is when someone obstructs the repossession of property when being caught in the act. This situation applies, for example, both when a person uses violence or threats of violence for the purpose of obstructing repossession, and when a person refuses to desist after being told to stop. A person is 'caught in the act' if he or she is arrested at the scene of the crime or if he or she is continuously followed from the scene of the crime. According to Swedish Supreme Court Case NJA [1994] 48, a person can also be regarded as being 'caught in the act' if the act of following starts a minute or so after the crime has been committed (i.e., a small time gap may be permitted).

Self-defence, according to Chapter 24 Section 1 Paragraph 2 Point 2, presupposes that the actor is allowed to repossess the property, for example on the grounds of rules on lawful repossession of stolen goods.

The third and fourth situations which give rise to self-defence are situations of unlawful entrance, which is criminalised either as unlawful entrance or violation of domicile under the Swedish Criminal Code Chapter

---

9   See Asp, Ulväng and Jareborg (n 2) s 3.2 and Lena Holmqvist, Madeleine Leijonhufvud, PO Träskman and Suzanne Wennberg, *Brottsbalken. En kommentar* (Norstedts juridik 2012) commentary to ch 24 s 1.

10   See Swedish Supreme Court Case NJA [1998] 48.

4 Section 6 and situations of violation of domicile committed by refusal to leave a dwelling upon order under Swedish Criminal Code Chapter 4 Section 6.

Whether or not a self-defence situation actually exists is assessed objectively, and there is no need for the defending person to act for the right reasons (a situation in which a person acts in a situation which does not constitute self-defence, but where that person believes that the circumstances are such that he or she has the right of self-defence, are treated as a special form of lack of intent).[11] Self-defence can also be invoked by a person who did not know that he or she was in a self-defence situation. Assume, for example, that A approaches B with a tennis racket (with the intent of striking B). If, when A approaches, B hits A just for the fun of it, B may nevertheless invoke self-defence (should it for some reason become known that A was just about to attack B).

The fact that the defending person has caused the self-defence situation does not exclude a right to self-defence. Thus, a person who has provoked the aggressor to commit the attack may nevertheless invoke self-defence.

An act committed in self-defence is only unlawful if the act is manifestly unjustifiable. This means that the person who acts in self-defence has rather a wide margin of action on his or her side. Another way of expressing this is to say that an act committed in self-defence may be lawful even when it is not justifiable provided it is not *manifestly* unjustifiable. The guiding principles as expressed in case law are (i) that the defence act must not deviate from that which was necessary, and (ii) that there must not be a clear disproportion between the defence act and the danger posed by the attack.

When assessing whether a defence act is manifestly unjustifiable one should, according to the law, pay special regard to the nature of the attack, the importance of its object and the circumstances in general.

The reference to the nature of the attack allows regard to be paid to the characteristics of the aggressor (strength, intoxication, age and any other factor that affects the degree of danger he or poses). Whether the attack came be surprise, in the dark, or in a place where there was no chance to get assistance may also be taken into account.

The object of the attack obviously has a great impact on the assessment. This should be read as a direct reference to the importance of the interest threatened by the attack. When defending one's life one is, for obvious reasons, allowed to do more than when simply defending one's property.

The circumstances in general should also be taken into account. For example, it may be of importance to consider whether the attack could be avoided by merely stepping aside (especially if the aggressor is drunk, mentally ill, etc.). There is, however, no general obligation to try to escape from or otherwise avoid the attack.[12] The harm brought about by, and the risks associated with the defence act are also of great importance. The Supreme Court of Sweden stated that the intentional use of a knife or other weapons which causes risk for life may be accepted only in exceptional circumstances.[13]

Intentional killing may, as a matter of principle, be justified with reference to the rule on self-defence. However, one must take into consideration that too extensive a right to defend oneself by taking the life of another may be contrary to Article 2 (right to life) of the European Convention on Human Rights and Fundamental Freedoms.

Self-defence may only be invoked to justify acts which are directed towards the aggressor or against an interest on his or her part. If A attacks B and B defends him- or- her-self by taking an ice hockey stick from C, then B's assault may be justified under the rules of self-defence, but the property offence committed against C cannot be justified under these rules since it is directed against the interests of C. The property offence can nevertheless be justified with reference to the rule on necessity.[14]

An act carried out in self-defence, but which is deemed clearly unjustifiable is always unlawful *per se*. This does not necessarily mean that the act constitutes a crime or that the actor will be punished. The actor may

---

11   See above on putative justification.
12   Cf Swedish Supreme Court Cases NJA [1969] 425 and NJA [1999] 460.
13   See Swedish Supreme Court Case NJA [1994] 48.
14   See below in the section on necessity.

under special circumstances be excused even though he or she has done more than was permitted according to the rules on self-defence.[15]

In cases where some of the provisions stating justifying circumstances (as mentioned in Chapter 24 Sections 1–4 of the Swedish Criminal Code or the Police Act (1984:387)) apply but where the actor has used excessive violence, force, etc., responsibility is excluded if the circumstances were such that he or she *had difficulty in coming to his or her senses*. The doctrine of excess is derived from the principle of conformity. The basic idea behind this principle is that a person should not be considered responsible for a crime if he or she was unable to conform to the law. Chapter 24 Section 6 states that a person who has done more than is permitted is completely excused 'if the circumstances were such that he had difficulty in stopping to think'.

In situations where people are exposed to danger, threats, or are forcibly compelled to act in certain ways, they generally do not have the same ability to make sound judgements about their actions as would normally apply. In other words: the ability to make sound judgements can, to some extent, be presumed to be impaired in such circumstances. When assessing whether the accused had such impairment the courts are instructed to consider the following:

1) the character of the danger,
2) the time available to the person to consider his or her actions and to restrain him or herself, and
3) the actor's individual capabilities.

For example, if a person suffers from anxiety, is easily scared or easily aggravated this could be relevant to the question of whether or not he or she can be excused. The assessment assumes the perspective of the accused and his or her particular disposition, and is thus strictly subjective.[16] It only focuses on the individual's general capabilities (character). The law does not (at least in theory) set particularly high standards for exercising self-restraint in these situations. This implies that we treat a person who acts excessively as someone whose abilities are diminished and that this could be interpreted as an extenuating circumstance. The person's difficulties in coming to his or her senses are more or less treated as a character trait relevant to the assessment of criminal responsibility.

However, such a depiction of excusable excess as indicating diminished capability due to bad character is somewhat misleading. The law concerning excess as an excuse must viewed in context, i.e., as a norm complementing primary rules concerning justification (self-defence, necessity, acting on orders, etc.). In cases of excess, we presuppose that the accused has been (more or less) forced to act in an extreme situation. The actions of the agent were partially justified, but he or she has exceeded his or her right to use force, violence, etc. The person can be excused under these (extreme) circumstances if he or she had certain difficulties in coming to his or her senses. The extent to which a court will really accept loss of self-control due to previous provocation, bad temper, stress, etc. as sufficient justification for a reduced ability to come to one's senses is an open question. There are reasons to suspect that courts are rather careful in their practices in this area and that the scope of application is rather narrow.[17] People are, as a general rule, expected to control themselves.

The law on justificatory defences (self-defence, necessity, etc.) only concerns situations of 'real' states of danger, attacks, etc. There are no corresponding statutory rules if a state of self-defence or necessity is imagined. However, the requirements of guilt (*dolus/culpa*) continue to apply to any justification as well as the underlying prohibition. Therefore, a person who mistakenly imagines that he or she is in a situation where

---

15   See Asp, Ulväng and Jareborg (n 2) s 5.3 and Holmqvist, Leijonhufvud, Träskman and Wennberg (n 9) commentary to ch 24 s 6.

16   In the assessment of whether the accused had difficulties in coming to his or her senses, Swedish law is not clear about whether a person's reasons (for having these difficulties) should relate only to the situation at hand (i.e., self-defence, necessity, etc.) and the circumstances surrounding it, or if other reasons can interfere (such as being drunk, angry with something else, etc.). One reason to focus solely on the circumstances that justify a certain use of violence is that the provision stating excuse is only applicable in cases when the deed is partially justified. On the other hand, the provision in Chapter 24 Section 6 of the Swedish Criminal Code does not mention any circumstances other than the defendant having difficulties in coming to his or her senses.

17   Compare Swedish Supreme Court cases NJA [1977] 655, NJA [1988] 495, NJA [1994] 48, NJA [1995] 661. Cf NJA [2009] 234.

justifying circumstances require defensive action to be taken, should be judged based on that person's actual perception of the situation at the time of his or her actions. (See above in the section on mistake of facts and defences.)

Necessity

The rule on necessity is found in Chapter 24 Section 4 of the Swedish Criminal Code. In common with self-defence, necessity is a justificatory defence (as opposed to an excuse) under Swedish law. The provision states:

> An act by a person, in cases other than those described previously in this Chapter, if committed out of necessity, constitutes a crime only if it is indefensible having regard to the nature of the danger, the injury caused to another and to the circumstances in general.

> Necessity exists when a danger threatens life, health, property or some other important interest protected by the law.

The preconditions for justification under this section can be summarised as follows:

1) there must be a necessity situation
2) the act committed in necessity must not be indefensible.[18]

Under Swedish law, no distinction is made between duress and necessity; both are covered by Chapter 24 Section 4 of the Swedish Criminal Code. A necessity situation always involves a collision between two interests which are both protected by the legal system. The necessity situation is characterised by the fact that protection of one of the interests intrudes on the other interest. A necessity situation arises when there is a threat against life, health, property or some other important interest protected by the law. Cases involving threats against life or health are the most frequent ones in case law.

'Other important interests' may concern vital public interests. For example, necessity may be invoked by someone who prevents a spy handing over information to a foreign state. By analogy (threat to life or health) it is arguably also applicable to cases of cruelty to animals, as per the Swedish Criminal Code Chapter 16 Section 13.

Necessity can only be invoked if the threatened interest is protected by the legal system. This means, for example, that it cannot be invoked by a person who has escaped from prison and steals clothes for the purpose of avoiding capture.

In common with self-defence, necessity can also be invoked by a person who has foreseen or brought about the danger concerned. A person who has started a fire may, for example, invoke necessity when breaking in to another person's house for the purpose of phoning the fire brigade. One important difference between necessity and self-defence is that necessity can be invoked when the danger is not brought about by a human being (i.e., one can still resort to the rule of necessity when confronted by a dangerous natural event, wild animal, etc.). The provision can also be applied in event of an attack from a human being which is not criminal (i.e., which does not fulfil all the requirements of an offence, for example due to lack of intent). Furthermore, necessity can be invoked when a person, in a self-defence situation, intrudes on the interests of an innocent third party.

Since the scope of application is described in a fairly broad way in Chapter 24 Section 4 (there are of course many situations in which important interests are threatened in some way), limitations on the right to invoke necessity is first and foremost set by the requirement of defensibility. In the legal literature this is often explained with the following example: if a person with expensive clothes is surprised by a heavy rain storm, he or she cannot invoke necessity to justify taking an umbrella from a person dressed in cheaper clothes.

---

18   See Asp, Ulväng and Jareborg (n 2) s 3.3 and Holmqvist, Leijonhufvud, Träskman and Wennberg (n 9) commentary to ch 24 s 4.

This is, however, not due to the absence of a necessity situation (the expensive clothes are threatened and property is an interest protected under the provision), but to the fact that the taking of the umbrella in such a circumstance is indefensible. This non-defensibility requirement will be considered in the next section.

The section on necessity, above, can be applied for the purpose of justifying virtually any criminalised act imaginable. It is not, however, possible to justify the killing of another person by reference to necessity. Thus, murder and manslaughter are offences that, at least in a practical perspective, are excluded from the application of the provision. (The fact that an act of murder and manslaughter is performed in a necessity situation may, however, be of importance for triggering application of the section concerning excessive necessity and also as a mitigating circumstance at time of sentencing.)

Since the necessity situation is described in broad terms in the law, necessity conceptually includes cases of self-defence. The reason that self-defence is nevertheless regulated separately is that the assessment of defensibility is much more favourable to the defendant when acting in self-defence. When a person acts out of necessity, he or she must be prepared to sacrifice his or her own interests to a larger extent than that which is required according to the section on self-defence.

When assessing whether or not an act is defensible, regard should be given to the character of the danger at hand, to the harm caused to other interests and to the circumstances in general. In general terms, an act performed out of necessity can only be justified if the interest protected is clearly more important (or valuable) than the one sacrificed. Thus, it may be considered defensible to sacrifice the property of others for the purpose of safeguarding life or to protect someone from severe injuries. If property stands against property, the rescued property must have a considerably higher value than the sacrificed one in order for the act to be justified with reference to necessity.

The fact as to whether or not an act taken in order to secure a threatened interest is strictly necessary is not formally decisive, but an act which is not necessary will normally be considered indefensible. In situations where there is a threat to life, the possibility to invoke necessity is not excluded by the fact that the person threatened does not wish to be saved. Thus, at least under certain circumstances, the section can justify coercive feeding or coercive treatment of a person or acts performed while saving a person who is trying to commit suicide. The fact that the person does not wish to be saved must, however, be considered when assessing defensibility. This is of special importance when the section on necessity is invoked by someone acting on behalf of the state, as the constitutional prohibition against bodily interference applies in such cases.

Such rules must generally be considered—as a normative standard—when applying the rules on necessity. For example, the prohibition against bodily interference arguably also excludes justification for torture in, for example, a case where it is known that a person has placed a nuclear bomb in a city centre and refuses to say where. However, the rules on excessive necessity may be applicable (i.e., the perpetrator may be excused) and if the person is convicted the punishment may be reduced by reference to the necessity situation.

The rules on excessive defence apply also in relation to necessity, i.e., a person who does something which is not defensible may be excused if the circumstances were such that he or she *had difficulty in coming to his senses*.

Duress by Threats/Circumstances

See the section on necessity (which is the defence that must be invoked when someone is coerced to do something prohibited by means of threats).

General Mental Condition Defences

Insanity
Sweden takes a rather unusual view on the relationship between insanity and criminal responsibility since Swedish law does not contain a requirement that the actor must have a sufficient mental capacity in order to be able to commit a crime.[19] Hence, insanity, insane automatism etc. is not a valid defence under Swedish law. Instead persons suffering from mental diseases are judged according to the general rules and principles

---

19   See Official Investigations of the State (SOU) 2012:17, 504 ff. for a short historical account.

of criminal law. In this respect, Swedish law adopts an almost unique position shared only with Greenland and a few states in the United States.

A general requirement of mental capacity existed in Swedish law until the mid-1960's, but was removed when the Swedish Criminal Code was introduced in 1965. Thus, anyone—even an infant or a person suffering from severe mental illness—can technically commit a crime as long as the *actus reus* and *mens rea* requirements are fulfilled and no justificatory or excusatory defences apply. The background to the Swedish position on this issue was a questionable rejection in the 1950s and 60s of the idea that people can be morally responsible for their actions. In the preparatory works, the legislator took the view that persons suffering from serious forms of mental illness would often not be held criminally liable for their unlawful deeds since they were not at fault because of lack of awareness, knowledge or intention. Whether or not the accused were found criminally responsible was anyway not considered a particularly important issue. Any criminal suffering from mental illness was to be sentenced to treatment in an institution. The main focus in criminal law was therefore placed on rehabilitation and treatment (and not on responsibility and just desert).

This special preventive ideology has turned out to have serious flaws. First it is manifestly false that persons with mental illness do not normally fulfil the *mens rea* requirement. A person suffering from, e.g., schizophrenia or some other form of psychotic state of mind can often sufficiently understand the implications of his or her actions, even when lacking the ability to control his/her behaviour or lacking understanding of the proper meaning of his or her actions. Furthermore, it is morally wrong to punish an individual by holding that person legally responsible for a crime, simply in order to be able to secure proper medical or psychiatric treatment.

The prevailing view within criminal law doctrine as well as with the legislator is that some sort of requirement of mental capacity ought to be (re)introduced into Swedish criminal law. Several proposals have been drafted and presented to the government.[20] The practical consequences of Swedish legislation as it stands today are the following:

Insanity: An insane person who commits a crime can be held criminally responsible, convicted of a crime and sentenced. Nevertheless, mentally ill people are, just as young offenders, given special consideration when being sentenced. As a main rule (and a legal presumption), persons suffering from *a serious mental disturbance* may not be sentenced to imprisonment under Chapter 30 Section 6 of the Criminal Code. Instead they are to be committed for forensic psychiatric care under Chapter 31 Section 3 of the Criminal Code. The diagnosis of 'serious mental disturbance' is interpreted in a rather broad manner. Thus the concept of 'insanity' in Swedish law includes different conditions of a psychotic character, conditions of impaired reality valuation and symptoms of type delusions, hallucinations and confusion. The condition can be either long-term/permanent (e.g., schizophrenia, mental retardation, Alzheimer's disease, etc.) or a short term, temporary loss of one's senses.

Forensic psychiatric care is formally a punishment and the offender is regarded as a criminal even though he or she is placed in a hospital (receiving treatment) rather than in a prison. The length of the sentence is indefinite and it is ultimately a psychiatrist (not a judge) who is responsible for discharging the criminal/patient from hospital. If there is a risk of relapse into serious criminality by reason of the mental disturbance, the court may decide that a special release inquiry shall be conducted during the time in care.

Other forms of diminished responsibility: Short-term states of mental confusion or temporary losses of one's senses, which fail to fulfil the criteria of being a 'serious mental disturbance', are treated differently than the cases of 'insanity' mentioned above. There is no statutory excuse for short-term loss of capacity or diminished responsibility. However, the general view is that an unwritten rule exists which functions as an excusatory defence. Provided that the short-term state of mind occurred without the actor's fault, then temporary loss of one's senses is regarded as a completely excusing circumstance.[21] For example, if A slips a narcotic substance into B's drink (without B's knowledge) and the substance causes B to become angry and violent, thereby attacking C, then B can plead temporary loss of senses as an excuse, thus securing an acquittal. It is imperative

---

20   See Official Investigations of the State (SOU) 1996:185, SOU 2002:3, and SOU 2012:17.
21   See Asp, Ulväng and Jareborg (n 2) s 5.2.

that the actor (B) is not responsible for the alteration to his/her state of mind. As will be elaborated below, Swedish law takes the view that a self-induced, temporary loss of the use of one's senses is never an excuse.[22]

Intoxication

According to Swedish law, any perpetrator who has committed an unlawful act whilst voluntarily intoxicated is to be judged according to the same rules as a sober person. Ordinary *mens rea* requirements must be fulfilled in order to convict a person of intentional crimes. Hence, mistake or ignorance of fact does not amount to a defence; although it may negate the requisite intention. Support for some kind of exemption from the ordinary requirements of *mens rea* can be found in many criminal codes. Usually the court is instructed to disregard ignorance which has arisen as a result of self-induced intoxication. Even though statutes of this kind do not clearly state that *mens rea* is to be feigned, the legal position is that any mistake of fact caused by self-induced intoxication is irrelevant to the question of whether an act has been committed with intent.[23] The classic example would be a person taking something from someone else, falsely thinking that he or she is the rightful owner of the property. In such cases, courts are permitted to convict the drunken perpetrator for (intentional) unlawful dispossession since the mistake of ownership (i.e., putative lack of intent) is caused by drunkenness.[24] Current Swedish law has no practice of foregoing the *mens rea* requirement in situations where the perpetrator was not at fault simply because of self-induced intoxication. However, until very recently (a possibility of) foregoing intent in cases of voluntary intoxication formed a part of the Swedish doctrine of guilt. Support for this previous interpretation of the law was taken from the preparatory works and the Swedish Criminal Code Chapter 1 Section 2, which states:

> § 2 If the act has been committed during self-induced intoxication or if the perpetrator has in some other way himself brought about the temporary loss of the use of his senses, this shall not cause the act to be considered non-criminal.

However, the Swedish Supreme Court has recently (2011) quashed this kind of interpretation of the Swedish statute, potentially rejecting voluntary intoxication as a defence.[25] According to the verdict, it was established that the statute does not specifically say that courts are supposed to forego the *mens rea* requirement. The law only says that self-induced intoxication does not preclude criminal responsibility. Furthermore, the Supreme Court of Sweden held that any principle that allows a lowering of fundamental requirements of criminal liability—for example, the *mens rea* requirement—clearly violates the principles of conformity, guilt and proportionality. If A did 'X' without knowledge, specific purpose or even foresight of the risk of the actual consequence of his or her action, then a meta-rule precluding the fault element would be practically equivalent to a presumption of guilt. Such a practice is morally questionable and may also be in conflict with the presumption of innocence found in ECHR Article 6. The only reasons for the previously espoused Swedish approach on crimes committed under intoxication were found in preventive utilitarian considerations (originally expressed in preparatory works from the 1920s when the government was attempting to reduce the general level of alcohol consumption in Sweden). According to the Supreme Court, such arguments could not challenge fundamental principles of criminal law. The Supreme Court found little evidence that courts have actually used the possibility to forego the *mens rea* requirement. Intoxicated persons are usually sufficiently

---

22 Swedish Criminal Code ch 1 s 2.

23 It should be emphasised that the practice of foregoing the mens rea requirement has nothing to do with prior fault or crimes of recklessness or negligence. According to Swedish law, a voluntarily intoxicated perpetrator could, until 2011, be convicted of *intentional* causing of harm even though he or she fails to meet the fault requirements. In theory, a totally drunk person could be convicted of attempted murder if, for example, he tried to stab a person in a fight, at a time when all evidence of intention or knowledge of the eventual consequences of his actions was missing. This approach can be compared with the solution in the German Criminal Code, according to which a person who has caused his or her state of mind to be altered by self-induced intoxication can be convicted of a special crime—crime committed in drunkenness (Rauschtat).

24 Exceptions from this practice are often made in cases of crimes with ulterior or specific intent.

25 See Swedish Supreme Court Case NJA [2011] 563.

aware of the circumstances surrounding their deeds in order to fulfil the *mens rea* requirement. Thus, there has been little practical need for a special rule on voluntary intoxication which offers an exception from the ordinary requirements of *mens rea*.

Mistake of Law

Just as in most other legal orders, Swedish law does not acknowledge ignorance—or mistake—of law as an excusatory defence (*Ignorantia juris non excusat*). Criminal law operates on the (fictional) premise that people have knowledge of all statutory offences. Mistake of law is thus often irrelevant for the *dolus/culpa* requirement. The criteria for intent focus on the actual deed itself and the prerequisites of the offence description, rather than on the existence of the prohibition.

It should however be noted that the distinction between 'being ignorant of the law' and 'to be ignorant of one's actions' is often subtle. The law is sometimes construed in a way which requires the actor to have some basic legal knowledge of the law in order to fulfil the *mens rea* requirement. Hence, mistakes about what the law requires can lead to situations where the actor wrongly qualifies his or her actions, which in its turn can lead to lack of intent. In such cases, the actor has not understood the true meaning of his/her actions. For example, if A is ignorant of the law on ownership and under the misapprehension that lost property is always abandoned and free for any finder to take, then this is normally irrelevant to the issue of liability. Let us assume that A finds B's bicycle in the park and brings it home with intention to keep it; as a consequence A is later charged with theft. The offence description for the crime of theft reads as follows:

> § 1 A person who unlawfully takes what belongs to another with intent to acquire it, shall, if the appropriation involves loss, be sentenced for theft to imprisonment for at most two years.[26]

A has unlawfully taken the bicycle with intent to acquire it. Nevertheless, A's mistake of law (on ownership) can lead to an acquittal on the ground that he lacks intent with regard to the requirement that the bicycle 'belongs to another'. It should be noted that A is acquitted on this ground (i.e., because A believed that the bicycle was abandoned and therefore did not belong to another) and not because his ignorance or mistake of law is excused.

Nevertheless, Swedish law does acknowledge mistake of law as a completely excusing circumstance in some rather extraordinary situations. In these cases mistake of law is irrelevant for the dolus/culpa requirement. According to the Swedish Criminal Code, Chapter 24 Section 9:

> [A]n act committed by a person labouring under a misapprehension concerning its permissibility shall not result in his being liable to punishment if the mistake arose by reason of an error in the proclamation of the criminal provision or if, for other reasons, it was manifestly excusable.[27]

The scope of this excuse is dependent on how the prerequisite 'manifestly excusable' is interpreted. In this regard, the legislator has been rather frugal and the preparatory works instruct courts to apply the rule restrictively. The statute only refers to one situation where a mistake of law can be excusable, namely error in the proclamation of the criminal provision (which occurs very rarely). However, the provision leaves open which other cases might suffice the requirement of being manifestly excusable. Three other situations are mentioned in the preparatory works.

The first concerns cases where the accused, for some reason, lacked the opportunity to know of a criminal prohibition. As an example, one can imagine a person who arrives in Sweden from abroad and is confronted with a prohibition that is completely foreign to him. In order to be manifestly excusable it is required that the person had no realistic way of knowing of the prohibition. This requires quite special circumstances. An

---

26   Swedish Criminal Code ch 8 s 1. The Ministry of Justice, Official translation of The Swedish Criminal Code, Ds 1999:36.

27   See Asp, Ulväng and Jareborg (n 2) s 5.4 and Holmqvist, Leijonhufvud, Träskman and Wennberg (n 9) commentary to ch 24 s 9.

example could be that consumption of a previously-authorised substance (for example, the khat plant) has been classified as a drug of abuse and thus prohibited, and someone who has been away from Sweden is caught using khat when unaware of the prohibition. However, people are normally expected to find out which rules apply in a foreign country and the statute is applied strictly. For example, if a person intends to drive a car in Sweden, he or she is expected to know all traffic rules.

The second concerns a situation where the legislator has failed in constructing a criminal statute which is sufficiently clear and unequivocal. If the prohibition, and its meaning, is significantly obscure, then anyone violating the law might be excused. This rule is derived from the principle of legality and the requirement for unambiguous legislation. The obscurity here only refers to the linguistic meaning of the law as drafted, and not that the law may be complex and inaccessible for people without legal training or education.

The final example concerns situations where a defendant violates a prohibition after having received incorrect advice or a wrong decision from an authority. It is assumed in these situations that the person concerned has made some effort to know the law. This, in its turn, requires that the person had reasons to expect that the authority would give authoritative information and that the persons involved in giving such information have themselves received data which is correct and complete.

Residual Catch-All Defences/Existence and Ambit of Statutory Defences

The division between the prerequisites for a criminalised act and the absence of a justification is not clear under Swedish law. Some argue that the division is merely for legislative convenience (i.e., it would be inconvenient to repeat exceptions which are applicable in relation to many or to all offences in each and every proscription). Others argue that there is, at least in theory, a difference in kind between the two levels: prerequisites which are necessary to depict whether the basic intrusion of the interest in question belongs to the criminalised act, while justifications provide special reasons that can be invoked to justify such an intrusion of an interest. Be that as it may, exceptions exist which are applicable only in relation to certain offences. For example:

- according to Chapter 5 section 1 paragraph 2 there is an exception in cases of defamation ('If he was duty-bound to express himself or if, considering the circumstances, the furnishing of information on the matter was defensible, or if he can show that the information was true or that he had reasonable grounds for it, no punishment shall be imposed'.)
- according to Chapter 6 section 14 a person who has committed an act which falls under the rules on statutory rape 'shall not be held criminally responsible if it is obvious that the act did not involve any abuse of the child in view of the slight difference in age and development between the person who committed the act and the child and the circumstances in general'.

There are also a number of sections in the Swedish criminal code which presuppose that an act has been performed without permission (for example, theft and, due to the requirement of coercion, etc., rape), without authorisation (for example, breach of domiciliary peace and unlawful intrusion) or was simply unlawful. In these cases consent on behalf of the other party or authority means that no criminalised act has been committed under the law. When the relevant proscription does not presuppose unlawfulness, authorisation by law is viewed as a justification, see below. The same applies in relation to consent.

Some provisions in the Swedish Criminal Code and the Swedish Tax Crime Act 1971 offer the possibility of refraining from imposing penalties in cases where a defendant has incurred criminal responsibility, but has voluntarily, and before any considerable inconvenience has arisen, averted the risk of further inconvenience or completion of the crime presented by the act.[28] A precondition is normally that the danger occasioned by the act was slight.

It is fairly obvious that these exceptions from responsibility are not 'excuses' *in strictu senso* since the actor has already fulfilled the requirements of the offence description. Criminal responsibility does not arise because of the actor's behaviour after the crime was committed. The 'excuse' must be viewed in a wider

---

28　See, for example, the Swedish Criminal Code ch 13 s 11, ch 14 s 12 and ch 15 s 14. See also Tax Crime Act 1971: 69, s 12.

context and in retrospect. The reason for accepting that such culprits are free from punishment are said to be that whoever has second thought and (tries to) redeem him or herself, ought to be encouraged to undo the damage (already done) or to at least minimise the harm. The law only applies to some specific offences, where the harm involved is aptly described as concrete or abstract endangerment, for example, crimes involving public danger or crimes of falsification where the harm of the act is described as 'jeopardising proof'. In such cases the offender has the possibility to remove the danger from the situation by retrospective action.

However, the Swedish Criminal Code entails a general possibility to refrain from punishing persons who have committed an inchoate offence (attempt, preparing or conspiring to commit a crime), but who have voluntarily—by breaking off the execution of the crime or otherwise—prevented its completion.[29]

Finally the law on perjury offers two excusatory defences.[30] First, a person who perjures him or herself under legal oath but corrects his/her statement before the interrogation is over is free from responsibility. Second, a special form of excuse exists in situations where a person has given untrue information or withheld the truth under legal oath, but where the information concerns something about which the person would— according to the law—have had the right to refuse to express him or herself about (for example, information that would reveal that he or she has committed a crime or was otherwise dishonourable). In these cases the actor is free from responsibility if the circumstances furnish him/her with a reasonable excuse.

If a person has been induced to commit an offence by the police or some other public official in a way which deprives that person from the right to a fair trial under the ECHR this shall, according to NJA 2007 Section 1037, be treated not as a justification or an excuse (an offence has still been committed), but as a factor which constitutes an impediment to punishment in a way analogous to the statutes of limitation. According to Swedish law the acquittal in these cases is 'lack of a material precondition for punishability', which do not form part of the offence structure, but which is substantive as opposed to procedural in character. Thus, there are beside justifications and excuses a third category of exceptions which do not concern the question of whether an offence has been committed, but rather the punishability of the act.

---

29   See the Swedish Criminal Code ch 23 s 3; see also Asp, Ulväng and Jareborg (n 2) s 5.5 and Holmqvist, Leijonhufvud, Träskman and Wennberg (n 9) commentary to ch 23 s 3.
30   Swedish Criminal Code ch 15 s 1.

Chapter 22
Turkey

R Murat Önok

General Issues

Justificatory and Excusatory Defences—Distinction and Seat in the Offence Structure

There are widely diverging views in Turkish academic writings as to the constitutive elements of crime. There is the classic understanding, drawing from nineteenth and twentieth century Italian and German penal law, based on the positivist classic criminal theory that was founded by *Beling* and *v Liszt*,[1] and which was largely dominant until the entry into force of the new Turkish Penal Code (hereinafter TPC) on 1 June 2005. This approach, which is still supported by some writers,[2] accepts that crime consists of four general or constitutive elements, without the existence of which it is not possible to define an act as a criminal offence. These elements are: a) the legal element or 'typicity' (*kanuni unsur/tipiklik*); b) the material element (*maddi unsur*); c) the moral/mental element (*manevi unsur*); and d) the unlawfulness of the act (*hukuka aykırılık*).[3] According to this understanding, the legal element can be defined as the requirement that a law that designates the act in question as a crime and indicates the corresponding punishment must exist at the time of commission of the act, and that the act in question must correspond to the statutory criminal definition. The material element (sometimes called 'act' (*fiil*)) consists of three sub-elements[4]: conduct (*hareket*); result (*netice*); and a causal link (causation—*nedensellik bağı*) between the two. According to this understanding, the moral (subjective) element of the crime is referred to as culpability.[5] Some name the concept 'guilt' when analysed from the viewpoint of the perpetrator, and 'culpability' when assessed with regard to the criminal conduct.[6] Culpability refers to the fact that the perpetrator, despite having had the opportunity to act lawfully, chose to enter into unlawful conduct, therefore that act can be subjectively imputed to the perpetrator and he can be blamed for it.[7] Therefore, it a characteristic of the criminal conduct in question.[8] In order for the moral element to be fulfilled,

---

1 Veli Özer Özbek, M Nihat Kanbur, Pınar Bacaksız, Koray Doğan, and İlker Tepe, *Türk Ceza Hukuku Genel Hükümler* (3rd edn, Seçkin 2012) 186–188.

2 Nur Centel, Hamide Zafer, and Özlem Çakmut, *Türk Ceza Hukukuna Giriş* (7th edn, Beta 2011), 205–206; Doğan Soyaslan, *Ceza Hukuku Genel Hükümler* (3rd edn, Yetkin 2005), 212 et seq.

3 For the leading exponent of this view during the period in which the previous Penal Code (Law no 765) was in force, see Sulhi Dönmezer and Sahir Erman, *Nazari ve Tatbiki Ceza Hukuku, Genel Kısım, Cilt: I* (11th edn, Beta 1994) 310–311 (the authors have influenced contemporary Turkish penal law academicians, and their views have been echoed in subsequent books written by all the other authors). Also see, for the classic view, Uğur Alacakaptan, *Suçun Unsurları* (2nd edn, Ankara 1975), 8–10. For a similar approach see Turhan Tufan Yüce, *Ceza Hukuku Dersleri – Cilt: 1* (Manisa 1982), 191–192 and Ayhan Önder, *Ceza Hukuku Dersleri* (Filiz Kitabevi 1992), 152–155 (the author lists the following general elements: conduct, 'typicity', unlawfulness, guilt/culpability).

4 Dönmezer/Erman (n 3) 368–9; Faruk Erem, Ahmet Danışman, and Mehmet Emin Artuk, *Ceza Hukuku Genel Hükümler* (14th edn, Seçkin 1997) 253 ('act' is also called 'objective element' by the authors); Nevzat Toroslu, *Ceza Hukuku Genel Kısım* (18th edn, Ankara 2012) 125; Centel/Zafer/Çakmut (n 2) 228; Soyaslan (n 2) 220–221; Hakan Hakeri, *Ceza Hukuku Genel Hükümler* (13th edn, Adalet 2012) 124.

5 Sulhi Dönmezer and Sahir Erman, *Nazari ve Tatbiki Ceza Hukuku, Genel Kısım, Cilt: II* (11th edn, Beta 1997) 143–144; Alacakaptan (n 3) 117–118; Toroslu (n 4) 189 ; Kayıhan İçel, *İçel Ceza Hukuku Genel Hükümler II* (5th edn, Beta 2013)173; Timur Demirbaş, *Ceza Hukuku Genel Hükümler* (8th edn, Seçkin 2012) 324; Centel/Zafer/Çakmut (n 2) 344; Zeki Hafızoğulları and Muharrem Özen, *Türk Ceza Hukuku Genel Hükümler* (5th edn, USA Yayıncılık 2012) 265; Soyaslan (n 2) 409.

6 Dönmezer/Erman (n 5) 197; Erem/Danışman/Artuk (n 4) 429.

7 Önder (n 3) 267; Özbek et al. (n 1) 340; Hakeri (n 4) 302.

8 Dönmezer/Erman (n 5) 206.

two elements must exist: criminal capacity (as a pre-condition), and guilt/culpability (*kusur/kusurluluk*).[9] Guilt can be manisfested either in the form of intent (*kast*) or negligence (*taksir*).[10] Finally, the act must not be legitimated by any grounds of justification. Hence, according to the classic view, crime can be defined as an unlawful and culpable act that is designated as a crime by law, which is realized by a person having criminal capacity.[11] Within this doctrine, excusatory defences would act on the criminal capacity of the perpetrator, and eliminate his culpability, thus negating the mental element. As for justifications, they would negate the unlawfulness of the act. In both cases, there would be no crime, and the perpetrator would have to be acquitted.

Since the beginning of this millennium, and especially after the entry into force of the new TPC which is strongly influenced by German academic writings, some recent academic works have adopted a new understanding of the notion of crime. As a result, the majority today adopts an approach based on a variation of the 'teleological system'. The writers adopting this view[12] do not make a distinction between the legal and material element of the criminal offence in that they do not list the two as different elements,[13] but argue that 'typicity'[14] (*tipe uygun fiil/eylem or tipiklik*) is amongst the constitutive elements. This approach[15] accepts that a crime consists of three elements: legal elements of the offence[16] ('typicity'), unlawfulness, and moral element/culpability. According to this approach, 'a crime is a conduct which fulfills the legal elements of a criminal offence and which is unlawful as well as culpable'[17]. Within this doctrine, excusatory defences would act on the criminal capacity of the perpetrator, and eliminate his culpability, thus negating the mental element. This would not lead to an acquittal in the technical sense, but the judge would declare that due to lack of guilt there is 'no need to punish' the perpetrator by virtue of Article 223(3) of the Criminal Procedure Code. As for justifications, they would negate the unlawfulness of the act, and this would lead to an acquittal.

Finally, there are those who argue that the new TPC is based on the understanding that the general elements of the crime are the following three[18]: material elements (*maddi unsurlar*), moral elements (*manevi unsurlar*), and the unlawfulness of the act (*hukuka aykırılık*). Within this approach, the material elements comprise the following:[19] act (*fiil*)[20], result, causation, perpetrator, victim, object of the crime, and qualifying circumstances.

---

9   Dönmezer/Erman (n 5) 144; Alacakaptan (n 3) 118; Önder (n 3) 271; İçel (n 5) 193 et seq.; Bahri Öztürk and Mustafa Ruhan Erdem, *Uygulamalı Ceza Hukuku ve Güvenlik Tedbirleri Hukuku* (12th edn, Seçkin 2013) 236; Demirbaş (n 5) 324; Centel/Zafer/Çakmut (n 2) 351 et seq.; Soyaslan (n 2) 388 et seq.

10   Dönmezer/Erman (n 5) 209; Alacakaptan (n 3) 153 et seq.; Erem/Danışman/Artuk (n 4) 429 et seq.; Yüce (n 3) 321 et seq.; Önder (n 3) 291; Toroslu (n 4) 197; İçel (n 5) 193; Soyaslan (n 2) 409; Demirbaş (n 5) 194; Centel/Zafer/ Çakmut (n 2) 380; Süheyl Donay, *Türk Ceza Kanunu Şerhi* (Vedat Yayıncılık 2007) 47; Hafızoğulları/Özen (n 5) 276 et seq. Results caused in excession of intent (*preterintenzione* in Italian), such as causing death as result of intentional wounding, and 'result-aggravated crimes' (combination of intent-negligence), such as turning a person blind as a result of intentional wounding, can be seen as a third category.

11   See Centel/Zafer/Çakmut (n 2) 206 for a similar definition.

12   See İçel (n 5) 6; Öztürk/ Erdem (n 9) 146; Demirbaş (n 5) 195; Özbek et al. (n 1) 196–199.

13   For example, İçel (n 5) 78 argues that typicity is not an independent formal element, but a characteristic of the criminal act.

14   This term does not actually exist in English law; however, it was created by the author to describe the term '*tipiklik*' (in Turkish) or '*tipicitá*' (in Italian). The German-oriented Turkish doctrine uses the term '*tipiklik*', although Articles 21 and 30 (1) of the new TPC uses the term '*legal definition of the crime*' instead of '*tipiklik*'.

15   Which is characteristic for German penal law, see Krey, *Volker, German Criminal Law, General Part, Volume II: Legal Elements of the Intentional Offence Committed by Action (Three-stage Structure of Crimes, Concept of Action, Causality, Objective Attribution, Intent)* (W Kohlhammer Publishing Company 2003) rn 210.

16   *Straftatbestand* in German, *typicité* in French, *tipicità* in Italian.

17   *Krey* (n 15) rn. 214.

18   İzzet Özgenç, *Türk Ceza Hukuku Genel Hükümler* (8th edn, Seçkin 2013) 160; for a similar variation see Mehmet Emin Artuk, Ahmet Gökcen, and A. Caner Yenidünya, *Ceza Hukuku Genel Hükümler* (7th edn, Adalet 2013) 201 (the writers add 'legal elements of the offence (*tipiklik*)' as a fourth element). Also see Hamide Zafer, *Ceza Hukuku Genel Hükümler* (TCK m. 1–75) (2nd edn, Beta 2011) 159 et seq., who argues that the lawmaker has identified the following as the elements of a criminal offence: typicity, act (in the framework pf the material/objective structural elements of the crime), the existence of intent or negligence (in the framework of the subjective structural elements of the crime), and unlawfulness. Culpability is not an element of the criminal offence.

19   Artuk/Gökcen/Yenidünya (n 18) 212.

20   In the system of the new TPC, the term '*fiil*' (act) refers to the 'conduct' alone. See, for example, Artuk/Gökcen/ Yenidünya (n 18) 212.

The moral elements refer to intention and negligence, as well as motive in certain crimes. However, as distinct from the classic view, the 'moral element of the crime' and 'culpability' do not have the same meaning.[21] Furthermore, intent and negligence are not regarded as types of guilt (manifestations of culpability), but as ways in which a wrongful conduct may be realised in criminal law.[22] In this system, culpability is not an element of the crime, but a judgment value regarding the conduct of the perpetrator.[23] In other words, it is an assessment as to whether the perpetrator is blameworthy, i.e., if he deserves to be condemned or reproached for acting in a certain way.[24] Thus, the new TPC recognises that intent and negligence are components of the mental elements of a crime, but they are not types of criminal culpability.[25] This understanding is a product of the finalist conduct theory developed by *Welzel*, and which resulted in intent not being considered within the framework of culpability, but as a matter of determining the wrongfulness of the act.[26] According to this view, crime refers to wrongful behaviour (wrongfulness—'*haksızlık*') violating a legally protected value.[27] A criminal act may be perpetrated by a person who cannot be deemed culpable (e.g., someone mentally ill or acting under duress). Even if such person is not culpable, the act will still constitute an intentionally committed wrongful conduct,[28] and, as such, a crime. However, the perpetrator who is not culpable will not be punished because he is not blameworthy, and does not deserve punishment.[29] Within this doctrine, excusatory defences would act on the criminal capacity of the perpetrator, and eliminate his culpability. The act would still constitute a criminal offence. However, the judge would declare that due to lack of guilt there is 'no need to punish' the perpetrator by virtue of Article 223(3) of the Criminal Procedure Code. As for justifications, they would negate the unlawfulness of the act, thus rendering the act lawful and not criminal, and this would lead to an acquittal.

Finally, there are also writers who analyse the elements of the crime according to other approaches.[30]

---

21   Özgenç (n 18) 227.

22   Özgenç (n 18) 227 et seq.; Artuk/Gökcen/Yenidünya (n 18) 289. Compare Mahmut Koca and İlhan Üzülmez, *Türk Ceza Hukuku Genel Hükümler* (6th edn, Seçkin 2013) 137 et seq (the writers consider intent (and negligence) within the framework of the 'moral (subjective) elements of typicity'); compare Özbek et al. (n 1) 341 (the authors argue that, according to Arts. 21–22 TPC, intent and negligence are manifestations of guilt (*kusur*), but culpability (*kusurluluk*) is a separate concept, as explained above). According to the recent German theory, many authors argue that intent is both a form of culpability (*Scholdform*) and a way of realization of a wrongful act (*Verhaltenform*), therefore it has a double function (Özbek et al. (n 1) 240). However, this view does not have other supporters in the Turkish doctrine. There are, however, certain provisions of the TPC which seem to espouse this view. Koca/Üzülmez (n 22) 144–145 (although the writers reject this approach).

23   Özgenç (n 18) 227; Artuk/Gökcen/Yenidünya (n 18) 288; Koca/Üzülmez (n 22) 282; Özbek et al. (n 1) 337. Krey (n 15) rn 219 (can the perpetrator be 'personally reproached with the act'?)

24   Özgenç (n 18) 227–229; Artuk/Gökcen/Yenidünya (n 18) 289; Koca/Üzülmez (n 22) 293; Özbek et al. (n 1) 337; Hakeri (n 4) 301–302. In Turkish academic writings there are diverging views regarding the scope of guilt. Certain writers prefer to determine guilt by assessing whether the perpetrator could have behaved differently, others prefer to determine its existence by assessing whether the conduct of the perpetrator manifests a way of thought which is disapproved by the legal order, see T. Zeynel Kangal, *Ceza Hukukunda Zorunluluk Durumu* (Seçkin 2010) 409 et seq. (the writer himself adopts *Roxin*'s theory based on the understanding that guilt refers to the fact that the perpetrator opted to enter into an unjust conduct despite the normative call to the contrary, at 423 et seq.).

25   Compare Özbek et al. (n 1) 239, 466 et seq. (the authors consider intent as a subjective element of typicity, and negligence as an atypical type of manifestation of the crime).

26   Koca/Üzülmez (n 22) 140. However, this theory is no longer prevalent in Germany, see Krey (n 15) rn 244.

27   Özgenç (n 18) 156 et seq.

28   Özgenç (n 18) 228; Artuk/Gökcen/Yenidünya (n 18) 289; Koca/Üzülmez (n 22) 143; Kangal (n 24) 165.

29   Özgenç (n 18) 227–9; Koca/Üzülmez (n 22) 145.

30   For a view that merges the classic understanding with the German-oriented one, the elements of crime are the following: typicity, material element (act), unlawfulness, moral element (intent or negligence). However, moral element does not have the same meaning as culpability, as the latter is not a formal element of crime, but a condition required for punishment. Hakeri (n 4) 101 et seq. According to another view (Koca/Üzülmez (n 22) 75 et seq.), criminal responsibility shall be determined by assessing the wrongfulness of the conduct and the culpability of the perpetrator. If, according to an objective determination which shall be made independently of the perpetrator's personal qualifications, the conduct is typical (fits the statutory definition) and unlawful, it will be wrongful (*haksız*). After that, it will be determined if the perpetrator can be held personally responsible (culpability – *kusurluluk*) for this wrongful act. In that vein, once it is determined that an act in the criminal sense exists, wrongfulness will be assessed by taking into consideration the following factors: 1) Typicity – a) the material (objective) elements of typicity (the perpetrator, victim, object of the crime, act, result,

Conceptual Foundations

It is nearly unanimously accepted in academic writings published subsequent to the entry into force of the new TPC that the unlawfulness of the act is a separate constitutive element of the crime.[31] Unlawfulness refers to the fact that the conduct in question is in contravention of the legal order.[32] It is unanimously accepted that unlawfulness should be assessed not only in light of penal law, but of the legal order as a whole.[33] If there is a ground justifying the act, there is no criminal wrong in the first place.[34] It might be said that typicity constitutes an indication (or presumption in favour) of the conduct's unlawfulness.[35]

According to the understanding of the new TPC, there is a difference between the act being unlawful (*fiilin hukuka aykırılığı*) and it being wrongful/unjust (*fiilin haksızlığı*).[36] Unlawfulness denotes the fact that certain conduct is in violation of the legal order[37]. Therefore, unlawfulness cannot be qualified in the sense that an act cannot be more or less unlawful—it is either lawful or not.[38] On the other hand, a criminal act constitutes wrongful behaviour. Therefore, this term denotes the criminal act itself. As a result, certain acts are more wrongful than others (e.g., robbery compared to theft, intentional killing compared to causing death by negligence). So the wrongfulness of the act can be qualified.[39]

In Turkish penal law doctrine a distinction is made between justifications (*hukuka uygunluk sebepleri*) and grounds excluding culpability/excuses (*kusurluluğu kaldıran sebepler*). In the former case, the act is no longer unlawful, in the latter case, it is unlawful (and it constitutes a crime according to the understanding of the new TPC), but the perpetrator does not deserve to be punished. The new TPC lays down those grounds under the same section which is entitled 'grounds for excluding or reducing criminal responsibility' (*ceza sorumluluğunu kaldıran veya azaltan nedenler*—Articles 24–34), but it is unanimously accepted that the distinction still exists.[40]

---

causality, qualifying circumstances), b) the moral (subjective) elements of typicity (intent, negligence, purpose/motive, mistake); 2) Unlawfulness (is there a ground of justification?). Once wrongfulness has been determined, one shall proceed with analysing whether the perpetrator can be reproached or condemned for the wrongful act. In this sense, culpability will be assessed by taking into consideration the following factors: 1) Does the perpetrator have criminal capacity; 2) Is there any ground (mental infirmity, minority of age, threat or duress, unjust provocation …) affecting culpability. Compare Toroslu (n 4) 119–121 for two elements (material (objective) element (material act) and moral (subjective) element (culpable will), this is a view based on the traditional Italian doctrine. Further compare Tahir Taner, *Ceza Hukuku Umumi Kısım* (3rd edn, Istanbul 1953) 82 (legal element, material element (act), moral element) and Nurullah Kunter, *Suçun Maddi Unsurları Nazariyesi* (Hareket-Netice-Sebebiyet Alakası 1954) 11 et seq. (legal elements (typicity- unlawfulness-conditions for punishability) and material elements (conduct-result-causality)). Further compare Hafızoğulları/Özen (n 5) 190 (act, violation, guilt).

31   Artuk/Gökcen/Yenidünya (n 18) 369 et seq.; İçel (n 5) 89; Öztürk/ Erdem (n 9) 194; Demirbaş (n 5) 254; Özgenç (n 18) 282; Özbek et al. (n 1) 261; Soyaslan (n 2) 346; Centel/Zafer/Çakmut (n 2) 279; Koca/Üzülmez (n 22) 250; Zafer (n 18) 255. In the opposite direction Toroslu (n 4) 149–151. For extensive debate refer to Tuğrul Katoğlu, *Ceza Hukukunda Hukuka Aykırılık* (Seçkin 2003) 127 et seq.

32   Katoğlu (n 31) 21–24; İçel (n 5) 90; Kangal (n 24),176–7.

33   Artuk/Gökcen/Yenidünya (n 18) 369. For extensive debate refer to Katoğlu (n 31) 21 et seq.

34   İçel (n 5) 95; Öztürk/ Erdem (n 9) 194; Demirbaş (n 5) 254–255; Centel/Zafer/Çakmut (n 2) 280; Soyaslan (n 2) 346–347; Özgenç (n 18) 282; Hakeri (n 4) 240.

35   In this direction Koca/Üzülmez (n 22) 253; Özbek et al. (n 1) 260.

36   Özgenç (n 18) 286; Artuk/Gökcen/Yenidünya (n 18) 370; Koca/Üzülmez (n 22) 255; Hakeri (n 4) 241.

37   Katoğlu (n 31) 36 et seq.

38   Kangal (n 24) 182; Koca/Üzülmez (n 22) 255.

39   Özgenç (n 18) 286; Koca/Üzülmez (n 22) 255.

40   Artuk/Gökcen/Yenidünya (n 18) 371; İçel (n 5) 85 et seq. and 222 et seq.; Öztürk/ Erdem (n 9) 194, Demirbaş (n 5) 248 et seq., Centel/Zafer/Çakmut (n 2) 287; Özgenç (n 18) 290–291; Soyaslan (n 2) 356 et seq.; Hafızoğulları/Özen (n 5) 237–238; Özbek et al. (n 1) 260 et seq., 344 et seq. Compare Erem/Danışman/Artuk (n 4) 552–553 (the authors categorise all these different grounds under the heading of 'excuses'). A distinction may be made between grounds excluding culpability, and excuses, where culpability is not precluded altogether, but the guilt of the perpetrator is diminished, thus rendering punishment unnecessary. Kangal (n 24) 432–433. However, this issue has not yet been dealt with in Turkish academic writings.

Whereas the objective existence of a justification was found sufficient for the perpetrator to be acquitted in the understanding of the previous penal code,[41] the perpetrator should be aware of the existence of such a ground and act with the requisite intention (for example, the will to act in self-defence) in order to escape liability according to the new TPC.[42] This is because, according to the German-oriented understanding, the conscience to realise a lawful act eliminates the negative value of the conduct, thus negating its unjust nature.[43] However, the act would still be intentional because, according to the understanding adopted by the new TPC, the knowledge about the unlawfulness of the act is not included into intent (strict intent theory), but it is a matter to be assessed in the light of culpability (guilt theory). In case the agent acts under the objective existence of a justification, but lacks the subjective element to do so, it is argued that he should be held responsible for an attempted crime.[44] Even so, many writers still consider the objective existence of a justification sufficient.[45]

Finally, certain provisions of the Penal Code specifically refer to the requirement that the conduct be unlawful.[46] In such case, unlawfulness is regarded as an element of typicity, and the result is that the perpetrator has to be aware of the unlawfulness of his conduct to be held responsible; hence, the judge must ascertain this when determining intent.[47] In this case, it is argued that typicity no longer constitutes an indication of the conduct's unlawfulness.[48] In addition, certain writers argue that in this case the crime may only be committed with direct intent.[49]

Cumulation/Cumulative or Alternative Pleading of Defences

In line with the understanding of the new TPC and CCP, a person shall be acquitted in case of relying on a justification (Article 223(2) CCP), whereas he shall not be punished due to lack of guilt in case of relying on a ground excluding culpability (Article 223(3) CCP). Hence, while it is possible to plead, as far as factually possible, different defences in the same case,[50] the defence should rely on justifications where possible. This is because in the case of relying on grounds excluding culpability the defendant would not be punished, but the act would still constitute a criminal offence. This would have the following consequences:

---

41 Dönmezer/Erman (n 5) 21; Önder (n 3) 222; Katoğlu (n 31) 105.
42 Öztürk/ Erdem (n 9) 198; Artuk/Gökcen/Yenidünya (n 18) 372; Koca/Üzülmez (n 22) 254; Hakeri (n 4) 243; Özbek et al. (n 1) 265; RB Erman, 'Yanılmanın Ceza Sorumluluğuna Etkisi' (PhD thesis, Istanbul University 2006) 392.
43 Koca/Üzülmez (n 22) 254; Kangal (n 24) 202.
44 Artuk/Gökcen/Yenidünya (n 18) 530; Koca/Üzülmez (n 22) 258. Cf *Erman* (n 42) 390–392 (the writer argues that with regard to Turkish penal law, in case of the objective existence of a justification, one may speak of 'impossible crime', hence the perpetrator cannot be punished at all. This is because, contrary to the German Penal Code (ss 22 and 23(3)) where attempt is defined purely subjectively, under the TPC, impossible attempts are not punished, and the provisions on attempt may not be applied anyway when the typical result has materialised).
45 Demirbaş (n 5) 256; Centel/Zafer/Çakmut (n 2) 289; Toroslu (n 4) 150; Kangal (n 24) 203; Devrim Güngör, *Ceza Hukukunda Fiil Üzerinde Hata* (Yetkin 2007) 63. Refer to Katoğlu (n 31) 81 et seq. and Erman (n 42) 388–393 for extensive debate.
46 This is called 'special unlawfulness' (however, see Katoğlu (n 31) 126 for criticism directed at the distinction between general and special unlawfulness).
47 Artuk/Gökcen/Yenidünya (n 18),373; Özgenç (n 18) 289; Özbek et al. (n 1) 263. In the opposite direction Öztürk/ Erdem (n 9) 197 (the authors regard this to be a useless repetition). Compare Centel/Zafer/Çakmut (n 2) 292 (the authors argue that this argument has lost its relevance by virtue of TPC Art. 30(4) on mistake concerning the wrongful nature of the act). Further compare Zafer (n 18) 231 (if the requirement of unlawfulness concerns a given material element of the statutory definition, then unlawfulness becomes part of typicity, and lack of knowledge concerning such unlawfulness eliminates intent. If, on the other hand, the requirement of unlawfulness qualifies the statutory definition as a whole, it is just a repetition and bears no particular relevance. Ignorance of the unlawfulness in this context shall be assessed in light of TPC Art. 30(4) concerning mistake on the wrongful nature of the act).
48 Demirbaş (n 5) 253.
49 Artuk/Gökcen/Yenidünya (n 18) 373; Öztürk/ Erdem (n 9) 197 n 686.
50 With regard to justifications, see in the same direction Koca/Üzülmez (n 22) 259 and Özbek et al. (n 1) 266.

a) In the case of the defendant pleading an excuse, an aider and abettor may still be held responsible for the excused crime. When a justification is pleaded, no participant to the act may be punished since the conduct at issue is not unlawful;

b) An action in self-defence by the victim of criminal conduct is allowed even if such criminal conduct may be excused (e.g., having to shoot a mentally ill person intending to kill one). However, self-defence may not be urged against an action that is made lawful by a justification;

c) In the case of pleading an excuse, the defendant may still be liable to pay compensation for any damage resulting from his misconduct. On the other hand, if the behaviour is legally justified, no such obligation would arise.

In the case of different justifications being applicable, they all have to be taken into account since each one is independent from the other.[51]

Provocation of Defence Situation

This is a matter discussed in more detail in the framework of self-defence. It is accepted in academic writings that in case of intentionally provoking an attack in order to be able to rely on self-defence, the person acting with such intention cannot benefit from this justification.[52] This understanding is applicable to all justifications.[53] On the other hand, where the person acting in self-defence has not acted with such intention, but merely caused the attack through his own initial and unlawful act, it is still possible to rely on self-defence, e.g., a wife who gets caught by her husband while committing adultery may act in self-defence against the husband who grabs his gun to shoot her.[54] In addition, it is also argued that it is possible to rely on self-defence against an act that was initially itself in self-defence, when that act has exceeded the permissible limits.[55]

As for state of necessity, because of the requirement that the danger must not be created wilfully, there can be no reliance on self-induced necessity.

Mistakes of Fact and Defences

Mistake may be divided into two: mistake in the legal elements of the crime, which negates intent; and mistake regarding the wrongfulness of the act, which precludes culpability.

TPC Article 30(3) regulates mistake regarding the grounds for excluding or reducing criminal responsibility: 'Any person who is inevitably mistaken about the existence of circumstances concerning grounds excluding or reducing criminal responsibility shall benefit from such mistake'.[56]

The first alternative falling under this provision is mistake concerning the existence of the material conditions of a justification.[57] In this case, the actual situation is not what the perpetrator thinks, e.g., as he runs at night through the woods, A comes across a bleeding man, and notices another man, M, holding a gun in his hand. A immediately grabs his own gun and shoots M. However, it turns out that a movie was being shot. According to the classic doctrine, the perpetrator will benefit from his mistake (and rely on legitimate defence of a third person) if his mistake is essential, and if the perpetrator is not culpable in being mistaken. Essential refers to the fact that the perpetrator would have been acting lawfully had the situation been as he believed. As for the German-oriented approach adopted by the new TPC, if the mistake is inevitable,[58] no criminal

---

51 Hakeri (n 4) 243.

52 Muharrem Özen, *Türk Ceza Hukukunda Meşru Müdafaa* (Ankara 1995) 88; Artuk/Gökcen/Yenidünya (n 18) 387; Özbek et al. (n 1) 266.

53 Hakeri (n 4) 244.

54 Artuk/Gökcen/Yenidünya (n 18) 386. Further see Özen (n 52) 84 et seq.

55 Zafer (n 18) 271.

56 Unless otherwise indicated, the translations are the author's own.

57 Güngör (n 45) 62–63; Kangal (n 24) 367.

58 Refer to Güngör (n 45) 69 for the meaning of 'inevitable' (the author argues that this refers to the perpetrator's lack of guilt in being mistaken, see in the same direction Özbek et al. (n 1) 420; Artuk/Gökcen/Yenidünya (n 18) 530; Hakeri (n 4) 376; Kangal (n 24) 369–70).

responsibility arises.[59] If the mistake was evitable, there are different views. According to one view (theory on negative elements of typicity), this mistake negates intent, thus the first paragraph of the article shall apply, and the perpetrator may only be held responsible if the act amounts to a crime which can be punished when committed negligently.[60] According to another view (strict guilt theory),[61] this mistake precludes culpability, but the conduct is still intentional and unlawful, therefore the perpetrator shall be held responsible for the crime, but the mistake shall be taken into account, according to Article 61 of the TPC, in the determination of the sentence.

The second alternative falling under Article 30(3) is mistake concerning the material conditions of a ground reducing or excluding culpability. A typical example is a mistake regarding the existence of unjust provocation, e.g., A mistakenly believes that B has insulted him before other persons, and, under the influence of a state of anger caused by the alleged insult, he stabs B. In this case, if the mistake is inevitable, A shall benefit from the provisions of provocation. If it is not, he shall be punished for the intentional crime he has committed without benefitting from the provisions of unfair provocation, but this mistake will be taken into consideration in the determination of the punishment.[62]

Mistakes concerning the existence of a justification in law (e.g., is euthanasia permissible?) concern the issue of 'mistake of law'. On this issue, a distinction may be made between 'abstract' or 'direct' mistake concerning the wrongful nature of the act, and 'concrete' or 'indirect' mistake concerning the wrongful nature of the act.[63] The former has no relevance by virtue of TPC Article 4 which provides that ignorance of the law is no excuse. As for the latter, Article 30(4) provides: 'Any person who makes an inevitable mistake regarding whether his act constitutes a wrong, shall not be subject to punishment'. Article 30(4) does not concern ignorance of law in the classical sense, but mistake regarding the wrongful nature of the act ('*haksızlık yanılgısı*' or '*yasak hatası*', *Verbotsirrtum* in German). The question is whether the perpetrator is aware of having engaged in wrongful conduct.[64] In order to be punished, the perpetrator should be aware of the anti-social character of his act and he should know that his action is disapproved by the legal order.[65] To put it in another way, the perpetrator should be conscious of the fact that the legal order does not permit such action.[66] If this is not the case, then the perpetrator cannot be blamed or condemned for such conduct.

A mistake about the wrongful nature of the conduct should be inevitable (unavoidable) for the perpetrator to escape punishment. Hence, although unlikely in most cases, a person acting in the belief that a justification exists might rely on this provision. The assessment whether the mistake was unavoidable should be made, taking into consideration the personal conditions of the perpetrator (his level of education, cultural and social background, etc.) by evaluating whether the perpetrator has shown the necessary endeavour to obtain the relevant information in order not to be mistaken.[67] However, the personal political, religious and ethical convictions and considerations of the perpetrator shall not relieve him from responsibility, as long as awareness exists as to the fact that the conduct was in violation of social and legal norms.[68] If the mistake was avoidable, criminal responsibility will arise but the mistake can be taken into consideration in the determination of the sentence since the act is still intentional but it may be accepted that culpability has been affected (guilt theory).[69]

---

59 Öztürk/ Erdem (n 9) 287.

60 Artuk/Gökcen/Yenidünya (n 18) 531; Özgenç (n 18) 431; Koca/Üzülmez (n 22) 287; Hakeri (n 4) 376; Güngör (n 45) 72; Kangal (n 24) 365, 369.

61 For the understanding of this view see Koca/Üzülmez (n 22) 283 and Kangal (n 24) 366. Compare Özbek et al. (n 1) 421 (the authors find this view acceptable but unjust); Güngör (n 45) 70.

62 Özgenç (n 18) 435; Artuk/Gökcen/Yenidünya (n 18) 531; Koca/Üzülmez (n 22) 329.

63 Koca/Üzülmez (n 22) 326; Zafer (n 18) 336–340.

64 Demirbaş (n 5) 399; Hafızoğulları/Özen (n 5) 319; Hakeri (n 4) 384.

65 Özgenç (n 18) 435–436; Öztürk/ Erdem (n 9) 288; Koca/Üzülmez (n 22) 325–328.

66 Koca/Üzülmez (n 22) 326; Donay (n 10) 48. So, the perpetrator should be conscious of the fact that he was violating the law, Artuk/Gökcen/Yenidünya (n 18) 534–536.

67 Öztürk/ Erdem (n 9) 289; Artuk/Gökcen/Yenidünya (n 18) 535–536.

68 Hakeri (n 4) 384; compare Donay (n 10) 48. You may think of 'honour killings', where the perpetrator knows that his conduct is unlawful, but acts in the belief that customs and tradition entitle, and indeed, oblige him to kill a certain person.

69 Özgenç (n 18) 438; Koca/Üzülmez (n 22) 327; Özbek et al. (n 1) 428.

Transferred Defences/Collateral Damage Defences

This issue has been discussed in the framework of justifications. The prevailing view in Turkish doctrine, based on the understanding that an act benefitting from justification is in compliance with the legal order, is that in cases of both mistake in person and *aberratio* (deviation), the agent shall still benefit from the justification.[70] Hence, it is possible to transfer the ground the offender may have had *vis-à-vis* his intended victim to the actual victim. According to the opposite view,[71] in case of error in person, TPC Article 30(3) shall apply.

In case of *aberratio ictus*, the assessment shall be made in light of whether the agent has acted with intent or negligence with regard to the result caused by the deviation. Even so, the Court of Cassation has relied on self-defence in acquitting the agent who misfired and shot dead a 12-year-old boy staring from the window.[72]

With regard to self-defence, it is argued that where both the aggressor and an innocent third person are harmed, the two results must be assessed separately: the harm inflicted to the third person may not be considered in self-defence, but an excuse based on necessity might be available.[73]

Individual Defences

Self-Defence and Excessive Self-Defence

TPC Article 25(1) provides that an act committed in self-defence shall not be punished subject to certain conditions. The first three of the following requirements are categorised as those concerning the attack; the ensuing three are classified under 'requirements as to the (act in) defence'.[74]

There must be unlawful attack. An 'attack' is an assault, by another person, which is prejudicial to any legitimate interest protected by law. It does not have to constitute a criminal offence. The attack may be constituted by an omissive or negligent action.[75] As long as the attack is unlawful, it does not matter if the attacker does not bear criminal responsibility due to lack of criminal capacity or culpability.[76]

The attack must be directed against a right to which the person acting in self-defence or a third person was entitled. The right in question does not necessarily have to be under the protection of criminal codes.[77] As a novelty, the new TPC permits self-defence for the protection of property. However, this right is circumscribed by the requirement of proportionality, and especially with regard to law-enforcement officials dealing with runaway criminals, the requirements of Article 2 of the European Convention on Human Rights.

In addition, defence of a third person is also covered by the provision. There was no such explicit provision in the previous TPC, however, it was accepted both in academic writings and judicial practice that defence of a third person would fall within the provision regarding self-defence.

The attack must be ongoing. A view defended in academic writings was that if an attack that has not yet been launched is certain to be carried out, or an attack which has terminated is certain to be repeated, this requirement is satisfied. This has now been explicitly incorporated into the provision.

Resort to the action which constitutes self-defence must be indispensable. In other words, there should be no other option than to act in such way in order to repel the attack. However, the generally accepted view is that if an agent who is in a position to escape in order to avoid the attack does not do so but prefers to confront

---

70 With regard to self-defence, in the same direction Demirbaş (n 5) 277; Koca/Üzülmez (n 22) 285 (however, the personal view of the authors is in the opposite direction).

71 Koca/Üzülmez (n 22) 286.

72 1st Chamber judgment of 24 April 1984 no 1827.

73 Hakeri (n 4) 265.

74 Court of Cassation, Criminal Section Grand Chamber, judgment of 26 February 2008 no 37.

75 Artuk/Gökcen/Yenidünya (n 18) 385; Zafer (n 18) 270.

76 Özen (n 52) 92; Zafer (n 18) 271.

77 Artuk/Gökcen/Yenidünya (n 18) 388.

the attack, he may still rely, in principle, on self-defence.[78] Hence, there is no duty to retreat.[79] On the other hand, it is also argued that where the agent facing an attack is in a position to protect himself without having to sacrifice any legally protected value, there is no right to self-defence.[80]

The act of self-defence must be proportionate to the assault. Proportionality is assessed both in terms of the means used and the legal interests at stake, in light of the situation and circumstances prevailing at the time. In general, if it is possible to repel the attack in various manners, the agent acting in self-defence must choose the method that is less harmful to the attacker.[81] In particular, there must be a proportion between the right sought to be protected, and the legal interest harmed by the act in self-defence. Hence, unless the attack threatens to harm his right to life, an agent may not kill an attacker in order to protect his property.[82]

The act in self-defence must be directed at the aggressor. In addition, in case of a reciprocal claim of self-defence by two agents attacking each other, the established case law of the Turkish Court of Cassation is not to apply the provision on self-defence to either of them if it cannot be conclusively determined who attacked first.[83] This approach is criticised in academic writings since it is argued that due to the principle of *in dubio pro reo* both agents should be able to rely on self-defence.[84] The Court of Cassation prefers to apply provocation as a general mitigating circumstance to both agents.

It is argued that, exceptionally, a person confronted with excessive self-defence might be able to rely himself on self-defence to contrast such excessive response.[85]

As for excessive self-defence, Article 27 provides that if the limits of grounds excluding criminal responsibility are unintentionally exceeded, and the act can be punished when committed negligently, the punishment imposed for the negligent crime shall be reduced by one-sixth to one-third. Despite its wording, the provision only applies to justifications.[86] It regulates exceeding the permissible limits of a justification as regards its material conditions, e.g., an agent acting under self-defence exceeds the limits of the requirement of proportionality, and causes the death of the attacker. If the person cannot be considered guilty, he cannot be held responsible whatsoever. However, if the limit has been exceeded due to negligence, such as firing four shots when one shot had already and clearly neutralised the attack, responsibility may result. Thus, if the penal code envisages that the crime which has resulted may be committed negligently (as is the case here—unintentional homicide), the perpetrator will be sentenced under the relevant provision, but the punishment will be reduced.

Exceptionally, and with regard to self-defence only, if the limits were exceeded as a result of excitement, fear or agitation that can be regarded as excusable, the offender shall not be subject to any punishment (TPC Art. 27(2)). This is another novel provision of the new TPC. An example may be where an elderly householder sleeping in her room wakes up to a noise coming from downstairs, she grabs her gun with the intention of checking the situation. As she opens her door she sees a shadow in the hall a couple of metres away from her, and in panic she fires multiple random shots killing the intruder. There is no mistake here concerning the permissible limits of self-defence, the agent knows that the response is excessive but, under the circumstances of the case, can be excused for acting in such way. Hence, this provision concerns culpability.[87] The requirement of proportionality in the response to an unlawful attack is infringed here.[88] If the excessive response is deemed as excusable under the circumstances of the case, no punishment shall be imparted.

Finally, where the material conditions for a justification do not exist at all, the provisions of Article 27 are not applicable. In this case, Article 30(3) shall apply.

---

78   See, for example, Centel/Zafer/Çakmut (n 2) 309; Demirbaş (n 5) 275–276; İçel (n 5) 129; Hakeri (n 4) 264.

79   See, in this direction, the judgments of 18 December 1991 (no. 1–4/39) and 26 November 1990 (no. 1–275/300) of the Grand Chamber (Criminal Section) of the Court of Cassation. For different views, see Zafer (n 18) 273.

80   Öztürk/ Erdem (n 9) 208.

81   Artuk/Gökcen/Yenidünya (n 18) 392.

82   Özen (n 52) 129; Artuk/Gökcen/Yenidünya (n 18) 395. For extensive debate, refer to Mustafa Ruhan Erdem, 'Malvarlığına Yönelik Saldırılara Karşı Meşru Savunma İçin İnsan Öldürme ve Yaşam Hakkı (AİHS m. 2)' in *Dokuz Eylül Üniversitesi Hukuk Fakültesi Dergisi* (2007 vol 9), 987 et seq.

83   See, for example, Court of Cassation, 3rd Criminal Chamber, judgment of 20 February 2011 (no. 18239).

84   Artuk/Gökcen/Yenidünya (n 18) 385. Compare Özen (n 52) 92.

85   Artuk/Gökcen/Yenidünya (n 18) 387; Zafer (n 18) 271.

86   Artuk/Gökcen/Yenidünya (n 18) 442.

87   Artuk/Gökcen/Yenidünya (n 18) 446.

88   Court of Cassation, Criminal Section Grand Chamber, judgment of 26 February 2008, no. 37.

Necessity

This ground is regulated in TPC Article 25(2),[89] and it prevents any punishment from being imposed upon the offender. Contrary to Germany where there is a distinction between necessity as a justification, and necessity as a ground for excluding culpability, TPC Article 25(2) is the only provision on necessity. Some writers argue that this ground constitutes an excuse; according to this view, the existence of state of necessity is a ground for precluding culpability.[90] Indeed, CCP Article 223(3)(b) refers to necessity as a ground for excluding culpability.[91] Thus, if a person acts under a state of necessity, he is not acquitted, but the judge shall decide that there is 'no need to inflict punishment because there is no guilt'. However, despite this provision, the majority opines that, because of the way it has been articulated, or due to its intrinsic nature, it constitutes a justification.[92] This is particularly so because the provision seeks a balancing judgment between the gravity of the danger and the means used in response.[93] However, in line with the provision of the CCP, the Court of Cassation has held that state of necessity no longer constitutes a justification but an excuse.[94]

Article 25(2) applies under the following conditions. First, there must be a serious and certain danger. 'Danger' refers to a situation that may give rise to a major harm to a person or object. The TPC refers to the danger being 'certain' (*muhakkak*). This is to mean that unless preventive measures are taken, the danger is highly likely to harm a protected legal interest.[95] There is no requirement that the danger be caused by forces of nature.[96] Seriousness shall be assessed *in concreto* by the judge.[97]

Second, the danger must be directed at a right to which the perpetrator, or a third person, is entitled. Any right or interest protected by any branch of law is within this scope. The provision clearly provides that it is possible to rely on this ground when the danger is directed to a third person.

Third, the danger must not have been knowingly caused by the perpetrator himself. If the danger is caused intentionally the agent may not rely on state of necessity to justify an act committed with a view to avoiding the danger in question ('self-induced necessity'). In cases of negligence, it is possible to rely on this provision.[98] It may be said that in case of advertent negligence, the agent should also be unable to rely on

---

89   There are also some provisions that provide for special instances of state of necessity, such as Art. 92 (1) regarding the trading of organs or tissues, art 99(2) on illegal abortion, and art 147(1) regarding theft. In these instances, the judge is free to impose a punishment, albeit a reduced one, whereas no punishment may be imposed when the general rule (art 25(2)) is applied.

90   Özgenç (n 18) 394; Artuk/Gökcen/Yenidünya (n 18) 459; Koca/Üzülmez (n 22) 304; Hakeri (n 4) 328; Recep Gülşen, *Ceza Hukukunda Sorumluluğu Kaldıran Nedenlerden Kaza, Mücbir Sebep, Cebir ve Tehdit* (Seçkin 2007) 206; further see Kangal (n 24) 36 n 27 for references.

91   In this case, it may be possible to act in self-defence against the agent acting under necessity. Hakeri (n 4) 245–246. Refer to Nevzat Toroslu, *Ceza Hukukunda Zaruret Hali* (Ankara 1968) 49 et seq. for extensive information on the view that necessity affects culpability.

92   See Kangal (n 24) 34 n 22 for references. Further see Toroslu (n 4) 167; İçel (n 5)136; Öztürk/ Erdem (n 9) 213, Demirbaş (n 5) 279, Centel/Zafer/Çakmut (n 2) 312; Soyaslan (n 2) 379 et seq.; Hafızoğulları/Özen (n 5) 247; Yener Ünver, 'YTCK'da Kusurluluk' [2009] 1 Ceza Hukuku Dergisi 59; Güngör (n 45) 66. Compare Özbek et al. (n 1) 382, who argue that it includes certain features from both institutions.

93   Öztürk/ Erdem (n 9) 212.

94   Court of Cassation, Criminal Section Grand Chamber, judgment of 26 February 2008, no 1–281/37. It is also argued that, depending upon the circumstances of the case, it may constitute either a justification or an excuse. *Kangal* (n 24) 48. Thus, there is a justification if the legal value confronted with the danger that is trying to be avoided is significantly superior to the legal value harmed by the protective act, there is an excuse if the protected legal value is equal to or not significantly superior to the harmed legal value belonging to a third person. In line with this view, the person acting under state of necessity should be acquitted in the former case, and it shall be decided that there is 'no need to inflict punishment' in the latter case.

95   Özbek et al. (n 1) 385; Zafer (n 18) 279.

96   Özgenç (n 18) 394; Artuk/Gökcen/Yenidünya (n 18) 463. Hence, a human behaviour may be the source of the danger. Toroslu (n 103) 83.

97   Toroslu (n 91) 114.

98   Toroslu (n 91) 127.

necessity.[99] There are diverging views on whether it is possible for the agent to rely on necessity to the benefit of a third person, when the danger was created by that third person, but the agent is unaware of this.[100]

Fourth, the perpetrator should not be under a legal obligation to confront the danger. This is a requirement that, although not explicitly stated in the provision, is inherent in the nature of necessity.[101] Certain professions impose on the person practising it the duty to face the danger, e.g., a doctor may not refuse to treat the patients and abandon the hospital because of the risk of an infectious disease. Obviously, in case of material impossibility, the agent may not be held responsible for the result he could not prevent.[102]

Fifth, there should be no other means of protection. In other words, it should be impossible to escape the danger without having to harm the right of a third person. Hence, it is argued that, contrary to self-defence, there is, where possible, a duty to retreat here.[103] This is because an innocent third person is harmed.

Finally, the means used must be proportionate to the gravity and object of the danger. It is argued that this condition must be assessed differently with regard to state of necessity as a justification and state of necessity as an excuse. In the former case, the legal value confronted with the danger that is trying to be avoided must be significantly superior to the legal value harmed by the protective act. In the latter case, the protected legal value must be equal to or not significantly superior to the harmed legal value belonging to a third person.[104] However, for those who regard the provision to constitute a justification only, the protected legal value has to be superior to the one harmed.[105] However, regardless of which view is accepted on the legal qualification of necessity, it is generally accepted that it suffices for the legal interests at stake to be at least equal.[106]

Duress by Threats/Circumstances

According to Article 28, no punishment shall be imposed upon a person who commits a criminal offence as a result of an irresistible or inevitable use of force or violence against himself. Similarly, in the case of having to commit a crime under the threat of being submitted to a certain and serious injury, no responsibility arises.[107] In academic writings[108] it has been argued that this last option refers to '*istenemezlik*', a ground for precluding culpability that has been called '*l'inesigibilità*' by the Italians and '*nichtzumutbarkeit*' by the Germans.

According to Article 223(3)(b) of the Penal Procedure Code, the judge shall decide that the person acting under such influence is not culpable, and that there is no need to inflict punishment upon him. In such cases, the person using material or moral compulsion to force another to commit the crime shall be deemed to be the offender (indirect perpetration).

As for duress by circumstances, this is not explicitly provided for in the TPC. However, it is accepted to constitute an excuse. Necessity as laid down in TPC Article 25(2) is widely regarded as a justification, whereas a state of necessity is considered an excuse understood as *force majeure* (*mücbir sebep*).[109] In the case of necessity, if a balance of interests reveals that the legal interest sought to be protected by the agent acting under duress is at least equivalent to the one sacrificed, there shall be no criminal liability due to lack of guilt.[110] In case of force majeure, no such balancing test is required since the agent was forced to act in the way he did.[111]

---

99   Toroslu (n 4) 168; Demirbaş (n 5) 287; Hakeri (n 4) 334; Özbek et al. (n 1) 387; Koca/Üzülmez (n 22) 309; Hafızoğulları/Özen (n 5) 249; Zafer (n 18) 280. In the opposite direction İçel (n 5) 141.

100   In the affirmative Hakeri (n 4) 334 and Demirbaş (n 5) 290; in the opposite direction Toroslu (n 91) 130.

101   Toroslu (n 91) 93.

102   In similar vein Koca/Üzülmez (n 22) 310.

103   Öztürk/ Erdem (n 9) 215; Demirbaş (n 5) 288; Hakeri (n 4) 336; Zafer (n 18) 281.

104   Kangal (n 24) 303 et seq., 469 et seq.

105   Öztürk/ Erdem (n 9) 216.

106   Toroslu (n 4) 170; İçel (n 5) 143; Artuk/Gökcen/Yenidünya (n 18) 467; Demirbaş (n 5) 289; Özgenç (n 18) 395; Koca/Üzülmez (n 22) 311; Zafer (n 18) 282.

107   Therefore, moral compulsion (duress/threat—vis compulsiva) and physical compulsion (violence—vis fisica) have been treated under the same provision and have been subjected to the same conditions. For a critical view of this approach, see Hafızoğulları/Özen (n 5) 324.

108   Hafızoğulları/Özen (n 5) 324–325.

109   Zafer (n 18) 317.

110   Özgenç (n 18) 395.

111   Zafer (n 18) 318.

This is what separates it from necessity, where the agent had, in fact, a choice.[112] In the case of *force majeure*, the agent is compelled by an irresistible force to act in the given manner.

General Mental Condition Defences

The TPC embodies the Classical School concept of the moral responsibility of the perpetrator. To be found guilty of a crime, a person must have both criminal capacity and, in principle, criminal intent at the time of commission of the crime. Only security measures may be imposed on a person without criminal capacity.

Criminal capacity refers to the whole of the personal characteristics that must be found in the perpetrator in order to impute him an act.[113] 'Culpability' (in intentionally committed crimes)[114] requires the existence of the capacity to comprehend (the capability of appreciating the legal meaning and consequences of one's own acts), and of the capacity to act wilfully (the capability to control one's own behaviour). If one of these elements is lacking, the act may still be intentional (and constitute a crime), but the perpetrator may not be blamed, and, as a result, cannot be punished due to the lack of culpability.

Insanity

With regard to mental disorder or infirmity, TPC Article 32 makes a three-fold distinction:[115]

a) If the perpetrator cannot comprehend the legal meaning and consequences of the act he has committed, no punishment shall be imposed.
b) If, in respect of such act, the perpetrator's ability to control his behaviour was significantly diminished, no punishment shall be imposed.
c) If the perpetrator's ability to control his behaviour in respect of an act he has committed is diminished, but not to the extent defined above, the sentence shall be reduced.[116] In this case, the punishment to be imposed may be enforced partially or completely as a security measure specific to mentally disordered persons (TPC Article 57), provided the length of the punishment remains the same.

Intoxication

TPC Article 34(1) regulates the situation of a person who is under the effect of a so-called 'transitory reason', or of involuntary intoxication. In such cases, if the agent is unable to comprehend the legal meaning and consequences of the act he has committed, or his ability to control his behaviour regarding the act is significantly diminished, he shall not be punished.

Transitory reasons are temporary conditions, such as acting under the effect of an illness, that cannot be considered as mental disorder in the sense of Article 32, but which eliminate or significantly diminish the capacity to comprehend or to control one's behaviour.[117] The perpetrator should not have any guilt in the emergence of such condition in order to benefit from it.[118]

---

112   Öztürk/ Erdem (n 9) 215.
113   Dönmezer/Erman (n 5) 145.
114   Artuk/Gökcen/Yenidünya (n 18) 451; Özgenç (n 18) 360; Hakeri (n 4) 303.
115   İçel (n 5) 185. Some writers (such as Demirbaş (n 5),335; Centel/Zafer/Çakmut (n 2) 372–376; Hafızoğulları/ Özen (n 5) 417–418; Soyaslan (n 2) 404; Donay (n 10),53) make a dual distinction between complete mental disorder and partial mental disorder. Others (Özgenç (n 18) 381; Artuk/Gökcen/Yenidünya (n 18) 508–510; Hakeri (n 4) 313; Koca/ Üzülmez (n 22) 338) argue that mental disorder either exists or it does not, and it may not be technically categorised as complete or partial. However, its effects on criminal capacity may be graduated.
116   25 years where the offence committed requires a punishment of aggravated life imprisonment; 20 years for crimes that require a punishment of life imprisonment; other penalties to be imposed shall be reduced by no more than one-sixth.
117   Önder (n 3) 287; İçel (n 5) 191; Artuk/Gökcen/Yenidünya (n 18) 514; Hafızoğulları/Özen (n 5) 421–2; Soyaslan (n 2) 407; Hakeri (n 4) 315; Koca/Üzülmez (n 22) 341; Özbek et al. (n 1) 367.
118   Dönmezer/Erman (n 5) 185; Toroslu (n 4) 388; Artuk/Gökcen/Yenidünya (n 18) 514; Öztürk/ Erdem (n 9) 237; Demirbaş (n 5) 342; Centel/Zafer/Çakmut (n 2) 379; Soyaslan (n 2) 407; Hafızoğulları/Özen (n 5) 422.

Residual Catch-All Defences/Existence and Ambit of Statutory Defences

TPC Article 24(1) provides that a person who carries out the provisions of a statute shall not be subject to punishment. This justification is part of the larger defence known as 'execution of duty'. TPC Article 24(2) provides that a person who carries out an order given by an authorized body shall not be held liable (superior orders defence) if the offences' execution is required as a matter of duty. To rely on this ground: (i) there must be a superior-subordinate relationship; (ii) there must be a binding order; and (iii) the order must be lawful. Article 24(3) clearly provides that an order amounting to the commission of a criminal offence 'shall never be executed in any circumstances. Otherwise, the person who carried out the order and the person who gave the order shall be liable'. This provision mirrors Article 137(2) of the Constitution, which determines that '[a]n order which in itself constitutes an offence shall under no circumstances be executed; the person who executes such an order shall not evade responsibility'. Therefore, where an order that constitutes an offence is carried out, both the superior who gave the order, and the subordinate who complied with it, will incur criminal responsibility.[119]

There is debate regarding whether execution of superior orders constitutes a justification,[120] or a ground precluding culpability.[121] CCP Article 223(3)(b) treats it as an excuse.

A novelty of the new TPC is that it explicitly provides for exercise of a right[122] and consent of the victim[123] as a justification. The previous TPC did not incorporate these grounds, but it was unanimously accepted in judicial practice and academic writings that these grounds constituted a justification.[124]

In any case, it is argued that the grounds of justification are not restrictive (*numerus clausus*), and resorting to custom for the purpose of creating justifications is not in violation of the prohibition of analogy since that principle aims at protecting the perpetrator.[125]

Minority of age is a ground concerning criminal capacity, thus culpability. According to TPC Article 31(1), minors under the age of twelve are exempt from criminal liability. While such minors cannot be prosecuted, security measures in respect of minors (TPC Article 56) may be imposed on them. Such measures, named 'protective and supportive measures' are laid down in the Children Protection Law (Law no 5395, Arts 5 and 11). With regard to minors older than twelve, but younger than fifteen at the time of commission of the crime, a distinction has to be made. If, at the time of an offence, (i) they are incapable of appreciating the legal meaning and consequences of the act; or (ii) the capability to control their behaviour is underdeveloped, they shall be exempt from criminal liability. However, such minors shall be subject to security measures specific to children. Their mental capacity has to be assessed by an expert in order to determine the applicable regime, and this determination has to be made in light of the specific crime in question.[126] Where the minor has the capability to comprehend the legal meaning and result of the act, and to control his behaviours in respect of his act, he/she shall be convicted but the sentence has to be reduced.[127]

---

119 Dönmezer/Erman (n 5) 94; Demirbaş (n 5) 267. Note, though, that art 41(2) of the Military Penal Code provides that where an order concerns an activity falling within the duty of the subordinate, he has to comply with it, and the responsibility arising from the order will only fall on the person issuing the orders. However, paragraph 3 of the same article provides for two exceptions: a) the subordinate will also be held responsible if he trespassed the orders given to him, or b) if he knew that the order of the commander regarded an act which involved a criminal purpose.

120 In this direction, Centel/Zafer/Çakmut (n 2) 296; Demirbaş (n 5) 263; Öztürk/ Erdem (n 9) 198 et seq.; İçel (n 5) 105; Toroslu (n 4) 153; Soyaslan (n 2) 369; Zafer (n 18) 265.

121 In this direction, Artuk/Gökcen/Yenidünya (n 18) 456; Özgenç (n 18) 396; Hakeri (n 4) 320; Koca/Üzülmez (n 22) 300; Özbek et al. (n 1) 389.

122 According to TPC art 26(1), an agent exercising his right shall not be punished. Various rights may be classified under this provision: freedom of the press, right to petition and right to denunciation, medical interventions, sporting activities, etc.

123 TPC art 26(2). This justification shall be the topic of a different volume.

124 Yüce (n 3) 278 et seq.; Önder (n 3) 256 et seq.

125 Öztürk/ Erdem (n 9) 198; Hakeri (n 4) 241; Koca/Üzülmez (n 22) 259.

126 Öztürk/ Erdem (n 9) 245.

127 TPC art 31(2). For offences requiring a punishment of aggravated life imprisonment, a term of twelve to fifteen years of imprisonment shall be imposed; for offences that require a punishment of life imprisonment, a term of nine to eleven years imprisonment shall be imposed. Otherwise the punishment to be imposed shall be reduced by half, and, in any case, for each act such punishment shall not exceed seven years.

The provisions which relate to minors under twelve years of age (at the time of commission of the crime) apply to deaf and mute persons under the age of fifteen. So, a deaf and mute person does not have criminal capacity unless he/she has completed 15 years at the time of committing the crime. The provisions which relate to minors who are over twelve years of age but under fifteen apply to deaf and mute persons who are over fifteen years of age but under eighteen years of age, as per TPC Article 33.

Some authors refer to the 'societal appropriateness' of the act (e.g., giving a gift of an insignificant value to a public official) as a possible justification or excuse.[128] These might rather be seen as instances where the gravity (the scope/substance of wrongfulness) of the act does not justify criminal intervention.[129]

In case of negligent crimes, where the agent is simultaneously confronted with two duties with the ensuing result that one has to be neglected, the ground known as 'conflict of duties (or obligations)' may apply. The agent may rely on a justification where the duty bearing less importance, in light of the legal interests at stake, is sacrificed.[130] In cases where the sacrificed legal interest is not of lesser importance, but the agent could not have been reasonably or materially expected to behave otherwise, it is possible to rely on an excuse since culpability is affected.[131]

Finally, the concept known as 'permitted risk'[132], which denotes certain inherently dangerous activities which are, however, permitted by the State,[133] may also constitute either a justification or a ground eliminating the objective imputability of the act to the perpetrator.[134]

---

128   Zafer (n 18) 260.

129   Hence, this is merely a restrictive interpretation of the criminal offence in light of its *ratio legis*. Öztürk/ Erdem (n 9) 231.

130   Demirbaş (n 5) 292. Others argue that it suffices for the two duties to be of equal importance to rely on a justification. Öztürk/ Erdem (n 9) 232.

131   Demirbaş (n 5) 293; Özbek et al. (n 1) 331.

132   Refer to Yener Ünver, *Ceza Hukukunda İzin Verilen Risk* (Beta 1998) 126 et seq. for extensive information on the legal nature of this ground.

133   Zafer (n 18) 260.

134   Zafer (n 18) 260.

Chapter 23
United States of America

Luis E Chiesa

General Issues

Justificatory and Excusatory Offences—Distinction and Seat in the Offence Structure

Anyone who engages in conduct that satisfies the elements of a criminal offence knows that he or she has some explaining to do. Conduct that satisfies an offence definition is inherently incriminating. That is, an act (or omission) that satisfies the elements of a criminal offence inculpates the offender and, therefore, calls for an explanation. Take, for example, the case of someone who intentionally kills another person. While such conduct does not necessarily give rise to criminal liability, it certainly requires the offender to explain to the authorities the reasons that moved the killing. Contrast the act of killing a human being with the act of tearing a piece of paper. While the former (killing a person) requires that the actor explain herself to governmental authorities, the latter does not. Nevertheless, if tearing a piece of paper is not an offence, no explanation is needed for engaging in the conduct. In other words, killing a human being is conduct that is relevant for the criminal law in a way in which tearing a piece of paper simply is not.[1]

Given that conduct that satisfies the elements of an offence incriminates the actor, criminal liability will be imposed unless the circumstances surrounding the actor's conduct reveal that she should be exculpated. General defences—the topic of this chapter—define and flesh out the scope of the claims that the government allows actors to plead in order to exculpate themselves from criminal liability. Self-defence, necessity (lesser evils), and insanity are paradigmatic examples. Those who kill in self-defence or pursuant to the necessity defence or while insane have engaged in conduct that satisfies the offence elements of homicide. The concurrence of these general defences reveals that—in spite of the fact that the defendant's conduct satisfies the offence elements of homicide—criminal liability is inappropriate either because of self-defence, necessity, or insanity.

While the claim underlying general defences is that the actor's conduct should be exculpated although it admittedly satisfies the offence elements, there is another type of claim that courts and lawyers frequently call a 'defence' which is not a true 'general defence'. These are claims in which the so-called defence serves to negate an element of the offence. Mistake of fact is the most obvious example. Properly understood, mistakes of fact demonstrate that the defendant's conduct failed to satisfy the subjective offence elements of the offence. In traditional common law terms, mistake of fact 'defences' actually amount to claims that negate the mental state, or *mens rea*, required by the offence. Suppose that Larry takes an umbrella believing it to be his when it actually belongs to María. Larry's mistaken belief amounts to a mistake of fact that defeats liability for the crime of theft. Note, however, that it does not defeat liability for conduct that satisfies the elements of the offence of theft, as a true general defence would do. Rather, Larry's mistake reveals that his conduct did not amount to theft in the first place. A taking amounts to theft only if it is done with the intent to deprive another of her property. Larry's mistaken belief that the umbrella he was taking belonged to him thus negates the intent element of theft. As such, mistakes of fact are claims that show that the defendant's conduct did not actually satisfy the (subjective) elements of the offence. This is why some scholars call such claims 'absent-element defences'.[2]

---

1   See generally Luis Chiesa, Why Is It a Crime to Stomp on a Goldfish? Harm, Victimhood and the Structure of Anti-Cruelty Offenses, 78 Miss. L.J. 1 (2008).

2   Paul H. Robinson, Criminal Law Defences: A Systematic Analysis, 82 Colum. L. Rev. 200, 204 (1982).

The distinction between true general defences and so-called absent element defences is of practical importance. Perhaps the most obvious practical import of the distinction is that it is essential to understanding the allocation of burdens of proof in America. In *In re Winship*, the US Supreme Court held that the prosecution has the burden of proving the culpability of the accused beyond a reasonable doubt.[3] In subsequent cases, the Court clarified that the Constitution only requires that the state prove the offence elements beyond a reasonable doubt. Given that general defences do not negate offence elements, the Court held that it is lawful for the state to shift the burden of proving such defences to the defendant.[4] Nevertheless, given that so-called absent element defences like mistake of fact actually negate an offence element, it is unconstitutional to shift to the defendant the burden of proving such 'defences'.[5]

General defences may be subdivided into justification and excuse defences. Justification defences exculpate the actor because they reveal that her conduct was, all things being considered, an appropriate thing to do under the circumstances. A person who breaks the window of a car to save a child who is suffocating inside the vehicle acts justifiably pursuant to the lesser evils defence. Such conduct is considered appropriate and correct under the circumstances, and, therefore, justified. Since justified conduct is appropriate conduct, such courses of action negate the wrongfulness (unlawfulness) of the act. Examples of justification defences are self-defence, necessity (lesser evils), law enforcement authority, and parental authority.

In contrast, excuse defences exculpate the actor without negating that her conduct is inappropriate and unlawful. An excused actor is acquitted in spite of the wrongfulness of the act because we cannot fairly expect the actor to conform his or her conduct to the mandates of law. The insanity defence is a classic excuse. The insane actor who kills is acquitted, not because killing is appropriate if the killer is insane, but rather because, in spite of the inappropriateness of such killings, we cannot fairly expect that those who fail to understand that their conduct is wrong will conform their acts to the requirements of law.

Several practical consequences follow from labelling a general defence a justification or excuse. First, justified conduct may be lawfully assisted by third parties, whereas excused conduct may not. If, for example, an actor is justified in using force against another pursuant to justifiable self-defence, a third party may use force to repel the aggression on behalf of the justified actor. On the other hand, if an actor's use of force is merely excused pursuant to insanity, a third party may not lawfully use force on behalf of the excused actor. In sum, justifications transfer to third parties, whereas excuses are personal to the actor. Another practical implication of the justification/excuse distinction is that justifications generally defeat both criminal and civil liability,[6] whereas excuses defeat criminal liability but do not generally negate civil liability. Thus, self-defence precludes both the imposition of punishment and tort liability. In contrast, insanity is a bar to the imposition of punishment, but does not usually defeat tort liability.

Legal systems that distinguish between justifications and excuses generally adopt a tripartite approach to criminal liability. They do so by distinguishing between claims that negate the existence of an offence (absent-element defences), claims that negate the wrongfulness of conduct that satisfies the elements of an offence (justification defences), and claims that negate the culpability for engaging in wrongful conduct (excuse defences). While the distinction between justifications and excuses and, therefore, the tripartite approach to criminal liability was generally ignored in America until the second half of the twentieth century, there has been renewed interest in the distinction during the last several decades. More importantly, the influential Model Penal Code distinguishes between justification and excuses. As a result, the current trend in American criminal law is to adopt a tripartite approach to criminal liability that distinguishes between absent element defences, justification defences and excuse defences.

---

3   In *re Winship*, 397 U.S. 358 (1970).

4   See, e.g., *Martin v. Ohio*, 480 U.S. 228 (1987) (self-defence); *Dixon v. United States*, 584 U.S. 1 (2006) (duress); *Leland v. Oregon*, 343 U.S. 790 (1952) (insanity).

5   See, e.g., *Mullaney v. Wilbur*, 421 U.S. 684 (1975).

6   Note, however, that the party harmed as a result of what American tort law calls justifiable 'private necessity' has a right to demand compensation for the damages caused by the defendant's justified conduct. See generally *Vincent v. Lake Erie Transportation Co.*, 109 Minn. 456 [1910].

Conceptual Foundations

Both justification and excuse defences have objective and subjective elements. The objective elements can be referred to as 'triggering conditions', whereas the subjective elements refer to a particular mental state that the defendant must have in order to qualify for the defence. The objective element of the justification of self-defence is the existence of an unlawful aggression. It is this unlawful aggression that triggers the defendant's right to use force in self-defence. In contrast, the triggering condition of the excuse of insanity is the existence of an objectively confirmable mental disease or defect. It is this mental disease or defect that triggers the insanity defence. As a result, if the defendant fails to suffer from such a disease or defence, the insanity excuse is simply inapplicable.

Justification defences have several objective elements in addition to the triggering conditions. As a general rule, the use of force is justifiable only if it is necessary and proportional. Force is necessary if it is the only way of averting the wrongful aggression. In the case of self-defence, force is necessary if it is the only way of averting the unlawful aggression. Force is not necessary if there are less harmful alternatives that could with equal success avert the wrongful attack. Regarding proportionality, force is proportional when it maintains a certain kind of relationship with the averted harm. The proportionality that is required by the different justification defences varies. Self-defence usually requires only that force not be grossly disproportional. As a result, an actor may inflict more harm that is threatened in order to avert a wrongful aggression. A person may, for example, kill in order to avoid suffering serious bodily injury. In contrast, the proportionality requirement in the case of the lesser evils defence is much stricter. As the name of the defence implies, force is justified pursuant to necessity (lesser evils) only if it inflicts less harm than the harm averted.

While force is generally justified only if it is necessary to avert harm and is in some way proportional to the harm averted, conduct is usually excused regardless of whether it is necessary to avert a harm or proportional to a harm averted. Insanity is once more the textbook example. An insane person who kills is acquitted because we could not fairly expect him to know that what he was doing was wrong, rather than because the killing was necessary to avert harm. This is true even in cases of duress. Properly understood, duress excuses criminal conduct if a person of reasonable firmness in the actor's situation would have also engaged in the criminal conduct. It is thus not necessary to demonstrate that the crime committed under duress was a lesser evil.

Regarding the subjective elements of justification and excuse defences, it is helpful to once again distinguish between justification and excuse defences. Justification defences usually require that the actor both (subjectively) believe that her conduct is necessary to avert a threatened harm and that her subjectively held belief be objectively reasonable. In the context of self-defence, the actor must believe that he or she is being wrongfully attacked. In addition, the actor's belief that he or she is being attacked must be reasonable. A similar analysis applies in cases of necessity. To successfully plead necessity, an actor must prove that he or she believed that the act was necessary in order to avoid an even greater harm. This belief must also be reasonable if the defence is to succeed.

The subjective elements of excuse defences vary widely. In the case of duress the actor must be aware of a threat that jeopardizes her wellbeing. In contrast, insanity or intoxication does not require proof of awareness of a threat. Instead, insanity generally requires that the actor be unaware of the wrongfulness of her conduct. Similarly, intoxication may generate an acquittal if it causes the defendant to be incapable of forming the mental state(s) required by the offence.

Cumulation/Cumulative or Alternative Pleading of Defences

In the United States there is no bar to pleading defences in the alternative. This is the case even if the defences are incompatible with each other. Thus, for example, a defendant is allowed to claim that his killing was justified in self-defence, but—if it was not—that he should be acquitted by reason of insanity. American criminal law is so flexible in this regard, that it even allows the defendant to alternatively claim that she did not engage in conduct that satisfies the elements of the offence, but that—if he did—he ought to be justified or excused pursuant to a general defence.[7]

---

7   See, e.g., *Matthews v. United States*, 485 U.S. 58 (1988).

Provocation of Defence Situation

It is often stated that the person who claims the right to use justifiable force must not have provoked the conditions that create her own defence. This, in turn, leads to broad statements such as that the person who purports to use justifiable force must be 'free from fault' if the force is to be ultimately justified.[8] In the context of self-defence, it has been stated that a person loses the right to self-defence if he engages in an 'affirmative unlawful act [that is] reasonably calculated to produce an affray foreboding injurious or fatal consequences'.[9] As a result, provoking or causing the conditions of one's defence can, and often does, lead to losing the opportunity to plead the defence. It is unclear, however, what amount of provocation is enough to deny the right to plead a particular defence. As was mentioned above, some courts like to assert that the defendant must be entirely free from fault. However, as one commentator has put it, this is very likely an 'overstatement'.[10] Other courts tone down the rhetoric, stating that self-defence situations often feature 'fault on both sides'.[11]

A further complication in this context arises because courts and statutes sometimes approach the problem of provoking the conditions that trigger the defence differently depending on which defence is being triggered. Thus, for example, the Model Penal Code denies a duress excuse to an actor who recklessly places himself in a position in which being subjected to duress is likely.[12] Under this approach, the person who joins a dangerous and ruthless street gang will lose the right to claim duress if the gang members threaten to harm him if he does not commit a crime. It can easily be argued that in such a case the actor recklessly exposed himself to the risk of duress by joining the dangerous and ruthless street gang. If such recklessness is found, the actor loses the opportunity to claim duress as an excuse to criminal liability. This approach is sensible, for duress defeats liability by negating that the defendant's commission of the crime is blameworthy. Since a defendant who recklessly creates the conditions of his own defence is not free from blame, he does not deserve to be excused.

While the Model Penal Code denies a duress defence when the defendant recklessly creates the conditions that give rise to the duress claim, it only denies a self-defence claim when the defendant 'with the purpose of causing death or serious bodily injury, provoked the use of force against himself in the same encounter'.[13] As a result, a defendant who recklessly provokes the use of force against him does not automatically lose the right to use force in self-defence under the Code.

Interestingly, the Model Penal Code approaches the lesser evils (necessity) defence in an entirely different way. According to the Code, a defendant who provoked the situation that led to causing harm pursuant to necessity or lesser evils is liable on the basis of the form of culpability with which she provoked the defence.[14] That is, if the defendant negligently provoked the situation that gave rise to necessity, he will be held liable for a negligent version of the offence charged, assuming that such an offence exists. Similarly, if the defendant recklessly created the situation that gave rise to the defence, he will be punished for a reckless version of the offence charged (once again, assuming that such an offence exists). The same analysis follows if the defendant knowingly or purposely caused the conditions of his own defence.

Mistakes of Fact and Defences

Sometimes a person believes that the triggering conditions for using force pursuant to a general defence exist when they actually do not. In the context of self-defence, for example, the actor may believe that he is about to be wrongfully attacked, when in reality he is not being attacked. Does such a mistake preclude the defendant from invoking self-defence? The common law answer to this question is straightforward. Force is justified pursuant to self-defence (and other justifications) as long as the defendant reasonably believes that the triggering conditions for the defence exist. Therefore, the law does not require the defendant's belief in the

---

8   *United States v. Peterson*, 483 F.2d 1222, 1231 (D.C. Cir. 1973).
9   Ibid. 1233.
10   Joshua Dressler, *Understanding Criminal Law* 266 (2006).
11   Dressler, ibid.; *State v. Corchado*, 453 A.2d 427, 433 (Conn. 1982).
12   Model Penal Code § 2.09(2).
13   Model Penal Code § 3.04(2)(b)(i).
14   Model Penal Code § 3.02(2).

existence of the triggering conditions to correct or accurate. Reasonable but mistaken beliefs in the necessity to use justifiable force thus generate full-blown justification for the conduct.[15]

Given that the law of general defences requires reasonable rather than accurate beliefs, the fact that the defendant is mistaken as to the facts that trigger the right to use force is legally irrelevant. If the belief is reasonable it qualifies for a full defence even if mistaken. If it is unreasonable, then the general defence is simply unavailable. The language of mistake does not do any work in this context.

The Model Penal Code takes a slightly different approach, at least with regard to the problem of mistakes of fact regarding the triggering conditions of *justification* defences. According to the Code, an actor is justified as long as he subjectively believes that the triggering conditions for the justification defence exist, regardless of whether his belief is mistaken. Nevertheless, the Code prescribes that the defendant should be liable for a negligent version of the offence charged if his mistake was negligent or for a reckless version of the offence if his mistake was reckless.[16]

Transferred Defences/Collateral Damage Defences

A particularly thorny problem arises when an actor uses justifiable force against a wrongful aggressor but ends up harming an innocent third party. Think of an actor who shoots at an aggressor but misses and the bullet ends up killing an innocent bystander. Does the justification defence transfer so that it justifies the killing of the third party, or is the killing unlawful because the third party was not a wrongful aggressor?

While there is not much authority on the subject, it seems that justifiable use of force that is directed at an aggressor but reaches an innocent third party is justified as long as the actor's conduct did not recklessly or negligently endanger the third party. If, on the other hand, the actor's use of force recklessly or negligently risked harm to the third party, the actor may be held liable for recklessly or negligently causing harm to the innocent bystander. This is the solution expressly prescribed in the Model Penal Code, which states:

> When the actor is justified under Sections 3.03 to 3.08 in using force upon or toward the person of another but he recklessly or negligently injures or creates a risk of injury to innocent persons, the justification afforded by those Sections is unavailable in a prosecution for such recklessness or negligence towards innocent persons.[17]

Individual Defences

Self-Defence and Excessive Self-Defence

A person may justifiably use force against a wrongful aggressor in order to protect her person, property, or habitation. Force may also be used against a wrongful aggressor in order to protect a third party from an unlawful attack. These cases share four elements in common. First, the use of force is triggered by the existence of a wrongful attack. Second, the use of force is justified only if it is necessary to avert the wrongful attack. Third, the use of force is justifiable only if it is in some way proportional to the averted harm. Finally, justification follows only if the actor reasonably believed that the use of force was necessary to repel the wrongful attack.

The triggering condition for a claim of defence of self, property, or others is a wrongful aggression. If the aggression is not wrongful, then the force used to repel the aggression cannot be justified as self-defence. Instead, the force will either be unjustified or justified pursuant to some other defence, such as choice of evils. When is an aggression wrongful? This question has generated considerable debate in the scholarly literature. While there are some cases in which it is unclear whether an aggression is wrongful, there are some instances in which attacks are obviously wrongful. If the attack amounts to a criminal offence, the aggression is clearly wrongful. There seems to be general agreement that conduct that satisfies the elements of an offence but

---

15 See, e.g., *People v. Goetz* 68 N.Y.2d 96 (N.Y. 1986).
16 Model Penal Code § 3.09(2).
17 Model Penal Code § 3.09(3).

is excused also counts as the sort of wrongful aggression that triggers a right to self-defence,[18] although a minority of scholars think that excused aggression should not trigger the right to use force in self-defence.[19]

Another particularly complicated case is that of an aggression that does not satisfy the voluntary act requirement. Think, for example, of a person who attacks you while sleepwalking or someone who violently thrusts their body toward you while they are having a seizure. These acts do not satisfy criminal law's venerable act requirement and thus do not give rise to criminal liability. Do they, however, count as wrongful aggressions that trigger the right to use self-defence? There is scant case law on the subject. Even if such 'acts' do not count as wrongful aggressions, using force to repel them should be justified pursuant to some other justification, such as lesser evils or necessity.[20]

In addition to being wrongful, it is usually held that the aggression must be imminent. Pursuant to this requirement, defensive force may be used only to avert an imminent attack. On the other hand, force used to avert an attack that will happen in the future, is generally not justified.

The imminence requirement has increasingly come under attack because of the outcome that it usually produces in battered women cases. The paradigmatic case is one in which a battered woman kills her husband while he is sleeping in order to prevent future attacks and to end years of severe physical and emotional abuse. The facts of *State v. Norman* are illustrative.[21] Judy Norman had endured decades of severe physical and mental abuse from her husband. He made her eat dog food, forced her to prostitute herself, cut her badly with glass bottles, and put out cigarettes on her skin. Sometimes the beatings were so severe that they would leave Judy unconscious. After enduring a brutal beating, Judy decided that she had to do something to end the abuse and prevent future attacks. She waited until her husband fell asleep, took out a gun, and fired it several times at her husband's head, killing him.

It is important to note that Judy unsuccessfully tried to summon help from local authorities several times prior to deciding to kill her husband. During the trial for the murder of her husband, Judy pleaded self-defence. Nevertheless, the trial court refused to instruct the jury on self-defence, ruling as a matter of law that no reasonable person could conclude that an actor poses an 'imminent' threat of wrongful aggression while he is asleep. Ms Norman was convicted of the lesser offence of voluntary manslaughter. She appealed, arguing that refusing to instruct the jury on self-defence was reversible error. The North Carolina Supreme Court ultimately affirmed the conviction, explaining:

> [S]tretching the law of self-defence to fit the facts of this case would require changing the "imminent death or great bodily harm" requirement to something substantially more indefinite than previously required and would weaken our assurances that justification for the taking of human life remains firmly rooted in real or apparent necessity.[22]

The *Norman* decision has been the subject of much discussion in the scholarly literature. Some agree with the core holding that self-defence should not apply when there is no imminent attack, but argue that courses of conduct like Judy Norman's ought to be excused.[23] Others argue that the outcome in *Norman* was mistaken and that self-defence ought to be construed broadly enough to justify killings in non-confrontational situations as long as the use of force was necessary to avert a future attack even if the aggression is not technically imminent.[24]

---

18   See, e.g., Luis E. Chiesa and G.P. Fletcher, Self-Defence and the Psychotic Aggressor, in *Criminal Law Conversations* (Paul Robinson, Kimberly Ferzan and Stephen Garvey eds. 2010).

19   See, e.g., Kimberly Kessler Ferzan, Culpable Aggression: The Basis for Moral Liability to Defensive Killing, 9 Ohio St. J.Crim. L. 664, 669 (2012).

20   Chiesa and Fletcher, supra note 18.

21   *State v. Norman*, 324 N.C. 253 (1989).

22   Ibid.

23   See, e.g., Joshua Dressler, Battered Women and Sleeping Abusers: Some Reflections, Ohio St. J.Crim. L. 457 (2006).

24   See, e.g., Richard Rosen, On Self-Defence, Imminence, and Women who Kill their Batterers, 71 N.C. L. Rev. 371 (1993).

Interestingly, the Model Penal Code adopted an intermediate position. While not entirely doing away with the imminence requirement as the critics of *Norman* would do, the Code relaxes the requirement by requiring merely proof that the force was 'immediately necessary' to preventing future harm.[25] The 'immediacy' requirement imposes some temporal limits on when force can be used, but the limits are considerably less rigid than what a strict requirement of imminence would impose.

Assuming that there is an imminent wrongful aggression, use of force is lawful only if it is necessary to avert the attack. Force is necessary when there are no less harmful alternatives that may avert the attack with equal possibility of success. The necessity of the use of force is often confused with the proportionality of the force. If a pickpocket steals your wallet, is running away from you, and the only way to stop him is to shoot him in the leg, shooting the pickpocket is necessary, although likely disproportional. It is necessary because it is the only means that you have available to stop the aggression. It is likely disproportional, however, because the harm threatened (loss of a wallet) is considerably less serious than the harm inflicted (serious bodily injury).

An issue related to the necessity of the use of force is the so-called 'retreat' doctrine. According to this doctrine, a person has a duty to retreat before resorting to the use of deadly force if retreating could safely avert the attack.[26] Nonetheless, the general rule is that there is no duty to retreat if non-deadly force is used to repel the aggression. The one glaring exception to the retreat doctrine is that there is no duty to retreat when you are attacked in your home. That is, a person attacked in her home may meet deadly force with deadly force even if retreating would avert the attack. This is typically called the 'castle doctrine'.[27]

Support for the retreat doctrine has waned considerably in recent years. Several state jurisdictions have now enacted so-called 'stand your ground' laws, which allow actors to use deadly force without having to retreat even if retreating would prevent the threatened harm from taking place. The oft-cited Florida 'stand your ground' statute is representative. According to this law:

> A person who is not engaged in an unlawful activity and who is attacked in any other place where he or she has a right to be has no duty to retreat and has the right to stand his or her ground and meet force with force, including deadly force if he or she reasonably believes it is necessary to do so to prevent death or great bodily harm to himself or herself or another or to prevent the commission of a forcible felony.[28]

Force used in defence of self, property, or others must also be proportional to the threatened harm. There is no requirement, however, that the force inflict a lesser evil than the one averted. An actor may thus inflict more harm than the harm with which he is threatened, as long as the force used is not grossly disproportional to the harm caused. A person may, for example, kill in order to prevent rape or serious bodily injury. With regard to defending property, a person may not use deadly force in order to prevent harm to property interests.[29] Furthermore, the use of trap guns or other contraptions that may endanger vital interests to protect property or habitation is generally deemed unlawful, for such mechanical devices are not able to discriminate between wrongful intruders and lawful visitors and the force unleashed by the devices may be grossly disproportional to the harm threatened by an intruder.[30] A trap gun that is triggered by the opening of a door cannot, for example, discriminate between the burglar who opens the door to commit a crime inside the dwelling and the firefighter who opens the door to put out a fire inside the home.

Finally, an actor may only use force in self-defence if he reasonably believes that the force is necessary to thwart a wrongful attack. As was mentioned in the section devoted to mistake regarding the triggering conditions of general defences, it is legally irrelevant to the American law of self-defence whether an actual attack takes place. Force is justified regardless of whether an actual aggression takes place as long as the defendant *reasonably believed* that an attack was about to take place and force was necessary to repel the aggression.

---

25 Model Penal Code § 3.04(1).
26 See, e.g., Model Penal Code § 3.04(2)(b)(ii).
27 See, e.g., Model Penal Code § 3.04(2)(b)(ii)(A).
28 Florida Penal Code 776.013(d)(3).
29 See, e.g., Model Penal Code § 3.06(3)(d).
30 See, e.g., Model Penal Code § 3.06(5); see also *People v. Ceballos*, 78 N.Y.2d 1074 (N.Y. 1991).

The actor's belief that force is necessary to repel wrongful aggression must be objectively reasonable. As a result, the defendant's subjective belief that force is necessary is not enough to justify defensive force. This is the lesson to be learned from the much-discussed case of *People v. Goetz*.[31] The defendant was riding the New York City Subway when he was approached by several black youths who asked him for 'five dollars'. The defendant refused to give them the money. Instead, he shot at the youths several times, seriously injuring some of them. A grand jury indicted Goetz for the commission of various offences, including attempted murder. Goetz sought the dismissal of the charges, contending that the prosecutor erroneously failed to explain to the grand jury that his conduct was justified pursuant to self-defence as long as it seemed *reasonable to him* that using force was necessary to thwart a wrongful attack.

Instead, the prosecutor had explained to the jury that defensive force is justified only if it is objectively reasonable, not if it is reasonable to the defendant. Lower courts accepted the defendant's view of self-defence and therefore dismissed the charges against Goetz. The state appealed, arguing that acceptance of the defendant's view would be tantamount to adopting a subjective standard of reasonableness, which is a contradiction in terms. The New York Court of Appeal agreed with the state and reinstated the charges against Goetz, concluding that the belief that justifies defensive force must be an objectively reasonable belief that force is necessary to avert wrongful aggression. A subjective belief that force is necessary will not do if it is deemed to be objectively unreasonable according to societal standards.[32]

The defendant in *Goetz* also argued that evidence regarding his prior experiences should be relevant to determining whether his belief that force was necessary was objectively reasonable. This was of particular importance in the case, for Goetz had been mugged several times in the past. The prior muggings were the reason why he bought a gun and also explain why he was afraid that the youths were going to mug him. The Court of Appeals agreed that evidence of prior experiences that are relevant to assessing the defendant's state of mind at the time of the use of force is relevant to determining whether his belief that force was necessary was objectively reasonable. The Court further explained that the standard that should be employed to assess whether the defendant's belief is reasonable is whether a reasonable person *in the defendant's situation* would have also believed that using force was necessary to thwart wrongful aggression. An assessment of what a reasonable person would believe 'in the defendant's situation' allows the fact finder to take into consideration past experiences of the defendant that are relevant to assessing his frame of mind at the time of the incident.[33] This is also relevant in battered women cases, where courts routinely hold that evidence of prior spousal abuse and battered woman syndrome is admissible to assessing the objective reasonableness of the woman's belief that force was necessary to avert a wrongful attack from her spouse.[34]

As a general rule, if the force used in defence of self or property is excessive, the defendant is precluded from raising the defence.[35] The defendant typically also has no right to mitigation of punishment when he uses excessive force. Excessive force may be unjustified because it is unnecessary to thwart the attack, given that less force would have been sufficient to avert the aggression. Excessive force may also be unjustified because it is grossly disproportional to the threatened harm, as when someone kills when it is the only way to prevent harm to property.

Although excessive force does not generally trigger a full or partial defence to liability, some courts do recognise a partial defence of 'imperfect self-defence' when the defendant is charged with murder and it is deemed that the force she used is excessive or unreasonable. The partial defence of 'imperfect self-defence' mitigates murder to the less serious offence of manslaughter.[36] The imperfect self-defence mitigation applies either when the defendant honestly but unreasonably believed that the force was necessary to avert wrongful aggression or when she reasonably believed that using some force was necessary but she unreasonably used more force than was necessary to thwart the attack.[37]

---

31 *People v. Goetz*, 68 N.Y.2d 96 (N.Y. 1986).
32 Ibid.
33 Ibid.
34 *State v. Norman*, 324 N.C. 253 (1989).
35 See, e.g., *Ross v. State*, 211 N.W.2d 827, 830 (Wis. 1973).
36 See, e.g., *Swann v. United States*, 548 A.2d 928, 930–931 (D.C. 1994).
37 See generally Dressler, supra note 10, at 249.

Necessity

Engaging in what would otherwise be criminal conduct is justified pursuant to necessity when engaging in the conduct is necessary to avert a more serious harm than the one brought about by the conduct. Necessity is frequently referred to as the 'lesser evils' defence, given that the claim succeeds only if the defendant causes a lesser evil than the one avoided. A paradigmatic example of justifiable necessity would be the case of a person who breaks the window of a car to save a child who is suffocating inside the vehicle. If the person is charged with criminal damages for breaking the car's window, he may successfully plead justifiable necessity, for his conduct was necessary to avert a harm that is more serious (death of the child) than the one he inflicted (damage to property).

The necessity defence applies if four requirements are satisfied. First, the defendant's conduct must avert an imminent harm. Second, the conduct must be necessary to avoiding the imminent harm. Thirdly, the harm caused by the defendant must be proportional to the harm averted. Finally, the necessity situation must not be one that the legislature had already anticipated and resolved in a way that is contrary to the defendant's conduct.

Force used pursuant to necessity is justified only if it is necessary to avert imminent harm. In *Commonwealth v. Leno*,[38] for example, the defendants established a needle exchange program to fight the propagation of AIDS. They were charged with the crime of distributing needles without a prescription in violation of Massachusetts state law. The defendants contended that their conduct was justified pursuant to necessity because distribution of clean hypodermic needles was necessary to save the lives of addicts who would otherwise likely acquire the AIDS virus from sharing needles. The Supreme Judicial Court of Massachusetts rejected the argument, explaining that necessity justifies what would otherwise be criminal conduct only when it is necessary to avert an *imminent* harm and that the possible future death of addicts who contract AIDS from sharing needles is speculative and—in any case—not an imminent harm. More specifically, the Court argued that:

> The prevention of possible future harm does not excuse a current systematic violation of the law in anticipation of the eventual over-all benefit to the public … . The defendants did not show that the danger they sought to avoid was clear and imminent, rather than debatable or speculative. The defence of necessity '[does] not deal with nonimminent or debatable harms … [it is inapplicable when] the hazards are long term, [and] the danger is not imminent'. … [39]

Causing harm is justified pursuant to necessity only if it is necessary in order to avoid an even greater harm. Inflicting harm is necessary only if it is the only way of avoiding an even greater injury. Causing harm is therefore not necessary if the defendant had other reasonable (and less harmful) alternatives that would have successfully prevented the threatened harm from taking place.

The case of *Stodghill v. State* is illustrative.[40] The defendant's girlfriend suddenly became very sick and was in clear need of immediate medical attention. After waiting for an ambulance, the defendant drove her to the hospital even though he had consumed a considerable amount of alcohol. The defendant was pulled over by a police officer and was subsequently arrested for driving under the influence of alcohol. At trial, the defendant argued that his conduct was justified pursuant to necessity, as it was necessary for him to drive his girlfriend to the hospital to prevent her from suffering serious injury. The trial court denied his defence, contending that the defendant had reasonable alternatives that would have prevented the harm. The Supreme Court of Mississippi affirmed, pointing out that the defendant could have easily asked his daughter or son-in-law to drive his girlfriend to the hospital. They were both sober. Had the defendant done so, he would have prevented harm to his girlfriend without having to drive while under the influence of alcohol.

The central element of the necessity defence is that the actor's conduct must avert a greater harm than the one that it causes. Sometimes it is difficult to determine whether the actor's conduct inflicts a lesser evil than the one prevented. In *People v. Unger*, for example, the trial court had to decide if the harm averted by

---

38 415 Mass. 835 (1993).
39 Ibid.
40 892 So.2d 236 (Miss. 2005).

escaping from prison is greater than the evil inflicted by the escape.[41] The prisoner escaped from prison in order to avoid being sexually assaulted by fellow inmates. Was escaping from prison a lesser evil than the harm inherent in a sexual assault? The question is complicated, for it is unclear what, precisely, is the harm inherent in escaping from prison. Even after the harm is appropriately defined, it is difficult to quantify it in a way that makes it possible to compare it with the harm averted by escaping from prison. Perhaps because of the complexities that answering this question entailed, the trial court refused to instruct the jury on necessity. The defendant was convicted and subsequently appealed his conviction to the Supreme Court of Illinois. While the Court did not actually explain how the competing harms should be balanced, it reversed the ruling of the trial court and ordered a new trial, explaining that the defendant was entitled to have the jury charged with an instruction regarding necessity.

Perhaps the thorniest problem regarding the balancing of evils required by the necessity defence is whether killing an innocent human being can ever be regarded as the lesser evil. This is the issue that the court faced in the (in)famous *Dudley and Stephens* case.[42] Following the sinking of their ship, the defendants were stranded in a boat with a young cabin boy. After several days without rescue, the defendants killed the cabin boy and ate him in order to stave off starvation. They were rescued several days later. Upon their arrival in Great Britain, they were charged with murdering the cabin boy. They argued that killing the cabin boy was justified because cannibalizing him allowed them to survive. The court rejected the argument. In doing so, the court expressed doubts about whether the comparative value of human lives could be determined objectively. Furthermore, the court pointed out that 'awful danger' inherent in 'admitting the principle' that it may sometimes be justified to sacrifice an innocent person for the wellbeing of many more.

In *U.S. v. Holmes*,[43] a ship struck an iceberg and started to sink. A group of passengers and crewmembers boarded a lifeboat. Unfortunately, the lifeboat started to leak. Several hours later, the defendant crewmember helped force 12 men out of the lifeboat in order to slow the sinking of the vessel. Upon reaching shore, the defendant was charged and convicted of murdering one of the persons he helped throw overboard. The conviction was upheld on appeal. In explaining their decision, the Circuit Court noted that the crewmembers did not draw lots or consult the people in the lifeboat as to how to proceed. This suggests that the result might have been different had the people who were thrown overboard agreed to some sort of procedure for randomly selecting which persons to sacrifice.

Finally, it is worthy of note that while no American case has ever concluded that the killing of an innocent human being amounts to the lesser evil and could thus be justified pursuant to necessity, the drafters of the Model Penal Code argued that sacrificing an innocent life to save many more ought to be justified under the Code's lesser evils justification defence.[44]

The necessity defence is often invoked by protesters who break a law by engaging in civil disobedience. Nevertheless, as the United States Court of Appeals for the Ninth Circuit explained in *United States v. Schoon*, the majority of acts of civil disobedience fail to meet most—if not all—of the elements of the necessity defence.[45] The imminence requirement is often not satisfied, for the acts that are being protested frequently threaten future rather than immediate harm. This is the case, for example, with protests against nuclear power plants, for the harm threatened by such plants will take place at some indefinite point in time, if at all. Even in the few cases in which the harm being protested against is imminent, it is unclear whether the acts of civil disobedience will actually avert the threatened harm. Finally, there are often legal alternatives available that may be used as a tool for preventing the threatened harm. Thus, engaging in lawful efforts to change the legislation authorizing such plants may curb the threat from nuclear power plants.

The court in *Schoon* distinguished between direct and indirect civil disobedience. A person engages in an act of civil disobedience if she breaks the law that she is seeking to change. This is what Rosa Parks did when she refused to take a seat in the back of the bus, for the law that she violated was precisely the law or policy that she was protesting against. In contrast, refusing to pay taxes as a way of protesting against a war being waged by the government in a foreign country is an act of indirect civil disobedience, for the law that is infringed

---

41   66 Ill.2d 333 (1977).
42   [1884] 14 QBD 273.
43   26 F.Cas. 360 (C.C.E.D. Pa. 1842).
44   Model Penal Code and Commentaries § 3.01.
45   971 F.2d 193 (9th Cir. 1991).

(tax law) is not the law or policy that is being protested against (the law authorizing military intervention in the foreign country). The court argued in *Schoon* that '[i]ndirect protests of congressional policies can never meet all the requirements of the necessity doctrine'.[46] Nevertheless, the court's holding leaves the door open for a subsequent finding that some acts of *direct* civil disobedience may meet the requirements of the choice of evils defence.

Duress by Threats/Circumstances

Self-defence and necessity are justification defences. That is, society acquits those who act in self-defence and those who cause a harm to prevent even greater harm because such courses of conduct are, all things being considered, appropriate under the circumstances. Given that self-defence and necessity are justification defences, they negate the wrongfulness of the conduct.

Duress, on the other hand, is usually classified as an excuse defence. We acquit those who act under duress because we cannot fairly expect such actors to behave differently. Nevertheless, given that those who act under duress do not generally prevent a greater harm than the harm they inflict, such conduct is typically considered wrongful. Suppose that a person is told that his son will be shot and killed if he does not cause serious bodily injury to an innocent third party. Assuming that the actor inflicts serious bodily injury to an innocent person in order to prevent harm to his child, his conduct would be excused pursuant to the duress defence. Note, however, that such conduct remains—all things being considered—wrongful, for the actor does not have a right to harm an innocent third party.

The excuse of duress is triggered when an actor faces a threat that originates in the acts of a human being. Although there is support in American scholarly literature for expanding the defence of duress to encompass 'situational' or 'circumstantial' duress that is the product of natural acts,[47] American courts and codes continue to reject broadening the defence in this manner. According to the drafters of the Model Penal Code, the rationale for limiting duress to cases of human threats is that it is still possible to prosecute the actor who issued the threat for the criminal conduct committed by the excused actor.[48] In contrast, when the threats originate in natural acts (i.e., 'situational duress'), excusing the actor who engages in the crime necessarily entails that no one would be prosecuted for the criminal conduct. This outcome is deemed unacceptable.

The *Dudley and Stephens* case illustrates this matter quite nicely. Since the threat facing the crewmembers (starvation) originated in natural events (capsizing of the boat), American duress law would not excuse the killing of the cabin boy. The result would be justified on the grounds that excusing the crewmembers would leave the killing of the cabin boy unpunished, which is an unwelcome outcome. In contrast, if a person had told the crewmembers that they would be shot and killed unless they kill the cabin boy, they would have a valid duress defence under the Model Penal Code and in many American jurisdictions. Excusing such a killing is acceptable to the Code drafters and many American legislatures because someone will still be held accountable for the killing of the cabin boy: the person who issued the threats.

The American reticence to expand duress to encompass situational or circumstantial threats that do not originate in the acts of human beings is objectionable. While it is true that excusing such conduct will leave the harm caused unpunished because there is no actor who can be held criminally liable for the conduct, it is also true that it is unfair (and probably inefficient) to punish someone for yielding to natural pressures that would prove insurmountable to an average person.

At common law, it was often stated that duress would only excuse conduct if the threat that triggered the defence was imminent. It was also frequently asserted that duress amounted to a defence only if the harm caused by the actor was less than the threatened harm. This, in turn, led many jurisdictions to hold that duress could never excuse homicide, for a person who kills an innocent human being to save herself does not cause less harm than the harm prevented. By doing so, such jurisdictions seemed to include a proportionality requirement to the analysis of duress.

---

46   Ibid.
47   See generally Dressler, supra note 10, at 342.
48   Model Penal Code and Commentaries § 2.09, 379.

In contrast, the Model Penal Code excuses what would otherwise amount to criminal conduct pursuant to duress if a 'person of reasonable firmness' in the actor's situation would have also yielded to the threat.[49] The Code provision does not require that the threat that compels the defendant to act be 'imminent', nor does it demand that there be proportionality between the threatened harm and the harm inflicted. Instead, it merely requires proof that a reasonable person in the actor's situation would have also committed the offence. As a result, the Code's duress provision may excuse the commission of a homicide, as long as a person of reasonable firmness in the actor's situation would have also committed homicide in order to avert the threat.

General Mental Condition Defences

Insanity

A person who commits a crime while she is legally insane is excused. Nonetheless, a person held not guilty by reason of insanity may be committed to a mental institution until she is no longer a menace to society. Two requirements must be satisfied in order for the insanity defence to apply. First, the defendant must suffer from a mental disease or defect at the time of the commission of the offence. Second, the mental disease of defect must prevent the defendant from understanding the nature of his act or from distinguishing right from wrong. In some jurisdictions, insanity also applies if the mental disease or defect prevents the defendant from conforming his conduct to the mandates of law.

Regarding the first element, it is generally held that an inclination toward antisocial behaviours is not a 'mental disease or defect' for the purposes of the insanity defence. This understanding found its way to the Model Penal Code, which expressly states that 'the terms "mental disease or defect" do not include an abnormality manifested only by repeated criminal or otherwise antisocial conduct'.[50] As a result, so-called sociopathic personality disorder will not generally trigger the insanity defence.

With regard to the kind of cognitive or volitional defect that insanity must cause, the majority of American jurisdictions continue to follow the rule laid down by English courts in the *M'Naghten* case.[51] According to the *M'Naghten* rule, mental disease or defect is a defence only if it prevents the defendant either from understanding the nature of his act or from comprehending the wrongfulness of his conduct.[52] A frequently cited example of the former is that of a person who is squeezing his spouse's neck while actually believing that he is squeezing lemons. If this belief was brought about by a mental disease or defect, it would preclude the imposition of liability under *M'Naghten* because it prevents the defendant from understanding what he is doing. An example of the latter would be the case of a paranoid schizophrenic who kills her spouse because she hallucinated that her spouse was poisoning her food. The defendant may be acquitted under *M'Naghten* because her mental disease or defect prevented her from understanding that killing her spouse was wrong.

There is some debate as to whether the defendant is entitled to an acquittal only if his mental disease prevents him from knowing that his conduct is legally wrong or whether it suffices to show that his disease caused him to be unaware that his conduct was morally wrong. Think, for example, of a mentally diseased father who drowns his son believing that doing so is against the law, but that it is not morally wrong because it is the only way of saving his son's soul. Should he be acquitted by reason of insanity? If the law requires that his disease prevent him from knowing that drowning his child was legally wrong, he will not be acquitted. Nevertheless, if the law merely requires proof that the disease prevented the father from knowing that drowning his son was immoral, he may be acquitted. The Model Penal Code drafters deliberately refused to take a position regarding the matter, leaving the resolution of the issue to state courts and legislatures.[53] Finally, some courts follow what is often called the 'deific decree rule', which holds that the insanity defence applies whenever a defendant believes that she was commanded by God to commit the criminal offence.[54]

The Model Penal Code's approach to insanity is broader than the *M'Naghten* rule, for it provides a defence both under the circumstances that trigger *M'Naghten* and when the defendant's mental disease or

---

49   Model Penal Code § 2.09.
50   Model Penal Code § 4.01.
51   [1843] UKHL J16.
52   Ibid.
53   Model Penal Code § 4.01.
54   See, e.g., *State v. Crenshaw*, 617 P.2d 1041 (Wn. App. 1980); *State v. Cameron*, 674 P.2d 650 (Wash. 1983).

defect prevents him from conforming his conduct to the mandates of law. This would provide a defence to someone who because of mental disease or defect is aware that his conduct is legally and morally wrong but is unable to control his acts. In the wake of the publication of the Model Penal Code, a significant number of jurisdictions adopted the Code's broader insanity provision. Nevertheless, the recent trend in jurisdictions that adopted the Code's insanity formulation has been to revert to the more stringent *M'Naghten* rule.[55] This was provoked, at least in part, by the massive public outcry in the wake of John Hinckley's acquittal by reason of insanity for attempting to assassinate then President Reagan. Not only did many jurisdictions revert to the *M'Naghten* rule in the wake of the controversial Hinckley acquittal, but a handful of states actually abolished the insanity defence altogether.[56]

Intoxication
American law distinguishes between involuntary and voluntary intoxication. Involuntary intoxication occurs when the defendant is not at fault for becoming intoxicated. This can happen when the actor is forced to intoxicate himself or when he mistakenly (and non-negligently) believes that he is not ingesting intoxicating substances when he in fact is.[57] So-called pathological intoxication is also involuntary. Pathological intoxication occurs when a person has a psychotic reaction as a consequence of a pre-existing mental condition that is exacerbated or triggered by the ingestion of alcohol.[58] On the other hand, voluntary intoxication occurs when the defendant chooses to ingest intoxicating substances.

Involuntary intoxication is admissible to negate the *mens rea* required by the crime. Although there is scant case law on the subject, it seems that involuntary intoxication is admissible to negate any kind of *mens rea*, including both what the common law calls 'specific' and 'general intent'.[59] Furthermore, involuntary intoxication is a defence if it alters the defendants mind to such an extent that he satisfies the jurisdiction's test for legal insanity.[60]

Strictly speaking, voluntary intoxication is not a 'general defence'. Rather, it is an absent-element defence that, when applicable, may negate the (subjective) element of the offence charged.

At common law, evidence of voluntary intoxication was admissible only to negate a specific intent. Therefore, evidence of voluntary intoxication is not admissible at common law if defendant is charged with a general intent crime. While the common law distinction between specific and general intent crimes is confusing, the best way of approaching the distinction is by discriminating between the following:

1) Crimes that merely require that the defendant intend to engage in the prohibited act (e.g. trespassing), and
2) Crimes that—in addition to the intent to engage in the prohibited act—require proof of an additional mental state that does not directly refer to the act proscribed by the statute (e.g., burglary = trespassing with intent to commit crime therein).

The former kinds of crime merely require a general intent, whereas the latter types of offences demand proof of a specific intent.

Given the confusing nature of the common law's general/specific intent distinction, the Model Penal Code abandoned it in favour of a more streamlined approach to *mens rea* that distinguishes between purposeful, knowing, reckless and negligent wrongdoing.[61] Pursuant to the Code, voluntary intoxication is admissible to negate 'purpose' or 'knowledge', but is inadmissible to negate 'recklessness' or 'negligence'.[62]

---

55   Dressler, supra note 10, at 372.
56   See, e.g., Idaho Code § 18-207 (2005).
57   Dressler, supra note 10, at 357.
58   Ibid. 358.
59   Ibid.
60   Ibid.
61   Model Penal Code § 2.02.
62   Model Penal Code § 2.08.

Mistake of Law

Sometimes an actor may believe that the law recognises a particular general defence when in it in fact does not. Suppose that a person believes it is lawful to kill another as long as the victim consents to the killing. In fact, consent is not a defence to homicide. Such mistakes regarding the existence of a defence are not relevant in American criminal law and therefore do not generate an acquittal. They are also not generally grounds for mitigation. The same can be said about mistakes as to the reach or scope of a defence. Thus, for example, an actor who mistakenly believes that he may inflict serious bodily injury to his child pursuant to parental authority is mistaken as to the scope of the justification of parental authority. He may lawfully use minor physical force to discipline his child, but inflicting serious bodily injury on his child as a way of disciplining him is categorically prohibited. Once again, the mistake is legally irrelevant under American law.

Residual Catch-All Defences/Existence and Ambit of Statutory Defences

American criminal law recognizes several other general defences not discussed in this Chapter. Perhaps the most prominent example is the defence of entrapment. Pursuant to this defence, an actor will not be held criminally liable when the police induced him to commit a crime by engaging in tactics that would likely cause a law abiding person to commit the offence. Courts follow two different approaches to the entrapment defence. Under the so-called 'subjective' view, a defendant is entitled to a defence only if he was not predisposed to committing the offence prior to being approached by the police. If, however, the defendant was predisposed to commit the offence prior to being contacted by the police, the defence automatically fails.[63] This is the view adopted by the United States Supreme Court. In contrast, the 'objective' view of entrapment affords a defence to criminal liability if the police conduct would have likely caused a law-abiding person to commit the crime.[64] Under this approach, the defendant's predisposition to committing the crime is legally irrelevant and, therefore, does not preclude him from pleading entrapment. This is the approach adopted in the Model Penal Code.[65]

Another general defence recognized in American criminal law is law enforcement authority. Force used pursuant to law enforcement authority is—along with self-defence and necessity—one of the classic claims of justification in the United States. Pursuant to this justification, police officers may generally use physical force to prevent a crime or to arrest a suspect. Nevertheless, officers may not use deadly force to prevent the fleeing of a suspect who poses no risk to the lives or limbs of the officers or third parties.[66]

---

63   See, e.g., *Sherman v. United States*, 356 U.S. 369 (1958).
64   *Grossman v. State*, 457 P.2d 226 (Alaska 1969).
65   Model Penal Code § 2.13(2).
66   See generally *Tennessee v. Garner*, 471 U.S. 1 (1985); *Scott v. Harris*, 550 U.S. 372 (2007).

Index